Introduction to
Social Work

Also available from Lyceum Books, Inc.

Introduction to
Social Work

The People's
Profession

Third Edition

Ira Colby
University of Houston

Sophia F. Dziegielewski
University of Cincinnati

LYCEUM
BOOKS, INC.

Chicago, Illinois

© Lyceum Books, Inc., 2010

Published by

LYCEUM BOOKS, INC.
5758 S. Blackstone Ave.
Chicago, Illinois 60637
773+643-1903 (Fax)
773+643-1902 (Phone)
lyceum@lyceumbooks.com
http://www.lyceumbooks.com

Photographs in Chapter three are reprinted by permission of the
Chicago Historical Society.

All other photographs are reprinted by permission of Mary Whalen.

Library of Congress Cataloging-in-Publication Data

Colby, Ira C. (Ira Christopher)
    Introduction to social work : the people's profession / Ira Colby,
Sophia Dziegielewski.—3rd ed.
        p. cm.
    Includes bibliographical references and index.
    ISBN 978-1-933478-53-1
        1. Social service—United States. 2. Social workers—United States.
I. Dziegielewski, Sophia F. II. Title.
HV91.C597 2010
361.3'20973—dc22   2009031194

Table of Contents

List of Boxes and Tables

Preface

Your career should be personally rewarding. Feeling a sense of accomplishment when you make a difference in someone else's life provides a natural high that is both uplifting and fulfilling. Social work is a profession that provides ample opportunities to make positive differences in others' lives and to help make our communities better and safer for all people.

In the pages that follow, you will be introduced to the social work profession—its obvious strengths as well as its limitations. You will see how social work started and how the field has grown from those humble beginnings working with poor and underserved populations to the worldwide profession of today. Each chapter introduces the beginning professional to what social work involves and the roles social workers perform. Although social work is an old profession, rich in tradition, it remains dynamic, flexible, and open to change. Indeed, with the field's focus on the "person-in-situation" or "person-in-environment," the need to address continuous and repeated change is ongoing. To facilitate this process, in addition to examining the field of social work in its present form, we make suggestions for future exploration and expansion. Taking into account the past, the present, and the future provides fertile ground for social workers to develop new services, allowing the best possible care for the client.

By presenting the many different facets of social work and the helping professional's helping activities that result is exactly why we titled this book the "people's profession." It is our goal to provide a realistic and varied presentation that will help you develop a more authentic understanding and appreciation of the profession. At a minimum, you will be exposed to what social workers do and the importance of considering the environmental context that surrounds all decisions. Social workers believe strongly in allowing ethical principles and a respect for cultural diversity to guide all practice decisions. Differences in individuals are acknowledged, and concepts such as dignity, worth, and respect, along with a nonjudgmental attitude, provide the cornerstone on which all intervention is built.

In part, it is our hope that the success of this book will be measured by whether it can help the beginning social work professional answer the following question: Is social work really the profession for me? If so, let the book introduce you to the field and what rewards and challenges lie ahead. If not, may you gain an understanding of and respect for the field, an awareness of the needs and struggles that people face, and the knowledge that most of these problems and issues are not self-perpetuated.

Part I provides abroad overview of the profession, in which we introduce professional terminology and acronyms. This is followed by a discussion of social workers' typical employment settings, responsibilities, and salaries. After that we explore, albeit briefly, the rich traditions within the field of social work, highlighting how the past clearly relates to the present, making predictions about what the future has in store.

In part II, the reader is introduced to the practice of social work and will learn the meaning of terms such as the micro, mezzo, and macro levels of practice. At each level of practice, we highlight concepts such as the client system and the notion that this system almost always involves more than one person. Although it is possible to view clients as individuals, they are most often addressed in terms of context or systems and this can involve individuals, families, groups, communities, or policies that either directly or indirectly affect client system well-being.

In the chapters in part III, several examples of the various practice settings where social workers are employed are presented. This section discusses current practice strategy as well as suggestions for expanding current activities while exploring areas for further development.

This book is unique in that it will challenge you to synthesize information about successes and events in the field. Activities are included to give the beginning professional a sense of hands-on learning. These activities will help you develop a more in-depth understanding of the profession. There is also an emphasis on the use of the Internet, a tool that is now part of all of our lives. Case examples are used throughout to help you see the interface between what is written in the text and actual practice.

On a personal note, we would like to say that putting together this third edition, selecting and updating the topics most germane to the social work field, was not an easy task—nor should it have been. This book represents more than fifty years of combined direct practice and teaching experience. We are both committed to using our passion for the profession to introduce others to this exciting and challenging field. As practitioners, we believe that much can be learned from the clients we serve. As administrators, we know the importance of recognizing system variables and remaining flexible in our current financially challenged environment. In fact, many of the examples we present have been drawn from our own practical, administrative, or academic experience. Using our actual experiences in direct practice, as administrators and as educators, helped us to decide how best to present information in a practical and informative way, one that is sensitive to students' interests and concerns while taking into account the expectations that social work programs have for a beginning social work course.

This book would not be complete if we did not acknowledge the individuals in our own support systems who have made this effort possible. Ira Colby thanks his wife and best friend, Deborah, who for thirty-four years has honestly critiqued his teaching, writing, and thinking. Sophia Dziegielewski thanks her husband, family, friends, and colleagues, who respect and support her passion for the field and tolerate her "workaholic" ways.

Foremost, however, we would like to thank all the social workers who graciously allowed us to use their biographical sketches. We are also grateful for our publisher, David Follmer, and his staff, all of whom take such great pride in the quality of their work, for their editorial assistance. We continue to appreciate and admire the work of our photographer, Mary Whalen.

Now, with all of that said, we invite you to begin this adventure in learning about one of the oldest helping professions ever developed. May this book and its description of the social work profession ignite a fire in you, as our careers in social work have done for us.

About the Authors

Ira Colby is Dean of the Graduate School of Social Work at the University of Houston; prior to this position he developed and directed the baccalaureate social work program at Ferrum College, taught at the University of Texas at Arlington, and directed a new school of social work at the University of Central Florida. He received his MSW from Virginia Commonwealth University and his PhD from the University of Pennsylvania. He is widely published and has presented papers at state, national, and international meetings and forums. His passions are golf and family, not necessarily in that order.

Sophia F. Dziegielewski is professor in the School of Social Work at the University of Cincinnati and editor of the *Journal of Social Service Research*. Previously, she served as Dean of the School of Social Work at the University of Cincinnati and had faculty appointments at the University of Central Florida, the University of Alabama, the Departments of Family and Preventive Medicine and Psychiatry at Meharry Medical College, the School of Social Work at the University of Tennessee, and in the U.S. Army Military College at Fort Benning, GA. She received her MSW and her PhD from Florida State University. In 2003, Professor Dziegielewski was noted in the national magazine *Social Worker Today* for her work in the field of social work. She has over 120 scholarly publications and lectures widely across the United States.

Part **I**

The Context of
Social Work

Social Work: The Profession

"CALL ME A SOCIAL WORKER" IS HOW HERMAN MELVILLE, SITTING at his desk in his summer home, in Pittsfield, Massachusetts, might begin a novel detailing his social work experience. As the central character, he describes his work as rewarding and exciting with no two days alike. His cases, he says, run the gamut from simple to complex; while many are successfully resolved, some do not reach a happy ending. Throughout the novel, Herman would clearly set forth the many challenges facing new and rising social workers.

Herman Melville's novel might not make it to the *New York Times* best seller list, but it would be an honest attempt to portray the life and commitment necessary for today's social worker. The profession of social work is an old one whose story begins in the mid-1880s, when professional helping and assistance, often referred to as "social work practice," was first introduced. At this time, social workers were active with all types of people regardless of age, color, or creed, and this helping activity involved individuals, families, groups, and communities, in both public and private social service settings.

These initial efforts at helping have come a long way. According to the United States Department of Labor 2008 labor force study, there are approximately 600,000 professional social workers nationwide. More than 140,000 of these workers are members of the National Association of Social Workers (NASW), the world's largest professional membership organization for social workers. In addition to NASW, there are more than 50 other professional social work membership associations in the United States that support specific interests or fields of practice such as research, gerontology, health care, and clinical social work. The memberships of these various associations comprise professional social workers in all walks of life, from those who work with the elderly to those who work with infants. For the professional education of all these social workers, there are slightly more than 700 social work education programs, ranging from the baccalaureate to the doctorate level. And that's just in the United States! There is no precise figure or estimate of the number of social work educational programs in the world; the International Association of Schools of Social Work (IASSW) will conduct a "global census" of social work education in 2010 that, hopefully, will result in a better understanding of the number and types of educational programs there are in the world.

Social work professionals are employed in more than 90 percent of the nations of the world. Schools of social work can be found on every continent. This

Name: Paul A. Gildersleeve

Place of Residence: Oyster Bay, Long Island, NY

College/University Degrees: Adelphi University, BSW, MSW, and currently I am taking the Advanced Clinical Practice Program at NYU.

Present Position and Title: Currently retired from Nassau County Department of Behavioral Health as a Psychiatric Social Worker who handled crisis situations at Nassau County Department of Social Services.

Previous Work/Volunteer Experience: My volunteer work began with my interest in helping others in the 1960s when I volunteered at the Oyster Bay East Norwich Youth Association. I then volunteered at the Long Island Association for AIDS Care (LIAAC) and for the Long Island Gay Lesbian Switchboard where I was a hotline operator. Because of my volunteer work at LIAAC, I was able to secure part-time work with Nassau County Department of Drug and Alcohol Addiction as an HIV/AIDS counselor/educator/phlebotomist (the county trained me as a phlebotomist). Realizing that I had a lot to learn about addictions, I enrolled at Professional Alcoholism Counseling Education (PACE) and eventually became a Credentialed and Substance Abuse Counselor (CASAC). I worked in two methadone clinics and at two inpatient drug and alcohol settings, one with 90-day treatment and the other a long-term treatment program (12 months or more). I also worked in a day treatment drug and alcohol setting and set up a new program at a day treatment facility as well as a program with the Nassau County Department of Probation. I gave an educational presentation at Nassau County Correctional Center and was subsequently asked to work at the correctional center as a drug and alcohol counselor.

I worked in the STOP DWI Program and had a caseload of 9 to 12 clients and also conducted educational lectures in a 60-man open dorm. I did an internship in an Alzheimer's facility where I learned that you may only be able to help someone enjoy a brief moment in their life, and I interned in GAMPRO where I learned how to work with and treat gamblers. Once I earned my MSW, I was transferred to DSS as a psychiatric social worker to build a program called Behavioral Health where I would assess and refer clients who had mental health issues and who were not taking medications or diagnosed as having a disorder. I also sat in on the "case of the week," where individuals from all parts of DSS as well as outside agencies worked on difficult cases to help the client in receiving needed treatment or assistance.

Why did you choose social work as a career? My interest in becoming a social worker began when I entered therapy with a local therapist after a friend tried to commit suicide. This was my first experience with anyone trying to kill himself or herself. I lost complete control of my life and needed help.

A friend recommended a book about suicide, the title of which I have since forgotten. I purchased the book and began to read. I was totally amazed to find the book recounted every feeling and stage I had gone through. It also talked about my friend's feelings about death and his suicide attempt. The author did not know me nor did he know my friend, so how could he know what was going on inside either of us? This was my first clue that there was more to therapy than I had previously believed. This caused me to think carefully about the impact this book and therapy had on me. It knew my feelings. It knew the emotions I went through from the beginning to end. Because of this experience I had, I knew that, with training and education, I could help others.

What is your favorite social work story? I remember a colleague, a person of color with whom I frequently was at odds, said to me at a staff meeting, "You are the only person I know who has no color." I don't think there could ever be a better achievement.

What is one thing you would change in the community if you had the power to do so? To provide treatment and therapy to everyone regardless of the ability to pay, just their need for assistance and to be able to extend the hand of help to those who would never be able to enter an office for treatment.

---

worldwide activity is represented by the International Association of Schools of Social Work, the International Consortium for Social Development, and the International Federation of Social Workers. In addition, social workers are able to join social work membership associations in their own countries, similar to those in the United States. In Canada, for example, social workers may join Association canadienne des travailleuses et travailleurs sociaux (Canadian Association of Social Workers); in the United Kingdom, the British Association of Social Workers is the largest professional social work group.

THE PROFESSIONAL SOCIAL WORKER

Considering the enduring popularity of the social work profession, you may ask how and why this interest began and why it continues to grow in scope within the global community. The answer is simple: people across the world and in our own neighborhoods face similar problems and need the assistance that social workers provide. When these problems are individual in nature they are referred to as microsystem problems. Responsibility for finding solutions to microsystem problems often rests squarely on the shoulders of the individual client or family.

Did You Know...According to the Substance Abuse and Mental Health Services Administration (SAMHSA), professional social workers are the nation's largest group of mental health services providers.

For example, when a single, elderly person falls at home and breaks an arm, he may need to be admitted to a local hospital for treatment. Often after admission, the emergency room physician refers the case to the hospital social worker, who is tasked with assessing the client's situation. Suppose that during the assessment process, the worker learns that the client has no immediate family and lives alone. Taking into account the needs of the client, the worker must help to develop a plan with the elderly client that ensures provision of the support and services needed.

In many cases, this includes arranging home health care so that the client can receive medical services in the home (Dziegielewski, 2004). It can also include ensuring that the client has access to nutritious meals by arranging contact with a Meals on Wheels program. To increase socialization and provide mealtime activity, referral to a local neighborhood center's senior citizen's program can be made. Further, individual or group supportive counseling can be provided directly or by referral within the community. The role of the social worker through the microperspective is essential because this role stresses the individual client's personal and social needs in the assessment and intervention processes.

Did You Know...The member countries of the United Nations maintain missions in cities throughout the United States. You can learn from them about particular customs and cultural nuances that may affect your work with clients. Also, many international laws that affect practice pertain to individual visitors. If you're not sure about a particular situation, contact the relevant UN mission. Finally, a UN mission can provide you with a great deal of information about its home country's welfare system.

A second system often addressed in social work is the mezzosystem. Through the mezzoperspective, social workers highlight the needs of the client by focusing primarily on the environmental systems that can assist the individual. The client is linked directly to support systems that enhance and maximize individual functioning. From a mezzoperspective, family and friends are paramount. This perspective also incorporates those social workers who work in administration. These social workers run many of the programs that a client will need and can either initiate or oversee service delivery. When a client's problems are found to be by-products of a larger social system, such as the family or a group, this mezzosystem is usually the primary target of intervention.

Unfortunately, many problems have much wider roots in broader community or social institutions. Social workers need to be well-versed in multiple roles ". . . from adding a few lines to a policy and procedures manual to altering the laws that guide how nations interact" (Ellis, 2008, p. 131). To address these problems a social worker would use what is called a macrosystem approach. From the macroperspective, solutions to the problems that clients face must be tied directly to larger systems.

For example, providing decent and safe places to sleep for people who are homeless may require advocacy with local and state government. The social worker may need to initiate and organize a citywide movement to open a shelter. Indeed, macrointervention for this population is not as simple to accomplish as an inexperienced observer may think. At a minimum, in order to initiate macrochange the social worker needs to understand housing policy as it affects the homeless. She must also be knowledgeable about housing options and shelter alternatives used elsewhere. In addition to this basic knowledge, the social worker must also be aware of and anticipate resistance from the community that she is trying to serve. It is important to work with the larger community to get everyone to understand why a homeless shelter is really needed and to mobilize agreement.

When working within the macrosystem, however, caution should always be exercised; providing a homeless shelter is much more complicated than simply securing the site and the funds to construct a building. In implementing this type of change, the social worker must be sensitive to current community concerns and political issues that can enhance or impede service assistance and progression.

Did You Know...More than 40 percent of all disaster mental health volunteers trained by the American Red Cross are professional social workers.

This list of some of the most serious macrosystem social problems—homelessness, HIV/AIDS, physical and emotional abuse, mental health, substance abuse, and community development—touches on only some of the areas that make up the domain of social work practice. As highlighted by Specht and Courtney (1994), the ultimate goal of the profession is to seek perfectibility of the community, whereby all people are given the opportunity to live their lives to the fullest and to achieve their own potential. On first sight, the concept of perfectibility of the community may be alarming, since it appears to represent a utopian goal that is unattainable. Evaluated more closely, however, the aim of perfectability is not that unusual. Helping clients to improve their life situations and their capacity to achieve their full potential has been one of the central forces driving the profession since its modest mid-nineteenth-century beginnings.

TOWARD A DEFINITION OF SOCIAL WORK

What exactly is social work? Interestingly, although it is a well-established profession, any ten people will probably give you ten different answers. One weekend morning at a donut shop in Orlando, Florida, we asked ten people to describe what social workers do. We received the following responses:

- Social workers give out food stamps and money to freeloaders.
- I dunno.
- Don't they work at the welfare office?
- They help abused kids.
- My mom had one while she was in the hospital. She really liked that young gal!
- They work in mental hospitals.
- One helped my wife and I when we adopted our baby. He helped prepare us for parenting and has stayed in touch ever since. Now, some four years later, he still stays in touch.
- It is helping poor individuals to get services.
- Social workers are liberal thinkers that support programs for the poor.
- Help private and public agencies to help individuals in need.

Activity...Select ten people either at a local mall or at any other shopping area and ask them, "what is social work?" Write down their answers. Also, take notes on their nonverbal reactions to the question.

The variety of responses illustrates two major points. First, the profession is a diverse one, and this diversity means that the roles and tasks that social workers perform are varied and often poorly defined. Second, members of the general public are often confused about the profession. Many people simply do not understand exactly what the mission of this diverse profession really is. This confusion is deepened when social work professionals themselves define what they do on the basis of their scope of practice, using job-specific descriptions such as health care social worker, community organizer, adoptions worker, or mental health counselor. Today, the profession of social work remains flexible as it reflects a society where expectations are influenced by a market-driven, business-oriented service delivery system (Franklin, 2001). The diversity and broad purview of social work practice makes it difficult to reach a simple, all-inclusive definition of exactly what social work is.

Social work is not the only profession that is difficult to define; however, professions whose tasks are easier to outline are generally received more positively by the community. For example, most people are able to describe accurately what a dentist, a nurse, or a physician does, or they can quickly describe the role of a stockbroker or a lawyer. Defining exactly what a social worker does and is expected to do is a lot more complicated.

There is so much confusion about what social workers do that you might experience something like this: A woman at a holiday party asked her niece what her college major was. The niece proudly announced, "social work." A disquieting hush spread over the room, and the party seemed to grind to a halt. Some of her relatives looked shocked and glanced around at other family members in astonishment. When her father noted the reaction, he simply shrugged his shoulders and said, "that's nice," secretly hoping this career choice was "just a youthful phase" and that she would change her major before year's end. Today, although she has become a successful university professor of social work, her father and other relatives still refer to her as "a psychologist"! When asked why they keep making this mistake, they reply that they can usually define to others what a psychologist does, but defining social work takes a lot more time and effort. "Besides," her father still asks, "is there really that much of a difference?" This question, although at first it may seem alarming, is one that those in the profession must face daily. What complicated this distinction further is the fact that many of these professions do perform many of the same functions, making it difficult to formulate an exact role for social workers, particularly those in what is generally referred to as "direct practice" (Franklin, 2001; Dziegielewski, 2004).

Did You Know…March of each year is designated "Social Work Month."

Many social workers, old and new, have at least one or two stories about how their families reacted when they announced that they had selected social work as a career, and many of the stories will be similar to the one above. The confusion surrounding what social workers do, as well as their "image" of working primarily with the poor and disenfranchised in our society, complicates efforts to define what social work is. Or, indeed, what people perceive it to be. Now, keeping in mind the difficulties of making a simple definition—just what is social work?

Let us start by considering some of social work's key attributes. First, the profession generally involves addressing the needs of at-risk populations in a community. Second, in our society there is a common belief that people need to be helped and that the community sanctions, that is, "approves," this helping activity. Third, most of the activity performed and services provided are agency based, where social workers provide client services but also possess business acumen capable of understanding diverse administrative and profit-driven human service systems (Franklin, 2001). Fourth, social work is a profession and therefore requires a professional education as well as clearly defined ethical standards for practice. Becoming aware of and understanding these ethical standards, which are embodied in a professional code of ethics, is crucial to approaching professional practice regardless of the employment setting (Freud & Krug, 2002a). Now, let's explore these ideas more fully to develop an understanding of the breadth and depth of the profession.

Thinking about helping people focuses our attention on what social workers actually do. Through programs and intervention services, social workers help people—individuals, families, groups, communities, and organizations—in their day-to-day life situations (see figure 1). A hallmark of social work helping is its focus

Figure 1: A mother with her children and stepchildren is outside of a Boys & Girls Club. The club offers after-school, weekend, and summer programs and opportunities for children from first grade through high school.

on the interaction between person and social environment. While a psychologist, for example, would consider primarily an individual's psychological state in trying to help, social workers go beyond this to include the interplay between the individual's life situation and social environment.

In the provision of social work services, at-risk populations comprise those people who, for any number of reasons, are vulnerable to societal threats. Children and the elderly are often viewed as at-risk populations. Other people considered at risk are those who may be victimized by a person or group through a series of life events that leaves these people susceptible to unwarranted pain and resulting problems. Certainly the larger context impacts how we define at-risk populations. For example, the 2009 economic crisis that has led to home foreclosures and increased unemployment has moved many families into at-risk situations.

Sanction refers to the community's "blessing" or recognition of the need for a service or program. Professional sanctioning of services comes in many forms; state licensing or state registration as well as professional certification requirements are among the more common types. Community funding agents, such as the United Way, can also sanction an activity by supporting it financially. When a funding entity such as the United Way supports a social service agency, it is indicating its belief that the services provided are important to the community good. This type of support is often called having "the good stamp of approval." Having the legitimacy that comes from such support is essential in gaining community approval. Formalized public (or community) sanctioning of the provision of social services can also protect the public by distinguishing between authorized and unauthorized service delivery.

Agency-based practice consists of social work services generally conducted by or delivered under the auspices of social welfare agencies. Agencies can be public, funded by federal, state, or local tax dollars; or agencies can be private, funded by donations or foundations. Most practicing social workers are agency based, that is, they are employed by a social services agency; however, a small percentage do engage in independent professional social work. Independent practitioners are generally educated at the master's degree level or beyond. You will find it common for social workers, both students and practitioners alike, to want to become private practitioners in mental health and other health-related settings. Most professionals working in this area agree, however, that the old notion of long-term therapy has been replaced with brief interventions that clearly focus the social worker–client relationship that results in a clear emphasis on outcomes that are obtained in the fastest most efficient means possible (Dziegielewski, 2004; Franklin, 2001).

Professional education involves the preparation of individuals in social work practice. It takes place in baccalaureate and graduate-level degree programs at colleges and universities. Professional education begins in the classroom setting. This is expanded and strengthened by agency-based experiences through what is commonly called field education or internships. In their internships, students work in a specific field agency where they practice the skills and apply the theories taught in school. To further advance their professional education most social workers, following graduation, begin working in a social work setting under the direct supervision of an experienced professional social worker while also completing continuing education programs each year.

The last area among the key components of social work practice has to do with ethics and expected conduct. Each profession is established and coordinated under a professional set of standards, often referred to as a "code of conduct," that is designed to govern the moral behavior of those in the field. In social work, NASW through the National Delegate Assembly is tasked with maintaining and updating this document for the profession. It has been said that the social work Code of Ethics is one of the most comprehensive ever written. It is often used as a model for comparison by related professions. A copy of social work's Code of Ethics is included in appendix A of this book, and because it is critical to understanding professional conduct, it will be discussed further in subsequent chapters (NASW, 2000). The latest revision to the NASW Code of Ethics was approved by the Delegate Assembly and published in 2008. In addition to the NASW Code of Ethics, you will find that most state licensing and registration boards for social work practice also have a specified code of ethics that social workers must abide. When social workers seek licensure in the profession, they will be expected to adhere to both state board regulations as well as the NASW Code of Ethics.

In general, when defining social work practice, ethical and moral issues should always be evaluated (Reamer, 2009). Social workers use the guidelines for professional practice given in the Code of Ethics to understand their moral and legal obligations in assisting their clients. Social workers entering the field must not only be aware of this document; they must also agree to adhere to the standards it sets forth. Any questions about moral and ethical practice should be addressed by using the guidelines it provides. Therefore, the centrality of the Code of Ethics to all practice decisions is crucial to formulating a moral vision within our field that will help to determine both peripheral and procedural practices within the professional helping activities (Freud & Krug, 2002b).

Did You Know...In August 1996, NASW delegate assembly met in Washington, D.C., and updated social work's previous Code of Ethics. This was the first major revision since 1979. This updated and revised Code of Ethics went into effect January 1, 1997. The present Code of Ethics most individuals use as a reference point was published by NASW in 2000, with the latest revision made by Delegate Assembly in 2007.

SOCIAL WORK DEFINED

A definition of social work is not easy to formulate or apply. Most would agree, however, that the field of social work involves working actively to change the social, cultural, psychological, and larger societal conditions that most individuals, families, groups, and communities face (O'Hare, 2009). The helping process emphasizes the use of advocacy to create societal conditions that lead to a stronger sense of person-in-situation or person-in-environment; this promotes the community good, which benefits all individuals. According to this perspective, social work is directed to two ends: first, to help resolve the micro- and mezzoissues that clients face, and, second, to create societal macrochanges that prevent or ameliorate such problems for all individuals, families, groups, or communities.

To initiate the helping process, a social worker may begin by working with an individual or family on an issue. This microlevel work will continue until the issue is resolved; however, the task of the social worker does not end here (see figure 2). This is especially true when the social worker recognizes that the causes of the client's problems are not unique to that client. Many seemingly individual problems have deep roots in the policies and procedures of larger institutions. When these problems have the potential to affect others in the community the social work practitioner must take a macroperspective. If current policies or programs may harm others unless certain changes take place, the social worker is called to action. The worker begins macrointervention and moves to promote changes in the larger system.

For example, Ellen, a social worker employed in a family agency, learned that her client had been evicted from his apartment. After helping the client to find a new apartment, Ellen discovered that the first landlord had not followed eviction procedures as outlined in the city's ordinances. Ellen must decide what to do next. For most social workers the task of helping the client would not be considered complete even though the client now has a safe place to stay. The social worker may feel the need to continue helping this client and future potential clients who may also fall victim to this failed system enforcement. In this case, Ellen could begin working on macroissues by contacting city officials to ensure that local ordinances are enforced and to make them aware of the problems that can occur when ordinances are not enforced. Her advocacy efforts could prevent other people in circumstances similar to her client's from becoming homeless.

Figure 2: A respite house client writing a note to a social worker who is leaving for a new job. The respite house offers services and weekend-away-from-the-family programs for persons with physical and emotional disabilities. These programs give caregivers and parents a break from their caregiving duties.

Box 1: Various Definitions of Social Work

National Association of Social Workers

The professional activity of helping individuals, groups, or communities enhance or restore their capacity for social functioning and creating societal conditions favorable to this goal.

International Federation of Social Workers and International Association of Schools of Social Work

The social work profession promotes social change, problem solving in human relationships and the empowerment and liberation of people to enhance well-being. Utilizing theories of human behavior and social systems, social work intervenes at the points where people interact with their environments. Principles of human rights and social justice are fundamental to social work.

Colorado Chapter of NASW

Social work practice means the professional application of social work theory and methods by a graduate with a master's degree in social work, a doctoral degree in social work, or a bachelor's degree in social work from an accredited social work program, for the purpose of prevention, assessment, diagnosis, and intervention with individual, family, group, organizational, and societal problems, including alcohol and substance abuse and domestic violence, based on the promotion of biopsychosocial developmental processes, person-in-environment transactions, and empowerment of the client system. Social work theory and methods are based on known accepted principles that are taught in professional schools of social work in colleges or universities accredited by the council on social work education.

The Social Work Dictionary (Barker, 2003)

The applied science of helping people achieve an effective level of psychosocial functioning and effecting societal changes to enhance the well-being of all people.

In sum, a social worker's immediate focus is usually on a particular client population, providing service to individuals, couples, or families. These immediate efforts take a micro- or mezzoperspective; however, the macroperspective should never be ignored. Service provision in the field of social work cannot be defined simply, because in order to be successful it often must go beyond the identified client and include the larger system. Social work is both science and art. A skilled social worker must be knowledgeable about all aspects and perspectives of client helping and flexible in their application. The best-prepared social workers are those who recognize the importance of helping as a multifaceted process and who can easily move between micro-, mezzo-, and macrosystems with and on behalf of the client populations they serve.

BECOMING A SOCIAL WORKER

People sometimes call themselves social workers even when they do not possess the professional qualification needed to be a social worker. Many times newspaper articles, television news broadcasts, and talk radio hosts refer to "a social worker" whose mishandling of a case led to very negative consequences for an individual or family. The two following case examples are typical.

In the first case, a child abuse report is made to the state child protective services agency, but the child is not removed from the home. A few days later the child dies after a severe beating by the caretaker. The media reports that the social worker responsible for the case did not follow through with a proper investigation and ignored a variety of information and signals. The community is given the impression that if the social worker had just done his job, the child would still be alive. Unfortunately, there is no simple formula for handling such situations or for avoiding them in the first place—even though we want there to be one. The glaring fact is that a child has died and no one was able to help. This is disturbing to everyone, and it is difficult to look beyond the initial fact. However, if the event is not examined more deeply, other children could be placed in harm's way. It is also important to look beyond the media's simplified portrayal of the situation: Due to cutbacks and limited funding, or for other reasons, the person responsible for the investigation may not be a social work professional at all. In fact, this person's college degree and professional training may not be in the area of social work. For example, his education and training might be in the liberal arts, and he may have no formal training in the problem assessment and intervention methods essential to social work practice. Similarly, he may not be familiar with establishing the micro-, mezzo-, and macroperspectives needed to address client situations and problems.

The second case, which involves a young mother reported for child neglect, comes from the authors' firsthand experience. The mother has been sending her children to school without their coats, and the weather is too cold for such attire. A state social service worker visits the house and agrees that the mother seems unfit to handle the needs of her children. The state worker reports that the mother's responses to questions are very basic and brief and that she does not appear to understand the seriousness of what she is allowing the children to do. The worker recommends that all the children be removed from the home before any harm comes to them.

Later the case comes to the attention of one of the authors, who is facilitating the discharge of a client from the hospital. This social worker learns that the client is asking to be released from the hospital against medical advice. When she goes to see the client to discuss the situation, he explains that he recently suffered a small stroke and was immediately taken from his home and admitted to the hospital. He fears that his wife cannot care for their children properly, and he has to go home immediately. His wife is moderately retarded, and he has always handled most of the childcare. After the social worker talks with the client and places several phone calls to help him secure childcare coverage, he agrees to stay in the hospital for the

Name: Nicole Todd

Place of residence: Brooklyn, New York

College/university degrees: Western Michigan University, BSW, University of Chicago, School of Social Service Administration, AM

Present position: I currently work as a Counselor/Social Worker at the Hetrick-Martin Institute, home of the Harvey Milk High School. The Hetrick-Martin Institute is a non-profit organization that provides comprehensive youth services for gay, lesbian, bisexual, transgender, and questioning youth between the ages of twelve to twenty one.

Previous work/volunteer experience: Some of my other experiences include working in mental health, working with the Boys and Girls Clubs, being a community organizer, volunteering as a big sister, working as a human rights activist, and being a childcare worker.

Why did you choose social work as a career? I have always been drawn to working with people, particularly youth. I chose social work because it is one of the few disciplines that focuses on empowering groups and individuals within the context of their environment.

What is your favorite social work story? One of the benefits to working in this field is the opportunity to work in a variety of settings with various individuals. While living in Chicago, I had the opportunity to work at a Boys and Girls Club in the Robert Taylor Homes. This area is notorious for gangs, drugs, and violence. Many of the youth with whom I worked were frequently stereotyped as gang members. Working with these kids and their families, I had the chance to see first-hand the inaccuracy of this stereotype. Most of the kids I encountered were just like the young people I worked with in other settings: they have families who loved and cared for them, they strive to be successful, they desire love and affection, and they like to laugh and have fun. People need to realize that most individuals living in poor areas are not violent; rather, they are hard working, loving family members attempting to survive in a society that often criminalizes poverty.

What would be the one thing you would change in our community if you had the power to do so? I would like to change the way our community approaches social problems. I think it is crucial that all people within our society take responsibility and recognize that everyone's lives are affected when social injustices exist. I believe that if all individuals approached social problems with the perspective that it is the community's responsibility to address the problem, regardless of whether they feel personally impacted, our society would be more effective in creating social change.

---

remainder of his treatment. He agrees to stay because the social worker was able to make arrangements with some members of his church who will watch the children until his return home. Later that day, the client becomes very upset when a family friend tells him that his children are about to be removed from home. After receiving permission from the client to release information about the situation, the social worker contacts the state worker and tells him about the plan to care for the children. The removal decision is reevaluated, and because support is in place the children are not removed from home or the care of their mother.

In discussing the case, the social service worker obviously is frustrated. His caseload did not give him time to explore disposition options. He was also concerned that a child had died several weeks before in a case very similar to this one. Because of the attention paid to that case, he felt it was best not to take a chance on this one. He also did not realize that the mother was mentally retarded; he thought she might be on drugs or merely resistant to intervention. In trying to understand why he made such a limited assessment, the social service worker reports that he just did not realize the significance of the client's behavior. The worker reports that he has limited on-the-job training and that he often uses opportunities for inservice provision to catch up on his paperwork. Moreover, although this state requires that all social service workers have at least a four-year professional degree, his degree is in physical education.

Cases like these are all too common. For whatever reason—be it a desire to cut costs or a lack of recognition for professional intervention—there is a widespread but false impression that anyone can be a social worker and that anyone can handle the tasks and responsibilities expected of a social worker. Some people even believe they can be their own social workers.

For example, a plumber working for one of the authors asked her what she did for a living. When he heard she was a social worker, he smiled and said, "Oh, never needed one of them before; always do my own social work." When asked what he meant, he said, "Don't need somebody else to solve my problems. I can solve them for my family and myself. I had a lot of training on how to deal with people in school, and that helped." Such comments are very disturbing because they show that many people just don't know what social workers do. Furthermore, it was very tempting for the social worker to reply with "Yes, I know—I used to do my own plumbing too, but your expertise is why you are here now." When people assume that social work is simply everyday problem solving, they conclude that anyone can do it and that becoming a social worker is open to all. The irony in this statement is as pronounced as believing that everyone can do their own plumbing. Yet, because social work is such a diverse field and not as specific as plumbing, generalizations like this can be all too common.

Confusion also exists among helping and counseling professionals about who can be a qualified social worker. For example, at a public hearing held by the Florida Board of Mental Health Counselors, Marriage and Family Therapists, and Clinical Social Workers, a board member opposed the licensing of BSW and MSW social workers who do not do clinical social work. A marriage and family therapist added, "Anyone can do social work. There is such a thing as social work with a small 's' and 'w'."

On the surface this statement seems to make sense, and it warrants serious discussion. Certainly, all helping individuals must have "good" hearts and be compassionate as well as willing to help others. But can these qualities alone make someone a professional social worker?

Let's make a comparison. Suppose you have a sore throat, feel somewhat congested, and have hot and cold sweats. Your roommate says, "You may be coming down with the flu. Why don't you take brand X over-the-counter cold pills, use some brand Y throat lozenges, and stay home and rest." This could be very good, helpful advice, but does this mean your roommate is a medical doctor, albeit with a small "m" and "d"? Of course not—it seems crazy to even suggest that. Everyone knows that to be a medical doctor you need a formal education and supervised experience in a medical setting. You can't hang out a shingle that says "MD" just because you think you can diagnose some physical ailments.

So what are the requirements for becoming a social worker? Certainly there are personal attributes that a social worker must have. First, a social worker must like working with people. A social worker is involved with people from all walks of life. These people, who come from widely varying backgrounds, can have ideas and expectations very different from the social worker's own. Being aware of and sensitive to the beliefs of others is not always a simple task to accept and achieve. In dealing with different people a social worker must really want to understand the troubles that others face. So first of all, a good social worker must genuinely like working with diverse individuals.

Second, a social worker must want to help people. A professional social worker encounters all sorts of client problems, ranging from abuse and neglect to homelessness, from mental health issues to community-based substance abuse problems. A good social worker wants to help his clients in their efforts to figure out what is going on and how best to resolve their problems.

Third, a social worker wants the community to be a better place for all people. Through her professional activities, a social worker helps a specific client while at the same time she tries to better the community for all people. For example, ideally social workers want to end poverty and its debilitating effects on people and communities. Social workers envision communities where all people have access to decent housing and health care. They also strive to end unfair treatment of individuals, the "isms" that face millions of people today—racism, sexism, and ageism. The personal traits that foster the desire to work with and to help individuals, families, and communities are critical ingredients in creating a social worker. To finish the mix, however, these personal traits must be complemented by professional education and training. In the United States, professional social work education takes place in baccalaureate or graduate-level degree programs at specific colleges and universities.

Did You Know…The Council on Social Work Education (CSWE) is the only national standard-setting and accrediting body for social work education. It was organized in 1952 through the merger of two associations that coordinated baccalaureate and graduate programs, respectively.

For any U.S. college or university to offer a recognized social work educational program, it must meet the accreditation standards, more commonly referred to as EPAS (Educational Policy and Accreditation Standards) of the Council on Social Work Education (CSWE). CSWE is authorized by the Council for Higher Education Accreditation (CHEA) to set and oversee educational standards for social work programs across the United States and is the sole social work accreditation authority in the United States. The Council on Social Work Education (CSWE) was first established in 1952; at its inception there were 59 graduate schools and 19 undergraduate programs (Watkins & Holmes, 2008).

Other countries have their own accrediting bodies for social work education. For example, the Canadian Association for Social Work Education is responsible for accrediting programs in Canada, the Joint University Council for Social and Public Administration oversees social work educational programs in the United Kingdom, Finnish programs of social work are associated with the Scandinavian Committee of Schools of Social Work, Brazilian schools of social work are members of the National Association of Schools of Social Work, and Indian social work educational programs are members of the Association of Schools of Social Work. Overall, international accreditation associations can be found in nineteen different nations, in addition to five regional associations (Kendall, 1984). Although there are numerous accrediting associations throughout the world, the International Association of Schools of Social Work, in 2000, implemented a joint initiative with the International Federation of Social Workers to create global standards (http://www.iassw.soton.ac.uk/en/GlobalQualifyingStandards/Globalstandards august2002.pdf). The standards are an attempt to develop consistency among social work educational programs around the world.

Regardless of where a professional social work program is located, it must withstand the rigorous scrutiny of an accreditation process, which entails the validation of explicit standards of practice (Barker, 2003). Curriculum format and delivery, which is the heart of the educational experience, must be coherent, built on a series of specific behavioral competencies, and a supervised field placement or internship experience; through an internship the social work professional learns to apply in the field environment what has been taught in the classroom. Standards require that the faculty members who teach students possess certain types of degrees and in addition have professional work experience that can facilitate the education process. Accreditation standards also specify that a variety of institutional (e.g., college or university) resources be available. Finally, an accredited program must identify specific behavioral outcomes that all graduates are expected to demonstrate at the end of their course of study.

Activity...Ask to review your social work program's latest "self-study" for accreditation. Compare the self-study to the CSWE's Commission on Accreditation Handbook and the CSWE Educational Policy Accreditation Standards found in appendix E. In order to be accredited, your program must conform to these standards. Being part of an accredited program is important for your future development.

Attending and graduating from an accredited social work program is crucial for the future social work professional. Remember that only a graduate of an accredited social work program is recognized as a professional social worker. Because CSWE accreditation standards apply nationally, the public recognizes that a graduate of a BSW program in California has completed the same minimum educational requirements as a graduate of a BSW program in New Hampshire or Georgia. Uniformity of content through the country means that social workers can be hired in any state and meet specific educational requirements for employment and subsequent licensing in the field. This is particularly important for employers and supervisors of social work professionals because they can then assume that a particular educational background implies familiarity with certain content. Many employers report that this standardization of course content across social work programs makes social workers predictable employees in regard to what they have and have not been trained to do. BSW education prepares individuals for entry- or beginning-level social work practice—commonly referred to as "generalist practice." Baccalaureate studies occur in the junior and senior years of study. MSW education prepares individuals for advanced practice, also called specialization or concentration practice. (We will explore advanced practice in more detail in chapters 5 and 6.) An MSW program requires two years of full-time study; a person with a BSW degree may be eligible for advanced standing in a graduate program thus bypassing up to half of the graduate work through mastery of foundation competencies. The number of courses waived or exempted as a result of BSW study is different for each graduate program; the waived courses range from a maximum of one full year of full-time study to no courses waived. The decision on how to implement an advanced standing program and what courses to waive is made by the faculty of a particular social work program, not CSWE.

> *Did You Know…The initials BSW stand for Baccalaureate Social Worker and MSW for Master Social Worker. BSSW and MSSW also signify degrees in social work, Bachelor of Science in Social Work and Master of Science in Social Work. The most advanced degrees in social work are the DSW and the PhD. In most circles the MSW or the MSSW is considered the highest level needed to practice in the field.*

A number of schools of social work offer academic programs leading to a doctoral degree, either a PhD or a DSW (Doctorate in Social Work); such programs are not accredited by the CSWE, however. As a result, doctoral education varies greatly from school to school, with a program's focus set by its faculty's values and beliefs. Individuals pursuing doctoral degrees in social work will for the most part be employed in academic settings, though some will work in agency settings, primarily in administrative, supervisory, or research-related positions.

Social work education is a very large enterprise in the United States. According to the CSWE Commission on Accreditation, in June 2009, there were 665 total accredited programs, of which 470 were at the baccalaureate level and 195 offering the master degree. These programs are found in all fifty states and an additional 33 programs are in candidacy status—that is, working toward initial accreditation

(CSWE, June 26, 2009) In 2006, CSWE reported that more than 32,457 junior and senior social work students were working toward BSWs, 39,566 toward MSWs, and approximately 2,554 toward doctorates (CSWE, 2007). According to the CSWE 2006 statistics more than 6,100 full-time faculty members were involved in social work education (CSWE, 2007). In addition, the Group for the Advancement of Doctoral Education (GADE, n.d.) identified 81 doctoral social work programs in 2006–2007 including six programs in Canada and one in Israel.

MEMBERSHIP ASSOCIATIONS FOR SOCIAL WORKERS

All professionals have the opportunity to belong to membership organizations or associations that represent their interests. An association provides professional self-identity and an opportunity to meet colleagues in order to discuss ideas and share innovations in practice. Some of the most familiar professional associations are the American Medical Association (physicians), the American Bar Association (lawyers), and the National Educational Association (teachers).

Activity…Gather information about your local unit of NASW. Ask one of your instructors or a social worker in the community when your local unit of NASW will be meeting. Try to attend the next meeting. Also, find out when the state board of directors of NASW next meets. These meetings occur several times each year and are held somewhere in the state. Try to attend one of these meetings to see the process firsthand.

The National Association of Social Workers is the largest membership organization for social workers. According to NASW, its membership in 2008 totaled approximately 150,000 persons. One important point to recognize is that membership is voluntary. Indeed, the federal government's Department of Labor in its annual publication Occupational Outlook Handbook, 2008–2009 Edition, estimates that in 2006 there were about 595,000 professional social work positions in the United States, which means that many fewer than one-third of all social work professionals are members of NASW.

NASW was first organized in 1955, when five special-interest organizations joined together. These five interest groups were the American Association of Group Workers, the American Association of Medical Social Workers, the American Association of Psychiatric Social Workers, the American Association of Social Workers, and the National Association of School Social Workers. In addition, two study groups also joined: the Association for the Study of Community Organization and the Social Work Research Group. The ideas of all these groups were merged: to unify the profession (Alexander, 1995). Today, the national offices of NASW are located in Washington, D.C., only a few blocks from the U.S. Capitol.

NASW regards itself as a bottom-up members' organization. What this means is that governance and direction are established from below and responsibility lies with the units and chapters in each state. Each state has its own chapter of NASW, and each chapter is further subdivided into units. Each local unit covers a geographical area small enough to allow members to attend meetings and programs together.

After joining NASW, each member is assigned to a state chapter and then to a local unit that reflects where the person lives. Most local units conduct quarterly or monthly meetings. These gatherings run the gamut of formality, from the very formal meeting with an invited speaker to the informal after-work get-together. Unit meetings offer social workers from the same geographical area an opportunity to meet on a regular basis and strengthen their professional networks.

The state chapter coordinates activities between the local units and offers ongoing educational opportunities, known as continuing education, around the state. It also brings to the attention of its membership issues in the state legislature that could affect the profession or clients being served. Most state chapters provide their members with a monthly newsletter as well as professional and social activities such as an annual or biannual convention. The state chapter is staffed by a paid employee, generally a social worker, and is governed by a board of directors elected by the membership of the state and serving for a prescribed term.

Did You Know...NASW News, the monthly newspaper of NASW, is the primary source of news about opportunities for social workers across the United States. Each issue includes a classified section that lists, by state, job vacancies.

The national office of NASW comprises divisions ranging from membership services to political advocacy to publications. The national office is responsible for carrying out the policy of the national board of directors, which is made up of elected social work members from across the country. The national office also publishes a monthly newspaper that provides an exhaustive overview of social work around the country. Other member benefits include opportunities to purchase life and malpractice insurance and reduced registration fees to national meetings (see box 2).

Box 2: Benefits of NASW Membership
✓ Subscription to Journal of Social Work
✓ Subscription to NASW News
✓ State chapter and local unit memberships
✓ Credit and loan programs
✓ Hospital indemnity option
✓ Toll-free telephone to the NASW Information Center
✓ Representation on Capitol Hill in Washington, D.C., and in state legislatures
✓ Discounts for NASW-sponsored continuing education programs
✓ Subscription discounts for specialty journals
✓ Car rental discounts
✓ Credit card option
✓ Term life insurance options
✓ Malpractice insurance
✓ Job link

Through local units, state chapters, and the national office of NASW, individual social workers have numerous opportunities to affect the profession. By holding leadership positions, serving on various committees, and attending local, state, and national meetings, individual social workers mold the profession and give direction to future activities.

Social workers belong to such groups in order to support specific interests. According to Tourse (1995), special interest associations provide professional identity and professional cohesiveness, monitor specialized practice, broaden the sphere of professional influence, and encourage development of specialized theory and practice. In addition to NASW, there are about 54 other national membership or professional social work associations in the United States, although the exact number is not known. These various groups are based on a variety of attributes ranging from race and ethnicity to practice interests (see box 3 for examples of pro-

---

Box 3: Other Social Work Membership Organizations

American Association of Industrial Social Workers: Social workers employed in employee assistance programs

Association for Community Organization and Administration: Community organizers and agency administrators and individuals interested in macro-related issues

Council on Social Work Education, CSWE (2007): A professional membership organization of more than 3,000 individual members and graduate and undergraduate programs in the field.

North American Association of Christians in Social Work: Interdenominational association to assist members to develop Christian faith in social work practice

National Association of Black Social Workers: Association to influence practice and policy that impact all black ethnic groups

National Association of Oncology Social Workers: Individuals working with cancer patients

National Association of Puerto Rican/Hispanic Social Workers: Association concerned with advocacy and human services issues that impact the Latino community

National Federation of Societies of Clinical Social Work: State and regional societies that focus on issues relating to clinical social work practice

National Indian Social Workers Association: Association that works to develop understanding of native Americans and Alaska natives in tribal and nontribal organizations

Rural Social Work Caucus: Individuals working in and concerned about rural and small community human services

Society for Social Work Administrators in Health Care: Individuals seeking to promote effective social work health care administration

fessional associations). In 2002, the National Association of Social Workers convened a meeting, known as the "Social Work Summit II," of the presidents and chairs of these various associations. The group agreed to hold periodic meetings in an attempt to coordinate on various common matters and to create formal lines of communication between and among the various associations.

Most special interest groups sponsor an annual meeting, and some publish a journal or newsletter. These organizations' membership rolls are much smaller than the NASW's, they often do not have state or local unit groups, and they generally do not have paid staff to run the organization.

In 2007, eight social work associations—NASW, CSWE, Baccalaureate Program Directors, GADE, the Institute for the Advancement of Social Work Research, St. Louis Group, Association of Social Work Boards, National Association of Deans and Directors, Society for Social Work Research—met at the Wingspread Conference Center in Racine, Wisconsin, to discuss unification of the profession. That is, is it necessary and possible for the various social work professional associations to come together as one. Referred to simply as "Wingspread," the meeting was historic in many ways. First, it provided a forum for open discussion on the social work profession and its relevancy in a turbulent world. Second, participants were forced to honestly assess their respective associations as well as those of others. And finally, participants had to move outside of their own interests and consider what was in the best interests of the profession and the clients served. Meeting participants unanimously agreed on and signed a resolution calling for professional unification by 2012. A small work group was established to begin working on the details to create a new professional association. Sadly, at the end of one year of work, the group concluded this would not happen as some associations felt their organizational structures were too complex to fold into a new association. So in 2009 the profession remains splintered into many special interest groups, some working together better than others.

SUMMARY

Social work is a diverse profession. It is not easily defined and, as a result, is often misunderstood by the general public and the greater community. One thing remains prominent: social work is a profession of people helping people. Despite possible confusion about the daily activities of social workers, there is growing recognition that social work plays an important role in today's society. Children, seniors, families, communities, the rich, the poor, and the middle class are all represented among the many clients who benefit directly from social work. Social work clients are found in all quarters of the country. Social work is a global profession, similar to other professions, with many of its efforts designed to assist and stimulate an enriched and informed practice strategy rich in methods designed to incorporate strategy at the grass roots level.

Today thousands of people studying in colleges and universities are striving to become professional social workers. The role of these new social work professionals is an essential one because it is these individuals who will steer the profession and support the mission of micro-, mezzo-, and macrointervention well into the twenty-first century.

Questions to Think About

1. What do you say to a friend who, after learning that you want to be a social worker, states, "You won't make any money doing that"?

2. What do you think a meeting of professional social workers, such as a local NASW unit meeting, would be like?

3. Do you know any professional social workers? What personal qualities do they have that you think might be useful for a social worker?

4. Do you think there should be one professional membership association, such as NASW, or a number of membership organizations as discussed in this chapter?

5. Why do you think there is a general misunderstanding of social work?

6. What are some ways social workers could help to educate family and friends about what it is they do?

Chapter 2

Social Welfare: A System's Response to Personal Issues and Public Problems

WHEN YOU HEAR THE WORDS "SOCIAL WELFARE" WHAT COMES TO mind? Many people think of cash assistance to the poor, child abuse, and low-income housing. Before we begin to explain social welfare, test your knowledge of the subject by taking the following quiz. We expect that as a beginning professional interested in this field, some of your answers will be correct and others will be wrong; just give it your best guess.

Welfare Quiz

1. What is the Supplemental Nutrition Assistance Program?
a) the former food stamp program
b) prenatal food program
c) federal government support for faith-based food programs
d) food program limited to seniors

2. Who makes up the majority (more than 50 percent) of people receiving public assistance?
a) Mothers and their children
b) Unemployed adults
c) Senior citizens
d) Single females

3. In the United States there are more black individuals than white individuals living in poverty.
a) True
b) False

4. Many individuals who receive welfare benefits have children just to get more money from the government.
a) True
b) False

5. When we talk about the unemployment rate we are referring to those people who are not working at the present time.
a) True
b) False

Name: Jon Kei Matsuoka

Place of Residence: Honolulu, Hawai`i

College/University Degrees: BA, Social Sciences, Humboldt State University; MSW, University of Washington; MA, Psychology, University of Michigan; PhD, Social Work and Psychology, University of Michigan

Present Position and Title: Dean, Asian Counseling and Referral Service

Why did you choose social work as a career? I decided on social work as a career path in large part because of where I grew up in Los Angeles and the era in which I grew up. It was an era of social turmoil and progressive social change. In the end, it was an existential decision regarding how I wanted to devote my life energy and to what cause.

What is your favorite social work story? My favorite social work experience was when I was engaged in a community organizing effort in a rural Pacific community. In the face of massive development, we organized residents around an effort to gain a greater share of power and control over community resources. The Commission rarely, if ever, handed down a negative decision, but in this case it ruled that the developer could not proceed unless they conformed to a whole set of mitigation measures to reduce social impacts.

What is one thing you would change in the community if you had the power to do so? I would like to see a change in societal values regarding economic growth and prosperity and the distribution of wealth across sectors. Gross National Product is the primary indicator of a living standard, but it doesn't represent human well-being and the most important aspects of life. As a standard, "happiness" that is drawn from family cohesion and support, social capital and exchange, spirituality, and environmental kinship should replace old notions that are generally reflective of accumulated personal wealth and gain. If such a change were to occur, social work would be at the core and less peripheral to society and determine the course of social development.

---

6. The amount given to the poor in a "welfare" check is the same in all states.
a) True   b) True, but prorated for family size   c) False

7. More than half the people who receive welfare could be working but choose not to.
a) True   b) False

8. Which of the following groups are not considered to be welfare recipients by the U.S. government (circle all that apply)?
a) Schoolchildren   b) Seniors receiving social security
c) Armed forces veterans   d) Food stamp recipients
e) College students receiving Pell grants   f) Medicare recipients

9. Aid to Families with Dependent Children is the only federal program that provides cash assistance to poor families.

    a) True   b) False

10. In your own words define "social welfare."

Now turn to the back of this chapter to find the correct answers and see how you did. You'll find no answer to question 10. After reading this chapter come back and answer question 10 again. Be sure to compare your two responses to see if your first response is different from your second.

Are you surprised by some of the answers? Think about which questions you got wrong and what you learned from this brief quiz. Clearly, social welfare is a very complicated system that is often misunderstood.

In this chapter we discuss the dimensions of social welfare—in particular, what is meant by the term. We also direct attention to the role of the social work profession as well as that of each individual social worker within our current social welfare system.

TOWARD A DEFINITION OF SOCIAL WELFARE

To begin our discussion of the current social welfare system, we would like you to try this exercise. To prepare, take a piece of paper and a pencil and get ready to write down some of your ideas. First, think of your hometown or where you were raised. Second, imagine that you have the ability to make it into what you consider the "ideal" place to live. What kinds of services are needed to improve this neighborhood or community, bringing it to the perfectability that Specht and Courtney (1994) suggest is the profession's goal?

Social Services for Respect and Dignity

Use the following list of questions to suggest possible ideas and guide your thinking on this topic.

Housing and Employment

Would everyone have safe and affordable housing?

Would everyone be able to find employment?

Would employment pay well and include social and health benefits?

Education and Services

Would the education of the young be given top priority?

Would the community help all schools to get the services and supplies they need (e.g., fully equipped classrooms and state-of-the-art technology)—public and private alike?

Would a safe learning environment be provided?

Community Safety and Security

Would senior citizens be protected from abuse and neglect?

Would senior citizens have access to the services they need to complete their activities of daily living?

Would children be protected from exploitation and abuse?

Would domestic violence be tolerated, and what options would be available to those who are victimized?

Would discrimination based on race, color, age, sexual orientation, and the like be tolerated?

Would food services be provided to those who cannot afford to buy their own?

Your own list probably includes many more considerations that you feel are essential to address. Nevertheless, we believe that if you compared your list with someone else's you'd be surprised at how similar the two lists are. Most people agree that in an ideal place, all people are treated with respect and dignity (see figure 1). Further, most people agree that for a community to be responsive, it needs

Figure 1: Students in a self-contained public school classroom for persons with emotional disabilities. Biweekly sessions with the social worker help the students to discuss their feelings.

to be a place where members are valued for who they are and what they can offer to their community.

Seems too simple, doesn't it? And, it's true, some issues are much more difficult to address. Most people cannot agree on what services are needed in a community, who deserves these services, and how many services need to be provided. To complicate things further, communities are not static entities. A community needs to shift and change in response to the social, political, and economic conditions that exist at the time. Changing times can create and worsen social problems. For example, in 2007, the U.S. Bureau of the Census reported that 38 million people, about 13 percent of the U.S. population, were in poverty (Bishaw and Semega, 2008, p. 19), and of those living in poverty many are women, children, and the elderly. These people are also at particular risk of abuse and neglect, both physical and emotional.

Social and Economic Justice

The United States is among the wealthiest countries in the world. It has abundant natural resources and technology, yet many American citizens battle daily with poverty as well as emotional and psychological difficulties that can impede their ability to function at home and in their communities. In 2007, the National Center for Children in Poverty reported that 39 percent (28.8 million children) of all children lived in low income families, defined as a family with an income that is 200 percent of the federal poverty level (National Center for Children in Poverty [NCCP], 2008). The Children's Defense Fund reports that in 2006–2007, one in six children were in poverty (Children's Defense Fund, 2008, p. 5) Every day millions of children are ill fed, live in unsafe environments, and have no access to high-quality health care services. And just who are these young people? The Children's Defense Fund offers the following portrait of America's children in poverty:

> There are more poor White, non-Hispanic children than Black children. However, Hispanic and Black children are about three times as likely to live in poverty than White, non-Hispanic children. Children who live in inner cities, rural areas, in the South or in female-headed families are more likely to be poor. Children under age 6 are more likely to be poor than school-age children. Poverty and race are the primary factors underpinning the pipeline to prison. In fact, Black juveniles are about four times as likely as their White peers to end up being incarcerated (Children's Defense Fund, 2008, pp. 5–6).

Furthermore, it should be of no surprise that in 2000, the former Surgeon General David Satcher reported that one of the greatest challenges for the United States health care system is to respond to both the physical and the mental health of our children (Satcher, 2000). Yet, children seemed to have slipped off of the nation's political and social agenda even in the face of the overwhelming problems that American communities face.

The U.S. Census Bureau reported that in 2007, 36 percent of people over age 65, approximately 13.3 million, had an income below 200 percent of the poverty threshold (U. S. Census Bureau, [Current Population Survey], 2008). Sherman and

Shapiro (2005) estimated that without social security benefits, the incomes of nearly one in every two seniors falls below the poverty threshold (p. 1); with Social Security, the income for some 13 million seniors rises above the poverty threshold. There is now virtually universal agreement that the federal Social Security retirement program will not be able to meet the growing financial needs of our aging society as the baby boomers, persons born between 1946 and 1964, move into retirement.

The list of social issues facing America today goes on and on. Education, health care, employment, and the environment are just a few but also think of our global relations and obligations. The economic crisis that hit America with a vengeance in 2008 reverberates around the world.

Thus we are left with a daunting question and task—how do we determine who should get service priority? Different people have different impressions about what is needed. With each member of a community asked for input, the list of suggestions will grow.

For social workers, where the primary mission is to help individuals in need, it is clear that challenging **social injustice** is critical. The goals for helping vulnerable populations include (1) assessing and enhancing social resources; (2) acquiring and increasing economic resources; (3) increasing self-determined behavior; and, (4) influencing the social policies and organizational and community practices that affect the lives of vulnerable groups (Eamon, 2008). The role of the social worker is crucial in challenging systems that do not treat all individuals fairly. If social justice equates to "fairness" in terms of human relationships within the society, then conditions such as unemployment, poverty, starvation, and inadequate health care and education are only a few of the problems that will need to be addressed. Furthermore, what remains central is that often the conditions that exist are beyond the control of the individual. From a social work perspective, the existing conditions should not always be perceived as the fault of the individual based on his or her bad choices. Often circumstances develop because of coercion by others due to outside political and economic influences and to the social order of systems.

Addressing social justice and encouraging social change is so important to the field of social work that the preamble to the National Association of Social Workers Code of Ethics (NASW Code of Ethics, revised 2008) clearly states that "social workers are sensitive to cultural and ethnic diversity and strive to end discrimination, oppression, poverty, and other forms of social injustice." Therefore, our purpose in this chapter is not merely to develop a laundry list of society's ills and social injustices; rather it is to identify how individuals within a community can begin to address these issues.

When a society strives for community betterment by developing methods and programs to promote social justice and address social needs, this effort is often referred to as **social welfare**. Our perceptions of social welfare vary. The term can bring to mind a myriad of pictures, ranging from the homeless person walking to the shelter to the tornado victim receiving assistance from the Red Cross. From the varied perceptions of social welfare, two common but opposed threads emerge.

On one hand, many people believe social welfare recipients are those who cannot make it on their own and need society's help and intervention. Some people also believe that most recipients are responsible for the misfortunes they are experiencing and, in some cases, have created their own problems. This misperception contributes to the view that welfare recipients are "not worthy" or lack the motivation to help themselves. It is important to note, however, that not everyone feels this way. Many people, on the other hand, believe that some of the problems facing welfare recipients are not of their own making. They think that these problems should be regarded as similar to unexpected crises or traumas. In times of crisis, almost everyone expects victims to seek government assistance; such help is considered a right of citizenship.

The varying opinions that people can hold about government assistance and the wide range of social welfare services that can be provided make an accurate definition of social welfare essential. If the concept is defined too narrowly, people may focus on a few programs that account for only a small portion of welfare spending and decide that welfare policy is too specialized. If social welfare is defined too broadly, people may decide that entitlements are being given too freely and that society's limited resources cannot sustain this policy.

SOCIAL WELFARE DEFINED

Let's approach the concept of social welfare by examining several existing definitions. Later we will formulate a definition of our own (see figure 2).

Figure 2: Students with emotional disabilities posing in front of a mural they created during their study of insects.

Social Welfare Is . . .

♦ The assignment of claims from one set of people who are said to produce or earn the national product to another set of people who may merit compassion and charity but not economic rewards for productive service (Titmus, 1965).

♦ "Collective interventions to meet certain needs of the individual and/or to serve the wider interests of society" (Titmus, 1959, p. 42).

♦ A system of social services and institutions, designed to aid individuals and groups to attain satisfying standards of life and health, and personal social relationships which permit them to develop their full capacities and promote their well-being in harmony with the needs of their families and community (Friedlander, 1955, p. 140).

♦ A subset of social policy, which may be defined as the formal and consistent ordering of affairs (Karger & Stoesz, 2010, p. 3).

♦ A nation's system of programs, benefits, and services that help people meet those social, economic, educational, and health needs that are fundamental to the maintenance of society (Barker, 2003, p. 221).

♦ An encompassing and imprecise term but most often it is defined in terms of "organizational activities," "interventions," or some other element that suggests policy and programs to respond to recognized social problems or to improve the well-being of those at risk (Reid, 1995, p. 2206).

♦ A concept that encompasses people's health, economic condition, happiness, and quality of life (Segal & Brzuzy, 1998, p. 8).

♦ Society's organized way to provide for the persistent needs of all people—for health, education, socioeconomic support, personal rights, and political freedom (Bloom, 1990, p. 6).

Close examination of these definitions shows that, while the phrasing differs, the content and focus are similar. Let's identify the common themes in these various statements as we develop a comprehensive definition of social welfare. First, social welfare includes a variety of programs and services that yield some type of benefit to their consumers. People participating in any type of welfare-based program benefit because they receive some form of assistance. Many times the assistance, or social provision, is given in cash. At other times social provision is given **in-kind**, for example, as clothes or counseling that the consumer did not have beforehand.

Second, social welfare, as a system of programs and services, is designed to meet the needs of people. The needs to be addressed can be all-encompassing, including economic and social well-being, health, education, and overall quality of life.

Third, the end result of social welfare is to improve the well-being of individuals, groups, and communities. Helping those systems in time of need will later benefit society at large.

RESIDUAL AND INSTITUTIONAL SOCIAL WELFARE

In their classic work *Industrial Society and Social Welfare,* Harold Wilensky and Charles Lebeaux (1965) attempt to answer a basic question: Is social welfare a matter of giving assistance only in emergencies, or is it a frontline service that society must provide? As part of their discussion, Wilensky and Lebeaux developed two important concepts that continue to frame and influence our understanding and discussions of social welfare: residual social welfare and institutional social welfare (see box 1 for examples). Wilensky and Lebeaux (1958) defined the terms as follows:

Residual: Social welfare institutions come into play only when the normal structures of supply, the family and the market, break down.

Institutional: Welfare services are normal, frontline functions of modern industrial society.

Box 1: Examples of Residual and Institutional Programs

Residual	**Institutional**
Food stamps	Social security
Medicaid	Medicare
Head Start	Libraries
Temporary Assistance for Needy Families (TANF)	Health departments
Homeless shelters	Veteran's benefits

Residual Social Welfare

The residual conception of social welfare rests on the "individualistic" notion that people should take care of themselves and rely on government support only in times of crisis or emergency. People are not considered eligible for help until all of their own private resources, which may include assistance from the church, family wealth and inheritance, friends, employers, and so on—have been exhausted. Only then do public welfare efforts at assistance come into play. Therefore, in order to access residual social welfare services, people must first prove their inability to provide for themselves and their families. As a result the help received often carries the stigma of failure.

Qualifying for this type of service is often referred to as **selective eligibility**. When eligibility is selective, social services are delivered only to people who meet certain defined criteria. When a person needs cash assistance as a service, the eligibility determination procedure is commonly called **means testing**. To access means-tested programs, people must demonstrate that they do not have the financial ability to meet their specific needs. When a residual type of program provides cash assistance, clients must recertify their eligibility every few months. The recertification process is designed primarily to ensure that clients are still unable to meet their needs through private or personal sources.

People who receive residual services are generally viewed as being different from people who receive other kinds of services. They are often regarded as failures because they do not show the rugged individualism that is a cornerstone ideal of our society. Many times beneficiaries of residual programs are labeled as lazy, lacking in morals, and dishonest. They are often accused of making bad decisions and of needing constant monitoring because of their untrustworthiness. In short, people in residual programs carry a **stigma**.

Imagine for a moment that you are standing in the checkout line of your local grocery store. The person in front of you is paying for some items with food stamps. Noting this, you feel compelled to look more closely at what is being purchased. In the grocery cart are potato chips, soda, some candy, and beer, as well as other food items. You have similar items in your own cart. On a piece of paper, write down your first thoughts about this. Be honest, and allow yourself to express any thoughts you might have. One response to this kind of situation is shown in box 2.

The response illustrated in box 2 is not unusual. In fact, it is characteristic of the way many people view and react to beneficiaries of residual programs, and it raises some interesting questions. Do people receiving assistance have a right to entertainment? Or when they accept public assistance do they give up their right to the luxuries available to others not dependent on this social welfare service? As we will see in chapter 3, the history of social welfare is marred by a reluctance to help others in need. Residual programs and services are stigmatized, and those who need these types of services are constantly scrutinized. Many people believe that such services, although necessary as temporary forms of assistance or as last-resort charity, reinforce negative behaviors rather than promoting rugged individualism and a strong work ethic.

In summary, residual programs highlight narrow views of helping. Assistance is minimal and temporary and designed only to help people survive immediate problems or crises. These types of programs provide support only when no other support options are available. In other words, a residual program is a program of

---

Box 2: Food Stamps and the Video Game

Dallas Morning News. Letters to the Editor. January 1, 1983.

Last week I was passing through the checking line at a supermarket. In front of me was a young woman with two children about 5 and 6. She paid for her groceries with food stamps. On their way out they stopped by the store's video game machines. All three played the game, once each. In other words, the woman squandered 75 cents while letting taxpayers pay for the groceries. That money would have bought a dozen eggs for that "poor" family. I wonder if their color TV and stereo are working? I never have objected to my tax dollars being spent to help the truly poor, but I protest vehemently the idea of helping them pay for their entertainment or luxuries.

(Name Withheld)

Dallas, Texas

Name: Dianne Harrison

Place of residence: Tallahassee, Florida

College/university degrees: University of Alabama, BA, MSW, Washington University, PhD

Present position: Associate Vice President for Academic Affairs, School of Social Work, Florida State University

Previous work/volunteer experience: Former Dean of the School of Social Work, Florida State University; social worker in mental health settings; social work researcher and academician; certified sex educator; designed HIV prevention interventions; member of numerous community agency boards (telephone crisis hotline, women's prison, teen pregnancy program, local high school)

What do you do in your spare time? Aside from watching both of my kids play soccer, I read, watch movies, play tennis, and cook.

Why did you choose social work as a career? I did not really know much about social work but I knew I wanted to work with people. I went into a graduate program in social work basically because they offered me a scholarship. Once I experienced the courses and my first internship (in a mental hospital), I knew I had found a career that would be incredibly interesting and rewarding.

What is your favorite social work story? As a dean, I spent a lot of my time talking with social work alumni about their education and careers. On occasion, I would talk with both men and women who received their social work degrees but who never practiced social work. To a person, they each claimed that their social work education was a key to their success in their chosen career (whether it was law, banking, real estate, or parenting). Why? Because as social work students, they had all learned good communication, problem-solving, and people skills.

What would be the one thing you would change in our community if you had the power to do so? I would eliminate prejudices that are based on race, gender, physical ability, or socioeconomic differences. These kinds of biases and subsequent discrimination are a waste of our human energy.

---

last resort. In the 1980s, American public welfare programs were categorized as essentially residual in nature. Collectively referred to as "the safety net," these programs could be accessed only after all other avenues of assistance had been exhausted.

There are three important points to keep in mind regarding residual programs. First, these programs are all means tested. To be eligible for benefits people must document their inability to care financially for themselves and their families. In a typical residual program, clients are routinely means tested or recertified for continued eligibility every few months.

Second, residual programs can create barriers for those who seek assistance. Numerous eligibility criteria, which often force clients to produce a variety of supporting documents and evidence, can be disheartening. Continual recertification processes can thus encourage clients to give up, forgoing assistance even when their needs persist.

Third, residual programs carry a stigma, and recipients are not proud to receive services. The Supplemental Nutritional Assistance Program, more commonly referred to as the **Food Stamp Program**, is a typical residual program (see box 1). Recipients must qualify to receive program services, they must be recertified every few months by the state, and they are not viewed positively in the greater community.

Recall the food stamp recipient in our hypothetical grocery checkout line. How often do we look at what the person ahead of us is buying? Do we spend more time scrutinizing the purchases of those who pay with food stamps? If another person had been purchasing exactly the same items and paying with cash would our reactions have been the same? Probably not. Why? Since both individuals would have similar buying habits, why is there a difference in how these two people would be viewed? The sad reality is that the food stamp recipient carries a stigma. Some people believe that beneficiaries of residual programs such as food stamps cannot be trusted, are morally weak, and do not make good decisions. Food stamp clients are often thought to be different from people who do not receive public aid.

Institutional Social Welfare

The second conception of social welfare described by Wilensky and Lebeaux (1965) is institutional social welfare. This definition of social welfare gives it much broader scope and function than the residual definition does. In the institutional conception, the community is expected to assist individual members because problems are viewed not as failures, but instead as part of life in modern society. This broader community responsibility allows members in need to be provided services that go beyond immediate responses to emergencies. Help is often provided before people exhaust all of their own resources, and preventive and rehabilitative services are stressed.

Therefore, an institutional program, as opposed to a residual program, is designed to meet the needs of all people. Eligibility is **universal**. Institutional programs have no stigma attached and are viewed as regular frontline programs in society. In fact, institutional programs are so widely accepted in society that many are not viewed as social welfare programs at all (see examples in box 1). Institutional programs are often called "**entitlement programs**," meaning that services and benefits are available because of a person's earned status.

In concluding our discussion of residual and institutional provision of social welfare as outlined by Wilensky and Lebeaux, we must note the primary weakness of this framework: not all programs and services are easily classified as one or the other; some programs have both institutional and residual attributes. The **Head**

Start program, for example, is institutional in nature but is means tested and restricted to a particular segment of the population. One solution is to expand the traditional dichotomy and classify social programs on a residual-institutional continuum. A program's position on the continuum reflects whether it is more residual or more institutional in design and to what degree. Some questions to help guide the classification process include:

1. Is the program short term or long term?
2. Is the program open to all people or a selected group of people?
3. Do program participants carry a stigma?
4. Does the public embrace the program?
5. Is the program controversial?
6. How would you feel if you were a program participant?

Activity...Ask fifteen to twenty people to define the term "social welfare." Then ask them to list five social welfare programs of which they are aware. Review these responses in light of the work of Wilensky and Lebeaux. Do you notice any patterns in the responses? How many of the responses would you identify as residual, institutional, or a mix of both types? In analyzing these responses do you find that people have a narrow or a broad view of social welfare? How do you feel about the responses you have received? Do you think your respondents' views are accurate?

Although there are ways to classify social programs, ensuring that social justice is addressed through recognizing social stigma, misperception, and its influence on clients cannot be underestimated. The public does appear openly to support some forms of social welfare, but these feelings and expectations seem to vary based on individual perception and the service that is being received.

IS EVERYONE REALLY ON WELFARE?

Richard Titmus (1965), a famed British social scientist, argued that social welfare was much more than aid to the poor and in fact represented a broad system of support to the middle and upper classes. In his model, social welfare has three branches:

Fiscal welfare: Tax benefits and supports for the middle and upper classes

Corporate welfare: Tax benefits and supports for businesses

Public welfare: Assistance to the poor

Abramowitz (1983) applied the Titmus model to American social welfare. She identified a "shadow welfare state" for the wealthy that parallels the social service system available to the poor. She concluded that poor and nonpoor alike benefit from government programs and tax laws that raise their disposable income. In other words, were it not for direct government support—whether through food stamps or through a childcare tax exemption—people would have fewer dollars to spend and to support themselves and their families.

So, is everyone really on welfare? To address this question, let's focus first on college students. Did you know that college students are probably one of the largest groups of welfare recipients in the United States today? The vast majority of college students first attended public school, which was provided at no cost to them. Why? Because our government subsidizes the public school system. It is important for all children to have nutritious meals, and the daily school lunch is relatively inexpensive to purchase for all school students. In fact, try to buy the same meal in a restaurant and compare costs—the school lunch is much cheaper. Why? Because the government subsidies given to public schools lower the cost of these meals for all students. Okay, that's what happens in public school. Now consider the role of government in a public college. Compare tuition fees at a private college or university with those at a state- or community-supported institution. Why are tuition costs at the public college so much lower? Once again, the answer is simple: because of government subsidies. The government is very involved in subsidizing the educational needs of students at both the elementary and secondary and the college levels. Students are very much in need and dependent on these subsidies in order to complete their educations.

With all the support provided and the need for continuing support, doesn't it sound like welfare? Why then is there no stigma attached to this form of social provision? Some people may say, "I paid for my 'welfare' through taxes on my earnings, which makes me different from those people who did not." There is no easy response to this statement, and such attitudes continue to disturb social work professionals who do not agree with the distinction between the worthy and the unworthy that is often applied to social services. Is there really a difference in the welfare service provided? Could most individuals and families afford to pay the full tuition for college or the costs associated with operating a good-quality public school, including lunch? Government subsidies are important to the maintenance of society and are used by all people.

PUBLIC SOCIAL WELFARE

Social welfare is found in both public and private settings. "Public" refers to programs within the purview of state, federal, or local (city or county) government; "private" refers to services provided for profit and voluntary services.

Federal Welfare

One would think it would be easy to find out how much money the government spends each year on social welfare. That is not the case, and to make matters even more difficult, the published information is often sorely out of date.

Why is it difficult to determine the government's welfare expenditures? The answer rests with how you define welfare and what programs you end up "counting" as social welfare. For example, do you count the reduced school meals program, veteran's affairs, and section eight housing? The budgets for these three programs are in three different federal agencies, not part of one major federal welfare budget. What about Medicare and unemployment insurance? As you can see, trying to identify *all* welfare programs and their budgets is problematic.

Why are data out of date? If you search for *federal welfare expenditures* on the Internet, you might find a link titled "Annual Statistical Report Social Welfare Expenditures." Go there and you will find the Social Security Administration's *2002 Annual Statistical Supplement*, the most recent public document that identifies welfare expenditures; the government may once again publish welfare expenditure data, but as of February 2009, the 2002 report is the most current federal information available. Even so, the Social Security Administration reported data in 2002 that covered a brief time period, from 1965 to 1995. In other words, the 2002 data were already seven years old.

The federal government classifies social welfare into seven broad areas: social insurance, education, public aid, health and medical programs, veterans' programs, housing, and other social welfare (see box 3).

Social insurance has been and continues to be the most costly area of federal welfare, followed by education. In fact, on average over the years, these two areas account for approximately 70 percent of total federal welfare expenses, whereas public aid accounts for only 14 percent of the federal welfare budget. It is interesting to note, however, that when "cutting welfare" is discussed, the emphasis is on public aid. But what would happen, for example, if the federal appropriation for

---

Box 3: Federal Social Welfare Programs

Social insurance: Old-age retirement, workers' compensation, disability, unemployment assistance, railroad retirement, public employee retirement

Education: Elementary, secondary, and higher education; vocational education

Public aid: Cash payments under TANF, WIC, general assistance, emergency assistance

Veterans' programs: Assistance to veterans and their families, burial, health and medical programs, education, life insurance

Housing: Public housing

Health and medical programs: Hospital and medical care, maternal and child health programs, medical research, school health, other public health, medical facilities construction.

Other social welfare: Vocational rehabilitation, institutional care, child nutrition, child welfare, OEO and ACTION programs, social welfare not classified elsewhere, food stamps

---

supplemental nutritional assistance program, for example, food stamps, were cut? Let's look at the last official reported data from the *2002 Annual Statistical Supplement*. In 1995, the last reported year, $25.3 billion was spent on food stamps; if we were to be aggressive and cut "food stamps" by 50 percent or by $12.7 billion, it would seem like a big cut and a lot of money, right? Reducing food stamps by $12.7 billion reduces the total federal welfare expenditures by a mere 0.8 percent.

On the other hand, reducing federal education expenditures by 50 percent saves the government $182.8 billion and reduces welfare expenditures by 12.1 percent.

Who would suggest cutting education by 50 percent to reduce our welfare expenditures? Probably not many. But any number of people and groups will advocate that we are overspending on food stamps and need to cut welfare to "balance the budget."

State Welfare

State welfare programs differ across the country. Each state is able to develop its own set of social programs to augment the federal government's initiatives. Typically a state establishes rules and provides funds for statewide social agencies. State social welfare agencies include protective services for children and juvenile justice. Funding for state services comes from two sources: **block grants** from the federal government and state tax revenues. A *block grant* is a lump sum of funds given to a state, which then has the authority to determine how best to spend the dollars. The federal government imposes few rules on block grants, allowing each state to determine how programs will be structured. A state can also supplement block grant funding in order to expand services.

Local Welfare

City and county welfare programs depend on local taxes for funding. Such funds are primarily used for community protection and support, such as police, fire, and other basic local services. Funding and provision of most of these types of local social services are considered mandatory. By contrast, many government officials and community leaders see social welfare provision as a minimal, "fill the gap" measure. Those in power are usually reluctant to develop and sponsor "costly" local services. As with state government programs, the types and levels of local welfare programs vary by municipality. Because of their "gap filling" status, local programs are generally residual in nature. Typical local programs include emergency food relief and housing and clothing vouchers.

PRIVATE SOCIAL WELFARE

Private social welfare consists of for-profit and not-for-profit agencies, also called *voluntary agencies* or *nonprofits*. Examples of nonprofits include the United Way, Red Cross, Salvation Army, Boys and Girls Clubs, Girl Scouts, YMCA, YWCA, Jewish Community Centers, Catholic Charities, and Family Services.

Activity…Go to your local (county or city) welfare office. Look around and try to get a feel for the setting. What messages does the physical structure send to the clients? Does this environment seem like a typical business setting? Do the setting and staff suggest an interest in serving the clients, and are the clients made to feel important? How does this facility differ from a physician's office? What sorts of informational brochures are available to read? How long do clients wait before a worker sees them?

After you've visited a public agency, visit a private social service agency. What differences, if any, do you see between the two agencies? If differences do exist, what are they and why do you think they exist? Should there be any physical differences between public and private agencies?

Karger and Stoesz write that "confusion exists" around the role of private social welfare and characterize it as "the forgotten sector" (p. 150). For the most part, American social welfare has rested within the public domain since the 1930s when the government implemented a series of welfare programs to combat the effects of the Great Depression. As the government took on greater welfare responsibility, the voluntary sector's activities lessened (Karger & Stoesz, 2010, p. 4). With financial cuts in federal welfare funding taken hold in the early 1980s and holding well into the twenty-first century, private welfare has taken on new importance. This forgotten sector is now recognized as a crucial player in the delivery of social services.

The nonprofit sector relies on donations from public foundations and, to a much lesser extent, federal, state, and local governments. In order for nonprofits to provide services, their fundraising efforts must be successful. The success of fundraising depends on three factors: 1) the agency's ability to provide a high-quality program, 2) the agency's ability to communicate its successes, and 3) the community's financial ability to support the program. Karger and Stoesz (2010) suggest that the voluntary sector, while well received by the public, faces many challenges including commercialization, an increase in faith-based services, and the growth of private, independent practice (pp. 159–163). Therefore, in most instances, the level of private social welfare programming available depends directly on the financial well-being of the surrounding community. This dependence on private funding is particularly problematic during periods of economic turmoil, such as recession and rising unemployment. During these periods people have less money and time to donate to private charities, which in turn forces these organizations to make critical choices about which programs to close or cut.

According to the Social Security Administration, the role of the private sector in financing social welfare continues to grow, and this growth is needed to complement public social welfare expenditures and programs. Hoeffer and Colby (1998) referred to the private sector as the "mirror welfare state," a system of services that reflect public programs but are more supportive of the middle and upper classes than the poor.

Private welfare can be categorized into four areas: health, income maintenance (retirement), education, and welfare services. The data on private welfare are old with no recent reports published by the Social Security Administration. The old data do, however, offer some insight into the private welfare arena and allow us to consider its size and complexity today. In 1994 private welfare expenditures totaled $921.5 billion, a 99 percent increase over the 1985 level.

As with federal welfare spending, it's illuminating to examine where private sector funds are going. In particular, it is not the case that most of the spending, or even most of the increase in spending, is going to millions of poor people to gain the services they need. Of 1994 private welfare expenditures, $528.6 billion was spent on private health care; $204.7 billion was spent on income maintenance services, that is, retirement support programs. Thus health and income maintenance together accounted for nearly 80 percent of all private welfare expenditures. By contrast, $86.2 billion, 9.4 percent, was spent on private welfare services. So although overall private expenditures have increased, the majority of these funds have gone to assist not the poor but rather the middle and upper classes.

SOCIAL WORK IN THE SOCIAL WELFARE SYSTEM

Social workers make up the primary professional group in the social welfare system. But social work is not the sole social welfare profession. Given the broad definition of social welfare used here and in the social work literature, many other professional groups are welfare providers as well. Although it is possible to lump the various professionals together and classify them all as welfare workers, it is more accurate to recognize that some professions are more concerned than others with people's social, health, wellness, and economic welfare needs. A useful way to differentiate among professions is to classify their level of involvement as either primary or secondary.

The primary category consists of professions whose principal efforts are in the provision of social, health, or economic services. The principal activities of professions in the secondary category are not directed toward welfare, but their work does at times involve social, health, or economic service provision (see box 4).

Box 4: Examples of Social Welfare Professionals by Primary or Secondary Classification

Primary	Secondary
Social workers	Police officers
Mental health counselors	Librarians
Schoolteachers	Recreational specialists
Marriage and family therapists	Road crews
Psychologists	Government officials
Psychiatrists	Military personnel
Nurses	
Sanitation workers	

Look at the professionals listed in box 4. What is your opinion of who is included and where they have been placed? Do you think the professionals listed would agree with where we have classified them? For example, how would an elementary schoolteacher react to being described as a welfare worker? We believe that many of the professionals listed above would openly disagree that they are welfare providers. It's possible that the stigma attached to programs and services offered under the rubric of "welfare" might influence their reactions. To explore this possibility, how do you think these professionals would reply to the following question?

> Do you as a professional provide a program, benefit, or service that helps people meet those social, economic, educational, health, and wellness needs that are fundamental to the maintenance of society?

We believe that as this question is framed—without addressing the concept of social welfare provision openly—the vast majority of the professionals listed in box 4, whether classified as primary or as secondary service providers, would answer yes. The simple truth is that although few professionals think of their activities in this way, providing welfare services is an integral part of their jobs.

Our broad definition of social welfare also suggests some rethinking of rigid ideas about social work. The social work profession has its roots in efforts to help the poor and disenfranchised (Hepworth, Rooney, & Larsen, 2002), neither of which is considered a desirable client population according to a narrow definition of social welfare. These efforts historically meant promoting and enhancing individual client well-being albeit in a societal or environmental context.

Over time, however, the traditional role of the social work professional has expanded. According to social work's revised Code of Ethics:

> The primary mission of the social work profession is to enhance human well-being and help meet the basic human needs of all people, with particular attention to the needs and empowerment of people who are vulnerable, oppressed, and living in poverty. A historic and defining feature of social work is the profession's focus on individual well-being in a social context and the well-being of society. Fundamental to social work is the attention to the environmental forces that create, contribute to, and address problems in living.
>
> . . . These activities may be in the form of direct practice, community organizing, supervision, consultation, administration, advocacy, social and political action, policy development and implementation, education, and research and evaluation. (NASW, revised 2008)

For the social work professional, social welfare methods and programs now address diverse populations, which can include those who are homeless, suicidal, homicidal, divorced, unemployed, mentally ill, medically ill, drug abusing, and delinquent, just to mention a few. Moreover, the term "client" is now used inclusively and can mean individuals, groups, families, organizations, and communities.

Adopting, in essence, the institutional perspective, the social worker must strive to restore and enhance client wellness and to provide preventive as well as basic, brief services. Strategies to assist clients must address all of these areas because often the factors involved are intertwined and interdependent (Dziegielewski, 2004; Skidmore, Thackeray, & Farley, 1997).

> *Activity...Now for a moment, pretend to be a United States Senator or a member of the United States House of Representatives. Your assignment is simple: balance the federal budget and eliminate the projected 2004 $307 billion deficit, which does not include the cost of the Iraq War. Go the following web site—http://www.budgetsim.org/nbs/shortbudget 04.html—and follow the directions. You will be asked to increase, decrease, or maintain expenditures for the federal government. Items you will consider include maintaining the 2001 and 2003 tax cuts, how you want to deal with the Iraq war, and the administration of justice.*

The Fading "Public" versus "Private" Distinction

Changes in the social welfare environment have blurred once-clear distinctions in social work—for example, whether an agency that employs a social worker is public or private. For simplicity, "public" agencies are understood to be primarily, if not totally, funded through tax-supported dollars. It is the public agency that is regarded as most representative of social welfare services and programs. Most people believe that these agencies have primary responsibility for residual or means-tested social welfare programs. "Private" agencies, on the other hand, are believed to be voluntarily supported and to rarely have tax-supported dollars as part of their basic budgets. If public and private agencies were distinctly different, these straightforward definitions would suffice. However, in today's social service environment nothing could be further from the truth. There is no longer any clear distinction between public and private agencies because their funding and the services they deliver so often overlap. Many private agencies now actively seek public or tax-supported funds, and many public agencies now contract with private agencies and individual providers to provide services to their clients. Because private agencies can specialize in a way that public agencies, with their broad responsibilities, cannot, such contracts allow public agencies to secure services that they do not have the budget or the skilled personnel to offer on their own.

In addition to this blurring between public and private agencies a dispersion of social workers across both the public and private sectors has placed social work practitioners in new roles. Traditionally, social workers served in the public sector because these agencies and programs assumed primary responsibility for the poor and the underserved. Today, however, social workers practice in many different agencies that have many different goals and allegiances.

Cost Containment versus Quality

For all social workers the current state of social work practice mirrors the turbulence in the general social welfare environment. There is little consistency in the delivery of social welfare services as primary emphasis is placed on cost containment. Social welfare program administrators, forced to justify each dollar billed for services, may reduce the provision of what some see as "expendable services" designed to promote the mental health and well-being of clients. They may be tempted to regard the role of social workers as adjunct to the delivery of care and to cut back on professional staff or replace them with nonprofessionals simply to lower costs. These substitute professionals have neither the depth nor the breadth of training that social work professionals do. The result can be substandard professional services.

The employment of these kinds of paraprofessionals, though cost effective, is not quality driven. When social services are rushed or minimized, issues such as the individual client's sense of well-being, ability to self-care, and family and environmental support may not be considered. The involvement of social work professionals is thus essential to ensuring that personal, social, and environmental issues are addressed and clients are not put at risk of harm.

For social workers, a client who is discharged home to a family that does not want him is at risk of abuse and neglect. A client who has a negative view of herself and a hopeless and hapless view of her condition is more likely to attempt suicide or come to some other harm. Many paraprofessionals and members of other professional disciplines differ from social work professionals in that they do not recognize the paramount importance of culture and environmental factors to efficient and effective practice. Their outlook may enable the delivery of "cheap" service, but the care provided is substandard.

As social service administrators strive to cut costs by eliminating professional social work services the overall philosophy of wellness can be sacrificed. It is important to note, however, that staff reorganizations and reductions in social welfare services are rarely personal attacks on social work professionals. The changes and cutbacks in services and those who provide them are responses to an immediate need-cost reduction. Fluctuating employment and downsizing of social work professionals, as with allied health professionals, simply reflects the fluctuating demands of the current market (Dziegielewski, 2004; Falck, 1990).

SUMMARY

So what is social welfare? The residual view suggests that welfare support should be temporary, only for the poor, and as minimal as possible. If we look at actual public welfare spending, however, it seems that social welfare as practiced is much broader. In fact, everyone in society is a welfare recipient of one type or another.

Similarly, the role of the social work professional is broader than many people expect. Originally, social workers served the poor and disenfranchised; however, over the years the role of the social worker has expanded tremendously. Many social work professionals now provide services outside of the traditional social welfare realm. This diversity of style, task, and approach makes defining exactly what social workers do difficult. Clarity of definition has been further complicated by changes in scope of practice, roles served, and expectations within the client-professional relationship.

In the turbulent social welfare environment social work professionals face a constant battle of "quality of care issues" versus "cost containment measures" for clients (Dziegielewski, 1996; 2004). In addition, they must strive to maintain a secure place as professional providers in the delivery of social welfare services.

Quiz Answers

1. a) the former food stamp program

2. a) Mothers and their children. Approximately 60 percent of all welfare recipients, according to the U.S. Bureau of the Census, are mothers and their children.

3. b) False. The majority of people in poverty are white.

4. b) False. Under federal welfare rules a family on welfare that has another baby will not receive any additional benefits.

5. b) False. The unemployment rate identifies only those people not working who actively looked for a job within the past thirty days.

6. c) False. Each state determines the amount a family receives on public assistance. As a result, a person in Florida receives a different amount from someone in Alabama.

7. b) False. According to reports by the U.S. Bureau of Labor Statistics, more than 70 percent of public assistance recipients are women with children, children, and senior citizens.

8. All the groups listed are participants in programs the federal government defines as "social welfare." As a result, all of the groups are welfare recipients.

9. b) False. Trick question—AFDC was replaced by TANF—Temporary Assistance to Needy Families in 1996.

10. Revise your answer to this question using the information presented in this chapter.

Chapter 3

How Did We Get Here from There?

TIME FOR A BRIEF HISTORY QUIZ:

1. Why is the year 1492 important in American history?
2. The New Deal was the name given to what set of programs?
3. What did the Emancipation Proclamation address?
4. What important event took place in Seneca Falls, New York, in 1848?
5. Where was an immigrant arriving at Ellis Island most likely to be from?
6. What is Salem, Massachusetts, perhaps best known for?
7. The United States acquired California, Nevada, Utah, and parts of Texas, Colorado, New Mexico, and Wyoming as part of what act or event?
8. What document preceded the U.S. Constitution?
9. What does the term "Seward's Folly" refer to?
10. What was at issue in the Dred Scott Case?

So, how did you do? (The answers are at the end of the chapter.) For most people taking this quiz the results are mixed. A few of the questions seem easy while others are complete mysteries. Yet each of these questions addresses a meaningful part of our American history. The importance of being familiar with such events is twofold: 1) it is important to know what has happened simply to be an educated citizen and 2) knowledge of the past can help us to understand both present and future societal developments.

In the field of social work, as in other disciplines, knowing the history of the profession is essential to understanding its past, present, and future (Alexander, 1995; 1997). Social work has come a long way from its early beginnings, transcending its origins within religious orders, to serving as good Samaritans (Leighninger, 2008). Unfortunately, however, studying history and looking at what happened in the past may not seem as exciting as learning about direct social work practice, policy, or social action. When history is discussed in the classroom or in less formal situations, it is almost always received with an air of indifference and reluctance. As one student remarked, "It's over and done with, so why should I be concerned about it? I want to learn how to help people. What happened two hundred years ago won't help me today."

Name: Rachel J. Blais, SC

Place of Residence: Morgantown, WV

College/University Degrees: BA, Psychology/Religious Studies, Merrimack College; MA, Religious Education, LaSalle University; MSW, West Virginia University

Present Position and Title: Home Visits, St. Mary Catholic Church; Vocation director, Sisters of Charity of Seton Hill

Why did you choose social work as a career? I come from a family of seven children. Both of my parents struggled to take care of us. We received help from different organizations. I was grateful for those organizations, and hoped that I too someday could help others and make a difference. For the past 20 years or so, I have been involved with peace and justice and doing social work indirectly. Many values were similar to the social work profession, so I decided to go back to school and work on a MSW. I'm hoping that with my MSW, I will be able to do more.

What is your favorite social work story? I arrived at my regularly scheduled appointment to visit an elderly woman who was on hospice care. Her sister answered the door and was pretty upset because her sister was dying. I stayed with the family for several hours, and we prayed with the dying person. My presence calmed the family, and the woman went into a coma and died peacefully the next day. I was honored to be able to be with the family during this difficult time.

What would be the one thing you would change in our community if you had the power to do so? I live in a college town where housing is expensive. It is very difficult for single parents or single people to find affordable housing. I would love to build several apartment complexes for these groups of people.

Is this statement really valid? It's true that in social work practice, regardless of the model or technique employed, the emphasis is on the here and now. Nevertheless, most social workers recognize the importance of history in their practice. For example, when first meeting a client, the social worker asks probing, thoughtful questions about the client's past. This systematic accumulation of information is referred to as gathering a social history or a **psychosocial history**. A social work practitioner would never consider the social history that he completes on each client useless information. In particular, the social history is important to understanding and exploring the client's growth and development process as well as to identifying possible effects of events and relations with others in the client's past.

The past offers valuable clues to interpreting the present and anticipating the future. History is essential to helping all of us better understand who we are and how we got here. It also influences our future decisions. Indeed, some people take

Activity...Contact your state NASW office and ask for names of local "Gold Card" members. These are people over age 60 who have been members of NASW for at least twenty-five years. Try to meet them to talk about social work twenty to thirty years ago. What do they see today that is different from when they started out in the profession? How do they think technology is influencing social work and social welfare?

the extreme position that we are so profoundly influenced by the past that it actually determines the future. This theory is called "determinism."

Whatever degree of importance we place on history, it is obvious that people—sometimes intentionally, sometimes unintentionally—use past experiences as a frame of reference for current and future experiences. For example, a baby only has to burn her hand once not to put it on a hot stove; in adulthood people rarely try this again because they know they can be painfully hurt. Although the causes and effects may not be clearly linked, a similar process can govern the relations we develop throughout our lives. Therefore, the importance of history should not be underestimated. We hope we have sparked your interest in history as a way to understand the roots of social welfare and general aspects of social work practice. In many cases considering the experiences of the past can teach us valuable lessons worth remembering.

Did You Know...Harry Hopkins, a social worker, was one of President Franklin D. Roosevelt's closest friends and was the administrator of a Great Depression program called the Federal Emergency Relief Administration.

This chapter will make a brief foray into social welfare history. In the past, comprehensive examinations of social welfare history have been undertaken by others (Axinn & Levin, 1982; Chambers, 1967; Jansson, 2004; Katz, 1986; Lubove, 1969; Trattner, 1989), and this area is well worth the effort of further investigation. We will briefly examine significant events and trends that influenced the emergence of our current American social welfare system.

THE ELIZABETHAN POOR LAW OF 1601

Most social work historians would agree that the watershed year for social welfare was 1601, when English poor laws were "codified" or brought together under one law. This codification is commonly called the *Elizabethan Poor Law of 1601*. Colonial America adopted the central tenets of this law, and many of its principles continue to underpin the design and implementation of our current social services.

An important note of caution: Let's not fall into a simple trap and believe that welfare began with the Elizabethan Poor Law of 1601. Karger and Stoesz (2010, pp. 41–42) tracked the development of the English poor laws back through a series of events to the mid-fourteenth century. Gilbert and Specht (1981, p. 17) noted that modern-day social welfare has roots in the Reformation period and the Middle Ages. And Trattner (1989), in his classic work *From Poor Law to Welfare State*, traced the roots of American welfare efforts to the ancient Greeks and Romans. In advanced social policy courses, you'll learn more about the rise of social welfare as a system, but for our purposes, we will begin with the Elizabethan poor laws.

Before 1601 in Europe welfare attempts to assist people in need were generally viewed as the province of the church. With the advent of the industrial era, great changes occurred in society. Many new and better paying jobs were created, and men and women of all ages were encouraged to apply. Rural communities began to decrease in population as people left the limited and shrinking opportunities of farm life for what the industrialized cities offered. Unfortunately, the promise of more jobs and a better way of life was not fulfilled for everyone, and many became unemployed and homeless. The newly destitute turned to the churches, the traditional providers of assistance to the poor. With the ranks of the poor growing to unprecedented levels, however, these urban churches did not have the resources or the expertise to cope with the swelling numbers of rural migrants and their assorted needs.

Faced with a growing population of urban poor, the English government implemented a series of sweeping reforms in an attempt to gain control of this problem. The result, the 1601 poor laws, radically changed the form, function, and scope of welfare assistance. First, the poor laws redefined welfare as no longer a private affair but a public responsibility. Second, the 1601 laws identified local government as the public entity responsible for the poor. Last, the poor laws denied relief if family resources were available (Katz, 1986, pp. 13–14).

In addition to setting the parameters for public aid, the 1601 poor laws divided potential recipients into two groups, the **worthy poor** and the **unworthy poor**. The worthy poor included the ill, the disabled, orphans, and elders. These people were viewed as having no control over their life circumstances. A second group of the worthy poor consisted of people who were involuntarily unemployed. Although they were seen as bearing some responsibility for their own situations due consideration was given to the fact that their misfortunes were beyond their control. The unworthy poor, on the other hand, included the vagrant or able-bodied who, while able to work, did not seek employment (Cole, 1973, p. 5).

Overall, when services were provided, assistance was first given to the worthy poor who were considered helpless to control their situations. Some assistance was provided to those who were involuntarily unemployed. No assistance was given to the unworthy poor, who were treated with public disdain.

COLONIAL AMERICA

The provision of public assistance in colonial America was tenuous at best. Influenced by strong Puritan and Calvinist views, most citizens regarded both the worthy and the unworthy poor as morally flawed. They believed that the poverty-stricken had somehow caused their own distress. This belief released society from any obligation to lend assistance and implied that it was the impoverished individual who was responsible for finding and providing a remedy. Aid or **charity assis-**

tance, in any form, was thought to lead to an "erosion of independence and self-respect; the spread of idleness and the loss of the will to work; the promotion of immorality in all its ugly forms; and the increase in public costs through the growth of poorhouses and jails" (Katz, 1986, p. 40). Benjamin Franklin, for example, strongly opposed public aid: "[The] 'natural state' of working persons was one of sloth, wastefulness, and dissipation. The Common people do not work for pleasure, but for necessity" (Williams, 1944, p. 83). Relief, Franklin felt, simply provided an opportunity for people to return to their natural state of laziness at the expense of others.

Did You Know…In 1931, Jane Addams, social worker and founder of Hull House, was the first American woman to win the Nobel Peace Prize.

Based on a weak commitment to a public welfare system, American colonists developed a dual system of relief that was modeled on the English poor laws of 1601. The resulting programs provided aid to the worthy poor, who in this case comprised the ill, seniors, orphans, widows, and veteran soldiers. The unworthy or able-bodied poor, who included the involuntarily unemployed, were provided little if any assistance.

Assistance to the worthy poor was grudgingly given, primarily in the form of **outdoor relief**, which provided minimal assistance to individuals and families in their homes. The unworthy poor were not provided aid in their homes and often were encouraged to move on to another county. If assistance was required, the unworthy poor were required to return to their counties of origin to receive it. The unworthy poor were eligible, however, for **indoor relief**—the poorhouse.

Funds to support the worthy and unworthy poor were collected by local taxes assessed by the local **overseer of the poor**. In many ways this overseer was a colonial version of a social worker. The overseer was responsible for identifying who constituted the poor, what their needs were, and what the community should do to address their needs (see figure 1).

In general, the availability and accessibility of colonial public services reflected Franklin's negative view of relief. These programs were often designed with a punitive intent, in an effort to shame people out of their poverty. Typical of this approach was the auctioning of the poor into apprenticeships and indentured service to the lowest bidder—that is, the person who would charge the community least for taking a pauper off its hands. Another example of this reluctant attitude toward helping the poor is the treatment of a widow in Hadley, Massachusetts. In 1687, this woman, who had no resources of her own, was forced to live for two-week periods with those families who were "able to receive her" (Trattner, 1989, p. 18). Further, in Pennsylvania those receiving aid were required to wear a scarlet letter "P" sewn on their right sleeves "with the first letter of the county, city, or place of his or her residence underneath" (Heffner, 1913, p. 11). Even more

Figure 1: A United Charities of Chicago caseworker or visiting housekeeper calling on a family about 1909. Formed when the Relief and Aid Society merged with the Bureau of Charities, United Charities of Chicago was the city's oldest private welfare organization. It was the best known of the family service agencies and worked on prevention, easing desperate social situations, and creating better living environments.

Box 1: Selected Dates in American Social Welfare History

1601	Elizabethan Poor Law enacted by the English parliament.
1642	Plymouth Colony enacts first poor law in the colonies.
1657	Scots Charitable Society, first nonprofit organization focused on the provision of welfare, founded in Boston.
1773	First public mental asylum opens in Williamsburg, Virginia.
1790	First public orphanage opens in Charleston, South Carolina.
1798	U.S. Public Health Department established.
1817	Gallaudet School, a school for the deaf, founded in Hartford, Connecticut.
1822	Kentucky opens first public asylum for deaf people.
1829	First asylum for the blind opens in Massachusetts.
1841	Dorthea Dix begins investigations into mental institutions in the United States.
1853	The Reverend Charles Loring Brace organizes Children's Aid Society.
1854	President Pierce vetoes federal legislation designed to use federal land for state asylums.
1865	Freedmen's Bureau is organized.

Check the *Encyclopedia of Social Work* under Distinctive Dates in Social Welfare History (Alexander, 1997) or the chapter by Leighninger (2008) for a comprehensive review of social work history and other dates and events. What events in social welfare history impress or surprise you? What do you think is the most important social welfare event on the list? Why?

extreme was a 1754 North Carolina law that allowed vagrants to be whipped in the public square simply because of their impoverished state (Rothman, 1971, p. 25).

Not all potential recipients of social welfare services were viewed negatively in colonial America. For example, veteran soldiers who had fought for the colonies were given a more honored status because, when poor, they were generally considered to be among the worthy poor (Axinn & Levin, 1982, p. 31). As early as 1624, veterans could expect to receive social welfare benefits as a right earned by the service they had provided. It was believed that since veteran soldiers had shown their willingness to risk life and limb in defense of their nation they deserved public aid if they needed it. Providing relief to veterans was not considered the responsibility of the town; rather it was the obligation of the colony. In addition, veterans did not have to satisfy residency requirements in order to receive aid (Axinn & Levin, 1982, p. 31). In summary, two of the primary components of colonial poor relief legislation—local responsibility and residency—did not apply to veterans because they enjoyed the status of the worthy poor.

Did You Know…Jeannette Rankin, a social worker, was the first woman elected to the U.S. Congress, representing Montana, in 1916.

NINETEENTH-CENTURY REFORM EFFORTS

Throughout American history, immorality and pauperism have been tightly linked by the idea that poverty is a direct result of an individual's flawed character. Nineteenth-century programs intended to help the poor sought to do so by changing their behavior and making them overcome their personal failings. At the same time public opinion turned hostile toward all those living in poverty. As Benjamin Disraeli lamented following passage of the punitive 1834 British poor law reform, it was "a crime to be poor" (Trattner, 1989, p. 49).

Despite the strong resistance to helping the poor, poverty was widespread enough that some form of relief was necessary. Welfare organizations became more formalized and commonplace, particularly in large urban areas. The most prominent agencies for the delivery of social welfare services and programs for the poor were almshouses and asylums, charity organization societies, and settlement houses.

Almshouses and Asylums

The roots of service provision for the poor and disabled can be traced back as far as the 1700s to the first **almshouses**. Almshouses, also called "poorhouses," were intended to be places of refuge for the poor, medically ill, and mentally ill of all ages. In colonial times, however, caring for the family and its members was considered a private matter, and people who had any kind of family support were kept at home. Therefore, the almshouse was an "option of last resort," providing shelter and relief for society's outcasts—those who were poor, incapacitated, or suffered from contagious disease. Severely underfunded, almshouses were dirty and disease filled, and the workers who staffed them, who can be regarded among the earliest practical social workers and health care providers, often became ill (Dziegielewski, 2004).

Did You Know...In 1713 William Penn founded the first almshouse, in Philadelphia. In 1736 a second almshouse was founded at Bellevue Hospital in New York. The almshouse in Bellevue usually housed the mentally ill and later became one of the most famous mental health hospitals in the country.

At one point, almshouses housed all of the poor. However, eventually children were removed from almshouses by the efforts of the Children's Aid Society and later placed in orphanages. In 1851 the mentally ill were also removed and sent to improved facilities and asylums primarily through the crusading efforts of Dorthea Lynde Dix. Basically, the almshouse as "holding tank" was replaced with more segregated forms of institutionalized care such as orphanages and other residential facilities, referred to as "asylums."

Asylums, the most common human service organizations in the 1800s, became the homes for the blind, deaf and dumb, and insane and developed regimented programs formed by a guiding trinity of work, religion, and education.

Tightly regulating an inmate's life with scheduled activities throughout each day, according to Rothman (1971, p. 145), reflected belief in the "therapeutic value of a rigid schedule." For example, in the Pennsylvania Hospital, patients were awakened at 5:00 a.m., "received their medicines at six, and breakfast at 6:30; at eight o'clock, they went for a physical examination, and then to work or to some other form of exercise. At 12:30 they ate their main meal and then resumed work or other activities until six, when everyone joined for tea" (Rothman, 1971, p. 145).

As can been seen from this cumbersome schedule, labor was a central component of asylum life. Inmates, as they were being taught jobs, learned the "value" and "importance" of work. This training, coupled with the regimented schedule, in theory imparted "habits . . . necessary for patients' recovery" (Rothman, 1971, p. 146). A poem allegedly written by a young woman in the Texas Asylum for the Blind reveals the negative side of work as the cornerstone of welfare programming:

> *Work, work, work*
> *till the brain begins to swim;*
> *work, work, work*
> *till the eyes are heavy and dim;*
> *seam, gusset, and bond,*
> *bond, gusset, and seam*
> *till over the buttons I fall asleep*
> *and sew them on in dream.*

Did You Know…The first American charity organization society was established in Buffalo, New York, in 1877.

Charity Organization Societies

A second innovative approach to combating poverty was the **Charity Organization Society (COS)**, founded in London, England, in the mid-1800s. Besides its significance as a social welfare development, the COS is important to the history of social work because some social work historians view its founding as the profession's birth event. The first American COS, modeled after the British program, was founded in Buffalo, New York, in 1877 by the Reverend Humphrey Gurteen.

In the mid-1800s, charitable efforts proliferated in American cities, resulting in many duplicated and uncoordinated programs. COSs sought to organize the various charities within a city in order to reduce program duplication. A second objective was for COSs to certify the needs and claims of clients in a systematic, investigative fashion. Thus only those in need could receive services from the various charities. Finally, COSs sought to change the lives of the poor through home visits by volunteers.

COSs subscribed to the philosophy that poverty was a consequence of moral decay and the eradication of the slum depended on the poor recognizing and correcting their personal deficiencies (Boyer, 1978, p. 144). The **friendly visitor**, a key volunteer in the COS movement, was to establish a personal relation with each client through "home visits" and by serving as a role model, to help the poor change their behavior. The 1889 Buffalo Charity Organization Society Handbook declared that the friendly visitor soon would be a power in the home.

> In a very short time the houses would be clean and kept clean for her reception. Her advice would be sought. . . . In a word, all avoidable pauperism would soon be a thing of the past when the poor would regard the rich as their natural friends. (Gurteen, 1882, p. 117)

Women volunteers, particularly those from middle and upper class families, were preferred for the role of friendly visitor. These women would be able to demonstrate and foster the values of the successful family to less fortunate individuals and families. In essence, by psychological and social osmosis, poverty and its companion evils would be uprooted through the kind works of middle class ladies. Specifically, Gurteen wrote,

> [All that is] needed to make our work a grand success . . . is hundreds of women from the educated and well-to-do classes, especially women of our city, who as mothers and daughters, coming from bright and happy homes—homes adorned by virtue and radiant with love, can impart to the cheerless tenement or the wretched hovel, a little of their own happiness. (1882, p. 116)

The COS movement also relied on female volunteers to staff the various organizations. As COSs became more accepted and formalized, the role of women changed. For example, COS women, by the end of the nineteenth century, were paid for their work, and COSs became a primary employment arena for women. It is interesting to note, however, that the first COS administrators were men and the first female administrator, Mary Richmond, was not appointed until late 1891.

Did You Know...Frances Perkins, a social worker, was the first woman appointed to the U.S. cabinet when in 1933 she was named secretary of labor.

In summary, the COSs were an important development in the history of social work because they provided the basis for the modern social service agencies of today. The workers they employed were some of the first to deliver social services in the home setting to poor and disenfranchised people. COSs provided an opportunity for systematic investigation of those in poverty and need. Home visitation, which today remains a highly valued social work intervention technique, allowed volunteers to learn more about individuals and their environments.

Did You Know...The first social work educational program started in 1898 as a summer training course at the New York Charity Organization Society. It later became Columbia University School of Social Work.

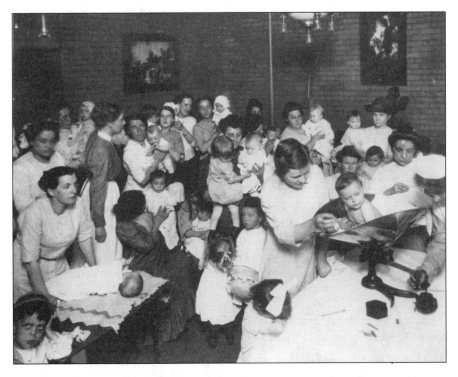

Figure 2: The Infant Welfare Society was founded in 1911 when the Milk Commission and the Children's Hospital Society joined forces. It trained nurses to staff milk distribution stations where they weighed babies, promoted proper nutrition, and provided mental and emotional guidance for women, children, and families.

Settlement House Movement

Another major British innovation also crossed the Atlantic during the mid-1800s and made a significant impact in the American social service arena. Known as the Settlement House Movement, its philosophy was remarkably different from that of the COSs. The Settlement House Movement sought the causes of poverty in macro- rather than microsystems. For example, poor education, lack of health care, and inadequate housing were considered the primary reasons for poverty. The settlement house was an actual house in a neighborhood where the workers lived year-round coordinating and providing programs, activities, and services directed to the needs of their neighbors.

The most famous nineteenth-century settlement house was Hull House, founded by Jane Addams and Ellen Gates Starr in 1889. Located in a poor west side Chicago neighborhood, Hull House forged a strong bond between neighborhood immigrants and social workers with its efforts to bridge the gulf between rich and

Name: Janina Henson-Dinio

Place of residence: Kitsap County, Washington

College/university degrees: St. Theresa's College, BA in Journalism; University of Washington, MSW

Present position: Therapist, Case Manager, Consultant/Minority Mental Health Specialist

Previous work/volunteer experience: Public Relations, Advertising and Training Manager, International Corporate Bank; teacher of Spanish and journalism; writer for local newspaper

Why did you choose social work as a career? I had always been sensitive to the need to help and provide human services. As an activist in my country of origin—the Philippines— I was part of a group that sought to address social inequity. When I migrated to the United States, I saw that the need to serve minority communities is just as great here. Even today, many services available to mainstream communities are not accessed by minority communities owing to lack of information and to language and cultural barriers. I see my role in the community as being a conduit of information from minority communities to professional and volunteer service providers and vice versa.

What is your favorite social work story? On many occasions, I have thought of going back to journalism due to the pressures of changing state and federal contract requirements and the unrelenting pace of change. At these times, I hesitated from taking that crucial step when people stopped me on the street and thanked me for the support and assistance I had provided them in a time of need. This "psychic income" compensates for a lot of the aggravation associated with clinical social work in the community mental health setting.

What would be the one thing you would change in our community if you had the power to do so? I have been in the helping profession for less than a decade. For social workers to survive stress and burnout, I would implement true outcome-based practice and decrease regulations. If bureaucrats are truly to manage by outcomes, social workers must be given the leeway to develop the objectives and programs necessary to achieve desired outcomes, guided by quality and service norms rather than regulations.

poor (Leighninger, 2008). By the beginning of the twentieth century there were more than one hundred settlement houses located in the United States.

The Settlement House Movement initiated the macromodel for social work practice, more commonly referred to as "community organization" and "group work practice." Problems were seen as resting not with the individual but at the larger organizational or community level. Poverty was the result not of an individual's lack of morality but of a system that kept wages low, did not enforce housing or health codes, and maintained a marginalized working class. Through client empowerment, problems could be confronted and social resources redistributed.

> *Did You Know…The Scots Charitable Society, organized in Boston in 1657, was the first voluntary society in the colonies to focus on welfare needs.*

THE TWENTIETH CENTURY

At the dawn of the twentieth century, the United States was poised to become a world economic leader. By the 1920s, economic prosperity seemed to come within reach of a growing number of Americans. Yet for blacks and immigrants economic gains were elusive. Blacks continued to suffer racism and discrimination under nineteenth-century Jim Crow laws. As immigration increased, laws inspired by xenophobia (fear of foreigners) framed social policy initiatives.

The prosperity of the first quarter-century quickly unraveled in the worldwide depression of the 1930s. By 1929, 1.6 million people were unemployed, and by the mid-1930s, nearly one in four Americans were unemployed.

Everyone knew someone—a brother, sister, father, mother, aunt, uncle, grandparent, or friend—who was out of work. Poverty was no longer a distant concept reserved for blacks, immigrants, and other minorities. Very quickly, the philosophy that the poor were morally depraved and had no work ethic became unacceptable because now more people had become poor who were never poor before. The new poor were everyone's friends and family and didn't fit the image of the lazy, immoral poor.

With the presidential election of Franklin Roosevelt, relief measures were immediately put in place, followed by the ambitious **New Deal** programs. These programs were funded and coordinated at the federal level and dramatically changed government's ambivalent role in social welfare.

The most important New Deal initiative was the Economic Security Act of 1935, which established the social security system to provide cash assistance to retired workers. This act—which also established the precursors of AFDC and unemployment insurance—became the organizing framework for the federal social service system. By the end of the twentieth century, it has been amended on numerous occasions to include cash assistance, health benefits, and services for the disabled, the blind, families, children, and seniors.

The New Deal included initiatives directed toward a variety of people. The Federal Emergency Relief Act, the Civilian Conservation Corps, and the Works Progress Administration formed the backbone of the New Deal. All of these programs were unprecedented in that they were developed and coordinated by the federal government, but like local relief efforts of the nineteenth century they made work a condition of relief.

> *Activity…Go to a library and read, generally on microfilm, newspapers from the 1930s. Try to get a feel for life during the depression. Then visit a local nursing home or senior center to meet people who lived during the depression. Ask them how the depression affected their families and neighbors and how did it influence the rest of their lives.*

The New Deal essentially affirmed the federal government's role in social welfare. The national effort was unparalled in American history, until the massive social movement of the 1960s.

Social Reform in the 1960s

By 1960, slightly more than one in five Americans lived in poverty. In 1962, Michael Harrington's classic work *The Other America: Poverty in the United States* helped the nation to rediscover this poverty in its backyard. The short book had a profound impact within the halls of Congress and reawakened nationwide debate on the role of government in combating poverty.

In the early part of his administration, President Lyndon Johnson declared a "war on poverty" that would make full use of the nation's resources. The resulting initiative—later referred to as the "Great Society" programs—brought a new federal presence into local communities far different from previous welfare program efforts. Guided by the phrase "maximum feasible participation" of the poor, welfare programs involved the poor in local decision making in their neighborhoods and communities.

The coordinating agency for the Great Society was the Office of Economic Opportunity (OEO). Typical new welfare strategies include assistance to newborn babies and their mothers (Women, Infants, and Children—WIC), preschool education (Head Start), health care for seniors (**Medicare**) and the poor (**Medicaid**), employment programs for young adults (Job Corps), community action programs that encouraged neighbors to marshal resources, legal services for the poor, food stamps, and model city projects that were designed to provide assistance to the poorest neighborhoods.

Did You Know...Social worker and civil rights trailblazer Whitney M. Young Jr. became the executive director of the National Urban League while serving as dean for the Atlanta School of Social Work. He also served as president of NASW in the late 1960s.

The Great Society was spurred by a newfound belief that the nation could fight and win any battle it chose, and the War on Poverty had no borders. The Peace Corps, developed in 1965, sent volunteers to nations around the world to work in poor communities. Volunteers in Service to America (VISTA) was a domestic version of the Peace Corps with volunteers working in low-income American neighborhoods.

By the end of the 1960s, the Great Society was under growing attack for being too costly with too few benefits to the larger society. During the presidential administration of Richard Nixon, the influence of the OEO was minimized, and numerous programs were scrapped. In their place Nixon proposed an innovative guaranteed annual income for the poor—a "negative income tax." Known as the Family Assistance Program (FAP), Nixon's plan would have subsidized a poor family by $2,400 a year. FAP required work or job training with the states eventually having full responsibility for program operation. This controversial proposal was ultimately rejected by Congress, but it was nevertheless a dramatic attempt to establish a minimum income based on work requirements.

The 1980s and 1990s: A Return to the Work Ethic

With the election of Ronald Reagan to the presidency and a more conservative Congress, the attacks on public service relief programs became more numerous and boisterous. Numerous federal public assistance programs were eliminated while others had their funding cut and their eligibility requirements tightened to weed out the unworthy poor. The results of this realignment were dramatic. Palmer and Sawhill (1984, pp. 363–379) found that 500,000 families were removed from AFDC and an additional 300,000 families received reduced benefits. One million people were eliminated from food stamp rolls. In 1985, the National Anti-Hunger Coalition charged that the federal government was not spending allocated funds for the WIC nutrition program, depriving thousands of pregnant women and newborn infants of health and nutrition services.

Children, women, seniors, and minorities were the primary victims of the Reagan welfare reforms. The message of the 1980s was clear: First, public assistance was contributing to the national debt. Second, only the truly needy, the poorest of the poor, would be helped with a "safety net" to ensure survival. Third, welfare was a state and a local, not a federal, concern.

The safety net approach places responsibility for helping the poor and disadvantaged at the doorstep of local government and private sources; the federal government becomes a resource of last resort. To achieve this purpose the Reagan administration adopted three overriding goals with regard to income security programs: 1) reduce short-term spending by implementing changes in entitlement programs; 2) turn over welfare responsibility to the states; and 3) promote reliance on individual resources rather than create and maintain dependence on governmental benefits (Storey, 1982). The result was

> a patchwork of programs at the federal, state, and local level that results in gross inadequacies in education. . . . We have developed too few resources to prevention and maintenance, and too many to picking up pieces after the damage is done. On the other hand, the United States has established a broad welfare system for the non-poor while the middle and upper classes and corporate America are able to take advantage of many benefits and, to a large extent, have become dependent on government support. (American Assembly, 1989, p. 34)

Welfare reform continued in the 1990s with the 1992 presidential election of Bill Clinton, who promised to "end welfare as we know it." His ambition came within reach with later developments in Congress. The midterm congressional election in 1994 brought a Republican sweep, and in their "Contract with America" conservative congressional Republicans made welfare reform a top priority.

In 1996 Congress essentially ended federal relief programs with the passage of the Personal Responsibility and Work Opportunity Reconciliation Act. In other words, Clinton's pledge "to end welfare as we know it" became reality. The new law abolished specific categorical programs and provided federal block grants to the states. Today, the federal government is no longer responsible for operating public welfare programs. No longer does the country have a national welfare program. Rather each state operates its own set of public welfare services, each with its own set of eligibility criteria, program rules, and benefits. Another way of looking at public welfare is to recognize that the nation has fifty different welfare programs, each operating under a different set of rules. Commonalities come from conditions placed on federal block grants: a lifetime limit of five years of relief, a work requirement, and participation in job-training programs.

According to the Federal Welfare Reform Act of 1996, all adult welfare recipients are required to work, be registered for work, or be participating in a job-training or educational programs. The food stamp program—now run by the states—has similar eligibility criteria; failure to follow these work guidelines results in program disqualification. This welfare reform act also ended the AFDC program, in place since the New Deal. It was replaced by Temporary Assistance for Needy Families (TANF), a short-term program that incorporates lifetime limitations and work requirements.

The Clinton administration can claim a number of achievements: lowest number of people receiving public welfare, an increase of child support payments by 80 percent, increased availability of housing vouchers, the creation of incentives to save, such as the *Individual Development Acccounts*, increased minimum wage, protected Medicare and modest health care reform, immunization rates raised to an all-time high, and the enactment of the largest health care act for children (Children's Health Insurance, CHIP).

COMPASSIONATE CONSERVATISM AND THE NEW MILLENIUM

Moving into the twenty-first century, President George W. Bush pledged a new approach to social welfare, which he referred to as "compassionate conservatism." Essentially this philosophy relies on the private, voluntary sector to provide assistance. Through volunteerism and private, nonprofit and faith-based organizations, people in need of help are provided with locally developed programs. At the same time, the compassionate conservative philosophy seeks out programs and policies that support the traditional two-parent family, strategies that encourage a rewards-based public education system, public assistance programs that are temporary in nature and support individual responsibility, and, when appropriate, providing assistance, both monetary and in people, to third- and fourth-world nations. What emerged was a federal welfare program that was almost 180 degrees opposite the 1930s New Deal program or the 1960s War on Poverty. President Reagan's stance that "government is not the solution but the problem" was almost completely realized under compassionate conservatism.

Obviously not supporting compassionate conservatism, comedian Robin Williams, in the character of Mork, said compassionate conservatism is like "a Volvo with a gun rack."

Yet, when looking at the Bush years, one must recognize that slightly less than eight months after he took office, the United States was attacked; eighteen months after 9/11, in March 2003, the United States invaded Iraq, and this war became the singular focus of the Bush administration. Others might argue that the Bush presidency was not preoccupied with Iraq, but we will leave that analysis to the historians.

By the time President Obama took office in 2009, the nation's economy was in dire straights—unemployment was rising, people were experiencing foreclosure on their homes, and businesses were collapsing. The pressures felt in the United States were reverberating around the world, and we experienced the impact of a global economy, albeit in a negative manner. People understood that Main Street and Wall Street were connected.

Compassionate conservatism suggests that the private sector should intervene and help those individuals and families who are caught up in the national financial tsunami. But the problems are so large, so complex, and so interwoven that the private, voluntary sector is not capable of intervening in such massive national unemployment and the negative impact of a declining economy. We will see whether the government moves to a more balanced approach to social welfare, one that marries the public and private sectors in a comprehensive, coordinated effort.

The Bush and Obama administrations are too recent for detailed discussion not fraught with emotion. Read the papers, stay informed, and watch to see what unfolds over these critical years. Make sure your debate is fair and accurate, no matter your position.

SUMMARY

American social welfare history is marked by a deep mistrust of the poor. Persistent beliefs that the poor are immoral and lacking either the ability or the desire to work have inspired repeated attempts to condition relief on work and improved behavior—and, above all, to make relief as difficult to obtain as possible. Social welfare and ensuring social justice is much bigger than simply programs to support the poor and disadvantaged such as Section 8 housing and food stamps. The federal government provides support to a variety of groups: banks requiring bailouts, farmers needing subsidies, and cities requiring federal loans to make payrolls are just some of the many acceptable forms of welfare. In these circumstances, however, bankers, farmers, and mayors do not consider themselves "welfare recipients"; rather, federal supports are viewed as necessary subsidies that benefit the community.

Workfare, training programs, and stringent program eligibility requirements, coupled with ongoing recertification in order to continue receiving even minimal assistance, are the punitive features of today's federal and state welfare systems. When it comes to poverty Americans are inclined to blame the victim as much as ever. Rather than maintaining a dignified helping system accessible to the poor, American welfare policy is designed to exclude people and to discourage clients by constantly setting hurdles to eligibility.

The 1996 welfare reform is an example where the knowledge of history can help us understand what is happening today. The philosophy that undergirds today's welfare provision reflects some of Franklin's admonitions. The reluctance to acknowledge government responsibility continues, and with a lifetime limit on years of eligibility for welfare, so do deep concerns about dependence. Recipients are to be forced into a totally independent and self-reliant mode of existence.

Throughout its history, finding the appropriate balance between public and private responsibility has plagued American social welfare. There is a clear record of national ambivalence and resistance toward welfare services and the poor. The current debate on welfare is an extension of a discussion threaded through the nation's fabric since colonial times. The lack of national consensus on who is to receive what type of social provisions for what period of time and on how these services will be funded means that the debate will continue well into the twenty-first century. Therefore, social workers are challenged to promote social justice by working toward increased and improved services for all groups within the society. This challenge supports the notion that social justice is a human issue and much more than just a legal or moral issue (Monroe, 2003). Primary importance needs to be placed on: (1) understanding the current social, political, and economic environment; and (2) using this knowledge to educate and mobilize the community and other stakeholders to work together to identify and address social problems and to develop effective programs designed to address these needs.

Movies to See

Movies on social welfare history rarely win Academy Award consideration or excite producers. The following videos, while not specifically detailing social welfare history, help us to better understand people and their conditions in the past.

Across the Sea of Time: 1920s New York City through the eyes of Russian immigrants.

All Mine to Give: Orphaned children in nineteenth-century Wisconsin are put in different homes in order to survive.

America, America: In the 1890s, a Greek youth immigrates to New York City; emotional presentation of an immigrant's challenges.

April Morning: A solid portrayal of a teenager's life in the American colonies immediately before the American Revolution.

Attacks on Culture: A brief, forty-nine minute, examination of the U.S. government's legislative attacks on Native Americans.

Autobiography of Miss Jane Pittman: An examination of life from the Civil War through the 1950s as remembered by a 110-year-old former slave.

Avalon: A Russian Jewish immigrant family moves to New York City.

Black West: An examination of African American cowboys, the unsung heroes of the West.

Grapes of Wrath: Classic John Steinbeck story of family's search for a better life than in 1930s depression Oklahoma.

The Molly Maguires: Interesting film set in the 1870s Pennsylvania coal country, as the Irish try to organize a union.

Roll of Thunder, Hear My Cry: Black teen copes with depression, poverty, and racism in 1930s Mississippi.

Separate But Equal: An examination of Thurgood Marshall as the NAACP attorney whose U.S. Supreme Court case led to the end of segregation.

Sounder: A sharecropper is forced to steal to feed his family; family deals with poverty and racism in the 1930s.

Wild Women of the Old West: The stereotype of the quiet housewife is broken with this analysis of women in the 1800s.

A Woman Called Moses: An examination of the life of Harriet Ross Tubman, a fugitive slave, founder of the underground railroad, and leader in the abolitionist movement.

Quiz Answers

1. In October 1492 Christopher Columbus reached the Bahamas, marking Europe's first documented contact with the Americas.

2. The New Deal was the name given to a set of social and economic programs established under the leadership of President Franklin D. Roosevelt in the 1930s to combat the depression.

3. The Emancipation Proclamation freed slaves in areas (rebellion states) no longer loyal to the union.

4. In Seneca Falls, New York, in 1848 women rights advocate Elizabeth Cady Stanton organized a convention that generated a declaration of women's rights.

5. Earlier immigrants arrived from northern and western Europe. By 1900, there was a significant rise in people from eastern and southern Europe.

6. In the late seventeenth century nineteen people were executed for witchcraft in Salem, Massachusetts.

7. In 1845 the United States annexed most of what is now Texas. Mexico ceded the remaining land in 1848 following the Mexican-American War.

8. The Articles of Confederation, adopted in 1777, united the colonies; it created a one-house congress.

9. In 1867, William Seward negotiated the purchase of land, now Alaska, from Russia for $7.2 million. It was called "Seward's Folly" because, until the discovery of gold, people saw little value in the far away purchase.

10. Dred Scott, a Missouri slave, sued for his freedom in 1847. The 1857 Supreme Court decision held that slaves were property and had no claim to the rights of citizenship.

Chapter 4

So You Want to Be a Social Worker!

THERE ARE NUMEROUS JOBS FOR SOCIAL WORKERS THROUGHOUT the country in cities, suburbs, and rural communities. According to the U.S. Department of Labor (DOL), through 2010 employment opportunities for social workers will be "faster than average" (http://www.bls.gov/oco/ocos060.htm). The growth in positions will be in both public and private agencies, large and small alike. Gerontology, long-term care services, health areas, substance abuse, school social work, and private practice are cited in the DOL's Occupational Handbook, 2002–2003 as having the greatest opportunities for social workers. On any given day social work job opportunities across the country are listed by a variety of sources including the national and state NASW offices, schools of social work, university career placement offices, and national magazines such as *Social Work Today*. Here is a small sample of job openings as listed by the University of Houston Graduate College of Social Work Web page in February 2009 (http://www.sw.uh.edu/alumni/jobboard.php)

Job Title: Staff Therapist—SPA
Employer/Agency: El Centro de Corazon
Job Description: Provides counseling/therapy services to children, adolescents, families and adults. Services include but are not limited to: individual, family and group psychotherapy.
Qualifications: Fluent in Spanish; licensed LPC, LPC-I, LMSW, LCSW, LMFT, LMFT-A
Salary/Hours: Competitive/8am–5pm

Job Title: At-Risk Youth Facilitator
Employer/Agency: Families Under Urban and Social Attack, Inc. (FUUSA)
Job Description: The At-Risk Youth Facilitator is responsible for delivery of program curriculum in school and after-school settings. Other responsibilities include: outreach and recruitment, gathering data and completing reports, developing and fostering community relationships and collaborations, and conducting program evaluation activities.
Qualifications: Undergraduate degree in social work, psychology or behavioral science.
Salary: Negotiable

Job Title: Domestic Violence Services Coordinator
Employer/Agency: Houston Area Women's Center

Name: Ariel Champaloux Heaton

Place of Residence: Satellite Beach, Florida

College/University Degrees: BSW, MSW, University of Central Florida; presently an LCSW intern

Present Position and Title: Emergency Department/ Trauma Social Worker, Holmes Regional Medical Center; Social Worker on inpatient unit, Circles of Care Psychiatric Hospital; Hospital social worker/discharge planner; Florida Hospital Orlando

What do you do in your spare time? I enjoy exercising, running, step aerobics, and lifting weights. I love going to church, shopping, going to the movies, and cooking.

Why did you choose social work as a career? My mother is an LCSW, and I have always been fascinated with her job and how she helped people. When I was a little girl, she would take me to her office, and I would wait in the waiting room. When she finished a session, I could see how her clients looked so much more relaxed and relieved compared to when they arrived.

At first, I thought that I wanted to be a nurse and was accepted into University of Florida's School of Nursing. During the first semester of the program, my educational experience included "clinicals," where you work to provide direct patient care. As I was on one of my rotations in the hospital and started seeing patients, I found myself talking to the patients and enjoying it more than just physically providing patient care. It was then that I realized I wanted to be a social worker. I left nursing school and was accepted to University of Central Florida, School of Social Work, where I completed my BSW and later my MSW degrees.

What is your favorite social work story? One of my favorite social work stories was when I was working in the hospital emergency room. One night a 48-year-old male was rushed to the emergency room because he was in severe respiratory distress. Sadly, despite the best efforts of the emergency room medical staff, shortly after arriving the patient passed away. Soon after his death, his family arrived in the waiting room, unaware of what had just transpired. His family included his parents and his fiancée, who said they were to be married that weekend. As the social worker, I took the family to a quiet area. I was able to answer their questions and support them once they were told the news.

His fianceé asked, "What is going on, I will be his wife on Saturday." The physician told the family the horrific news. The family was devastated, and we sat and talked for quite some time about what had happened and to support them in terms of what they would do next. I will never forget how much it meant to this family and that I was able to provide support to this patient's family during one of the most tragic days of their life.

What is one thing you would change in the community if you had the power to do so? If I could change something in the community, I would advocate for more resources for mental health. I see so many people who suffer from debilitating mental illness who do not have access to proper treatment because of the limited resources in the community.

Job Description: Counsel adult survivors of domestic and/or sexual violence on-site and coordinates day-to-day counseling services for the nonresidential program.

Essential Functions of This Position: 1. Provide crisis intervention to adult survivors of domestic and sexual violence (and children when needed). 2. Provide direct services, individual and group counseling, case management and childcare (on an as needed basis) to clients. 3. Coordinate day-to-day counseling services for NRS program. 4. Hire, supervise, train, evaluate and mentor counselor positions. 5. Supervise and train volunteers and interns. 6. Maintain accurate records and appropriate documentation of services. 7. Assist in planning phases that will result in client empowerment. 8. Provide referral information, counseling and emotional support in a non-judgmental, non-directive manner to clients. 9. Flexibility in schedule need to work some evenings for PM sessions.

Qualifications: Bachelor's degree in social sciences or equivalent experience and minimum of three years counseling experience in a social service agency with adults and children. Minimum of one year experience in a supervisory role. Speak, write, and understand English and preferably Spanish as well. Skilled in crisis intervention counseling and case management with adults (and children on an as needed basis) in individual and group formats.

Hours: Tuesday–Saturday w/some evenings.

Salary: Based on experience.

Job Title: Coordinator, Domestic Violence Programs

Employer/Agency: Anti-Violence Project (New York)

Job Description: *PRIMARY FUNCTIONS*

Manage all aspects of AVP's Domestic Violence Programs, including Rape and Sexual Assault, and services in collaboration with the Deputy Director who coordinates Programmatic Services. Provide clinical and administrative supervision of DV and Rape/SA staff counselor advocates and provide direct services to clients. Provide some direct coverage of crisis hotline during office hours and staff back-up support to volunteers after-hours on a rotating basis with other Client Services Staff. Provide community outreach and education concerning the Domestic Violence and Rape/SA Programs as well as AVP services in general. Responsible for program development and evaluation as well as managing contracts that support these programs. Participate as a member of related community committees and working groups/task forces.

Qualifications: Master's degree and certification in Social Work (LMSW or LCSW) required. Supervisory experience and clinical experience with crisis intervention, violence and victimization with LGTBH clients required. Training or experience in work with domestic violence and sexual assault required. Experience in work with HIV preferred. Certification in social work field instruction preferred. Demonstrated ability to work collaboratively with others. Ability to facilitate working alliances between diverse groups within and beyond the LGTBH communities. Strong verbal, public speaking, writing and computer skills needed. Knowledge of available social service resources in New York City helpful. Must be available to work flexible schedule as needed. Fluency in languages other than English, including

Spanish, is strongly preferred. NYC AVP is an Equal Opportunity/Affirmative Action employer. Excellent benefits, including health insurance and vacation time.

Job Title: Case Manager for Older Refugees
Employer/Agency: Catholic Charities
Job Description: Catholic Charities is seeking a highly qualified Case Manager for Older Refugees to serve within our Refugee Resettlement and Cabrini Center teams. This position is shared between both programs. The person that fills this position will be responsible for recruiting eligible refugee clients to enroll in case management program; intake and assessment; and outreach to refugee communities about case management services. In addition to the refugee duties, this position will also be responsible for preparing client legal intakes, translating clients documents, preparing immigration forms for citizen applications, and performing legal case management.
Qualifications: Applicants should have: 1) A Bachelor's degree from an accredited university or equivalent work experience; 2) A minimum of one year experience in immigration law, legal casework, refugee resettlement, or social service agency experience with an emphasis on refugees/immigrants; 3) Proficiency in English and Vietnamese—verbal and written; 4) Proficiency in MS Office applications, especially Word, Excel and Power Point; and 5) Reliable transportation, valid Texas driver's license and evidence of insurability.
Hours: Full Time.
Salary: Based on experience and bilingual status.

Do these prospective jobs sound interesting to you? There is an array of employment opportunities for BSW, MSW, and DSW or PhD practitioners in every state. What is probably most exciting to the job seeker is that social work positions offer a variety of challenges working with individuals, groups, families, organizations, and communities.

This chapter explores the nature of employment opportunities in the field of social work. We first discuss the educational requirements to become a social worker and the role that accreditation standards play. Then we take an overview of prospects for social workers today, presenting salary and employment projections into the twenty-first century. We conclude with tips on finding that first social work job.

THE EDUCATION OF A SOCIAL WORKER

What educational criteria are needed to make a person a social worker? The answer is simple: a baccalaureate or master's degree in social work—that is, a BSW, BSSW, or BA or BS in social work or an MSW, MSSW, or MA or MS in social work—from a program accredited by the Council of Social Work Education, more commonly referred to as "CSWE." When students graduate from either of these kinds of degree programs in social work, they are considered to have professional practice degrees. A degree in sociology, psychology, anthropology, or any other "ology" does not make a person a social worker. The major difference between a degree in social work and these degrees is that sociology, psychology, and anthropology are science-based. People who major in these fields may specialize in practice or complete practice-based courses, but they are not based in practice as social work graduates are. It is also important to note that working in a social agency for ten years, even under the tutelage of a degreed social worker, does not alone make a person a qualified social worker. Further, a doctoral degree in social work, a PhD or a DSW is not recognized as a practice degree. These programs are not regulated by CSWE, and their graduates are considered researchers, administrators, educators, or scientific practitioners. As a result, entry into the social work profession is limited, and those interested in becoming social workers must pass through at least one of the two doors.

Having said this, maybe it's not quite that simple. Not to muddy the waters, but in some states, it is possible to be licensed to practice social work without having a degree in social work. For example, some states may choose to "grandfather in"—or make exceptions for—certain individuals to practice or sit for a qualifying exam. Generally, each state sets its own criteria and deadlines for this type of exception so it is best to contact the state licensing board directly to find out if and how these exemptions are made. For example, in Alabama certain client protection workers for the state have been grandfathered in and are therefore eligible to be licensed as baccalaureate-level social workers; these individuals do not have BSWs, a standard requirement in most states. West Virginia has also used a similar practice. Caution should be exercised, however, because people who use this nontraditional door into the field of social work may be disappointed if they move from the granting state. Other states may not honor their designated status, and no appeal based on reciprocity is possible. Remember, the best way to ensure entry into the field of social work is the traditional way: earning a baccalaureate or master's degree in social work from a program accredited by CSWE, and as of June 2006, CSWE had accredited 635 social work programs across the country (Watkins & Holmes, 2008). Since grandfathered exceptions are so rare and policies vary from state to state, based on state need and requirements, we'll operate on the premise that a bachelor's or master's degree is the only way to enter the profession.

The difference between someone who simply wants to help and someone who is trained in the professional skills to give help is pronounced. Nevertheless, some professionals from other disciplines feel the strong requirements that must be satisfied to qualify as a social worker are unfair. That most states require a professional social worker to have either a bachelor's or a graduate college degree in social work strikes them as elitist. In fact, they might say, a lot of good people carry out important activities on behalf of individuals in need, and these helping workers should also be considered social workers. Most professional social workers would disagree because they believe that social work is indeed a profession and, as such, must have clear rules and requirements for entry. Social workers believe that within the field professionals are expected to confront the full range of human problems and do so in multiple practice settings (Burger & Youkeles, 2004); this requires professional education as a generalist.

To support this position, let's look at some professions and see what they require for entry:

Law: Completion of a baccalaureate degree in any discipline; graduation from a law program, accredited by the American Bar Association; passage of a state bar examination. At one time, a person was able to "sit" for the bar exam without graduating from a law program. In such cases, the individual was required to have worked in a law office, under the mentorship of a board-certified lawyer, that is, one who had passed the bar exam, for a number of years. This practice is no longer allowed.

Medicine: Completion of a baccalaureate degree, preferably in the hard sciences; graduation from a medical school, accredited by the American Medical Association; passage of a state medical examination. As with law school, medical school was in the past not a requirement for practice, but that too is no longer the case.

Nursing: Education in the scientific basis of nursing under defined standards of education and concern with the diagnosis and treatment of human responses to actual or potential health problems (PDR: Medical Dictionary, 2005). Most nurses have completed their education in accredited programs and can practice at the level appropriate to their educational qualifications. For example, a licensed practical nurse has graduated from an accredited school of practical (vocational) nursing (one year of training), passed the state exam for licensure, and is licensed to practice by the state authority. Similar requirements with varying education exist for the other levels of nursing at the associate, bachelor's, and graduate levels. An individual without a degree in nursing may assist a nurse in daily routines; often this individual is called a "nurse's aide." Regardless of education nurse's aides are not nurses and cannot perform the traditional duties of nurses licensed at different levels of skill acquisition.

Physical Therapy: Completion of a baccalaureate degree, with emphasis on biology, chemistry, physics, and social sciences, or graduation from a graduate physical therapy program, accredited by the Commission on Accreditation in Physical Therapy Education and in January 2009, 451 programs were accredited nationwide'.

Lawyers, physicians, nurses, and physical therapists are only a few of the professions that require professional education which is regulated by a professional accrediting body and, usually requires passage of a state examination to practice. Up to the nineteenth century, people were not required to complete any formal education in order to enter particular professions. Rather, someone hoping to enter a profession studied and worked as an apprentice under a practicing member of that profession who was recognized as experienced. This mentoring model was acceptable for three main reasons. First, at that time the relatively small number of colleges and universities were geographically inaccessible to many. Second, since there were fewer schools, the number who could participate in higher education was limited by the availability of educators and seats. Third, few families could afford the costs of a college education. Higher education was reserved for the elite and, for the most part, white males. With these limits on access to formal education most aspiring professionals found it productive to learn under the watchful eye and guidance of a successful practitioner.

With the spread of the public state college system and the democratization of all higher education the historical barriers were slowly chipped away. As formal education became more accessible many professionals moved their courses of study from the practical to the academic setting. Social work was no exception.

Did You Know...In 2008, New York had more accredited BSW and MSW programs (43) than any other state. Following New York were Pennsylvania (40) and Texas (39), while Montana and Wyoming (2 each) had the fewest BSW and MSW programs (www.CSWE.org).

The first documented educational training program in social work was a six-week-long summer institute offered in 1898. Sponsored by the New York Charity Organization Society, this program is credited with helping to found the Columbia University School of Social Work. Before this summer institute was held almost all social work training took place within agencies and was provided by agency staff. In the years that followed social work education became a fixture of higher education. The February 2009 report of the Commission on Accreditation identified a total of 665 accredited social work programs including 470 at the baccalaureate level and 195 MSW programs. In addition, the membership for the Advancement of Doctoral Education in Social Work (GADE) totaled 81 in 2007 (see table 1). There are scores of social work programs found in all regions of the world; there is no reliable estimate of the total number of social work programs worldwide, but the conservative consensus is that there are a minimum of 1,500 programs.

Table 1: Number of Accredited BSW, MSW, and PhD Programs

Year	BSW	MSW	PhD	BSW and MSW in Candidacy
2009	470	195	81	33
2008	465	191	NA	38
2007	462	186	NA	35
2006	458	181	69	36
2005	450	174	NA	37
2004	446	268	NA	36
2003	437	159	78	36
2000	420	139	67	51
1998	410	126	62	53
1996	388	117	56	52
1994	382	112	55	45
1992	374	106	53	41

Source: CSWE, Accreditation. Retrieved June 30, 2009 from: www.cswe.org.

> *Did You Know...In 2009, of all social workers, a master's in social work is the pre-dominant social work degree for licensed social workers (79% of active practitioners).*

The twentieth century was critical for the developing field of social work. During this time social work was transformed from a volunteer activity into an established profession requiring a clearly designed education. When apprenticeship occurs now it is intertwined with or follows a competency-based education provided within the rigorous setting of baccalaureate or graduate study.

ACCREDITATION AND WHY IT MATTERS

As an aspiring social work professional you should be aware of the accreditation standards your social work program must meet. By meeting these standards your program assures you, and others, that when you complete its requirements you will be well prepared for your future career. Because of the importance of this information we present an overview of accreditation and explain how it relates directly to your development as a professional in the field of social work.

Council on Social Work Education

The Council on Social Work Education is the primary national organization that oversees and provides guidelines for social work education in the United States. The council was organized in 1952 with the merger of the National Association of Schools of Social Administration (NASSA), which had coordinated baccalaureate education, and the American Association of Schools of Social Work (AASSW), the membership body for graduate programs (Beless, 1995). In 2009, the number of CSWE member schools included 470 baccalaureate and 195 master's accredited programs (see table 1). In addition, 33 programs were in **candidacy**, or pre-accreditation status. While not regulated by CSWE, there were 81 social work doctoral programs. Overall, approximately 74,577 full-time and part-time students were enrolled in BSW, MSW, and doctoral programs (see table 2).

Table 2: Number of BSW, MSW, and PhD/DSW Students and Graduates of Accredited Programs

Year	2006	2000	1998	1997	1996	1995	1994
BSW students	32,457	35,255	42,443	48,050	56,038	42,974	45,604
BSW degrees awarded	12,845	11,773	11,435	12,356	10,305	10,511	10,288
MSW students	39,566	33,815	31,759	35,559	35,468	32,283	33,212
MSW degrees awarded	17,209	15,016	13,660	15,058	14,484	12,976	12,856
MSW applications made, first year	36,715	30,262	34,533	40,075	44,968	43,024	46,247
PhD/DSW programs		67	62	58	56	56	55
PhD/DSW students	2,554	1,953	2,102	2,436	2,087	1,949	2,097
PhD/DSW degrees awarded		229	266	286	258	279	294

Source: CSWE, Accreditation. Retrieved June 30, 2009 from: www.cswe.org.

Activity...Visit the CSWE Web page at www.cswe.org and look for the listing of schools, colleges, departments, and programs of social work. Compare and contrast programs from around the country; compare urban and rural programs, large and small colleges/universities. What difference, if any, do you find? What kinds of electives do programs offer? How do BSW and MSW programs differ? What patterns of interesting educational activities do you find?

Although the CSWE was formed by the merger of two organizations that concentrated on baccalaureate and graduate education respectively, undergraduate education over time appeared to take a back seat to graduate studies (Leighninger, 1987). It wasn't until 1974 that CSWE implemented accreditation standards for baccalaureate programs. As Gardellia (1997) noted, BSW and MSW educational programs were never fully integrated—that is, they have never viewed each other as equal partners—which has created tension between the groups. Moreover, the CSWE board of directors initially included ten seats for BSW educators and twenty seats for MSW educators (Gardellia, 1997, p. 39). But over time, the disproportional number of board seats changed to reflect the dominant view that BSW education is important and central to the social work profession. In 2009, the CSWE board included equal representation by BSW and MSW educators. Even so, there are some BSW and graduate educators, although their numbers are very

Figure 1: Middle school students meeting with a social worker to discuss various school and family issues.

small, who continue to foster unnecessary tension between graduate and undergraduate educators.

For social work students, knowing how CSWE business is conducted can be helpful in understanding why their educational programs are organized in a particular manner. CSWE is governed by five commissions: Accreditation, Curriculum and Educational Innovation, Diversity and Social and Economic Justice, Professional Development, and Global Social Work Education. Working with each commission are "councils," which focus on a specific interest area. For example, three councils work with the Commission on Diversity and Social and Economic Justice and these are (1) Council on Disabilities and Persons with Disabilities; (2) Council on Sexual Orientation and Gender Expression; and (3) Council on Racial, Ethnic, and Cultural Diversity. Go to the CSWE Web site through the following link and explore the various councils and commissions—http://www.cswe.org/CSWE/ about/governance/. Look at the important work each is doing to promote, enhance, and strengthen social work education. You will discover that social work educators are tackling a variety of issues, and they do this for free! That's right, social work educators volunteer countless hours serving on the board of directors, commissions, and councils. They do this because we social workers understand the importance of working on behalf of our entire professional community.

Did You Know...Social workers' most frequent specialty practice areas are mental health (37%), child welfare/family (13%), health (13%) and aging (9%).

Now let's explore one commission in detail to learn more about its work and significance to you.

Commission on Accreditation. One of the most important functions of CSWE is the accreditation of baccalaureate and master's degree programs. Social work accreditation is coordinated by the **Commission on Accreditation**, a twenty-five-member committee that includes social work educators representing both BSW and MSW faculties, BSW and MSW students, and social work practitioners. These commissioners are volunteers who are appointed by the president of CSWE for three-year terms; a commissioner may serve no more than two consecutive terms, or a total of six years. A professionally paid staff supports the commission. The commission influences the direction of social work education through such activities as maintaining and updating accreditation standards; conducting commissioner **site visits** to programs in candidacy; voting on candidacy status, initial accreditation, and **reaffirmation**; and ensuring the quality of social work education and of the commission's functions.

Educational Policy and Accreditation Standards. The **Educational Policy and Accreditation Standards (EPAS)**, written by the Commission on Curriculum and Educational Innovation, is a critical document to social work educators and program developers. The EPAS describes in broad terms the essence of social work education at the undergraduate and graduate levels. The document is so important to education that accreditation standards require social work students to be familiar with it. As a social work student you need to be aware of this policy statement, and if your program is being reaccredited, you might be asked to tell the site visit team what you believe it says.

Did You Know…Social workers spend the majority of their time providing direct client services (96%), followed by consultation (73%) and administration/management (69%).

The EPAS addresses a number of different subjects, including the curricular design and educational context to prepare students for professional social work practice. The core of EPAS is the focus on competencies that a social work student must acquire in their course of study. All students, BSW and MSW alike, must master and demonstrate the ten core competencies, but more on that later. According to the EPAS, the BSW is the entry-level degree, and a BSW practitioner's interventions are developed within a **generalist practice** framework. The MSW is the advanced practice degree, and an MSW practitioner's interventions are developed within a **specialist practice** framework.

Generalist and specialist social workers can be characterized as follows:

Generalist: A social work practitioner whose knowledge and skills encompass a broad spectrum and who assesses problems and their solutions comprehensively. The generalist often coordinates the efforts of specialists by facilitating communication between them, thereby fostering continuity of care.

Specialist: A social work practitioner whose orientation and knowledge are focused on a specific problem or goal or whose technical expertise and skill in specific activities are highly developed and refined. (Barker, 2003)

Accreditation Standards for Social Work Programs

Educational Content for Baccalaureate and Master's Programs. The EPAS requires all social work educational programs to be grounded in the liberal arts from which the professional education grows. The liberal arts perspective, according to the Commission on Accreditation,

enriches understanding of the person-environment context of professional social work practice and is integrally related to the mastery of social work content. . . . It provides an understanding of one's cultural heritage in the context of other cultures; the methods and limitations of systems of inquiry; and the knowledge, attitudes, ways of thinking, and means of communication that are characteristic of a broadly educated person. (CSWE, 1994, pp. 99–100, 138)

That is why before you were allowed to enroll in your social work classes you were required to complete several courses in certain liberal arts. The completion of these courses satisfies part of the social work program's liberal arts educational requirement. Content areas completed most often are English, additional electives in the arts and humanities, science, history, political science, sociology, anthropology, and psychology. A point to remember: accreditation standards do not specify liberal arts courses that must be completed; rather it is your program faculty who have identified courses they feel will prepare you for the social work program's course of study.

Did You Know...With 12% of respondents planning on leaving the workforce in the next two years and the increasing need for social work services, there will likely not be enough social workers to meet the needs of clients.

According to the EPAS, "the explicit curriculum constitutes the program's formal educational structure and includes the courses and the curriculum. . . . The explicit curriculum achieves the program's competencies through an intentional design that includes the foundation offered at the baccalaureate and master's levels and the advanced curriculum offered at the master's level. The BSW curriculum prepares its graduates for generalist practice through mastery of the core competencies. The MSW curriculum prepares its graduates for advanced practice through mastery of the core competencies augmented by knowledge and practice behaviors specific to a concentration" (CSWE, Commission on Accreditation, 2009).

The key component is the "mastery of the ten core competencies" (see table 3). All programs, BSW and MSW alike, must insure that students address and are able to demonstrate the ten competencies. As a result of this mandate, we recognize that a BSW student in New York addresses the same core competencies as a BSW student in Austin, Texas. This results in a common ground for all social workers whatever their individual agency settings, client populations, practice functions, or practice methods. This common educational content is a real asset. In particular, this competency model helps supervisors and coworkers know what new social workers are able to do as a result of their formal professional education. No such uniformity in educational content exists for some related disciplines such as the various counseling specialties.

Activity...Meet with a social work advisor to discuss your program's admission process. Is the program a limited access program? What is the application process? Are all applicants accepted into the program? What are some of the reasons people are denied admission to the program? Explore with the advisor the program's liberal arts requirements. Why are these specific courses required? Are you surprised by some of the required courses?

Baccalaureate in Social Work (Educational Model). The typical baccalaureate social work program begins in the sophomore year of college and requires four to five semesters of study. Accreditation standards require some form of admission process into the BSW program and these standards are established by the program's faculty. Limited access programs require a formal application and review process for admission. Admission may depend on such criteria as cumulative grade point average (GPA), successful completion of the liberal arts requirements, reference letters, and a narrative statement. In programs that are not limited access,

Table 3: EPAS Ten Core Competencies for Social Work Education

Specific Competency	EPAS Explanation of Competency	Examples of Competencies
Identify as a Social Worker and Act Accordingly	Social workers serve as representatives of the profession, its mission, and its core values. They know the profession's history. Social workers commit themselves to the profession's enhancement and to their own professional conduct and growth.	◆ advocate for client access to the services of social work; ◆ practice personal reflection and self-correction to assure continual professional development; ◆ attend to professional roles and boundaries; ◆ demonstrate professional demeanor in behavior, appearance, and communication; ◆ engage in career-long learning; and ◆ use supervision and consultation.
Apply Social Work Ethical Principles in Practice	Social workers have an obligation to conduct themselves ethically and to engage in ethical decision-making. Social workers are knowledgeable about the value base of the profession, its ethical standards, and relevant law.	◆ recognize and manage personal values in a way that allows professional values to guide practice; ◆ make ethical decisions by applying standards of the National Association of Social Workers Code of Ethics and, as applicable, of the International Federation of Social Workers/International Association of Schools of Social Work Ethics in Social Work, Statement of Principles; ◆ tolerate ambiguity in resolving ethical conflicts; and ◆ apply strategies of ethical reasoning to arrive at principled decisions.
Apply Critical Thinking in Making Judgments	Social workers are knowledgeable about the principles of logic, scientific inquiry, and reasoned discernment. They use critical thinking augmented by creativity and curiosity. Critical thinking also requires the synthesis and communication of relevant information.	◆ distinguish, appraise, and integrate multiple sources of knowledge, including research-based knowledge, and practice wisdom; ◆ analyze models of assessment, prevention, intervention, and evaluation; and ◆ demonstrate effective oral and written communication in working with individuals, families, groups, organizations, communities, and colleagues.

Table 3: EPAS Ten Core Competencies for Social Work Education—(*Continued*)

Specific Competency	EPAS Explanation of Competency	Examples of Competencies
Engage Diversity and Difference in Practice	Social workers understand how diversity characterizes and shapes the human experience and is critical to the formation of identity. The dimensions of diversity are understood as the intersectionality of multiple factors including age, class, color, culture, disability, ethnicity, gender, gender identity and expression, immigration status, political ideology, race, religion, sex, and sexual orientation. Social workers appreciate that, as a consequence of difference, a person's life experiences may include oppression, poverty, marginalization, and alienation as well as privilege, power, and acclaim.	◆ recognize the extent to which a culture's structures and values may oppress, marginalize, alienate, or create or enhance privilege and power; ◆ gain sufficient self-awareness to eliminate the influence of personal biases and values in working with diverse groups; ◆ recognize and communicate their understanding of the importance of difference in shaping life experiences; and ◆ view themselves as learners and engage those with whom they work as informants.
Advance Human Rights and Social/Economic Justice	Each person, regardless of position in society, has basic human rights, such as freedom, safety, privacy, an adequate standard of living, health care, and education. Social workers recognize the global interconnections of oppression and are knowledgeable about theories of justice and strategies to promote human and civil rights. Social work incorporates social justice practices in organizations, institutions, and society to ensure that these basic human rights are distributed equitably and without prejudice.	◆ understand the forms and mechanisms of oppression and discrimination; ◆ advocate for human rights and social and economic justice; and ◆ engage in practices that advance social and economic justice.
Engage in Research Informed Practice and Practice Informed Research	Social workers use practice experience to inform research, employ evidence-based interventions, evaluate their own practice, and use research findings to improve practice, policy, and social service delivery. Social workers comprehend quantitative and qualitative research and understand scientific and ethical approaches to building knowledge.	◆ use practice experience to inform scientific inquiry and ◆ use research evidence to inform practice.

Apply Knowledge of Human Behavior in the Social Environment	Social workers are knowledgeable about human behavior across the life course; the range of social systems in which people live; and the ways social systems promote or deter people in maintaining or achieving health and well-being. Social workers apply theories and knowledge from the liberal arts to understand biological, social, cultural, psychological, and spiritual development.	◆ utilize conceptual frameworks to guide the processes of assessment, intervention, and evaluation; and ◆ critique and apply knowledge to understand person and environment.
Engage in Policy Practice to Advance Social and Economic Well-Being	Social work practitioners understand that policy affects service delivery, and they actively engage in policy practice. Social workers know the history and current structures of social policies and services; the role of policy in service delivery; and the role of practice in policy development.	◆ analyze, formulate, and advocate for policies that advance social well-being; and ◆ collaborate with colleagues and clients for effective policy action.
Respond to the Contexts that Shape Practice	Social workers are informed, resourceful, and proactive in responding to evolving organizational, community, and societal contexts at all levels of practice. Social workers recognize that the context of practice is dynamic, and use knowledge and skill to respond proactively.	◆ continuously discover, appraise, and attend to changing locales, populations, scientific and technological developments, and emerging societal trends to provide relevant services; and ◆ provide leadership in promoting sustainable changes in service delivery and practice to improve the quality of social services.
Assess, Evaluate, and Intervene with Individuals, Families, Groups, and Communities	Professional practice involves the dynamic and interactive processes of engagement, assessment, intervention, and evaluation at multiple levels. Social workers have the knowledge and skills to practice with individuals, families, groups, organizations, and communities. Practice knowledge includes identifying, analyzing, and implementing evidence-based interventions designed to achieve client goals; using research and technological advances; evaluating program outcomes and practice effectiveness; developing, analyzing, advocating, and providing leadership for policies and services; and promoting social and economic justice.	◆ The Council on Social Work Education (CSWE) was first established in 1952, and is the accrediting body for Colleges, Schools and Departments of Social Work. With its original inception there were 59 graduate schools and 19 undergraduate programs.

Source: CSWE. Commission on Accreditation, 2009.

admission depends on successful completion of the liberal arts requirements. Whether access to a program is limited or not depends on school policy.

Accreditation standards require that students receive at least 400 hours of field education, though a particular program may demand more than this minimum. Programs currently use a number of models to address the **field placement** requirement. One option is "block placement," in which the student is assigned to an agency full time, forty hours a week, for an entire semester. A second approach, "concurrent placement," assigns the student to an agency one to three days a week while the student takes courses, usually for two semesters. A third approach combines concurrent and block placements: concurrent placement is made in the student's junior year of study and block placement in the senior year. This approach allows the student to be assigned to different agencies. What's more important to remember is that whatever field model your program uses, you must complete at least 400 hours in the field practicum. Because this requirement is set forth in the accreditation standards, your program is very unlikely to allow modifications or exceptions.

Master of Social Work (Educational Model). Professional education at the master's level requires the equivalent of two academic years of full-time study and combines two components, foundation and specialization in a particular area of study.

The professional foundation content is the same as for baccalaureate programs and is most often studied in the first year. Specialization takes place during the equivalent of the second year of full-time study and builds on the foundation education. According to the social work educational model, specialization must be firmly rooted in the foundation content. A specialization can be designed around different areas of social work practice (see box 1); second-year courses and field education should reflect this specialization area. Accreditation standards require that MSW students complete at least 900 field hours. Students complete two placements, one in the foundation year and another in the specialization year, and together these must total to a minimum of 900 hours.

Box 1: Specialization Models

Methodology: Specialization by intervention, such as critical social work, community organization, or group work

Setting: Specialization by agency setting or type, such as child welfare, mental health, criminal justice, rural practice, or gerontology

Population group: Specialization by a specific client population, such as children, families, women, and seniors

Problem area: Specialization by a focused problem, such as alcohol, tobacco, and other substances, mental illness, family violence, and poverty

Combination: Combination of specialization, such as methodology and population growth, for example, clinical social work with children.

Name: Maryann Petri

Place of residence: Palm Bay, Florida

College/university degrees: University of Central Florida, BSW, MSW

Present position: Counselor/Educator

Previous work/volunteer experience: Alzheimer's Association, Case Management and Guardianship Services

What do you do in your spare time? I enjoy playing water sports, bowling, and karaoke.

Why did you choose social work as a career? I chose social work because I enjoy engaging in social change activities and advocating for better conditions for the aged. Many times elderly individuals may be left to feel helpless and useless and I enjoy helping them and their families to prepare for the future and adapt to existing social conditions.

What is your favorite social work story? My favorite social work story is one that involved a homeless man suffering from pneumonia. The man was admitted to a nursing home for short-term care while he recovered. Although he did not need long-term care, he remained at the facility for approximately three years because he had no one able to support his return to the community. He had a married daughter who lived out of state with her new husband. Her husband felt that the responsibility of caring for his elderly father-in-law was overwhelming and awarded power of attorney and limited guardianship to the agency where he resided. I worked for many months to reunite my client with his family. I advocated for his veteran benefits and helped the family work through the issues that were preventing reunification. He was later reunited with his daughter and son-in-law.

What would be the one thing you would change in our community if you had the power to do so? I would acquire a state-mandated allotment of funds to provide parenting classes to all pregnant mothers- and fathers-to-be.

A common complaint among newly enrolled first-year graduate students is that their field placements are not in their intended areas of specialization. Students need to remember, however, that first-year field placements are intended to be generalist in nature and to allow students to demonstrate the acquisition of the core competencies. Competencies for specializations are developed in the equivalent of the second year of study; it is at this point that specialization placements occur.

Did You Know...The Department of Veterans Affairs—the largest employer of social workers in the country—employs more than 6,000 social workers to assist veterans and their families with individual and family counseling, client education, end of life planning, substance abuse treatment, crisis intervention, and other services.

Students choosing a graduate program should know that not all programs offer the same choices of specialization and some limit the advanced study to only one specialization. A colleague has remarked that when reviewing admission folders for her graduate program, she feels that students know little about the program they are applying to. One student, for example, wanted to study administration, but the school only offers a clinical specialization. The student had a GPA of 3.8 and a Graduate Record Exam (GRE) score of 1,175. The admission committee, nevertheless, rejected the student's application because the student's career interests did not match the school's mission and curriculum. The applicant was very angry and complained about his rejection. Even when the committee's rationale was explained to him, he did not accept the decision, saying "What I want to do professionally has nothing to do with the type of program I want to apply to." The moral of this story: Make sure that your career goals match the school's mission and educational program.

> *Did You Know…Forty percent of mental health professionals working with the Red Cross Disaster Services Human Resources system are social workers.*

Advanced Standing (Educational Program). Some graduate programs offer "advanced standing." Advanced standing, which is limited to graduates of CSWE baccalaureate programs, allows these students to have certain graduate courses waived because they mastered the content in their baccalaureate studies. Advanced standing reflects the EPAS stipulation that a graduate program not require course work to be repeated once it has been mastered.

Social work is the only profession that offers an advanced standing option in its educational model. Even within social work advanced standing is very controversial in both theory and practice. The profession's ambivalence toward advanced standing is seen in its inconsistent application. Some programs waive the entire foundation year of study while others limit the exemption to one or two courses, some require successful completion of content-specific examinations, and some programs do not offer an advanced standing option at all. Some programs require BSW practitioners to enroll in the graduate program within a specific time period from the time of their BSW graduation, typically ranging from four to seven years; otherwise, they are not eligible for advanced standing and are required to complete the regular two-year curriculum.

PhD/DSW (Educational Program). CSWE does not regulate doctoral study. As a result, doctoral programs differ in required courses, program structure, and specialization. Generally, a doctorate is required for people who teach in BSW or MSW programs. While not required for agency practice, there is a small, but growing trend in agencies to hire upper level administrators who hold doctoral degrees.

Two types of doctoral degrees are associated with social work, the PhD and the DSW. The PhD is the familiar Doctorate of Philosophy; DSW designates a Doctorate in Social Work. Basically, the two degrees are more similar than different. When doctoral programs first originated in the field of social work, the DSW was awarded. As time passed and social workers were hired as educators, schools changed the doctorate to a PhD, and today that is the more common designation in academia. Both degrees require approximately the equivalent of two years of full-time study, passage of a comprehensive qualifying examination, and successful completion of a written dissertation. It is important to remember, however, that because doctoral-level programs, unlike master's and bachelor's programs, are not accredited by CSWE, careful exploration to find the right match between student and program is essential.

SOCIAL WORKERS TODAY

According to U.S. Department of Labor (2008) employment projections through the year 2016, social work is projected to be among the fastest growing professions with lower unemployment and steady pay. The Department of Labor (2008) identified 595,000 social work jobs in 2006; 30 percent of these jobs are in state, county, or local government, but as the government contracts for more and more services from the private sector, many jobs will shift to private agencies (http://www.bls.gov/oco/ocos060.htm). A much earlier study (Gibelman and Schervish 1997, p. 5) estimated the number of people employed in social work and holding social work degrees ranging from 645,000 to a high of 693,000.

The bottom line: no single information source provides a detailed overview of social work employment. We know social workers are employed in a variety of settings, both public and private, and employment prospects continue to be sound.

Activity...Contact your state's department of labor. The agency is usually located in the state capital and may have an 800 number. Find out the department's employment projections for social workers in your state. Do the data match national trends?

What Are Social Workers Paid?

Probably of most interest to people considering social work as a career is salary: how much can I make? Well, you won't be poor, and you'll be able to live a comfortable life. Current information on salaries is not available, but in the recent past the average income, while modest, was comfortable. Trying to identify "average" salaries or answer the question "what can I expect to earn" is plain hard to answer. A social worker in New York City will, on average, earn more than a social worker in Reno, NV. Not that there is salary discrimination in Reno but the cost of living is much less. So be careful when comparing salaries (see table 5).

The best source on salaries is right in your own city or town. Go to a local NASW unit meeting and ask the social workers what the salaries are in your community. Some social work programs have their own career services office and collect salary information. So check around and see what you find. You can also get a feel for salaries by reading your local newspaper's classified advertisements (Sunday classifieds are your best bet for finding the most advertisements).

But let's at least create some parameters on general national average social work salaries. Remember that salary is a function of degree (MSW or BSW), agency setting, and location. In 2006, the Department of Labor reported that child welfare social workers averaged $37,480; medical social workers earned on average $43,040; mental health and substance abuse social workers averaged $35,410; and salary average for all others was $46,370 (http://www.bls.gov/oco/ocos060.htm).

Activity...Check out the New Social Worker Online *Web page (www.socialworker.com). You'll find a number of discussion boards and chat rooms dealing with a variety of topics, including careers, ethics, student forums, general items, announcements, and resource recommendations. Questions about jobs and salaries are hot topics on this Web site.*

Where Do Social Workers Work?

To better understand where job opportunities might be, let's look at social work practice from four interrelated perspectives: job function, auspices, setting, and practice area:

Function: What Do I Do?

Direct service	Supervision
Management/administration	Policy development/analysis
Consultant	Research
Planning	Education/training

Auspices: Where Do I Work?

Public, local	Private nonprofit, sectarian
Public, state	Private nonprofit, nonsectarian
Public, federal	Private for profit, proprietary
Public, military	

Setting: What Type of Agency Do I Work In?

Social service agency	Nursing home
Private practice, self-employed	Criminal justice system
Private practice, partnership	College/university
Membership organization	Elementary/secondary schools
Hospital	Non–social service organization
Outpatient facility	Group home

Practice Area: What Is My Practice Area?

Children and youth	School social work
Community organization/planning	Services to the aged
Family services	Alcohol and other substance abuse
Criminal justice	Developmental disabilities
Group services	Occupational
Mental health	Public assistance

Any set of choices, one from each list, defines a social work position. For example, you can be a supervisor (function) in a private nonprofit, sectarian (auspices) nursing home (setting), providing services to the aged (practice area). Or you might provide direct service (function) in a public, local (auspices) outpatient facility (setting) as an alcohol and substance abuse counselor (practice area). The thousands of potential combinations demonstrate the versatility of social work employment opportunities.

Did You Know...There are hundreds of social workers in national, state, and local elected office, including two U.S. Senators and seven U.S. Representatives.

Source: http://www.socialworkers.org/pressroom/swMonth/2009/swfacts.asp

Another way to discover the breadth of the social work profession is to examine CSWE studies of social work education programs. Each year the Council collects these data in order to track the state of the profession and to detect possible trends in education. In its 2002 study the Council identified fourteen different practice area concentrations in most social work schools (see table 4). The data in table 4 reinforce the impression of diversity in social work, although mental health, child welfare, and family services stand out as the three most popular concentrations among students.

Table 4: Fields of Practice among 32,214 Graduate Students in 2000 in Social Work Education

Field	Percentage of Students 1996	Percentage of Students 2000
Aging	2.7	1.7
Alcohol or substance abuse	1.5	.7
Child welfare	7.8	7.4
Community planning	1.0	1.5
Corrections	1.0	.6
Family services	7.4	6.8
Group services	.4	.4
Health	5.1	4.3
Mental health	11.0	9.7
Mental retardation	.3	.2
Occupational social work	.8	.5
Public welfare	.2	.1
Rehabilitation	.2	.2
School social work	3.5	3.1
Other	3.7	7.1
Combinations	2.6	2.4
Not determined	21.6	17.9
None (methods only)	29.2	35.3

Source: Lennon (2002).

GETTING A SOCIAL WORK JOB AFTER GRADUATION

There's no secret to finding a job, whether in social work, law, nursing, or any other profession: it takes a great deal of hard work and a lot of patience on the part of the job seeker. While jobs in general are available, it takes time to find the one that is right for you. A rule of thumb is that it takes three to four months to find a job from the time you begin your search in earnest. So if you want to have a job by June, you'll need to have your resume prepared and your search strategy developed and implemented no later than the preceding February.

A note of caution: Be prepared not to get the one job you've always wanted. Even for the most experienced social worker a job rejection letter hurts. Great jobs are waiting for competent social workers—the key is finding a position in which you can make full use of your knowledge, skills, and potential.

Prepare Your Resume Carefully

Be sure your resume is up to date. You can get an easy-to-use resume software program at the college bookstore or computer store. There are also any number of books on resume writing that you can review. Ask your academic advisor or some other social worker for tips and ideas about what to highlight. Consider taking advantage of your school's job placement office by attending a resume-writing workshop. But recognize that most helpers in the resume-writing process are not well versed in social work; their work is geared to a general audience and does not reflect the nuances of social work. The key is to ask social workers in the field what they did and what they listed on their resumes.

Be sure your resume is clean and as error free as possible—no spelling errors, no photocopies with wrinkled edges, and so on. Your resume is your introduction to a potential employer, and you want to make the best impression possible. Consider writing an initial goal or objective for the type of work you want to do in the field. Be sure to link the contents of this statement with the job you are applying for. You may not have much paid clinical or administrative experience, so be sure to highlight volunteer experiences and start with your most recent field placement. For other tips and suggestions present a draft of your resume to a favorite social work instructor or a social worker in the field. Listen to their suggestions carefully because they have been through the employment process; hearing their "words of wisdom" first might save you a great deal of time and effort later.

Attend Local NASW Meetings or Meetings of Other Professional Groups

To facilitate your job search, attend local NASW meetings as often as you can. You can begin to network by attending meetings and becoming active with this group as soon as you declare your major. Dues for a student are a real bargain! Simply contact your state NASW office for information about your local unit and for the name of a contact person. You should be able to get an NASW membership application from your school's social work office or through the state NASW office.

While attending local NASW unit meetings you'll make new friends, begin to develop a professional network, and keep abreast of issues within your new social work community. Moreover, the monthly or bimonthly meetings often include time for members to announce job opportunities. Most people would be surprised at how much information about job openings and availability is spread by word of mouth and through these types of informal networks. For example, you may even get firsthand information on a position that has just become available from the contact person within the agency.

Activity...Attend a local NASW meeting. Talk to members about finding jobs and see what hints they can give you.

Get on the World Wide Web and see what kind of jobs you can find in at least five different states. Try looking in large cities as well as small towns.

Read a number of job announcements and look for qualifications that are minimum requirements versus those that are preferences.

Visit your school's job placement office. See what the staff recommend about putting together a job search packet. Remember, it's never too early to begin collecting material for your resume.

Put together a draft resume and pass it around asking for suggestions on how to make it better.

Use Your Field Placement Experience

Each student must complete a field placement. Don't be surprised if your field agency offers you a position following graduation. The field site has the luxury of assessing your work; if you do an excellent job the agency may ask you to consider moving into a regular position. An agency benefits from hiring a field placement student who has already worked in the agency, because this "new" employee can be moved into a regular position more quickly and with less orientation time. Furthermore, there is little need for an initial skill and knowledge assessment period because the agency, through the internship experience, is well aware of the student's practice abilities and thus the level of supervision needed. Employment in a field placement agency also has advantages for the student accepting the job. The student already knows the agency and how she will fit into the overall organization. Based on direct experience the student knows that it is the setting in which she wants to start a social work career.

Read Local and National Newspaper Advertisements

Local newspapers, *NASW News*, and your state NASW chapter newsletter publish countless employment announcements. Familiarize yourself with the range of jobs that are available as well as the jobs that interest you the most. Read each advertisement carefully, and when you apply for a job be sure to follow the instructions; if it asks for a resume and the names of three references, provide just that— no more and no less.

Look closely at the words used in the announcement. Words such as "must have" or "minimum" or "required" signal baseline qualifications that the successful candidate must possess. For example, if the announcement requires an MSW degree and five years of post-MSW experience, don't apply if you are a newly graduated BSW or an MSW with three years of experience. On the other hand, words such as "should have" or "preferred" signal not minimum criteria but preferences. These words introduce the agency's wish list for the desired candidate, and employers understand that they often don't get everything on their wish lists. Let's say you find an interesting job for which you meet the minimum requirements but not the preferences, go ahead and apply.

Use the Internet

If you'd like a job outside of your local area, the World Wide Web and the Internet are your best friends. Through the Web you can locate newspapers, state NASW offices, and employment services across the country. Use the Web's search engines to identify employment opportunities.

Get to Know Your Social Work Faculty Advisors and Instructors

One of your best sources of employment information and strategies is your program faculty. They are very interested in your success, they have years of experience, and they know people in the field in the surrounding community who can help you. Your social work teachers have probably had contact with most local agencies, and a good word, phone call, or reference letter from a faculty member can be one of your greatest aids in getting your first job.

Don't forget that many programs use adjunct or part-time faculty to supplement their full-time faculty. Adjunct faculty members who are employed full time in the community can help you in your job search because they are tied into the local informal social work network.

Did You Know...All states have some form of licensing or regulation of social work practice, but in many states such regulation is limited to MSW or advanced practice and does not apply to BSW practice. Be sure to check with your academic advisor to learn more about your state's particular licensing requirements.

NASW also regulates MSW and advanced social work practice through the Academy of Certified Social Workers (ACSW). A practitioner with an ACSW certification meets the following criteria: 1) NASW membership; 2) MSW degree; 3) two years or 3,000 hours of post-MSW experience; and 4) passage of a multiple choice examination, given after the experience requirement is satisfied. A social worker does not need to have the ACSW, but state law may require a practitioner to be licensed.

Explore Your Social Work Student Association or Club

Your program's social work student association or club can help in your job search. The association can invite area agency directors to provide workshops or panels on finding a job. The club can also sponsor a job fair on campus at which area agencies set up booths, distribute agency information, and recruit potential employees. The fair can be coordinated with the program's field office and the local NASW unit. Probably the best time to hold a job fair is in the spring, when most potential graduates are looking for jobs.

A job fair is a win-win-win situation. Students win because they have immediate access to potential employers. Agencies win because the fair is a cost-effective recruiting mechanism that reaches a large pool of potential job applicants. The social work program and university win because the job fair is a positive public relations tool that strengthens ties between the university and the community.

Last Thoughts about Your Job Search

We often get caught up in salary and look for the best-paying jobs. Yes, salary is important, but consider other aspects of the job as well. Who works at the agency? What kind of colleagues will you have, and can you learn from them? Your first job will be a major source of knowledge and experience. Will the job be exciting and offer you a variety of learning opportunities? What kinds of benefits are in place? These can range from health care and vacation time to pets—one organization allows staff members to bring their pets to work each Friday. (Now what does that say about the organization?)

A few years ago, a student came into the office very excited about a job offer she had received in New York City as a childcare worker. She said, "I'm getting a great salary. They're going to pay me $55,000!"

But what does $55,000 mean to a new, twenty-one-year-old social worker? Sounds like a great deal, but not really. Use the Web to find salaries for comparison purposes; the easiest way is to search for "salary converters." For example, as you can see in table 5, $55,000 in one city means something quite different somewhere else.

Remember that you need to be happy with what you find. Make sure the setting offers you an opportunity for continued professional growth and self-fulfillment. Don't focus only on the salary—there is much more to a job than money!

Table 5: A Salary of $55,000 in Houston, Texas, in February 2009, Is the Same As . . .

City	Salary
Hartford, CT	$72,728
New York City (Manhattan)	139,490
Orlando, FL	63,026
Chicago, IL	71,736
Los Angeles, CA	91,948
Albuquerque, NM	60,723
Portland, OR	70,927

Source: http://cgi.money.cnn.com/tools/costofliving/costofliving.html

SUMMARY

Students entering social work will find the field rich in opportunities. The profession's future is bright.

In embarking on a professional career in social work the selection of an educational program is important. A social work career should begin with either a baccalaureate or a master's degree, and this degree must come from a CSWE-accredited program. Request admission information directly from the programs you are interested in attending. Programs are located in every state in the United States and throughout the world. Be sure to gather information early so you have plenty of time to prepare what is required. Some baccalaureate programs have open admission, while others use a formal admission process. Admission to graduate programs, on the other hand, is usually competitive, and about 40 percent of applicants are turned down.

Employment possibilities for social workers can be found in both public and private settings. They involve a wide range of activities and tasks and a variety of practice areas. Simply stated, practice opportunities for social work professionals are open and diverse.

The key to a successful work experience in social work is planning your education carefully—whether BSW or MSW—and making the most of it. Take advantage of your educational opportunities to develop new knowledge, theories, and skills that will make you more competent. Remember, before you can help the individuals, groups, families, and communities that you will serve, you must first help yourself to be the best equipped professional, with the best foundation of education and training possible.

Part **II**

The Practice of Social Work

Chapter 5

Social Work Practice

STEVE, AN UNDERGRADUATE SOCIAL WORK STUDENT, STOPPED BY to see one of the authors in his office. Steve was enjoying his introduction to social work class, had not missed a session, and believed his final grade would be high. Steve often asked questions and really enjoyed taking part in class discussions, so it was no surprise when he asked, "So, how do you do it?" Not quite sure what he meant by "it," the instructor asked Steve to clarify what "it" meant. Very seriously, he said, "You know, social work. How do you 'do' social work?" Today, some twenty years after this visit, Steve, who now holds an MSW along with his BSW degree and is employed in a public mental health facility, laughs about that question. "I guess I was looking for that magical pill you give a client, the one thing we do to help a person in pain. I just believed that social workers had a bag of tricks that 'poof' solved the person's problems. How wrong I was."

Pondering how exactly to "do" social work is where most professionals start, and even for seasoned practitioners, the quest never ends. Steve, like so many beginning social workers, was unsure of what to do in social work practice and hoped for a simple answer. Wouldn't it be wonderful if the unique and ambiguous challenges of human life could be easily addressed by giving a pat answer, taking a simple pill, or using a standard procedure? It's tempting, but wholly unrealistic. If social work practice required nothing more than simple prescriptions, then there would be a limited need for formal education beyond the basics, for supervision, or for continuing education.

In fact, the practice of social work stems directly from the mission of the profession, which is neither simple or standardized. Furthermore, market forces, whether academic, governmental, or private in origin, can also affect practice (Witkin & Iversen, 2008). If you look at the definition of social work set forth in chapter 1, you'll be looking in the right direction for practice guidance. Social workers seek to enhance social functioning, promote social justice, and help people to obtain resources.

> *Did You Know...The number of social work jobs doubled in the 1930s, from 40,000 to 80,000, as public sector income maintenance, health, and welfare programs were created in response to the depression (NASW, 1993).*

Changes in the detailed definition of social work have occurred over time, yet the basis for social work practice has not changed. Today there are several definitions that outline the profession of social work but all follow a similar theme

Name: Ellendeer Berkowitz

Place of Residence: Lima, New York

College/University Degrees: BS, S.U.C. at Brockport; Collaborative MSW Program of Brockport and Nazareth Colleges, Rochester, NY

Present Position and Title: I am a social worker at St. John's Nursing Home, in Rochester, NY. My heart's passion is most reflected in my work as a comfort care social worker, and I also work with elders needing rehabilitation, as well as those who have dementia. Monthly, I facilitate a dementia support group for families. I have also done presentations for staff in regard to quality of care and providing compassionate care at the end of life.

Previous Work/Volunteer Experience: I worked for 23 years for Hillside Children's Center in Rochester, NY. I supported children and teenagers who had experienced abuse in their lives and who had suffered from different learning impediments. In this position, I learned to measure success not only by the completion of tasks or by improving grades but by the smiles and heart connections I was able to foster.

Why did you choose social work as a career? The difficult challenges that I experienced as a child and as an adolescent transformed into passion, within my heart, and I developed a sincere desire to help others in a meaningful way. Once my own healing journey began, I learned never to underestimate the power of love and compassion. I also learned that true healing occurs when you are able to help someone find their heart's connection or strength, as this helps enhance the healing process in beautiful ways. (Validating feelings and instilling hope is also very important.) I am very grateful to all my teachers for their inspiration, especially Shaman-Brant Secunda, M. Howden, and B. Allardice.

What is your favorite social work story? There have been many special moments. One of them was when my supervisor asked me to assist with an elder who, since admission, had not made eye contact and who hadn't spoken a word. I thought long and hard about how to help her. I remembered my teachings. After spending some supportive time with her and placing a compassionate hand on her shoulder, she turned her head and her eyes met mine. She then spoke some words to me, the last words she spoke so clearly were "thank you."

What is one thing you would change in the community if you had the power to do so? I would like to continue to empower people and help others to learn to be respectful and accepting of those who are different from us. This includes uniting all people regardless of race, culture, faith, or age. Though idealistic, I believe that the lack of this type of unification has resulted in a lot of pain and suffering in our world, as well as land, air, and water pollution. In addition, I would alleviate the barriers that prevent elders from having dignity and respect as they approach the end of their lives here on earth.

highlighting the importance of addressing the "person in situation" or the person in environment. According to the National Association of Social Workers (NASW, 1993), social work is the professional activity of helping individuals, groups, or communities enhance or restore their capacity for social functioning and create societal conditions favorable to their goals.

Furthermore, as outlined in the preamble of the NASW Code of Ethics, social work is also engaged in promoting and empowering the needs of individual well-being of all human beings within the context and environmental forces that influence problems related to their condition (NASW, 1996, updated 2008). Barker (2003) further elaborates that "social work is the applied science of helping people achieve an effective level of psychosocial functioning and effecting societal changes to enhance the well-being of all people" (p. 408).

In examining these different interpretations of the profession it is easy to see how the definition has evolved but still remains relevant to the early definition written by Boehm (1959) which defines the profession this way: "Social work seeks to enhance the social functioning of individuals, singly and in groups, by activities focused on their social relationships which constitute the interaction between man [individuals] and his [or her] environment. These activities can be grouped into three functions: restoration of impaired capacity, provision of individual and social resources, and prevention of social dysfunction" (p. 54).

Reflective of the revised (2008) NASW Code of Ethics, all of these definitions highlight the tasks that social workers undertake, the agencies in which they work, and the social policies they support. These helping efforts are all aimed toward three overarching goals: to enhance client social functioning, remedy client dysfunction, and promote social justice (Hepworth, Rooney & Larsen, 2002). The professional education a social worker acquires, whether at the BSW or the MSW level, through academic classes and course work as well as the experiences gained through the field practicum, help the new social worker to develop the necessary value-driven knowledge and skills to support social work practice.

UNDERSTANDING DIVERSITY

Although today's definition of social work may seem simple, recognizing the diversity, uniqueness, and complexity in what constitutes individuals, groups, or communities needs further exploration. As a professor of social work and a practicing clinician, one of the authors was asked by a student, "how come in class you rarely give case examples of what might be considered the traditional family?" The response was simple: "If you mean the traditional family as constituting the biological parents with 2.4 children, who have never been divorced or separated, I rarely see them in my practice." At first, this statement may seem shocking, but these changes remain reflective of our current social times. In fact, today's traditional family may be better characterized as yesterday's nontraditional family. Diversity of family includes blended or step-families and those units headed by a single parent, by gay or lesbian partners, or by a grandparent or other relatives.

Today in practice, it has become evident that the basics of what has traditionally constituted social structure and expectations within individuals, family groups, and communities has changed.

When seeking to understand individuals and families, the uniqueness of each situation that takes into account the worth and dignity of each individual and family system must be acknowledged. Social workers are expected to recognize these differences through a nonjudgmental lens or perspective that embraces diversity rather than discourages it. This requires that social workers become familiar with what is considered ethical practice as well as implement practice strategy that highlights client self-determination in the most nonjudgmental way possible. From this perspective, individual dignity and worth stand at the forefront of all helping activities. Social workers will actively be engaging with many individuals of different social classes, genders, races, ethnicities, and sexual orientations as well as differing belief systems and spiritual views. Furthermore, the awareness of this type of diversity will be coupled with varying personal problems, including individual health and mental health problems, and family issues as well as various social problems such as racism, sexism, and violence, to name a few. Therefore, effective individual practice must be transactional. In transactional practice, each event is viewed in multiple dimensions, and case-specific factors, practice models, ethical principles, and issues of power must all be considered (Mattaini, 2001). Furthermore, as the funding for agencies responsible for assisting clients in need becomes more competitive, an emphasis on client outcomes is expected to grow. From this perspective agencies and thus the services they provide will become increasingly more accountable with success being measured by helping clients to move forward and gain their desired outcomes (Poertner & Rapp, 2007). This new focus on the measurement of client outcomes is shaped by contextual factors such as agency competition for funding, agency practices, natural networks, and social institutions. Social workers must not only be aware of this changing climate but also learn how to prepare for what is currently happening or could happen. In being prepared for current changes and future trends taking place in the surrounding environment this knowledge can be used to help individuals, families, groups, and communities enhance or restore their capability for social functioning.

So often, under the guise of "diversity," we lump or group entire populations and from this limited perspective broad and sweeping assumptions can be made. For example, consider the term "Hispanic": what comes to mind when you hear someone refer to a person or family as "Hispanic"? From a U.S. Census perspective, "Hispanic" includes people of Latin or Mexican descent or origin. As a result, people from Cuba, Mexico, Argentina, Brazil, and Spain would be "Hispanic." Yet, would you say the culture with its traditions, mores, and folkways is the same for each of these nations? Do you think a person from Cuba is different from an Argentinean? Of course, Cubans are very different from people from Argentina as from Mexico, Brazil, and Spain.

Consideration of human diversity in social work practice requires reflection on and consideration of how such diversity impacts our worker-client relationship and ensuing problem-solving process.

Although there are numerous potential examples highlighting the need for the recognition of diversity which expands beyond traditional definitions of family and race, the African-American child provides a case in point. Children learn to use their cultural experiences to interpret their immediate surroundings and interact with others. From this growth and development perspective the interpersonal patterns that will shape the child's lifetime are developed. Similarly, culture and family are the first two powerful influencing determinants of how children understand, internalize, and act on the expectations of their family, community, and larger society (Dziegielewski, Leon & Green, 1998; Morales & Sheafor, 2006).

In the case of African-American children, frequent discriminatory experiences provide these children with additional information and feelings to decipher and understand. During times of emotional or psychological turmoil, human nature requires that African-American children strive for meaning in their lives, using their "cultural lens"—their values, beliefs, and experiences. In social work practice, these children present a rich and complex biopsychosocial picture requiring examination of the biological, psychological, and social factors within a historical and cultural framework (Austrian, 2009; McAdoo, 1997). In order to address issues of individual diversity and to carry out this task efficiently, culturally sensitive social workers must be aware of their own values, the African-American child's values, and how both relate and integrate with the larger society in which all must coexist. Ridley (1995, p. 10) noted that even the most sincere, caring, and ethical practitioner can be guilty of "unintentional racism." Therefore, all helping professionals providing services to African-American children need to be sensitive to the culture of these children.

To address diversity, develop cultural sensitivity, and provide effective services, social work practitioners need to recognize, understand, and appreciate geographic and regional differences among children of color (Gonzalez-Ramos, 1990). Regardless of the child's race or creed, social workers must also learn to look critically and carefully inside at their own feelings, while confronting their own expectations and cultural biases (Sue & Sue, 2008). Although the primary experience of the African-American child today may reflect the influence of American society, the impact of the family's place of origin and sense of connectedness and belonging should not be minimized. The African-American family today may have values and traditions from northern states, southern states, or Caribbean areas. Similarly, family values may reflect differences in urban versus rural expectations and traditions and the first step in combating racism could be as simple as acknowledging that it exists and learning more about it (Miller & Garran, 2009).

Congress (1994; 1997; 2009) recommends that social workers identify appropriate tools to conduct culturally sensitive assessments. One such tool is the culturagram which takes into account different cultural aspects and empowers families to perceive their specific culture as important within larger society. Congress (2009) believes that creating a culturagram can help the clinician to get a better understanding of the family by examining the following areas: reasons for relocation; legal status; time in community; language spoken at home and in the community; health beliefs; impact of trauma and crisis events; contact with cultural and religious institutions, holidays, food and clothing; oppression, discrimination, bias and racism, values about education and work; and values about family structure, power, myths and rules (p. 970). Once these factors can be identified and understood families can become empowered to examine their problems as stemming from cultural clashes between their culture and that of mainstream society.

THE BASICS OF PRACTICE

It is important to recognize, however, that you will be introduced to practice in only general terms in parts II and III of this book. You will not be qualified to "do" social work after reading these chapters. Remember, your career in social work is just beginning and numerous courses and field experiences are before you. It is these studies and your professional learning experiences put together that will provide you with the foundation for social work practice. This chapter will provide a basic overview of the central concepts related to the delivery of social work services and examine the helping process as it can be applied to the practice of social work.

Before we begin to explore the "doing" of social work, however, we need to remind ourselves that the practice of social work is a professional activity intended to achieve the profession's purpose of helping clients. In examining your own motivation for entering this profession a question that must be explored is: Why have you decided that this is the profession for you? Be honest with yourself as you explore the areas of social work practice, examining and confronting your own biases and using this knowledge to decide which area of practice holds your interest the most. Don't be surprised if you find that, as for many helping professionals, your initial motivation comes from wanting to learn more about yourself and your own family. This is not unusual nor is it particularly problematic. However, when this is your motivation for choosing this field, you must be highly aware of the fact that the professional helping services you provide are not designed to help you—

Activity... Is Social Work Practice Really For Me? *On a piece of paper write the following questions and answer them individually. For this exercise you may at first feel more comfortable answering them by yourself. Later you may choose to discuss your answers with your instructor or academic advisor. Feel free to add questions to this list. You might also want to save your answers and revisit them later in your professional career.*

What first attracted you to the profession of social work?

What needs of your own are likely to be met by serving as a social worker?

Who in your life has been instrumental in helping you choose this career?

Have you ever received help from a social worker? What did you like most about this person? What did you like least?

What do you believe you can contribute to the field of social work?

In what ways do you believe this profession can help to make you feel like a better person?

What is evidence-based social work, and how will this trend affect the services you provide?

they are for the client. Other typical reasons for choosing a helping profession include the need to be needed, the desire to give something back to society and humankind, the need to care for others, and the desire for prestige and professional status. As you embark on a helping career, it is essential first to examine what motivated you to select this career and what you want to accomplish. As you explore this motivation do not be shy about asking for feedback from other professionals who know you, particularly your social work teachers and professionals experienced in the field. Remember, choosing a career path is not simple or quick. Nor is staying in the field automatic. For many of us, the pressures created by the kind of work we do require constant self-examination throughout our educational and professional careers. Some students decide relatively early that this is not the work for them. This realization should never be considered a personal or professional failure as a career in the helping professions is not for everyone. It is a good idea to establish and reaffirm this decision as early as possible especially before investing a great deal of time, effort, and expense into pursuing it.

CONCEPTS ESSENTIAL TO SOCIAL WORK PRACTICE

We have described social work practice as an art and science. The art of social work involves the sensitive coordination of complex activities to help clients. The science entails selecting, merging, and understanding potentially voluminous amounts of information and applying the conclusions to a specific case situation. While many are successful in learning the science of the profession, the art is always more difficult to acquire. The interplay of art and science means that effective social work practice grows from the relation between knowledge, skills, values, and ethics (see box 1). Social work practice requires unique skills, either

Box 1: Dynamic Interplay of Knowledge, Values and Ethics, and Skills

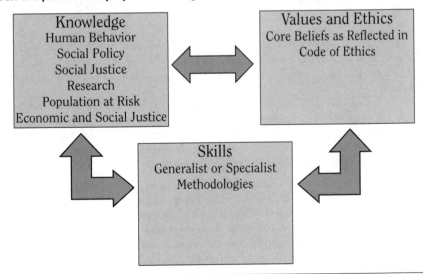

specialized or generalist in nature, derived from specific knowledge areas and guided by a clear, fundamental set of values and ethics.

Skills

"Doing" social work implies that a social worker has a set of specific skills used in practice. These skills, which are inseparable from the helping process, include the ability to perform critical tasks in working with clients: basic communication, exploration, assessment and planning, implementation, goal attainment, termination, and evaluation of the services rendered (Hepworth, Rooney, & Larsen, 2002).

Skill building and acquisition are the bridge between values and knowledge and all subsequent social service activities (Vass, 1996). Unless knowledge and values underlie skills, the practice of social work is undefined and vague. Social workers must have basic competencies in the following skill areas:

◆ *Cognitive skills*, including analytic skills and the capacity to evaluate and understand research
◆ *Administrative skills*, including record keeping and report writing
◆ *Interpersonal skills*, including verbal and nonverbal skills, understanding, self-awareness, use of authority, working with diversity, working in partnership, and the ability to make and sustain positive working relationships
◆ *Decision-making skills*, including authority and responsibility
◆ *Use and management of resources* (Vass, 1996, p. 63)

A social worker must be able to balance many critical aspects of the practice relationship with each client. For example, the worker must first establish and then maintain a worker-client environment of trust. In this environment, the client can feel safe revealing emotions and thoughts that might disturb an untrained practitioner; for the skilled worker, the ethical values of client worth, dignity, and self-determination are paramount. When counseling culturally diverse

---

Did You Know...Often you will hear social workers discuss "an empathetic relationship" or read in the social work literature about the importance of "empathy" in the social work process. What is the difference between empathy and sympathy? It was once described as follows:

Sympathy is what you feel when you begin actually to feel the pain of the client. In a sympathetic relationship the helping professional cannot be objective or render the nonjudgmental intervention required. Say, for example, you wear a size 8 shoe and your client wears a size 7. If you actually put the client's shoes on your own feet, your feet will be so squeezed that you cannot concentrate on the issues the client is facing.

Empathy, on the other hand, is what you feel when you remain in your own shoes while imagining what it is like for the client in his or her situation. The client's situation is assessed based on direct observation and information provided by the client or people from the client's environment. In an empathetic relationship the helping professional uses objective and subjective information and professional helping skills to truly understand the client's situation and the pain that the client is experiencing.

individuals, an awareness and respect for the client's beliefs, values, and lifestyles is central to creating an atmosphere of sensitivity and trust (Sue & Sue, 2008). The worker also must know how and when to approach those of the client's problems that need further explanation and exploration. The skilled social worker is well versed in empathetic communication and helps the client to clarify and confront what may be difficult issues to address. In short, the skilled professional social worker is an expert at establishing a positive worker-client relationship in which problem identification, helping, addressing, and subsequent healing can take place.

Knowledge Base

The practice of social work is based on a specific body of scientifically tested knowledge. Practice evolves from the knowledge base, as social work skills first developed in the academic curriculum later mature through field experiences and continuing education. Without the appropriate knowledge base and awareness of the theoretical constructs that undergird professional practice, skills would be nothing more than a series of unrelated actions that cannot address total person-in-situation who is at the heart of professional social work practice. Conversely, knowledge evolves from current practice through practice-based research and evaluation of social work interventions. Without such research and evaluation, social work knowledge would quickly become static, outdated, and unfounded.

In many ways, knowledge drives a professional's daily actions with and on behalf of clients. Knowledge supports practice in its efforts to be client centered and directed to the unique situation of each client. The knowledge base of professional practice premises, skills, and techniques allows social workers to choose the specific set of skills clearly embedded in a theoretical framework best applied to a particular client situation. In other words, to achieve client-centered practice, the professional knowledge base must come first. Once this is established the development of critical thinking skills will help the new social worker address situations that otherwise might be considered challenging or filled with multiple problems. The field's recent emphasis on evidence-based practice (EBP) has started to address this. From this perspective the social worker is taught to use skills to clearly identify problem areas and express the probabilities of addressing them (Shlonsky, 2009).

Therefore, to create a consistent and comprehensive knowledge base of professional practice, the Council on Social Work Education (2001/2004), which accredits social work programs, requires that all social work educational programs provide mastery of foundation content in ten areas: social work practice, human behavior and the social environment, social welfare policy and services, social policy, field practicum, research, diversity, social work values and ethics, populations at risk, and promotion of social and economic justice (see table 3 in chapter 4). Be prepared, as the courses you take and the social work program you complete will most assuredly include this information and it will be infused throughout the courses you take.

Knowledge needs to be directed toward three areas for the development of integrated, competency-based social work practice:

◆ *Knowledge that informs the social worker about the client*: Psychology, sociology, social problems, social policy, and antidiscrimination.

◆ *Knowledge that helps the worker plan appropriate intervention*: Social work practice theory and models of intervention, methods of social work intervention, and processes involved in social work intervention.

◆ *Knowledge that clarifies the worker's understanding of the legal, policy, procedural, and organizational context in which practice occurs*: Federal, state, and local public legislation; social welfare policy and procedures; and organizational contexts (Vass, 1996).

Values and Ethics

Values and ethics are the third critical component of social work practice. These humanistic concerns, based on human well-being and justice, help to solidify and provide unification for the field (Hopps & Lowe, 2008). At the start of your social work education, perhaps during the application procedure itself, you were probably introduced to our professional Code of Ethics. This document can be called an "ought to" guide: it specifies how social workers "ought to" conduct themselves and their helping activities in the professional setting. We cannot emphasize enough the importance of becoming familiar with this code from the very start of your career and learning its applicability to your practice activities (Reamer, 2009; Strom-Gottfried, 2007).

Activity…As a class or by yourself, look at the NASW Code of Ethics, in appendix A, and think about how it will shape your practice experiences. Which parts of the code do you find comforting and compatible with your beliefs? Which parts are more difficult for you to understand or support?

All professionals embrace specific values. All clients embrace specific values. Having certain values, however, may not always be consistent with how an individual behaves (Twohig & Crosby, 2009). Personal values belong to the individual, but professional values are governed by the profession and constitute a professional promise that governs professional conduct and behavior. Although social work values are spelled out in a number of documents, the primary reference for the profession's value base is the NASW Code of Ethics (reproduced in appendix A). The code establishes a set of clear beliefs which defines ethical social work practice and thus act as a unifying force among all social workers (Reamer, 2001; 2009). The way we work with and on behalf of others, how we view social issues, and the remedies we consider for individual, group, or community ills are all firmly rooted in our value base. All social workers need to be versed with the code and aware of key duties and obligations (Reamer, 2009). Using awareness and knowledge makes ethical decision-making a planned and objective process. Reamer (2001; 2009) identified the following core values for the social work profession:

◆ Individual worth and dignity of people
◆ Respect for people
◆ People's capacity for change
◆ Client's right to self-determination
◆ Client's right to confidentiality and privacy
◆ People's right to opportunities to realize their own potential
◆ Social change
◆ People's right to adequate resources and services to meet basic needs
◆ Client empowerment
◆ Equal opportunity
◆ Antidiscrimination
◆ Diversity
◆ Willingness to transmit professional knowledge and skills to others

As you read the code and consider Reamer's points, several common themes emerge, but let's look at three in particular.

First, all people, no matter who they are or what their circumstances, should be treated with respect and civility. Respect and civility are cornerstones of a just society. We show respect in any number of ways: being on time for appointments, and apologizing to clients when tardy; calling people Mr. or Ms. until asked to do otherwise; listening without interruption, and without looking at our watches during interviews. In these sessions, maintaining client confidentiality and privileged communication should always be at the forefront of all helping efforts (Reamer, 2009). When the term "confidentiality" is used, it generally relates directly to the information shared in the counseling session. When the term "privileged communication" is used, it generally relates to information that will be released in the context of legal proceedings. Be sure that as a beginning professional you discuss this with your supervisor to help make you keenly aware of what information can be shared and how best to do it. Also, one general rule that may help you if this situation ever arises is to make sure you have tried to secure written client permission to release information even if it is ordered to do so through a court.

Second, when given the opportunity, people may have the ability to participate in solving their own problems in a way of their own choosing. We understand that not all people can participate fully in such processes, but we recognize that everyone should be encouraged to participate as much as possible. We support client self-determination when we help them to figure out ways to identify and deal with their problems; we do not say, "If I were you, I would. . . ." Clients have strengths, and we must help them to discover and use these as energy sources for change. The only exception to this practice principle involves what has been referred to historically as a danger to self or others. In these situations, if a client's action poses an imminent threat or danger to himself or herself or others, the social worker may be forced to take action to protect the client or those in danger. To interfere with this process and not allow clients to make their own decisions with the intention to stop and protect them from self-harm is referred to as *paternalism*. According to Reamer (2009) paternalism is when a social worker decides to withhold information from clients or misleads them. It can also involve lying or coercing clients to do what the social worker rather than the client feels is best. Prior to beginning your professional practice, discussions related to topics such as this need to be discussed. It is always best to address this before you are faced with a situation. When situations such as this come up and it is too late to do this, the new social worker should immediately seek guidance on how best to continue and address this type of situation with the intent of protection of all involved.

Third, although not stated explicitly in the code or among Reamer's points, we can infer the basic principle that we do no harm to people. Our work is to help not harm. We cannot hold back any professional efforts or strategy if we believe they will help our clients. But with that said, we should never work beyond our scope of practice and dabble in areas we are not yet trained to address.

As you become more familiar with the Code of Ethics, compare it with other value statements, such as that of the International Federation of Social Workers (appendix B). What similarities do you find? The words and phrases may be different, but the respect for the human condition and the goal of social change are the same.

As professionals, social workers must pursue the art of helping within a context shaped by values and ethics. Practice that is not guided by values or ethics has no meaning because it fails to recognize the unique circumstances of our clients, their individual needs, and appropriate change strategies. Unless we operate within an ethical framework, our clients might as well be telling their problems to a computer!

DIFFERENTIATING BETWEEN GENERALIST AND SPECIALIST SOCIAL WORK PRACTICE

Social work practice is organized around two principal service delivery conceptual models: the generalist and the specialist. Generalist social work is more broadly defined and targeted toward a wider variety of clients and problem areas. Specialist social work is more narrowly defined with a sharper focus on specific issues or a particular client population.

Generalist Practice

Landon (1995) has asserted that regardless of how hard the profession has tried, there still is no completely agreed upon definition of generalist practice—although he did believe consensus existed on key elements of the definition. First, most professional social workers agree that generalist social work practice is primarily reserved for BSW social workers, although this view has changed as some graduate programs now offer a specialization reflective of additional course work in the area of advanced generalist practice. This advanced generalist would occur at the master's level and go into more depth in certain areas of practice. Second, generalist social workers are prepared for entry-level social work practice. Last, in generalist practice social workers most often apply some type of "systems approach" to professional practice and subsequent intervention. According to the

Social Work Dictionary, a social work generalist is a practitioner "whose knowledge and skill encompasses a broad spectrum and who assesses problems and their solutions comprehensively" (Barker, 2003 p.176).

The broad-based generalist approach to social work practice integrates clients' needs with those of the environment. In accepting the importance of the person-in-situation, social workers are leaders in understanding and interpreting the interaction between behavioral, psychological, and social factors in the client's condition with environmental factors faced daily.

Generalist social work follows a multilevel integrated process for addressing the interplay between personal and collective issues applied to a variety of human systems, such as societies, communities, neighborhoods, complex organizations, and formal groups, as well as individuals and families (Miley, O'Melia, & Dubois, 1998). According to Miley, O'Melia, and Dubois (1998), generalist practice depends on four major principles: First, generalist practice recognizes the importance of human behavior and the connection between this behavior and the social and physical environments that surround each human being. Second, generalist practice understands that changes in the client's environment must include changes in systems interactions that better the environment for all affected. Third, generalist practice works at every level of a system to assist in bringing about needed changes. Last, generalist practice assists in macropractice while also conducting research on the efficacy and effectiveness of the approaches used. Therefore, it is highly possible the generalist-level social worker may be working directly in a non-clinical setting and is expected to have developed skills reflective of this type of practice environment (DeAngelis, 2009).

Specialist Practice

The specialist social worker provides a more focused, higher level of intervention. A specialist possesses an MSW degree and is also prepared for advanced social work practice. According to the *Social Work Dictionary,* a specialization is "a profession's focus of knowledge and skill on a specific type of problem, target population, or objective" (Barker, 2003, p. 415). Social work specializations have developed in a number of ways over the years. One comprehensive scheme categorizes the various social work specializations into eight different types:

Models
- *Methods*: casework, group work, community organization
- *Fields of practice*: school, health care, occupational social work
- *Population groups*: children, adolescents, and elderly people
- *Problem areas*: mental health, alcohol and drug abuse, corrections, mental retardation

Specific Factors
- *Geographic areas*: urban, rural, neighborhoods
- *Sizes of target*: individual (micro), family group (mezzo), and community (macro)

Name: Sandra F. Brown

Place of residence: Cape Elizabeth, Maine

College/university degrees: Colorado College, BA; Simmons College School of Social Work, MSW

Present position: Clinical social worker for Scarborough Schools, and private practice in Portland, ME.

Previous work/volunteer experience: Clinical social worker, outpatient department, Jackson Brook Institute; licensed clinical social worker, Child Abuse Treatment Team, Somerville Mental Health Clinic; licensed clinical social worker, Italian Home for Children. Fund-raising for Center for Grieving Children, Hurricane Island Outward Bound School, Kids First Center.

What do you do in your spare time? Run, play tennis, ski, hike, kayak, and garden.

Why did you choose social work as a career? I was certified to teach in undergraduate school, but found that I was more interested in the student's lives, struggles, and families, and how I might help on that level.

What is your favorite social work story? I worked with a family who had two children who were placed in residential treatment for several years. This father had never been considered as a viable parent for these children, and when given the opportunity, worked hard and became a consistent, loving parent to his children. This father worked hard to learn parenting skills and how to manage on a day-to-day basis with his boys, in spite of his own challenges. Both children were able to leave residential treatment and live with their father.

What would be the one thing you would change in our community if you had the power to do so? I would increase the mental health services for both children and adults and get rid of the stigma that is often attached to those seeking mental health services.

◆ *Specific treatment modalities*: behavior modification, ego psychology, Gestalt therapy, cognitive therapy
◆ *Advanced generalist* (Hopps & Collins, 1995, p. 273)

After an extended period of MSW practice, the specialist worker is eligible for independent practice. Through state licensing laws (see chapter 15 for a fuller discussion of licensing and regulation of social work practice) and professional practice certifications, the MSW practitioner can move into private practice or practice independently within the agency context.

Social work is one of the most diverse fields of practice imaginable. Specialist social workers are found in numerous settings: public and private agencies, public and private hospitals, clinics, schools, extended care facilities, private practice, private business, police departments, courts, and countless other workplaces too numerous to name. But the multiplicity of practice specializations has created a major weakness, a professional Achilles' heel if you may. Meyer (1976) said it best when she wrote, "[Whereas] other professional specialists become expert by narrowing their parameters, social workers have had to increase theirs." This diversity in practice and settings makes it difficult for the broader community to understand what social workers do. And given the wide range of our specializations, any attempt to reduce or narrow our efforts will, as Hopps and Collins (1995) suggested, create tension, conflict, and fragmentation within the profession.

In summary, generalist and specialist social workers have different focuses. Specialization of social work practice usually occurs at the master's level. Specialist social workers are first trained in the generalist approach to practice and later embark on more specialized career tracks by choosing more concentrated areas in which to apply their skills. It is also in specialization that many professional educators believe "real" training as counseling professionals and therapists occurs. MSW social workers, with supervised experience (and certification or licensure), are usually free to engage in full non–clinically supervised counseling activities. In the field of social work, the master's degree is generally considered the terminal practice degree. For those studying at the doctorate (DSW or PhD) level, the focus is on research or science rather than clinical practice.

THE EMERGENCE OF EVIDENCE-BASED SOCIAL WORK PRACTICE

It is safe to say that the public expects high-quality service and "state of the art" care (Shortell & Kaluzny, 1994). Whether we pay for services directly through out-of-pocket costs or indirectly with our tax dollars, we want to receive the best services possible. These expectations extend to social workers, and indeed, the profession itself expects all services and activities performed on behalf of clients to be of the highest quality. Yet how do we demonstrate to the public that our activities are effective?

Social workers have historically been accused of avoiding the use of empirical techniques to establish practice efficiency and effectiveness. According to Rubin and Babbie (2008), this gap still exists today, and the gap is so large between research and the practice community that this lack of connection extends into the educational classroom as well. As we move into an era of professional accountability and client rights, however, the pressure remains high for continued progress toward change, highlighting the importance of assessment, intervention, and evaluation in all activities completed (O'Hare, 2009). Challenges made to the profession to prove service effectiveness and ensure that interventions are germane to client issues continue to be embraced.

The challenge to tie evidence-based research and evaluation to practice is not new. For example, in 1978, Fischer wrote the following:

> It seems to be difficult to avoid the conclusion that unless major changes are made in the practice methods—and hence, the effectiveness—of casework, our field, if not the entire profession of social work, cannot long survive. Indeed, unless such changes are made, it is not clear that as a field,

we deserve to survive. On one hand, we have the option of choosing—and building—a new revitalized future for social casework, one rooted in the superordinate principle that our primary if not our sole allegiance is to serve our clients with demonstrable effectiveness. On the other hand, we can continue our outmoded practices, denigrate and resist new approaches to practice, and bury our collective heads in the sand when confronted with the vaguest hint of a threat that we may not be doing all in our power to provide effective services. (p. 310)

The new revitalized casework that Fischer envisioned is today called **evidence-based social work practice**. All social workers, generalist and specialist alike, are expected to apply its principles to their activities. The *Social Work Dictionary* defines empirically based social work practice as: "a type of intervention in which the professional social worker uses research as a practice and problem-solving tool; collects data systematically to monitor the intervention; specifies problems, techniques, and outcomes in measurable terms; and systematically evaluates the effectiveness of the intervention used" (Barker, 2003, p. 141).

Furthermore, Barker goes further to define evidence-based practice (EBP) as: the use of the best available scientific knowledge derived from randomized controlled outcome studies, and meta-analyses of existing outcome studies, as one basis for guiding professional interventions and effective therapies, combined with professional ethical standards, clinical judgments, and practice wisdom (2003, p. 149).

For the beginning social work professional, it is important to understand that in evidence-based social work practice, the application of clear-cut research and evaluation models is guided by four broad ideas. First, research findings must be relevant to practice by assessing the change in a client's level of effectiveness after a specific intervention directed at a specific problem. Second, applications, practice and evaluation models, and findings are to be drawn from research reports. Third, research findings are to be disseminated so that the results are known in the practice community. Finally, other social work professionals should be able to interpret, understand, and apply what they read to what they do. Evidence-based practice mandates that in developing a practice intervention with a client, the practitioner include systematic research activities that provide feedback on the intervention's effectiveness, controlling for bias, while being potentially replicable (Bronson, 2009; Sackett, Rosenberg, Gray, Haynes, et al., 1996; Shlonsky, 2009; Thyer, 2001; 2004; Thyer & Meyers, 2007). In addition, the practice intervention may give additional information on how the client's ability to resolve the problem can be strengthened.

THE STEPS IN PROFESSIONAL HELPING

Work with clients in social work practice has five steps. These are illustrated in box 2. Note that evaluation is not a distinct step but rather takes place throughout all steps of the social work process.

Box 2: Social Work Process

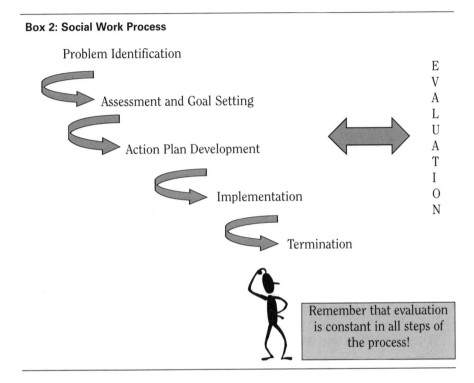

Problem Identification

Assessment and Goal Setting

Action Plan Development

Implementation

Termination

E
V
A
L
U
A
T
I
O
N

Remember that evaluation is constant in all steps of the process!

Step 1: Problem Identification

The first step involves problem identification. The social worker helps the client to identify and concretely define the problem(s) to be addressed by the intervention process.

The role of the worker is clear: apply logical thinking to identify the beginning, end, and the dynamics of the problem (Ragg, 2001). The client's problems are discussed thoroughly, and the client is made aware of the social worker's serious and dedicated efforts to help. It is in this initial step of the helping process that the rapport established will characterize the remainder of the practice experience. A working alliance is developed allowing the client to begin to feel comfortable yet eager to embark on change. The practitioner avoids simply giving advice to the client. It is here that the social worker utilizes empathy, where the social worker is able to understand what the client is experiencing within the context of the other person's perspective (Koerner & Linehan, 2009).

The social worker is a professional who at all times remains objective in educating, advocating, facilitating, and intervening on behalf of the client. In establishing rapport and giving feedback validation, active communication that the client's perspective makes sense is often used (Koerner & Linehan, 2009). Moreover, as ironic as it may sound, the social worker always begins plans for termination of the practice encounter early. In fact, as explained in chapter 6, termination should be discussed and decided in the first session. The client is thus well aware of what is coming and what needs to be accomplished by the end of the therapeutic term.

At the end of each session, the technique of "summarization" is used. The client is asked to state what was covered in the session and what progress was made in regard to the identified goals and objectives. Never summarize the session content for the client: it should always be done in the client's own words. Letting the client state what he or she got from the session helps the social worker to determine what really was accomplished and whether both client and social worker are aiming toward the same intervention outcomes. When relevant the social worker should acknowledge what a client is feeling and validate emotions and change efforts that support the changes desired (Koerner & Linehan, 2009). Clients often need this feedback and reinforcement that understanding has occurred and progress is being made.

It is also during this initial step that the social worker decides how accountability or practice effectiveness will be evaluated after the intervention is completed. Exactly what will be measured, and how, varies from case to case. No "magic pill" ensures evidence-based practice. We hope, however, that knowing its importance piques your interest in the research course you have yet to take.

Step 2: Assessment and Goal Setting

The second step involves helping the client to set goals and objectives that can be accomplished (Dziegielewski, 2002; Gilgun, 2005). Worker and client assess the client's need for assistance and how specifically the problem can be addressed. The "goal" is the overall end that the client wants to accomplish and the "objectives" are the concrete steps that the client will take to get there and that allow for measurement of the outcome (Dziegielewski, 2002; 2008a; 2008b; Gilgun, 2005). Setting goals and objectives, when done adequately, has the following valuable consequences:

- Ensures agreement between worker and client on intervention focus and purpose
- Provides to the client knowledge about how to address the problem, while providing a basis for continuity of session content across the intervention process
- Provides a basis for selecting appropriate treatment strategies
- Assists the social worker to structure session content and monitor progress of the intervention
- Gives outcome criteria (the objectives) for measurement of intervention effectiveness

When setting goals and objectives, the following always apply: First, the goals and objectives must relate to what the client wants to achieve at the end of the intervention. Second, the goals and objectives must be defined in explicit terms so that the client knows what is expected of him or her. Third, the objectives must be feasible; clients must believe they can succeed in the process, otherwise they may become disheartened and drop out of the intervention process. Fourth, the goals and objectives must be consistent with the skills and abilities of the helping professional. Social workers should never try to address medical problems they know little about. For example, if the social worker becomes unsure of one's abilities, supervision, consultation, and continuing education options should be explored before going any further in the intervention process. Ensuring quality of services in this manner is important for the client and the social worker.

Fifth, whenever possible, goals and objectives should be stated positively rather than negatively. Sixth, all goals should be mutually negotiated with the client; however, if you have reservations you must state these. Clients desire your input in their decision making. Be sure, though, that your hesitation reflects concern for the client's good rather than your personal bias.

Step 3: Action Plan Development

Once goals and objectives have been clearly identified, the social worker helps the client to develop a plan of action. The role of the social worker is paramount in identifying strategies for action and change. The worker may be able to provide the direct supervision or consultation necessary to implement the plan. Often, however, the social worker does not have the required expertise—he may be a generalist when a specialist is needed—and will contract with another provider or use work strategies to assist the client in meeting the objectives.

The action plan may include a task or a series of tasks. Each task is specific, clear, and supported by a time frame monitored by both worker and client. Each task builds on previous efforts, which together lead to the goals and objectives identified. As with goal setting, each task must be understood by both client and worker and, most important, within the client's ability to achieve.

Every action plan must have clearly established contingency plans. These plans specify the rewards for completion of the practice strategy agreement and the consequences for noncompliance. Clients participate in this part of the change process because they will accept the consequences of their actions or inactions.

Step 4: Implementation

Implementation takes place when the client is ready to put the plan into action. During implementation, the worker and client together monitor the progress; this activity is part of the evaluation that is the empirical side of our practice. Therefore, practice evaluation is basically a determination as to whether there has been useful improvement with the problem situation (Corcoran, Gingerich & Briggs, 2001). Through monitoring, worker and client are able to assess progress toward the goal, judge the effectiveness of the intervention and/or tasks, examine the client's reactions to the progress or lack thereof, and enhance motivation (Gilgun, 2005; Hepworth, Rooney & Larsen, 2002). Ongoing monitoring also allows worker and client to identify barriers as well as strengths in the process. New strategies can be built to overcome or cope with the barriers. And most important, monitoring provides the client with feedback on positive experiences that in turn reinforce the change efforts.

Implementing an action plan can be intimidating for a beginning social worker. Social work practice knowledge is essential because the social worker will be expected to use multiple practice strategies to assist the client. These can involve the application of planned skills such as modeling, behavioral rehearsal, role playing, or simply the use of paper-and-pencil exercises in which the client writes down feelings experienced as well as steps to be completed in the action plan. Referrals for additional help and assistance should also be considered and discussed at this time—for example, additional individual therapy, group therapy, couples therapy, or family therapy.

Step 5: Termination

The last step in the social work process involves termination. Client and social worker end their working relationship and describe how any change strategy developed will be continued. Many clients realize at termination that they want additional help. If this happens, the social worker informs the client of options for continued intervention and emotional growth by giving appropriate referrals. Referrals for group therapy, individual growth-directed therapy, couples therapy, and family therapy can be considered.

Evaluation and Follow-up

Successful practice intervention achieves significant changes in a client's levels of functioning and coping. Measures that can substantiate these changes are essential to evidence-based practice. Measuring intervention effectiveness can be as simple as making a follow-up phone call to discuss how things are going, or as structured as scoring the client's behavior on a standardized scale at the beginning and end of treatment and then comparing the two. Scales that measure depression, trauma, and so forth, are readily available. If more advanced methods of measuring practice effectiveness are expected, more advanced training and planning are warranted.

Planned practice evaluation and follow-up at the termination of intervention is essential, but these are steps which have historically been forgotten. As a matter of fact, when you consider the five steps in the social work process, research and evaluation seem to be missing. And if these are missing, how does the process we've outlined lead to empirically based social work practice? In fact, they're not missing—it's simply that they're not a separate step: research and evaluation should be included at each step of the helping process.

PRACTICE APPLICATION: THE ROLE OF THE MEDICAL SOCIAL WORKER

Ms. Martha Edda had been living with her family for approximately a year. Before then she had lived independently in her own apartment. Ms. Edda had to leave her apartment after a neighbor found her unconscious. The apartment was unsafe, with rotted food, urine, and feces throughout. Upon discovery, Ms. Edda was immediately admitted to the hospital. Originally, she was believed to have suf-

Figure 1: An elderly man leaves a rural West Virginia home after a visit from a home healthcare worker. In many such rural areas there is a shortage of physicians and medical facilities.

fered a stroke; later she was formally diagnosed with a neurological condition called "vascular dementia." Doctors believed that she was in the moderate to advanced stage of this condition because, at age 62, she had pronounced movement and memory difficulties.

After discussion with the hospital social worker, it became obvious that Ms. Edda needed a supervised living arrangement. Joan, Ms. Edda's daughter, admitted how guilty she felt about what had happened to her mother, but felt she could not handle her mother at home. The social worker reminded Joan that the family would benefit from Ms. Edda's receiving services from a home health care agency and that a community daycare program could be explored. After convincing her family to give it a try, Joan took her mother home.

Once in Joan's home, Ms. Edda did receive home health care services. However, much to her daughter's surprise all services stopped after just two months because Ms. Edda's physical therapy was discontinued. Joan relied heavily on these services, particularly the nurse's aide who helped to give Ms. Edda a bath. Ms. Edda weighed 170 pounds and could not help herself in or out of the tub. Joan recruited the help of her husband, who reluctantly agreed. Unfortunately, Ms. Edda could not get into the adult daycare center in the area because no spaces were available, and she was placed on a waiting list. She required help with all of her activities of daily living, and her daughter was afraid to leave her at home alone during the day. So Joan quit her job to help care for her.

On the morning of January 12, Joan found her mother lying face down in her bed. She had become incontinent of bowel and bladder, unable to speak, and the features appeared distorted on the left side of her face. When Joan could not rouse her mother, she panicked and called an ambulance. Ms. Edda was immediately transported to the emergency room.

In the emergency room, the staff began to administer numerous tests to see if Ms. Edda had suffered a stroke. Plans were made to admit her to the hospital, but no beds were available. Because Ms. Edda needed supervised monitoring, and a hospital bed could become available in the morning, an agreement was made to keep her overnight. In the morning, she was admitted to the inpatient hospital where she remained incontinent and refused to eat. She was so confused that the nurses feared she would get out of bed and hurt herself; she was placed periodically in restraints throughout the day.

After two days, most of the medical tests had been performed and determined negative; Ms. Edda's vital signs remained stable. The physician felt that her admission to the hospital could no longer be justified, and the social worker was notified of the pending discharge. On placing the call to prepare Ms. Edda's family for her return home, the social worker was told that the family would not accept her and wanted her placed in a nursing home. The social worker was concerned about this decision because Ms. Edda did not have private insurance to cover a nursing home stay and was too young to be eligible for Medicare. This meant that an application for Medicaid would have to be made. This state-funded program had a lower reimbursement rate, with most privately run nursing homes drastically limiting the number of Medicaid clients accepted. After searching for nursing home services, the social worker was told of the lack of bed availability.

When the social worker explained the problems with facilitating discharge plans to the physician, he simply responded, "I am under pressure to get her out, and there is no medical reason for her to be here. Discharge her home today." Since it was after 4:00 p.m. and the administrative offices were closed, the social worker next attempted to secure an out-of-area placement for the following day.

When the physician returned at 6:00 p.m., he wanted an explanation as to why the client has not been discharged. The nurse on duty explained that a nursing home bed could not be found; angry, the physician wrote an order for immediate discharge. The nurse called Ms. Edda's family at 6:30 p.m. and notified them of the discharge. Ms. Edda's family was angry and asked why she had not being placed in a home. The nurse explained to the family that discharge orders had been written and she was only trying to do her job. Ms. Edda's daughter insisted on speaking to the discharge physician prior to picking up her mother. A message was left for him, and at 8:00 p.m. her call was returned. The physician, sounding frustrated, told Joan that all medical emergencies had been addressed and Ms. Edda would have to leave the hospital immediately. Furious, Joan yelled, "If she is still incontinent and in restraints, how do you expect me to handle her?" Listening to Joan's distress, the physician softened his voice and said, "I will put the nurse on the phone to update you on her condition. In addition, the social worker will call you in the morning to arrange home health care services."

Upon arriving at the hospital, Joan found her mother hooked to an IV, wearing a diaper, and still placed in restraints. Pleased to see a member of Ms. Edda's family, the nurse sent for a wheelchair, unhooked the intravenous tubing, removed the restraints, and placed Ms. Edda in the wheelchair for transport to the family's car.

Discussion. Unfortunately, situations like this one continue to exist. This case example is a true depiction of events. The social worker was responsible for discharge planning, but many other issues needed to be addressed to best serve the client and her family. With perseverance, and the help of the hospital social worker, Joan eventually (several months later) placed her mother in a nursing home. However, the strain on Joan was so severe that she requested medication to combat her depression. Joan also began to fight with her husband and children over numerous issues related to the time, care, and loss of their second family income in caring for her mother. As in most American families, her earnings not only supplemented basic necessities (rent, food, etc.) but also paid for family luxuries (movies, eating out, etc.). Clearly in such situations, the price of the "cost effective" managed care strategy far exceeded the dollar value placed on it, and the client and her family became silent victims. The role of the social worker—officially labeled a "discharge planner"—involved considerably more than just finding a place for the client to go. Referrals, counseling, and openness to service flexibility make the social work professional an invaluable member of any interdisciplinary team. (The case scenario is adopted from Dziegielewski, 2004.)

SUMMARY

Social work practice evolved from mid-eighteenth- and nineteenth-century efforts to assist the poor. In those early years activities were carried out by volunteers, with few organizational supports and limited training. Today the profession has a well-established knowledge base, a clearly articulated value orientation, and diverse practice methodologies and interventions, which are transmitted to the new practitioner through formal educational processes.

The practice of social work is generally conducted in one of two major venues: the generalist and the specialist. The generalist works with a wide range of clients and services, whereas the specialist can complete the same duties but can also focus more distinctly on particular groups of clients, making this one of our greatest strengths as a profession. This is the reason we find social workers in a variety of different types of social agencies and organizational settings.

Social work practice has never been static. It has evolved dramatically since its conception and will continue to change in the future. To grow and adapt, practice must be conducted within a systematic, well-thought-out process that allows the use and production of scientifically tested knowledge and skills, and is founded on a clear and coherent set of professional values.

Chapter 6

Recognizing Diversity and Applying It to Generalist Practice

IN HIS FIRST FIELD PLACEMENT JUAN, A SOCIAL WORKER WORKING with older people, often found himself struggling. He joked that he was waiting for the single-problem client to come in so that he could carefully choose the very best method of helping. Although he sincerely wanted to help his clients address their problems, remembering what had been taught to him in school, the thought of applying this knowledge was frightening. In school Juan learned numerous intervention methods which supported his generalist approach to practice, yet he was concerned that he would not interpret the client's problems correctly or make the wrong decisions when beginning helping activities. Ideas such as always remembering to respect the "individual worth" and "dignity" of each client and maximizing self-determination were strong in his memory. He knew that he should never compromise his professional values or show lack of respect for the client's culture, values, or beliefs. For Juan, as for many beginning social work professionals, discovering the best thing to do is never easy.

Furthermore, Juan was never exactly sure who his client was. Was it the person suffering from the problem? Was it the family? Was it the group the person associated with or the community in which the person lived? Was the "client" even more extensive—was it the policy or legislation leading to the client's problem that required change? Or was it all of the above?

Juan's experience is quite normal for a beginning social worker. As we've commented, social work is not purely a science. Many aspects of helping have much more to do with art than science and creating the best fit for the client in his/her situation. The skills required to practice this art take time and experience to develop and, in fact, also depend on continual updating of what many professionals would consider the science of social work, where we prove that what we do does indeed make a difference. In this way, we can show the evidence of improvement reflective of clear goals and guidelines within the practice structure.

Deciding how best to handle a client's situation is never easy, nor should it be. The best practice interventions require constant assessment, reassessment, evaluation, and collaboration with other professionals (O'Hare. 2009). Furthermore, on any professional team, options will vary on how to interpret, select, and apply best helping strategies. Remember, applying helping skills to problem situations is an

Name: Sharon R. Williamson

Place of Residence: Walton, KY

College/University Degrees: BA in Sociology, University of Florida (*Go Gators!*)

Present Position and Title: Medicaid Waiver sponsored Case Manager for MRDD Population; Supports for Community Living Case Manager; MSW student at the University of Cincinnati.

Previous Work/Volunteer Experience: Case Management for various oppressed populations and Supportive Employment for MRDD population for over 20 years; previous work with Special Olympics.

Why did you choose social work as a career? My undergraduate degree is in sociology and has allowed me the opportunity, over the past 20 years, to assist and learn from various oppressed populations such as the elderly, the mentally ill, and mostly from the MRDD population. The main thing I have learned is that to truly be effective in creating change (and not just providing assistance), you need to have the foundation in the profession of social work. I feel that social workers not only provide the assistance and advocate for self-empowerment to help oppressed populations, but they have the ability to help change society so that the numbers of oppressed people needing assistance and/or empowerment can be reduced.

My life partner and two of my dearest friends are LCSWs and have had a great influence on me. They have been excellent role models (thanks Jan, Jill, and Sophia) and have taught me that no matter what happens, you need to be ethical in all of your dealings with people. They have set a very high standard that I hope to be able to follow. If I can be half the social worker my life partner is, I feel that I will have accomplished something very rare and special.

What is your favorite social work story? I was recently doing an assessment on an individual who was newly assigned to my caseload. He and I were discussing how he views himself in terms of positive attributes. He told me that he was "sexy and some peoples knows it." He went on to say that he is a nice guy and that "peoples should like him." It was so enlightening to see this positive self-description from this young man when so many of our MRDD individuals have such poor self-esteem.

I have had the privilege and pleasure of working for a great many individuals whose self-esteem was a major barrier in their lives. To have this young man feel so confident that others should like him and find him attractive gave me hope that, with the right supports, other individuals on my caseload can feel that good about themselves, too.

What is one thing you would change in the community if you had the power to do so? I am and will continue to be a strong advocate for realistic normalization for every individual with MRDD. I also believe that we must instill a sense of personal responsibility and accountability in the training we provide to this population. I have seen regulations from state departments of mental retardation in three states stress that caregivers must provide the same privileges and rights to the MRDD population as is provided to the nondisabled. However, I have failed to see regulations that emphasize the need to provide training to help this population become more accountable and responsible for their own actions, as much as is realistically possible. I feel we do a disservice to these folks when we only stress the privileges and do not teach them about being a responsible member of society, too.

---

art; situations vary and options are diverse. From an ecological systems perspective, practice strategy and intervention must occur on multiple levels to achieve treatment goals and objectives (Franklin, Jordan, & Hopson, 2008). This diversity is one strength of social work, and an important part of the helping process is identifying and supporting alternatives and innovative strategies. The goal is not chaotic improvisation. The general practice consensus is that all client-based interventions take place within a practice framework with clear theoretical foundations. When working in the practice environment it remains clear that the expectation is to have good problem identification, contracting, and case planning skills (Dziegielewski, 2008a; 2008b).

In this chapter we explore the concept of diversity and how it relates to generalist social work practice. From this orientation all clients (individuals, families, and groups) are viewed through a culturally sensitive "lens"; this means that client strengths are recognized and supported at each step of the helping process (Diller, 2004). We also discuss the three most common approaches to social work practice: micropractice, mezzopractice, and macropractice. Social workers must be well versed in all three, though their efforts to assist clients may be concentrated at only one or two of these.

DIVERSITY AND SOCIAL WORK PRACTICE

A distinguishing hallmark of the social work profession is its insistence to view practice within a specific context, commonly referred to as "**contextual practice**." As a client-centered approach, contextual practice suggests that all practice methods consider a variety of unique attributes or characteristics, which in turn, influence what we do with and on behalf of clients. One type of intervention may work for one person or group, but not necessarily for another. The characteristics that an individual, family, group, or community bring to the relationship are powerful influences shaping and molding the client-centered intervention.

Why? Because we are all different, from different backgrounds, with different experiences, ideas, philosophies, and traditions. A simple way to start to understand that basic differences in thinking and responding can occur is to read John Gray's classic book, *Men Are from Mars, Women Are from Venus* (1992), which details gender differences. Think back to your introductory sociology course: we learn from sociology that norms, mores, and folkways create our individual skeletal system from which our character and behaviors take shape.

The first step toward understanding differences is recognizing the life experiences of each individual. For example, a lesbian womaen, or a person with HIV/

AIDS, or a person with a disability might not experience an event in a similar way compared to someone who does not have these conditions or circumstances. In the case of the lesbian woman, common experiences with a history of marginalization, stigmatization, and discrimination can clearly affect the social context that surrounds the disorder (Dodd & Booker, 2008). The person with a disability may have to contend with beliefs that socially marginalize them; Mackelprang and Salsgiver (2009) use the term *albeism* (often interchangeably with the term *disableism*) to describe the belief that people with disabilities are inferior to nondisabled people because of their differences (p. 9). Furthermore, people with disabilities may be left vulnerable, requiring the help and assistance of others simply to meet their daily needs (Fitzsimons, 2009).

What makes this more complicated to understand is that there are "differences within differences." For example, to label certain diverse peoples as Hispanic can ignore the fact that there will always be cultural differences between those who are designated "Hispanic" among those that are Mexican, Cuban, Puerto Rican, or Spanish, just as there are differences between Asian Americans who are Chinese, Filipino, Japanese, Korean, Vietnamese, or Samoan. And, to complicate matters further, is it fair to say all Mexicans will act one way and all Puerto Ricans another way? Also, be careful not to assume, for example, that if you have a Muslim student in your group, he or she represents all Muslims (Nadir & Dziegielewski, 2001; Rehman & Dziegielewski, 2003). Nothing could be further from the truth, and this type of attitude can be frustrating for all involved. Yet at times the unfortunate mistake is made that places all individuals in certain groupings together, and they are assumed to be alike. It is critical always to remember that individual differences will always exist in all attempts at grouping.

This makes the second step in understanding and recognizing diversity which involves the factoring of individual differences and life experiences as part of the intervention strategy. In this way, we recognize the uniqueness of the individual and understand the influence and power of these unique dimensions on the human experience. Therefore, before we talk about the types of practice utilized in social work, it is crucial to understand diversity, what are the similarities and differences, taking an individualized approach and recognizing how shared perceived "differences" influence practice. And, once identified, we must understand how this information can be integrated into generalist practice strategy.

Understanding, recognizing, and integrating diversity into practice strategy is so important in the field that often social work programs, undergraduate and graduate alike, require students to complete one or more courses that cover this topic. In addition, elements related to diversity are generally covered in almost every course you may take in your undergraduate or graduate program. So don't be surprised if in several if not all the chapters in this book this topic in one form or another may continually resurface. Sue and Sue (2008) discuss a concept called cultural universality and how it relates to cultural relativism. The term *etic* relates to what is culturally universal whereas the term *emic* relates to what is culturally specific. The new social worker should always operate from the emic position where everything is challenged and explored. From this perspective it is important to outline how cultural values, lifestyles, and worldviews can affect how our clients think and respond. Space limits our discussion and focus; so although not all groups can be included in our discussion, we expect that by the end of this chapter you will understand three key points: first, the importance of understanding your own cultural perceptions and potential biases; second, that cultural, racial, or ethnic dimensions are critical elements of successful professional helping to consider when working with clients; and last, not ALL people who constitute certain similar groups are the same.

MEASUREMENT OF DIVERSE PEOPLE—THE U.S. CENSUS

Since 1790, the United States census has been taken every ten years. The "count" gives the government direction in a variety of matters, such as the number of U.S. Representatives assigned to a state or the amount of funding a state receives from the federal government for certain programs. Census data are used by public and private agencies to chart population trends and shifting mobility patterns. These planners then interpret data and project need and response to "changing demographic patterns." For example, at the turn of the twentieth century, census data revealed significant migration streams of people from rural communities to the nation's urban areas, and within a few short years the majority of the nation's population lived in urban areas. In terms of employment and business forecasts, the recently released 2006 census data also support an increase of no-employee or small businesses that do not hire employees. This can include family-run businesses or husband-and-wife teams but definitely shows a changing demographic.

Activity...Visit the United States Census Bureau web page (www.census.gov) and download a copy of the short and long forms for the 2000 census. Which do you think provides information that gives a better picture of the United States? Why?

According to the 2000 census, the United States population was 281,421,906. According to the U.S. Census Bureau current figures for the 2007 census, our nation's population was 305,931,227 as of December 21, 2008 (retrieved from http://factfinder.census.gov/home), although by the time you read this number, the statistic will already be out of date! This is because the actual survey was conducted several years ago and the population continues to grow, and therefore the growth related changes that occurred after the numbers were recorded are not reflected. In addition, regardless of when the information is collected, it still remains difficult to count every person in the United States. For example, how would you count the homeless population, in particular those who do not live in shelters but stay on the street? How do you count the migrant worker population? And how do we know where every house, home, or shelter is in the United States where people stay can be recorded? Although numerous controls are in place to help with this, the basic problem in recording the total picture can affect many aspects of the numbers being reported. For example, as of 2007, all people living in poverty totaled 298,699 with 73,996 of these individuals under the age of 18 and 36,790 age 65 or older (U.S. Census Bureau, Current Population Survey, 2008 Annual Social and

Economic Supplement). Although you may find these numbers helpful, caution should always be used and dated census information and undercounting of the poor and underserved in the population are just two reasons why the numbers generated by the census data are not an absolute measure.

In terms of data related to health insurance coverage in the United States based on information collected from the Current Population Survey (CPS) and the Annual Social and Economic Supplement (ASEC), which support the work of the Census Bureau, estimates show that the median household income for 2006 and 2007 continued to increase, the poverty rate has not changed significantly, and both the number and the percent of people without health insurance coverage decreased between 2006 and 2007.

DIVERSITY BY RACE AND ETHNICITY IN THE UNITED STATES

The United States is a patchwork quilt of people with males, females, old, young, multi-race, single race, an array of ethnic groups, rural and urban—these being just a few ways to identify diversity. However, the most common denominator when thinking about diversity seems to be race and/or ethnicity.

Essentially one determines his/her race by self-identification, which may be sociopolitical in nature rather than anthropological by design (Mulroy, 2004; Wallerstein, 2002). In 1997, the federal government's Office of Management and Budget identified five racial categories that remained the key organizing groups to identify diversity for the ten-year census categories starting with the 2000 census. These groups include: American Indian and Alaska Native, Asian, Black or African American, Native Hawaiian and other Pacific Islander, and White. The term *Hispanic origin* was denoted as ethnicity. This category on the 2000 survey was different from those before it as individuals were given the choice to use one or more racial categories to identify their racial identities. This major change in categorization that occurred in 2000 has really affected our ability to compare the 2000 and after surveys with those that came from the 1990s and before. In addition, for those who could not fit into any of the above categories an additional category, "some other race," was added; in this category, a respondent could simply check this box and write in a more specific race group.

Within these groupings are subgroups. For example, Asian includes Asian Indian, Chinese, Filipino, Japanese, Korean, Vietnamese, Cambodian, Hmong, Laotian, Thai, and other Asian. Within these subgroups are additional identifiers: Hmong, for example, includes people who categorize themselves as Hmong, Laohmong, or Mong. For Hispanic individuals, a self-identification question was used. These individuals were asked if they were persons of Spanish/Hispanic/Latino orgin. Further classification of this group included Mexican, Puerto Rican, Cuban, as well as others that indicated they were from Spain, the Spanish-speaking countries of Central or South America, other Hispanic, or from other Spanish or Latino origins (U.S. Census Bureau, Statistical Abstracts for the United States, 2009). As you can see in table 1, the majority of the population clearly speaks only English at home, followed by the second-largest number speaking Spanish or Spanish Creole.

Table 1: Languages Spoken at Home, 2006

The American Community Survey universe includes the household population and the population living in institutions, college dormitories, and other group quarters. Based on a sample and subject to sampling variability; language number in 1,000s.

Total population 5 years old and over	**279,013**
Speak only English	224,154
Spanish or Spanish Creole	34,045
French (incl. Patois, Cajun)	1,396
French Creole	602
Italian	829
Portuguese or Portuguese Creole	683
German	1,136
Yiddish	153
Other West Germanic languages	255
Scandinavian languages	130
Greek	353
Russian	823
Polish	640
Serbo-Croatian	271
Other Slavic languages	312
Armenian	217
Persian	349
Gujarathi	299
Hindi	505
Urdu	325
Other Indic languages	613
Other Indo-European languages	394
Chinese	2,493
Japanese	475
Korean	1,061
Mon-Khmer, Cambodian	184
Hmong	187
Thai	140
Laotian	147
Vietnamese	1,208
Other Asian languages	609
Tagalog	1,416
Other Pacific Island languages	356
Navajo	176
Other Native North American languages	205
Hungarian	97
Arabic	733
Hebrew	225
African languages	697
Other and unspecified languages	122

Source: U.S. Census Bureau (2008) information from 2006 American Community Survey; B16001. Language Spoken at Home by Ability to Speak English for the Population 5 Years and Over; using American FactFinder®; http://factfinder.census.gov.

In looking at the application and understanding of diversity in regard to generalist practice it is crucial to remember that diversity is not limited to racial identity, but also includes a variety of other attributes. All of which, including differences in language, can make communication difficult for those who are not aware of how these differences can impair communication. Knowledge and recognition about these "differences" is important and can help the social worker better understand and develop effective practice intervention plans.

THE GENERALIST SOCIAL WORKER AND DIVERSITY

Generalist social workers are employed in a variety of agencies, both public and private, and must develop helping relationships with all kinds of clients. Generalist work therefore, as articulated in the CSWE Curriculum Policy Statement, requires a broad range of knowledge and skills allowing problems and their solutions to be assessed comprehensively (Barker, 2003). Furthermore, the definition that we as a profession use to represent diversity goes beyond that outlined in the U.S. Census. In social work, we are very concerned about enunciating a commitment to improving practices and policies, whether intentional or nonintentional, related to racism, immigrants, and refugees as well as lesbian, gays, bisexual, and transgendered people. Moreover, generalist social workers often extend beyond what would be considered clinical services bridging the person-and-situation/person-and-environment stance allowing for the coordination and expansion on the work of other professionals. In such cases the generalist is an invaluable member of the helping team, not only bridging the person and the environment but also facilitating communication and fostering continuity of care (Barker, 2003; Dziegielewski, 2004).

Did You Know…In 1998 the field of social work in the United States celebrated a century of professional social work education and recognized more than 100 years of contributions to the well-being of individuals, groups, families, communities, and the natural environment. This was such an important event that Volume 43, Number 6, of the NASW journal Social Work *was dedicated to accomplishments in social work practice.*

Taking an Empowering Approach to Practice

In today's social work practice environment, the idea of "empowerment" and using client-oriented resources and support systems should not be underestimated. It is the uniqueness of the individual, group, or community that we must accentuate in each step of the helping process, whatever method of practice we select. This needs to be tied to self-maintenance where the changes made are fostered for continuance within the system. To put it simply, when the formal intervention ends the effects and changes made are self-sustaining. These changes need to be fostered in such a way that they continue long after the social worker is gone. Almost all clients respond favorably when they are acknowledged for their strengths and challenged to achieve their full potential. Also, when they feel there is a plan that will allow the changes to continue, they can feel secure in what can and will continue to be accomplished.

Empowerment, as a central theme of social work practice, reflects the profession's emphasis on strengths and suggests that the client has the ability to make decisions and pursue change. So often in looking at a problem we focus on the "pathology" rather than on the strengths that the client brings to the situation. For example, when addressing the needs of a disabled client, we can focus on his inability to participate fully at the workplace. This narrow view, however, can ignore valuable information. The client experiencing trouble functioning may have been unsuccessful in some ways, but what about the ways in which success has been achieved? The disabled often overcome barriers that the nondisabled may not notice. Social workers must ask what strengths the client has and how the client has overcome obstacles in his/her life. The emphasis is placed on the client's strengths, resiliency, and coping style, with a clear focus on the client's ability to succeed. What makes more sense if you want to motivate and support someone: focusing on strengths and successes or on problems and failures?

Empowerment also requires providing access to the resources and information necessary for success (Fitzsimons, 2009). We cannot expect clients to succeed if they don't have the resources nor do they know how to get them. Just providing resources without the knowledge to make it self-sustaining yields limited positive results.

> *Did You Know…The Hollis-Taylor report, a study conducted in 1951, showed that the social work profession was becoming increasingly specialized and fragmented in the delivery of services. Many social workers were treating client problems on a case-by-case basis. The report emphasized a more generic orientation to social work practice, with greater concern for social issues and social action. Many objectives set in this report were accepted by the profession and now form the basis of what is taught in many schools of social work today (Barker, 2003).*

Trust, respect, and treating the client with civility are all part and parcel of empowerment. Without these core ingredients, we cannot foster the client's sense of self-worth and ability to look realistically at resolving a problem. People often say, "Social workers empower their clients"—as if social workers have a bag of magic dust that we sprinkle on clients. Poof, we empower the client! In reality, empowerment comes from within. Social workers help clients to find and sharpen the skills and tools they possess and to look for the resources they may need. Social workers facilitate the empowerment process, but it is clients themselves who make it happen. In addition, the cornerstone of all intervention efforts rests in the social worker's ability to understand his or her own values, while not imposing those values and beliefs on others (Hodge, 2003; Sue & Sue, 2008). From this perspective the social worker recognizes the importance of not encouraging the client to change his or her views to reflect that of the social worker and thus achieves client-centered empowerment.

The Systems Perspective

Social work's mission is to engage in a helping activity that enhances opportunities for all people in an increasingly complex environment. From a systems perspective, the essential realization is that human systems are different from other types of systems (Forder, 2008). Social work professionals deal with a variety of human systems—individuals, couples, families, groups, organizations, and communities. In its simplest form a "system" consists of parts that interact so that a change in one part affects all others and the relations among them.

In future social work classes and texts, you'll come across the term "client system." The addition of the word "system" to "client" indicates that an individual, her family, her group, and her community are all interrelated; all are part of the individual's "galaxy" of relations, where each relation influences the others. In considering the client system we focus on the individual within his/her relations with and to other parts of his/her system and seek to understand the extent to which these influence the client.

Activity…Look at yourself as a system. Identify the components of your "galaxy"— family, friends, associations, workplace, and other aspects of your life. Imagine arranging these items with "me" in the middle and drawing a circle around each one to indicate the portion of your environment that it makes up. Do any of the circles overlap? For example, do you work with any members of your family? Is one circle more influential than the others? Why? Do any of the circles influence the others?

Although a client may initially seek individual help, the social worker may assess that expanding and including a spouse or a significant other may increase the chances of positive change. Consider the case described in box 1: the social worker was given a referral to see one client, Don; but after meeting and talking with him, the social worker realized the importance of including Don's wife and his dietitian. A basic assessment, intervention plan, and referral process initiated by the social worker with Don's permission and participation helped to harness the strengths of the client system, thereby helping Don to promote his own physical health.

In addition to addressing Don's particular needs, the social worker believed that advocacy might be needed in order to help other clients like Don. The social worker talked with other professionals in the hospital to inquire about similar prior occurrences. It soon became apparent that Don's situation wasn't unusual. The discussions initiated by the social worker led to the issue being brought before the hospital's quality care management team and the development of a new protocol which required the interviewing and assessment of all diabetic clients regarding their living situations. This advocacy did not benefit Don directly, but it benefited others who could be prevented from landing in a similar situation.

For the generalist social worker using a system's perspective, the helping activity assumes four roles: education, advocacy, facilitation, and intervention.

Box 1: The Case of Don: The Systems Perspective

Don, a 54-year-old Hispanic male who was not following his diabetic diet, was referred to a social worker for discharge planning. Don's medical condition was worsening and his physician had become very frustrated with Don's noncompliance with his assigned treatment. According to the physician, Don was well aware that he was causing himself harm and might actually lose his eyesight if he did not change his behavior. In the interview with the social worker, Don appeared resistant. He stated that he was trying but that he found it hard to stick to his diet. He was too busy and tired when he got home from work to worry about the food he ate. He said his wife worked hard to cook what he liked, and he also did not want to disappoint her.

During the interview the social worker explored Don's situation by asking questions about his lifestyle, his job, and whether he lived alone. Don stated that he had been married for 30 years and had no children. Don's wife was a homemaker who prepared most of the meals, which included packing him a sack lunch to take to work every day. In an attempt to find out more about Don's support system the social worker asked Don if his wife had participated in the dietetic counseling he was provided. Don seemed surprised and said no, she had not. When asked why his wife had not participated in any of the educational sessions about his condition, Don replied that she had not been invited. Also, since she was such an excellent cook he was not sure this type of class would interest her anyway.

With Don's permission, the social worker called his wife to talk about their both coming in. The social worker also asked Don if he would come back and bring his wife so that they could discuss his diabetic condition with the dietitian and his physician. At Don's request the social worker agreed to join them in these meetings, helping Don and his wife to explore what they needed to do to safeguard his health. In the discussions that occurred it became apparent to the social worker that Don's wife felt she may have caused his condition with her cooking. Don's wife had been told by her mother-in-law that her cooking was what caused his health to get worse. Education in regard to the probable causes of the condition was explained and the social worker provided the wife with written materials about the condition to bring back to the mother-in-law. A meeting with the dietician was also arranged, asking for copies of meal plans that could be shared with relatives if needed to assure them they were working together on his health issues. The counseling the social worker provided helped the couple feel more secure with the immediate needs as well as how to address the concerns of other family members. After this intervention and at a six-week follow-up Don continued to follow his diet regime. He even joked that his wife was enjoying the cooking classes that she had attended and now he never knew what he was going to eat for lunch or supper. He also stated he wished he could get his mother to attend as well.

Through this perspective the social worker serves as enabler, broker, mediator, advocate, resource person, gatekeeper, educator, and trainer (Chan & Law, 2008). While performing these functions that often overlap the helping activities, social workers often go beyond working with the originally identified client.

First, education of the client is essential. Education is intended to increase awareness of the services needed and to empower clients to address problems that previously seemed insurmountable. The social worker's practice activities often involve helping clients to secure the information they need and fostering connections that link clients to services and resource systems contributing to resolving their problems.

Social workers can educate clients in many different areas. In Don's case the social worker provided education in the meeting with Don and his wife while bringing to the forefront the concerns the wife had about family blaming her for making him ill. The couple needed to be educated about the condition in an atmosphere where they were comfortable asking questions about the causes of diabetes. The social workers can work with the couple to facilitate communication by exploring questions or having them write down the questions to ask the physician at the next visit. The social worker also saw the frustration the wife felt with the family and suggested she take home written information to show them she was taking care of her husband as expected and, as she put it, "following orders." Facilitating the meeting with the dietitian was important to discuss the medical need for Don to maintain the proposed diet and the consequences if he does not. Getting copies of the meal plans helped to formalize what the wife was trying to do in terms of cooking differently. The worker facilitated the dialogue between the dietitian and the family and helped to support both in asking questions and clarifying discussion. After the meeting, Don's wife understood what was needed from her, and Don's diet compliance improved dramatically. This case demonstrates how a social worker can assist by educating the entire client system—the client, his family, and other members of the delivery team.

Education is important in all practice settings. Child abuse, domestic violence and incest dynamics, parent-child relations, caregiving, homemaker services, and health care, just to name a few, are areas where education commonly takes place. Social workers understand the importance of going beyond the traditional bounds of counseling. They can assist in educating clients to better maintain the safety, security, and wellness not only of themselves but of their families.

Activity...Go to the library and find the journal Social Work, Volume 43, Number 6. *Think about what the articles in this special issue tell you about the following questions:*

1. What types of contributions did social workers make in micro-, mezzo-, and macropractice?

2. How do social workers feel about the Code of Ethics, and what does it mean to each area of social work practice discussed in this chapter?

3. What issues in the history of social work do you believe helped to make the profession what it is today?

4. What issues in the field of social work need the attention of today's workers?

Indeed, social workers are uniquely placed to participate in education, particularly in the areas of prevention and continued health and wellness: "As a go-between of services, the social worker is the linkage between the person and a sys-

Name: June Martin Perry

Place of residence: Milwaukee, Wisconsin

College/university degrees: North Carolina Central University, BA in Sociology; University of Wisconsin-Milwaukee, MSSW; University of Wisconsin-Milwaukee, PhD student in the Department of Urban Studies

Present position: CEO and co-founder of New Concept Self Development Center, Inc.

Previous work/volunteer experience: Employee in the Protective Service Unit, as a Family Counselor, and as a Purchase of Service Coordinator in the Milwaukee County Department of Public Welfare. More recently, a seat on the Board of Directors for many schools, non-profit, and charitable organizations, Associate Steward at St. AME Church, Chair of the Mayor's Commission on Crime-Youth and Mental Health Committee, and Co-chair of the 2000 Census project for the city of Milwaukee.

Why did you choose social work as a career? I grew up in a community in South Carolina where those who had more reached out to their neighbors and shared what we had with the less fortunate. Volunteerism was a way of life that has led me to a very rewarding career.

What is your favorite social work story? Over the years, I've met many people who say to me, "You don't remember me but. . ." This is the best part because these are people who I served as a case worker who feel I have impacted their lives positively. I also am proud to be able to hire people who used to be New Concept clients!

What would be the one thing you would change in our community if you had the power to do so? Gun deaths are ravaging our community and creating a culture of violence that is beginning to be tolerated. I would remove access to fire arms.

---

tem of support that maintains health, or that may be the means of detecting illness early, or of preventing deterioration of the problem" (Dziegielewski, 2004; Skidmore, Thackeray, & Farley, 1997).

Second, advocacy helps clients to identify their own strengths and use individual and community resources to support their efforts to change. Advocacy does not always mean doing something for the client; it often means helping or teaching the client how to do things for herself. Issues of individual worth and dignity must always be considered. Therefore, every social worker must know how to maintain cultural integrity while fostering change, allowing diversity to flourish.

Third, facilitation consists of making connections among different resource systems which enhance responsiveness and usefulness. The social worker may contact agencies to support and mobilize the client and others in the client system. It is here that direct intervention is found, whereby the social worker actually makes the connections needed to help the client (e.g., arranging transportation services to a medical appointment, or registration with programs such as Meals on Wheels). Direct intervention occurs when the client is unable to intervene on his/her own behalf or simply needs assistance to do so successfully.

PERSON-IN-SITUATION: GUIDING THE PRACTICE FRAMEWORK

Generalist practice is more than simply combining methods of practice such as casework, group work, and community organizing. It requires a theoretical practice framework involving structured ideas and beliefs that provide a foundation for helping. Within this framework, the applied knowledge and theory is consistent with social work values and ethics from a person-in-situation context. This person-in-situation or person-in-environment context differentiates social work from other helping professions. Additionally, most professional social workers feel strongly that practice should be guided by theory. Therefore, engaging in a theory-absent practice is deficient, helping efforts are decreased, and the client system is deprived of needed professional helping activities.

The systems perspective is part of the conceptual framework used to understand and assess human relations in context in social work. It reflects the person-in-situation or person-in-environment stance that has always underpinned social work practice, focusing attention on an individual, a collective, a policy, a program, a practice, or any concrete or abstract unit in dynamic interaction with an environment.

A practice framework always addresses issues of human diversity. As we have stated throughout this book social workers always recognize and respect human diversity when forming and maintaining professional relations. Furthermore, social workers are committed to promoting social justice and professional ethical conduct. Social work has historically been concerned with oppressed and disadvantaged populations. The profession's focus on human diversity and social justice reinforces its ethically driven commitment to serving people who do not receive an equitable share of social resources. The commitment and adherence to a professional code of conduct is essential for any type of professional practice, be it generalist or specialist.

Did You Know...Lee Frankel (1867–1931) was an early social work educator and developer of family casework theories and practice. He established the Training School for Jewish Social Work in New York and became a national leader in early health and welfare organizations (Barker, 2003).

For beginning social work professionals, deciding where and how best to engage the client can be difficult because this choice must be linked to the theoretical principles that underlie certain types of helping activity. To accomplish this goal, the social worker reviews the client's situation and based on the client's needs decides what theoretical perspective to use. In other words, the client, not the worker's comfort with or allegiance to a particular practice theory, drives the choice of perspective. The theoretical practice approach and helping strategy employed are firmly based in the reality of the client's environment.

At times making this link may seem too difficult or time-consuming, but acknowledging the relation between environment and the selected practice method is critical. For example, one of the authors worked with an elderly male client with a history of alcohol abuse who received treatment only to be discharged back into an environment that encouraged him to relapse. The return to his previous environment negated much of the influence of the intervention and started a pattern of repeated rehabilitation attempts with numerous admissions to treatment centers. He always seemed to respond well while in the program but on discharge quickly relapsed into alcohol abuse. After numerous failed interventions, he was referred to a social worker. The social worker assessed his situation thoroughly and examined the type of home environment to which he was returning. The social worker discovered that because of his instability and troubles with alcohol the client was unable to maintain a bank account. Therefore, when it came time to cash his social security check, he used the local bar as his bank. His check arrived each month, he would pick it up, and there was only one place he knew was willing to cash it—that local bar. To complicate matters, the bar would cash checks upon purchase only. It's clear what the consequences were. Assessing the client's discharge environment was critical to applying a helping strategy. To assist the client, the social worker initiated a supervised living arrangement and helped the client to acquire his own bank account where his social security check was directly deposited.

In formulating a helping strategy the method chosen must be congruent with the needs and desires of the client system being served as well as reflective of the values and ethics of the social work profession. Beginning social workers often feel trapped within a system driven by social, political, cultural, and economic factors so powerful that they influence the practice techniques and skills that are utilized. In addressing the needs of the poor, the disadvantaged, and those who are culturally different from the majority culture, it is the diversity of problems and of people who experience them that makes social work practice an art. How can social workers constantly evaluate what is happening to the client and whether societal factors—race, sexual orientation, and so forth—affect the way a problem is viewed? How can the beginning professional take into account all system variables that affect the helping relationship? How does a social worker maintain the dignity and worth of each client served and ensure that her own feelings and prejudices never enter the helping relationship? Furthermore, if a client has values or beliefs that could lead to hate crimes and actions, the social worker must be able to identify these feelings and help the client address them before a potential hate crime erupts (see box 2).

There are no easy answers to these questions. To address each of these questions and give it the attention it deserves would take several books just to begin. Yet it is critical that each client system be treated individually, no matter how similar a case may be to one the social worker has already encountered.

Box 2: Hate Crimes a Consequence of Diversity

The social work profession celebrates all forms of diversity and recognizes that differences among people provide valuable opportunities and tools in the helping relationship. At the same time, there is another side to diversity that we must address—fear of others and their differences. Sociology refers to this as xenophobia, a fear or hatred of foreigners or strangers. Hate crimes are a direct by-product of xenophobia and are directed at people who are "different"—differences are based on any characteristic(s) such as race, gender, sexual orientation, religious affiliation, or political views. Simply stated, there is no logic to a hate crime other than fear. Social workers recognize that clients are often victims, or at-risk of being victims, of hate crimes.

All too often, diversity is associated with "hate crimes"—any of various crimes . . . when motivated by hostility to the victim as a member of a group, as one based on color, creed, gender, or sexual orientation (http://www.infoplease.com/spot/hatecrimes.html).

The Southern Poverty Law Center (http://www.splcenter.org/) is a nationally recognized organization that tracks and combats hate crimes in the United States. According to the Center, there are in the United States 602 active hate groups and 158 "Patriot Groups," that is, organizations that define themselves as opposed to the "New World Order" or advocate or adhere to extreme antigovernment doctrines (http://www.splcenter.org/intelligence-project/ip-index.html; http://www.splcenter.org/intelligenceproject/ip-index.html). Examples of hate crimes and their location are listed below. Using intimidation through emotional, physical, or psychological means, hate crimes are a mechanism to oppress individuals and groups.

Examples of hate crimes in the United States:

JOHNSTON COUNTY, N.C.

After getting a tip about a plot to blow up the local sheriff's office, the county jail, and the sheriff himself, federal and local law enforcements officers arrested Xxxx, fiery leader of the Nation's Knights of the Ku Klux Klan, on July 19. After the arrest, a search of Xxxx's home uncovered an Uzi and an AK-47, two homemade bombs, and bomb-making materials. In January, Xxxx pleaded guilty to weapons charges. While he awaited sentencing, his wife and three other local Klan members were charged with the murder of an unidentified man. The victim was allegedly killed because he knew about threats against law enforcement officers supposedly made by Xxx, grand dragon (or state leader) of a Klan faction based in nearby Robeson County.

BOSTON, MASS.

Two members of a neo-Nazi terror cell, Xxxx and Xxxx, were convicted on July 26 in a conspiracy to bomb Jewish and African-American landmarks and leaders.

SEMINOLE, FLA.

When police answered a domestic dispute call on Aug. 22, they ended up searching the townhome of podiatrist Xxxx, uncovering plans and ammunition for a series of attacks on

Box 2: Hate Crimes a Consequence of Diversity—(*Continued*)

Islamic targets in Florida. Xxxx, who was reportedly seeking to retaliate for the Sept. 11 attacks and the Palestinian intifada, faces up to 30 years in prison. His wife, xxxi, charged in October with being his accomplice, agreed to cooperate with prosecutors in a plea bargain.

LEWISTON, IDAHO

On Oct. 3, FBI agents seized pipe bombs, homemade land mines, 13 firearms, and 13,000 rounds of ammunition from antigovernment activist Xxxx, who was arrested on seven federal counts and held without bond. A member of the Idaho Mountain Boys militia group, xxx is also a co-conspirator in a plot to kill U.S. District Court Judge xxx.

PHOENIX, ARIZ.

When an Oct. 16 brawl spilled out of the River City Pockets pool hall, police say three white supremacists viciously attacked 20-year-old Xxxx., who was standing nearby waiting for a taxi after applying for a job at the club. The three allegedly chased, tackled, and stomped Bailey to death while yelling "white power."

LOS ANGELES, CALIF.

Jewish Defense League (JDL) National Director Xxxx, charged with plotting to bomb a mosque and a congressman's office, was declared brain dead on Nov. 4 after slashing his throat and then plunging from a balcony in an apparent suicide in federal prison.

REDDING, CALIF.

Xxxx, a devotee of the anti-Semitic Christian Identity religion who teamed with his little brother to firebomb three California synagogues and an abortion clinic, killed himself in Shasta County Jail on Nov. 17. His trial for murdering a gay couple—a crime he said was "God's will" in a confession to newspaper reporters—had been scheduled to start this January.

SANTA ANA AND LONG BEACH, CALIF.

Three of Southern California's most active neo-Nazis were arrested on Nov. 18. Xxxx and boyfriend Xxxx, members of Blood and Honor, were charged with possessing bomb-making materials. Xxxx founded Women for Aryan Unity, a group closely affiliated with the neo-Nazi World Church of the Creator, and launched an "Aryan Baby Drive" to distribute food and clothing to poor white families. Xxxx, head of the "Brandenburg Division" of the Aryan Nations, was arrested on weapons charges. During a search of his apartment, investigators said they found a letter advocating that the Aryan Nations partner with Islamic extremists.

CHEROKEE COUNTY, N.C.

Federal authorities searched more than a year before nabbing Xxxx, a white-supremacist shortwave radio operator and former stalwart of the Kentucky State Militia, on Nov. 22. Anderson had fled into the woods in October 2001 after allegedly firing 25 shots with an automatic at a sheriff's deputy who had stopped him for a traffic violation.

Box 2: Hate Crimes a Consequence of Diversity — (*Continued*)

OLYMPIA, WASH.

Xxxx, a former member of the antigovernment Jural Society who had recently attended a meeting of the anti-Semitic Christian Identity movement, was arrested this Jan. 18 on firearms charges.

LEESBURG, VA.

On Jan. 23, armed FBI and Secret Service agents raided the home of Xxxx, a former National Alliance staff member who owns the neo-Nazi Web site www.tightrope.com. Calvert, who was not arrested, sent an e-mail message to supporters saying the agents seized "10 shitloads" of stuff under the pretext of a copyright infringement for Nike/Nazi shirts he had made.

MACON, GA.

Xxxx, founder and leader of the black supremacist hate group Nuwaubian Nation of Moors, pleaded guilty on Jan. 23 to 77 state charges of molesting 13 children of his cult members.

PHOENIX, ARIZ.

White supremacist Xxxx was sentenced to death on Jan. 24 for murdering his two housemates in 2000. Prosecutors said Xxxx killed one of the housemates, Xxxx, because he believed her unborn baby had been fathered by a black man.

SANTA FE, N.M.

Former Minutemen Militia member Xxxx was arrested on Feb. 14 in connection with two anti-environmental crimes: putting a pipe bomb in an environmental group's mailbox and setting a forest fire in June 1998 that scorched more than 5,100 acres of the Jemez Mountains and nearby Pueblo land. It took more than 800 firefighters and $3.5 million to contain the blaze.

Source: http://www.splcenter.org/intelligenceproject/ip-index.html

SELECTING A PRACTICE METHOD

A multitude of factors must be considered in selecting the most appropriate practice method. Who makes up the client system? What is the target of change? What resources are available to the client system? What is the probability of success given the many elements that can affect the situation? This already sounds complicated, and in fact, it is only a small part of what needs to be considered when choosing a practice method. You'll learn more about these factors, and others, in future social work practice classes.

Although it is beyond the scope of this book to explain the many theoretical and practice frameworks available to social workers and how to use them, we explain the most common practice methods: micro-, mezzo-, and macropractice:

Did You Know...The term "homophyly" acknowledges that people derive comfort and support from people who are like themselves. Culturally sensitive social work practice recognizes this phenomenon. It is one reason why social workers are always encouraged to use a client's own naturally occurring support network whenever possible. Clients are more likely to achieve needed changes when they can work within a system that is familiar to them.

Microlevel practice: More commonly called direct or clinical practice with target populations including individuals, families, and groups; primarily uses face-to-face interaction with client. Since people deliver services, not programs, emphasis is placed on the highly trained case manager or clinical social worker. It is at the microlevel where the emphasis remains on ensuring ongoing supervision training and continuing education designed to improve individual skills and strategy (Walsh & Holton, 2008). From this perspective it is often assumed that the greatest interest lies in the for-profit sector and private practice (Segal-Engelchin & Kaufman, 2008).

Mezzolevel practice: Involves environmental system variables, agency administration with minimal client contact; examines agency effectiveness and policy implementation. It can also evaluate quality programming, systematic organizational barriers, and organizational management functions, including trends with respect to market stabilization of human capital stressing employee maintenance and well-being (Cabrera & Raju, 2001; Everhart & Wandersman, 2000). When agencies offer adequate material supports such as compensation packages, agreeable working conditions, and adequate agency material supports, workers are more likely to stay and support the programs offered (Walsh & Holton, 2008).

Macrolevel practice: Defines client more extensively to include the community or organizations; often deals with broader social problems that impact the community (Hepworth, Rooney & Larsen, 2002; Jansson, 2004; Mulroy, 2004). Here the greatest emphasis is often working in social change agencies and the application of skills designed to change social programs and policies for the betterment of all involved (Segal-Engelchin & Kaufman, 2008).

In the broadest of terms, micropractice is undertaken with individuals, families, and groups; mezzopractice directs our attention to organizational administration; and macropractice involves change within larger systems, such as communities and organizations. You might be thinking that we're playing semantic games, that micro, mezzo, and macro are just new names for casework, group work, and community practice. This is not really true because all three perspectives—micro, mezzo, and macro—apply a systems perspective to analyzing the presenting problem. For example, there are not foci in micropractice; the individual's system is the focus—note the use of singular versus plural. Micropractice involves an individual client with a presenting problem, and our work includes assessment of the system's role in creating, sustaining, or solving the problem—in fact, the system may play all three roles.

As we discussed in a number of places in this book, social work has two significant professional goals. The first is to help people to achieve their potential and to adjust more effectively to the demands of their environment. The second is to make social resources more responsive to people's needs, particularly for poor and disadvantaged people, who often are avoided or neglected. Incorporating these goals into the helping process reinforces social work's dual focus on personal and social problems and emphasizes the importance of linking micro-, mezzo-, and macrochange efforts.

Micropractice

In box 3 we present the case of Maria, who became a client but not through her own choice. Following her rape, she became almost immobilized, unwilling to leave her apartment or see others. A victim's advocate social worker proved instrumental. She was a constant presence for Maria during the critical time following the rape. The advocate explored issues from Maria's childhood and identified unre-

---

Box 3: The Case of Maria: Micropractice

Maria, at age 22, was a victim of rape at her workplace. At the outset of the criminal investigation she met a victim's advocate, who was a BSW social worker employed by the police department. The advocate brought Maria to the hospital and became a major support person for her in the following days. During one of their conversations, the advocate learned that Maria had been a victim of sexual abuse during her childhood. The rape, compounded with her childhood experiences, now had put Maria in a very vulnerable emotional and psychological state: she was unable to go to work or meet family or friends, saying that she would rather just stay at home. Maria was blaming herself for the rape, stating, "I deserved it. Look at my whole life. I deserve it all." The BSW advocate quickly recognized that Maria needed more in-depth help. She referred Maria to a family service agency, where Maria first took part in individual sessions with an MSW social worker.

After a month, the social worker asked Maria how she felt about joining a group of women who had been raped. At first Maria refused, but with gentle, persistent encouragement from the social worker she reluctantly joined the weekly group. Maria's group included seven other women aged 18 to 52. All of the participants reached out to Maria and welcomed her. The social worker, who facilitated the group, told Maria that she did not need to talk unless she wanted too. Discussion at Maria's first group meeting focused on a particular topic: "The Court Hearing." Women shared their fears about the hearings, and some who had been through the courts shared their experiences. Subsequent sessions looked at anger control, relationship building, and becoming a survivor. Maria became an active member of the group and after one year joined the police department as a volunteer victim's advocate.

solved feelings which resurfaced following the rape. Rather than trying to provide in-depth clinical help to Maria, the advocate referred her to a more advanced, MSW social worker, who had expertise in violence against women. The skilled worker was able to help Maria by using a mezzointervention model that employed a variety of processes, education, and therapeutic techniques. Group sessions helped to validate Maria's experiences and those of the other group members as well as to consistently examine the broader system's impact on each of their lives.

In micropractice, as in all social work methods, social worker and client work together to establish goals and objectives and to develop the steps that must be taken to reach these goals. A typical microapproach has social workers dealing with clients, family members and significant others, and at times other groups of people. In this micro approach, the first step is always deciding what the clients wants and taking the action needed to help make it happen (Lanci & Spreng, 2008). Thyer (2008) warns, however, that in addressing the needs of the client all information gathered should be based on empirical data that clearly outline what has been done and the treatment gains that have been made (Thyer, 2008). Maria, for example, was first seen as an individual and later referred to the group setting to continue the intervention process. Had Maria's family lived in the same geographic area they too might have become directly involved in the healing process.

Mezzopractice

Mezzopractice involves minimal face-to-face client contact, focusing rather on administrative intervention within the agency organization. Typical administrative titles include supervisor, unit director, director, executive director, chief executive officer, and president. When the social service agency has a more positive work and service environment, staff turnover will be less and the delivery of higher quality services can result (Glisson, 2008).

Don't leave this chapter with the impression that micro workers do not engage in mezzo activities. In fact, any competent social worker will be knowledgeable and possess basic abilities in mezzo-level tasks. Organizing your workload, preparing monthly reports, conducting policy analysis, supervising staff, and making public presentations to service groups are all mezzo tasks that micro workers will find themselves undertaking.

Did You Know...Hull House is the most famous of all settlement houses, founded in Chicago in 1889 by Jane Addams. Settlement houses were community centers where poor and disadvantaged residents of the area could go for help. These centers were major innovators in social reform.

Individuals in mezzo roles develop expertise in a number of areas but particularly the following:
- Policy formulation and implementation
- Program development
- Funding, budgeting, and resource allocation
- Management of internal structures

♦ Staff and professional supervision
♦ Organizational and professional representation with internal and external groups
♦ Community presentations
♦ Ongoing evaluation of agency effectiveness (Hepworth, Rooney & Larsen, 2002).

Generally, you will find MSW workers assigned to mezzo positions in agencies, while BSW workers are limited to direct service lines. This may not be the case in rural and small communities, however, where with fewer MSW professionals available, the BSW worker is more likely to find an administrative assignment. Although their knowledge and skills may not be as broad and as deep of those of MSW practitioners, baccalaureate practitioners do possess beginning knowledge and skills in mezzo work.

Macropractice

Macropractice directs the worker's attention to change in the larger community, organizational, and policy arenas. Similar to "community organization," macrowork involves helping individuals, groups, and communities with common interests to deal with "social problems and to enhance well-being through planned collective action" (Barker, 2003, p. 84). Typically, micro- or mezzopractice identifies problems, needs, concerns, or issues needing to be addressed that require intervention or change strategy at a much higher level (Jansson, 2004; Mulroy, 2004; Netting, Kettner, & McMurtry, 1993; Sakamoto & Pitner, 2005). Just as micropractitioners and mezzoworkers have specialized knowledge and skills, so too does the macroworker. The macroworker has expertise in the following areas:
♦ Communities, their composition and type—for example, geographic or professional
♦ Power structures within communities and influence within communities
♦ Policy-making procedures
♦ Human service organizations, their purposes, functions, and constituencies
♦ Dynamics and nuances of social problems
♦ Macro-specific tasks such as collaboration and capacity building, negotiation, task group dynamics, marketing, research and analysis, and teaching

Macropractice builds on private issues that become public matters. Substance abuse, for example, involves individuals. Yet the abuse quickly becomes a public matter when it leads to increased crime related to the selling of drugs, lack of workforce participation or missed work due to drug abuse, poor school grades and eventual dropout, and family dysfunction. In the example described in box 4, the macroapproach involved a not-so-subtle nonviolent confrontation with a local storeowner. The owner wasn't sure which would be worse: the wrath of the drug dealers or the lack of neighbors who would purchase items from his store. He decided the latter, and with help from the local police department, drug sales disappeared from the area. An interesting note: when the group's organizer was told

Box 4: The Case of a Drug-free Community: Macropractice

A drug-related shooting took place in the middle of the day in a poor area of town. A few people gathered that evening in a local church and decided that they had had enough, but they didn't know what to do. One of the participants was a social worker from the local neighborhood center. She suggested that the group in fact knew what it wanted—a drug-free community—but now needed to figure out where to begin in order to make this happen. The group expanded and created a neighborhood drug-free task force to act as a "conduit" for the community. Neighbors were invited to share their frustrations at meetings held in churches, school halls, and the neighborhood center. Local social service agencies and elected and appointed officials were asked to come and listen to the neighbor's concerns.

Out of these meetings came a plan for a march through the neighborhood, with the police leading the parade and marching with citizens. The group decided to include a social action activity by marching to the primary spot where drugs were sold, a mom-and-pop convenience store, one block from the public elementary school. Once at the store, the marchers, about two hundred people, formed a long single-file line, and each walked in without saying a word and left one dollar on the counter. The police stood in front of the store and within minutes there was a noticeable disappearance of the drug pushers! Over the following weeks, the storeowner worked with the local task force and police; the drug pushers stopped selling in the neighborhood and moved out of the community. The storeowner joined the task force when it took on other substance abuse issues in the community.

that the dealers were only going to another neighborhood, he responded, "Then that's their problem and they will have to organize them out of the community like we did."

In this application of macropractice the social worker helped the group to develop a plan of action and supported the group as it organized itself. The worker facilitated the process, helped to mobilize significant agencies and local leaders, and provided background research—essentially providing the neighborhood group with the tools it needed to become successful. What began as an individual problem ended up as a community macroissue whose resolution brought about significant changes in the daily lives of individuals, families, and organizations in the neighborhood.

Did You Know...Mother Jones was Mary Harris Jones (1830–1930), a community organizer and labor union advocate who led many strikes against inhumane treatment of children and adults. She advocated better child labor laws and less dangerous working conditions in the mining and steel industries (Barker, 2003).

In Brief: Short-Term Intervention Approaches

Having looked at micro-, mezzo-, and macropractice, we would not be helpful if we didn't touch on one major issue facing social workers who practice at the microlevel.

Whether we like it or not, current social work practice is now dominated by brief, or short-term, practice models (see, for example, figures 1a, b). There are also many different approaches that could fall in this category, but regardless of the methods that are used there are two tasks that seem to overlap. The first is that the helping process needs to occur quickly (short duration) and the second is to prove it works. This means clearly identifying what the client wants to accomplish and working out a system to measure the accomplishments of the goals and objectives outlined. There are many reasons for this trend, but the major influence is money: getting the "biggest bang for the buck." Our current environment is limited in terms of financial and human resources, and there is little chance this will ever change (Ligon, 2009). Insurance companies, as third-party payers (those who pay a provider for services for another person, thus "third party"), and health care organizations limit the time during which a client system may receive a service. Simply stated, third-party payers will not underwrite long-term intervention if a short-term model will help, even if the end is less desirable than what a longer term approach may yield. Social workers therefore employ time-limited approaches as a major practice model.

In other cases clients simply don't have the time, desire, or money for long-term social work microservices. People today are working more hours, sometimes two jobs, and have less time to devote to the "self." With less time available, they are unwilling to commit extra time and energy to go beyond simply addressing the cause of the problem. Practitioners can become frustrated when the presenting problem and the underlying issues clearly require a long-term model but the client system, for any number of reasons, is only willing or able to look at the surface issue.

Figures 1a, b: Scenes in a migrant farm worker camp in Michigan. Workers come to Michigan in June to pick strawberries and leave in late fall after the apple harvest. The workers travel in vans and trucks as they move from one region of the country to another, following the harvest cycles.

So often, new social workers aren't all interested in social welfare policy. Students taking policy courses often complain, "Why do I need this course? It has nothing to do with social work!" The ongoing national debate about health insurance and resulting services shows one reason why we need to understand policy and how to influence its scope and design. Our practice grows out of policy: Change policy and you can change practice. Change the ways that third-party payers reimburse for service and you can change your practice. These days insurance rarely covers long-term encounters, and short-term, time-limited practice is the norm.

So what do we mean by short-term, or brief, practice? Short-term practice generally ranges from six to eight meetings (Wells & Phelps, 1990); however, as many as twenty have been noted (Fanger, 1995). For many social workers only seeing a client system once is becoming commonplace. Dziegielewski (2004) refers to this as intermittent therapy, where the most is done in the available time.

We must realize social work practice encounters are going to be brief. Planning for this short duration in implementing a helping strategy is critical; lack of planning can result in numerous unexpected endings for the client (Wells, 1994) and can also contribute to feelings of failure and decreased job satisfaction for the social work professional (Dziegielewski, 2008a; Holliman, Dziegielewski & Datta, 2001; Resnick & Dziegielewski, 1996). Limited time and service provision restrictions can result in increased job complexity and fewer defined procedures for achievable successful outcomes. These practice constraints can lead to decreased job satisfaction and exit from the job market (Cabrera & Raju, 2001).

WE ALL MAKE MISTAKES!

A number of years ago a t-shirt often worn at social work gatherings had a Superman logo on the front; but rather than a big "S" the yellow and red lettering spelled out "Super Social Worker." The apparent exaggeration was ironic because at times the efforts of social workers really did seem Herculean. No one can dispute, however, that social workers are human beings and therefore, unlike Superman, are vulnerable and capable of making mistakes. However hard we try, everyone of us is subject to err. Social workers are only human!

Therefore, all social workers must try to minimize the number of mistakes made and, of course, mitigate any potential harm to the clients served. Moreover, a mistake should be viewed as a "learning moment." A natural reaction may be to act defensively and try to blame others; however, professionals take responsibility for what they do. When in supervision with a trained professional, the beginning social worker has the opportunity to explore a mistake and replay what happened, as if watching it on videotape. It is important to evaluate what actually happened and what might have happened had some other strategy been implemented. Social workers use professional supervision as a forum for these detailed discussions so that the same or similar mistakes can be avoided in the future. The most powerful resource that a social worker has is the ability to seek supervisory help or peer consultation about a problem.

CULTURALLY SENSITIVE PRACTICE

Social workers must help clients to maintain cultural integrity and must respect diversity. The term "ethnic identity" is generally defined as common heritage, customs, and values unique to a group of people (Casas, 1984; Fong, 2009; Queralt, 1996; Worden, 1999). Social science researchers often gather information on race and ethnicity, yet the difference between the two concepts is pronounced. Race is partially based on physical characteristics of genetic origin (Helms, 1990). Ethnicity embraces a much broader range of commonalities, such as religion, customs, geography, and history. These commonalities between individuals and within a community define and bond members, thereby giving an ethnic backdrop to everyday life. Ethnicity can thus influence thinking and feeling and can pattern behavior in both obvious and subtle ways (Leon & Dziegielewski, 1999; Sakamoto & Pitner, 2005). It is easy to overlook the deeper influence of ethnicity because it often appears to be natural and to consist simply of daily behavior—for example, what individuals eat or how they react.

Activity...Ethical, culturally sensitive social work practice emphasizes the concepts of "respect," "self-determination," and "remaining nonjudgmental." Together with a fellow student, and without using any references, outline briefly what you understand each of these ideas to mean. Then consult a social work resource such as the Social Work Dictionary *or the* Encyclopedia of Social Work *and define them again. Compare your first set of definitions with the second. Were there any differences? If so, what were they?*

The development of ethnic identity occurs on a continuum determined by acceptance of one's ethnicity (Helms, 1990; Sakamoto & Pitner, 2005). Clients may either embrace or reject their ethnicity, depending on how it relates to personal identity or to identity ascribed by a particular reference group dictating behavior and decision-making practices (Helms, 1990). Personal identity is how an individual sees herself/himself, whereas ascribed identity is how society values or perceives her/him. Crucial to understanding the concept of ethnicity is realizing that although it is a potent factor in the professional helping relationship, it is not easy to identify and the degree to which it influences life decisions and behavior is not the same for every client.

When providing culturally sensitive practice social workers must avoid applying a narrow cultural "lens" that can interpret client system traditions and problem-solving processes as abnormal or dysfunctional. In mental health, for example, social workers must thoroughly understand, appreciate, and assess cultural differences in order to enable providers to develop culturally compatible services. For example, the social worker who works with an Asian client needs to be aware of Asian customs and expectations. In Asian cultures, there may be resistance to outside intervention as family matters are viewed as private. In the mental health area in particular, there is shame and stigma attached to needing these types of services (Ofahengaue-Vakalahi & Fong, 2009). It is important for the social worker to be aware of and to respect this cultural tradition, and to know how it can affect the helping relationship. Culturally sensitive services must extend beyond the general task of making services more accessible and include specifically relevant therapeutic interpretations to guide the framework being used (Leon & Dziegielewski, 1999).

One last issue in providing culturally sensitive practice from a systems perspective is that the beliefs and values of social workers and other helping professionals generally reflect those of the greater society. These workers may view client systems differently through their own cultural lens, consequently overlooking the need to help the client and his system to maintain cultural and ethnic heritage as well as feelings of integrity throughout the intervention process. It is therefore the role of the social worker to acknowledge and facilitate family adjustment and acculturation whether working with Asians, Latinos, African Americans, or any other diverse groups (Earner & Garcia, 2009; Logan, 2009; Ofahengaue-Vakalahi & Fong, 2009).

Professional helpers must be aware of the probable tendency to assess clients based on their own values, beliefs, biases, and stereotypes (Dupper, 1992; Dziegielewski, 2002; Sakamoto & Pitner, 2005; Sousa & Eusebio, 2005). Lack of awareness of ethnicity and culture may distort perceptions of clients and of their family dynamics (Dziegielewski, Leon, & Green, 1998; Sakamoto & Pitner, 2005). The potential danger here is that the client's right to self-determination may be violated (Reamer, 2009). Providing ethnically sensitive practice requires social workers to assess clients and client systems very clearly in regard to the effects that culture, environment, and family can have on behaviors and responses. Being aware of ethnicity and culture and accepting diversity are essential in culturally sensitive practice.

Did You Know…Examinations such as those used to measure intelligence can be "culturally biased" and thereby inaccurately depict an individual's intelligence or aptitude. For example, a test may ask questions about American history that place immigrants at a disadvantage. Social workers need to be aware of this potential problem and must work with each individual client to ensure that he or she is represented fairly and accurately.

In closing, culturally sensitive practice requires that the social worker:

- ◆ Be aware of the family's identity, values, and norms and note problems related to acculturation or immigration
- ◆ Identify and discuss the impact of psychological problems than can result from adaptation to a new situation or environment
- ◆ Encourage the development of positive and supportive peer relations
- ◆ Encourage relations outside of the client system that can help to reduce feelings of isolation and facilitate transition
- ◆ Help the client to develop new coping skills with which to negotiate the new environment

◆ Explore ways in which culturally sensitive measurements can be conducted and ways that these standardized measures can take into account multicultural differences.

Today, in our global society so much of what is considered learned is measured through testing for competence. Testing is used now from the earliest grades to later in life. For a complete list of articles and discussion related to measurement instruments and providing relevant and accurate psychoeducational assessments, see *Multicultural Psychoeducational Assessment*, edited by Grigorenko (2009). Since it is beyond the scope of this book to address the specifics of how these types of measurements are used, the reader is urged to see the chapters in Grigorenko's book. This book can help to break down this complex area and help to link multicultural assessment across multiple languages as well as multiple domains of functioning.

SUMMARY

To understand the practice of social work within a culturally sensitive framework you must appreciate the broad range of activities and areas that practice involves. Choosing from among the varied roles and tasks that social workers perform, as well as identifying what constitutes the client system, is not easy within the dynamic social work practice environment. So it is not uncommon for beginning professionals to struggle with basic practice principles and how best to help the client they serve. Our advice is simple: Don't worry! This can happen even with the most experienced MSW practitioner. Deciding what helping approach to use and when to apply it requires a delicate balancing act among the needs of the client, the demands of the environment, the skills and helping knowledge available to the social worker, and the sanction of the social welfare agency.

Social workers assist a variety of people, groups, and communities whose issues, concerns, and needs more often than not are unique to their particular status. The information gleaned from diversity and differences strengthens the social worker's ability to be an effective practitioner and helps develop a specialized intervention reflecting the client system's specific needs.

So where does the social worker begin with matters of diversity? From a social work perspective, diversity first must be recognized; second it must be understood; and third, this knowledge needs to be applied in providing ethnic-sensitive practice. Once we take hold of diversity from these three venues, we then integrate this information into practice strategy. Recognizing the importance of diversity with the populations we serve, incorporating this knowledge and awareness into our practice skills, and supporting the provision of a diversity of services and programs stands at the forefront of all professional helping (Carlton-LaNey, 2008).

In closing, realize that recognition, understanding, and acceptance of another person, in this case a client, does not mean abandoning one's personal values and beliefs. In the professional helping relationship, our personal beliefs are set aside as we embrace those of the client system. The new and experienced professional social worker both struggle with difference and diversity: *"Why do they do that"*; *"That life-style is not for me"*; *"Their views are very different from mine."* Such subjective reactions are human and natural. As a professional, however, the client is always our primary concern, and this should never require that the client match the worker's individual value and belief system. At the same time, our personal values and beliefs may be in such conflict with those of a particular client that we are not able to help that client. At that time, the most important thing to do is to recognize this and transfer the case to a supervisor or another worker who can effectively work with a client—this is in the client's best interests and reflects the professional's ability to determine his or her own level of effectiveness.

When confronted with a new culture or experience, it is of paramount importance that the social workers learn about the culture. Pieces of the human experience cannot be disregarded simply because the social worker is not familiar with it. Discovery comes through many venues—including processing with your supervisor and talking with other colleagues who may be better versed with the culture. Always allow clients to help you learn and develop sensitivity to those matters with which you are unfamiliar. Remember, helping is a two-way street and reciprocity is commonplace in a just society.

The numbers from the Census Bureau provide important information regarding the breadth of diversity. The numbers, however, do not illustrate the latent issues such as racism, prejudice, and discrimination. Disproportionate levels of poverty, individual and family incomes, and high school and college graduation rates are just some of the indicators that demonstrate that diverse people can be "treated" differently than others.

Recognizing and understanding diversity can help the social worker understand how clients can develop anger, hostility, passivity, low self-esteem, poor self-worth, and a sense of hopelessness. The social work relationship considers these may be "some of the baggage" that a client outside the mainstream brings to a social work relationship.

Recognizing the strength in client system diversity can assist in the helping process. For example, strong family and, in particular the extended family, is a hallmark in the African-American community. Acknowledging this strength will allow the social worker working with an African-American client to consider the possible role of the family or extended family in the helping process. Recognizing and understanding diversity is the essence of "contextual practice"—seeing each client

---

Box 5: Helpful Resources

Profile of general demographic characteristics, Washington, DC: U.S. Census Department: http://www.apa.org/pi/

http://gamapserver.who.int/mapLibrary/Files/Maps/Global_HIVPrevalence_ITHRisk Map.png

NASW Standards for Cultural Competence in Social Work:

http://www.socialworkers.org/practice/standards/NASWCulturalStandardsIndicators 2006.pdf

---

as an individual who is set within a specific culture, and whose decisions and actions result from his or her life experiences.

Today's society suffers from a multitude of complicated problems that need to be addressed, and social workers, like other helping professionals, are being pressured to assess and address them as quickly and as effectively as possible. Varied social work roles and fluctuating environmental influences reinforce the ongoing need for educational preparation and training in practice. Even after receiving a degree, every social worker needs to enhance his knowledge and skill bases while developing new areas for more effective practice. We must all continue learning and growing in order to anticipate the needs of our clients.

Social workers believe that competent ethical practice is more than simply helping clients by using what is known. It also involves knowing the client, respecting cultural diversity and the uniqueness of the individual, assessing the environmental situations and resources available, and recognizing the strengths and limitations of the intervention strategy employed. The social worker must decide what method of change to use and at what level—micro, mezzo, or macro—the client will best be served.

Microapproaches to social work practice help clients, whether individuals, families, or groups, to feel better about themselves and to address previous relationship experiences affecting new or current relationships. Mezzopractice strengthens an agency's ability to respond more congruently with worker practice needs and client issues. And macropractice confronts larger issues affecting individuals, families, groups, or communities.

In this chapter and in chapter 5, we have tried to explain as briefly as possible the basics of social work practice. We have presented a few case scenarios that exemplify how different social workers have tried to help their clients. These cases offer a glimpse of the exciting, challenging, and often frustrating world of the practicing social work professional.

Social workers are needed in the practice arena to address the wide array of social problems. And yes, while social workers face numerous external pressures from funding groups, we cannot allow these to limit our practice strategies. Clients need and continue to want supportive services; as the number of people suffering from anxiety and depressive disorders, self-destructive behavior, and life-threatening illnesses continues to grow, so too does the need for social workers who engage in professional practice.

Part **III**

Settings for
Social Work
Practice

Chapter 7

Poverty and Income Maintenance

THROUGHOUT ITS HISTORY THE CORE FUNCTION OF THE SOCIAL work profession has been service on behalf of those who are economically, socially, or politically disadvantaged. From the earliest efforts of the COSs and settlement houses of the nineteenth century, social workers have always tried to help people to achieve their potential and participate in the development of their communities.

As we entered the new millennium, the United States experienced unparalleled economic growth. There were more millionaires and billionaires than at any time in U.S. history. The stock market boomed to new and unexpected heights. Unemployment and inflation reached their lowest levels in decades, and new job opportunities abounded, while institutes such as the Carter Center report that reducing poverty for all is a possibility (Carter, 2000). All of these developments showed signs of a growing, prospering economy. And then the walls came tumbling down in 2008 and 2009. Banks collapsed, people lost their homes due to foreclosures, businesses and companies closed. Everyone knows someone who has been impacted by this economic crisis. The pain is shared and felt by many, yet one group of people remain the hardest hit, and those are people in poverty.

What do we mean by poverty? Poverty is determined primarily by income because it is income that allows the purchase of necessary material resources (Coulton & Chow, 1995, p. 1874). Closely tied to poverty and income is the ability, or inability, to purchase or access quality health care, decent and safe housing, and an adequately nutritious diet. As Darby wrote, "Being poor hurts. By itself, poverty diminishes the quality of life" (1996, p. 3). Certainly, many heroic examples exist of people and families who have risen above the limitations of poverty by taking full advantage of public welfare programs and services. For the vast majority of people in poverty, this is not the case. Living in poverty far more often is associated with negative life experiences that can leave deep scars. Crime, low educational attainment, inadequate health care, substandard housing, and minimum wage employment with little opportunity for promotion are among the many debilitating experiences faced by the poor. For the economically disadvantaged—that is, people who cannot financially support themselves and their families—life is not easy.

Imagine what it would be like not to have enough money to feed, clothe, or house yourself and your family. Now imagine what it would be like if, in addition to these troubles, you are viewed negatively and treated differently simply because your income is low.

Name: Terry Werner

Place of Residence: Lincoln, Nebraska

College/University Degrees: BSW, Magna Cum Laude, University of Nebraska

Present Position and Title: Executive Director of the Nebraska Chapter of the National Association of Social Work

Previous Work/Volunteer Experience: I was an at-large member of the Lincoln City Council and City Council Chairperson, and still am President/Owner of Werner Family Business Inc. In 1991, I opened a Dairy Queen and later expanded to a second fast-food restaurant. I opened and operated Nebraska Discount Travel. In 1997, I sold my restaurants and concentrated on the travel business. I have been Vice President of Baker Hardware Co., Lincoln, Nebraska.

Why did you choose social work as a career? When I discovered what social work is about, it was an "aha" moment. I was drawn to the profession because it was a way to contribute to and advocate for people less fortunate than I. My orientation was business and much of my career has been in business, but my social work degree allowed me to succeed because all careers are about human relationships. I can think of no better college education for nearly every profession. This career has allowed me to continue my life's work of serving the public in a capacity that reflects my personal philosophies and beliefs. What I learned in social work school has enhanced my ability to be a public servant, a personnel manager, a volunteer, an executive director, a political advocate, and a business manager.

What is your favorite social work story? While serving on the Lincoln City Council, I was able to pass an initiative called Ride for Five. This program allowed people living in poverty to have unlimited rides on the bus for $5.00 per month. When I was running for reelection, I received a campaign contribution in the mail from a man with mental illness and living on disability. In the envelope were three one-dollar bills and a note. The note simply said that he wanted to support the person who started the Ride for Five. I was extremely moved by his contribution, knowing that he was truly giving until it hurt.

What is one thing you would change in the community if you had the power to do so? There are so many to list only one, but I'll limit it to one. Nebraska has over 63,000 children living in poverty, our third largest city. We consistently rate in the top five states with children in poverty where at least one parent is working full time. I would love to see Living Wage legislation pass in our state so that parents can raise their families with dignity.

Poor people are often regarded as contributing less than their share to society. Indeed, with our society's emphasis on rugged individualism, it's difficult not to view the poor in a negative light. Well-educated people who we believe should know better sometimes make statements like "Poor people are disadvantaged because they don't work or try hard enough to better themselves." Many people also believe that recipients of social welfare services are immoral because they often have live-in partners while maintaining single-parent families. These misconceptions about the poor are more than just a matter of perceptions—these false assumptions often determine how poor people are treated and what services they are given.

Think about it. Can you remember any discussions you've had with friends or family about people who are impoverished? How were these people characterized? How often have discussions of this type become emotionally charged? Did your friends or family members feel strongly about what they'd seen or believed to be the case? Now think about pronouncements you've heard politicians make in the heat of political campaigns. How did the politicians present the issue of poverty, and what kinds of plans were proposed to address it? Why do you think people who want to hold office seem constantly to attack poverty-related social programs? We believe the reason is that most of the time politicians wish to please their constituents, so they pander to widespread beliefs and attack these programs as costly and wasteful.

Regardless of your opinion about people who live in poverty, it is clear that the poor and disadvantaged inspire strong emotions. Views and expectations about those living in poverty are founded on myths and stereotypes that unfortunately are assumed to be fact. We actually know quite a lot about poverty, however, particularly that the state of poverty is persistent. Poverty affects all races and ages. Poverty affects both men and women. Poverty is found in urban, suburban, and rural communities. Those who live in poverty are often disadvantaged or disenfranchised by the greater society. Finally, poverty cannot be isolated within a particular segment of society. Through its effects on educational performance and crime, poverty affects everyone in society and the quality of life for all people (see figure 1).

Did You Know…In 1995, in the United States 36.4 million people, 13.8 percent of the population, were living in poverty.

In this chapter, we first try to cut through many of the myths that surround the poor and impart critical information to make you a more informed helper. We then look at several important social programs and assess their effectiveness within a framework of facts rather than mythology.

POVERTY DEFINED

According to the *Social Work Dictionary* **poverty** is *"the state of being poor or deficient in money or means of subsistence"* (Barker, 2003, p. 333). Other definitions similarly stress the link between resources and livelihood: Poverty is a *"condition of being without basic resources"* (Segal & Brzuzy, 1998, p. 78). According to Karger and Stoesz (2010), similar to Coulton and Chow (1995) poverty is defined as deprivation.

Figure 1: The children in this photo are siblings. They live with their parents in this trailer and another the same size. The trailers are in a parking lot at the edge of a large city in Ireland.

Two ideas further refine the concept of poverty: **absolute poverty** and **relative poverty** (Southwell, 2009). Absolute poverty is determined by comparison with a fixed numerical standard that is applied in all situations and usually reflects bare subsistence. Basically, "absolute poverty refers to a set of resources that an individual must attain to reach some standard of living threshold" (Southwell, 2009, p. 318). Relative poverty is determined by comparison with some normative standard that may reflect a living standard far higher than subsistence. Absolute measures are usually income based. For example, if a person's annual income is below a certain figure, then the individual is regarded as poor. On the other hand, a relative measure—though still income based—would compare the individual with someone else. A single person with a $45,000 annual income is not absolutely poor but is poor relative to Bill Gates, one of the richest persons in the world. A second kind of relative measure is based on the ability, or inability, to meet a standard set and approved by the community. For example, if immunizations are expected but a family cannot afford them for its children, then that family is considered poor by this measure. Absolute measures make it easy to count people and minimize subjective variables. The key is identifying a threshold below which people are counted as poor. Relative measures are much more difficult to formulate or to reach consensus about. They are also difficult to use. For example, people sometimes say that poor people in the United States have it easy compared to poor people elsewhere. But this is like trying to compare apples with oranges. Different countries have different beliefs, values, and economic and social systems, all of which affect the standards by which people are judged to be poor.

Measuring Poverty

The U.S. government measures poverty using a standard called the **poverty threshold**. Mollie Orshansky, director of the Social Security Administration in 1963, conceptualized the poverty threshold as an absolute measure so that statistical processes could be used to simply count the number of poor. Orshansky's formula is based on the amount of money that a family must spend on food and on the portion of overall income that this expense constitutes. Orshansky assumed that a family spends one-third of its total income on food. After calculating the cost of a minimum, or economy, food plan as determined by the Department of Agriculture, she multiplied that amount by three to establish the poverty threshold. This value, which is essential in determining benefits, is updated annually and adjusted for inflation, family size, and age, and to reflect the increased cost of living in Hawaii and Alaska. Its application is simple: a person or family whose gross income falls below the poverty threshold is counted as being in poverty.

Did You Know...According to the National Center for Children in Poverty in 1998, 23.2 percent of the children under age 6 live in poverty in the United States.

Having explained the poverty threshold calculation, let's complicate matters a bit. The poverty threshold was the government's original attempt to establish a poverty measure, under the oversight of the Social Security Administration, and its purpose is to establish a basis for counting retrospectively the number of people who live in poverty. Each year, however, another branch of the federal government, the Department of Health and Human Services (HHS), is responsible for issuing poverty guidelines (see table 1). These prospective guidelines, which closely approximate the poverty threshold, are used in determining financial eligibility for certain federal programs.

An important point to remember: the HHS poverty guidelines are used for determining eligibility for many federal programs but not for all of them. Examples of federal programs that use the HHS guidelines are Head Start, Low-Income Energy Assistance Program, Supplemental Nutritional Assistance Program, National School Lunch and School Breakfast programs, Legal Services for the Poor, Job Training Partnership Act, WIC, and Job Corps. Some of these programs use a percentage multiple of the guidelines, such as 125, 150, or 180 percent. For example, a program may use 125 percent of the HHS guidelines to determine eligibility. In 2008 this eligibility standard for a four-person family was $22,050 x 125%, or $26,460—in other words, a family of four was eligible for the program if its income was below $26,460. The percentages of the HHS guidelines used by different programs are established by congressional committees and, predictably, can create a great deal of confusion between programs. Moreover, several well-known programs are not tied to the HHS guidelines: Supplemental Security Income, Social Services Block Grant, Section 8 housing, the Earned Income Credit, and Temporary Assistance for Needy Families.

Activity...Using the 2009 poverty guideline for a family of four, $22,050, imagine what life is like. You'll have $1,837.50 each month for expenses. Using Orshansky formula's assumption, one-third of your income, $611.88, goes for food, leaving you $1,225.62 for other expenses including housing, transportation, health care, clothing, recreation, and so on. Put together a monthly food menu—what type of meals, and so forth—with the $611.88. Find a place to live and set up other expenses with the remaining $1,225. The two children are ages 5 and 13, and the two adults are the biological parents.

Now, how realistic do poverty guidelines seem to be? What does this exercise tell you about the level at which poverty guidelines are set? If this were your family of four and these were the resources you had available, could you make ends meet?

One last point about "counting people in poverty"—not all people are actually counted. The Census Bureau does not include or attempt to estimate the poverty status of the following groups.

♦ Unrelated individuals under age 15 (such as foster children); income questions are asked of people age 15 and older; if someone is under age 15 and not living with a family member (maybe a runaway, throwaway, or pushout teen), they are not counted.

♦ Those who live in institutional group quarters (such as prisons or nursing homes), college dormitories, military barracks, and living situations without conventional housing (and who are not in shelters)—the homeless.

So when looking at the poverty numbers and related rates, recognize that these are underestimates of the real numbers. The extent of the undercount is not known; it might be small, less than 100,000 persons, or it might be large, more than 1,000,000 persons. So what we do know is that the official federal numbers are at best a low number and do not accurately reflect the true number of persons in poverty.

Did You Know...A single parent with two children making the minimum wage and working forty hours a week will not make enough money to raise this family above the poverty threshold. This parent, in 2002, would need to make $8.67 per hour to be above the poverty threshold.

Other Considerations in Measuring Poverty

Setting poverty thresholds and thus establishing exactly who will be counted as poor is very controversial. Orshansky's definition, when examined closely, has all sorts of limitations. First, it doesn't consider geographical differences in cost of living, other than for Alaska and Hawaii—and this is an important consideration in the United States. Go back to table 5 in chapter 4 to see how far the same amount of money goes in different cities. Second, the threshold is based on food costs but does not adjust for the different nutritional needs among children, women, women of child-bearing age, and men. Last, assuming that one-third of a family's income is spent on food purchases is itself problematic. Over the years this has not proved to be a well-founded assumption.

Did You Know...In statistics the mean, median, and mode are indicators of how a set of numbers tends to focus around central values. Applied to income, the mean income is the average income of a population—50 percent of the population has income above median income and 50 percent below—and the mode income is the most frequently occurring income.

Beyond problems with the formula used to determine poverty is the question of what should or should not be counted as income. For example, should federal cash subsidies such as social security retirement payments be counted as income? Should income be established as the pretax or the post-tax amount? Should the cash value of in-kind benefits from federal subsidy programs such as food stamps and Section 8 housing be counted as part of a family's income?

As exhibited in table 1, how income is defined affects actual poverty estimates. Moving down the table, income is adjusted in steps so that we can observe the effects on the poverty rate: first, government cash benefits are removed—then

Table 1: 2000–2009 HHS Poverty Guidelines

Year	First Person	Each Additional Person	Four-Person family
2009	$10,830	$3,740	$22,050
2008	$10,400	$3,600	$21,200
2007	$10,210	$3,480	$20,650
2006	$ 9,800	$3,260	20,000
2005	9,570	3,260	19,350
2004	9,310	3,180	18,850
2003	8,980	3,140	18,400
2002	8,860	3,080	18,100
2001	8,590	3,020	17,650
2000	8,350	2,900	17,050

Source: United States Department of Health and Human Services, http://aspe.hhs.gov/poverty/figures-fed-reg.shtml

private non-wage income is added, federal tax payments are removed, the primary antipoverty tax credit is added, state tax payments are removed—and finally government benefits are added successively. Critics of the federal government's income maintenance programs argue that the poor are receiving numerous supports and these should be "counted" as income, which in effect raises a number of individuals above the poverty threshold. For a moment, what do you think would happen to the number of people in poverty if you do a combined "count" that includes Earned Income Credit (EIC), means-tested cash transfers, food stamps, non-medical non-cash transfers, and rent subsidies? Will the number of people in poverty increase or decrease? If you think decrease, you are correct—but will this "net" number portray a realistic picture of the nation's poverty level?

The data presented show that federal programs do improve income levels and thus remove individuals from poverty. The data also show, however, that people who rely on federal benefits for large parts of their income are extremely vulnerable to the slightest modifications in program eligibility conditions and benefit levels.

So, are we really doing a disservice to all poor people when we count such uncertain income? What rate do you believe most accurately reflects existing poverty: the 11.3 percent determined by definition 1 or the 9.5 percent determined by definition 14, or one of the other rates? Does it really matter which definition is used? If the official poverty rate declined slightly because governmental subsidies were added to income calculations don't you think this information would be used to justify reductions in welfare programs? And, if welfare programs actually were reduced, wouldn't the poverty rate rise again?

Nevertheless, agency administrators and welfare advocates often argue that data produced by a standardized process applied consistently from year to year, even if the process is rife with potential measurement flaws, are essential. Such numerical measures allow a community to follow trends in poverty and to assess the effects of different attempts to reduce poverty among its citizens. In other words, even though the poverty rate itself may have little intrinsic meaning it is nonetheless important because its fluctuations over time serve as a barometer of economic well-being.

Number in Poverty versus Poverty Rate

Note that our discussion of measuring poverty started with counting the number of people in poverty but is now framed in terms of the poverty rate. The poverty rate is a more illuminating way to quantify poverty because it provides context by expressing the number of people in poverty as a percentage of the total population. This context is important for two reasons. First, the scale of poverty is difficult to judge if we know only the number of poor people: One thousand people in poverty is a far more serious problem if the total population is 2,000 than if it is 100,000. The poverty rates, 50 percent and 1 percent, show how different the two situations are. Second, trends in poverty cannot be judged by changes in the number of poor people alone. Suppose over a decade the number of people in poverty rises from

1,000 to 2,000. If the total population remains stable at 100,000, the poverty rate has doubled from 1 to 2 percent; if, however, the population grows from 100,000 to 200,000, the poverty rate is unchanged at 1 percent—the rate distinguishes between worsening poverty and population growth.

Examine table 2, and remember that the U.S. population has grown every year since the nation's founding. You can now "read" different eras in the recent history of poverty. In the 1960s the number of people in poverty actually declined, a dramatic development, as evidenced by the sharp drop in the poverty

Table 2: Poverty Status, 1959–2007

Year	Number in Poverty (in thousands)	Poverty Rate	Year	Number in Poverty (in thousands)	Poverty Rate
2007	36,460	12.3%	1981	31,822	14.0%
2006	36,460	12.3%	1980	29,272	13.0%
2005	36,950	12.6%			
2004	37,040	12.7%	1979	26,072	11.7%
2003	35,861	12.5%	1978	24,497	11.4%
2002	34,570	12.3%	1977	24,720	11.6%
2001	32,907	11.7%	1976	24,975	11.8%
2000	31,054	11.3%	1975	25,877	12.3%
			1974	23,370	11.2%
1999	32,258	11.8%	1973	22,973	11.1%
1998	34,476	12.7%	1972	24,460	12.5%
1997	35,574	13.3%	1971	25,559	12.5%
1996	36,529	13.7%	1970	25,420	12.6%
1995	36,425	13.8%			
1994	38,059	14.5%	1969	24,147	12.1%
1993	39,265	15.1%	1968	25,389	12.8%
1992	38,014	14.8%	1967	27,769	14.2%
1991	35,708	14.2%	1966	28,510	14.7%
1990	33,585	13.5%	1965	33,185	17.3%
			1964	36,055	19.0%
1989	31,528	12.8%	1963	36,436	19.5%
1987	31,745	13.0%	1962	38,625	21.0%
1986	32,221	13.4%	1961	39,628	21.9%
1985	32,370	13.6%	1960	39,851	22.2%
1984	33,700	14.4%			
1983	35,303	15.2%	1959	39,490	22.4%
1982	34,398	15.0%			

Source: U.S. Census Bureau, Population Division (2008). Income poverty and health insurance coverage in the United States, Current Population Reports. U.S. Department of Commerce, Economics and Statistics Administration, U.S. Census Bureau. Release date August 2008, Retrieved December 21, 2008, from www.census.gov/prod/208pubs/p60-235.pdf and www.census.gov/prod/2008pubs/09statab/pop.pdf

rate from 22 to 12.1 percent. This decrease was achieved primarily through the federal government's activist War on Poverty. Over the following years the poverty rate fluctuated, peaking at 15.2 percent in 1983, 11.3 percent in 2000, and 12.5 percent in 2007 while the number in poverty trended steadily upward with the growing population. Indeed, although poverty rates are far below the 1959 level, the numbers in poverty were not far different and most troubling, poverty continues.

WHO ACTUALLY CONSTITUTE THE POOR?

Poverty cuts across all races, ethnic groups, and ages and darkens the lives of both men and women. In this country there has always been a myth that the poor are almost all nonwhite. Yet this is far from true (see table 3). Numerically there are more whites in poverty than any other single race. However, poverty rates for blacks and those of Hispanic origin are much higher than that for whites. In 2007, 37.3 million people were in poverty, up from 36.5 million in 2006. Poverty rates in 2007 were statistically unchanged for non-Hispanic Whites (8.2 percent), Blacks (24.5 percent), and Asians (10.2 percent) from 2006. The poverty rate increased for Hispanics (21.5 percent in 2007, up from 20.6 percent in 2006). The poverty rate in 2007 was lower than in 1959, the first year for which poverty estimates are available, while statistically higher than the most recent trough in 2000 (11.3 percent). The poverty rate increased for children under 18 years old (18.0 percent in 2007, up from 17.4 percent in 2006), while it remained statistically

Table 3: Profile of Persons in Poverty, 2007

	Number in Poverty (in thousands)	Poverty Rate in Subpopulation
Total	36,460	12.3%
White	24,416	10.3
Black	9,048	24.3
Asian and Pacific Islander	1,353	10.3
Hispanic	9,243	20.6
Under 18 years	12,827	17.4
18 to 64 years	20,239	10.8
65 years and over	3,344	9.4
In families	25,915	10.6
Northeast	6,222	11.5
Midwest	7,324	11.2
South	14,882	13.8
West	8,032	11.6
Lives in metropolitan areas	29,283	11.8
Lives outside metropolitan	7,177	15.2

Source: http://www.poverty/poverty07/table3/pdf

unchanged for people 18 to 64 years old (10.9 percent) and people 65 and over (9.7 percent). The data in table 3 also challenge the idea that most poor people should be supporting themselves. Children, those under age 18, account for almost 36 percent of all poor, and seniors, those age 65 and over, account for more than 10 percent.

Did You Know...In 2002, the number of people living below the poverty threshold totaled 32.9 million, or 11.7 percent of the U.S. population. To think about how large this number actually is, consider that the total population of the Northeast—Maine, New Hampshire, Vermont, Massachusetts, Connecticut, Rhode Island, and New York—is slightly smaller. Or consider that the total population of the following states approximates the number of people in poverty: Idaho, Montana, North Dakota, South Dakota, Wyoming, Colorado, Utah, Nevada, Arizona, New Mexico, Nebraska, Oklahoma, Iowa, Louisiana, and Arkansas. That the United States is one of world's most technologically advanced societies and has one of the highest standards of living makes it difficult to comprehend the number of Americans who live in poverty.

Poverty and Location

In 2007, the U.S. Census Bureau reported the number of people in poverty living in metropolitan areas totaled 22.9 million (11.9%) compared to 7.4 million (15.4%) of those living outside of metropolitan areas (DeNavas-Walt, Proctor, & Smith 2008, p. 15). Few Americans think of the poor living in rural areas or small communities, which are generally associated with tranquil places for vacation or weekend escapes. Creating successful programs for the rural poor is a significant challenge; certainly what works in New York City may not work in northwest rural Wyoming.

Poverty and Race

As table 4 clearly shows, poverty rates for blacks and Hispanics have been about twice that for whites for years. Averages by decade show that over time the differences have lessened, but they remain extreme. In 2007, 10.3 percent of the Anglos were in poverty compared to 24.3 percent and 20.6 percent for African Americans and Hispanics, respectively.

Did You Know...The term "Hispanic" is unique to the United States? No other nation uses this word. "Pertaining to the culture of Spanish- and Portuguese-speaking people . . . this term is often applied to people of Latin American ethnic background. . . . Some people prefer the term 'Latino' " (Barker, 2003, p. 216). According to the U.S. Bureau of the Census, which first used the word in 1980, a person of Hispanic origin can be of any race. This means that people who describe themselves as Hispanic can have diverse backgrounds and very different mores and cultural expectations.

Table 4: Poverty Rates by Race and Hispanic Origin: 1959–2007

Year	All Persons	White	Black	Hispanic
2007	12.5	10.5	24.5	21.5
2006	12.3	10.3	24.3	20.6
2005	12.6	10.6	21.9	21.8
2004	12.7	10.8	24.7	24.9
2003	12.5	10.6	24.3	22.5
2002	12.1	10.2	24.1	21.8
2001	11.7	9.9	22.7	21.4
2000	11.3	9.5	22.5	21.5
1999	11.6	9.7	23.1	22.1
1998	12.7	10.5	26.5	27.1
1997	13.3	11.0	29.3	30.3
1996	13.7	11.2	28.4	29.4
1995	13.8	11.2	29.3[b]	30.3[a]
1994	14.5	11.7	30.6[b]	30.7[a]
1993	15.1	12.2	33.1[b]	30.6[a]
1992	14.8	11.9	33.4[b]	29.6[a]
1991	14.2	11.3	32.7[b]	28.7[a]
1990	13.5	10.7	31.9[b]	28.1[a]
1989	12.8	10.0	30.7[b]	26.2[a]
1988	13.0	10.1	31.3[b]	26.7[a]
1987	13.4	10.4	32.4[b]	28.0[a]
1986	13.6	11.0	31.1[b]	27.3[a]
1985	14.0	11.4	31.3[b]	29.0[a]
1984	14.4	11.5	33.8[b]	28.4[a]
1983	15.2	12.1	35.7[b]	28.0[a]
1982	15.0	12.0	35.6[b]	29.9[a]
1981	14.0	11.1	34.2[b]	26.5[a]
1980	13.0	10.2	32.5[b]	25.7[a]
1975	12.3	9.7	31.3[b]	26.9[a]
1970	12.6	9.9	33.5[b]	22.8[a]
1965	17.3	13.3	41.8[b]	
1959	22.4	18.1	55.1[b]	NA
1990–95	14.3	11.5	31.8[b]	29.7[b]
1980–89	13.8	11.0	32.9[b]	27.6[b]
1970–79	11.8	9.0	31.6[b]	23.1[c]
1960–69	17.5	13.7	37.11[d]	NA

Source: Baugher and Lamison-White (1996); http://www.censusbureau.gov/prod/2003pubs/
p60-222.pdf. U.S. Census Bureau 2003–2008): Current Population reports, income,
poverty, and health insurance. Washington, DC: U.S. Government Printing Office.

[a]Data for 1972.
[b]Data for 1966.
[c]Data for 1972–79.
[d]Data for 1966–69.

Poverty and Gender

Gender historically plays an important role in income distribution and continues to do so today. Simply stated, women are more susceptible to poverty than men. Even social workers, members of a profession that proudly advocates for social and economic justice, work in organizations and agencies that discriminate against women. Gibelman and Schervish (1997) found that in 1995 the median income for female social workers was $34,135, compared with $37,503 for their male counterparts. A 2003 salary study provides evidence that the more a service profession is dominated by women, the lower the worker's average weekly salary (Gilbelman, 2003). The median salary for men compared to women, between 2005 and 2007, was $43,948 to $33,969, a 23 percent difference (U.S. Census Bureau 2009). And when looking at the percent of men and women who earned over $100,000, the discrepancy is even more glaring: 12.1 percent of all men compared to 4.6 percent of all women (U.S. Census Bureau, 2009).

During the twentieth century, American family structure underwent significant changes. Two-parent families declined while single-parent families increased; birthrates declined for the general population but rose dramatically among teenagers; and women entered the workforce in great numbers. The United States now has many single-parent families that depend on the wages of a female head of household for their income.

Female-headed families are three times more likely to be in poverty than all families. Even more disturbing are the data for black and Hispanic female-headed households. The three-year average, 2005–2007, found that 36.3 percent of black female-headed families and 38.1 percent of Hispanic female-headed families were in poverty—more than one in three families (U.S. Census Bureau, 2009)!

This hierarchy of poverty faithfully reflects income inequalities. The nation's median income for all households for 2005–2007 was $50,007. For married couples with children it was $90,835 compared with families that have just a female head of household. Again race and ethnicity make a difference. Ethnic and gender discrimination together generate extremely low salaries for minority women and "impair women's ability to support themselves and their children" (Landrine & Klonoff, 1997, p. 8):

> If a job paid White men $20,000, then White women received $15,000, Black women $12,200, and Latinas $11,000 for the same work.
>
> If a job paid White men $35,000, then White women received $26,250, Black women $21,350, and Latinas $19,250 for the same work.
>
> If a job paid White men $50,000, then White women received $37,500, Black women $30,500, and Latinas $27,500 for the same work. (p. 8)

One group greatly at risk for poverty include teenage parents and their children. According to the Child Welfare League of America 2009 Fact Sheet, in 2006, 6,405 babies were born to girls younger than age 15. Another 435,427 babies were born to girls aged 15 to 19. This statistic is of particular importance because although it represents a 3% decline since 2005, teen births cost taxpayers approximately $9.1 million as often these children end up in foster care or child protective services.

Poverty and Age

The younger the person, the more likely he or she is to live in poverty. In 2007, 18.0 percent of children were in poverty and the age cohort with the next largest poverty rate was young adults, ages 18 to 24 (table 5). In the primary work years, ages 25 to 54, poverty rates decrease. Finally, for people in retirement and relying on fixed incomes, poverty rates fluctuated but remain slightly below 10 percent (see table 6).

Did You Know…Children have been getting poorer as our nation grows richer. American children are twice as likely as adults to be poor. Children in the United States are 1.6 times more likely to be poor than those in Canada, 2 times more likely than those in Britain, and 3 times more likely than those in France or Germany. What is most astonishing is that the United States is the wealthiest of these nations and has the lowest unemployment levels (Children's Defense Fund, 1998).

Despite a rise in poverty rates with retirement the percentage of seniors in poverty is lower than the rate for the whole population—9.7 percent in 2007 (retrieved June 15, 2009, www.census.gov/hhes/www/poverty/histpov/hstpov3.xls). This was not always the case. In 1959, 35.2 percent of seniors lived in poverty compared with 27.3 percent of all people—and between 1966 and 2000, the senior poverty rate declined from 28.5 to 9.9 percent, compared with a range of 17.6 to 16.2 percent for the whole population. The sharp decline in the poverty rate for seniors was a result of specific federal legislation (Jansson, 2004). The Older Americans Act of 1965, the Supplemental Security Act, and the indexing of social security retirement checks in the early 1970s all helped to raise seniors' fixed incomes above the poverty threshold. It's important to recognize that the reductions in senior poverty are primarily due to federal support that pushes income levels slightly above the poverty threshold.

Table 5: Poverty Rates by Age Group and Ethnicity, 2007

	Percentage below Poverty Threshold		
Group	18 and under	18–64	65 and over
All	18.0	10.9	9.7
White	14.9	9.4	8.1
Black	33.7	19.8	23.3
Asian	11.9	9.4	11.2
Hispanic	28.6	17.9	17.1

Source: http://www.census.gov/hhes/www/poverty/hispov/hstpov3.xls

Table 6: Poverty Rates Based on Age, 1980–2007

Year	Children under 18		People 18 to 64 years		People 65 and older	
	Number	Percent	Number	Percent	Number	Percent
2007	13,324	35.7	20,396	54.7	3,556	9.5
2006	12,827	35.2	20,239	55.5	3,394	9.3
2005	12,896	34.9	20,450	55.3	3,603	9.8
2004	13,041	35.2	20,545	55.5	3,453	9.3
2003	12,866	35.9	19,443	54.2	3,552	9.9
2002	12,133	35.1	18,861	54.6	3,576	10.3
2001	11,733	35.7	17,760	54.0	3,414	10.4
2000	11,587	36.7	16,671	52.8	3,323	10.5
1999	12,280	37.4	17,289	52.7	3,222	9.8
1998	13,467	39.1	17,623	51.1	3,386	9.8
1997	14,113	39.7	18,085	50.8	3,376	9.5
1996	14,463	39.6	18,638	51.0	3,428	9.4
1995	14,665	40.3	18,442	50.6	3,318	9.1
1994	15,289	40.2	19,107	50.2	3,663	9.6
1993	15,727	40.1	19,783	50.4	3,755	9.6
1992	15,294	40.2	18,793	49.4	3,928	10.3
1991	14,341	40.2	17,586	49.2	3,781	10.6
1990	13,431	40.0	16,496	49.1	3,658	10.9
1989	12,590	39.9	15,575	49.4	3,363	10.7
1988	12,455	39.2	15,809	49.8	3,481	11.0
1987	12,843	39.9	15,815	49.1	3,563	11.1
1986	12,876	39.8	16,017	49.5	3,477	10.7
1985	13,010	39.3	16,598	50.2	3,456	10.5
1984	13,420	39.8	16,952	50.3	3,330	9.9
1983	13,911	39.4	17,767	50.3	3,625	10.3
1982	13,647	39.7	17,000	49.4	3,751	10.9
1981	12,505	39.3	15,464	48.6	3,853	12.1
1980	11,543	39.4	13,858	47.3	3,871	13.2

Note: numbers in thousands.
Source: U.S. Bureau of the Census, Current Population Survey, Annual Social and Economic Supplements.
For information on confidentiality protection, sampling error, nonsampling error, and definitions, see http://www.census.gov/apsd/techdoc/cps/cpsmar08.pdf
Footnotes are available at http://www.census.gov/hhes/www/poverty/histpov/footnotes.html.

Of all the figures we have discussed so far, those that probably disturb people the most are the ones that involve our nation's children. For the better part of twenty years, poverty rates for children hovered around 20 percent—that is one in five children being poor. But in the mid-1990s, these rates began to decline. By 2000, poverty among children declined to 16.2 percent. According to the Children's Defense Fund, the percentage of children living in poverty grew to 18.1 percent (13.3 million children) in 2008—this was the beginning of the economic turmoil that engulfed the United States (Children's Defense Fund, November, 2008).

We know that poverty has negative consequences for those who live in it. As of April 2009, the Child Trends Research Brief concluded, "that poverty is one of the factors that negatively affects children's development, especially deep, long-term poverty. Research also suggests that a combination of parental effort and social programs—correctly designed and implemented—*can* improve the lives of poor children and their families" (Moore, Redd, Burkhauser, Mbwana, et al., 2009). But what specific effects does it have on children? What exactly does it mean to be a child raised in an impoverished home? Some facts can help to answer these questions:

1. Poor children are twice as likely as non-poor children to have stunted growth, iron deficiency, and severe asthma.

2. Low-income children are three times more likely to die during childhood.

3. According to the Centers for Disease Control and Prevention (CDC), poor children are more likely to die before their first birthdays than children whose mothers smoked during pregnancy.

4. Every year spent in poverty increases the chances that a child will fall behind grade level by age 18.

5. Three out of four poor children live in a working family (Children's Defense Fund, Child Poverty research Data, retrieved June 30, 2009, from http://www.childrensdefense.org/child-research-data-publications/child-poverty.html).

We've seen that race and ethnicity affect poverty rates for women and for the general population, so we shouldn't be surprised to learn that race and ethnicity also affect age-specific poverty rates. In 1995 poverty rates were 41.5 percent for black youths and 39.3 percent for Hispanic youths, compared with 16.2 percent for white youths. Poverty rates were 25.4 percent for black seniors and 23.5 percent for Hispanic seniors, compared with an overall senior poverty rate of about 10 percent (Baugher & Lamison-White, 1996, pp. C-5–C-7). These numbers represent long-standing inequalities.

WHY IS THERE POVERTY IN A WEALTHY NATION?

Entire university courses are devoted to studying how poverty can exist in the midst of great wealth. Countless books and articles also attempt to answer this question. The breadth of this topic allows us only to review some theories put forth to explain why poverty continues to exist.

Karger and Stoesz (2010, pp. 110–112) identified three theories of poverty: the culture of poverty, eugenics and poverty, and the radical school of poverty. Each

Figure 2: Subsidized housing in a small midwestern city. These units were built for low-income working-class families and are located on the edge of the city.

differs markedly from the others, and depending on your philosophical and political views you may have strong reactions, positive or negative, to some or all of the theories:

Culture of poverty: Poverty and its traits are transmitted from one generation to the next. Behavior is learned and repeated. There is a sense of hopelessness, indifference, and dependence and a focus on the present rather than the future. Impulse control is lacking, and resignation and disintegration of the family is pervasive. In the development of an underclass, the population is clustered around similar behaviors and beliefs and is outside the dominant or majority section of society. Its neighborhoods deteriorate, employment opportunities diminish, and marriage rates decline. The underclass is on the outside looking in and is not able to access society's opportunity structure.

Eugenics: Poverty is tied to genetics. Accumulation of wealth depends on ability, which is directly related to intelligence, which is inherited. The "most capable" citizen should receive the greatest benefits, which in turn will stimulate this group to take greater leadership in society.

Radical school: Poverty is exploitation of one group of people by another. The purpose of poverty is to provide a source of cheap labor—the cheaper the labor, the greater the profits. A second purpose of poverty is to provide the middle class with a group to whom it can feel superior, which moderates tension between the middle and upper classes.

Name: Dana Kaplan

Place of residence: Burlington, Vermont

College/university degrees: University of Vermont, BSW

Present position: Case Manager

What do you do in your spare time? In my spare time, I do what I am doing right now . . . I sit in a coffee shop and write, or read books, or the local newspaper. I am in an indie-pop band, so we spend a lot of time either practicing, or playing shows. If I am not with them, I'm usually listening to music or playing the guitar. I love spending time with my friends, cooking, being outside, and going for bike rides. I grew up in New York City, so I like to people watch. I also take photographs and love a good yard sale.

Why did you choose social work as a career? I happened upon the field of social work more than anything else. I didn't know what the term meant until I visited the University of Vermont and saw it was an option for a major. I thought it was fantastic because it was doing what I knew I already loved—working with people—but on a professional level. I've come to view it as less of a "career" choice, and more of just something I am involved in, something that's important to me to do as an active member of my community.

What is your favorite social work story? I was recently working with a client who was sleeping in his car with his two dogs. The client was reluctant to come in for regular case management sessions, but would drop by when the need arose. One of his dogs got an eye infection, and the client was without the money to pay for the care. This was case management outside the box. I was able to network with a local veterinary office that provided the medical care needed. That afternoon I found myself driving to a local pet store who graciously donated two dog sweaters to the client. Currently, they are living in a motel and both dogs are healthy and warm. I like this story because the situation was unique. Practicing social work can encompass such a broad range of services, depending on each individual's particular needs and desires. This time it was case management for a dog—who knows what it will be tomorrow.

What would be the one thing you would change in our community if you had the power to do so? I'd create more affordable housing, and a livable wage. I'd bridge the gaps that exist between different sub-groups of people: the university students, the locals, the mentally ill, the queer and the straight, the wealthy, and the economically challenged. If we could all listen to each other's stories a bit more, and be open to the differences that do exist between us, we might have a better understanding of one another, and I bet things would run more smoothly. Now where's the magic wand?

Each of these theories is much more elaborate than the brief summaries we give here. At the end of the chapter we list further reading on these four theories.

Setting forth another perspective, Darby (1996, p. 20) listed five factors that have produced poverty:

Decline in low-wage jobs: Fewer jobs are available for the labor pool.

Immigration: New immigrants take low-paying jobs away from unemployed residents.

Decline in labor force participation and work effort: Work effort among men is down over the long term.

Breakdown of traditional family structures: The number of single-parent families has increased, particularly among blacks.

Drugs: Alcohol, tobacco, and other drugs (ATOD) continue to plague the most disadvantaged populations. ATOD use among inner city youth is increasing.

According to Darby, these five factors are intertwined. Therefore, efforts to address poverty that are limited, in that they are only aimed at one of these five areas, can be futile. Rather, efforts must be coordinated to target all of these areas.

Johnson and Schwartz (1988) divided the causes of poverty into three broad areas: economic, social, and political. Economic causes relate to unequal distribution of income across society, inadequate income supports in public assistance programs—TANF and food stamps, for example—and unemployment and underemployment rates. Social causes of poverty refer to negative views the public holds of the poor, the strong belief in self-reliance, and discrimination against people based on race, ethnicity, and gender. Political causes include lack of participation in the political process by the poor and unjust social policies. Poverty and welfare programs are not popular in political circles and seem to be more vulnerable to public scrutiny and cutbacks than other public programs.

PROGRAMS TO AID THE POOR

It is time to examine current programmatic responses to poverty in the United States and to consider how these programs are viewed and how their recipients are treated. This section presents a brief overview of major public assistance programs.

In chapter 3 we learned that the modern welfare system has its roots firmly planted in the Great Depression of the 1930s and the passage of the Economic Security Act of 1935. A second major federal welfare initiative occurred in the 1960s with the advent of President Johnson's War on Poverty. Finally, a third, dramatic shift in federal social welfare programs for the poor took shape with the passage and implementation of the Personal Responsibility and Work Opportunity Reconciliation Act of 1996.

This act was a sweeping reform of the role of the federal government in welfare provision. This 1996 act dramatically restructured programs to aid the poor and ended the nation's six-decade-old guarantee of cash assistance to poor families.

Temporary Assistance for Needy Families

The 1996 Welfare Reform Act, also known as the Personal Responsibility and Work Opportunity Reconciliation Act or PRWORA, created a new federal program, Temporary Assistance for Needy Families (TANF), which replaced AFDC, the AFDC Emergency Assistance program, and the Job Opportunities and Basic Skills Training (JOBS) programs. TANF, which is commonly referred to as "welfare," is the monthly cash assistance program for poor families with children under age 18. TANF funds come to the states as a block grant, and the states are given broad discretion in determining how TANF funds are spent as long as they address one of the following four goals:

(1) Assist needy families with children so that children may be cared for in their own homes or in the homes of relatives;

(2) Reduce dependency on government benefits by promoting job preparation, work, and marriage;

(3) Reduce and prevent out-of-wedlock pregnancies; and

(4) Encourage formation and maintenance of two-parent families.

The federal government's 2008 fiscal year appropriations authorized that TANF be funded at $16.5 billion for each year through 2010. TANF benefits differ by state and the grant awards are not that large. For example, the maximum TANF grant for a family of three living in Washington, D.C., is less than $14 a day. Even with food stamps, Washington, D.C., families live well below poverty with the total benefits being about $800 for a family of three or 58 percent of poverty. In New Mexico, the maximum benefit for a three-person family is $389, a little less than $13 per day.

Did You Know...To qualify for TANF aid a parent that is a minor must live at home with parent(s) or in a home supervised by an adult. Also a teen mother must attend school or a training program once her baby is twelve weeks old.

Some specific aspects of TANF:

1. States no longer have to help all families judged by the federal government to be in poverty but can use their own definitions of poverty and eligibility.

2. Parents must work within two years of receiving their cash benefits, and the option to shorten this two-year period is given to each state.

3. States must impose a sixty-month (five year) lifetime limit on TANF aid, and although states can shorten this length of time, they are not allowed to expand it. Therefore, five years is the lifetime limit.

4. Funds are given to states in block grants, which allow each state significant discretion in how to use the funds (Children's Defense Fund, Child Poverty Research Data, retrieved June 30, 2009, from http://www.childrens defense.org/child-research-data-publications/child-poverty.html).

Implementation of state discretion and time limits. No longer is cash assistance to the poor an entitlement, it is now short term and variable (Ginsberg, 1998, pp. 188–189). Taking advantage of the flexibility allowed by the federal legislation, some states modified TANF services by setting stricter time limits on how long someone in poverty could receive cash assistance. The U.S. House of Representatives, in its reauthorization of the Personal Responsibility, Work and Family Promotion Act of 2003 (H.R.4), called for increasing the number of hours a parent/caretaker must work in order to receive benefits; the House bill proposed a required 40 hours, up from 30 hours, per week. Of this time, a minimum of 24 hours must be in "core" activities, which may be paid or unpaid with the remaining hours spent in unspecified activities, such as education or training (Children's Defense Fund, August 26, 2008). H.R.4 is severely underfunded, with a five-year appropriation of $1 billion compared with a Congressional Budget Office estimate of $8 to $11 billion needed just to cover child care costs (Children's Defense Fund, August 26, 2008)!

TANF provides states the flexibility to structure its programs within broad and flexible guidelines set by the U.S. Congress. As a result, states have different names for the programs, time limits, program requirements, and cash benefits. Essentially, a person living in Florida is treated differently than a person living in Wisconsin. Even with this flexibility, this variation takes place within an iron constraint. The lifetime limit of 60 months is a national limit. If a person receives TANF aid for 50 months in one state and then moves to a state with a lower time limit, such as Florida, then the second state's limit has already been exceeded and the person receives no further TANF aid there. Even if the person had moved to a state that had not lowered its time limit, only a further 10 months of TANF assistance would be available.

Work requirements. TANF requires adults to work, a significant departure from the AFDC program and the philosophy behind the War on Poverty of the 1960s. The law mandates that a person must work a minimum of thirty hours each week and a child's benefits can be reduced or eliminated if the parent is not participating fully in the program. A further example of TANF's decentralized state-centered approach is reflected in the various names for the state's programs. As shown in table 7, names for the programs vary across the country, which leads to confusion by the general public.

Few forms of preparatory education and job training meet the work requirement. For example, adults over age 20 attempting to earn GEDs and most people working toward college degrees are not eligible for TANF. Community service may be used in place of work, but this option is left to the discretion of individual states. All social workers are aware, however, that work alone and providing employment

Table 7: Names of State TANF Programs

State	Name
Alabama	FA (Family Assistance Program)
Alaska	ATAP (Alaska Temporary Assistance Program)
Arizona	EMPOWER (Employing and Moving People Off Welfare and Encouraging Responsibility)
Arkansas	TEA (Transitional Employment Assistance)
California	CALWORKS (California Work Opportunity and Responsibility to Kids)
Colorado	Colorado Works
Connecticut	JOBS FIRST
Delaware	ABC (A Better Chance)
Dist. of Col.	TANF
Florida	Welfare Transition Program
Georgia	TANF
Guam	TANF
Hawaii	TANF
Idaho	Temporary Assistance for Families in Idaho
Illinois	TANF
Indiana	TANF, cash assistance; IMPACT (Indiana Manpower Placement and Comprehensive Training), TANF work program
Iowa	FIP (Family Investment Program)
Kansas	Kansas Works
Kentucky	K-TAP (Kentucky Transitional Assistance Program)
Louisiana	FITAP (Family Independence Temporary Assistance Program), cash assistance; FIND Work (Family Independence Work Program), TANF work program
Maine	TANF, cash assistance; ASPIRE (Additional Support for People in Retraining and Employment), TANF work program
Maryland	FIP (Family Investment Program)
Massachusetts	TAFDC (Transitional Aid to Families with Dependent Children), cash assistance; ESP (Employment Services Program), TANF work program
Michigan	FIP (Family Independence Program)
Minnesota	MFIP (Minnesota Family Investment Program)
Mississippi	TANF

without supportive services simply may not be enough. Providing supportive services designed to address self-esteem and self-efficacy, especially for minority populations, can play an important role in program success and transition (Bruster, 2009). Just providing employment alone is not enough, and the importance of supportive services should not be ignored.

As with most TANF implementation issues, states can establish their own guidelines on how soon a person must be working to avoid elimination from TANF rolls (State Policy Documentation Project, 2005). Virginia requires a person to be employed within ninety days; other states demand employment within twenty-four months.

Table 7: Names of State TANF Programs—(*Continued*)

State	Name
Missouri	Beyond Welfare
Montana	FAIM (Families Achieving Independence in Montana)
Nebraska	Employment First
Nevada	TANF
New Hampshire	FAP (Family Assistance Program), financial aid for work-exempt families; NHEP (New Hampshire Employment Program), financial aid for work-mandated families
New Jersey	WFNJ (Work First New Jersey)
New Mexico	NM Works
New York	FA (Family Assistance Program)
North Carolina	Work First
North Dakota	TEEM (Training, Employment, Education Management)
Ohio	OWF (Ohio Works First)
Oklahoma	TANF
Oregon	JOBS (Job Opportunities and Basic Skills Program)
Pennsylvania	Pennsylvania TANF
Puerto Rico	TANF
Rhode Island	FIP (Family Independence Program)
South Carolina	Family Independence
South Dakota	TANF
Tennessee	Families First
Texas	Texas Works (Department of Human Services), cash assistance; Choices (Texas Workforce Commission), TANF work program
Utah	FEP (Family Employment Program)
Vermont	ANFC (Aid to Needy Families with Children), cash assistance; Reach Up, TANF work program
Virgin Islands	(FIP) Family Improvement Program
Virginia	VIEW (Virginia Initiative for Employment, Not Welfare)
Washington	WorkFirst
West Virginia	West Virginia Works
Wisconsin	W-2 (Wisconsin Works)
Wyoming	POWER (Personal Opportunities With Employment Responsibility)

Source: www.acf.hhs.gov/programs/ofa/tnfnames.htm. As of 9/04/2002.

Child care. An important component of TANF is the requirement that communities provide childcare to TANF participants. As adults, in unprecedented numbers, are now required to work, there will be large increases in demand for childcare program slots—children cannot be left at home, unattended and unprotected. Funding is required for childcare services to support low-paid employees passing through the TANF system. Social work professionals will be needed to assist these parents in finding low-cost childcare so that they can maintain their jobs.

TANF and Native Americans. There is a different set of protocols that govern public programs for Native Americans. The federal office of the Division of Tribal

Management, which is part of the HHS Administration of Children and Families, is a central point for assisting in implementation and coordination of ongoing consultation with tribal governments relating to TANF. Essentially these regulations recognize the unique cultural attributes and needs of tribal communities and allows for tribes to develop and administer TANF programs. In 2006, there were 53 Tribal TANF programs serving 265 tribes and Alaska Native villages and the non-reservation Indian populations of 104 counties and the Municipality of Anchorage, Alaska.

Food Programs

Supplemental Nutritional Assistance Program (SNAP). More commonly known as "food stamps," the federal Supplemental Nutritional Assistance Program is designed to fight hunger and malnutrition. The program name was changed from "Food Stamps" in 2008 to reflect a focus on nutrition. But note, this is the federal name and states have the option to call the program by another name. Another significant change is that the program no longer will give out paper coupons; beginning June 2009, a client can only use an EBT card (Electronic Benefit Transfer).

Prior to the Great Depression, no national coordinated effort addressed these fundamental issues. The problem was largely left to the states and local communities to deal with. For the most part, anti-hunger programs distributed actual food items. This practice moved to the national level when, in 1933, the Federal Surplus Relief Corporation was created to distribute surplus food.

Did You Know...In 1997 the average amount of food stamps per person per meal was less than $.80.

The first Food Stamp Program project, which ran from 1939 to 1943, used two types of stamps: blue and orange. Blue stamps could be used only for surplus commodities, while orange stamps allowed the purchase of any type of food.

In 1961, a demonstration Food Stamp Program was started. It led in 1964 to the passage of the Food Stamp Act. Under the auspices of the Department of Agriculture, clients received stamps that allowed them to purchase certain American-grown or -produced food at certain supermarkets. The current program structure was implemented in 1977 with the goal of alleviating hunger and malnutrition by permitting low-income households to obtain a more nutritious diet through normal channels of trade.

The 1996 welfare reform efforts included a $27 billion cutback in the Food Stamp Program over six years, to be achieved primarily by reducing, denying, or ending assistance to needy families.

Participation in SNAP in 2008 (the latest data available) totaled 28.4 million persons with an average monthly benefit of $101.53 (http://www.fns.usda.gov/pd/SNAPsummary.htm). The maximum monthly allocation for a family of four in 2009 was $588.

Eligibility for SNAP is based on financial and nonfinancial factors. The application process includes completing and filing an application form, being interviewed, and verifying facts to determine eligibility. With certain exceptions, a household that meets the eligibility requirements is qualified to receive benefits.

The following 2006 data best illustrate the type of people who are accessing SNAP and certainly shows that this program targets the poorest and most vulnerable people in our communities (http://www.fns.usda.gov/snap/faqs.htm#9).

- 49 percent of all participants are children (18 or younger) and 61 percent of them live in single-parent households.
- 52 percent of SNAP households include children.
- 9 percent of all participants are elderly (age 60 or over).
- 76 percent of all benefits go to households with children, 16 percent go to households with disabled persons, and 9 percent go to households with elderly persons.
- 33 percent of households with children were headed by a single parent, the overwhelming majority of which were women.
- The average household size is 2.3 persons.
- The average gross monthly income per SNAP household is $673.
- 43 percent of participants are white; 33 percent are African-American, non-Hispanic; 19 percent are Hispanic; 2 percent are Asian; 2 percent are Native American, and less than 1 percent are of unknown race or ethnicity.

The basic SNAP income eligibility requirements for 2009 include the following, but do note these are subject to change and often do, so the best bet is to check for the most recent information on the Department of Agriculture's web page (http://www.fns.usda.gov/snap/faqs.htm#9).

- Households may have no more than $2,000 in countable resources, such as a bank account ($3,000 if at least one person in the household is age 60 or older, or is disabled). Certain resources are not counted, such as a home and lot. Special rules are used to determine the resource value of vehicles owned by household members.
- The gross monthly income of most households must be 130 percent or less of the federal poverty guidelines ($1,907 per month for a family of three in most places, effective Oct. 1, 2008, through Sept. 30, 2009). Gross income includes all cash payments to the household, with a few exceptions specified in the law or the program regulations.
- Net monthly income must be 100 percent or less of federal poverty guidelines ($1,467 per month for a household of three in most places, effective Oct. 1, 2008, through Sept. 30, 2009). Net income is figured by adding all of a household's gross income and then taking a number of approved deductions for child care, some shelter costs, and other expenses. Households with an elderly or disabled member are subject only to the net income test.
- Most able-bodied adult applicants must meet certain work requirements.
- All household members must provide a Social Security number or apply for one.

Also, SNAP does limit what may be purchased. Eligible items include breads and cereals; fruits and vegetables; meats, fish, and poultry; and dairy products. Additionally, seeds and plants which produce food for the household to eat may be purchased with SNAP. Conversely, one cannot purchase beer, wine, liquor, cigarettes or tobacco; pet foods; soaps, paper products, and household supplies; vitamins and medicines; food that will be eaten in the store; and hot foods.

School lunch and breakfast and other food programs. Other federal food programs we need to consider include the National School Lunch and Breakfast Program, WIC, and Meals on Wheels. Targeted toward the poor, these programs were developed as supplements for specific vulnerable population groups.

The National School Lunch Program (NSLP), which provides school children in the United States a lunch every school day, was created by Congress following World War II. At that time, the military draft showed a strong correlation between physical deficiencies and childhood malnutrition.

Schools are required to serve meals at no charge to children whose household income is at or below 130 percent of the federal poverty guidelines. Children are entitled to pay a reduced price (a maximum of 40 cents for lunch, 30 cents for breakfast, and 15 cents for a snack) if their household income is above 130 percent but at or below 185 percent of these guidelines. In the 2008–2009 school year, the annual income for a family of three to receive reduced lunch prices (the 185% level) was $32,560; eligibility for a three-person family for "free" meals required an annual income (130% of poverty) less than $22,880. In fiscal year 2007, more than 30.5 million children each day got their lunch through the National School Lunch Program and the program cost $8.7 billion in FY 2007.

The National School Breakfast program was established by Congress as a pilot program in 1966 in areas where children had long bus rides to school and in areas where many mothers were in the workforce. The program was standardized as a permanent entitlement in 1975 to assist schools in providing nutritious morning meals to the nation's children. Research clearly shows that beginning each day with a nutritious breakfast results in better and stronger learning outcomes. Studies conclude that students who eat school breakfast increase their math and reading scores as well as improve their speed and memory in cognitive tests. Research also shows that children who eat breakfast at school, in particular closer to class and test-taking time, perform better on standardized tests than those who skip breakfast or eat breakfast at home.

Any child at a participating school may purchase a meal through the School Breakfast Program. Children from families with incomes at or below 130 percent of the federal poverty level are eligible for free meals, similar to the school lunch program. The number of children participating in the breakfast program has grown slowly but steadily over the years: 1970, 0.5 million; 1980, 3.6 million; 1990, 4.1 million; 1995, 6.3 million; 2002, 8.2 million; 2004, 8.9 million; 2008, 10.6 million. In 2008, almost 1.3 billion free breakfasts and 176 million reduced-price breakfasts were served.

The Special Supplemental Nutrition Program for Women, Infants, and Children (WIC) was enacted in 1972 to provide nutritional counseling and basic food supplements to prenatal and postpartum low-income women and their children. According to the Children's Defense Fund (1998, p. 43), every $1 spent on WIC saves $3.50 in future federal supports including health, education, and cash assistance. Pregnant or postpartum women, infants, and children up to age 5 are eligible. They must meet income guidelines, a state residency requirement, and be individually determined to be at "nutritional risk" by a health professional.

Women generally receive food vouchers that entitle them to certain items including milk, eggs, cheese, infant formula, cereals, and fruits and vegetables. The type and amount of food is specified, limiting the adult's selection. Income guidelines require that a family's income must fall below 185 percent of the U.S. poverty threshold, or $32,560 in 2008 for a three-person family. In 2008, approximately 8.7 million persons participated in WIC with an average monthly per person benefit of $42.42.

Targeted to supplement and improve the nutritional needs of seniors in poverty, the Meals on Wheels program began in 1972. In some instances, meals are provided in the senior's home, while in other cases, meals are provided at a central location such as a senior center. An important and unintended benefit of the program is that seniors, many of whom are isolated, are provided daily contact with others. Volunteers who deliver meals to seniors are able to check on the elderly and ensure that all is fine with them.

Supplemental Security Income

Supplemental Security Income (SSI) was enacted in 1972 by combining three categorical programs that had been part of the Economic Security Act: Old Age Assistance, Aid to the Blind, and Aid to the Totally and Permanently Disabled. Prior to 1972, these three programs had been run by the states. With the creation of SSI, operations were transferred to the federal government. SSI recipients are also eligible for other social services including SNAP, Medicaid, assistance paying Medicare, and other social services.

SSI is a means-tested public assistance program. Age is not an eligibility requirement. Potential clients include the mentally retarded, those over age 65 who have little or no income, those who are legally blind, those disabled because of physical or mental impairment, some people who are visually impaired but do not meet the requirements for blindness, addicts and alcoholics in treatment, and children under age 18 who have an impairment comparable to those that determine eligibility for adults.

In 2008, the maximum federal benefit rate was $637 for an individual and $956 for a couple. Some states supplement the federal SSI benefit with additional payments. As of January 2009, those states that do not supplement SSI benefits included Arkansas, Georgia, Kansas, Mississippi, Tennessee, and West Virginia.

In January 2009, SSI participants totaled 7.5 million who received an average monthly payment of $504.08 (U.S. Social Security Administration, n.d). To be eligible for SSI, an applicant's resources must be minimal. Assets were limited to $2,000 for an individual and $3,000 for a couple, excluding a home; the value of a car was limited to $4,500.

Not all resources are counted in determining whether an applicant meets the resource limit. The following are excluded (that is, not considered to be personal resources):

- *A home* regardless of its value.
- *Personal effects or household goods* with a total value of $2,000 or less are not counted. If the total value exceeds $2,000, the excess counts.
- Typically the value of *one car* does not count.
- *Life insurance policies* with a total face value of $1,500 or less per person are not counted.
- *Burial plots or spaces* for an individual and immediate family generally do not count.
- *Burial funds* for an individual and spouse do not count if they are specifically set aside for burial purposes and do not exceed $1,500 per person.
- *Resources* held under the Uniform Gifts to Minors Act or held in trusts that are administered by custodians or trustees may not be counted.
- *Property* essential to an individual's self-support is not counted. Such property may include nonbusiness income-producing property and property used to produce essential goods and services.
- *Resources* that a person who is blind or disabled needs to fulfill an approved plan for achieving self-support are not considered.
- *Disaster assistance* and certain Native corporation stocks held by natives of Alaska also are excluded.
- *Any retroactive SSI payments or retroactive Social Security benefits* paid to a recipient are not counted as resources for six months after they are received.
- *Crime victims' compensation payments* are not counted.
- *State and local government relocation assistance* is not counted as a resource for nine months after it is received (see www.ssa.gov/pubs/11015 .html).

Legal Immigrants

One of the most radical changes introduced by the 1996 welfare reform act was the sweeping elimination of legal immigrants from all public programs. Legal immigrants become eligible for public assistance only when they become citizens or have worked for forty calendar quarters (ten years). A public outcry led to the amendment of the law to allow legal immigrants receiving SSI on or before August 26, 1996, to continue to receive payments. Yet this wasn't the case for all programs. As a result of the legislation approximately 300,000 legal immigrant children were removed from SNAP (Children's Defense Fund, 1998, p. 7).

Ginsberg (1998, p. 192) suggests the rationale behind this decisive move against immigrants is to force legal immigrants to seek and obtain citizenship. Until then new immigrants are expected to support themselves or find assistance from private sources, including family or sponsors.

Earned Income Credit

The Earned Income Credit (EIC), also called the Earned Income Tax Credit (EITC), is a tax credit for working families with low incomes. One of the Clinton Administration's major welfare initiatives, it was developed to stimulate work among the poor. The EITC is a federal income tax credit for low-income workers who are eligible for and claim the credit. The credit reduces the amount of tax an individual owes, and may be returned in the form of a refund.

Eligible working families, either with or without children, pay less federal income tax or receive a larger tax refund. To claim the EITC, you must meet certain rules. Income and family size determine the amount of the EITC. To qualify for the credit, both the earned income and the adjusted gross income for 2008 must be less than $38,646 ($41,646 married filing jointly) with two or more qualifying children; $33,995 ($36,995 married filing jointly) with one qualifying child; or $12,880 ($15,880 married filing jointly) with no qualifying children.

In most cases, the EITC benefit does not affect other program benefits such as housing supplements, TANF, SNAP, Medicaid, and SSI.

SUMMARY

Poverty cuts across all races and ethnic groups, both genders, and all age groups. Indeed, more whites are poor than members of any other group. Nevertheless, poverty rates reveal that some groups are especially vulnerable (Carter, 2000). Women, minorities, and children suffer disproportionately from poverty. One in six of all children are in poverty and one in four of children under age 6.

No consensus exists about causes of poverty, and theories to explain it are diverse and controversial (O'Gorman, 2002). The ideas proposed range from an individual's genetic makeup to deep, complicated structures of society. Also, considering the popularity of terms such as "family empowerment," it is time to do more than use these terms and to address the long-term effects of such concepts and how they can be measured (Bartle, Counchonnal, Canda, & Staker, 2002).

All social work professionals need to be aware that 1996 was a pivotal year in redirecting 61 years of entitlement programs and that as a result governmental antipoverty strategies have changed dramatically. Public programs are now time limited with greater state discretion in imposing limits. In most cases, once a family exhausts its TANF lifetime limit it is left to its own devices. TANF represents a new direction in welfare programming that stresses employment and penalizes clients who do not work or are unable to meet program requirements on a consistent basis.

As social work professionals, what does this mean for us? The social worker's role in public assistance programs is not as clear as it once was. A visit to your local food stamp or TANF office reveals that few, if any, of the workers are professional social workers. The public may believe that social workers run these programs, but the reality is that we do not. The need to assist the poor remains, however, and many people still believe that this is where social workers as professionals need to be.

McPhee and Bronstein (2003) outline four central implications for social workers in this area. First, social workers are encouraged to find ways to include the opinions and wishes of program recipients in future changes and continued implementation of the program. Second, the common myths about the poor and women on governmental and state subsidy in particular need to be identified and addressed based on evidence not opinion. Third, adequate resources need to be provided to front line workers to assist them to do their jobs. Fourth, if TANF is going to claim that it supports families, then the disproportionate concentration on work needs to be addressed, as in many ways this can be counter-productive to basic family reunification.

Poverty and its ravages can't be washed away by finding people jobs and wishing them well. Nor will it occur through providing minimum wage jobs for women and children living in poverty, because unfortunately no matter how hard you work raising a family out of poverty from these types of efforts will never work (O'Gorman, 2002). Clients need to be linked with appropriate resources—they need workers who understand the emotional and psychological toll that poverty takes and who can suggest how best to respond to this personal turmoil. Someone with a personal problem expects the best possible professional service from the social worker at the local mental health center. A patient in the hospital expects high-quality care from the hospital's social worker (Dziegielewski, 2004). Why should a poor person expect and receive a lower level of care?

A probably more important question concerns the sixty-month limit on welfare. What happens at the end of five years? Do we really believe that people forced without proper education into low-paying jobs will be self-sufficient within sixty months? And remember, a number of states have shorter time limits, some as short as twenty-four months. Where will these people go? Will they simply disappear? Of course not. They will remain in our communities—some more visible than others. Some people will say that they were given a chance and we shouldn't do anything else. But what will happen when the first child dies on the streets because a parent's TANF time expired? This question is extremely relevant because for TANF, positive effects depend on improved income, not just the ability to increase employment (O'Gorman, 2002). What will happen when our country experiences an economic recession and jobs are just not available?

The poor will always be part of our society, and we must have public policies in place that protect them rather than cause them harm. Social workers can and should take the lead in promoting just social policies that create opportunities for all people to achieve their full potential and gain economic independence.

Further Readings

DeNavas-Walt, C., Proctor, B. D., & Smith, J. C. (2008, August). U.S. Census Bureau, Current Population Reports, P60-235, *Income, Poverty, and Health Insurance Coverage in the United States: 2007*. U.S. Government Printing Office, Washington, DC.

Internal Revenue Service (2003). Forms and Publications. Retrieved from: www.irs.gov/formspubs/page/0,,id%3D104425,00.html#T3.

U.S. Census Bureau. (2009) American fact finder. http://factfinder.census.gov/servlet/ DatasetMainPageServlet?_program=ACS&_lang=en&_ts=143471788982.

Culture of Poverty
Banfield, E. C., & Lewis, O. (1966). *The unheavenly city.* Boston: Little, Brown.

Underclass
Auletta, K. (1982). *The underclass.* New York: Vintage.
Wilson, W. J. (1987). *The truly disadvantaged.* Chicago: University of Chicago Press.

Eugenics
Jensen, A. R. (1969). How much can we boost IQ and scholastic achievement? *Harvard Educational Review, 39,* 1–23.
Shockley, W. (1976). Sterilization: A thinking exercise. In C. Bahema (Ed.), *Eugenics: Then and now.* Stroudsburg, PA: Doidon, Hutchinson and Ross.

Radical School
Gil, D. (1981). *Unraveling social policy.* Boston: Schenkman.
Piven, F., & Cloward, R. (1971). *Regulating the poor.* New York: Vintage.

Chapter 8

Child Welfare Services

CHILDREN CONSTITUTE A GROWING PORTION OF THE U.S. POPULA-tion with a 50 percent increase since 1950. In 1995, over 70 million children under age 18 made up 26.8 percent of the U.S. population (Baugher & Lamison-White, 1996, p. C-5); in 2002, this number rose to 72 million (U.S. Census Bureau, 2003); and as of 2006, the number continues to rise to 73.7 million (U.S. Census Bureau, 2006). With the median income for American households being $46,300 for non-Hispanic White Americans in 2002, the latest figures confirm a slight rise of 1.1 percent to an estimated $46, 326 occurring between 2004 and 2005. The poverty rate in the U.S. is approximately 12.6 percent and approximately 46.6 million people do not have health insurance (U.S. Census, November 17, 2008). Therefore, supporting and caring for these millions of children, taking into account the limited incomes most parents have, is the single most important investment we can make in the future of our society. In twenty years, people now in their mid-40s will rely heavily on the children of today to keep the United States prosperous.

We cannot overestimate the importance of today's children to tomorrow's society. We can all agree that we need the best and brightest people leading our country. Don't you want competent and self-assured people in the labor force that can take over and move us beyond what has been accomplished? In order to plan for the future, we need to start raising these bright and competent people early. Through current investment in support and intervention we can avoid a future in which millions of undereducated and at best minimally competent Americans continue to suffer from personal and social problems deeply rooted in their childhood.

The importance of nurturing children is not a new idea. Indeed, a complex child welfare system exists to give children the opportunity to grow and reach their full potential. Karger and Stoesz have asserted, however, that child welfare programs and services are controversial because many people see them as an intrusion: "they sanction the intervention of human service professionals in family affairs that are ordinarily assumed to be private matters related to parental rights" (2010, p. 338). Most of us can remember being told that being a child should be "fun." Many adults long to return to a simpler time in their lives when cares and responsibilities were few and far between. For many, Norman Rockwell's images of small-town America capture the ideal childhood. Television too has actively promoted the idea of families as caring groups always having fun, even during hard times. Older shows such as *Father Knows Best, Good Times, The Brady Bunch,*

Name: Syprenia M. Bonner, BSW

Place of Residence: Montgomery, Alabama

College/University Degrees: BSW, Alabama State University; Certified Medical Assistant, Capps College

Present Position and Title: Public Health Social Worker

Previous Work/Volunteer Experience: Therapeutic Foster Care Social Worker, Macon County DHR Child Protection Worker/CA/N investigator, Referral Nurse, Medical Assistant for Cancer Care Treatment Center

Why did you choose social work as a career? My mother was a homemaker with nine children in the home. My farther provided for the family on a construction worker's salary. I grew up in a community of people who did not have much but learned to share what they had with each other. I learned as a young child the value of people coming together as a whole and making life better for all. Communities joining together in changing the situations and conditions of others and by sharing, respecting the dignity and worth of others, and in loving one another.

What is your favorite social work story? Working as a therapeutic foster care social worker, I was honored to work with a group of energetic, smart children as well as a group of caring and loving foster parents. There was one situation that stood out the most regarding my role as a social worker. I worked with a 17-year-old African American female who had many problems and hurdles causing her to fail. My efforts at helping her were for her to develop self-confidence in seeing her value and her worth as a person. I began helping her to prioritize and focus on her goals and teaching her consistency in hard work and making good decisions. The process was slow but successful. She learned a life lesson, graduated from high school with honors, and got a good paying job.

What is one thing you would change in the community if you had the power to do so? As I grew up in a community of caring people working together as a whole for change, if I had the power to make changes in communities today, I would start by creating programs that would empower people at making changes within their communities as a whole. I would hope to bring a sense of community pride and a strong desire to change that circumstance of their environment by working together as a whole.

and *The Cosby Show* illustrated life in suburbia and the city within a happy and caring family. When outside help was required, it often came from extended family members, friends, neighbors, religious organizations, and even membership associations.

In this society we expect, and the media encourages us to expect, that no child will face the horrors of poverty, homelessness, abuse and neglect, and inadequate health care, or live in an environment where crime, alcohol, tobacco, and drug abuse are the norm. This is a worthy goal, but we have to be careful as such an ambitious goal can sometimes be satisfied by simply denying that such problems exist. Few sponsors, if any, would want to be the ones to tell America that all is not well with its children. When looking specifically at children, it is critical to know how many children do not have their needs adequately met (Southwell, 2009). But the simple fact is that all is not well with America's children. Even in the United States, considered one of the most advanced of the developed countries, for millions of children life is filled with turmoil. These children are repeatedly forced to face crises that may eventually lead to chaos and tragedy. In this chapter, we look in depth at America's children. We examine what life is like for many of them and explore the laws, programs, and services geared toward helping them. In addition, we discuss how the public and voluntary child welfare systems work together. The role of the social worker in protecting and advocating for the child is highlighted, and concepts such as mandatory reporting are explained.

CHILD WELFARE DEFINED

Let's begin by looking at how **child welfare** has been defined. The *Social Work Dictionary* defines child welfare as

> programs and policies oriented toward the protection, care and healthy development of children. Within a national, state and local policy and funding framework, child welfare services are provided to vulnerable children and their families by public and non-profit agencies with the goals of ameliorating conditions that put children and families at risk; strengthening and supporting families so that they can successfully care for their children; protecting children from future abuse and neglect; addressing the emotional, behavioral, or health problems of children; and when necessary providing permanent families for children through adoption or guardianship. (Barker, 2003, p. 69)

Heffernan, Shuttlesworth, and Ambrosino, like Barker, offer a very broad view of child welfare that encompasses "programs and policies that address the needs of children, youth, and families as diverse as the type of needs experienced" (1988, p. 167). Berzin, Thomas, and Cohen (2007) go so far as to say that involving the family and community in decision making for the best practices related to child welfare services is not just innovative—it is our standard for practice. This type of inclusive definition was reflected in the writings of Linderman (1995) who highlighted how the formal organizational aspects of child welfare need to remain inclusive of the interrelated aspects of family and community action. His definition of child welfare characterizes it as both a public and a voluntary effort to coordinate seven interrelated objectives:

- ◆ Protect and promote the well-being of children
- ◆ Support families and seek to prevent problems that may result in neglect, abuse, and exploitation
- ◆ Promote family stability by assessing and building on family strengths while addressing needs
- ◆ Support the full array of out-of-home care services for children who require them

◆ Take responsibility for addressing social conditions that negatively affect children and families, such as inadequate housing, poverty, chemical dependence, and lack of access to health care
◆ Support the strengths of families whenever possible
◆ Intervene when necessary to ensure the safety and well-being of children

Dobelstein (1996), however, omits the voluntary sector from his discussion and concludes that child welfare involves a broad range of public activities undertaken on behalf of children. Mirroring Dobelstein's view, Chelf describes family and child welfare policies as "covering a broad spectrum of public efforts . . . [and] closely interwoven with several other policy sectors such as health, nutrition, education, and income maintenance, making them somewhat a confusing patchwork of policies and programs" (1992, p. 108).

The work of Kadushin and Martin is especially important in understanding social welfare because they view it from a social work perspective. For them, "child welfare is concerned with the general well being of all children. It encompasses any and all measures designed to protect and promote the bio-psycho-social development of children" (1988, p. 1). Gil gives another straightforward definition of child welfare: "In the simplest terms, as well as in a most profound sense, child welfare means conditions of living in which children can 'fare well," conditions in which their bodies, minds, and souls are free to develop spontaneously through all stages of maturation" (1985, p. 12).

Over the years, the definitions have changed slightly; some include public and private responsibilities, others do not, but all of these definitions of child welfare have several points in common. First, the child welfare system is firmly established within the public sector; whether or not private sector involvement occurs, it clearly will have a less prominent role. Second, child welfare policy is closely tied to and directly influenced by family policy. The importance of the family and community connectedness is always a central part of the integration. Third and probably most important is that all policies, services, and programs included in child welfare cover a broad range of interventions and services, but all efforts aim to improve child well-being. In this way the child's resilience, an ability to cope, is maximized and the child is provided with as safe a nurturing environment as possible, one that fosters positive growth and full development. Taking into account all of these commonalities, we define the child welfare system as the system of services and programs that protect, promote, and encourage the growth and development of all children in order that they can achieve their full potential and function at their optimal level in their communities.

AMERICA'S DIVERSE CHILDREN AND THEIR FAMILIES

Although there are more white children than any other racial or ethnic group, population increases for blacks and Hispanics have been far greater than for whites (see chapter 7). The Hispanic population in the United States has grown quite dramatically, but it is important to note that these rates may be inflated. The term "Hispanic" is difficult to define. In the U.S. census Latinos can classify themselves as Hispanic, black, or white; in other cases, they might be listed as both Hispanic and black. Part of the growth in the Hispanic population may actually reflect resolution of this confusion as individuals switch affiliations.

Just as American children have become more diverse so too have their families. The family is a critical institution in shaping and transmitting from generation to generation the values and rich traditions of culturally and ethnically diverse Americans. The kaleidoscope of families includes those whose roots are Anglo-European, Native Indian, African, Latino, Asian, and Middle Eastern, to mention a few. American families, whatever their ethnic heritage, are expected to respond to

---

Box 1: Child Fact Sheet

- 11.7 million American children younger than 18 lived below the poverty line.
- More than half the children born in the 1990s will spend some of their childhood in a single-parent family.
- Only one in four children in a single-parent family receive child support payments.
- The average monthly child support payment to a child in a single-parent family is $168 or $2,000 per year.
- Over 2.5 million households with children live in substandard housing.
- Children account for 40 percent of the nation's homeless.
- One out of every six American children (16.3 percent) was poor in 2001. By race and ethnicity, 30.2 percent of Black children, 28.0 percent of Hispanic children, 11.5 percent of Asian and Pacific Islander children, and 9.5 percent of Non-Hispanic White children were poor.
- Three out of four poor children live in a working family. 74 percent of children in poverty live in a family where someone works full or part time for at least part of the year. One out of three poor children (34 percent) lives with someone who worked full time year round.
- There are more poor White Non-Hispanic children (4.2 million) than poor Black children (3.5 million) or poor Hispanic children (3.6 million), even though the proportion of Black and Hispanic children who are poor is far higher. More poor children live in suburban and rural areas than in central cities.
- Poor families have only 2.2 children on average.
- Most child poverty is not temporary: 80 percent of children poor in one year are still poor the next year.
- Poor children are at least twice as likely as nonpoor children to suffer stunted growth or lead poisoning, or to be kept back in school.
- Poor children score significantly lower on reading, math, and vocabulary tests when compared with otherwise-similar nonpoor children.
- A baby born to a poor mother is more likely to die before its first birthday than a baby born to an unwed mother, a high school dropout, or a mother who smoked during pregnancy, according to the Centers for Disease Control.

Source: www.childrensdefense.org/fs_cpfaq_facts.php

the expectations and norms of this society, even though many have very different cultural traditions, values, beliefs, norms, folkways, and mores. Some families hold their distinctive beliefs so strongly that they refuse to change; instead, they pass the same set of rigid expectations from one generation to the next. The key challenge for families is to balance the rich traditions and customs of their cultural heritage with the values and beliefs of the dominant society.

Family structures are also becoming more diverse. No longer do families mirror the traditional stereotype of a two-parent household in which the father works and the mother maintains the home. Nontraditional families are growing in number, and it is no longer uncommon to be raised in a single-parent household or by lesbian, gay, or transgendered parenting couples. Regardless of the type of family or whether the parents are heterosexual, research does appear to suggest that two-parent families appear to be more successful in child-rearing (Mallon, 2008). For many couples raising children, however, one parent staying at home with the child has clearly become a luxury as often both parents work outside of the home. For so many of these parents, working outside the home, and in some cases having a second job, is not a choice—it is a necessity.

Divorce rates are increasing, and more children are seeing their parents split up than ever before. In the thirty-two years between 1960 and 1992, the number of divorces tripled from 400,000 to 1,200,000 annually, with nearly 50 percent of all marriages ending in divorce (Lindsey, 1994, p. 73). Although these numbers have been challenged, the rate appears to remain at 48–50 percent in 2003 (Americans for Divorce Reform, n.d.). Current statistics quote the rates as high as 60 percent of all marriages ending in divorce, whereas second or third marriages have only about 20 percent of couples remaining happily married (Robbins, 2008). What is of the most concern about these high rates of divorce is the effect it can have on

Activity…Discussion of factors. Listed below is a complete list of the circumstances Robbins (2008) cites as affecting children after their parents divorce. Do you agree with these and are there any others that you believe should be added? Be sure to say why you agree or why you don't and what supporting information you have on which to base your opinions.

According to research, children of divorced parents:
 ◆ Are more often involved in abuse or neglect.
 ◆ Have more health, behavioral, and emotional problems.
 ◆ Are more involved in crime and drug abuse
 ◆ Have more incidents of suicide.
 ◆ Perform poorly in reading, spelling, and math.
 ◆ Are more likely to repeat a grade, drop out, and be unsuccessful at completing college degrees.
 ◆ Will likely earn less as adults than children of intact families.
 ◆ Lose their virginity at a younger age.
 ◆ Are less likely to have children of their own.
 ◆ Are more likely to divorce as adults.
 ◆ Are more likely to grow up in a level of poverty.

children under the age of 18. Robbins (2008) reports that although some children do just fine and adapt to the divorce, some of the problems that become more likely include: abuse and neglect, health, behavioral health and emotional problems, crime and drug abuse, incidents of suicide, performing poorly in school and less success in school-related goals and activities, and growing up in a level of poverty.

Another significant force shaping family structure is the growth in the number of children born out of wedlock to single parents. Between 1950 and 1991, the number of such births increased almost nine-fold from 140,000 to 1,200,000 annually (Lindsey, 1994, p. 74). Although the birthrate for adolescents—that is, the number of children born per 1,000 adolescents—declined in the early 1990s, 518,389 babies were born to teenage mothers in 1994 (Children's Defense Fund, 1998, pp. 81, 82). In that year, 36 percent of children lived with a single parent who had never married the birth partner (Brunner, 1997). Increased divorce rates and high out-of-wedlock birthrates have together fueled an increase in the number of single-parent households. When looking specifically at the number of births outside of marriage, the estimates are as high as 70 percent involving women over the age of 20 (Sawhill, 2001). This increased number of out-of-wedlock births has clearly changed how we define the traditional family. This high level of unprecedented out-of-wedlock births, however, does not seem relevant to teenagers. For example, in 2002, the birth rate for teenagers was 5 percent lower than it was in 2001 and 10 percent lower than it was in 2000 (Centers for Disease Control [CDC], 2003). The exact reason for this decline is not known, but it is possible that these lower numbers may be related to a decrease in the overall number of births and to preventive education. In 2006, however, for the first time in 14 years the numbers of teen births actually rose (Reinberg, 2007). Since this is only evident in this one year, this trend and the potential increase will need to be monitored over the years to come. What is very clear from these birth patterns, however, is that the traditional family structure is changing rapidly.

Have you ever wondered why so many people worry about the growing number of single-parent households? Why does it matter whether a family is single-parent or two-parent? The primary reason is that two-parent families usually have a greater income and therefore greater resources with which to carry out their parenting obligations and responsibilities. Simply stated, by pooling their income two parents have more money for the family to spend on goods and services. Lindsey (1994, p. 87) estimated that the difference between two- and one-parent families is so great that a single parent earns only 25 percent of what two parents can earn. Underlying this figure is the fact that most single parents are women, who have income levels much lower than average. A two-parent family allows for more flexibility in child care and supervision. With two adults available, one parent can take a break when the relationship gets too stressful, and whether taking turns or caring for children jointly, more nurturing parent-child time is available. The single parent often has no one to help ease the childcare burden, as well as being often forced to face the many day-to-day problems and circumstances alone, while having to manage a lower family income and singlehandedly maintain a safe and nourishing home environment (Lindsey, 1994).

A third significant development changing family structure is the rise in "blended families." A blended family is one in which the primary caretakers did not give birth to one or more of the children who live in the household. Such families are most often the result of divorce and remarriage. With the high rate of American divorce and lifestyle adjustment, blended families are becoming more common. These families often face a difficult task because supportive relations may need to be developed even before they can be nurtured. Becoming a blended family requires adjustment because members may enter and reenter the family at various times throughout their lives. These adjustments intensify the need to establish and maintain family unison and support. Although all family systems need constant negotiation to maintain equilibrium, blended families face the added struggle of keeping their balance as family members come and go.

The growing diversity and changing structure of American families is the focus of much attention. The kind of family situation regarded as *ideal* is often shaped by a *political lens*. Think about political candidates and their campaign rhetoric and advertisements. How often have you seen "the family" play a starring role in a local, state, or national election? The Republican Party's *Contract with America* (Gillespie & Schellhas, 1994) and the Christian Coalition's (1995) *Contract with the American Family* placed the family as the centerpiece of all political activities. Why have children and families become such hot political items? Two reasons come to mind immediately:

Every human being was once a child: Having been a child and had experiences that influenced the way you think and feel about things as you aged helps raise your consciousness in this area. Most of us identify with children's issues simply because of our own experiences. All of us had positive and negative childhood experiences. Most of us cherish the good times and wish we could have avoided the bad ones. Few, if any, adults believe it is in a child's best interest to suffer physical or emotional pain. Therefore, social workers and other professionals will continue to support and encourage programs and services that prevent and alleviate unfair treatment of all vulnerable groups (Eamon, 2008). Since children are considered a vulnerable population, most adults agree that all children should be protected and have a safe environment in which to grow. Adults are responsible for ensuring that children are shielded from various risks.

Everyone has a family: Just as all of us were children once, we were all raised in some kind of family. Our families probably differed vastly. Some people had two parents; others come from single-parent homes. Some people were raised with siblings, others without. Some were raised in foster homes or were adopted; others had aunts, uncles, or other relatives as their primary caretakers; and for some, institutions played the family role. No matter what our family background, our experiences mean we have strong feelings about what families should be like.

THE RIGHTS OF CHILDREN

Children have fewer rights than adults (Wineman, 1995, p. 465). From this perspective there are two counterbalancing forces at play. On one hand, we recognize that children generally are not able to make mature decisions. This is not a negative statement about young people but rather refers to their inexperience. For this reason, children's rights are limited and critical decisions about and responsibility for their lives rests, not with them, but with their caregivers. On the other hand, we also recognize that children need protection—sometimes from their own caretakers. As a result, we have established a complex system of child protective services.

The interesting history of children's rights thus for the most part reflects ambivalence. From a legal standpoint children are treated differently than adults. Children can face "status offenses"—that is, crimes based on status, in this case age. For example, a child can be arrested or detained for drinking alcohol, smoking cigarettes, being truant, or being a runaway. An adult cannot be arrested merely for smoking or drinking (unless doing so causes a public disturbance) or for running away from home or being truant.

Figures 1a, b, c: These photographs were developed in an Arts Outreach project for teenage mothers. The program, "My Life, My Lens, My Child," was part of an effort to help the mothers to finish high school. The program, staffed by social workers and teachers, taught photography skills, provided enrichment, and offered a positive school experience. The mothers photographed their children in various settings and created collages.

The overriding principle of ***parens patriae*** [which is Latin for "father of the people"]—under which children can become wards of the state—guided interpretations of children's rights. This principle supported creation of a broad range of juvenile services including parent-child relationships (Crosson-Tower, 1998, p. 270). Taking this basic position, child advocates were able to argue that children should be viewed in a different light from adults and offered rehabilitation rather than punishment.

In 1899, the first juvenile court was established in Chicago based on the principle of *parens patriae* and the belief that children could be rehabilitated, which required a legal system far different from the punishment-based adult system. By 1925, all but two states—Maine and Wyoming—had juvenile courts; by 1945 all states had such courts. Prosecution took a back seat to treatment as the primary focus of the juvenile justice system. Hearings were closed to the public to protect the child's right to confidentiality, and all juvenile legal records were sealed once the child reached the legal age of maturity, generally age 18. The juvenile court operated very informally. Attorneys were rarely provided for child offenders, and trial by jury and the right to appeal a decision were not available options. In these courtrooms hearsay evidence was admitted. Remember, the court's purpose was twofold: 1) to identify the problem and 2) to develop and implement an appropriate treatment plan.

The juvenile court changed dramatically as a result of U.S. Supreme Court decisions in the 1960s. Juveniles were given many of the legal protections enjoyed by adults. Courts were required to allow attorneys to be present; witnesses could be cross-examined; defendants had the right to refuse to incriminate themselves; and guilty decisions (or, in some states, "not innocent" decisions) had to meet the legal standard of reasonable doubt.

In recent years, as violent juvenile crime has worsened, people have begun to ask whether children should also face some of the same penalties as adults. Horrific crimes committed by children in 1998 alone left many people in shock. Two young boys, age 8 and 9, in Chicago, Illinois, murdered a young girl in order to ride her bicycle; two teenagers in Arkansas shot and killed schoolmates; another teenager walked into a school hallway and indiscriminately murdered his junior high school peers. The Chicago youth were released to their parents because state law forbade the incarceration of a child under age 10; these cases sparked a national debate over whether the teens should be tried in adult courts and, if found guilty, should serve their sentences in adult prisons or even be subjected to the death penalty. Is there an answer? At what age do we stop trying to rehabilitate young people? As you have probably guessed there are no clear-cut answers to these questions.

In a nutshell, historically children have had few rights, and there has been little agreement on what further rights, if any, they should be granted. In the past, the courts have primarily defined children's rights with regard to criminal proceedings against them. In addition, children have the right to financial support and education (Gustavsson & Segal, 1994, pp. 4, 6). Today, the United Nations continues to bring the rights of children to the forefront. The UN Convention on the Rights of the Child adopted in 1989 a declaration of children's rights. By 2003, 192 countries had formally ratified this Act, and the two remaining countries, the United States and Somalia, had announced agreement to do so (Convention on the Rights of the Child, 2003).This important declaration is very specific in identifying the issues facing children:

> Preamble . . . Childhood is entitled to special care and assistance. . . . The child . . . should grow up in a family environment, in an atmosphere of happiness, love, and understanding. . . . The child, by reason of his physical and mental immaturity, needs special safeguards and care, including appropriate legal protection.
>
> Article 3 (1). In all actions concerning children . . . the best interests of the child shall be a primary consideration.
>
> Article 18 (1). . . . Both parents have common responsibilities for the upbringing and development of the child. Parents or, as the case may be, legal guardians, have the primary responsibility for the upbringing and development of the child.
>
> Article 19 (1). State parties (government) shall take appropriate legislative, administrative, social and educational measures to protect the child from all forms of physical or mental violence, injury or abuse, neglect or negligent treatment, maltreatment or exploitation, including sexual abuse, while in the care of parent(s), legal guardian(s) or any other person who has the care of the child (United Nations, 1989).

THE DESIGN OF THE AMERICAN CHILD WELFARE SYSTEM

Formal child welfare programs and services are found in both public and private settings. Government programs—local, state, and federal—are augmented by both for-profit and nonprofit agencies. Together, these programs form a complex system that starts with prenatal care and ranges to opportunities for teenagers. As we start this section, look carefully at table 1 as it provides a snapshot of children most at risk of needing services from our welfare system. Programs are varied, but they can generally be categorized as child protective services, family preservation, out-of-home services, and other services.

Child Protective Services

Child protective services (CPS) is probably the best known as well as the most controversial children's program. The intent of CPS is to protect children from abusive situations in order that they can grow and develop. We've all heard stories about abusive CPS workers responding to unfounded charges, taking children from their parents, breaking up families, and ruining the lives of countless people. In fact, the CPS worker investigates each allegation of abuse or neglect and determines whether the charges are founded or unfounded. A case is opened if the investigation demonstrates that abuse or neglect is indeed occurring. A child is only

Table 1: America's Most Vulnerable Children: A Snapshot

Estimated referrals of possible child abuse and neglect (2006)	3,300,000
Children substantiated/indicated as abused or neglected (2006)	905,000
Children who died as a result of abuse or neglect (2006)	1,530
Children living in out-of-home care (2006)	510,885
Children adopted from the public foster care system (2006)	50,705
Children waiting to be adopted (2006)	139,064
Children living in poverty (2007)	13,247,238
Children living in low-income families (2007)	28,803,055
National Poverty Rate (2007)	12.5%
National Poverty Rate for children under age 18 (2007)	18.0%
National Poverty Rate for children ages 5-17 (2007)	16.8%
National Poverty Rate for children birth to age 5 (2007)	21.2%

Taken from Child Welfare League of America. (2009). National Fact Sheet 2009. Retrieved July 2, 2009, from http://www.cwla.org/advocacy/nationalfactsheet09.htm

removed from the home if his life is in immediate danger. An open case may receive direct services from the agency or from other contract agencies, such as a family service agency. The case is reviewed by CPS staff and is closed once all goals are achieved. All states provide some form of CPS. In 1962, a study of battered children in hospitals recommended that suspected cases be reported so that protective measures could be taken. By 1966 all states had passed legislation concerning abuse (Lindsey, 1994, p. 92).

Box 2: The Beginning of CPS: The Case of Mary Ellen

In 1873, Mrs. Etta Angell Wheeler, a church visitor in New York City, learned from people in a neighborhood about a 9-year-old girl, Mary Ellen Wilson, who had been whipped and left alone for hours on end. Neighbors in her apartment building heard the child's cries time and again. The New York City Department of Charities had placed Mary Ellen in this home when she was 18 months old. There had been no follow-up by the agency to assess the placement. Mrs. Wheeler sought help from a number of charitable organizations and the police to protect Mary Ellen, but no agency was willing to intervene and no CPS organization existed. She turned for help to Mr. Henry Bergh, president of the New York Society for the Prevention of Cruelty to Animals. The society intervened with court action and Mary Ellen was removed from the home.

The court found the home to be abusive. The foster mother, Mrs. Mary Connolly, was arrested and found guilty of assault. The court decided that Mary Ellen was to move to a group home, but Mrs. Wheeler asked that the child be placed in her care. Mary Ellen moved in with Mrs. Wheeler's mother and stayed with her until the mother's death. Within a few months of the reported abuse, the New York Society for the Prevention of Cruelty to Children was founded, the first such organization in the world (Watkins, 1990).

As of 2007, approximately 3.2 million referrals of child abuse and neglect were received, involving approximately 5.8 million children (U.S. Department of Health and Human Services, Administration on Children, Youth and Families, 2009). In the screening process, of the 61 percent of the received reports of child abuse and neglect, 38.3 percent were able to be screened-out because they did not meet the state's standards for investigation. More than half of these reports were submitted by professionals who are termed "mandatory reporters" such as teachers, police officers, legal staff, and social service staff workers. Nonprofessional reporting, which made up approximately 27 percent of the reports, came from sources including parents, family and other relatives, friends, neighbors, and other interested individuals. Nearly three-quarters of the children (75.4%) in these reports had no previous history of victimization.

Nearly 32 percent of the victims of maltreatment were under the age of 4; 23.8 percent were in the age group 4–7 years; and 19 percent were in the 8–11 age range. Of all the ages combined, 48 percent were boys and 51 percent were girls (U.S. Department of Health and Human Services, Administration on Children, Youth and Families, 2009).

According to the Children's Defense Fund the number of abuse and neglect cases continues to rise. It reports that between 1985 and 1995, the number of reports rose by 61 percent and the number of confirmed reports by 31 percent. The Children's Defense Fund also believes that these numbers undercount the true incidence of abuse and neglect, a claim it supports by citing a note that the number of abused and neglected children was actually triple the number reported by the U.S. Department of Health and Human Services (Children's Defense Fund, 1998, pp. 51, 53).

According to the Child Maltreatment 2001 (Children's Bureau, 2003), approximately 903,000 children were found to be victims of child maltreatment. Maltreatment categories typically include neglect, medical neglect, physical abuse, sexual abuse, and psychological maltreatment.

During the Federal fiscal year of 2006 there were an estimated 1,530 child fatality victims and over 78 percent of these were under 4 years old (U.S. Department of Health and Human Services, Administration on Children, Youth and Families, 2008).

Family Preservation Services

Family preservation services seek to stabilize troubled families in a short period of time (Linderman, 1995, p. 424). They require intensive, direct social services with the entire family. The goal of family preservation is to prevent child removal from the parental home when direct services may avoid the need for such out-of-home placement, to keep families together, and to strengthen family bonds (Tracy, 1995, p. 973). Gaining popularity in the 1970s and 1980s, these services received a boost in 1980 with the passage of the Adoption Assistance and Child Welfare Act (P.L. 96–272). The 1980 act called for reasonable efforts to be made to keep children within their families and to minimize family disorder.

The Convention on the Rights of the Child (2003) identifies important issues for children. Work in this area is intensive, requiring anywhere from six to ten hours of direct worker-family contact each week. The typical case requires four to twelve weeks of contact, and a worker's caseload should range between two and six families. In addition, the worker is on call twenty-four hours a day, providing a mix of services (Edna McConnell Clark Foundation, n.d.).

Research on family preservation has shown some positive outcomes. The first study examined Homebuilders, a program in Washington. The research findings revealed that out-of-home placement was avoided in 97 percent of cases (Lindsey, 1994, pp. 41–43). The Edna McConnell Clark Foundation reported that family preservation workers are extremely positive about this form of intervention. Clients too are strong supporters of family preservation programs: 99 percent are satisfied with services, 87 percent rated services as helpful, and 97 percent would recommend family preservation to other families in similar situations (Edna McConnell Clark Foundation, n.d.). Tracy (1995, p. 978) wrote, however, that not all reports reveal such high success rates, and in fact much more research is needed to establish the validity of family preservation.

Out-of-Home Services

Out-of-home services are programs for children no longer living with their biological or legal guardians, whose parental rights have been or may be terminated. Typical out-of-home programs are foster care, residential care, and adoption.

Foster Care. The *Social Work Dictionary* defines foster care as physical care for children "who are unable to live with their natural parents or legal guardians" (Barker, 2003). The goals of foster care include 1) maximum protection for the child, 2) permanency, and 3) family preservation. Foster care is generally organized through state or county social services and services may be provided within foster family homes, residential group homes, or institutions (Everett, 2008).

> *Did You Know…*Neglect *is maltreatment through the failure to provide needed, age appropriate care. Physical abuse is physical injury resulting from punching, beating, kicking, biting, burning, or otherwise harming a child (National Resource Center on Child Abuse and Neglect).*

In 1997 the Adoption and Safe Families Act (ASFA) was passed with the intention of addressing some of the preexisting problems in the foster care system related to the adoption of special needs children, and later its interpretation emphasized the importance of keeping families together (Public Law 105-89, Federal Register, January 7, 1997). Thereafter states were expected to implement ASFA with the emphasis on safety, permanency, and well-being of children who are found to be abused and neglected. In doing this, ASFA outlined the need for evaluation of the safety of children in foster care and the need for the measurement of child well-being. From this perspective, well-being is a multidimensional construct involving

Box 3: Myths and Facts about Out-of-Home Placements

Myth: Foster care is in the best interests of children who have known the hurt of abuse and neglect.
Fact: In some cases, when the child is at great risk, removal from the home is necessary, but it is not necessarily the solution. The devastating norm for foster children is multiple moves, extended stays, and no stable permanent family ties.

Myth: Foster care is principally a problem of poor and minority families.
Fact: Problems leading to abuse and neglect know no race or class boundaries. Of all children entering foster care and substitute care, almost 55 percent are white, 22 percent are black, and 10 percent are Latino.

Myth: Children placed in foster care are typically younger than 5 years of age.
Fact: Roughly half the children in out-of-home care are over age 10. However, the greatest growth in such placements is for infants under 1 year of age.

Myth: Most children in foster care are placed there because of physical or sexual abuse.
Fact: More than half of child removals are for neglect.

Myth: Child abuse is on the rise.
Fact: While the number of reports has increased, the evidence does not clearly substantiate that the actual incidence is on the rise. The growing number of reports may be a result of the public's growing awareness of child abuse and of resources to contact.

Myth: Parents whose children are removed from the home do not want their children, do not deserve their children, and cannot or will not change their behavior.
Fact: Experts working with troubled families find that their problems are more extreme versions of similar issues confronting any family. Troubled families often lack resources, knowledge, and skills that most take for granted. Most parents want their children and really want to be good parents. Proper help can help many families, but it must be timely.

Myth: Child protective service workers are well-trained professionals but have little authority to protect children.
Fact: The child protective service worker position is an entry-level job requiring minimal education. Most states do not require education in social work and allow a person to work in this position with a degree in music, math, and other non–human service disciplines. Caseloads are usually high, pay and morale low, and employee turnover high. Child protective service workers have a wide range of authority, including the power to remove a child from a home, in some instances without supervisor or court approval. (Edna McConnell Clark Foundation, n.d.)

the child's overall functioning levels in terms of health, mental health, and education (Jacobs, Bruhn & Graf, 2008). Therefore, if protection is needed to ensure the child's safety, a child may need to be placed in a foster home temporarily. Immediate placement decisions may be needed if at the start of a CPS investigation the worker assesses that the child's life is in immediate danger. This decision is never made lightly as every effort is made to keep families together whenever possible. If the child is to be removed, however, the family is entitled to a court hearing, in most states within twenty-four to seventy-two hours of the time of removal if the child was removed without a court order. In other cases, placement may occur after a court hearing, if a CPS investigation finds that this action is in the best interests of the child. Any placement must be in the least restrictive setting. For example, a foster home is less restrictive than a residential treatment center; placement with a relative is less restrictive than removal to a nonbiological foster home.

Children in foster care are provided with certain protections including the following:

- ◆ A detailed written plan that describes the appropriateness of the placement, the services to be provided to the child, and a plan for achieving permanence
- ◆ Periodic case review at least once every six months, though a jurisdiction may review a case more often
- ◆ A state inventory of children who have been in care for more than six months in order to track these children and the goals related to their placement
- ◆ Procedural safeguards that involve parental input in the development of case plans
- ◆ Reunification or permanency planning services, which programs include day care, homemaker services, counseling, parent education, adoption services, and follow-up (Everett, 2008).

For example, in 1994, an estimated 41,161 children were in substitute care in the state of Illinois (Department of Children and Family Services, 2003). For the most part, all states are similar in that most children in foster care are placed in foster family homes (Everett, 2008). As of July 2003, the Department of Children and Families in the State of Illinois estimated 20,508 children in substitute care. This decreasing number has been credited to early intervention efforts and permanency services such as adoption. According to the National Child Abuse and Neglect Data System approximately 794,000 children were found to be victims of child abuse and neglect in 2007, and this resulted in about 3.8 million children needing preventive services. Furthermore, an estimated 271,000 children received foster care services and, as a result of assessment and intervention, preventive services were provided (U.S. Department of Health and Human Services, Administration on Children, Youth and Families, 2009).

How are foster parents selected? What is their motivation—money? What about reports that children in foster homes are often subjected to more abuse?

(Mushlin, 1991, pp. 102–104). Kantrowitz and King (1991, p. 98) defended foster parents by stating that most have a calling, a sense of altruism, for the work. People choose to be foster parents because of their love for children. Their decisions to take children into their homes have to be for something more than the money because reimbursement rates are so low (Kantrowitz & King, 1991, p. 98). At the time daily reimbursement rates ranged from $5.00 to $12.00 (remember, this article was written in 1991, so reimbursement figures are higher today).

We need to keep in mind that children in foster care are coming from terrible home situations. Because permanency planning interventions are preferred, only those children in the most unbearable situations are removed. Most foster children are burdened by a unique set of complex problems that requires understanding and compassion. Being a foster parent is not easy, and it does require a special person.

Residential care. Residential group care, also called institutional care, takes place in physical settings apart from the natural parents or legal guardians. Residential settings include residential treatment centers, state hospitals, detention centers, runaway shelters, and halfway houses. All have a common theme: caring for groups of special needs children, twenty-four hours a day (Whittaker, 1995, p. 451).

Did You Know...The first residential program for children was established in 1729 in New Orleans. The program was developed by Ursuline nuns to care for children orphaned as a result of the battle with Native Americans at Natchez.

A number of trends in residential care have been consistent over time:

- ◆ The number of residential facilities is increasing though the actual number of youth in care has declined.
- ◆ The two main types of new facilities are juvenile delinquent centers and mental health centers.
- ◆ The average number of children in facilities has declined to fewer than thirty per facility.

Did You Know...The terms runaway, throwaway, *and* push-out *describe youths (under age 18), who no longer live at home with their legal guardians. A* runaway *is a person running away from home. A* throwaway *is a person forced or thrown out of home by the caretaker. A* push-out *is a person who with the agreement of the caretaker decides it is in everyone's best interest that he or she leave home.*

Residential programs are also available for children who no longer live with their legal caretakers. Typically such programs are shelters that provide temporary housing and counseling. The purpose of the runaway shelter is to get youths off the streets, provide protection, and attempt to reunite children with their families. Social service providers recognize the importance of getting runaways off the streets and into services as quickly as possible. Colby (1990, p. 282) reported that after living on the streets for two weeks, 75 percent of runaways turn to theft, drugs, prostitution, or pornography for support.

Activity...Contact your local runaway shelter and ask about the rules of admission and length of stay. Ask what happens to youths who leave the shelter but do not return home.

A state-established limit on the length of time that young people may reside in shelters generally restricts these settings to homeless youths. Some programs require parental consent for children to remain in shelters. What happens to the youth whose parents do not grant permission for her to remain in the program? And some programs do not allow disruptive youths or youths with mental health problems to enter shelters. What types of community programs, if any, are available for these youths?

Adoption. The *Social Work Dictionary* defines adoption as *"accepting and treating a child legally as though born into the family."* (Barker, 2003). Adoption creates a *"legal family for children when the birth family is unable or unwilling to parent"* (Barth, 1995, p. 48).

Massachusetts is credited with being the first state to enact an adoption law, in 1851 (Cole, 1985, p. 639), though some cite Mississippi, in 1846, and Texas, in 1850, as having earlier adoption statutes (Crosson-Tower, 1998, p. 356). Whichever state was first, there is consensus that the Massachusetts legislation served as the model for other states (Kadushin & Martin, 1988, p. 535; Crosson-Tower, 1998, p. 639). By 1929 all states had enacted some form of adoption law.

During the nineteenth and much of the twentieth centuries most children in need of homes lived in orphanages. Young people were placed in orphanages for any number of reasons, including having poor parents who couldn't afford to raise them, having been born to unwed mothers, or having no parents because of death or abandonment (Crosson-Tower, 1998, p. 357).

Charles Loring Brace, a minister and organizer of the Children's Aid Society in New York City, led one of the more compelling child welfare efforts of the nineteenth century. Brace developed what became known as the Orphan's Train, through which some 50,000 to 100,000 urban orphans were placed on midwestern and western farms (Quam, 1995, p. 2575). The children, picked up on the streets of New York City, were put on a wagon train heading west. In town after town, city after city, the train would stop and put the youths up for adoption. Brace believed that moving waifs off city streets, away from the temptations of urban life, to more rural, tranquil lives of work and family, would allow them to be prosperous and productive (Brace, 1872).

The Orphan's Train was a manifestation of the nation's prevailing belief, no less strong today, that children should live in wholesome environments where caretakers can provide for their needs. Remember the basic child welfare principle: in the best interests of the child? Brace's program and other child-saving programs, including orphanages, were built on this ideal.

Today, adoption takes place in many different ways. These include placing children through child placement agencies and through direct agreements between two parties sanctioned by the courts.

"Agency-based adoption" occurs in government, nonprofit, and for-profit family welfare settings. It entails a rigorous and time-consuming process, which generally includes the following steps:

Identification of suitable children ensures that all children in need of adoptive homes are identified.

Freeing for placement is the legal process by which custody of the child is removed from one set of parents in order that it can be assigned to the adoptive parents.

Preparation for adoption involves working with the child before adoption to prepare him for his new family. Potential adoptive parents are closely scrutinized by the agency to ensure they have the resources needed to raise a child in a loving, caring environment.

Selection of adoptive parents is conducted by the agency after close review of applications and supporting materials. The agency's goal is to match a child with the adoptive parent who can best meet her unique needs.

Placement with adoptive family is characterized by many social workers as one of the most exciting days for worker, family, and child. It is a time of joy as the new family begins its life together. Everyone involved often sheds tears!

Post placement services include a variety of agency-based supports to the family as it makes the transition to a new system of relations. By placing a child with a specific family, the agency is affirming that the placement is in the best interests of the child. To increase the likelihood of success, the agency offers the family continuing supports ranging from individual and family counseling and support groups to social worker home visits. Although the exact types of intervention may differ, within the home visit the target of intervention is generally characterized as child and family focused (Cook & Sparks, 2008). These home visits can support the parent by providing education, training, and information, helping the adjustment process. Again, the agency wants as few disruptions as possible with the adoption. Nevertheless, sometimes the child is removed from the adoptive parent's home. When this happens, the social worker does not blame anyone or refer to the original placement as a failure but instead looks again at what supports are needed for the child and what type of child is best suited for that particular family.

Legal finalization of the adoption takes place after a period of time following initial placement. There is a popular myth that adoption is final when the child is placed with the family. Not so for agency-based adoptions. The final legal assignment of custody is made after an extended period of time. The period varies among agencies; the norm seems to be six months to one year following placement. The court is the final authority in legally assigning custody of the child to the adoptive parent. The court's decision is reached after review of the agency's reports and recommendations.

Post adoption services provide children with any needed supports such as counseling, and parents with educational or ongoing counseling sessions. Agencies recognize that it may be in the best interests of the child for support services to be provided for extended periods beyond the legal adoption phase (Cole, 1985).

Have you seen advertisements in your college or local newspaper that read something like this?

> Loving couple with a great deal to give looking to adopt a newborn. Will pay all fees, including prenatal, delivery, hospitalization, legal, and follow-up costs. Please call. . . .

Some families resort to private sources, also called "independent adoption," rather than use agency-based adoption services. Agreements are reached between the two families involved, and the courts, assisted by attorneys, finalize the legal arrangements. These adoptions can take place much faster and with less red tape than the agency-based process. The prospective adoptive parents usually provide financial support for the pregnant mother and her family, cover all related health costs, and often add a financial stipend—that is, a salary.

Independent adoption is costly, running to tens of thousands of dollars. For-profit adoptions are against the law. Recognize that with independent adoptions there is less scrutiny and follow-up than with agency-based services. Cole suggested that problems with independent adoptions could be reduced if the following steps are taken:

◆ Courts require a detailed statement of all monies that change hands relating to the adoption.
◆ Violators are vigorously prosecuted and subjected to severe sanctions.
◆ Communities provide enough financial support to adoption agencies that they can offer the same level of health and maintenance care that takes place with independent adoption (1985).

There are three potential pools for adoption: healthy infants, children with special needs, and children from foreign countries (Kadushin & Martin, 1988). Fewer healthy infants are available for adoption because of the increased availability of birth control and abortion (Crosson-Tower, 1998). Unfortunately, it is not uncommon for a couple to be told the waiting period for a healthy infant may be up to ten years!

A special needs child has unique characteristics that can include "race and ethnicity, medical problems, older age (over age 3), attachment to a sibling group, developmental disabilities, and emotional difficulties" (Crosson-Tower, 1998, p. 374). Such children are much harder to place because of their special needs and are more available than healthy infants for adoption.

In recent years, more and more people are looking to the international community for children to adopt. Children born in areas of civil strife or extreme poverty are the main subjects of such adoptions. Latin America, Vietnam, Korea,

Name: Xan Boone

Place of Residence: Cincinnati, Ohio

College/University Degrees: University of Cincinnati, Bachelor of Science, political science, 1998; University of Cincinnati, Masters in Social Work, 1995

Present Position and Title: Field Service Instructor at the School of Social Work, University of Cincinnati and Trainer for the Ohio Child Welfare Training Program, conducting caseworker and foster parent training required by the state.

Previous Work/Volunteer Experience: Child Welfare Professional from 1989 to 2007. Two years as a dependency investigator for Lucas County Juvenile Court, two years as an ongoing caseworker for Hamilton County Children's Services, one year as a family preservation caseworker, four years as a family conference facilitator, nine years as a new caseworker trainer for Hamilton County Children's Services.

Volunteer experience includes a mission trip to rebuild homes for hurricane Katrina victims; travel to Ukraine to assist their government in development of an updated child welfare system; and Sunday school teacher, fellowship committee, vice president, president and pastoral liaison committee at Lutheran Church of the Resurrection.

Why did you choose social work as a career? Like many career child welfare professionals before me, I did not choose child welfare as my career initially. I planned to be a juvenile probation office. I did not get the job that I had hoped to get, but the Lucas County Court offered me another position. This would be to work in conjunction with the local child welfare agency to place children in safe family homes. I conducted the investigation of those families for the court and testified regarding their appropriateness to raise a child. I never looked back. Twenty-one years later I am still in child welfare. I feel that social work is a calling and that social work really comes from the heart as much as it does from the head. I was inspired to get my master's degree and am very proud to call myself a career social worker.

What is your favorite social work story? I remember running into a family on the streets of downtown Cincinnati on a sunny Saturday. There was something familiar about them. As they approached, I realized that this was a family with whom I had worked when I was doing family preservation several years back. They stopped and looked at me. I know that the mother recognized me immediately. She ran over to give me a hug. The daughter just kept staring at me. Finally she recognized me. She said, "I remember you, you helped me make my mom a birthday cake when we didn't have any money." It had been several years, but, yes, I helped her brother and her make her mom a birthday cake. This family was being torn apart by anger, poverty and mental health issues. When I saw them again, the mother was working, the kids were in school and they appeared to be doing well. There are few times we see the results of what we do to help us in the field of social work. This was a rare, but wonderful glimpse of both the formal and the informal work we do to help others. When successes happen, we might not even know it! I still smile when I think of baking that cake.

What is one thing you would change in the community if you had the power to do so?
I wish people in the world could spend a day walking in the shoes of another. It might be a first step to truly eradicating racism as well as addressing issues related to poverty and other environmental factors.

---

the Philippines, India, and other Asian countries have been the principal nations and regions sending children to the United States (Crosson-Tower, 1998).

CHILDREN WITH SPECIAL NEEDS

As of September 30, 2005, there were approximately 513,000 children in the foster care system (U.S. Children's Bureau, 2007). In 1998, 36,000 of the approximately 120,000 children adopted in the United States were adopted from the public foster care system. In 1999, the number of children adopted from foster care was 47,000; in 2000 and 2001 it was up to 51,000; in 2002 it was at 52,000, and in 2003 it went down to 50,000; in 2004 it went up from the year before to 51,993; and it was at 51,323 in 2005 (Child Welfare League, 2006).

Many of these children in foster care have suffered abuse, abandonment, and/or neglect. Due to a history of trauma, these children are considered "special needs" and require special parenting once placed into permanent homes. The term *special needs* is often associated with children within the United States' welfare system. Each state's specific criteria may vary slightly, but in general, these children are identified as special needs because they meet one or more of the following criteria: 8 years of age or older, emotionally handicapped, physically handicapped, a member of a sibling group, minority heritage, mentally handicapped, history of physical abuse, sexual abuse, or neglect (Florida Administrative Code, 2002; Groze, 1996). Due to their trauma histories, special needs children can be difficult to parent.

Adoption is the permanent legal transfer of full parental rights from one parent or set of parents to another parent or set of parents (Henry & Pollack, 2009, p.1). The social stigma of adoption has a long history in our society with disparaging community attitudes toward adoptive kinship, and for the most part Americans still consider adoption second best to having children by birth (Wegar, 2000). This prevailing mindset continues to leave adoptive parents to experience social stigmatization in their everyday lives (Miall, 2000). Adoptive parents of children that have special needs, in particular, do not start with a clean slate; they adopt not only the child of the present, but they also adopt the experiences of the child's past. The experiences imbedded in these children often make adoptive parenting a serious challenge that can compromise the child's ability to become part of the immediate family as well as the extended family system (Smith & Howard, 1999). Given the extensive needs of these children, adjustment for the adoptive parents can also be difficult. These new parents may go through their own grieving process, experiencing feelings of shock, denial, anger, depression, and physical symptoms of distress and guilt as the dreams of the child wished for or expected are soon replaced by the realities of the actual child.

After a brief honeymoon period, the adoptive parents of a special needs child may experience a shocking realization that the new child is unhealthy, either physically or emotionally. Despite the information provided prior to the adoptive placement, many adoptive parents cannot comprehend the full realm of the behaviors and difficulties of the child prior to placement. Consequently, the parents, especially the mother, may experience being in shock and having feelings of bewilderment and may start making excuses for the child's behavior. After living with a child who is unresponsive to the parents, anger and rage can often surface. The adoptive mother may discover feelings of guilt for not truly loving her adoptive child and for feeling ambivalent or angry toward her child (Forbes & Dziegielewski, 2003).

Many times the biases of society are as strong, if not stronger, within the nucleus of the immediate family and extended family. Adoption of a special needs child involves integrating their adopted children into the entire family social system. Therefore, Henry and Pallack (2009) outline the importance of preplacement training where the family and extended family are educated about adoption issues and feelings that may surface and including them as part of the preadoptive process for families. Rosenthal and Groze (1990) found that the approval of extended family members was directly correlated to the success of an adoptive placement. Conversely, Rosenthal wrote in a later paper that a key predictor of increased risk for adoption disruption is "low levels of support from relatives or friends" (Rosenthal, 1993, p. 81). Therefore, it is important to realize that a lack of support from the extended family can work to undermine the legitimacy of the adoptive placement for the adoptive mothers. This makes participation in post-placement services a necessary part of practice for professionals to encourage (Henry and Pollack, 2009).

In summary, a final but controversial point about adoption is that our discussion has been framed by the notion of placement in the best interests of the child. Yet one practice in adoption may run counter to this central tenet of child welfare: there is strong pressure to place children with adoptive families of the same race or ethnicity. Among the many types of adoption, transracial adoptions, also referred to as interracial, biracial, multicultural, or multiracial adoptions, have gained increased attention (Henry & Pollack, 2009). The justification is that the cultural needs of a child far outweigh other placement considerations. For example, the National Association of Black Social Workers does not support the placement of African-American children in nonblack homes. Or consider the 1978 Indian Child Welfare Act, which places responsibility for adoption of Native American children within tribes rather than with traditional public child welfare agencies. The 1978 law requires Native American children to be placed with extended family members as a first option and then with other tribal families, regardless of the wishes of the parents.

Should adoption be constrained by race and ethnicity and other cultural factors? Does the compelling need for permanency over-ride the cultural needs of a child? Can a child develop cultural competence and identity in a home of different racial or ethnic origin? What about religion? In Judaism, for example, the religion's law is that a child born to a Jewish mother is always Jewish. Should a Jewish child always be placed in a Jewish home? Should Catholic children always be placed with Catholic families? Is it best to keep a child in a temporary foster home if no culturally similar family can be found? There are no easy answers to these questions and they may require individual evaluation that clearly takes into account the best interests of the child.

Other Services

A number of other child welfare services meet additional needs of children. It is impossible to discuss all of them, but we touch briefly on two important program areas.

Youth programs. Most of us at one time or another have participated in youth programs sponsored by such groups as the YMCA, YWCA, Boys Clubs, Girls Clubs, Blue Birds, Girls Scouts, Boys Scouts, Brownies, Little League baseball, and so on. Many agencies in our communities work with young people through an array of programs ranging from gym-and-swim to therapeutic prevention.

The YMCA, for example, offers parent-child programs called Y-Indian Guide and Y-Indian Princess. The parent and child meet with other parents and children one evening each week. Ostensibly providing recreational opportunities, these programs also ensure that the parent and child have at least one evening each week of quality interaction. In addition, the parent and child carry out tasks and activities in the home between group meetings. These activities strengthen relations when time is limited.

Youth programs have four important functions in our communities:

◆ Youths have positive peer experiences in a formal supervised atmosphere.
◆ Youths learn to interact with others in groups.
◆ Youths are able to develop their own extended networks outside of the family.
◆ Through the programs youths find a safe haven, particularly with after-school, weekend, or evening activities, which take place when caretakers may be at work and unable to supervise their children.

CHILD SEXUAL ABUSE AND TRAUMA

According to the U.S. Department of Health and Human Services, *sexual abuse* is a type of maltreatment involving a child in sexual activity that provides sexual gratification or financial benefit to the perpetrator. This includes involving children in contracts for sexual purposes, prostitution, pornography, exposure, or other sexually exploitative activities (Gil, 1996). Sexual abuse of children is a difficult area for most people to talk about because of the emotional reactions it causes.

For years, acknowledgment of sexual abuse was avoided and considered an issue not to be discussed (Karp & Butler, 1996). As society's awareness of children's issues grew, so did awareness about child sexual abuse. It is estimated that by the time children reach age 18, one out of every four females and one out of every six males has been confronted with sexual abuse (Darkness to Light, 2009; Deblinger & Heflin, 1996). This means that by the time many children reach adulthood their lives have been affected by some type of sexual abuse.

By being aware of the different signs of child sexual abuse the social worker can best select from the many techniques for assessing the presence of sexual abuse in children (Karp & Butler, 1996). Most social workers use techniques such as play therapy, and look for and document the physical indicators of sexual abuse (Dammeyer, 1998). Physical indicators include difficulty walking or sitting, torn or bloody underclothing, bruises or bleeding in the external genital or anal areas, and venereal disease and pregnancy (Miller, Veltkamp, & Raines, 1998). Behavioral symptoms can also help assess sexual abuse in children. They include: sleep disturbances; withdrawal, regressed behavior; age inappropriate, sophisticated, or unusual sexual knowledge or behavior; extreme self-blame or fear; and poor interpersonal skills (Miller et al., 1998). With the apparent increase in cases of child sexual abuse, social workers need to be skilled at assessing children who are victims or suspected victims of child sexual abuse (Cohen-Liebman, 1999).

Mandatory Reporting

Who Is Expected to Report?

Social workers, similar to other professionals, are considered mandatory reporters. There are numerous professionals that are responsible for mandatory reporting, including all licensed or registered professionals of the healing arts and any health-related occupation who examine, attend, treat, or provide other professional or specialized services including, but not limited to, physicians, including physicians in training, psychologists, social workers, dentists, nurses, osteopathic physicians and surgeons, optometrists, chiropractors, podiatrists, pharmacists, and other health-related professionals. This also generally includes

- Employees and officers in both public and private schools;
- Employees or officers of any public or private agency or institution, or other individuals providing social, medical, hospital, or mental health services, including financial assistance;
- Law enforcement agency officials including courts, police departments, correctional institutions, and parole or probation offices
- Individual providers of child care, or employees or officers of any licensed or registered child care facility, foster home, or similar institution
- Medical examiners or coroners.
- In some states, employees of any public or private agency providing recreational or sports activities are also included.

As you can see there is a diverse group of professionals expected to care for and ensure the safety of our children (Department of Human Services, 2007; U.S. Department of Health and Human Services, Administration on Children, Youth and Families, 2009).

What are we expected to report?

As a professional social worker, we are mandatory reporters, and as a mandatory reporter we are expected to report any situations in which it is believed that child abuse or neglect will occur in the reasonably foreseeable future. All social workers regardless of where they work need to be aware of what is considered reportable and how to make a report. When a report is indicated, it must be made to the child welfare services office or the police department. If a social worker, similar to other professionals, fails to make a report of an incident involving child abuse or neglect, or who knowingly fails to provide additional information, or who prevents another person from reporting such an incident, can be found guilty of criminal charges.

What types of incidents need to be reported?

◆ Substantial or multiple skin bruising or any other internal bleeding;
◆ Any injury to skin causing substantial bleeding;
◆ Malnutrition;
◆ Failure to thrive;
◆ Burn or burns;
◆ Poisoning;
◆ Fracture of any bone;
◆ Subdural hematoma;
◆ Soft tissue swelling;
◆ Extreme pain;
◆ Extreme mental distress;
◆ Gross degradation;
◆ Death; and such injury is not justifiably explained, or when the history given concerning such condition or death is at variance with the degree or type of such condition or death, or circumstances indicate that such condition or death may not be the product of an accidental occurrence; or
◆ When the child has been the victim of sexual contact or conduct, including, but not limited to, rape, sodomy, molestation, sexual fondling, incest, or prostitution; obscene or pornographic photographing, or filming, or depiction; or other similar forms of sexual exploitation, or
◆ When there exists injury to the psychological capacity of a child as is evidenced by an observable and substantial impairment in the child's ability to function; or
◆ When the child is not provided in a timely manner with adequate food, clothing, shelter, psychological care, physical care, medical care, or supervision; or
◆ When the child is provided with dangerous, harmful, or detrimental drugs . . . this does not apply to drugs that are provided to the child pursuant to the direction or prescription of a practitioner.

Source: A Guide for Mandatory Reporters (November 2007). Department of Human Services, Honolulu, HI

What do I need to prepare to make a report?

Before you call the child welfare services office in your state to make a report of abuse or neglect, you will need to gather certain information. If you are concerned that the report is not needed or if you are not sure if you should make the report, call anyway and confer with the intake worker. It is not your responsibility to prove that abuse or neglect has occurred, only that you suspect it. If you make a report and it is found that the report was made in good faith, you will be immune from liability. In the best-case scenario, the family will not find out your name as having made the report but this can never be completely assured. If you do not want your name released, be sure to tell the intake worker that this is your preference. Also, many experienced social workers debate whether they should tell the child or the child's parents that they are making a report. For the most part, it is best to tell them, but never tell them if you feel it could put you in danger. Your safety is an important priority that should not be underestimated. Be sure whether you tell the child's parents or not about the report you are going to make concerning the abuse of their child—you still need to make the report. As you prepare to make the report, be sure you gather information about the details related to the situation and refer the case as soon as possible. Time is always of the essence, and the sooner you report the case, the less likely the child will have to be subjected to any further abuse or neglect or subjected to numerous interviews where the information will have to be repeated numerous times if the case is accepted.

Every state in the United States may vary slightly in procedure but for the most part the social worker will want to obtain as much of the following information as possible before referring the matter for investigation:

- Name and address of the child victim and his/her parents or other persons responsible for his/her care
- Child's birth date or age
- Names and ages of other persons who live with the child and their relationship to the child if known
- Nature and extent of the child's abuse or neglect (including any evidence or indication of previous abuse or neglect)
- Date, time, and location of incident
- Child's current location and condition
- Identity of the alleged perpetrator
- Whereabouts of the alleged perpetrator and any history if available
- Any other information that may be helpful in determining the cause of abuse or neglect and whether or not there is a family member who can protect the child

Source: A Guide for Mandatory Reporters (November 2007). Department of Human Services, Honolulu, HI

Once the report is filed, the social worker may be called on to provide the department any information relating to the incident of abuse or neglect that needs clarification or was not contained in the original report. When the intake worker arrives, facilitate the assessment as much as possible by making sure the intake worker has a private place to meet with the child. The intake worker will almost always want to meet with the children alone without the parents present. It will be up to the intake worker to decide if police intervention is needed. If it is not an emergency situation and the child is in a protected environment, the police may not need to be called. This type of decision will depend on the time and the circumstances that follow the situation, but be prepared for what could happen. The social worker may also be asked to testify in court; again this will depend on the individual situation.

The families and the children involved will be assessed and offered services to assist them in addressing and remedying the problem. The ultimate goal is to protect the safety and integrity of the child. There are varied services that can be provided and what is offered will be directly related to the needs as determined on the intake and follow-up interviews. Services that can be offered can range from diversion services, counseling services, childcare/daycare, chore services, emergency help such as food, clothing, or rent, referrals for other services not offered by the department as well as foster care and foster care–related costs, e.g., clothing for the child. If it is determined that harm does exist, a case plan will be developed and implemented. The case plan will outline the safety issues, the goals and objectives to be accomplished to ensure the protection of the child, and the desired outcomes. Indicators and consequences related to success or nonsuccess of the plan will be clearly identified. It is important to find out the reporting procedures for your state before an issue occurs. This way you are well aware of what is expected and what needs to be done to facilitate the situation and protect the child.

SUMMARY

Children are an essential part of our country's future development. What we do with and for them benefits all of us. Homer Folks, in 1940, wrote, "The safety of our democracy depends in large measure upon the welfare of our children" (White House Conference, 1942). Our nation's history shows an open sense of caring and responsibility for children and while we want to protect them—even from themselves—we also want to ensure they are provided as many opportunities as possible. How we care for our children tells us a great deal about our society's beliefs, hopes, and aspirations. We do a great deal to care for our nation's children, but we need to do more. We need to find ways to guarantee every child a healthy, caring home. A stimulating environment that encourages growth and development should be the norm for all children. We can accept nothing less.

Child welfare is an exciting field. It is in constant flux, though always under the watchful eyes of the public and of policymakers. Social workers have been, are, and will continue to be significant players in child welfare.

Chapter 9

Health Care

FOR MANY OF US, STARTING ONE CAREER IN THE HELPING PROFES-sions and changing to another is not that unusual. This was Liz's experience when she began her professional career as a nurse but after several years decided to switch to social work. Liz felt that her knowledge of the medical aspects of a client's condition blended beautifully with mental health considerations. Liz's belief is not unique; most health care social workers quickly agree that for intervention to be successful the link between mind and body needs to be clearly made. From this perspective, the contention is made that mind and body cannot be separated, therefore, each client must be treated individually with a focus on continued wellness and prevention. The health care social worker, who often works as part of an interdisciplinary team, brings knowledge and understanding of the importance of focusing on more than just the medical condition a client is suffering from. Each client is part of a system, where the social worker uses his or her knowledge and skills to link the client to the environment. This emphasis is central to discharge planning and case management.

Health care social workers face great challenges in the new century. Issues of behavioral-based managed care, downsizing and reorganization of hospital social work staffs, limited availability of services to insured and uninsured populations, and increased demand for brief interventions make health care a formidable setting for creative social work practice (Dziegielewski, 2004).

For many of the nonprofit organizations, the mere struggle for survival has caused social workers serving as administrators to explore sound fiscal management strategy (Burke, 2008). Questions such as: Do we provide health care to the homeless—and if so, to what extent? What about people in prison: do we provide health care to those serving life sentences with no possibility of parole? How do we ensure that people in rural and sparsely populated areas have access to high-quality health care? Should we continue to move efforts toward a national health insurance model? Should we finance alternative, nontraditional health interventions? Health care is costly. You know that from your own experiences buying medication or paying for medical treatment. Health insurance is also costly. Social workers have an important role in helping clients identify and get the services they need.

For reporting purposes, the U.S. Census Bureau describes health insurance broadly, and this definition includes numerous forms of private insurance as well as those eligible for government coverage (U.S. Census Bureau, 2008). It is

Name: Dodie M. Stein

Place of Residence: Indianapolis, IN

College/University Degrees: PhD, The University of Iowa; MSW, Indiana University; MA, University of Southern California; BS, Syracuse University; LSW Indiana (LCSW pending)

Present Position and Title: Medical Social Worker, Clarian Home Dialysis, Clarian Health Partners

Previous Work/Volunteer Experience: Medical social worker, in-center hemodialysis, hospice social worker, Fellow, Fairbanks Center for Medical Ethics, Clarian Health; clinical and educational audiologist in private practice and university, special education, community speech and hearing center, and medical practices; adjunct faculty, Technical Communications, School of Engineering Technology, Indiana University Purdue University Indianapolis; development professional in community organization and higher education; small business technology development consultant; human resources consultant; independent consultant/contractor, grant & document preparation. Volunteer: Planning Committee, Renal Support Network Patient Lifestyle Meetings; Scholarship Committee, National Council of Jewish Women; St. Vincent's Hospice; a variety of professional organizations in audiology, social work; grant reviewer, U.S. Department of Education; editor & reviewer, Sertoma, various professional journals and publishers in communication disorders; committee & board activities in audiological organizations, Kentucky technology assistance projects, National Governors Association

Why did you choose social work as a career? I was in an allied health field working with babies, young children, and older adults ("womb to tomb" as they say) for many years. After leaving the field and doing other things, I found I missed health care. This was about the time I spent a last year with a friend dying from breast cancer, and I volunteered for hospice at a local hospital. That's what inspired me to go into social work—working with hospice patients and folks with life-threatening chronic diseases, having the honor of helping them manage their illnesses, whether they are in a transition in their lives (starting dialysis) or at the end of their lives (hospice).

What is your favorite social work story? The series of events that I see every day as a renal social worker are inspiring: Patients waiting for years, then finally getting a transplant; patients feeling better and feeling like they have more control over their lives with home dialysis; patients who are depressed and not coping well getting better with appropriate meds and counseling and feeling more a sense of control and contentment. These are patients who have to constantly deal with dialysis as their lifeline, their many co-morbidities, the many meds they take to manage the renal disease and those co-morbidities . . . not to mention the financial aspects of insurances, high monthly co-payments or having to pay full-price for very expensive meds, juggling work and dialysis if they are well enough, multiple physicians' appointments, family demands, transportation difficulties, other activities. I have enormous respect for them and all they do cope with and juggle. I always wonder if I could do it if I were faced with all of it. At least I know I can help them learn to manage, "stay steady," and get back to enjoying what they used to enjoy before renal disease changed their lives.

What is one thing you would change in the community if you had the power to do so?
Universal health care (as in health care for all living in this country), preferably single-payer health care, to provide "health," not "sick" care, including preventative care at all ages. This also assumes physicians and other health care providers making decisions with their patients, not insurance or government bureaucrats "practicing medicine without a license"!

---

believed that the overall spread and accessibility of health insurance alone that occurred between 1950 and 1990 is what has caused at least a 40 percent rise in per capita health spending (National Bureau of Economic Research [NBER], n.d.). More individuals are now able to have access to health insurance and many can now purchase private insurance as a co-payment with an employer or purchased separately by the worker. Forms of government health insurance include: Medicare, Medicaid, military health care, and individual state insurance plans.

To be considered "uninsured," the individual would not have access to any private or government health insurance coverage for the year being measured. As of 2007, the estimated number of individuals in the U.S. with health insurance was 202.0 million. Of this number, an estimated 67.5 percent (177.4 million) had private insurance of some type with approximately 59.3 percent being employer subsidized (U.S. Census Bureau, 2008). The number covered by government subsidy programs was 27.8 percent with Medicaid recipients receiving about 13.2 percent of this subsidy.

According to the U.S. Census Bureau (2008), 15.3 percent of the U.S. population or 45.7 million people in 2007 were without health insurance. This put the number of children under the age of 18 without health insurance at 8.1 million or 11 percent of the uninsured population.

One reason why so many Americans have no form of health insurance is the sheer expense! And there is no reason to believe that costs will decline or even level off in the near future.

In this chapter we provide an overview of the numerous opportunities open to social workers who choose to practice in health care. Working in the health care field is one of the more complex arenas for social work because of the many external issues and constituencies that affect the delivery of health care social work. Miller (2008) outlines our health care system as "complex, under-funded, disparate, inconsistent, state of the art, miraculous, successful, unjust, illogical and more" (p. 219). Taking into account this complexity and all the challenges, however, the rewards from helping others in their time of need can be great.

HEALTH CARE SOCIAL WORK DEFINED

Health care social work, historically called "medical social work" and today "clinical social work" (not to be confused with the work of the private practitioner also referred to as a "clinical social worker") is one of the oldest, best-established fields of professional social work practice. Simply stated, health care social work practice deals with all aspects of general health. It enhances, promotes, and restores the highest level of social functioning for clients, families, and small groups when their abilities to do so are affected by actual or potential stress caused by illness, disability, or injury (Poole, 1995). This type of integrated care requires taking into account all aspects of a person's physical health as well as their mental well-being (Dziegielewski, 2004).

In health care practice, as in other areas of social work, the tasks performed are collaborative yet diverse and unique. Social workers serving in health care settings must be well trained in providing services to clients because they are competing in a service provision environment over-crowded with health care professionals. Moreover, today's health care social workers are exposed to all the turbulence and change of managed health care (Dziegielewski, 2004). In this environment, the insurance company dictates the level of service; no longer are recommendations from physicians or other professionals treated as "written in stone." Pressures to cut costs mean that health care service must be provided in the briefest, most effective manner possible (Dziegielewski, 1997; 2004; 2008a; 2008b).

There is also a movement to provide what has been termed wrap-around services. This involves a collaborative process for the implementation of "individualized" care plans capable of addressing the needs of each individual (generally children) and/or families in need (Walker, Bruns & Penn, 2008). This system of care highlights the importance of the "client in situation" or the client in the environment. From this perspective, the client's problems are addressed taking into account the supports that are available upon their return home, such as family and friends and other resources clients have in the community (Summers, 2001). As a result of interdisciplinary approaches, all health care providers including social workers must work in a versatile, flexible manner to complete tasks with limited resources. The varied tasks coupled with the dynamic environment and limited fiscal resources complicate our simple definition of health care practice.

Did You Know...In 1918, the National Conference of Social Work in Kansas City helped to form the American Association of Hospital Social Workers. This was the first professional social work organization in the United States.

Tom Carlton, a major social work thinker and advocate in health care social work during the 1970s and 1980s, defined health care social work in its broadest sense as "all social work in the health field" (1984, p. 5). Carlton felt that social workers interested in this area must be prepared to do more than engage solely in direct clinical practice. His vision of health care practice includes program planning and administration; preparation, supervision, and continued training for social workers and other health care professionals; and social research. It is not surprising that the term *health care social work* has historically been used interchangeably with the term *medical social work*. Mixing these two terms, however, can obscure a subtle difference in meaning.

In the *Social Work Dictionary, medical social work* is defined as a form of practice that occurs in hospitals and other health care settings. This type of practice facilitates good health, prevention of illness, and aids physically ill clients and their families in resolving the social and psychological problems related to disease and illness (Barker, 2003). Health care social work is more encompassing, indicating a type of practice that can take place in more than one setting.

Health care social workers often serve as members of professional **multidisciplinary** and **interdisciplinary teams**. As part of a multidisciplinary team, the social worker can help link together the services provided by each of the helping disciplines. In the interdisciplinary team, the shared roles and responsibilities allow the social worker to share his/her expertise as part of the team. Regardless of the type of team effort utilized to help the client, the role of the social worker is essential in sensitizing the other team members to the social-psychological aspects of illness (Barker, 2003). Health care social workers are expected to address the psychosocial aspects of client problems. They are also expected to alert other team members to the psychosocial needs of clients and to ensure adequate service provision within the discharge environment. In performing these functions, social work professionals not only represent the interests of clients but often become the "moral conscience" of the health care delivery team. According to Leipzig, Hyer, Ek, et al. (2002), although provider satisfaction with interdisciplinary teamwork was often high, client satisfaction was low. Information such as this further reinforces the role of the social worker as one of the primary providers responsible for increasing communication and understanding for all involved.

The struggle to define exactly what health care social workers are expected to do reflects the changing nature of the health care system. Part of the struggle is trying to establish concrete cost-containing goals and objectives that clearly represent the diverse and often unique service provided. This inability to document a concrete service strategy has long been a thorn in the side of health care administrators, who need this information to justify and compete for continued funding. Nevertheless, simple descriptions of service provision vary, depending on the client population served and the services needed.

Health care social workers practice in a setting where doctors are expected to fix "what's broken" and do so with incredible speed and competence. This has resulted in the push for quick and not always complete solutions such as a "pill" to address a situation rather than implementing behavioral types of treatment interventions (Dziegielewski, 2006). As a result these workers are often expected to do the same. Given the complexity of the human situation, however, this task is not at all straightforward. In adapting to their diverse clients while anticipating changes in the health service environment, social work professionals must employ flexible and constantly updated skills.

A BRIEF HISTORY OF HEALTH CARE SOCIAL WORK

Medical social work can be traced back to the nineteenth-century public health movement. With urban growth, a result of industrialization came overcrowding and the spread of disease. In Trattner's (1989) graphic words:

> American cities were disorderly, filthy, foul-smelling, disease-ridden places. Narrow, unpaved streets became transformed into quagmires when it rained. Rickety tenements, swarming with unwashed humanity, leaned upon one another for support. Inadequate drainage systems failed to carry away sewage. Pigs roamed streets that were cluttered with manure, years of accumulating garbage, and other litter. Slaughterhouses and fertilizing plants contaminated the air with an indescribable stench. Ancient plagues like smallpox, cholera, and typhus threw the population into a state of terror from time to time while less sensational but equally deadly killers like tuberculosis, diphtheria, and scarlet fever were ceaselessly at work.

All in all, not a great place or time to live. It soon was evident that public sanitation programs were needed. The resulting laws and health care efforts helped doctors and related medical professionals to gain in stature (Segal & Brzuzy, 1998, p. 108).

Hospitals too changed dramatically during this era. Once a haven for the poor, the hospital became a "scientific center for the treatment of illness" where physicians provided oversight and subsequent control of the helping activities and services provided (Popple & Leighninger, 1990, p. 436). Medical social work was first practiced in 1900 in Cleveland City Hospital, when the workers helped to discharge from overcrowded wards patients with chronic conditions and homeless Civil War veterans (Poole, 1995). It subsequently developed as a specialization through the efforts of Dr. Richard Cabot and shortly thereafter Ida Cannon, a new graduate from Simmons College. Cabot in 1905 set up the first social service (work) department in a hospital. Though trained as a physician, Cabot recognized the unique and important contributions of social workers when he served as director of the Boston Children's Aid Society. The social worker's skill in linking social environment to disease, thought Cabot, would be extremely helpful in medical diagnosis. The social work department established at Boston's Massachusetts General Hospital is regarded as the debut of medical social work.

Activity...Have you ever been admitted to a hospital? While you were there did you see a social worker? If you didn't, would you have liked to? If you did, what services did he provide? Make a brief list of the services that you believe social workers can provide in the hospital setting.

Health care social work today, as in Cabot's time, takes place in a "host" setting—that is, an organization whose primary purpose is something other than providing social work services. You'll find social workers in hospitals (a hospital accreditation requirement), neighborhood health centers, health maintenance organizations (HMOs), city public health departments, and nonprofit and for-profit health-related organizations. Our new aspect of today's health care social work is that it is now team based and interdisciplinary in nature. Health care social workers need to be invested in both the process and the structure of the services that are to be performed. Each discipline needs to be competent in the practice and approach utilized. Competency involves being able to link the knowledge, values, and skills the professional has to help the client directly to the practice approach selected and the outcome that results (Damron-Rodriquez, 2008). In interdisciplinary collaborations social workers can serve to help the team of professionals communicate with one another and the client to be served. The social worker can help to connect those clients entering the system with the supports that are needed while in the system and upon discharge. This intervention from start to finish builds continuity of care and links the client to their own helping networks that can continue long after the service has ended. Social workers are part of a professional team that may include physicians, nurses, vocational rehabilitation workers, psychologists, and psychiatrists. Today's social worker must therefore understand and value the contributions that other professionals offer. For our clients and ourselves, we can no longer see matters solely through our individual professional lens.

UNDERSTANDING THE CURRENT HEALTH CARE ENVIRONMENT

Throughout the last quarter of the twentieth century, spiraling costs and growing numbers of uninsured people challenged the American health care system. And the crisis is hardly abating. According to Dziegielewski (2004) several reasons of direct interest to social workers have been cited:

1. The aging population needs more costly health care services.
2. Americans are resistant to paying additional fees for medical services.
3. The insurance industry is highly fragmented, with managers trained under different environmental conditions.
4. There is excessive pressure to fill an oversupply of hospital inpatient beds.
5. There is a focus on treating acute illness rather than a more holistic, wellness, or preventive perspective that could lead to more costly treatment.
6. Insufficient medical outcome data impair decision making.
7. Too many heroic attempts are made to implement expensive procedures without regard to quality of continued life.
8. Professionals try to be cautious and can order unnecessary tests and procedures to avoid the potential of malpractice suits.

Even though many of the underlying factors are difficult to change, predictions of vastly increased health care urgently require a response of one type or another.

During the early 1990s, politicians were responsive to the American public's demand for health care reform. During his first term in office, President Clinton, who had made a campaign promise to address this issue, formed a major task force chaired by his wife, Hillary Clinton, which began to develop a national health care policy (Mizrahi, 1995). The task force considered numerous proposals for health care reform from single-payer systems to limited forms of universal coverage. The eventual proposal was not a single-payer approach but rather a type of "managed competition" in which purchasing alliances were formed that would have the power to certify health plans and negotiate premiums for certain benefit packages (President's Health Security Plan, 1993). Payment for these plans is financed by employer-employee premiums. The actual consumer out-of-pocket cost would vary based on the benefit package chosen. The Clinton proposal eventually failed after concerted attacks by the health care industry and conservative members of the Congress. Some political commentators felt this had been the last chance to change the health care system, yet during the 2000 presidential campaign, health care resurfaced as a hot topic, with arguments over insurance coverage and a "patient's bill of rights."

Today, health care affordability continues to remain a significant problem. According to Mills and Bhandari (2003), the key demographic factors noted in limiting health care coverage are age, race, false beliefs and naivete, and educational attainment. In terms of age, individuals between the ages of 18 and 24 were least likely to have coverage with only 70.4 percent having coverage in 2002, and as of the 2006 census this trend remains (DeNavas-Walt, Proctor & Smith, 2008). For uninsured individuals, Hispanics constituted 32.4 percent in 2002 and uninsured Blacks who reported a single race were 20.2 percent. For the foreign-born population those without health insurance (33.4%) were more than double those who were U.S. born (12.8%). In terms of education, it makes sense that the likelihood of being insured increases as educational levels increase.

As managed health care takes a firm grip on our delivery of health care, social workers who participate in these types of reimbursement schemes must continue to deal directly with managed care plans (Dziegielewski, 2004). Such dealings typically involve preauthorization for service by qualified providers; precertification for a given amount of care with concurrent review of treatment and services rendered; continued determination of need for hospitalization through a process of utilization review; and pre-discharge planning to ensure that proper aftercare services are identified and made available (Hiratsuka, 1990).

In addition, service reimbursement is linked clearly to performance indicators. This means linkage must be clearly made to consumer outcomes, service events, resource acquisition, and efficiency (Poertner & Rapp, 2007). We don't want to paint a bleak picture but rather a realistic one. The continual changes and swirling controversies contribute to a turbulent health care environment. Declining hospital admissions, reduced lengths of stay, and numerous other restrictions and methods of cost containment are common threats that unite all health care social workers.

Did You Know...In current health care practice the term "patient" is being replaced. Originally, the adoption of the word "patient" by the medical community caused many social workers to stop using words such as "client" when referring to the people they served. The use and acceptance of the term "patient" is obvious when we read articles in the health care social work literature (Dziegielewski, 2004).

Today, with the shift away from the "medical sick role model" to the "wellness, concrete service, cost-effective approach," the term "patient" is in conflict with the wholeness and prevention strategy marketed by host health care organizations. Replacement terms include "client" (a term familiar to social work), "consumer" (to represent those receiving a service), and "covered persons" (reflecting those who have some type of medical insurance coverage). Those in favor of the euphemism "covered persons" argue that it is not used just to denote medical coverage but rather to convey a universal care perspective indicative of the security of medical coverage.

In summary, it is beyond the scope of this chapter to identify all issues central to health care reform. Probably the most daunting fact in terms of access to care is that "the United States is the ONLY industrialized nation that does not have a system of health care with access to services for all of its citizens, regardless of race, ethnicity, gender, age, employment status, and income" (Moniz & Gorin, 2003, p.75). Five areas are presented to further help delineate and provide fuel for thought about where reform efforts need to be focused.

First, to reform the overall health care system meaningfully, there is a need for enhanced state-of-the-art information technology in all health care settings. For the most part, the health care sector has languished behind almost all other industries in adopting information technology. For example, many caregivers still record client data on paper documents that cannot be easily accessed by other providers in different settings—or sometimes even the same setting—which can result in errors and costly duplication of effort. Or to increase service delivery options using online education and support information as well as online group participation and networking as an option for increasing service delivery (Nicholas, Darch, McNeill, et al., 2007). With all the electronic technology available, it is surprising how little is used in standard care and delivery of services.

A second issue and probably the most daunting of health care challenges is the number of uninsured Americans, which now exceeds 40 million people and underinsured Americans. Some ways of increasing inclusion for the uninsured involve extending health coverage to all residents through the provision of tax credits designed to offset the costs of eligible participants' insurance premiums. Another way to confront this issue might be to consider expanding Medicaid and the State Children's Health Insurance Program to cover a broader range of participants. Among anticipated benefits is coverage of families under a single plan and access to a personal clinician, both of which increase the likelihood that patients will receive appropriate, timely care in the right setting.

To measure the number of underinsured and assist to gain better access to care is a much more complicated concept. What we mean by underinsured are people who have medical insurance but whose employers try to save dollars by cutting back policy coverage or benefits. These employers, in an effort to save costs, can eliminate benefits, reduce benefits for family members, or increase the employees' contributions to insurance benefits. This is also complicated by the fact that health insurance coverage is also relative to how many hours a person works. Part-time and temporary workers or those on contract are less likely to have health insurance (Moniz & Gorin, 2003).

A third area is malpractice reform. It has become commonplace to see debates over malpractice insurance and how some physicians are refusing to provide care based on what they perceive to be unreasonable rates. This debate and subsequent refusal to provide services has resulted in limited access to care for patients in some communities. On the other side, this professional fear of liability has impeded efforts to identify sources of error so that they can be prevented. Moreover, the tort system frequently does not result in injured patients getting compensated; those who do often experience long delays. One way to address this issue might be to have states create injury compensation systems outside of the courtroom that are client-centered and focused on safety. These systems would set reasonable payments for avoidable injuries and provide fair, timely compensation to a greater number of clients, while stabilizing the malpractice insurance market by limiting health care providers' financial exposure.

Another area of growing concern that needs attention has to do with changing times and the recognition of the quality and appropriateness of patient care, given the rising prevalence of chronic conditions such as diabetes and heart disease. Roughly 120 million Americans have one or more chronic conditions, many of which could have been prevented or delayed through education or other interventions that promote healthy behaviors. Studies have shown that counseling of lifestyle behaviors can be effective in reducing risks in diabetes and other chronic conditions (Tabenkin, 2004); evidence such as this makes counseling that includes behavior change a crucial component of any intervention designed to assist individuals suffering from chronic disease (Gross, Tabenkin, Heymann, et al., 2007). The physical and psychological implications are that living with a chronic condition can disrupt every area of a client's life. From the moment a client is diagnosed with the condition, the social and psychological factors will become a key area for the health care social worker to recognize and help the health care delivery team to access (Zabora, 2009).

As stated earlier, all too often health care practices generally focus on the physical symptoms. Whether these symptoms are acute and reflective of episodic problems, this type of focus cannot effectively provide the ongoing treatment and coordination among multiple care providers and settings needed by those with chronic ailments. Moreover, health care still focuses largely on treatment of the physical symptoms rather than the psychological ones. In addition a focus on treatment that lacks an emphasis on prevention could be equally problematic. For example, many diabetics still do not receive foot examinations to check for nerve damage, and smokers fail to receive counseling about quitting smoking and the health benefits that quitting can bring.

Last, the need remains to enhance primary care facilities as this is where the majority of clients enter the health care system and where most of their health care needs are met. The reliance on the primary care facility and receiving care in this way is critical to achieving goals related to treatment of acute and chronic conditions, prevention, and health promotion. For example, in order to improve delivery, community health centers need to undertake initiatives to reinvent and substantially enhance primary care through new models of care delivery, support for patient self-management, and other strategies. These centers as access and transition points need to build on their existing innovations in electronic record-keeping and management of chronic diseases, and they should also consider new incentives, such as enabling centers and their staffs to share in the rewards of the cost savings they generate by eliminating waste.

For the most part it is easy when confronted with challenges to unequivocally state "we are at a crossroads" or "we are facing a crisis." Yet social work is full of challenges, no matter what the workplace, whether it is health care or some other area of practice. And even the most experienced health care social worker has felt that no matter how hard they try health care organizations can represent large bureaucracies that seem impossible to change. As such, we can become mired down at the crossroad, never moving, feeling others control our destiny—or we can begin to understand and identify what the problems are and explore potential solutions for change.

ROLES AND TASKS OF THE HEALTH CARE SOCIAL WORKER

According to the *Social Work Dictionary* health care workers can be defined in a generic sense as all "professional, paraprofessional, technical and general employees of a system or facility that provides for the diagnosis, treatment and overall well being of patients" (Barker, 2003, p. 192). Nevertheless, a clear distinction must be made between *health care workers* and *allied health care professionals*. Health care workers are nonprofessional service support personnel such as home health aides, medical record personnel, nurse's aides, orderlies, and attendants (Barker, 2003). Allied health care providers, by contrast, are generally professionals such as social workers, psychologists, audiologists, dietitians, occupational therapists, optometrists, pharmacists, physical therapists, and speech pathologists, among others.

It is as allied health care professionals that you will find social workers practicing in health care settings. Health care social workers appear to serve this area well because of their broad-based training in evaluating based on behavior the biological, psychological, and social factors that can affect a client's environmental situation—that is, the behavioral biopsychosocial approach. The beginning generalist

(BSW) and advanced specialist (MSW) levels of education help to make the social work professional an invaluable member of the health care delivery team. The services that health care social workers provide can be divided into two major areas: direct practice and support or ancillary services.

Did You Know...The U.S. Veterans' Bureau, now the Department of Veterans' Affairs, began hiring social workers to work in its hospitals in 1926.

Where do physicians and nurses, the most recognizable health care providers, fit in? Physicians and nurses are not considered *allied* service providers. Because their services are necessary to any type of medical care, they are called "essential health care providers"—they are the major players in the host environment (Dziegielewski, 2006).

Direct Practice

Today, the role of the health care social worker is clearly established, and they can be found in every area of our health care delivery system. These practitioners typically provide a wide variety of services to clients and their families:

Case finding and outreach: Assist client to identify and secure the services they need

Preservice or preadmission planning: Identify barriers to accessing health care services

Assessment: Identify service needs and screen to identify health and wellness concerns

Direct provision: Secure concrete services such as admission, discharge, and aftercare planning

Psychosocial evaluation: Gather information on client's biopsychosocial, cultural, financial, situational factors for completion of the psychosocial assessment or social history

Goal identification: Establish mutually negotiated goals and objectives that address client's health and wellness issues.

Counseling: Help client and family to deal with their situation and problems related to health interventions needed or received

Short- and long-term planning: Help client and family to anticipate and plan for the services needed based on client's current or expected health status

Service access assistance: Identify preventive, remedial, and rehabilitative service needs and assist client and family to overcome potential barriers to service access

Education: Instruct client and family on areas of concern in regard to their health and wellness

Wellness training: Help client to establish a plan to secure continued or improved health based on a holistic prevention model

Referral services: Provide information about services available and make direct connection when warranted

Continuity of care: Ensure that proper connections are made among all services needed, taking into account the issue of multiple health care providers

Advocacy: Teach and assist clients to obtain needed resources, or on a larger scale advocate for changes in policy or procedure that directly or indirectly benefit the client.

Case management and discharge planning: Where clients are connected to the services they need after leaving general health care facility (Dziegielewski, 2004).

Did You Know...In the 1920s and 1930s the U.S. military started to add social workers to its ranks. Military social workers usually work in mental health, health, and protective service settings.

The clinical services that health care social workers provide have clearly expanded far beyond the traditional core of **discharge planning**. Health care is a changing environment where even the classic definition of discharge planning has been altered. Social workers not only coordinate discharges, they also oversee the multidisciplinary or interdisciplinary teams of which they are members to be sure that clients are getting the services they need. Since discharges can involve numerous individual, family, and community factors, counseling services often must accompany these placements (Summers, 2001). Social workers are often called upon to provide this type of service. Furthermore, once the team agrees that a client is ready for discharge, it is often the social worker who is responsible for ensuring that transfer forms are completed, client and family education has been done, and the records that support continued care are ready for transfer (Mankita & Alalu, 1996).

Support Services

Social workers can also provide health-related services that are not considered direct practice. These support or ancillary services include staff supervision, administration, and community-based services:

Direct supervision: Provide direct professional social work supervision through direction, guidance, and education on case services and counseling

Consultation: Provide consultation services to other social workers and multidisciplinary and interdisciplinary teams

Agency consultation: Provide consultation to agency administrators on how to enhance service delivery to clients and organizations

Community consultation: Provide consultation services to communities to assist with the development of community-based services

Policy and program planning: Assist in formulation and implementation of health care policies and programs that will help to meet client needs

Program development: Assist the agency to refine and develop new and improved programs

Quality improvement: Assist the agency to ensure that continuous quality services are provided that meet standards of professionalism and efficiency

Service advocacy: Assist the agency to recognize the needs of clients

Service outreach: Identify unmet needs and services that are not available to clients; advocate for improved programs and services

At-risk service outreach: Identify clients at risk of decreased health or illness; advocate securing services for them

Health education: Participate and instruct communities on developing and implementing health education programs

Activity...Cultural Diversity in the Medical Setting

Break into groups and discuss the following case. Prepare a plan on how to best assist the client situation described.

The social worker arrives in a client's hospital room to gather some routine admission information when she walks in on a couple having a very heated discussion. Jon is a 40-year-old Hispanic male who is in the hospital for routine same-day exploratory surgery. Jon's wife is visibly upset and crying. The social worker feels a bit awkward for intruding and asks if the couple would like her to leave. Jon motions that he would like her to stay, and begins to tell her that he is furious that his wife has decided to go on a trip alone to see her mother. When questioned as to whether he is disappointed because he wants to go with her, he quickly says no. He is angry because she made plans without getting his permission first. His wife states that she is sorry for not asking him first but she felt the decision had to be made quickly. The couple asks the social worker what her opinion is.

Taking into account a respect for cultural diversity and maintaining professional integrity, what types of responses and/or assistance could the social worker provide? What types of responses should be avoided?

Agency liaison: Serve as liaison to the agency on behalf of the client; ensuring connections are made between client, supervisor, and community

Community liaison: Serve as a contact or connection between client, family, and community

Support services go beyond what we generally consider to be the core of health care social work. We must, nevertheless, recognize the importance of all practitioners who do this type of work day in, day out. These tasks and functions cannot be overemphasized, particularly in this era of managed care (see figure 1).

Direct Supervision. Staff supervision is a major support activity with a long and rich history in health care social work. Supervision requires specialized knowledge that builds on years of practice. As a result, you will find that most social workers performing supervision, whether it is clinical or administrative oversight, have an MSW degree. On occasion, you may find a BSW worker in a supervisory role, but this is the exception.

Supervision is a complicated activity, but it is necessary for the professional growth of all social workers. Supervisors are mentors, teachers if you will, who can be sounding boards, share practice frustrations, and look at different ways of working with a particular client or group. Kadushin gave a more formal definition:

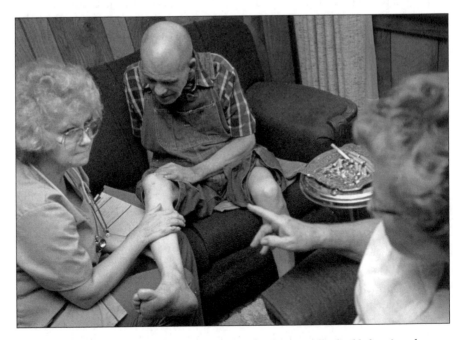

Figure 1: Home healthcare worker examining a developmentally disabled senior who lives with his sister.

An agency administrative staff member . . . is given authority to direct, coordinate, enhance, and evaluate on-the-job performance of supervisees for which work he [or she] is held accountable. In implementing this role the supervisor performs administrative, educational, and supportive functions in interaction with the supervisee in the context of a positive relationship. The supervisor's ultimate objective is to deliver to agency clients the best possible service, both quantitative and qualitatively, in accordance with agency policies and procedures (1976, p. 21).

Kadushin's definition applies to the field of health care social work, though with one very important addition. In health care work flexibility must be part of both practice and supervision. Repeated policy changes, and consequent organizational instability, often lead to reorganization, cutbacks, and ultimately reductions in the workforce (Braus, 1996). For the social worker, whether a new or an experienced practitioner, such uncertainty can be difficult to handle. Let's be honest—no one likes to be in an unsure work environment, where the rules may change from one day to the next. In health care, social workers must continually modify details of their practice. The health care social work supervisor also mediates, advocates, and brokers as part of staff supervision (Berkman, 1996).

In social work, supervision is viewed as a tool to help the new social worker develop and refine skills by a more senior professional knowledgeable and skilled in the area (Gelman, 2009). In mediating between supervisees and clients, coworkers, or the larger community, the supervisor should always try not to adopt the opinion of any side. Supervisors must be sensitive to their staff's ongoing struggles to create proactive client-directed services within the constraints set by payers. Supervisors too must balance the demands of their jobs with those of third-party payers. To say the least, the supervisor's role is difficult. Flexibility and the time to provide proper oversight, then, is central to competent supervision as well as good practice skills. The need to be flexible, however, and the environment that creates this need, is a major source of stress. Stress and its management are, therefore, important issues for both supervisor and staff.

Supportive supervision addresses such issues as stress, staff morale, and work-related anxiety and worry, which if left unattended, can lower job satisfaction and commitment to the agency. Supportive supervision builds worker self-esteem and emotional well-being. In the long run, it can reduce stress levels and thus the dissatisfaction that ultimately results in employee burnout (Resnick & Dziegielewski, 1996; Sheafor, Horejsi, & Horejsi, 1997).

As if system uncertainty were not enough for the health care supervisor, let's add another challenge to the job: lack of clarity in staff roles and responsibilities. In particular, what are the differences in the work carried out by BSWs and by MSWs? Guidelines differentiating practice responsibilities between the BSW and the MSW are rarely clear (Levin & Herbert, 1995). You may find that what BSWs do in one setting is done only by MSWs in another. This lack of clarity about functions means that supervisors must be careful in assigning cases and tasks. Without clear definitions it is possible to assign tasks that are beyond the competence of the social worker, which compromises client care and worker well-being (Levin & Herbert, 1995). Supervisors must ensure that tasks assigned to BSWs are within their scope of practice. That another organization assigns a particular task to BSWs is no guarantee that the activity is appropriate for an entry-level practitioner. Rather, that organization may not be able to assign or even hire an MSW; but the task must be done, so it must be given to a BSW. Though professionally unsound, this task assignment can be made less so if the BSW is given consistent and persistent supervision.

Mediation, Advocacy, and Brokering. The health care social work supervisor also mediates, advocates, and brokers as part of staff supervision (Berkman, 1996). In mediating between supervisees and clients, coworkers, or the larger community, the supervisor remains neutral and does not adopt the opinion of any side (Shulman, 1992). Advice and direction are given on the best way to handle client care for the supervisee, the multidisciplinary or interdisciplinary team, the agency, and the community. Mediation requires the supervisor to recognize that conflicts are not intentional and to help supervisees to address them in the most ethical, moral, and professional way possible.

The second role, advocacy, requires willingness on the parts of both supervisor and supervisees to assist with the development of needed services for clients, their families, and significant others, while not losing sight of the common ground that links them to administration (Shulman, 2002).

Did You Know...In the early days, hospital nurses generally performed medical social work services. These nurses were convenient choices for this employment because they were easily accessible, already knew agency procedure, and were aware of community resources. Later, however, when it was established that more specialized training in understanding social conditions was needed, the employment of social work professionals began.

Brokering, the third role, requires supervisor and staff to link the client with community services and other agencies. Remember, when most people come into a medical setting, such as a hospital, their stay is limited. The social worker must elicit a great deal of information on the client's environment and do this quickly and concisely. Information on social, emotional, and physical factors and their relation to the illness is a critical factor in understanding the person in his/her situation. From the early days of medical social work Dr. Cabot saw this as the most important role of social work practice in health care. The social worker may discover that a client needs a variety of follow-up support services to sustain her or her family through the recovery period or through ongoing illness. Brokering is how the social worker seeks out these community-based services and develops a case plan that is tailored to the client.

Health Education and Health Counseling. Social workers were part of the nineteenth-century public health education movement, also called the "Sanitation Movement." Therefore, providing education and instruction is not new to social

Name: Roni Levine

Place of residence: West Chester, PA

College/university degrees: West Chester University, BSW

Present position: Supports Coordinator for Chester County MH/MR Supports Coordination Unit

Previous work/volunteer experience: Devereus Kanner Center, American Red Cross, Pottstown Memorial Medical Center

Why did you choose social work as a career? I chose social work as a career to help other people. Seeing a smile on someone's face is my personal reward. Going through my first two years of high school I had no idea what I wanted to do. I started taking classes in psychology and sociology in order to find out what these fields would offer. I joined groups like peer counseling, drug, and alcohol prevention teams so that I could reach out to other students. I wanted to choose a major that offered services that would help others. I visited several schools, but decided that West Chester University was the right choice for me. They made me feel wanted and accepted in their program. I was treated by the school's professors the same way I had hoped to treat others.

What is your favorite social work story? When spending time thinking about my "favorite social work story" different situations come to mind. My most memorable story that I would like to share was about working with a woman in her late fifties who was dually diagnosed with mental retardation and mental health disorders. She was living in a group home with four other women and had displayed many behaviors that were getting worse over time. She was verbally and physically aggressive toward others. She was hospitalized six times in a six month period due to her behaviors. Each time she would go to the hospital the doctors would discharge her as they could not find anything wrong with her. Searching for placement in her county became very difficult as her reputation preceded her. Finally after everyone else turned her down I started to look for a placement outside her county. I found an agency that accepted her for who she was, and didn't judge her on her past actions. She has been there for three years now and has been very happy.

What would be the one thing you would change in our community if you had the power to do so? One of the things I would change in my community is the lack of compassion that exists for people that have mental health disorders. Working with people with these disabilities has given me a greater understanding of what their lives are like. I would have been better prepared to deal with these situations if the textbooks had offered more information about mental health disorders. All the knowledge and training I have received comes through on the job training with the population I work with. The way the general population look and stare at the mentally retarded show how they lack the knowledge about them. They do not take the time to get to know them as individuals as I do.

work—though recognition and emphasis on the importance of health care counseling was limited. Attention wasn't directed toward counseling until training became institutionalized in colleges and moved to an educational model.

Psychoeducation involves a wide array of services, but in health care, similar to other areas of practice, this type of supportive intervention involves helping clients identify the challenges they are facing and develop social support and coping skills to address them (Walsh, 2009). Health care counseling is especially important with the increased participation of social work professionals as educators in new health care areas that we might call "nontraditional social work." These include smoking cessation and weight reduction, for example. The worker continues to teach new patterns of behavior but then employs counseling theory and skills to help the client negotiate the period of change. The worker calls on a range of skills and strategies ranging from support to confrontation. According to Strom-Gottfried (2009), effective educational practice relies on six essential components:

1. the development of clear and appropriate objectives;
2. an understanding of the learner's needs and abilities;
3. an atmosphere that is conducive to learning;
4. knowledge of the material to be conveyed;
5. the skill to select and use teaching methods appropriately; and,
6. the ability to evaluate one's performance and the learner's acquisition

of the educational outcomes (p. 721).

Administration. Administration and related tasks have not been considered core practice areas of health care social work. In fact, most prospective social workers shy away from studying administration, focusing instead on client-related courses. Don't believe us? Ask your classmates how many of them plan to major in or develop a specialization in administration. You'll probably find that everyone agrees someone should study administration—"but not me." Yet administration, particularly in health care, directly affects the types of services that are offered in a setting. The role that administration plays in strengthening direct practice cannot be overstated. For the social worker serving as an administrator, training in time management, organizational management and operations, and sound fiscal awareness are only the start of what is needed.

Social work administrators, like other health care administrators, must respond to often competing management philosophies. These conflicting styles can affect the provision of client care. For example, the social work administrator may receive a directive from the hospital central administration "to increase the participation of professional staff members in the organization's decision-making processes." The idea behind this directive is that greater involvement will strengthen commitment to the hospital. The social work administrator decides that "quality circles" and "total quality management" (TQM) will best achieve the culture that central administration is seeking. While the social work administrator is attempting to put TQM in place with quality circles among staff members, central administration announces that reimbursement from third-party payers and census data (e.g., patient-bed days) are down. The announcement is an unmistakable signal of financial pressure—remember, a hospital is a business and, like all businesses, needs to make a profit. So now the social work administrator must be concerned with generating significant patient numbers to justify and sustain the department. The goal is now to maximize reimbursement potential. If numbers are not increased, then the department will be forced to cut back on staff while raising workloads for those who stay. A "more with less" mentality takes hold while the edict to develop staff loyalty remains in place.

Sound frustrating? Does it seem unfair, or that it simply does not make sense? You now understand why so many health care social work administrators become frustrated and feel trapped. Double-edged and conflicting messages sent by central administration or insurance companies make administration the most difficult, frustrating, and challenging aspect of health care work. However, the situation is not as dismal as it seems. Health care social work administrators can balance these pressures and influence the agency's **policy** decisions. Miller (2008) reminds us that all policy drives practice, so being a part of the policy-making can help to bring about needed changes. Therefore, serving on agency committees or boards allows the administrator to help construct new policy directions and provides an opportunity to meet funding bodies in order to explain practice realities and discuss ways to enhance service delivery. This strategy is called *practice policy*. It reflects the understanding that social work activities are born of policy decisions. As social workers, we must be informed about and involved in the development of organizational policy—our clients are stakeholders in the policy-making process. Our practice, knowledge, advocacy skills, and ability to mediate between conflicting parties are all contributions we social workers can make to the health care policy-making process.

Acute and Long-Term Care Settings

Social work has long been at the forefront in providing health care services to clients in acute care and long-term care settings (Beder, 2006; Chapman & Toseland, 2007). We find that the skills and theory that social workers bring to the workplace, again Dr. Cabot's observation holds true, are needed in today's acute care setting (Berkman, 1996). The health care social worker's roles and responsibilities in the acute care setting are clear:

- ◆ Provide assistance with treatment plans and compliance issues
- ◆ Assist clients and families with discharge planning and referral
- ◆ Provide counseling and support for clients and significant others in the areas of health, wellness, mental health, bereavement, and so forth
- ◆ Assist clients and their families ethically to make difficult decisions that can affect physical health and mental health
- ◆ Educate clients, their families, and significant others about psychosocial issues and adjusting to illness; assist in resolving behavioral problems

- Assist in identifying and obtaining entitlement benefits
- Secure nonmedical benefits; assist with risk management and quality assurance activities
- Advocate for enhanced and continued services to ensure client well-being

Did You Know...In 1928, the American College of Surgeons developed and included a minimum standard of service provision for social service—that is, social work—departments.

Long-term and restorative care settings may not be that familiar to you. Let's try some other names that you're more likely to recognize: rehabilitative hospitals and clinics, nursing homes, intermediate care facilities, supervised boarding homes, home health care agencies, hospices, and hospital home care units. These settings are usually multidisciplinary, and social workers provide services within the areas of assessment, treatment, rehabilitation, supportive care, and prevention of increased disability of people with chronic physical, emotional, or developmental impairments. Poole (1995) called for such health services to 1) be provided in the least restrictive environment possible, 2) support clients in autonomous decision making, and 3) maximize a client's level of physical, social, and psychological functioning and subsequent well-being.

Poole's recommendations may seem like common sense, and they are. They reflect the core values and ethics set out in the Code of Ethics, which remind us of how important it is to maintain sensitivity and respect for people served, to be aware of the individual's right and ability to make decisions for himself (in most situations), and to focus on client strengths and resources that can be maximized.

The phrase "long term" indicates that the client has a chronic condition that may affect his abilities. Unfortunately, many chronic conditions are unlikely to improve. But that doesn't mean the social worker and other team members give up hope or stop trying to ensure that the client receives the highest quality of professional treatment. We must be realistic, but optimistic. We should not hide information from clients or discount their feelings. Remember, we are all people who think, feel, and care.

Health care social workers employed in long-term care must develop specialized knowledge of various chronic conditions and learn to identify and assess signs and symptoms of the expected progression of various diseases (Dziegielewski, 2004). Such information is critical to being an effective practitioner with the client, family, and friends. They (family, friends, and significant others) often need assistance to participate in the care of their loved ones (see, for example, figure 2). Many people don't know what to say or how to say it and, as a result, feel overwhelmed and even useless. We should never underestimate the importance of "others" in the healing or sustaining process. Considerable evidence exists that the involvement and support of family and friends contributes greatly to the overall wellness and satisfaction of all involved (Dziegielewski, 2004; Rubinstein, Lubben, & Mintzer, 1994).

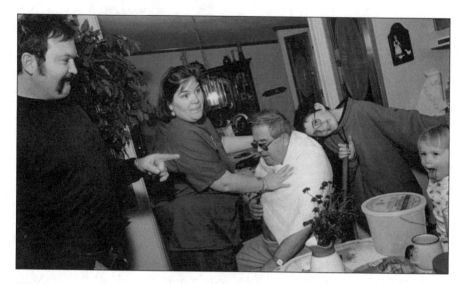

Figure 2: A daughter is about to give her father a haircut. The father and an adult son who was injured in an auto accident live together. Neither is able to drive and the other adult children take turns dropping by and helping out. Both the father and the son gain a sense of responsibility and accomplishment by taking care of each other.

One last thought: when addressing the needs of a client who suffers from a chronic condition the beginning professional should strive not to be afraid. Rely on what you have learned in school, and always be a compassionate person who uses skills and theory grounded in values and ethics that allow for the celebration of the entire human experience.

Did You Know...Johns Hopkins Hospital established its first social work program in 1907. The first social worker to be employed there was Helen B. Pendleton (Nacman, 1977).

Hospital Emergency Room Social Work

Social work services are offered in many hospital emergency rooms across the country; yet, in this fast-paced environment the actual services provided can differ greatly. For the social worker assigned to the emergency room, this employment setting is generally perceived as a fast-paced setting. In this setting, crises, deaths, and severe client problems need to be assessed and addressed as quickly and efficiently as possible. Once the emergency medical crisis is stabilized, the social worker needs to assist with the psychosocial protocol (Boes & McDermott, 2005). For the person being admitted to the hospital, the social worker can provide psychosocial services such as education and support to the client as well as the client's family and friends (Beder, 2006).

The pressure for immediate action in this setting is intense, and the social worker must remain in a constant state of readiness prepared for whatever might come through the door next. According to Van Wormer and Boes (1997), working in emergency room settings is different from other settings in the hospital because of the speed and intensity of which services must be assessed and provided. According to Ponto and Berger (1992) referrals to the emergency room social worker often involve complex problems. Specific cases included: 1) acute psychiatric episode involving suspected or threatened self-inflicted injuries, anxiety attacks, or emergent psychotic episodes; 2) acute medical crisis involving long-term mental illness, chemical dependent individuals, homeless, or transient patients; 3) cases of domestic violence or rape; 4) suspected cases of child abuse or neglect, including sexual abuse; and 5) any traumatic injury or illness that involved the police or other agencies, including assault, sexual assault, domestic violence, intoxication, or temporary disabling conditions.

For many social workers in the emergency room setting, it is not uncommon to work as part of an interdisciplinary or multidisciplinary team (Dziegielewski, 2004). Teamwork in this setting often involves a variety of professionals comprised of physicians, nurses, respiratory technicians, health unit coordinators, x-ray technicians, nurse case managers, social workers, and other health care professionals. Furthermore, some emergency departments divide this team further into what is often termed *a case management sub-team or dyad* that utilizes the combined services of a nurse and a social worker (Bristow & Herrick, 2002). In this setting, the case management sub-team members work together to provide social services and discharge planning, and to ensure that continuum of care needs are met for each client served.

Historically, the presence of a social worker in the emergency room setting has been important from a supportive/clinical perspective as well as to provide direct case management and discharge planning services (Beder, 2006). Supportive services for helping clients include discharge planning or counseling services for the family support system of the identified client. In the emergency room, the problems clients seek treatment for are multifaceted and complex and the types of problems addressed are diverse, ranging from auto accidents to other types of accidental and non-accidental injuries. Many individuals may have acute or chronic episodes of an illness, first or repeated episodes of a physical or mental illness, or suicide attempts related to health and/or emotional issues.

According to Bristow and Herrick (2002), the services that social workers provided in this setting include psychosocial assessments, bereavement counseling and support, substance abuse assessment and referral, discharge planning, referrals for community resources, emotional support, and educating and advocating for patients. In addition, the emergency room social worker can assist with case management by gathering contact information for family and friends as well as finding additional means for meeting the client's health needs. Unfortunately, some believe the emergency room has become a dumping ground for those that lack insurance or are homeless. This group of individuals has a very unique set of circumstances requiring short-term intensive support designed to facilitate the discharge process and decrease the chance of recidivism (Dziegielewski, 2004). Since many individuals who seek care in the emergency room often lack or have inadequate health care coverage, this factor may force clients to seek emergency rooms as a means for obtaining non-emergency or episodic care (Spitzer & Kuykendall, 1994). Social work in the emergency department plays an important role in providing for the psychosocial needs of the patients in a time of crisis. Although this role is important, emergency room social workers warn that medical staff may overlook social work services because of their focus on the medical needs and not the psychosocial needs of the client being served. Thus, to utilize the services of social workers in the emergency department better, it is vital that the emergency room staff as well as hospital administrators be educated about the role of the social worker in their department.

Home Care Services

Home care agencies have been providing high-quality, in-home services to Americans for more than a century and have remained an integral part of the provision of health services since 1905. Health care social workers help patients and their families cope with chronic, acute, or terminal illnesses and handle problems that may stand in the way of recovery or rehabilitation.

Home care refers to health care and the social services that are provided to individuals and families in their home or in community and other homelike settings (Dziegielewski, 2004). Home care includes a wide array of services including nursing, rehabilitation, social work, home health aides, and other services. This rapidly expanding area of health care social work can be traced back as far as the early nineteenth century (Cowles, 2003; National Association for Home Care, 2000). In 1955, the United States Public Health Services endorsed a physician-oriented organized home health care team designed to provide medical and social services to patients within their home. The team consisted of a physician, nurse, and social worker (Goode, 2000). Since that time social workers have continued to provide social services in the home care setting, and this area of health care social work remains a diverse and dynamic service industry. The demand for home care services is increasing as hospital stays are decreasing.

For the most part, the majority of home care services are considered third party and reimbursable by Medicare, Medicaid, private insurance policies, health maintenance organizations (HMOs), and group health plans. These types of payments are determined by several factors, including client diagnosis and the types of services required. Medicare recipients are the largest group of clients needing home health care services. More frequently than not, the services they need involve social as well as medical supports, making the role of social work crucial in the field of home care. When psychosocial needs go unmet, clients are at risk of further health problems that can lead to physical deterioration, reduced independence, and eventually to the need for more intensive and expensive services (Berkman, Chauncey, Holmes, et al., 1999, p. 9). Cowles (2003) identified six categories of home care client problems: (1) barriers to service admissions; (2) service adjustments; (3) diagnosis, prognosis, or treatment/care plan adjustments; (4) lack of information to make informed decisions; (5) needed resources are lacking; and (6) service barriers related to discharge. Rossi (1999) described home care social workers' duties as the following: "(1) helping the health care team to understand the social and emotional factors related to the patient's health and care; (2) assessing the social and emotional factors to estimate the caregiver's capacity and potential, including but not limited to coping with the problems of daily living, acceptance of the illness or injury or its impact, role reversal, sexual problems, stress, anger or frustration, and making the necessary referrals to ensure that the patient receives the appropriate treatments; (3) helping the caregiver to secure or utilize other community agencies as needs are identified; and (4) helping the patient or caregiver to submit paperwork for alternative funding" (p. 335). McLeod and Bywaters (2000) validate the need for social workers in health care and report that there is substantial scope for social work involvement by working toward greater equality of access to existing health and social services. Equally important is to participate in shaping how social workers are viewed, establishing their role as a knowledgeable, positive, and supportive resource to support staff, co-workers, and administration (Neuman, 2000).

Hospice Social Work

Hospice care is a special way of caring for people who are terminally ill and their families. The goal of a hospice is to care for the client and the family with open acknowledgment that no cure is expected for the client's illness. Hospice care includes physical, emotional, social, and spiritual care; usually a public agency or private company that may or not be Medicare-approved provides this service. All age groups are serviced including children, adults, and the elderly during their final stages of life, and the majority of this care occurs at the client's home (Facts and Figures, 2008). When working in the hospice setting, both in-patient and in-home services can be provided. In this setting the individual is prepared for a dignified death that is satisfactory to the person and to those who participate in the person's care (McSkimming, Myrick, & Wasinger, 2000).

In hospice the role of the social worker is crucial to the family planning process, and efforts are made to help family members deal with the client's illness and impending death in the most effective way possible. The social worker tries to facilitate open communication between patient and family and assess levels of stress—especially the ones that affect coping and prognosis. In addition, special attention is given to assessing the spiritual needs of the client and his/her family, and helping them continue to adjust and accept. In the hospice setting there is a strong interdisciplinary focus with a team approach that will continually assess environmental safety concerns. One of the first tasks of the social worker is to address grieving with an initial *bereavement risk assessment* for the caregiver, thereby assisting the patient and family to identify strengths that help cope with loss (Dziegielewski, 2004). Families are supported as time is allowed for the patient and family to progress through stages of grieving. Other duties of the hospice social worker involve updating bereavement care plans and assessing the type of bereavement program to be initiated upon the death of the patient. Referrals are also provided for bereavement support services.

Life-Threatening Conditions and People with HIV/AIDS

According to the Centers for Disease Control and Prevention (CDC) (2007) the prevalence, which is the number of people living with HIV/AIDS in a given year, at the end of 2003 was an estimated 1,039,000 to 1,185,000 persons in the United States. In 2006 alone, the estimated number of persons living with HIV/AIDS in the United States gathered through confidential name-based reporting was 509,681. In addition, an additional 24 to 27 percent are undiagnosed or unaware of their HIV infection. First recognized in 1981, by the U.S. CDC, today there are over one million people in the United States who are living with HIV or AIDS, and according to the UNAIDS Report (2007) over 32.2 million people worldwide. Accordingly, for the year 2006, the top five states in the United States with the highest reported levels of AIDS are: New York (5,495 cases), Florida (4,932 cases), California (3,960 cases), Texas (2,998 cases), and Pennsylvania (1,893 cases) (UNAIDS, World Health Organization, 2007).

Did You Know...HIV is a worldwide illness. At the end of 2002, UNAIDS and the World Health Organization estimated adults and children living with AIDS in the following regions:

North America	*980,000*	*Eastern Europe and Central Asia*	*1.2 million*
Caribbean	*440,000*	*South and South-East Asia*	*6 million*
Latin America	*1.5 million*	*Central Asia*	*1.2 million*
Western Europe	*570,000*	*East Asia*	*6 million*
North Africa and Middle East	*550,000*	*Australia and New Zealand*	*15,000*
Sub-Saharan Africa	*29.4 million*		

Source: http://www.who.int/hiv/facts/en/plwha_m.jpg

So just what is HIV? HIV, which is an acronym for *human immunodeficiency virus,* is a virus that damages the human immune system. When the immune system is compromised, the body is left in a weakened state and the individual becomes susceptible to opportunistic infections and tumors. How one acquires the disease is related to direct contact with a mucous membrane or the bloodstream or a body fluid that contains HIV. Body fluids that can contain HIV include: blood, semen, vaginal fluid, preseminal fluid, and during birth or from the breast milk of an infected mother.

AIDS or *acquired immunodeficiency syndrome* is the most advanced stage of HIV infection. Treated primarily through a drug regimen, the annual costs of treatment in 1998 were $18,300, and of this, 55 percent was for medication, 15 percent for outpatient services, and the remaining 30 percent for hospitalization (U.S.

Did You Know...In the United States,
  Every 13 minutes: Someone is infected with HIV.
  Every 13 minutes: Someone is diagnosed with AIDS.
  Every 34 minutes: Someone dies from AIDS.

Department of Health and Human Services, 2003). The federal government's primary legislation that focuses resources and funding on HIV/AIDS is the Ryan White Care Act, which was first enacted in 1990. HIV and AIDS cases can cut across all gender, racial, and ethnic boundaries. In 2000, less than 40 percent of the cases were related to men having sex with men (U.S. Department of Health and Human Services, 2003).

People with HIV/AIDS are vulnerable to economic threats as well. For example, in 2000, 63 percent of people in care were unemployed; 72 percent had annual household incomes of less than $25,000, and 46 percent had incomes of less than $10,000; only 32 percent had private health insurance; and 20 percent had no insurance at all, either public or private.

From a social work perspective, we recognize that HIV and AIDS is a life-threatening disease and that the worldwide medical community continues to search for a cure. In our practice we must ensure that the client with HIV/AIDS follows a strict medical regimen. As a mandatory reporter, it is crucial for all social workers to research the particular laws related to reporting and testing in his or her state. Some states allow for anonymous testing that is not name based. In this type of testing no one but the person taking the test will know that he or she tests positive. Other states utilize confidential testing sites where the name is recorded but kept confidential unless policies state otherwise. Many times in these situations the reporting of all confidential HIV tests may be released to the state health department or when a specific agency includes test results as part of the patient's medical record (NASW, 2008). As a social worker, be sure you contact your health department and verify what are the latest laws pertaining to mandatory reporting of infectious diseases such as AIDS/HIV, especially if someone who is infected is acting in a way that could put a partner or loved one at risk.

WHY DO IT?

By now you may be wondering why anyone would want to work in the changing, often unsettling, health care system. This is a fair question, so let's try to find an answer.

Social workers are among the many allied health professional groups that make up the health care "army." Given the interdisciplinary nature of today's work, it is incumbent for the social work profession to promote a clear understanding of its purpose and role in order to maintain a place in health care delivery. What we bring to the health care arena is vital. History shows this. Nevertheless, we must always define our role and be players in this process. Social workers cannot afford to let others decide what we can do with and on behalf of clients and their families. The roots of health care social work, as part of the social work profession, lie in serving the poor and disenfranchised. As the medical arena has changed over the years so too has the role of the health care social worker.

And now, as the social environment changes, expectations for health care are becoming clouded. Is health care a right or a privilege? Should the government guarantee a minimum standard of health care for all people? Who would establish such a standard? What role should the insurance industry have in such deliberations? Should we develop a "patient's bill of rights" as a new initiative? (FYI: In New York City taxicabs you will find a "rider's bill of rights." Interesting that taxicab riders are provided certain guarantees but not people in the health care system!) While the public debates these issues, the day-to-day work of the social worker in health care is daunting. Flexibility is a prerequisite for helping our clients and for adjusting to the constantly renegotiated health care environment.

All health care social workers—whether in the role of clinical practitioner, supervisor, or administrator—face the challenge of understanding and anticipating health care trends. Social workers need to know how society operates as well as having an appreciation for the causes of diseases and an understanding of psychological processes (Rosenberg, 2008). Each worker's skills must therefore be current, flexible to change, and proactive with clients. And yes, all health care social workers must also understand macroeconomics, and its influence on health care delivery. The current economic environment is characterized by a shifting tension between quality of care and cost containment. While the goal of the social work profession is to provide high-quality care, these services are shadowed and ultimately influenced by cost containment strategies. Health care social workers are expected to include cost containment among their practice principles whether they serve as direct practitioners, professional supervisors, administrators, or community organizers (Caper, 1995; Dziegielewski, 2004).

The viability of health care social work rests on two points. First, medical settings must place greater emphasis on the macroperspective in health care. Policy and practice are clearly linked (Miller, 2008). The social work profession must work actively to help the larger community understand its responsibility to create a cradle-to-grave health care system. Believing that the health care system will eventually solve its own problems is ludicrous. Health care social workers, whatever roles they choose for practice delivery, must take the lead in developing a more humane health care system that meets the needs of all people, regardless of their financial capabilities.

The second point that must be ingrained into all areas of health care social work practice is that advocacy leads to client empowerment. Health care social workers must change the mindset that managed care and the policies dictated by it are all bad. Social workers must recognize that there are benefits in a managed care system for both clients and providers. The strengths of managed care include enhanced and accountable mental health treatment; more positive client outcomes through concentration on specific goals and objectives in therapeutic treatment; time limits that can force emphasis on identifying external and environmental supports to allow continued therapeutic gains; avoidance of long-term therapy, with resulting decreases in long-term medication supplementation; and reduced health care costs for American businesses, which can only benefit the larger society (Browning & Browning, 1996).

We must recognize, however, that managed care also has many pitfalls. Health care social workers are therefore needed to advocate for clients. Workers must always stress development of new and needed services within the managed care framework. They must also teach clients how to obtain needed resources and help them to do so. On a larger scale, social workers are required—by our Code of Ethics—to advocate changes in policies or procedures that will directly or indirectly benefit clients.

Working as a health care social worker is far from easy. If you decide, nonetheless, that it's the area for you, the question is: How do you best respond to the challenge? You will often be tempted to switch areas and collect a paycheck in a less volatile setting. Health care social work is suited to people who will relish the changing environment, want to maximize resources for clients, look to serve on boards and committees to influence policy and practice, and enjoy the idea that every day will be different. If that's you, the health care setting is worth considering.

SUMMARY

Health care social work is a dynamic, exciting, constantly changing field of practice. The past ten years have brought things never seen before. Experienced social workers are forced to address specific issues in an environment where the "rules" are evolving. Health care social work's history is an extensive one, deeply rooted in the activities of pioneers such as Ida Cannon and Richard Cabot. These early practitioners directly linked social work practice to the medical model considered the core of health care practice.

Today health care social workers continue to strive to restore the highest level of functioning for each client, family, small group, and community served. Health care social work remains central in building the profession. Starting long ago, to this day health care social work remains an important and vital force both in the profession and in communities across the country and around the world. People with medical illnesses often have other related problems and may need help reestablishing their routines once they arrive home from the hospital, or they may have trouble paying their bills. Families who lose a loved one may need counseling to process their grief, and those with hereditary conditions may need help sorting through their fears and concerns about the future. Health care social workers use a wide range of skills in all of these settings, employing both a family- and a systems-oriented approach to psychosocial care. They provide counseling, help families develop strengths and resources, and run programs for patients who have diseases such as AIDS and heart disease. The settings these workers occupy vary from acute short-term settings to extended care long-term settings. Regardless of the type of clientele served, or the area of practice, health care social work is a challenging and essential area of practice.

Today's health care system is imbued with knowledge, expertise, equipment, and technologies never before even dreamed of or thought possible. Within our lifetime we have seen transplants go from headline news to no news; diseases have been eradicated; life expectancy has dramatically increased. Yet we all know the health care system is challenged. Costs have risen, and continue to rise, to levels that require health insurance to help make care affordable. Even so, more than 40 million people are without health insurance. Scores of individuals and families are often forced to weigh the importance of simple decisions such as, "Do I put food on the table tonight or buy the prescription for my child?"

Let's for a moment consider what the health care system might be like—reflecting on Ida Maude Cannon's ideals and see how they would translate to a health care system at the outset of the twenty-first century. One way to consider "what might be" is to identify core principles that you feel are central to your organization's purpose. These principles are jelled together without bias or consideration of who is favored or not favored, and we need to begin to think about what is in the best interest of the whole. Some areas for future thought include:

1. Health care needs to be affordable to individuals and families, businesses, and taxpayers, and financial barriers to needed care need to be removed.

2. Health care needs to be as cost efficient as possible, spending the maximum amount of dollars on direct patient care.

3. Health care needs to provide comprehensive benefits, including benefits for mental health and long-term care services.

4. Health care needs to promote prevention and early intervention.

5. Health care provisions and services need to eliminate disparities in access to quality health care.

6. Health care needs to address the needs of people with special health care requirements, particularly for those within underserved populations in both rural and urban areas.

7. Health care needs to promote quality and better health outcomes.

8. Health care services need to be inclusive by having adequate numbers of qualified health care caregivers, practitioners, and providers to guarantee timely access to quality care.

9. Health care needs to provide adequate and timely payments in order to guarantee access to providers.

10. Health care services need to be comprehensive, fostering a strong network of health care facilities, including safety net providers.

11. Health care services need to maximize consumer choice in terms of health care providers and practitioners.

12. Health care services need to ensure continuity of coverage and care.

Chapter 10

Mental Health

SOCIAL WORKERS ARE THE NATION'S LARGEST PROVIDERS OF MENtal health services. In the United States in 2006 it is estimated that there were 166,000 psychologists, 100,000 mental health counselors, 25,000 marriage and family therapists, and approximately 595,000 social workers (U.S. Department of Labor, 2008). If simply for no other reason, social workers clearly outnumber the other counseling disciplines working in the field of mental health. According to the Occupational Outlook Handbook, 2008–2009 edition, there are now 595,000 social workers as of 2006. Of these positions five out of 10 social work jobs are in the area of health care with approximately 122,000 in the area of mental health and substance abuse and another 124,000 in the area of medical and public health. Furthermore, social workers in the area of mental health and substance abuse are expected to grow 30 percent which is an accelerated pace over the 2006–2016 time frame. It is clear that health and mental health are two areas in the field that are expected to grow. In mental health practice social workers are essential service providers helping individuals meet their daily needs. Services provided include treating individuals with mental illness and other mental health and substance abuse–related problems. Social workers in the area of substance abuse treat many individuals suffering from abuse of alcohol, tobacco, and numerous other legal and illegal substances. Social workers practicing in this area engage in numerous services and functions, including mental health counseling in community mental health centers, private practice, psychiatric hospitals and psychiatric units, long-term care facilities, mental health courts and prisons; case management; discharge planning, intake or admission evaluation; high social risk case finding; patient education, support, and advocacy; crisis intervention; and interdisciplinary collaboration (Dziegielewski, 2004). Assessment and diagnostic services are considered an essential part of social work education and practice (Munson, 2009; Williams, 2009). Services are provided to all clients and their families, and all the major psychiatric disorders are addressed, including schizophrenia, affective and mood disorders such as depression, neuropsychiatric disorders, eating disorders, personality disorders, phobias, substance abuse, childhood disorders, and organic psychoses (Dziegielewski, 2002; Munson, 2009).

The mental health social worker has either a baccalaureate or a master's degree from an accredited school of social work. Social work in general is not a highly paid profession, but of all the practice areas, those who work in the hospital setting seem to fare the best. For example, 2004 U.S. Department of Labor

Name: Carole Zugazaga

Place of Residence: Auburn, Alabama

College/University Degrees: PhD, University of Central Florida; MSW, University of Central Florida; BSW, Florida State University

Present Position and Title: Associate Professor, College of Liberal Arts Engaged Scholar, Department of Sociology, Anthropology & Social Work, Auburn University, Auburn, Alabama

Previous Work/Volunteer Experience: Social Worker at Orlando Regional Medical Systems, Emergency Department Social Worker at Orlando Regional Medical Center, Sand Lake Hospital, and Arnold Palmer Hospital for Women and Children, Medical Social Worker; Director of Social Services and Admissions, Orlando Care Center; and Director of Social Services, Liberty Intermediate Care Center for the Mentally Retarded.

Why did you choose social work as a career? I chose social work as a career because I wanted to help people in a very practical, tangible way. I wanted to be able to help people in the "here and now" to obtain resources and support, and to problem solve and clarify options. Most importantly, I wanted to convey to my clients, one person at a time, that they were valued, worthy, and had something to contribute to their families, their community, and to society.

What is your favorite social work story? One of my favorite social work stories is about the homeless family I met while the wife was a patient in the hospital. The wife was thirty weeks pregnant and due to pregnancy complications she was required to spend the remainder of her pregnancy in the hospital. The family had recently experienced a series of setbacks and the patient, her husband, and their three-year-old child had been living in their car for the previous six weeks. The husband was employed full time but did not earn enough money to adequately provide for his family's needs. I was consulted to help the family arrange care for the child while Mom was in the hospital.

I walked into the patient's room, pulled up a chair, sat down and spent some time getting to know the family. Together we brainstormed and identified possible options for the child during the time Mom was hospitalized and unable to provide full-time care. The couple gradually took control of the situation and, with a little help from me, was able to make successful arrangements for their child. Later that evening as I left work for the day, I ran into the father in the parking lot. He came up to me and with tears in his eyes told me that he and his wife both wanted to thank me for treating them with dignity and respect. He said that I was the first person in the entire hospital who made eye contact with them and did not look down upon them because of their lack of housing and financial resources. This family helped me to understand the significance of treating people with dignity and respect—no matter what their situation—and how something so basic could have such a significant impact. Being treated respectfully helped the couple to feel better about themselves (to feel that they were worthy of our care) and to understand that while their *situa-*

tion may be devastating, it was temporary and that it had nothing to do with who they were as parents, as a family, and as citizens of society,

What is one thing you would change in the community if you had the power to do so?
The one thing I would change would be that everyone would have a home. In a country as rich and powerful as ours, I find it shameful that we cannot find the resources and the will to provide a safe, clean place to live for *all* of our citizens. Before addressing secondary needs of the homeless such as substance abuse problems, unmanaged mental health conditions, and unemployment, individuals and families must first be provided stable, secure housing. After basic human needs such as food, shelter, health care, and clothing are met, then higher order needs may be more successfully addressed.

Statistics (2008) place median annual income for child, family, and school social workers at approximately $34,820, and medical social workers at $44,920, with median earnings for mental health and substance abuse social workers at $33,920. Lower salaries are noted for social workers in mental health, substance abuse, and mental retardation related residential facilities ($29,110). In 2006, the median income for social workers in mental health and substance abuse was slightly higher at $35,410, with the top ten percent of the category at $57,630. Unfortunately, the labor statistics do not break down income by degree; however, according to NASW, social workers at the BSW level who work in mental health earned about $20,000 to $30,000 a year (NASW, 1998); those with MSWs earned a salary of approximately $41,290 to $45,660 in 1999 (Linsley, 2003).

Did You Know...Massachusetts General Hospital in Boston pioneered hospital and psychiatric social work, starting a social service department in 1905, and hiring social workers to work with patients who suffered from mental illness in 1907 (NASW, 1998).

When a social worker employed in a local mental health clinic outside of Orlando, Florida, was asked how she felt about her job, she said she could describe it best as "challenging, rewarding, and most of the time quite frustrating." She believed that the role of the mental health social worker is complicated because allegiances must be divided, and always placing the needs of the client first forced her to maintain a delicate balance between the needs of the family, the society, and the agency. Clients who are mentally impaired often cannot handle their own affairs, making it essential for the social worker to ensure that the client's rights in terms of respect for individual dignity, worth, and self-determination are not violated, thereby finding a balance between autonomy while minimizing risk (Scheyett, Kim, Swanson, Swartz, et al., 2009).

The mental health social worker must also be well aware of "duty to warn." If a client is perceived as a "danger to self or others," action is taken to protect any person or persons who may be at risk (Fox, 2009). "Duty to warn" may force a social worker to violate the confidence of the client in order to protect others in the immediate environment or, if threatening suicide, to protect the client. Therefore, mental health social work practitioners must always strive for balance between the *rights* of the client and the needs of the client and her family. Social workers must be advocates for clients who are mentally impaired; these clients will often be provided services through facilitation and referral especially when they are not capable of representing themselves.

Many beginning social work professionals are attracted to the area of mental health because they aspire to do therapy with the clients they serve. NASW (1990) described the essential components of psychosocial psychiatric services as 1) the completion of timely psychosocial screenings, 2) timely psychosocial assessments, 3) comprehensive psychosocial assessments, 4) timely contacts with family and significant others, 5) teamwork on interdisciplinary or multidisciplinary teams. These highlight how important it is for the social work professional to understand diagnosis and assessment, particularly because most social workers serve as advocates, facilitating and ensuring as part of the interdisciplinary team that the client gets the services needed.

In this chapter we introduce the role of social worker in mental health. In particular, we introduce the completion of a multidimensional psychosocial assessment that allows the social worker to gather information needed to understand the client and her environment. In closing we examine several potential areas of practice for the social worker interested in working in the area of mental health.

MULTIDIMENSIONAL PSYCHOSOCIAL ASSESSMENT

In the area of mental health the profession of social work did not develop in isolation. In order to survive and compete in the mental health practice environment many social workers have adapted to the dominant culture. This means that the practice approaches and methodologies employed by social workers at all levels meet the same expectations as other mental health professionals address. These expectations generally relate to reimbursement for service. For example, outcome measures, which dictate service reimbursement, have become mandatory (Dziegielewski, 2004); and, the more client-focused these measures can become the better (Pike, 2009). Moreover, it is not uncommon for social workers to feel forced to reduce services to some clients, focusing their efforts instead on those covered by insurance or able to pay privately. For those who cannot pay, services may be terminated if they seem too costly (Dziegielewski & Holliman, 2001; Ethics Meet Managed Care, 1997). Accurate psychosocial assessment is therefore a critical tool for all mental health and health care social workers because it documents a client's needs and can support the efficiency of a chosen intervention. Such assessments not only open the door for services, they also determine who will receive them and what will be provided.

Currently, many social workers work with clients who suffer from mental illness, from the BSW-level practitioner who is active in case management, initial assessment, and discharge planning to the master's-level social worker who is an active participant in completing assessments and diagnoses. Whatever his level of practice, a social worker must be aware of the tools and expectations characteristic of the field. The importance of the initial psychosocial assessment should not be underestimated; it provides the foundation and the framework for any future intervention.

Box 1: Mental Illness Can Strike Anyone and the Consequences Can Be Devastating: A True Case Story

Fort Worth—Jane fell so far so fast. A woman of education with a soft spot for the underdog, Jane combined a master's degree in social work with a compassion for the homeless that propelled her into Austin's power circles. She drove an expensive car, lived a full life, and was devoted to a loving family.

And she lost it all as a victim of mental illness.

The petite, blue-eyed blonde who once turned heads was beaten to death Saturday, left alone on a dirty sidewalk among those she once helped. At age 43, she died penniless and homeless, all her worldly goods in two plastic grocery bags.

For those who knew Jane, the tragic end was no surprise. Jane suffered from bipolar and personality disorders that left her without a family, unable to work, and on the street. "It is sad to say, but we feared something like this would happen," said her friend for 12 years. "She was so out of control, and no matter how hard we tried to help, she wouldn't take it."

Early Saturday, Jane was found slumped over in front of Mental Health–Mental Retardation Services day resource building. An autopsy showed she died from blunt force injuries to her head. Her killer remains a mystery, and there are no new leads in the case. Witnesses told police they saw Jane talking to an unidentified man about an hour before she was found dead, said the homicide detective.

A composite of the man has been posted on fliers and tacked up around the shelters and known hangouts for local indigents. "He could be a witness or a suspect, and right now we just want him for questioning."

Jane's daughter said the fact that her mother wouldn't accept help from loved ones adds to her sadness. "A lot of people ask me, 'Why didn't you help? Why didn't you do anything?' Well, what they don't know is that it is harder than that," her daughter said.

Jane's former social work professor, who taught and served as a mentor, said Jane is proof that mental illness can tear apart lives. "I don't think the general public knows just how vicious mental illness is. It can destroy you. . . . It destroyed her to the end."

Her daughter stated that most of her family hadn't seen Jane for two years. Her mother had avoided seeing loved ones but managed to keep in touch through phone calls and letters. She described her mother as someone who had inner and outer beauty, a person with a great sense of humor who was articulate and who made sure the family went to church. "During the summer she used to make me volunteer. She was just that way. She really cared about others. But the mental illness tore our relationship apart," her daughter said.

"I had a real good conversation with her, a week ago," her daughter continued. "It was the best we had in a long time. I was beaming for days afterward. . . . I think, since it was the last time we talked that it was a gift from God."

News about Jane's slaying unnerved the night shelter residents, who expressed fear that the killer might be among them.

"Women who are street-wise know how to protect themselves," said the executive director of the shelter. "Unfortunately, Jane didn't. Jane did not fit the stereotypes of a homeless person. She was educated and not addicted to drugs or alcohol. But the mental illness left her destitute. Jane didn't say anything to anybody. She kept to herself and roamed all over the city. I was really crushed when I heard what happened to her. She didn't deserve this."

"About 60 percent of the homeless in this country suffer from some form of mental illness, and about 40 percent have a substance abuse problem," said the chief of mental health and addiction services. Jane was first diagnosed with depression when she was about 18, relatives and friends said. She was in and out of treatment facilities much of her life, beating the illness long enough to fall in love, get married, and raise a family.

At some point, Jane, who was adopted, sought out her birth mother. The reunion proved devastating when her mother rejected her, friends said. The illness resurfaced and her marriage failed. She divorced her husband and lost custody of her daughter.

She remarried and enrolled in college while in her 30s. Her friend remembered the days when they went to the state capitol to lobby for welfare reform and how easily Jane fit into the social work community and the jobs that followed.

But Jane left the work she loved in 1993, when she learned she was pregnant with her second child. After the birth, manic depression took its toll, relatives and friends said. The marriage failed and her second husband took custody of her son, who is now 4.

Those close to her said those events may have triggered her depression and mood swings. And by the spring of 1996, Jane found comfort living on the streets, traveling between Fort Worth, Las Vegas, and San Diego.

Her friend tracked her down at a psychiatric facility in Fort Worth and found Jane staring blankly at daytime television through a fog of medication. She said, "Hi, what are you doing here?" And I said, "To see you. What are you doing here?" And she said, "Well, this is where I belong." This memory left her friend feeling helpless and frustrated.

"Jane used to work hard to help people who had fallen through the cracks and were unemployed or near homeless," her friend said. "She was a good person who took everything to heart. . . . To me, this is proof that if it can happen to Jane, it can happen to the rest of us." (Modified from Craig, 1998; names were either deleted or changed and text was abridged.)

Assessment is defined as "the process of determining the nature, cause, progression and prognosis of a problem and the personalities and situations involved therein; the social work function of acquiring an understanding of a problem, what causes it, and what can be changed to minimize or resolve it" (Barker, 2003, p. 30). Social workers assume that assessment is a key component to the start of any intervention and always begins with the first client-worker interaction (Austrian,

2009). The information that the social worker obtains determines the requirements and direction of the helping process. The mental health social worker gathers information about the present situation, elicits history about the past, and anticipates service expectations for the future. This assessment should always include creative interpretations of alternatives to best assist the client to get the services needed (Dziegielewski, 2002).

In mental health assessment, as in all social work assessments, the client is regarded as the primary source of data. In most cases, the client is questioned directly, either verbally or in writing. Information about the client is also derived from direct observation of verbal and physical behavior and interaction patterns between the client and other interdisciplinary team members, family members, significant others, or friends. Viewing and recording these patterns of communication can be extremely helpful in later identifying and developing strength and resource considerations (see figure 1). In addition, background sheets, psychological tests, and tests to measure health status or level of duty functioning may be used.

Furthermore, in keeping with social work's traditional emphasis on including information about other areas, the worker talks with family members and significant others to estimate planning support and assistance. It might also be important to access secondary sources such as the client's medical record and other health care providers.

Figure 1: This woman was previously hospitalized for schizophrenia. With family support she was able to live outside of an institution, enjoy her grandniece, and live a fuller life.

To facilitate assessment, the social worker must be able to understand the client's medical situation or at least know where to go for information and help. Knowledge of certain mental health conditions, as well as common accompanying medical conditions, can help the social worker to understand the breadth of what is affecting the client's behavior. Referrals for a complete medical checkup should always be considered (Dziegielewski, 2002). All social workers should not hesitate to ask for clarification of medical problems and the complications they can present in regard to a client's care, especially when unsure about how the information may enhance your understanding of the client's situation.

Five expectations guide the start of the assessment process in the health and mental health setting (Dziegielewski, 2004).

1. Clients must be active and motivated in the treatment process: As in almost all forms of intervention, the client is expected to be active. The client must often expend serious energy in attempting to make behavioral changes. Clients therefore must not only agree to participate in the assessment process but must be willing to embark on the intervention plan that will produce behavioral change. Social workers usually practice verbal therapy; however, clients who are unmotivated or unwilling to talk or discuss change strategies may require more concrete goals and objectives to bring about specific behavior change.

2. The problem must guide the approach or method of intervention used: Social workers need to be aware of different methods and approaches to practice. It is crucial to make sure that the approach favored by the social worker is not what guides the intervention that follows. The approach that best addresses the client's circumstance should be what guides the choice of the intervention. Sheafor, Horejsi, and Horejsi (1997) also warned about the opposite extremes, however: social workers becoming overinvolved and wasting valuable time in trying to match a particular problem to a particular theoretical model or approach. Health and mental health social workers must never lose sight of the ultimate purpose of the assessment process, that is, to complete an assessment that helps to establish a concrete service plan that addresses the client's needs.

Activity...Review the definition of assessment, and look at the reasons given for social workers to participate in this function. Discuss these issues with your classmates and decide where you believe it is essential for social workers in health care and mental health to participate in assessment. Explain both what you see as reason for participation and what you see as problems that might be caused by taking this active stance as a member of an interdisciplinary team.

3. The influence of values and beliefs needs to be made apparent in the process: Each one of us, professional or not, is influenced by her own values and beliefs. These beliefs are the foundation of who we are. In the professional practice of social work, however, it is essential that these personal beliefs and values do not affect the assessment and subsequent intervention process. This makes it essential for the social worker to clearly identify from the onset of treatment his or her personal values, beliefs, and practices and to be aware of how these beliefs can influence prac-

tice strategy. Professional helping strategy should never be led by personal assumptions or beliefs. For example, what if an unmarried client in a psychiatric hospital has tested positive for pregnancy? The social worker assigned to her case personally believes that abortion is wrong. She also realizes that this client probably does not have the capability to be a parent. The social worker feels so strongly about this belief that she cannot in good conscience or objectively discuss abortion as an option. Yet, the client is unsure about what to do although she realizes she cannot stop taking her medications and this will put the baby at risk. She also feels she would not be a good parent and states she knows this because she cannot take care of herself without help. She asks the social worker what she can do and what her options are. For the social work professional this can be a difficult case, but the ultimate assessment and intervention strategy must be based on the client's needs and desires, not the social worker's. Therefore, guided by the profession's Code of Ethics, the social worker does not tell the client of her personal feelings and refers her to someone who can be more objective in exploring all potential courses of action including abortion.

Most social work professionals agree that clients have the right to make their own decisions. Clients exercise this right especially when they are aware of their situation and want to participate in their own individualized health care plans. Whatever their own feelings, social workers must do everything possible to ensure this right and to keep their personal opinions from impairing a proper assessment.

In addition, the beliefs and values of the members of the interdisciplinary team must be considered. Social workers need to recognize value conflicts that arise among the other team members and make team members aware of how their personal feelings and opinions might keep them from exploring all possible options for a client. This is not to suggest that social workers are more qualified to address this issue or that they always have an answer; it means that social workers should strive to assist these professionals and should always keep before the team the goal, which is how to best serve the client in a nonjudgmental way. Furthermore, social work has a very comprehensive code of ethics, and at times this may be different or have a different emphasis from other professionals on the team. Good sound ethical decision making is expected, and educating other professionals about ethical conduct in social work may be warranted (Strom-Gottfried, 2008).

4. Issues of culture and race should be addressed openly in the assessment and treatment: The understanding of racial identity and the effect it can have on psychological well-being should not be underestimated (Woods & Kurtz-Cotes, 2007). In addition, social workers need to be aware of their own cultural heritage as well as the client's to create the most open and receptive environment possible. Dziegielewski (1997) suggested that the social work professional:

1. Be aware of her cultural limitations
2. Be open to cultural differences
3. Recognize the integrity and the uniqueness of the client
4. Use the client's learning style, including his own resources and supports
5. Implement a behavior biopsychosocial approach to practice within an integrated, nonjudgmental format (Austrian, 2009).

Did You Know...The fourth edition of the Diagnostic and Statistical Manual of Mental Disorders (DSM-IV), *the major reference for the diagnosis of mental disorders and related mental health conditions, stresses that cultural factors must be considered before establishing a diagnosis. DSM-IV emphasizes that delusions and hallucinations may be difficult to separate from general beliefs or practices related to a client's culture or lifestyle. Social workers do not take behavior arising from a client's cultural beliefs, however "socially inappropriate" it may seem, as evidence of mental disorder. To help professionals deal with the cultural aspects of mental health, an entire appendix of the DSM-IV-TR describes and defines culturally bound syndromes that might affect the diagnosis and assessment process (American Psychiatric Association, 2000). All social workers must know how cultural and ethnic factors can affect assessment.*

5. Assessment must focus on client strengths and highlight the client's own resources: Clients have enormous difficulty identifying and planning to use their own strengths. People in general tend to focus on the negative and rarely praise themselves for the good they do. Also, to admit someone has a mental health problem may also carry stigma the client may not want to accept. In addition, this stigma may be carried over to family and friends, referred to as "courtesy stigma," and this in itself may disturb the supportive helping networks the client needs (Rosenzweig & Brennan, 2008).

To empower the client use of a **strengths-based assessment** is considered critical (Morales & Sheafor, 2006). For so many clients, especially those with mental health problems, their judgments of the world around them as well as what they think of themselves can become clouded. An all-or-nothing approach may result in them feeling lost, alone, and ineffective in what they have done or tried to do. Therefore, it is the role of the social worker to assist the client in identifying positive behaviors and accomplishments. Some social workers also feel strongly about the importance of teaching life skills and how expanding upon this area can increase psychosocial functioning (Reddon, Hoglin, & Woodman, 2008).

In today's high-pressure health and mental health environments, social workers cannot spend time exploring issues and the related behaviors that don't contribute to the client's well-being. They must quickly utilize a strengths-based assessment by helping the client to identify her own strengths thereby maximizing skill-building potential. Most treatment is time-limited these days, so individual resources are essential for continued growth and maintenance of wellness after the formal treatment period has ended. Although there are many different time-limited approaches to practice, most social workers agree that their first task is to clearly identify the client's strengths to use them as part of the treatment planning process. Focusing on a client's strengths helps to empower the client to make changes in her life.

Person-in-Environment: A Systematic Approach to Assessment

In mental health practice today many forms of formal assessment can assist in the development of a treatment plan. One system of assessment that has recently gained favor with social workers is the **Person-in-Environment Classification Sys-**

Figure 2: Members of the Berrien County Association of Retarded Citizens (ARC) gather for a photo after a Fourth of July field trip with a social worker to a town on Lake Michigan. These citizens live either in group homes or with families.

tem, also known as "the PIE." Designed primarily for advanced MSW-level practice, the PIE was underwritten by an award given to the California chapter of NASW from the NASW Program Advancement Fund (Whiting, 1996). Knowledge of the PIE is relevant for all mental health social workers regardless of educational level because of its emphasis on situational factors (Karls & O'Keefe, 2008; 2009).

In the PIE the process of assessment is built around two major premises that are basic to all social work practice: recognition of social considerations and the person-in-situation stance. The PIE responds to the need to identify the problems of clients in a context that mental health and health professionals can easily understand (Karls & Wandrei, 1996a, 1996b):

> [It] calls first for a social work assessment that is translated into a description of coding of the client's problems in social functioning. Social functioning is the client's ability to accomplish the activities necessary for daily living (for example, obtaining food, shelter, and transportation) and to fulfill major social roles as required by the client's subculture or community (Karls & Wandrei, 1996a, p. vii).

The PIE provides the following:

- ◆ A common language with which social workers in all settings can describe their client's problems in social functioning
- ◆ A common capsule description of social phenomena that can facilitate treatment or ameliorate problems presented by clients
- ◆ A basis for gathering data to be used to measure the need for services and to design human service programs to evaluate effectiveness

---

Box 2: Tips on Information Recording and Documentation

Social workers must document their assessment plans clearly. Although it is beyond the scope of this book to discuss documentation techniques in detail, the following tips introduce the most important aspects of accurate and timely record keeping.

1. Always document justification for the "service necessity" of what you do.

2. Be sure to document clearly purpose, content, and outcome in every note you write—regardless of the type of note or reason for making the entry.

3. Always sign your name, credentials, and so forth, at the end of every note you write. Be sure to include the date and time the service was provided in every note. Don't forget to put in the record the amount of time spent with the client.

4. All those who review records for billing say that the biggest problems are lack of information and inaccurate information in the record.

5. Always document problem behaviors in terms of frequency, intensity, and duration.

6. Always be able to benchmark progress.

7. Use a black or blue pen (whose ink does not run), and never reproduce notes for others.

8. If you do not document it, it did not happen.

♦ A mechanism for clearer communication among social work practitioners and between practitioners, administrators, and researchers

♦ A basis for clarifying the domain of social work in human service fields (Karls & Wandrei, 1996a)

The PIE is an excellent tool for advanced social workers; beginning professionals are not ready nor will they be expected to use this complex assessment tool. As you progress through human behavior and practice courses you will become more familiar with this technique, its advantages, and its uses in mental health practice. It's enough now to observe that PIE provides an important vehicle to understanding the many factors that affect a client's behavior, which is an important part of the assessment process.

The PIE system is user friendly because it classifies clients' problems into four distinct categories, or "factors." For the purpose of this chapter we have presented an abbreviated version of this assessment system. This information is not meant to be all-inclusive; rather it is intended to help introduce beginning social work professionals to the knowledge base underlying the use of the PIE and to its relevance to formalized mental health assessment (Karls & O'Keefe, 2008).

DSM-IV-TR

Another important tool for social workers in the mental health arena that you should be aware of is the *Diagnostic and Statistical Manual of Mental Disorders* (DSM-IV-TR; American Psychiatric Association, 2000). The DSM is considered an advanced tool for social work practice. Its use is covered in graduate courses, and in some schools, entire courses are devoted to the study of the DSM. For a more detailed explanation of the DSM-IV-TR and its relation to the PIE in practice see Dziegielewski (2004) or Karls and O'Keefe (2008).

THE BEHAVIORAL BIOPSYCHOSOCIAL APPROACH TO SOCIAL WORK PRACTICE

Social work practice in assessment and intervention should recognize three factors: the *bio*medical, the *psycho*logical, and the *social* (Carlton, 1984; Dziegielewski, 2004). A social worker that understands the **biopsychosocial approach** to health and mental health practice strives to ascertain for each client the appropriate balance among biomedical, psychological, and social considerations (Austrian, 2009). Balance, however, doesn't mean that these factors are treated as equal for every client. The particular situation experienced by the client determines where emphasis must be placed and what area must be addressed first. In today's practice environment, with its insistence on an observable, measurable outcome, the mental health social worker addresses the biopsychosocial factors in the client's life through the *behavioral* aspects of the client's condition. One of the first aspects that needs to be addressed is completing a careful risk assessment. Since the most significant risk factors for suicide are suffering from a severe mental disorder or a mood disorder combined with substance abuse, this type of assessment should always come first (Yeager, Roberts, & Saveanu, 2009). This involves creating a culture of safety assessing the client as well as the physical environment. Yeager, Roberts, and Saveanu, (2009) stress that to assess for suicidality the social worker needs to identify psychiatric signs and symptoms, as well as past and current suicidal ideation, past attempts, and any current plans.

For example, if a client is newly assessed as having schizophrenia while also being HIV positive, many issues must be addressed. At first the emphasis may be placed on the biomedical or biological area. The client needs immediately to be told that the medical test for HIV is positive and to be given information about what a positive test means. The task can be complicated by the client's mental condition. The schizophrenia may produce periodic breaks from reality, such as hallucinations and delusions that keep him from accurately interpreting medical information. The client may have difficulty understanding how far the disease has progressed and what can be expected medically, for example. Nevertheless, every attempt must be made to help the client to understand the medical aspects of his condition and what being infected with this virus actually means. It is critical to ensure the client understands terms such as "t-cell count" and future self-protection from illness and opportunistic infectious diseases. While information such as this about the medical condition is shared, a constant vigil is needed relating to client safety with the assessment and reassessment for continued safety (Yeager, Roberts, & Saveanu, 2009).

Once the biomedical situation and support for what the client is experiencing emotionally are addressed, emphasis may shift to the social and psychological aspects of the client's condition. Since HIV is clearly communicable, the client

Activity...Here is a sample treatment plan for a client who is suicidal. Taking a behavioral biopsychosocial approach, what do you think of this plan? What are its strengths and its limitations for the client being served?

Sample Treatment Plan for Suicidal Ideation/Behavior

Definition: Suicide is a human act of self-inflicted, self-intentional cessation. Simply stated, it is the wish to be dead with the act that carries out the wish.
Suicide ideation: thinking about suicide. *Suicide verbalization*: talking about suicide.
Parasuicide: attempting suicide.

Signs and Symptoms to Note in the Record (be sure to document any of these signs in the record):
Changes in eating and sleeping; changes in friends and social programs.
Changes in grades, job status, or love relationships; changes in usual daily activities.
Constant restlessness or unshakable depression; neglected appearance or hygiene.
Increase in drug or alcohol use; giving away of material possessions.
Recurrent thoughts or preoccupation with death; recent suicide attempt.
Ongoing suicidal ideation and any previous or present plans; history of suicide attempts in the family.
Sudden change in mood that is not consistent with life events; past suicide attempts and what was done.
History of drug abuse.

Goals:
1. Stabilize suicidal crisis.
2. Place client at appropriate level of care to address suicidal crisis.
3. Reestablish a sense of hope to deal with the current life situations.
4. Alleviate suicidal impulses and intent and return to higher (safer) level of functioning.

Objective	Intervention	Time Frame*
Client will report no longer feeling the need to harm self.	Assess for suicidal ideation and concrete plan of execution. Then make appropriate disposition/referral.	
Client will discuss suicidal feelings and thoughts.	Assist client to develop awareness of negative self-talk patterns and encourage positive images and self-talk.	
Identify positives in current life situation.	Complete no-suicide contract. Address behaviors to complete when having suicidal thoughts or impulses.	
Help client to identify consistent eating and sleeping patterns.	Educate client in deep-breathing and relaxation techniques. Assist client in developing coping strategies.	
Take medications as prescribed and report any inconsistencies or side effects.	Monitor for medication use and misuse, and confer with treatment team on a regular basis.	
Complete assessments of functioning.	Arrange or complete administration of the test. Determine level of depression or suicide precaution. Assess and monitor suicide intervention.	

*Time frame is to be individualized to the client.

must realize quickly that his behavior could have significant effects on people in his support system. Early education about how the virus is transmitted can be critical. Since HIV is most often sexually transmitted, the client's past and present sexual partners must be considered. Himself or with help, the client must face telling loved ones about what has happened and what it will mean for future social relations.

Furthermore, the client may be frightened by the changes in his mental status and be unsure of how to control the symptoms related to schizophrenia. First, the client must understand what is happening. Second, the client must be helped to realize what schizophrenia means for him and for those he comes in contact with. Important information must be shared with family and friends. The social perspective of the biopsychosocial approach focuses on the individual client together with his family, significant others, and friends, on how best to protect them but also to involve them in problem solving. The psychological perspective focuses directly on the fears and concerns of the individual, on how to help him to understand his mental health and the emotions he exhibits.

As you can see, if a client is dual diagnosed helping can become very complicated. In our example, the dual diagnosis of HIV and schizophrenia means that the client may be losing touch with reality and how his behaviors can harm others at a time when this knowledge is especially important.

Once the immediate needs of the client and his family have been addressed and a risk assessment has been completed, the focus of intervention should shift to the functional/situational factors affecting the individual client. A functional assessment allows the social worker to determine the level at which the client is capable of responding to a concrete intervention-based plan.

It is essential that assessment and intervention be related to the needs and abilities of the client. The social worker begins with exploration where the unique aspects of the client are examined and organized (Austrian, 2009). A complete assessment is designed to help the client better understand himself, and the

---

Box 3: Biomedical or Biological Factors to Be Considered in Mental Health Assessment

Area	Explanation
General medical condition	Describe the physical illness or disability from which the client is suffering.
Overall health status	Client is to evaluate her self-reported health status and level of functional ability.
Overall level of functioning	Describe what the client is able to do to meet her daily needs. Concrete tasks are assessed and documented for focus on future change effort.
Maintenance of continued health and wellness	Measure the client's functional ability and interest in preventive medical intervention.

Box 4: Social Factors to Be Considered in Mental Health Assessment

Area	Explanation
Social/societal help-seeking behavior	Is the client open to outside help? Is the client willing to accept help from those outside her immediate family or the community?
Occupational participation	How does the client's illness or disability impair or prohibit functioning in the work environment? Is the client in a supportive work environment?
Social support system	Does the client have support from neighbors, friends, or community organizations (church membership, membership in professional clubs, etc.)?
Family support	What support or help can be expected from relatives of the client?
Support from significant other	Does the significant other understand and show willingness to help and support the needs of the client?
Ethnic or cultural affiliation	If the client is a member of a certain cultural or religious group, will affiliation affect medical treatment and compliance issues?

---

factors identified during the procedure are shared with the client to assist in self-help or continued skill building (Eamon, 2008). At first, the assessment process is used to examine the situation and initiate the helping process; later it contributes to an intervention plan.

MENTAL HEALTH AND WORKING WITH THE FAMILY IN ACUTE CARE SETTINGS

As early as 1903 at Massachusetts General Hospital, Dr. Richard C. Cabot realized the importance of addressing psychosocial factors in medical illness. From this early perspective the assigned duties of the medical social worker included focusing on the economic, emotional, social, and situational needs of patients and their families (Cabot, 1913). To accomplish the assigned tasks in the late 1800s and early 1900s, health care social workers were required to have adequate medical knowledge, an understanding of disease and factors that affected mental health, and a firm comprehension of public health. With the medical advances of the late 1950s the social worker was expected to bridge ". . . the gap between the hospital bed, the patient's home and the world of medical science" (Risley, 1961, p. 83).

In the area of health and mental health today the role of the social worker continues much along the same path, with extensive consideration being placed on

---

Box 5: Psychological Factors to Be Considered in Mental Health Assessment

Area	**Explanation**
Life stage	Describe the development stage in life at which the individual appears to be functioning.
Mental functioning	Describe the client's mental functioning. Complete a mental status measurement. Can the client participate knowledgeably in the intervention experience?
Cognitive functioning	Does the client have the ability to think and reason about what is happening to her? Is the client able to participate and make decisions in regard to her own best interest?
Level of self-awareness and self-help	Does the client understand what is happening to her? Is the client capable of assisting her level of self-care? Is the client capable of understanding the importance of health and wellness information? Is the client open to help and services provided by the health care team?

---

also meeting the needs of client and his or her family members. Although the family members are not the actual client being served, it is not uncommon for services to be provided to them that include education, supportive interventions, and referrals as well as reporting problematic social conditions, assisting and ensuring treatment compliance with the established medical regime, and providing linkages between the acute care setting and the appropriate community agencies. Often times it is the family that first recognizes the problem and seeks help for the client (Brennan, Evans, & Spencer, 2008). Other areas of service provision in these acute health care settings include case consultation, case finding, case planning, psychosocial assessment and intervention, case consultation, collaboration, treatment team planning, group therapy, supportive counseling, organ donation coordination, health education, advocacy, case management, discharge planning, information and referral, quality assurance, bereavement, and research (Dziegielewski, 2004; Holliman, 1998; Holliman, Dziegielewski, & Datta, 2001).

In this fast-paced environment, all health care professionals are being forced to deal with numerous issues that include declining hospital admissions, reduced lengths of hospital stay, and numerous other restrictions and methods of cost containment (Braus, 1996; Dziegielewski, 2002). Struggling to resolve these issues has become necessary based on the inception of prospective payment systems, managed care plans, and other changes in the provision and funding of health care (Lens, 2002; Ross, 1993; Simon, Showers, Blumenfield, Holden, & Wu, 1995). The concern for reducing expenditures in an environment that also

Name: Elizabeth Hosnedl

Place of residence: Sodus, Michigan

College/university degrees: Eastern Michigan University, BSW

Present position: Assistant to MSHDA Section 8 Housing Agent in Berrien County; Instructor for Basic and Advanced Drunken Driving Courses at the Berrien County Health Department

Previous work/volunteer experience: Home Health worker, SW for Area IV Agency on Aging, Program Coordinator and Director of ARC (Association for Retarded Citizens), Berrien County, Assessment Specialist for Shoreline Consultation assessing indigent and MA persons for drug and alcohol treatment. Volunteer at Benton Harbor Soup Kitchen and ARC Bowling League.

Why did you choose social work as a career? Actually, social work chose me! After a ten-year hiatus, I was working on finishing my English degree while working as an apartment manager. I was not really enthused about teaching, and didn't know what else I could do with an English degree, so I tried an introductory social work class. The types of work described and the different situations we discussed in that class were a very good fit to my personality, and I knew that was where I belonged. In the last seventeen years, I have been very fortunate to have worked with several different populations. I'm a very hands-on person, and social work gives me the opportunity to work one-on-one with clients in very practical ways that show immediate change.

What is your favorite social work story? One gentleman came in to Shoreline very reluctantly looking for treatment. He was forty-seven years old but looked seventy. He was forty pounds underweight, had no teeth, and had a broken jaw that could not be repaired, because they could not get him sober long enough to sedate him for surgery. His skin was waxy and yellow, and my co-workers and I thought he would be dead before he made it to treatment a week later.

Six months later, a good-looking man walked in the door, smiling and the picture of physical health. None of us recognized him, but it was the same man! Obviously, he had done the hard work, but I was in the right place at the right time to set him on the path.

What would be the one thing you would change in our community if you had the power to do so? If I could change one thing in Berrien County, it would be to give all levels of government from the city council on up to the governor the experience I have had with the recovery community. Drugs and alcohol have devastated large segments of this county, and it's only getting worse. In terms of man hours and money dedicated to programming, recovery is at the bottom of the list. It seems that the funders don't realize the multitude of problems they could solve if they would just work on reducing addiction.

requires maximizing scarce and dwindling resources continues to be prevalent (Yeager & Latimer, 2009). Yet, previous research has linked not receiving services to increased rates of high-risk patient relapse (Christ, Clarkin, & Hull, 1994; Lockery, Dunkle, Kart, & Coulton, 1994). Therefore, it should come as no surprise that some researchers question why so many people are dying because they simply do not receive preventive services in one of the most technology advanced countries in the world (Miller, 2008).

When a client is discharged from a facility, an important part of discharge planning is ensuring for the arrangement of an appropriate follow-up service plan for return to a lesser level of care. In the past, the role of the social worker was often expected to end once the client was discharged from the facility (Simon et al., 1995). Today, however, social workers are finding that these traditional roles have expanded to cover a broader function linking the client to other systems of care as well as developing specific care plans with a clear focus on continuity of care (Yeager & Latimer, 2009).

A significant issue to consider when dealing with mental health issues of the client is the psychological and social burden that is often placed on the client's family. This burden can in turn either lead to or exacerbate higher rates of mental health problems. From an environmental or situational (mezzo) perspective, the families of the client are left at increased risk for psychological disturbances. Mental illness and its chronic nature can strain family relationships at a time when clients may not realize they are becoming ill and in need of help (Marshall & Solomon, 2009). Often family members may have different expectations of what they perceive as their role in the inpatient and discharge process (Blumenfield & Epstein, 2001; Davidson, 1990). When dealing with the family of a mentally ill client, the role of the social worker needs to be flexible and diverse. Special challenges when working with families include finding treatment goals and objectives that are found to be effective for the identified client, while also of interest and importance to the members of the family (Jordan & Franklin, 2009). Helping to make all goals and objectives mutually negotiated for all is central because at times different expectations may lead to blurring and overlap of the services provided.

It is crucial for the social worker to examine the family member's sense of personal well-being, ability to self-care, or level of family and environmental support because many times these factors become essential to the discharge of the client. If these personal/social and environmental issues are not addressed, the mentally unstable client may be put at risk for harm. When a client is discharged home to a family that does not want him or her, the mentally ill client is more at risk of abuse and neglect. Family members can feel a situation is hopeless, placing them at greater risk for depression or even suicide.

The social worker must always recognize the importance of culture and environmental factors as paramount to efficient and effective practice. When cultural differences exist, they can clearly influence the therapeutic process (Duckworth, 2009). For example, depression that results in suicide can be viewed differently in some societies and by certain ethnic and racial groups. Culture as an important variable in suicide is modest at best, but understanding culture can help the clinician to gain a more robust assessment of suicidal reasoning and purpose (Leach, 2006). Another example of a situation wherein cultural and environmental factors play a part in patient care is when the family members of a sick infant object to a blood transfusion for religious reasons or when the family refuses life support because it is viewed as disturbing the natural life progression. The de-emphasis or denial of this consideration can result in the delivery of substandard care.

In today's environment of behavioral-based managed care, capitation, fee for service, and decreased number of hospital inpatient beds, health care social work continues to hold a place in the acute care hospital setting. According to Kadushin and Kulys (1994) and Dziegielewski (2004), the challenge for acute medical hospitals is to combine the humanitarian objective of practice with the hospitals' agenda for cost control and rationing of resources.

In addressing the mental health needs of family members the current focus on health and wellness and the decreased stigma associated with the treatment of mental health problems has clearly created and increased in-service requisition (Epstein & Aldredge, 2000; Lyons, Howard, O'Mahoney, & Lish, 1997; NASW, 1996).

Often family members need assistance and the acknowledgment and addressing of family problems can help to improve and maintain quality of life for the mentally ill client and his or her support system (Marshall & Solomon, 2009). The functions of the mental health social worker in this setting include psychosocial evaluations (assessment for the treatment plan), casework (counseling and supportive intervention), group work (education and self-help), information and referral, facilitation of community referrals, team planning and coordination, and client and family education, as well as advocacy for clients on their behalf within the setting or beyond that with local state and federal agencies (NASW, 1995). In addition, with the numerous service cutbacks and cost-effectiveness strategies, many social workers are now being required to expand their duties (Yeager & Latimer, 2009). Many are being asked to serve as financial counselors to ensure that the client and the service agency will receive adequate reimbursement for services needed. These services can involve assisting clients to apply for outside insurance carriers to cover additional services not directly covered under current policy.

Berkman (1996), Holliman (1998), and Dziegielewski (2004) all believe that social workers have essential skills and practice techniques that are needed in today's acute care mental health settings. The social worker remains integral in providing assistance with:

- ◆ treatment plans and compliance issues;
- ◆ assisting clients and families with discharge planning and referral;
- ◆ providing counseling and support for clients and significant others in the areas of health, wellness, mental health, bereavement, and so on;
- ◆ assisting clients and their families to make ethical and morally difficult decisions that can affect health and mental health;
- ◆ educating clients, their families, and significant others to psychosocial issues and adjusting to illness;

- assisting in resolving behavioral problems;
- assisting in identifying and obtaining entitlement benefits; securing non-medical benefits;
- assisting with risk management and quality assurance activities;
- advocating for enhanced and continued services to ensure continued client well-being.

DEINSTITUTIONALIZATION AND THE MENTALLY ILL IN THE CRIMINAL JUSTICE SYSTEM

The practice of deinstitutionalization, which resulted in the closing of many federal and state mental health facilities, has had devastating effects on the provision of mental health services, including those in the criminal justice system. More and more social workers interested in the area of mental health have begun to

---

Box 6: Functional/Situational Factors to Be Considered in Mental Health Assessment

Area	Explanation
Financial status	How does the health condition affect the financial status of the client? What income maintenance efforts are being made? Do any need to be initiated? Does the client have savings or resources to draw from?
Entitlements	Does the client have health, accident, disability, or life insurance benefits to cover her cost of health service? Has insurance been recorded and filed for the client to assist with paying of expenses? Does the client qualify for additional services to assist with illness and recovery?
Transportation	What transportation is available to the client? Does the client need assistance or arrangements to facilitate transportation?
Placement	Where will the client go after discharge? Is there a plan for continued maintenance when services are terminated? Is alternative placement needed?
Continuity of service	If the client is to be transferred to another health service, have the connections been made to link services and service providers appropriately? Based on the services provided has the client received the services she needs during and after the treatment period?

---

accept positions in this area. What is most concerning is that an alarming 16 percent of those in state prisons and local jails have been diagnosed as mentally ill (Ditton, 1999). Additionally, these individuals are 53 percent more likely to be incarcerated for a violent offense, and, according to year 2000 population statistics, this would equate to 296,176 incarcerated individuals with a diagnosed mental illness. Furthermore, extending this trend into the year 2002, incarcerated individuals could exceed 718,000 individuals suffering from a diagnosed mental illness. Beck and Maruschak (2001) also found a large incarcerated population with mental illnesses utilizing a survey that found that, in 1,394 of 1,558 U.S. adult correctional facilities, 1 in 8 state prisoners were receiving mental health services and 1 in 10 were provided with psychotropic medications. The majority of the facilities were able to provide psychiatric assessment (65 percent), therapy and/or counseling by trained mental health professionals (71 percent), and the distribution of psychotropic medications (73 percent).

For social workers, the greatest challenge yet to come is how to help these facilities to recognize and address the medical needs as well as mental health treatments needed for those diagnosed mentally ill. Furthermore, the problem can actually extend beyond the prisons, as what will happen to the mentally ill persons once they are released from jail or prison either through probation, parole, or their own recognizance? Prison systems designed purely to house rather than also treat mentally ill inmates will fall short when the mentally ill offender is finally released back into the community.

The implementation of deinstitutionalization provides a perfect example of how a political and economic proposal that is not thoroughly explored prior to implementation can have devastating effects on those caught in the system. Many professionals in the area firmly believe that deinstitutionalization has put tremendous pressure on families to care for their loved one as well as bear the stigma that they have done something wrong or, worse yet, were the cause of the problem (Olson, 2006). For some, the inability of the family and community to address the needs to these individuals has resulted in utilizing the prison system as a holding tank for those with serious mental disorders. From this perspective the prisons have become a replacement for the mental hospitals that have been closed (Butterfield, 1998). Furthermore, the mental health services that are provided within the prison system are limited because of the lack of public concern for rehabilitation with offenders. Regardless of the exact reason, the number of mentally ill offenders is growing in our prisons and jails and within the probation and parole system.

Moreover, this movement to close state mental health facilities and treat chronic offenders in the community has left many mentally ill homeless and without care (Grob, 1995). Additionally, individuals with mental illness may also be unfairly arrested and jailed because their behaviors present a danger or risk to those around them. This is further complicated by the fact that the most appropriate placements, such as mental health centers in the community, may be either unwilling or unable to help due to the chronically mentally ill's indigent status and subsequent inability to pay for services (Harrington, 1999). This problem requires the joining of law enforcement officers and mental health professionals.

To help address this issue, social workers have advocated for the development of case management services as a humane, effective, and efficient way to address the growing issue of the mentally ill offender in the community (Mechanic, 1998). Additionally, through assertive case management, and through collaboration between mental health providers and the criminal justice system, joint problem solving is encouraged. Social workers are taking a more active role in police departments as well as correctional facilities. In the police departments, social workers can assist with multiple types of crimes, assisting trauma victims, survivors, and family members (Knox & Roberts, 2009). Whether working in the police departments or other types of correctional facilities, this type of professional activity and coordination can lead to reduced hospital stays, improved living situations, and improved social relationships for the mentally ill offender (Calsyn, Morse, Klinkenberg, Trusty & Allen, 1998). Mechanic and McAlpine (1999) further support this stance by seeking more appropriate placement for the mentally ill through assertive case management with the presumption that this type of service could bring about beneficial results at a low cost (compared with the cost of incarceration) to the community.

Similar to problems occurring in the health care system, recidivism or the readmission of individuals within the penal justice system has presented a serious concern (Hiller & Knight, 1996). Hiller and Knight asserted that the rates of mental illness within the community-based setting were consistent with those of the rest of the correctional system, and that some offenders may be more at risk than others for re-arrest (especially those with comorbidity involving depression and substance abuse).

For mental health social workers in this area a partnership between criminal justice professionals and social workers is blossoming. This collaboration could result in early identification and treatment of the mentally ill, which ultimately lessens the burden on the criminal justice system (Conly, 1999; Harris & Koespell, 1998; Lovell & Rhodes, 1997). Without such a partnership, mentally ill offenders will continue to be rotated from mental health centers to jails in a cycle that causes further disease deterioration and increased criminality (Harrington, 1999). Jails are not trained to be mental hospitals, and the short period of incarceration compounds the problem because the mentally ill offender has no chance to stabilize or receive necessary treatment (McDonald & Teitelbaum, 1994). Therefore, planned efforts to achieve better community treatment would result in fewer costly hospital stays and less jail time for the mentally ill offender. With this in mind, mental health courts have become an emerging strategy designed to avoid placing the mental ill directly into the criminal justice system. These courts are based on the drug court model and seek to assist clients that suffer from severe mental illness (Hodges & Anderson, 2005).

Another important concept leading to this advocacy for service unification of the two disciplines revolves around societal cost, financial and otherwise. Spending for behavioral health care is falling behind other types of health care, and the quality of care is suffering (Mechanic & McAlpine, 1999). With deinstitutionalization, many of the mentally ill were diverted into substance abuse programs, which the federal government funded because the community programs were unprepared to handle the influx of patients (Grob, 1995). Those seriously mentally ill individuals who were not placed in residential treatment facilities were criminalized because the mental health providers were actively involved with treating societal coping skills (Harrington, 1999).

Yet this union of the disciplines will never succeed unless both disciplines acknowledge the importance and strongly advocate for collaboration and information sharing between the various professionals as well as the organizations involved in the process (Dawes, 1996). Since there is no single system or organization that can meet all of the conditions needed for optimal treatment of the mentally ill (Schnapp & Cannedy, 1998), sharing information is critical. Collaboration fosters more supportive and integrated planning as well as policy development and facilitation of the highest degree of complete and accurate information for decision making (Dawes, 1996).

SPECIAL CONSIDERATIONS: MENTAL HEALTH AND THE DUAL DIAGNOSIS

No matter what the population or field of practice in which social workers are employed, they are increasingly confronted with the dually diagnosed client. This means that clients can have more than one mental health problem and each must be equally addressed in the intervention process. In order for mental health social workers to work successfully with dually diagnosed clients, they must be cognizant of client problems, diagnostic assessments, clinical interventions, and current case studies. For example, clients with psychiatric and comorbid substance use disorders often exhibit extremely poor compliance for outpatient treatment (Booth, Cook, & Blow, 1992; Daley & Zuckoff, 1998; Matas et al., 1992). This leaves these individuals vulnerable to a variety of negative clinical ramifications, including problems with relapse and re-hospitalization that in turn could relate to higher service utilization and cost (Bartels et al., 1992, 1993; Clark, 1994; Cournos et al., 1991).

Although addressing the needs of a client with more than one mental health problem will be covered in more depth in your clinical courses, the client with a dual diagnosis can often be misdiagnosed and/or given inadequate treatment due to the limited time-frame allowed for inpatient care. Resources and at times intervention strategy is shaped and influenced by cost containment, with an emphasis placed on time-limited, outcome-oriented interventions (Dziegielewski, 2002; Moggi et al., 1999). In managed health care, adequate funding is rarely made available for treatment programs specializing in integrated treatment models.

Daley and Zuckoff (1998) highlight the following adverse effects that can transpire for noncompliant, dually diagnosed clients:

♦ Poorly compliant clients are more likely to experience clinical deterioration of their psychiatric condition, relapse to alcohol or other drug use, and return to the hospital as a result of severe depression, thoughts of suicide or homicide, mania, or psychotic decompensation.

♦ Missing outpatient appointments often leads to failure to renew medication prescriptions, which in turn contributes to exacerbations of psychiatric and substance use symptoms.

♦ Poor treatment compliance causes the loss of supportive relationships and contributes to frustration among family members and professionals, who find themselves watching helplessly as the client deteriorates.

♦ Due to increased risk of hospitalization, poor outpatient compliance leads to increased costs of care as a result of more days spent in expensive inpatient treatment facilities.

A clear assessment on the impact of trauma and other life events that could affect the performance of the mentally ill individual needs to be conducted. It is important to assess for conditions that could make the current situation worse, such as sexual abuse, medical emergencies, car accidents, overdoses from prescribed medications or illegal drugs, and other events and sudden losses that could complicate the mental health condition (O'Hare & Sherrer, 2009).

Mental health social workers must be educated and trained in the treatment of clients who suffer from more than one mental health problem and/or condition. For the dually diagnosed client, treating one condition without recognition of the co-morbid or contributing factors is not considered acceptable.

SUMMARY

Whatever we call them, diagnosis, assessment, or the diagnostic assessment, the psychosocial assessments performed by mental health and health care social workers are essential (Dziegielewski, 2002). Assessment is the critical first step in formulating a plan for intervention. It thus sets the tone and framework for the entire mental health social work process. In order to compete in today's mental health environment social work professionals must play a twofold role: 1) to ensure that high-quality service is provided to the client and 2) to ensure that the client has access and is given an opportunity to see that her mental health needs are addressed. Neither of these tasks is easy, nor will they make a social worker popular in today's environment. Mental and other health services must now be delivered with limited resources, and the pressure to reduce services is intense. Social workers must know the assessment and treatment planning tools that are used in the field and be able to use them. Assessment and treatment planning are together the first step in providing services, a step that social work professionals cannot afford to neglect.

Numerous tools and methods exist to assist social workers in the mental health assessment process, and the PIE is only one example of what is available. These forms of systematic assessment can provide social workers with frameworks for practice. We should always use such tools cautiously, however; as you will learn in practice courses yet to come, many social workers fear that these methods can place labels on clients that are very difficult to remove. These fears are well founded, but they shouldn't cause social workers to shun assessment. Indeed, the fact that social workers are aware of such dangers makes their participation in assessment essential. In addition, the social worker brings a wealth of information to the interdisciplinary team about a client's environment and family situation. Social workers, who focus on building on the skills and strengths of the client, are well equipped to help design a treatment plan that is realistic and effective. Although assessments completed today appear to have a more narrow focus, it is essential that utility, relevance, and salience be maintained (Dziegielewski, 2004). Because social workers practice in numerous health and mental health settings and perform many different duties, it is not surprising that the processes of assessment and treatment planning show great diversity. Assessment and subsequent treatment plan development depend on a multiplicity of factors, including client need, agency function, practice setting, service limitations, and coverage for provision of service. Many times the scope of assessment and intervention must be narrowed in response to reductions in economic support. Therefore, overall practice in the mental health setting must continually be examined to ensure high quality. If the process of helping is rushed, superficial factors may be highlighted

---

Box 7: Mental Health Social Work Practice in the New Millennium

Questions to guide assessment and intervention success:

1. Are you able to document a DSM-IV multiaxis diagnosis?

2. Can you show that the identified condition is treatable with a realistic chance of success?

3. Have you developed specific goals and objectives for the treatment of the client?

4. Do you provide a clear rationale for the level of care, modality, types of intervention, and duration of treatment?

5. Is there a process for updating and periodic review of goal and objective attainment?

6. Is the client involved in the treatment development process?

7. If treatment is to be longer than originally expected, is a rationale for extension provided?

8. What specific things will happen to indicate that treatment goals and objectives have been met?

9. Is the intervention plan utilized consistent with social work values and ethics?

and significant ones overlooked. All social workers regardless of the mental health care setting must establish services that are quality driven, no matter what the administrative and economic pressures may be.

Questions to Think About

1. Based on the information provided in this chapter, what do you see as the future role for mental health social workers in the assessment process?

2. Do you believe that the PIE will continue to gain in popularity in health and mental health settings with practitioners other than social workers?

3. Do you believe that a complete assessment and treatment planning framework is needed to guide social work practice and will continue to be required for reimbursement in order for social work services to increase?

Further Reading

Adkins, E. A. (1996). Use of the PIE in a medical social work setting. In J. M. Karls & K. M. Wandrei (Eds.), *Person-in-environment system: The PIE classification system for social functioning problems* (pp. 67–78). Washington, DC: NASW Press.

Fischer, J., & Corcoran, K. (2000). *Measures for clinical practice: A sourcebook* (3rd ed.). New York: Free Press.

Contact Information and E-mail Addresses:

National Association of Social Workers, 750 First St. N.E., Suite 700, Washington, DC 20002-4241. Internet: http://www.socialworkers.org

For a listing of accredited social work programs, contact:

Council on Social Work Education, 1725 Duke St., Suite 500, Alexandria, VA 22314-3457. Internet: http://www.cswe.org

Information on licensing requirements and testing procedures for each state may be obtained from state licensing authorities, or from:

Association of Social Work Boards, 400 South Ridge Pkwy., Suite B, Culpeper, VA 22701. Internet: http://www.aswb.org

Chapter 11

The Elderly

LET'S BEGIN BY EXPLORING YOUR THOUGHTS ABOUT AGING. TO start, answer these questions about getting older and let us explore your impressions of aging and what this means.

1. For me, getting older means . . .

2. Close your eyes and imagine yourself at various ages. What do you see?
    a) At age 60, I am . . .
    b) At age 70, I am . . .
    c) At age 80, I am . . .
    d) At age 90, I am . . .
    e) At age 100, I am . . .

3. Name a person age 65 or older whom you admire or have admired.
   What is so special about this person?
   How can this person be a role model for you?

No one escapes the aging process. In fact, from the moment we're born we all begin to age. During the aging process, as in all phases of human growth and development, people must adjust to changes in their life circumstances. Unfortunately, many of these changes are viewed negatively in our society. Declines in physical functioning, changes in physical appearance, loss of income, retirement, and loss of partner and social supports are all associated with aging. But not everyone experiences these shifts. Most professionals agree that to understand aging, we must look at more than just a person's chronological age—that is, how old he is. The study of the elderly therefore embraces varied life circumstances and issues and must consider physical and psychosocial factors (Dziegielewski, 2002, 2004; Dziegielewski & Ricks, 2000; Segrin, 1994; Strawbridge, Camacho, Cohen, & Kaplan, 1993; Zarit & Zarit, 2007).

Did You Know...One myth about aging is that "all older people are alike" and should therefore display predictable patterns of age-related behavior. However, this has not been proved; if anything, the opposite appears true—as people get older they are less alike (Peterson, 1994, p. 46).

Name: Panu Lucier

Place of Residence: Anchorage, Alaska

College/University Degrees: University of Alaska, Anchorage, BSW

Present Position and Title: Executive Director, Alaska Children's Trust & Friends of the Alaska Children's Trust

Previous Work/Volunteer Experience: Director, Rose Urban Rural Exchange; youth worker; Court Appointed Special Advocate; member, National Advisory Committee for the National Quality Improvement Center on Early Childhood

What do you do in your spare time? Outside of work, I have continued my role as a volunteer CASA. I enjoy the beauty of Alaska, spending time with my three grandchildren, traveling, gardening, reading and relaxing in my tipi.

Why did you choose social work as a career? Social work offered me a flexible and professional degree guided by a code of ethics, values, and theories that are very compatible with the values of Alaska native cultures, specifically, our relationship with and respect for all living things.

What is your favorite social work story? I helped convince the court to return four little boys to their village after they were taken into state custody while visiting Anchorage with their mother. I escorted them home. From them I learned courage and never to give up hope.

What is one thing you would change in the community if you had the power to do so? I would break down the social and political barriers that contribute to the division of the "haves" and "have-nots" so that all people have access to education, health, and social services, which are essential to the integrity of a healthy community.

Over the years, however, use of a chronological age cutoff has been the most common way to decide who is "elderly." You may know people who shortly after their 50th birthdays began to receive retirement information from various groups. A number of major airlines offer "senior discounts" to people age 55 or older. The Senior Golf Tour minimum age is 50, as is the entry age to various states' senior games, that is, athletic contests. Most professionals agree that the definition of "senior" status began with the Economic Security Act of 1935 and was based on the German precedent, which established 65 years as the appropriate age for benefits to begin (Brieland, Costin, & Atherton, 1980). And indeed, this simple definition is administratively useful because it establishes clear eligibility standards for programs such as Social Security.

As of 2000 there were an estimated 35 million people aged 65 or older in the United States (Federal Interagency Forum on Aging-Related Statistics, 2000). Therefore, earlier predictions of life expectancies that people who reach age 65 will live to be approximately age 83 for women and age 80 for men remains realistic (Morgan & Kunkel, 1998). Between 1900 and 1994, the elderly population increased elevenfold, whereas the remainder of the population only increased threefold (U.S. Census Bureau, 1994). According to the 2000 census the greatest population increases occurred in 50- to 54-year-olds (55 percent), 45- to 49-year-olds (45 percent), and 90- to 95-year-olds (45 percent). Furthermore, each five-year age group 75 and over has increased 20 percent (U.S. Census Bureau, 2001). This trend has continued and as of the 2006 U.S. Census the current number of those over 65 is 35,505 million, with the second largest number of elderly being in the 55- to 59-year-old age range at 17,827 individuals. What is most astonishing about these numbers is the total of all elderly age 55 and older equating to 66,485 million individuals, with the majority of them living in the South (U.S. Census Bureau, 2007).

Did You Know...When the Economic Security Act was passed in 1935, age 65 marked the 95th percentile of the U.S. age distribution. By 1986, age 65 marked the 76th percentile (Wolinsky & Arnold, 1988). Therefore, the share of the U.S. population age 65 and over has increased and it is expected to continue growing dramatically.

It is clear that the aging of our population has had far reaching effects and just based on the sheer numbers has attracted attention (Zarit & Zarit, 2007). In striving for a simple way to define old age, looking at the sheer number and using chronological age is the simplest approach for administrators and policy planners. This simplistic definition, however, is deficient when used alone because it cannot reflect changes in the composition of the aged population. These changes have made the elderly a much less homogeneous group. One long-term change is based on gender. As Americans continue to enjoy longer and longer life spans and lower death rates, the numbers of elderly women living longer than men has continued to increase. About sixty years ago there were equal numbers of men and women age 65 and over; since then, however, the proportion of men in this population has declined (Rhodes, 1988). Population projections support that this trend has continued. As of 2006, U.S. Census Bureau statistics record the number of females 65 years of age and older as constituting 20,320 individuals whereas males constitute 15,185. Of all the age breakdowns of those 55 and older, this is the biggest difference in gender noted, with more than double the number of females to males in the 85 and older bracket. From these numbers alone it is clear that women live longer than men and in doing so can be subject to many of the problems that result from living to an advanced age. Since women outlive men by approximately five years of age, it is no surprise that 70 percent of nursing home residents are reported to be women and the average admission age is 80 (American Association of Long Term Health Insurance, 2008). Women also tend to be the primary caregivers of a family unit which can put additional stress on the aging couple. The statistics that 70 percent of women age 75 and older are widowed, divorced, or never married may at first seem shocking. Yet, we all are aware that living on a single income is more likely to result in poverty and therefore it correlates to the recorded numbers that in 2005 the median income for these elderly women was $14,600 as opposed to $35,000 for married couples (American Association of Long Term Health Insurance, 2008).

There are many factors that complicate a simple definition of the "elderly" including the simple fact that there is such a wide range of ages of people who can be included in this designation (Belsky, 1988). Some people, for example, live well into their 90s and even beyond. Richardson (2009) reports that Americans age 85 or more are one of the fastest growing population segments and this astounding factor in itself requires attention. As this oldest age group continues to age they are more likely to have significant health problems than the younger elderly age 55 through 65 and even those in their 70s. This makes it very difficult to compare all groups equally and lump them into one category. To help further clarify age-related concerns the elderly population has been divided into the young-old, the medium-old, and the old-old (Rhodes, 1988). For purposes of simplicity we will use the terms "elderly" and "aged" to refer to all people age 65 or older.

During the late 1990s, the social work community was encouraged by the John A. Hartford Foundation, a national foundation that supports gerontological efforts, which financially supported the development of both MSW and BSW educational initiatives in aging (http://www.jhartfound.org/). In schools and departments of social work, gerontology field placements, elective courses, and concentrations (at the graduate level) were developed as a direct result of the Hartford support. The Council on Social Work Education has developed a national gerontological project, SAGE-SW (Strengthening Aging and Gerontology Education in Social Work), which in turn has supported national social meetings focusing on gerontology, and gerontological educational modules. And in 2001, a second major national foundation, the Randolph Hearst Foundation, awarded five schools of social work each a $500,000 endowment to support scholarships in gerontology. These efforts continue, and endorsed by CSWE and supported by the Hartford and Hearst Foundations, social work programs and their educators have been spurred to embrace gerontology as a key educational area and practice domain. In this chapter we introduce you to the topic of aging, a normal and universal stage of human development. As the number of elderly citizens rises today, so does the need for social work services. Fortunately, many services provided to the aged are considered human rights and are not subject to the means testing so common elsewhere in the social service arena. We highlight issues and trends essential to an understanding of the elderly population.

AGING: WHAT CAN BE EXPECTED

Constable and Lee (2004), Galambos and Rosen (2000), Richardson (2009), and others are clear in pointing out the implications for practice that the increasing numbers of elderly individuals will have in the twenty-first century. Reasons suggested for the increase of this population group include the following. One factor contributing to this increase is the simple fact that there is a really large portion of the population that will fall into the category of "old age"; this segment of the population has often been referred to as the baby boomers. Prior to World War II, large numbers of young immigrants came to America, most legally, and as such reflected in the national statistics, and others illegally, and therefore not counted. Many of these immigrants (legal and illegal) are now reaching retirement age. This group will be augmented as people born after World War II between 1945 and 1955, the "baby boomers," age into retirement (Rhodes, 1988). According to the U.S. Census (2000) these numbers continue to rise, and it is estimated that in 2030 one out of every five people living in the United States will be over the age of 65 (Council on Social Work Education/SAGE-SW, 2001). This means that one in every five individuals will be 65 years or older (Morgan & Kunkel, 1998). In particular, the proportion of the total population that is age 75 and over is expected to grow well into the twenty-first century. The increase in the numbers of elderly people is evident throughout the American population and currently the elderly make up the fastest growing age group in the United States.

Activity...Explore the concept of aging by visiting the Census Bureau web site www.census.gov/population/www/socdemo/age.html. Compare trends on the national level and in your home state or county. For information from an international perspective try www.census/gov/ipc/www/idbnew.html.

Another factor underlying the growth in the number of aged individuals is the number of births in relation to the number of deaths. The trend in recent years has been fewer births and longer and healthier lives resulting in lower death rates (Morgan & Kunkel, 1998; Rhodes, 1988). It is predicted that death rates will continue to decline, leaving more aged individuals in society, especially among the old-old, or those over age 75.

The third, most obvious reason for growth in the elderly population is the strides made by the scientific community in understanding and promoting the factors that support longer and healthier life spans (Belsky, 1988; Mosher-Ashley, 1994; Rhodes, 1988). Social workers have become keenly aware of the need for providers to look carefully at the needs of the elderly to ensure that quality of life is maximized for both the elderly and their caregivers (Gellis, 2009).

Aging and working with the elderly as a field of study, known as gerontology, did not become popular until the end of the 1930s (Shock, 1987). This increased attention to the elderly was related to three major events: 1) the implementation of the Economic Security Act, 2) the development of a scientific basis for the study of the aged, and 3) the dramatic population trends involving elderly people.

To track this development, it is important to recognize that in the 1930s, the United States was experiencing the aftermath of many major social changes. As World War I had ended many people were thrust into poverty. The Great Depression made destitute so many people who had never been poor before. Faced with these newly and "unusually" impoverished fellow citizens, American society showed increased willingness to help certain disadvantaged groups. This sentiment was felt particularly toward older people and young children (Frank, 1946). At the same time, the country still held a strong work ethic; regardless of age or

Figure 1: Rosa is an older woman who lives with her daughter and receives help from a visiting social worker.

circumstances every person was expected to be a productive part of society. It was during this period that the public, among whom social workers were active, began to insist that government take the necessary steps to ensure that the elderly and children did not, through their inability to work, become burdens on society (Axinn & Levin, 1982).

The Economic Security Act of 1935 was a societal response to the problem of widespread unemployment caused by the Great Depression. The act mobilized an unprecedented redistribution of income within society. As a result of this legislation, elderly citizens were provided with a government-assisted income, because they were officially designated as unemployable (Axinn & Levin, 1982). Their new guaranteed income helped to make this "worthy" group prosperous enough to command additional professional and societal attention.

Also in the 1930s, an improved scientific basis for the study of the aged developed. The year 1942 saw the publication of *Problems of Aging* by E. Cowdry, a collection of papers by eminent scientists from many disciplines that represented the first compilation of "scientific data on aging" (Shock, 1987, p. 34). It is interesting to note that following Cowdry's publication, the first issue of the *Journal of Gerontology* appeared in January 1946. This journal claimed to be the first in the field of gerontology designed "to provide a medium of communication and of interpretation in our efforts to gain a much surer knowledge of human growth and development" (Frank, 1946, p. 3). It represented the Gerontological Society, whose primary interest was to assist the elderly "against the present almost brutal neglect of the aged, by which many have been misused" (Frank, 1946, p. 3). These two publications highlighted the point that science and technology could assist in preventing the loss of this valuable resource. Now, over a half-century later, a large body of literature reflects the popularity of aging as a subject of study. Numerous books, textbooks, and classes are offered in this area. Furthermore, such professionals as chemists, physicians, economists, dentists, psychologists, and social workers have all contributed to existing knowledge about the aging population.

Did You Know...The social work profession has a long-standing interest in aging. This interest was expressed as early as 1947 at the National Conference of Social Work. Issues in aging were also included in the 1949 Social Work Yearbook *(Lowry, 1979).*

One last reason for the increased attention toward recognizing the needs of the elderly was that data collection had reached such a level of sophistication that it was now clear from tracking population trends within the 1930s that this population group was sure to grow. It was clearly documented that the late 1930s saw growing numbers of elderly individuals (Axinn & Levin, 1982; Morgan & Kunkel, 1998), which caused much concern because these people were not always considered capable of contributing to the national economy in terms of work (Axinn & Levin, 1982; Frank, 1946). Today, this fear has taken on a new light as many professionals now worry that these early attempts at meeting the needs of elderly individuals and the resulting programs may simply not be enough. Subsequently, the programs born of good intention under the Economic Security Act to assist this population may no longer suffice. This fear is inspired primarily by expected increases in the elderly population and the extended life spans that these elderly people will enjoy. Given the open advocacy and concern expressed for the elderly today, among severe financial constraints a sense of cautious optimism has developed. Resistance to providing these services continues as the problems that surround elderly individuals are often complex and involve an integrated approach to care that highlights the health and mental health as well as the social and cultural dimensions (Dziegielewski, 2004; Morris, 1993; Richardson, 2009).

THEORETICAL FRAMEWORKS FOR PRACTICE WITH THE ELDERLY

A cornerstone of all social work programs is the acknowledgment of the influence of human growth and development theory. This theoretical framework became popular in the 1970s because its broad approach takes into account the benefits and challenges that individual's encounter as they mature in life. The personality of an individual is assumed to be consistent with the way life tasks are developed and managed throughout his lifetime (Rhodes, 1988). For older adults the need to be accepted and participate fully within families and communities is great (Podnieks, 2006). For social workers borrowing from this psychological theory, the most comprehensive and widely used work is that of Erikson (1959). Erikson described eight different stages of human development:

Basic trust vs. mistrust

Autonomy vs. shame and doubt

Initiative vs. guilt

Industry vs. inferiority

Identity vs. identity diffusion

Intimacy vs. self-absorption

General activity vs. stagnation

Integrity vs. despair

Box 1: Disengagement Theory

Disengagement theory was introduced by Cumming and Henry (1961) and focused on the "normal" process of withdrawal from the social environment to which an aging person belonged. The aging person initiates withdrawal from the usual life events and acknowledges his impending death, reduced physical energy, or poor health. The process of disengagement is considered beneficial to both the individual and society. According to proponents of this theory, the role of the social worker is to help the client to disengage from mainstream society. This allows a natural transition by physically separating the individual from mainstream life, thus fostering an adjustment period to his absence. Disengagement is viewed as an inevitable process that every aging individual must undergo. Further, if a person resists this natural process of "letting go," then problems in adjustment to the elderly years would develop (Cumming & Henry, 1961).

To date, most social workers, although aware of this theoretical perspective, do not embrace it wholeheartedly. This is especially true since the research on disengagement theory has been controversial and contradictory. The relationship between disengagement and the activity level the elderly individual will engage in after leaving mainstream society is unclear (Rhodes, 1988). Previous studies suggested that the role elderly individuals assume after disengagement depends on the behavior patterns they had established over their lifetimes (Maddox, 1964; Sills, 1980). Furthermore, some individuals do not separate but instead stay engaged by changing the focus of their activities. In closing, more research is needed to determine whether disengagement really is a natural part of the aging process.

Erikson believed that once an individual had completed all of these stages successfully, she would accept her self and take responsibility for her own life. In the last developmental stage, integrity versus despair, an individual's life goals reach finalization, and reflection and contemplation become important tasks. Ryff (1982), among others, expanded on Erikson's last developmental stage by including such tasks as adjusting to the fact that the individual no longer supplements the sense of identity through work. Therefore, the individual becomes accepting of the physical limitations imposed by the aging process, and learns to cope with the concept of death while embracing spirituality.

Taking this perspective into account, the role of the social worker is an important one that allows for elderly people to maximize the positive experiences in their lives while minimizing the negative ones. To assist with this transition social workers help to create an environment where successful aging can occur. Unfortunately, we all have to face objective losses in the body and the mind, but the way we feel about and react to these losses helps to lay the foundation for future acceptance (Marsiske, Franks, & Mast, 1998; Roberts & Dziegielewski, 1995). As individuals age it is common for them to become frustrated with what their bodies can and cannot do and to be frustrated with the lack of ability to complete tasks that used to be so much easier. When an elderly individual loses his or her ability to act and manage affairs independently, family and supportive networks are sure to be affected and often strained (Constable & Lee, 2004).

Box 2: Activity Theory

Activity theory assumes that the elderly have the same social and psychological needs as middle-aged people. The concepts of activity theory were introduced before disengagement theory, but activity theory was not formalized until 1972 with the work of Lemon, Bengston, and Peterson. These authors were among the first to test activity theory in relation to reported life satisfaction. They hypothesized that as activity increased, life satisfaction would also increase; and conversely, as role loss increased, life satisfaction would decrease. Basically, getting older is characterized by the desire to remain middle aged. Therefore, in order for aging to be successful, the elderly individual needs to continue activities similar to those that were important in middle age (Lemon, Bengston, & Peterson, 1972).

Proponents of this theoretical framework believe that professional intervention involves helping the client to continue an active existence. For example, a social worker might encourage an elderly person to do volunteer work as a way to replace previously paid employment. To date, most social workers working with the elderly are aware of this theory and of its influence on ideas about the aging process; however, most agree that more research is needed before activity theory can be used as a framework for practice. In particular, additional research is needed to establish a direct link between level of activity and life satisfaction (Hoyt, Kaiser, Peters, & Babchuk, 1980; Rhodes, 1988).

Whatever theoretical practice framework is used, more empirical research is needed to establish the utility of developmental theories in working with all populations including the elderly (Dziegielewski & Powers, 2000; Dziegielewski & Roberts, 2004; Dziegielewski, Shields, & Thyer, 1998; Rhodes, 1988). Ryff (1982) argued that research must attempt to isolate the factors that result in accomplishment of Erikson's developmental stages and to examine the factors that actually allow elderly individuals to achieve optimal levels of performance. It is important to add another caution about these theories, namely, their apparent middle-class and sexist biases.

Human growth and development theories have largely displaced older theories about how the elderly adjust to their changing societal role. Historically, in our quest to understand the aging process and the milestones that elderly people attain, social workers entertained the concepts of disengagement and activity. These theories postulate that activity and disengagement from traditional life experiences are normal and natural parts of the aging process. While research has not proved these theories to be comprehensive enough to explain all life changes experienced by the elderly (Rhodes, 1988), their influence on social work practice remains. Furthermore, although many interventions that were originally developed for younger persons may work well with older ones, there are modifications needed for certain older individuals (Richardson, 2009). Social workers need to be aware of the different treatments that are used, but most of all how societal perspectives on aging can influence all treatment outcomes. Whether these theories are valid or not, the fact that many professionals and lay people believe them may strongly affect their expectations and behavior. Keeping an open mind, and avoiding uncritical adherence is central as to do so might keep practitioners from thinking about alternative explanations for clients' behavior and from trying innovative problem-solving techniques.

HEALTH, MENTAL HEALTH, AND THE ELDERLY

How often have you heard someone describe an aged loved one as dying "of old age"? How often have you heard professionals encourage this notion? How often have you seen or heard of an elderly person who consulted a physician about a certain ache or pain only to be told that the pain was simply related to old age?

Box 3: The Pain in My Elbow

A 90-year-old man visits a physician for pain in the elbow joint of his right arm. After the client explains his symptoms to the physician, the physician says, "You are 90 years old. It's possible that the pain is merely related to your age, and there may be no plausible medical explanation for your pain." After hearing this theory the patient thought for a moment and asked, "If your idea is tenable, why doesn't my other elbow hurt? After all, it's the same age."

Dying of old age is a myth that should not be propagated. Social work professionals must give elderly clients the respect they deserve, allowing them to state their concerns in a nonjudgmental atmosphere. No one ever died of old age. There are many causes of social isolation in elderly persons, including such serious conditions as chronic illness and visual, hearing, or cognitive impairment (Eamon, 2008) or decreased physical functioning and medical frailty such as heart disease, cancer, and stroke (Rhodes, 1988). When death occurs due to a medical condition, however, such a careless use of words that attribute death due to these or other medical conditions should never be dismissed as dying of old age. This attitude can lead to actual diseases going undetected because symptoms characteristic of disease may be attributed by both client and physician to the aging process itself (Anderson & Williams, 1989; Sadavoy, Jarvik, Grossberg, & Meyers, 2004). It is actually this recognition of how functional decline is attributable to medical or mental disorders rather than normal aging that has made it easier for certain disorders and subsequent treatments modalities to be given. Older adults deserve the same professional treatment as any other age group, and social work professionals have a role in educating and helping elderly individuals to secure the specific health services they need.

Did You Know...In an archival study of records on 298 clients treated by a mental health center, three types of issues predominated among elderly clients: 1) family conflicts, 2) poor physical health, and 3) feeling that they were not in control of their lives (Mosher-Ashley, 1994).

The U.S. Senate Special Committee on Aging (1981) reported that 45 percent of elderly people experience limitation of activity due to some type of chronic condition. As a result the elderly are important consumers of health care. Tan (2009) warns, however, that with all the research on the subject, when comparing studies there is no clear consensus on what measures service use. For the most part, service use is generally defined by the type of service utilized. For example, hospital use by the elderly received a strong boost in 1965 with the initiation of Title XVIII (Medicare), which provided health insurance for the elderly, a high-risk group in terms of vulnerability to illness and poverty (Axinn & Levin, 1982). Medicare was one of the amendments to the Economic Security Act of 1935.

To date, Medicare remains one of the largest health insurance programs in the world with an estimated annual cost of $260 million (National Bureau of Economic Research, n.d.; Nesvisky, 2006). Medicare's introduction in 1965 was, and remains to date, the single largest change in health insurance coverage in U.S. history. Medicare is the closest program we have in the United States to universal health insurance providing services to the elderly as well as many disabled. It is estimated that Medicare accounts for about 17 percent of U.S. health expenditures, one-eighth of the federal budget, and 2 percent of gross domestic production (Nesvisky, 2006).

Obviously, as people get older they are more likely to need health care services. Since 1965 and the implementation of Title XVIII, however, regardless of trouble defining what is meant by services, it is clear the increase in health care consumption at age 65 has been dramatic. Medicare brought health care benefits to many elderly people who could not afford them otherwise; physicians and hospitals also benefitted from the greater assurance of payment for providing needed health care services. The benefits to health care recipients and providers, however, came at a particularly high price for the federal government. As the cost of services continued to escalate, the government became determined to control Medicare expenditures (Starr, 1982).

In 1983, Congress mandated a radical change in the payment structure for hospital care to rescue the Hospital Insurance Trust Fund from imminent bankruptcy (Lee, Forthofor, & Taube, 1985). The original system required Medicare to pay whatever hospitals charged for a particular service. Faced with these various and fluctuating costs the government wanted to achieve uniformity and predictability. To control costs and develop an equitable payment system, Diagnostic Related Groups (DRGs) were developed (Begly, 1985).

The DRG system groups together individuals who have similar diagnoses, regardless of age or general health status. Each diagnostic category is assigned a particular standard of care, including length of stay, for which the government is willing to pay—for example, gallbladder removal is allowed seven days of hospital treatment. This new system thus has a fixed payment schedule and hospitals know how much money they will receive for each individual. Unfortunately, for elderly people, who are more fragile and often have chronic or complicating conditions, this system is problematic. Little incentive exists for hospitals to accept patients who might require extended stays. When hospitals do accept elderly patients, many social workers have noted that they are discharged as quickly as possible. Quick discharges are problematic because many of the sick elderly have low incomes and few supports in the community for extended care assistance (Blazyk & Canavan, 1985). Facilities such as nursing homes are often reluctant to take these recently discharged individuals, in their less medically stable conditions. Nursing home professionals are strained when these new patients require much more care and observation; in many cases an increase in staff to accommodate the additional needs of these new patients never occurs. The result in the long run can be readmission, which is costly for the individual and for the hospital (Berkman & Abrams, 1986).

Medicare—and insurance reimbursement in general—is of particular interest to social workers because they are the ones who generally handle the discharge and placement of elderly clients in both nursing home and hospital settings. Social workers must be aware of community supports for discharge back into the community and the availability of any special treatment or services. Discharging elderly people home may place great stress on the family and extended care staff. In discharges back to the community, family stress is often a major contributing factor to long-term care admission (Pratt, Wright, & Schmall, 1987). Measures should be taken to allow families to communicate needs, problem solve, and participate in support groups. Social workers provide an excellent entry point for supportive and educational services to both elderly clients and caregivers. Similarly, placing an elderly client who needs a great deal of individual care into a long-term care facility can create great stress for the staff. Support groups and regular in-service training on how to treat these clients is mandatory. If additional staff is needed to facilitate placement, social workers should recommend such support.

For so many elderly individuals, developing a chronic health condition is generally an elderly person's worst fear because it can impair activity and unaided mobility (Rhodes, 1988). The chronic conditions from which the elderly often suffer are either physical (biological or physiological) or mental (psychological) in nature. We make this distinction only for simplicity's sake; it is important to note that physical and mental health conditions are often related and interdependent. For example, a physical event such as a stroke may develop into the mental health condition dementia. Also, there are a number of stress-related conditions that can complicate the medical condition an individual is suffering from.

Did You Know…A "chronic" condition is generally defined as a disease of long duration, following a long, drawn-out progression (Taber's Cyclopedia Medical Dictionary, 1977). An "acute" condition, on the other hand, generally has a rapid, severe onset and a short duration (Taber's Cyclopedia Medical Dictionary, 1977). Elderly people are affected more often by chronic than by acute conditions.

Physical Health Conditions

"Probably no factor is of more immediate concern to older people than physical health" (Maldonado, 1987, p. 99). Many elderly people fear the loss of individual, unaided activity, or perceived independence. When an elderly person is assessed, it is critical to first look carefully at the signs and symptoms that occur and whether these symptoms could be explained by medically related factors (Woo & Keatinge, 2008). For example, has the individual been placed on a new medication? For all individuals, medications should be monitored carefully but in the elderly with slower metabolisms this is a critical factor to be considered (Dziegielewski, 2006). Be sure that a general medical practitioner has been consulted and a general medical exam has been conducted.

Of all physical health conditions, heart disease remains the leading cause of death among those age 65 or older, followed by cancer, stroke, chronic obstructive lung disease, pneumonia and influenza, and diabetes. For those individuals aged 85 or older heart disease was responsible for 40 percent of all the deaths (Federal Interagency Forum on Aging-Related Statistics, 2000). Although these conditions (excluding cancer) are considered acute, patients often gradually fall prey to chronic conditions such as paralysis and mental impairment resulting in some type of dementia, making dementia the sixth leading cause of death among the

Name: Ramsi Wilkes

Place of residence: Birmingham, Alabama

College/university degrees: University of Montevallo, BSW

Present position: Admissions Coordinator, Galleria Oaks Guest Home

Previous work/volunteer experience: Discharge planner in a rehab hospital (Healthsouth) and retirement community

What do you do in your spare time? I participate in church activities, and I like music.

Why did you choose social work as a career? It was a way to act compassionately for others and make a difference. I was drawn to geriatrics from personal experience and I believed service in this area represented my Christian beliefs.

What is your favorite social work story? I will never forget working with a terminally ill client who was receiving hospice services. She lived in the supervised housing facility where I worked. I was with her when she was dying, and she told me what she was seeing and experiencing. She told me she saw angels in her room while she breathed her last breaths. She described everything about them and pointed them out. Spine tingling!

What would be the one thing you would change in our community if you had the power to do so? I would encourage more people to work with seniors and to learn to respect them more.

elderly (Federal Interagency Forum on Aging-Related Statistics, 2000). Other major chronic conditions that result in the restriction of activity include rheumatism and hearing and vision impairments.

Among vision conditions, cataracts and glaucoma are most common. Social workers should always encourage elderly clients suffering from vision impairments to receive regular check-ups to aid in detecting such conditions before permanent damage results. It is also important for social workers to consider how decreased vision can affect the counseling relationship (Dziegielewski, 2002). For example, an elderly client may not want to admit that he cannot easily read written material or navigate in a particular setting.

Special attention should also be paid to possible hearing loss in clients. Someone who seems withdrawn and unresponsive to conversation may simply be suffering from hearing loss and may be hearing only part of what is said and hypothesizing the rest (Dziegielewski, 2002). If the response is not appropriate, it can seem like confusion. Family members, in particular, may believe their aged relative is becoming confused or simply ignoring them, and confusion in the elderly tends to increase the stress felt by family members about their aged relative (Dziegielewski, 1990; 1991; Smallegan, 1985).

In closing, social work professionals should always be aware that the elderly are often shocked and embarrassed by changes in their health, and these feelings may lead to denial. All of us can understand reluctance to admit individual inadequacy. Counseling and interviewing should include initial assessment to determine whether health concerns are affecting the interview process.

Mental Health Process

Elderly individuals suffer many life circumstances that can affect their mental health. It is virtually impossible to age and not have traumatic life-changing experiences (Richardson, 2009). Common stressful life events include widowhood, social and occupational losses, and physical health problems. In addition, criminal victimization is listed as a critical factor in the area of health risks (Federal Interagency Forum on Aging-Related Statistics, 2000). Taking the sheer number of life tragedies that elderly people have faced, it would seem logical that they would seek more mental health services than other population groups; however, this is often not the case. Many elderly individuals do not openly seek mental health services. One reason is the method of delivery. When living in the community elderly psychiatric clients generally go to community mental health centers for check-ups and medication; many of the elderly refuse these services because they don't want to leave their homes (Dziegielewski, 2004).

Depression. For many social work practitioners, clients who report symptoms of depression are commonplace. Nearly 30 million of the U.S. adult population may be affected with major depression and approximately one-third are classified as severely depressed (Nemeroff, 2007). Furthermore, it is reported that approximately 16 percent of the population will suffer from depression at some point in their lifetime (Capriotti, 2006; Hansen, Gartlehner, Lohr, et al., 2005). When looking specifically at older adults, about 25 percent of people over the age of 65 with a chronic medical illness suffer from depressive symptoms and approximately 15 percent suffer from major depressive disorder (Sheikh, Cassidy, Doraiswamy, et al., 2004). Because they are reported so frequently during routine medical visits and throughout the course of psychological treatment, these types of symptoms can seem like the common cold of mental health.

Therefore, it comes as no surprise that depression is a common mental health problem of the elderly, one frequently associated with physical symptoms and illness. According to the 2000 conference report by the Federal Interagency Forum on Aging-Related Statistics, women between the ages of 65 and 84 are more likely than men to have severe depressive symptoms. Once an individual reaches the age of 85, however, the levels of depression seem to become equal regardless of gender. Although it is obvious that depression exists, there is little consensus among researchers regarding the prevalence of this condition and how to recognize it in the aged (Ban, 1987; Dziegielewski, 2002; Reynolds, Small, Stein, & Teri, 1994). The existence of depression among the elderly is especially unfortunate, because although it is often treatable, it has been noted that few of the elderly actually seek treatment for this or any other mental health condition (Belsky, 1988; Maldonado,

1987). Furthermore, depression is believed to be related to the disproportionately high suicide rate among the aged population (Ban, 1987; Perkins & Tice, 1994).

Common signs and symptoms of depression include feelings of sadness, loneliness, guilt, boredom, marked decrease or increase in appetite, lack or increase in sleep behavior, and a sense of worthlessness (American Psychiatric Association, 2000). When depression arises in response to life circumstances, it is called "situational." Situational depression is a particular risk for the elderly because they generally endure many tragedies including loss of loved ones, jobs, status, and independence and other personal disappointments. Feelings of depression can be triggered by such experiences as bereavement for a deceased loved one or frustration with a medical condition (Dziegielewski, 2002; Marsiske et al., 1998). Of particular concern when working with the older adults are the increased problems that can come from increased mortality and chronic medical conditions. Elderly individuals who have increased limitations in mobility and the ability to carry out activities of daily living, self-perceived poor health, life dissatisfaction, and cardiac problems are at the highest risk for poor outcomes and recovery (Woo & Keatinge, 2008).

Social work intervention and counseling can help elderly clients to deal with situational depression and achieve greater life satisfaction. For example, social workers can teach elderly people how to control the frequency of their depressive thoughts and to use relaxation techniques, such as imagery and deep muscle relaxation, to calm down during anxious times. Concrete problem solving and behavioral contracting can be used to help the elderly client change problem behaviors. Whenever possible, family members should be included in treatment contracting because they can provide support and assist in recording and observing behaviors that the elderly client is seeking to change.

Caution should always be used, however; not all cases of depression in the elderly are situational. Some cases of depression may arise directly from internal causes; this is called "endogenous" depression. Furthermore, the etiology of depression in the elderly is not always distinct; depression may be the result of a combination of situational and endogenous factors. For example, many chronic medical conditions are often accompanied by depression. These include hypothyroidism, Addison's Disease, Parkinson's disease, Alzheimer's disease, and congestive heart failure. It is also possible that symptoms of depression are by-products or side effects of medication taken for another condition (Belsky, 1988; Dziegielewski & Leon, 1998) or are, in fact, symptoms of something else. The American Psychiatric Association (2000) has warned that the diagnosis of depression in the elderly can be particularly problematic because the symptoms of dementia in its early stages and those of depression are very similar. Symptoms such as loss of interest and pleasure in usual activities, disorientation, and memory loss are common to the two conditions. There is one big difference, however. Although many signs and symptoms are the same, the person in the early stages of dementia will rarely improve as a result of treatment.

For the beginning social work professional, working with clients who are depressed can be frightening. You may feel very uncertain about what to do and also worry greatly that the client might try to harm herself. This makes it a practice necessity to gather as detailed a social, medical, and medication history as soon as possible. In addition, depressed elderly clients should always be referred for medical examination in order to rule out any physical reasons for depressive symptoms. Depression is most dangerous when it is unrecognized. When implemented, treatment for depression in the elderly is as effective as with other age groups (Dziegielewski, 2002; Reynolds et al., 1994).

Discharge Options. The current trend is for many mentally impaired elderly who cannot be handled at home or in the community to be discharged to long-term care facilities. This practice has increased as a result of the deinstitutionalization that over the past thirty-three years has shrunk state mental health hospitals to one-third their former capacity, and thus reduced one important placement option (Dziegielewski, 2004; Talbott, 1988). In response to the consequent need for more constricted placement, many privately run long-term care facilities, including adult congregate living facilities (boarding homes) and intermediate- and skilled-level care nursing homes, have been opened. In the past thirty years the number of nursing homes alone has increased dramatically in the United States (Dziegielewski, 2004; Morgan & Kunkel, 1998). These homes provide a discharge option for mentally impaired elderly clients that other population groups do not have. Most patients admitted to long-term care facilities are over age 65.

Dziegielewski (2004) warns that long-term care facilities, although convenient, are inappropriate placement options for the mentally impaired elderly because they generally do not provide mental health services. Dziegielewski (1990 and 1991) along with Talbott (1988) argued that very few long-term care facilities provide psychosocial interventions, and medication is often the sole method of treatment. Beginning social work professionals must exercise caution when placing a client in a long-term care facility, especially if the client needs mental health services. Each facility is different. Social workers need to be aware not only of what long-term facilities exist in an area but which services these different facilities offer to the mentally impaired elderly client. Since many elderly people fear functional activity loss, social workers must be aware of this fear, regardless of whether such loss has actually occurred. Such worries have a real foundation. Since many elderly individuals suffer from chronic conditions, the probability that their condition will improve is low.

Our society tends to deny that problems may be terminal. Family members, and some professionals, may tell aged people that they'll get better rather than helping them to develop ways to cope (Dziegielewski, 2004). It is important for social work practitioners to be knowledgeable about common chronic conditions, their signs and symptoms, their expected progression, and when and where to refer clients for additional treatment. Furthermore, there is considerable evidence that the involvement and support of family members is important in creating a general sense of well-being in the elderly (Dziegielewski, 2004; Rubinstein, Lubben, & Mintzer, 1994). Therefore, the role of the social worker is essential in educating aged clients and their family members to cope with and understand changes that will occur. A comprehensive assessment of the individual, taking into account health conditions and environmental factors, is critical.

EMPLOYMENT CHANGES OF THE ELDERLY AND SOCIAL WORK PRACTICE

Today, problems associated with unemployment in the United States are inspiring social work professionals to look seriously at the social and economic consequences of being without a job (Rife & Belcher, 1994). At the same time, a growing abundance of low-paying and minimum wage jobs are not being filled. Having to address these problems has brought to the attention of the public the specific experiences of certain groups such as older adults. Currently, the trend toward early retirement, in conjunction with the diminishing number of youths entering the workforce (as a result of lower birthrates), has created interest in the elderly as a potential source of labor to help fill this gap. Elderly people, who are living longer and healthier, remain viable employees and constitute an underutilized labor pool that should not be ignored (Federal Interagency Forum on Aging-Related Statistics, 2000). In addition to societal need, many elderly individuals who enjoy good health see continued employment as desirable. For example, an archival study conducted by Mosher-Ashley (1994) on 298 mental health outpatient records found those elderly men between ages 60 and 98 described loss of "work role" as a major area of personal concern. Furthermore, with today's economic turbulence and changes in traditional family structure, elderly people may be expected to take more active roles in supporting their extended families (Duke, Barton, & Wolf-Klein, 1994). Staying active is so important that at the 2000 conference forum the Federal Interagency on Age Related Statistics found that social activity and staying active was a key factor in continued health status.

The Working Elderly

Over the past forty years, elderly individuals are better educated and wealthier than previous generations, and it is expected that this trend will continue and future generations will have even more education (Zarit & Zarit, 2007). Many individuals may not want to retire and see employment as a way to supplement income as well as an opportunity for continued meaningful engagement (Zarit & Zarit, 2007). Sadly, if an elderly person does decide to return to work there is no guarantee that a job will be obtainable. Even with the protective legislation that exists, such as the ban on mandatory age-based retirement, age discrimination can and does take place (Sterns, Barrett, Czaja, & Barr, 1994). This can occur when prospective employers refuse to make necessary adjustments for elderly employees (Sterns et al., 1994). In addition to finding a job, complications can occur in that many jobs now require an application and search process that involves use of a

Figure 2: An 80-year-old at the ecumenical social center after an exercise class. This is a drop-in center that offers seniors lunch and a variety of activities.

computer and access to the Internet. The expectation for online applications has increased and now many front-end nonprofessional level positions have also moved to an Internet application process (Mueller & Overmann, 2008). For elderly individuals, particularly those of low income, this can be problematic, serving as a block to seeking employment.

Box 4: Social Security Retirement Benefits

At one time people used to talk about retiring at age 65. Well, retirement age has increased for most people, as seen in this table. Can you retire at any age? Sure, but if you retire earlier than "full retirement age" your monthly social security check will be reduced. An eligible person may begin receiving retirement checks at age 62 or delay receiving checks while working past retirement age. Note that the longer you wait to collect your benefits, the larger your monthly checks will be.

Year of Birth	Full Retirement Age (years)	Total Reduction of Benefits If Retire Early[a]
1937 or earlier	65.5	20%
1940	65.5	22.5
1943–54	66.5	25.5
1960 and later	67.5	30.5

Source: See www.ssa.gov.

[a]Early retirement is age 62. An advantage of early retirement is that you collect your benefit for a longer period (if you live). The disadvantage is that your monthly check is permanently reduced by some percentage for the remainder of your life.

Until recently, social security rules created an unnecessary barrier for seniors who wished to work. Seniors who worked full or part time and earned income over a certain level were penalized for working by having their social security checks reduced. The U.S. Congress continues to address this issue while proposing strategies that would decrease and/or eliminate this penalty and allow seniors to earn as much as they can while maintaining their retirement checks.

To assist elderly clients returning to the workforce social work professionals strive to perform the following two tasks. First, social workers must encourage elderly clients to update or learn new skills so that they can remain competitive throughout their careers. This consideration is especially important with the rapid technological advances occurring today, as well as the use of computer and automation technologies in most occupational settings. For an elderly client learning and maintaining these types of skills can be frightening. This apprehension creates the need for the next point of social work intervention.

Second, social workers must work with employers to make job sites more worker-friendly while linking elderly clients to larger support systems. Programs are often needed to accommodate older workers. These may include work schedule modifications such as sharing one job between two or more workers, flextime schedules, and reduced work weeks. Furthermore, programs that are designed to build worker skills, motivation, and self-confidence need to be made available either by the employer through in-house programs or in community through community-based programs. Assistance programs such as the "job club" described by Rife and Belcher (1994), which utilized a specialized job assistance strategy, provide an excellent practice environment in which social workers can help older workers to become reemployed.

Caregiving in the Community

Social workers must be aware that caregiving assistance may be needed to allow elderly clients to leave the home and continue working. Caregiving can be as serious an issue for elderly couples as for younger couples. In addition, often the family member identified for this caregiving role is the female (Conway-Giustra, Crowley & Gorin, 2002). Other studies have found that caregiving supportive services are valuable in easing the burden on caregivers (Dziegielewski & Ricks, 2000). For all extended families, the need for eldercare services will become a reality (Dziegielewski, 2004). Provision of elder daycare services similar to child daycare services can help these families. Social workers should advocate for companies to consider adding eldercare as a standard option in employee benefit packages.

The Elderly in Retirement

Retirement from the workforce has been viewed in different ways over the years. Attitudes toward retirement have changed with changes in social, emotional, political, and cultural climates. To illustrate how the view of retirement has changed, we present a brief history of the role of the aged in the labor force, drawn from Dziegielewski and Harrison (1996).

Figure 3: This couple has just celebrated their 50th wedding anniversary. It is often difficult for them to make Social Security income cover all their expenses and they get help from their children.

The early twentieth century saw a shift from an agrarian to an urban industrial economy in the United States (Axinn & Levin, 1982). In agrarian society, all family members were viewed as contributing members of a cohesive unit. The family was responsible for meeting all the needs of its individual members, including elderly family members. Industrialization, however, changed this perspective, establishing different expectations and roles. The decline in individual business and farm ownership meant that many people had to obtain incomes from outside sources (Atchley, 1976).

Activity...Go to the Social Security Administration web page www.ssa.gov and using the on-line retirement planner estimate your monthly social security benefit check. What do you find? Is this what you thought you would get? Can you live on this amount of money?

During these years (1890–1912), one member's income was not enough to support the entire family, and often work outside of the home by all family members, including women, children, and the aged, became mandatory (Axinn & Levin, 1982). The participation of all these groups in the labor force did not last long, however. Family members left the workforce for primarily two reasons: 1) With industrialization fewer workers were needed in the production of output. 2) An

Activity...Retirement involves both endings and beginnings. Take a look at your own retirement and think about your endings and beginnings.

Endings: *What will your life be like when you retire? Think about your paycheck, alarm clock, commute . . .*

What Will End	Will You Miss It?	
	Yes	No
1. _____	_____	_____
2. _____	_____	_____
3. _____	_____	_____
4. _____	_____	_____

Beginnings: *What will you miss from your work environment and what can you replace it with? For example, you might miss managing projects, and replace it with volunteering in a program that requires management skills.*

Miss	Replace
1. _____	_____
2. _____	_____
3. _____	_____
4. _____	_____
5. _____	_____

Source: Arnone, W. J., Kavouras, F., & Nissenbaum, M. (2001)

influx of new immigrants made far more workers available (Morrison, 1982). Women, children, and the elderly were therefore no longer needed in the workforce. It was in this era that elderly people began to receive attention from the public. Morrison (1982) attributed this increased interest to the growth in the elderly population and to worries that this large population might compete for limited jobs with younger workers.

The Economic Security Act of 1935 was the first time the government had acknowledged responsibility for providing the elderly with an income that did not depend on continuing participation in the labor market. "The Social Security Act . . . set up a national system of old age insurance . . . which legitimized retirement at age 65" (Morrison, 1982, p. 9). This act supported limited, although permanent, economic guarantees to elderly individuals. Social security helped to ensure that retirement benefits would moderate the reduction in income that workers faced when they left the labor market, and it helped to establish 65 years as the encouraged or expected retirement age (Morrison, 1982).

The lives of the aged have not changed radically over the past fifty years; what has changed, however, is our view of the elderly and how society acts upon this view. In working with elderly clients, social workers need to be aware of the following aspects of retirement, and how they can affect the lives of the aged. Over the short span of forty years, retirement has become an important concern of the

American people; almost every day, articles and commentaries appear in publications throughout the country on the economic, social, and psychological consequences of retirement. In the past, it was clear that this interest in retirement was heightened by the rising costs of public and private retirement benefits and by doubts as to whether these costs can be sustained in the future (Dziegielewski & Harrison, 1996; Morrison, 1982). Today, this reason remains true but added to it is the fear that many individuals have that they will not be able to afford to retire because of the rising cost of living and health care expenses (Iftekhar, 2008).

Helpful Point...When working with clients approaching retirement have them contact the Social Security Administration to get a copy of their lifetime earnings report. They should do this each year to verify the amount earned and credited toward their retirement. Any problems can be corrected with documentation of salary. But it's best to catch errors early rather than waiting until retirement.

As baby boomers approach retirement age, fiscal concerns increase related to whether the Social Security system can handle the inevitable growth in the number of beneficiaries compiled with the recent downturns in our economy. Social work intervention can be critical in helping an aged client make a successful transition from the role of worker to the new role of retiree. It is important, however, that the social worker clearly communicate to elderly clients what role he will play in the delivery of services, because the provision of such services may be poorly understood (Scharlach, Mor-Barak, & Birba, 1994). For example, preretirement planning is just one of the services a social worker can provide to assist in the transition process. Through counseling and more specific assistance the social worker can help aged clients to plan for the role adjustment they will face. It is important to remember that many people gain their status or identity through working (Mosher-Ashley, 1994). They enjoy the work they do and don't want to give up the internal and external rewards they derive from it. Some elderly people can afford to retire but choose not to because of the value placed on working for money in this society (Davidson & Kunze, 1979). Ekerdt (1986) concurred that the importance of the work ethic in our society should not be underestimated. He recommended that elderly people reaching retirement plan their leisure time as carefully as they planned their work time; otherwise, their self-esteem may suffer. Social workers need to be sensitive to this aspect of work in order to help elderly individuals to find other activities that they will find fulfilling.

In planning leisure time, the degree and type of activity that a client can perform (and afford) must be considered. Worker and client can together create a list of possible options and discuss each option in a problem-solving, decision-making manner. Once they have chosen an appropriate leisure activity they can develop an individual contract. The contracting of leisure time activity can give the client "permission" to engage in something that does not work and can provide structure to an otherwise ambiguous period in life.

Finances are another factor that may deter an elderly individual from entering retirement (Dziegielewski & Harrison, 1996). Fear of not having enough income or of being inundated with medical bills and having difficulty securing health insurance may cause an elderly person to avoid facing retirement. In terms of suicide, there has not been a clear link between suicide and retirement, but the economic, social, and emotional contexts that change in a client's life can be severe, causing difficulties in any transitions that are yet to come (Zarit & Zarit, 2007). A social worker must be aware of the resources available to his elderly client and must help the client to obtain adequate financial counseling. Places of employment often will provide such counseling on request. Insurance brokers can be consulted about health and life insurance. These brokers are usually able to discuss numerous policy options because they represent several different companies.

Always remember when conducting retirement counseling that people often resist change and avoid what they cannot predict. Many people approaching retirement have grown comfortable in their careers and established job patterns that are integral parts of their lives. Elderly clients need to be made aware of the options available to them in retirement, especially in regard to leisure activities.

Preretirement services offered to prospective retirees is an area of social work intervention that should probably be expanded because currently many people preparing to retire avoid or do not engage in this type of planning (Rhodes, 1988) and social work practice offers few preretirement services (Dziegielewski & Harrison, 1996). Most social work interventions in this area come after the fact and are supportive in nature. Montana (1985) stated that preretirement counseling is necessary because it can help elderly people to decrease their anxiety about what retirement will bring. Social workers can take a more active role in preretirement counseling by telling clients about its importance, as well as about how to plan for the future and what to expect in the way of benefits and activities. Attitude toward retirement can be very important in determining life satisfaction during retirement (Rhodes, 1988).

COMMUNITY CARE AND CASE MANAGEMENT WITH THE ELDERLY

Case management is a collaborative process that assesses, plans, implements, coordinates, monitors, and evaluates the options and services required to meet an individual's health needs, using communication and available resources to promote quality, cost-effective outcomes (Mullahy, 1998). Case management services for elderly individuals are considered an important and necessary service for the continuity of care (Austin & McClelland, 2009). Case management services with elderly individuals, similar to all age recipients, seek to ensure that all clients receive the services that they need in a system that sometimes appears fragmented and difficult to navigate. The tasks in case management can vary; for the most part, however, for the elderly these services can include the concrete tasks of completion of psychosocial assessments, initiation and implementation of advanced directives, assistance in connecting to resources and insurance verification for hospital stays, provision of community resources, and completing referrals for services and durable medical equipment. Case management also includes more supportive services such as crisis intervention support services and assisting clients with medication understanding and compliance (Hawkins, Veeder, & Pearce, 1998). All of these services are designed to help the individual maintain his or her current status in the community.

Did You Know...Two general terms are often used in the medical community to describe the process of getting older. The first, "aging," is defined as the condition of growing older regardless of chronological age; the second, "senescence," is used to characterize the later years in a life span (Peterson, 1994).

Furthermore, normal aging can be divided into two types: "intrinsic aging," which refers to the characteristics and processes common to all elderly people of a given gender, and "extrinsic aging," which refers to the factors that influence aging in varying degrees and that can affect individuals differently—for example, lifestyle patterns and exposure to environmental influences. "Normal aging is defined as the sum of intrinsic aging, extrinsic aging, and idiosyncratic or individual genetic factors in each individual" (Peterson, 1994, p. 46).

For the elderly, community-based care and case management services often begin with assessing the "person-in-situation." For example, to stay in the community safely, what type of support system does the elderly individual have? When support systems are severely limited or do not exist, a client can refuse to consider more restrictive care. Therefore, it is a delicate issue when a client living in the community refuses to go to a nursing home when they are unable to handle their own activities of daily living (ADLs) or their own affairs.

In the broadest sense, the social work case manager is the person who makes the health care system work, influencing both the quality of the outcome and the cost (Mullahy, 1998). Roles are diverse but perhaps the case manager can facilitate an earlier more supported and stable discharge when a client has been hospitalized, negotiate a better fee from a medical equipment supplier, or encourage the family to assume responsibility for assistance with the day-to-day care for their elderly relative. In addition, the social worker can serve as a catalyst for change by seeking solutions that promote improvement or stabilization rather than simply monitoring patient status (Mullahy, 1998). Often the social worker may have to arrange home health care for the patient, for nursing home placement, for medical equipment, for hospice, transplants, or simply transportation for the patient (Nelson & Powers, 2001). To ensure that individual worth, dignity, and safety are always maintained, the social worker must take into account the client's desires, the client's family's desires, the needs of the client, and the potential for future growth in this environment.

ABUSE, NEGLECT, RISK OF EXPLOITATION, AND AGING

Elder abuse and neglect remains a significant concern of practitioners as well as policy makers and program planners (Nerenberg, 2006). The definition of exactly what constitutes elderly abuse can vary widely. According to Nerenberg (2006) these circumstances appear the most problematic for treatment, similar to child abuse situations that involve physical abuse, sexual abuse, verbal or psychological abuse, and the violation of basic human rights including abduction and abandonment. In addition to this is elder domestic violence, homicides against elders, elder homicide-suicides, and financial abuse. The term "elder justice" is used to signify the connection between adult protective services (APS) and the criminal justice system and making sure that when victimization rises to a criminal standard it is addressed and, if needed, prosecuted to the fullest extent of the law (Dubble, 2006). The process of taking reports of elder abuse, assessing and substantiating the reports, and providing intervention rests with the APS agencies.

Individuals with cognitive impairment disorders such as dementia are at increased risk of elder abuse. These disorders and others that disturb cognitive functioning can be the most difficult for APS workers to assess because of an elder's right to choose. This is very different than when working with children, where intervention is expected regardless of choice. Elders that are mentally competent are capable of making their own decisions, and for workers it can be difficult to decide what to do if the older adult does not want any intervention. Generally, there is only one reason usually cited by APS workers for when they would disregard a client's right to choose and that is when they are deemed to be mentally incompetent (Bergeron, 2006). As mandatory reporters, social workers must make sure every effort has been made to protect the client and determine whether the client who is refusing services is capable of rational thought.

Violent behaviors between caregivers and care recipients can occur as well as self-neglect, requiring the case be reported to adult protective services. Bomba (2006) suggests three essential questions to address when elder abuse is suspected:

1. Is the patient safe?
2. Does the patient accept intervention?
3. Does the patient have the capacity to refuse treatment?

Drifthnery (2000) examined abuse, neglect, and exploitation of the elder population and found that factors such as self-imposed neglect, endangered behaviors, financial mismanagement, and environmental dangers as well as physical illness and/or disability, with a mental health conditions such as alcohol or other substance abuse could increase cases of elderly abuse. Since social workers are in a unique position throughout the different levels of care, they are also in the perfect position to recognize and assess on behalf of this vulnerable population.

Choi and Mayer (2000) believe that one way to decrease this problem is to open up more community-based care opportunities such as case management. In the community care setting, social workers are encouraged to provide education to the elderly, their families, and the public to prevent elder maltreatment. Also, greater advocacy to increase funding for prevention, detection, support, and intervention in elder abuse and neglect is needed. This trend is just beginning, as law enforcement agencies have just begun to see the need to develop programs to investigate and identify crimes against the elderly. According to the U.S. Department of Justice Bureau of Justice Statistics, in 1999, 3.8 of every 1,000 persons 65 and older were victims of elderly crime. An elderly person swindled out of more than $50,000 is a typical financial crime of the aging population. Unfortunately, many elderly victims, especially those who live alone, worry that reporting crime could bring embarrassment, along with additional harassment. Even worse, victims think concerned family members could use the incident as leverage to put them in a nursing home. Social workers need to review warning signs, such as when the elderly withdraw large sums of money from bank accounts, and family members or financial institutions should watch for these transactions. Agencies and victim support services are ill prepared to deal with an increase in victims. Advocacy against crimes against the elderly is necessary and urgent.

ASSESSING SUICIDE AND PLANNING FOR DEATH

Today, suicide rates among the elderly are on the rise, particularly among elderly men, and some authors believe these rates are underreported. Perkins and Tice (1994) reported that among the general population, the suicide rate is 12.4 per 100,000 persons; the suicide rate for older people is higher than in the general population with a rate of 20 per 100,000 being recorded in 1990. Persons aged 65 and older compromise 12.5 percent of the population and account for 20.9 percent of the suicides annually (Perkins & Tice, 1994, p. 438). As of 2000, the American Association of Suicidology continues to support this contention, reporting that this rate is approximately 18.1 percent. This organization also reports that in 2000 suicide rates ranged from 12.6 percent or 100,000 persons aged 75 to 84. For the elderly, this makes the rate almost double when compared to the overall U.S. rate. Leach (2006) reports that today European American elderly individuals have the highest suicide rates among all age groups with the highest rate among people in their 80s. Depression seems to be a key factor leading to these decisions. This statistic alone is hard to believe: while older Americans constitute 15 percent of the population, those over age 65 also constitute 25 percent of all suicides.

Did You Know…Suicide is the eighth leading cause of death in the United States and accounts for over 30,000 deaths each year.

Why are the rates so high in this group, and will they continue to grow? There is probably no conclusive reason for these trends, but one possibility is that stress levels among the elderly are so high that usual methods of coping and problem solving are ineffective (Canetto, 1992). Another is that religious organizations and family and friends may be uncomfortable discussing this with a loved one as they fear it might make the situation worse (Leach, 2006). Furthermore, it is clear that many elderly appear to be more dissatisfied with their functional abilities because of ill health and its effects (Reynolds et al., 1994). Finally, the tremendous number of life stressors that the elderly may experience in a short amount of time—for example, death of spouse, relatives, or friends and changes in social status and employment status—cannot be overemphasized (Dziegielewski, 2004).

Suicide rates are usually considered indicative of the mental health, satisfaction, and well-being of a population. But society doesn't always view suicide among the elderly in the same way as suicide involving young people. For example, the increase in suicide rates among adolescents has raised much alarm and led many to a call for solutions. At the same time, however, suicide is sometimes accepted as an understandable option for elderly people who feel lost, trapped, and alone (Kastenbaum & Coppedge, 1987). As proposed by Kastenbaum and Coppedge (1987) it remains the case that suicide for the frail and sick elderly may even be encouraged by the reduction of health care benefits and the rationing of "limited health care options" to aged individuals. For the most part, the methods for completion of suicide are similar in the young and old, including methods such as inappropriate use of prescription medications or alcohol, delaying medical treatment for a life-threatening condition, or risk-taking behavior such as driving recklessly (Zarit & Zarit, 2007). In the elderly, however, the self-destructive behaviors tend to be more subtle and range from taking too much prescription medication to none at all (Zarit & Zarit, 2007).

The death of a partner presents a particular coping problem because it may require the elderly survivor to assume new, unfamiliar duties: balancing a checkbook, driving, shopping for groceries, and so forth. These new tasks and the adjustments they imply, in conjunction with the loss of a life partner, can place unbelievable stress on the elderly. They may feel isolated from married friends and fear possible dependence on family or friends. Widowhood particularly affects elderly women because they generally outlive their male partners (Federal Interagency

---

Box 5: A No Harm–No Risk Agreement

Social work professionals often help clients to complete these professional agreements even when clients have no actual plans to harm themselves. This is not a legal contract; it is merely done to help the client feel that there is a plan and that the plan is being monitored. It can also provide a standard of practice and documentation of a plan.

I _____ agree that I will not harm myself or someone else in any way and that I do not have any plans to do so. If I start to feel as though I might want to try to harm myself or someone else, I agree to immediately seek help at [insert the name and address of a 24-hour emergency room that handles indigent clients where the client can report to be seen].

Signed [client's name signed here]

Witness [social worker's name here] [phone number for agency/social worker]

Family Witness [get permission from the client for a family member to witness]

Forum on Aging-Related Statistics, 2000). Female widowhood may not be directly linked to suicide, however, because suicide rates are higher for elderly men than for elderly women (Zarit & Zarit, 2007). Nevertheless, Zarit and Zarit (2007) warned, widowhood is likely to have negative effects on the survivor, including impairment of physical, psychological, and social well-being. Suicide among the elderly is almost always a result of major life stresses and accumulated losses; therefore, widows and widowers have a high probability of committing suicide. Research indicates that the first year after the death of a spouse is the hardest time of adjustment (Erlangsen, Jeune, Billie-Brahe, & Vaupel, 2004). During this especially stressful period, social workers should keep aware of a client's abilities or problems in coping with grief.

The social worker plays an essential role with potentially suicidal elderly clients. First, if a client, young or old, expresses a wish to commit suicide and has a concrete plan, steps to ensure hospitalization must be taken immediately. The person needs to be in a safe place. Unfortunately, criteria for hospital admission are not always clear, and the social worker may not know how likely the client is to turn thoughts into actions (Dziegielewski & Harrison, 1996). In any case, some type of counseling must take place. For dealing with aged clients Perkins and Tice (1994) emphasized a counseling strategy that focuses on client strengths. In this method client and social worker identify the client's preexisting coping and survival skills in order to help the client to accept the role of survivor. This approach, in conjunction with crisis services and bereavement counseling, can help the elderly client to regain control of her life.

Much of the confusion in our society regarding death can be linked to the atmosphere of denial, secrecy, and fear that we have created around this inevitable part of life (LaRue, 1985; Leach, 2006). Many people attempt to ignore or avoid this fact, at least until it affects them indirectly. For example, have you prepared for your own death? Do you have a will? Is your family aware of your wishes? For most of us the answer is no. Our reasons vary from "I'm too young to worry about that now" to "I have plenty of time." Now consider, if you the helping professional said no, what do you think your clients will answer? By the way, if you did say no, you're not alone; but don't take too much comfort in this—it's evidence that you need to address these issues in your own life.

No one rationally desires to be dying or to have a terminal illness. Indeed, most people resist even the idea of being ill. For some people, however, regardless of age, there comes a time when they truly do want to die (High, 1978). Among the elderly, many fear the chronic conditions that can make them dependent on family and/or friends. Family members too fear this new relation, daunted by the prospect of making decisions about a loved one, especially in regard to continuing or terminating life. The elderly person and family members often turn to science and medicine for the answers. Physicians, as representatives of the scientific and healing community, are sought out and expected to supply answers and make decisions. Unfortunately, many physicians, taught from the day they enter medical school to preserve life, may feel unprepared to deal with the psychosocial aspects of dying (Nolan, 1987). Trained to help people avoid death, many health care professionals see their role as avoiding death (Dziegielewski, 2004). It is the social worker, often as part of an interdisciplinary team, who will be asked to help the client or family to cope with death.

Before a social worker can successfully help a client and her family to deal with death, several issues should be addressed. First, the social worker must explore his own feelings about death. Many social work practitioners, like their medical counterparts, are uncomfortable with the subject of dying (LaRue, 1985). It may help for the social worker to discover how death is viewed in other countries and religions (Dziegielewski & Harrison, 1996). The Roman Catholic Church, for example, has been very responsive in helping individuals to prepare for death (LaRue, 1985). By examining alternative conceptions of death and the legitimization of the role of death, social workers can disperse some of the mysticism that surrounds death in this country. Once the social worker feels comfortable talking about death these concepts need to be discussed with the client as well as family members.

Second, the social worker must know what resources and services available in the community might assist elderly clients in preparing for death. One example is the Hospice program (Facts and Figures, 2008). Hospice, which is funded by Medicare, offers services to people suffering from terminal illnesses who are expected to live six months or less (Dziegielewski, 2004). This and similar programs do not focus on prolonging life beyond its natural end. In providing services through such programs the social worker serves on an interdisciplinary team designed to help the client and family members to prepare for natural death.

Finally, the social worker should learn about living wills and decide whether such a measure is appropriate for the client. Most people are aware of the need for, and some do complete, a will that declares who is to receive their money, property, and other possessions. However, the concept of a living will is less familiar (Dziegielewski, 2004; Paterson, Baker, & Maeck, 1993). Simply stated, a living will allows a person to document, in advance, his or her preferences relating to the use or avoidance of life-sustaining procedures, in the event of a terminal illness. This type of documentation is especially helpful to family members burdened with making such decisions when an elderly relative is mentally incapacitated. Without it, they may avoid making any decision because they feel that doing so gives them too much control and responsibility.

SUMMARY

We all face the prospect of growing old. Yet the elderly often suffer as the result of societal attitudes that devalue old age. Our society fears aging and promotes any number of attempts to beat the effects of old age on the human body and the mind. Such prejudices spring from both rational and irrational fears. Rational fears about worsening health, the loss of loved ones, and declining social status can be intensified by negative stereotypes of the elderly. And irrational fears about changes in physical appearance, loss of masculinity or femininity, and perceived mental incompetence are not unusual. For elderly people, misinformation and myth, as well as real biological, psychological, social, and economic challenges, can impede self-help and the pursuit of individual contentedness.

Aging in today's society creates complexities both in policy and in the human experience. Advances in medicine allow people to live longer. You will find many families that have three generations of "seniors": the granddaughter in her late 50s, the father in his early 80s, and the grandmother in her 100s. Talk about perplexing family dynamics!

As we age and live longer, we will spend more years in retirement. Once a short period of time, maybe ten to fifteen years, retirement now can last forty and even fifty years. Income, health care, socialization, loneliness and happiness, and support are among the many areas that policymakers and senior advocates struggle with today.

The good news is that older people are turning more often to mental health professionals to address the problems they are facing (Zarit & Zarit, 2007). At a minimum, social workers need to examine their own attitudes about aging and how these attitudes can affect their practice with elderly clients and their families. As mandatory reporters, we should be familiar with our roles and what we need to do to protect those who cannot protect themselves. We should be keenly aware of the types of discrimination that can occur, and we must never contribute, directly or indirectly, to any discriminatory practices based on age. All helping professionals need to recognize that each aged person is a valuable resource in our society. Our role is to provide services and advocacy that will help the elderly to maximize their life satisfaction and well-being.

Chapter 12

Domestic Violence

CONSIDERABLE ATTENTION HAS BEEN PAID TO THE FACT THAT OUR society is "violent." In 1994, the cover page of *Time* magazine showed a bruised and battered woman and the subsequent article reported that women are as likely to be killed by their partners as by any other kind of assailant (When Violence Hits Home, July 4, 1994, p. 21). Today, as the population continues to increase so does the incidence of domestic violence against women (Walker, 2009; Wilke & Vinton, 2003). According to Miller (2008) domestic violence is the leading cause of serious injury to women in the United States and adversely affects 1.7 million women at any given moment; every nine seconds a woman in the United States is beaten by her husband or her boyfriend; and, in their lifetime, 20 percent of women will experience physical violence, over 7 percent are raped by their intimate partner, and almost 5 percent are stalked (p. 210).

Statistics say that more than 20 percent of all couples have experienced some form of domestic violence over the previous year (Miller, 2008). In these couples there may be mutual battering but statistics seem to show that in heterosexual couples the male is more likely to be the abuser. In support of this contention, Rennison and Welchans (2000), after utilizing the National Crime Victimization data, estimated that the abuse is so much more common on the male side that five times as many women as men were victims of domestic violence. Each year it is estimated that 8.7 million women will be abused by an intimate partner, and two million will be victims of severe violence (Green & Roberts, 2008).

Domestic violence and the abuse that occurs is not always limited to males, nor is it always extremely violent. It is not uncommon for less severe forms of abuse to be perpetrated and for these abuse patterns to be mutual by both males and females within intimate relationships (Wilke & Vinton, 2003). Furthermore, there is a growing body of research that has linked threats and coercion by the batterer as a means of keeping the individual from leaving the situation. Threats can include harming children, relatives, or even the individual's pets (Faver & Strand, 2003). Nevertheless, many women who experience abuse by partners still remain resistant toward pressing charges (Green & Roberts, 2008; Siegler, 1989).

Did You Know...Domestic Violence and the treatment of such has been recognized as a public health problem. In a 2003 study of 522 individuals in California, 79.4% of the participants agreed and supported the need for more domestic violence prevention programming (Sorenson, 2003).

Name: Magaly Ortiz

Place of residence: Miami, Florida

College/university degrees: Barry University, BS in Psychology; University of Central Florida, MSW

Present position: MSW intern/student and MSW Student Association President

Previous work/volunteer experience:
Case Manager for a sexual trauma recovery center

What do you do in your spare time? I like to exercise, dance, and spend time with family and friends.

Why did you choose social work as a career? One of the things that helped me decide to become a social worker was my parents' divorce, which was a very difficult experience for me. While technically my parents were not taken away from me, I can relate to the fear of losing one's family. In this way, I can empathize and relate on a more personal level with clients who are children of divorced parents.

What is your favorite social work story? I have not been in the field long enough to have many stories, but one that comes to mind occurred when I was an intern working with sexually abused children. I remember the satisfaction of watching a child begin and end her healing journey. It was exciting for me to see the progress and success that children can make with treatment. It was at this time that I knew I was in the right field.

What would be the one thing you would change in our community if you had the power to do so? I would like to change the decision-making power that managed care has on the treatment that our clients receive. Insurance companies make the decisions about how much time a client needs to recover from a mental illness or trauma; however, they do not have the education to determine the medical attention necessary. Therefore, if I had the power to change anything, I would like medical doctors and professionals to be the evaluators in determining the treatment a client should receive.

Although domestic violence is not purely a crime against women, millions of women are affected by this cyclic pattern of abuse. The numbers are astounding as each year at least 2,000 women are beaten to death by a domestic partner, and what is most sad is that women are more likely to killed by a domestic partner than a stranger or anyone else (Miller, 2008). Studies indicate that in any given year anywhere between one-third and one-half of women murdered in the United States have been killed by a boyfriend, spouse, or ex-mate (Litsky, 1994; Schneider, 1994) whereas 10 percent of the men murdered in America have been killed by a female partner, usually in self-defense (Statman, 1990). Gelles's (1979) prediction seems to remain true when he said that as many as half of the couples living in the United States are estimated to have experienced violence in their relationship.

Domestic violence is not unique to heterosexual couples as partner violence can also affect gay, lesbian, and transgendered couples. Just as in heterosexual couples, it is no easier to leave an abusive relationship and the love, caring, and remorse remain a part of all relationships (Shernoff, 2008). Although the violence patterns may be similar, these couples face the additional burden of social stigma or the fear that they will not be believed or, worse yet, that their concerns will not be given adequate attention by law enforcement or the judicial system (Miller, 2008).

According to Green and Roberts (2008), recorded on a yearly basis for the past 20 years, approximately 1.5 to 2 million women have needed emergency medical attention as a result of domestic violence. Social workers that work in the emergency room setting are sure to see this type of case. To these social workers, it comes as no surprise that approximately 20 percent of female visits to emergency rooms are the result of battering, and more generally, assault by a partner— domestic violence, date rape, and so forth; these numbers are so high they could account for incidents severe enough to account for 70 percent of all admissions. With abuse being addressed more and more in hospital emergency rooms, many states now allow the police to arrest a suspected abuser without a warrant when evidence exists of an injury serious enough to require emergency medical care (Statman, 1990). The legal treatment of domestic violence can be complicated because laws in regard to domestic violence vary from state to state and often differ between municipalities in the same state (Statman, 1990). Over the past fifteen years the problem of domestic violence and legal system intervention, as well as the roles of assessment and social work practice, have gained wide recognition within the social work profession. Walker (2009) warns that many women involved in the legal system, especially those incarcerated, may settle as soon as possible simply so they can return home to care for their children. On the other hand, Walker (2009) describes a recent case in her book where the client actually preferred jail, viewing it as a relief from the abuse she was forced to sustain at home with her partner.

Did You Know...In 1883 the state of Maryland outlawed wife abuse after acknowledging that violence against women was assault. In 1910 thirty-five states followed this lead and adopted the view that the battering of women is equivalent to assault (Siegler, 1989).

Domestic violence and its relationship to women being considered as subordinate to men has deep roots. Numerous theological teachings, Judeo-Christian as well as Moslem, foster the belief that women must submit and answer to their male counterpart. Roman law defined the status of women as subject to the wishes and desires of their husbands because women were regarded as personal possessions of men (Siegler, 1989). Throughout history father-to-son transmission of wealth has been common, and a woman's property has fallen under the control of her husband after marriage. Under English common law, a woman had no legal existence apart from the relation with her spouse. For example, if a woman was raped, only her father or her husband could claim compensation from the perpetrator (Siegler, 1989).

The advent of the feminist movement in the 1960s and 1970s greatly altered the perception of violence perpetrated against women. The prevailing psychoanalytic view, which asserted that battered women were masochistic and gained sexual excitement from beatings, was challenged (Constantino, 1981; Gelles & Harrop, 1989). Other theories of violence toward women take the view that battering is rooted in patriarchal society (Srinivasan & Davis, 1991) and that imbalances in power between men and women leave women vulnerable to abuse. The problem is thus redefined as a social issue rather than an individual pathology. Sociological perspectives investigate domestic violence in the context of social stress, learned violent response, and cycles of perpetuated family violence (Gutierrez, 1987). Feminist perspectives identify battering as a means of obtaining social control and maintaining social oppression (Gutierrez, 1987). Indeed, it wasn't until the feminist movement of the 1970s that the battering of women was recognized as a problem that required attention (Siegler, 1989).

In this chapter we discuss the problems related to domestic violence and the role social workers hold in addressing this problem. Recognizing the signs and symptoms of domestic violence and supporting and protected the survivor is essential. With each assessment and intervention provided, we emphasize that social workers must never blame those involved—and must teach others as well, to never blame those involved in domestic abuse. It is a nationwide problem that can affect anyone, of any age, race, creed, or income. Interventions with survivors of domestic violence must be interdisciplinary in nature. Social workers must cooperate closely with other service providers, including members of the criminal justice system.

DOMESTIC VIOLENCE DEFINED

What exactly is domestic violence? We use the word "violence" because "this is not a question of minor arguments or disputes but, rather, intentional hostile and aggressive physical or psychological acts" (Dwyer, Smokowski, Bricout, & Wodarski, 1996). Definitions of violence range from "the use of physical force by one person against another" (Siegler, 1989) to "pushing, slapping, punching, kicking, knifing, shooting, or the throwing of objects at another person" (Gelles, 1987, p. 20). In its most simple form **domestic violence** is defined as any physical act of violence directed at one partner or the other (Edleson, 1991). A broader concept, **abuse** refers to any behavior that harms the target, including psychological, emotional, and nonviolent sexual abuse (Green & Roberts, 2008; Siegler, 1989). Some researchers differentiate domestic violence into two main types. The first is known as intimate terrorism where the partner tries to control the other using a variety of coercive strategies (Miller, 2008). The second is known as situational couple violence, which is less coercive and results from certain situations where physical aggression arises and cannot be controlled. Many victims refer to this as "losing it," where the anger cannot be controlled. Although the magnitude and severity of domestic abuse varies, it generally also involves violent acts perpetuated against a partner in a relationship, oftentimes in the presumed safety and privacy of the home (Dwyer et al., 1996).

CHARACTERISTICS OF THE ABUSED AND THEIR ABUSERS

In discussing survivors of abuse two points must be emphasized. First, social workers must be careful never to blame the victim for domestic violence. Unfortunately, both society at large and the abuser may assert that the violence itself is evidence that the victim must have done something wrong (Walker, 2009). It is important to ensure that both the victim and her family understand that blaming the victim for what is happening simply reinforces the problem. Second, social workers need to be aware that female abuse survivors may blame themselves for the abuse. They may have illusions of being able to control the abuser's behavior and so feel great shame at allowing themselves to be abused (Dziegielewski & Resnick, 1996).

Several studies—admittedly on small samples—indicate that women who are battered have experienced childhood family violence, witnessed parental abuse, and were often abused as children (Gelles & Cornell, 1990; Siegler, 1989; Tolman & Bennett, 1990). There is also the assumption that the abuser has been physically abused themselves by parents, caretakers, or others. As adults, the abusers do not know how to control their anger and thus take it out on the intimate partner (Glicken & Sechrest, 2003). Another factor to consider involves entering childhood and adolescence with recruitment into the sex industry, where out of economic need and limited financial and social supports, women can become trapped, creating a pathway to violence-prone situations (Willison & Lutter, 2009).

Box 1: Blaming the Victim and the Case of Hedda Nussbaum

Societal contempt was clear in the case of Hedda Nussbaum, who made the cover of *Newsweek* in 1988. Her live-in boyfriend, Joel Steinberg, charged with murdering the couple's adopted 6-year-old daughter, had beaten her face and body. The abuse in this relationship was documented as beginning in March 1978 and ending November 1987, when Hedda asked Steinberg for permission to get help for their abused child. Unfortunately, the child was already dead from the beating she had received. In the aftermath many people blamed Hedda for her failure to save the child. The *Washington Post* described as sickening that the state and its key witness could collude to use "victimization" as an excuse for Hedda's lack of judgment and inaction (Jones, 1994, p. 175). Many people could not believe that the beatings that Hedda received and the fear she developed as a result of the abuse left her incapable of intervening for the life of her daughter, let alone her own.

Characteristics of women who feel trapped in abusive relationships include 1) low self-esteem, 2) lack of self-confidence, 3) a tendency to withdraw from marital disputes and stress, 4) increased feelings of depression, hopelessness, and frustration, 5) proneness toward drug and alcohol abuse and dependency, and 6) suicide attempts and successful suicidal and homicidal behavior (Liutkus, 1994). It is unclear how this feeling of being trapped can affect the children in these homes. Yet for women, violence often occurs in the home with mothers acting alone being considered responsible for approximately 40 percent of the child abuse and neglect cases (U.S. Department of Health and Human Services, 2007).

No one knows exactly why a victim stays in a violent relationship, but numerous reasons have been postulated. Probably one of the most sobering statistics outlines the very real danger that can occur in leaving or escaping the violent relationship. One in five women are severely injured or killed by a partner without warning. Oftentimes the fatal or life-threatening incident was the first of its kind, and in 45 percent of the homicides the partner was trying to leave the relationship (Green & Macaluso, 2009). So once a decision to leave is made, it should never be done on the spur of a moment or used as a threat. Leaving requires a well-developed safety plan that allows for the safe exit of the partner and his or her children. Devising a safety and escape plan is often the first order of business in the initial interview (Walker, 2009).

In many cases the victim simply believes that the abusive partner will reform, and promises that it will never happen again can be very seductive. The victim may doubt her ability to manage alone or fear the stigma of divorce and of being left "alone." The realization that you will have to live on one income and accept full responsibility for the children can be very frightening. Also, the victim may worry about what will happen to her and her children if she leaves—poor employment options and the possibility of homelessness (half of homeless women in this country are fleeing from domestic violence; Mullins, 1994), as well as difficulty finding and affording adequate daycare for her children (Dziegielewski, Campbell, & Turnage, 2005; Dziegielewski & Resnick, 1996; Dziegielewski, Resnick, & Krause, 1996; Gelles & Cornell, 1990). Family ties may be strained and support networks limited.

Among all these possibilities, it has been speculated that the greatest deterrent for women is the fear of economic hardship and inadequate care for their children. For women in this situation, this fear is very well founded. Many women, by accepting primary responsibility for home and children, place themselves at a disadvantage as wage earners. Their economic dependence can serve to preserve abusive situations by reducing opportunities for leaving them. On average for all women, not just abused women, marital separation often leads to a significant drop in a woman's standard of living within the first year. To complicate this further, child support payments are often not made regularly, and consistent alimony payments are rare even when they are awarded. Economic disparity alone amply explains why women stay in abusive relationships. Social and economic factors overall clearly indicate the need for therapeutic intervention that is progressive and addresses protection, prevention, and economic support.

A high correlation exists between substance abuse and domestic violence (Liutkus, 1994; Siegler, 1989; Stith, Williams, & Rosen, 1990; Tolman & Bennett, 1990). Furthermore, it appears that women who use substances report a higher level of exposure to trauma and dangerous situations (Cohen, Hien, & Batchelder, 2008). To further complicate this situation, spouse abuse is often mutual. Husbands and wives have both been found to initiate repetitive, violent interactions; however, the consequences of male physical violence are usually more profound (Siegler, 1989; Stith et al., 1990). Men who physically abuse their partners expect their partners to be subordinate to them (Stith et al., 1990). Abusive males generally adhere to traditional, stereotypic gender or sex roles and use violence to maintain power and control over the family (Petretic-Jackson & Jackson, 1996).

For many of the male abusers, their own low self-esteem, low assertiveness, and a low sense of self-efficacy and the possibility of being exposed to childhood family violence limit their coping skills (Green & Roberts, 2008; Tolman & Bennett, 1990). These men are especially prone to feelings of helplessness, powerlessness, and inadequacy. Abusers are often pathologically jealous, prone to addiction, and passive, dependent, and antisocial (Gelles & Cornell, 1990). Histories of sexual aggressiveness and violence toward others, poor impulse control, isolation, and poor relationship skills are also common traits (Finkelhor et al., 1988). Educational level, occupational status, and income are customarily low, and in fact, unemployment or underemployment increases the likelihood of battering (Gelles & Cornell, 1990; Siegler, 1989). Alcohol and other drug-related problems were identified in two-thirds of the offenders who committed or attempted homicide (Green & Macaluso, 2009).

Green and Roberts (2008) identify what they refer to as red flags and outline twenty-three warning signs of a potentially abusive partner. The most prominent of these signs include: the abuser is jealous and possessive; intimidates and raises fear in the partner by raising a fist or kicking a pet; exhibits poor impulse control and explosive anger; needs immediate attention and responses; violates personal boundaries; often tells the partner what to wear; uses extreme control tactics; attacks self-confidence of partner; is emotionally dependent and only wants to spend time together; becomes hostile after binge drinking; never takes responsibility for the role he/she has in a problem; cannot control anger; has poor communication skills; has a history abusing a previous partner; threatens to hit, slap, or punch when angry; acts in ways that are highly impulsive, self-punitive, moody, resentful, and tense (p. 116).

Pregnancy can put a tremendous stress on a relationship, and is indeed also a factor that increases the rate of battering (Rizk, 1988; Siegler, 1989). In an abusive relationship, pregnancy might escalate potentially assaultive behavior patterns (Green & Roberts, 2008). Liutkus (1994) reported that 37 percent of pregnant women seeking obstetrical care reported battering during the term of their pregnancies. Those who abuse often tell social workers that they were provoked to violence (Edleson & Tolman, 1992). Although claims that "she drove me to it" are often made to justify abusive behavior, research suggests that such provocation is rare (Ganley, 1989). Many professionals believe that these claims likely reflect the abuser's denial of responsibility for his actions and must be challenged and refuted in order for him to progress in treatment (Edleson, 1991).

Did You Know...Although there is no consensus about the causes of domestic violence, Straus (1980) identified the following characteristics in cases of spousal abuse:
- *Husband employed part time or unemployed*
- *Spousal concerns about economic security*
- *Two or more children*
- *Spousal disagreements over children*
- *Spouses from violent families*
- *Couples married less than ten years*
- *Spouses under 30 years of age*
- *High levels of family and individual stress*
- *Spouses verbally aggressive*
- *Frequent alcohol use*
- *Residence in a neighborhood less than two years*
- *Family not part of an organized religion*
- *Wife a full-time homemaker*

When working with batterers there are two primary types of intervention often used. The first is perpetrator groups and the other is couples counseling. In the groups designed specifically for men who batter, relationship issues and the power and control relationship is clearly defined. For example, Pence and Paymar (1993) use a tool called the "Power and Control Wheel," which helps the individual identify methods of coercion such as threats, economic abuse, intimidation, emotional abuse, minimizing, denying and blaming, isolation, male privilege, and children. In couples counseling, nonviolence and equality are stressed. In this type of equality, Pence and Paynar (1993) stress negotiation and fairness, nonthreatening behavior, respect, honesty and accountability, trust and support, responsible parenting, shared responsibility, and economic partnerships.

HELPING SURVIVORS OF ABUSE

To this point we have stressed that domestic abuse is a societal and a family problem and thus needs attention from social workers trained in both macro- and micropractice. Walker (2009) states that the best way to understand domestic violence is to listen to the stories of those who have experienced it. However, no practitioner should forget that domestic violence can also involve the committing of a crime; therefore, to best help survivors of abuse social workers must be skilled in cooperating and coordinating with representatives of the criminal justice system, from police officers to prosecutors and judges.

Providing Direct Clinical Services

Social workers often provide direct clinical services for survivors of abuse. Oftentimes group sessions are offered, whether these take place in a shelter or in a safe house. Providing group as well as individual counseling for the survivor is designed to empower the survivor and help her make a decision about the future and whether to stay or leave. Guiding principles for all intervention with the survivor include first and foremost ensuring client safety and, if children are involved, the children's safety as well. A safety plan will always be part of the intervention process. It is also crucial to respect the survivor's choices and not to judge or blame the victim (Green & Macaluso, 2009). The social worker needs to accept what the client says is the truth as the truth and help her explore choices and courses of action that will ensure safety for all involved.

Dziegielewski, Campbell, and Turnage (2005) believe that in providing support a type of reality-based questioning is needed. This type of therapy does not place blame on the many occurrences of abuse that may have been endured but rather focuses on the present and what can be done about keeping the client and family safe. From this perspective, the social worker leads the domestic violence survivor through a reality-based process highlighting self-forgiveness, which often starts the healing process. Concentration on the "here and now" is highlighted, placing emphasis on future healthy relationships and not dwelling on the negative painful relationships of the past. From this perspective, the social worker helps the survivor to explore four reality-based questions:

1. What do you want?
2. What are you doing to get what you want?
3. How will you keep yourself and your loved ones safe while planning to achieve what you want?
4. How will you know if what you are doing is working?
5. What will you do once you get what you want?

In answering these questions, a structured safety plan will develop. The survivor thereby accepts responsibility and does not blame herself for her activity in the relationship. Destructive anger can be addressed and plans for how to create a healthier relationship are highlighted. Through educational and supportive interventions, the role of the social worker is essential in helping the client to understand the physical and psychological challenges and coping strategies needed to overcome the obstacles these survivors must face.

Children: The Forgotten Victims

Probably of greatest concern is how does watching the repeated violence and domestic abuse occurring in a family affect the child who is viewing it? Whether abused or just witnessing the abuse, can this have a lasting effect on the children being raised in such a home? The sad fact is that studies seem to support that it does indeed affect the child. Children raised in these homes seem to be more vulnerable and can exhibit a range of problems related to adjustment difficulties and anxiety (Green & Roberts, 2008). Since children get many of their reaction cues from their parents, being in this type of a chaotic environment can leave a deep and lasting impression. There is also the risk that occurs when witnessing abuse, and this child is more likely to grow up and enter abusive situations or become abusive in his or her own relationships.

Furthermore, there is a myth that children under the age of three are generally not affected by this type of behavior. Yet at this age children develop the capacity to experience, regulate, and express emotions as well as learn from the environment and develop trusting and secure relationships (Kamradt, Gibertson & Jefferson, 2008). Regardless of the age of the child, the social worker should always explore the effects this may have on the children and ensure that they too receive intervention and assistance. As much as possible, the parents should be involved in this process because adult pathology may continue to be reflected in the parent-child relationship (Novick & Novick, 2005).

The Criminal Justice System

To understand how the legal system treats intimate partner violence, three major areas merit consideration (Parker 1985, presented in Siegler, 1989). The first is the ideology of privacy, whereby an individual's home is viewed as a private place. Acts that happen in the home are considered to have occurred in a sacred place. As long as the couple stays together in the same house the husband cannot be ordered to change his behavior (Siegler, 1989). Many victims fear that if their case does go to court, judges will not evict a man from his home. The old adage that "a man's home is his castle" still remains and even the victim may be concerned that if the abuser is evicted from his home, he will have nowhere to go and will end up homeless (Mullins, 1994; Walker, 2009).

Did You Know…A woman could not legally refuse her spouse conjugal rights until the 1970s, when some states legally recognized the concept of marital rape.

The second area is the gap between written law and contemporary practice. Traditionally, the justice system has been unwilling to intercede or intrude in family matters, and society has preferred it that way. Survivors of abuse can feel helpless trying to persuade police officers and the courts to take action to control their partners if violence has not occurred; police officers, for their part, are often frustrated by the situation and how to intervene, and this is often complicated by a victim who refuses to admit that abuse occurred or does not want to see their partner arrested. In recognition of this weakness in the law, the federal **Violence Against Women Act** of 1994 (VAWA) was designed to improve the response of the criminal justice system to violent crimes against women (National Resource Center on Domestic Violence and Battered Women's Justice Project, 1994).

The purpose of the VAWA is to create policies to prevent domestic violence. The VAWA treats domestic violence as a major law enforcement priority and funds improved services to victims of domestic violence. Title II of the bill, the Safe Homes Act, increases federal funding for battered women's shelters and related programs. It also provides a federal crime statute for spouse abuse committed during interstate travel (Mullins, 1994). By creating emergency and long-term solutions for battered women's housing and survival needs, the VAWA is an important step in the government's commitment to preventing domestic violence. Today, police officers have mandatory arrest policies and must arrest either party if it is believed that either has committed an assault (Miller, 2008). Therefore, if a domestic assault has occurred, an arrest will be made regardless of whether the victim wants the arrest made or not. If the abuse is mutual, both may be arrested.

The third area is the complexity and lack of integration of existing legal remedies. The laws that currently exist are complex, contradictory, and at times unenforceable. The law regards property division, divorce, child custody, financial obligations, and criminal culpability as separate matters. Just as marriages can be deemed as successful, so can divorces. Unfortunately, in many of these cases, divorces go badly and children are forced to face parental conflict, aggression, and anger (Johnston, Roseby, & Kuehnle, 2009). In domestic violence cases, however, many of these issues overlap, yet because they must be addressed separately important considerations are overlooked. Although new domestic violence statutes have reduced this confusion and increased integration between jurisdictions, an abuse survivor should still have a legal representative to successfully negotiate the system (Siegler, 1989).

The assistance police provide at the domestic violence scene is critical. As first responders, officers must be aware of mediation, listening to the events as presented by both sides, restating key points, and suggesting possible solutions (Miller, 2008). Once done, the officer must ensure that there is agreement and follow through by all parties. If an assault has occurred, processing charges must be completed. Policies that favor the arrest of abusers may address the immediate situation but do little to stop future incidents of abuse from occurring (Roberts, 1996a). Frisch and Caruso (1996) warned, however, against the opposite extreme: even the most complete legal plan to address an abused woman's needs is useless if those responsible for carrying it out have no enforcement power.

The Role of the Social Worker

Mullarkey (1988) identified five areas in which social workers can join the criminal justice system and prosecutors to assist domestic violence survivors. Mandatory arrest policies and warrantless arrests can detain the abuser, but they do not address the entire problem (Roberts, 1996a). First, the social worker can help the system to understand the client by completing a detailed and accurate assessment, thus providing more information about the type of abuse, the history of abuse, and the circumstances and repercussions of the abuse. Using this additional information the social worker can attempt to identify the most dangerous cases, screen survivors for treatment, and evaluate and predict potential treatment outcomes (Saunders, 1992). The social worker can also help the client to understand the system. Abused women have varied needs for legal services, social services, and psychological services. A well-documented community-wide approach, coordinated by the social worker, can help to integrate the efforts of mental health, social service, judicial, and law enforcement agencies for the benefit of abused women (Roberts, 1996a).

Name: Joya Hovde

Place of residence: Cumming, Georgia

College/university degrees: Georgia State University, BSW

Present position: Child Protective Service Investigator with Hall County DFCS

Previous work/volunteer experience: 2003 Council on Social Work Education Member, 2002 NASW GA Legislative Action Committee, 2002 Georgia State University, College of Health and Human Services, Student Services Committee, 2001 Georgia State University, BSW Social Work Club, Director of Fundraising, and Philanthropy and President in 2002. 1999 MOMs Club of Smyrna, Subcommittee Chair, Community Outreach and Administrative Vice President in 2000.

What do you do in your spare time? In my spare time, I race remote controlled gas powered cars with my husband and son, play with our four dogs, make homemade jams and jellies, research the current social work literature, and attend conferences.

Why did you choose social work as a career? For me, social work just made sense. I enjoy empowering individuals to look beyond the reality of today and embrace the possibility of tomorrow.

What is your favorite social work story? February 18, 2002 in Atlanta, GA. It was NASW GA Student Lobby Day at the capital. Approximately 200 students, teachers, and other professionals from around the state of Georgia presented a united front at the capital. At noon we gathered together on the capital steps awaiting the end of the daily legislative session, in order to take a picture with the Speaker of the House Terry Coleman, Representative Nan Orrock, and Representative Sally Harrell. At the bottom of the steps was Governor Perdue. I walked up to Governor Perdue, introduced myself and asked him if I could introduce him to 200 voting social workers from around the state of Georgia, all of whom were representing NASW Georgia. The look on his face was priceless. Even though it was not on his schedule, Governor Perdue graciously took a picture with the members of NASW Georgia chapter represented on the capital steps that day.

What would be the one thing you would change in our community if you had the power to do so? I would change the perception of the individual members of the community and help them realize that the power within a democratic society lies with the voting majority.

My favorite quote is: "It is not the hand that signs the law that holds the power, it is the hand that casts the ballot." —*Harry S. Truman*

The second type of assistance the social worker can provide is education, support, and psychosocial adaption strategies to help get through the crisis situation (Green & Roberts, 2008). These clients can suffer from self-esteem problems as well as concerns related to their own safety and survival of themselves and their children and this can affect any action or reaction they can have (Dziegielewski, Campbell, & Turnage, 2005). Working closely and supporting and educating the client each step of the way is essential to helping them request and access the services that they need.

Social workers have an obligation to educate their clients, and in turn to be educated by system participants such as police telephone operators and dispatchers, police officers and staff, prosecutors, judges, and those directly involved such as the survivors, the abusers, and family and support system members. They need to be aware of pro-arrest and mandatory arrest policies and what they involve, as well as the potential of electronic monitoring as part of a coordinated community effort (Roberts, 1996a).

In addition to helping the client, social workers also need to educate and train police telephone operators, dispatchers, and police officers. Operators and dispatchers are the first to receive the call for help and the officer is usually the first on the scene. This education and training should include telephone training for screening and assessment, basic techniques of police safety, and dispute management and crisis intervention techniques, as well as the ability to provide referral links with the social service worker (Fusco, 1989). Training sessions in these skills can influence police officers to take seriously their role in protecting the abused woman (Roberts, 1996a).

When conducting training the social worker is responsible for creating an atmosphere for a team intervention that reflects respect, support, cooperation, and feedback. Moreover, the social worker plays a crucial role in advocating for the rights of the client, particularly in ensuring equality of access, discouraging sex-role stereotyping, explaining the social and emotional effects of discrimination, and identifying the dynamics of victimization and other relevant psychosocial factors (Martin, 1988). Working in this area can be very stressful for the social worker, and special care should always be given to recognizing feelings of apathy, frustration, and cynicism, often referred to as compassion fatigue or professional burnout (Knoll, 2009).

In addition to training frontline workers, education and training also should be provided to court clerks, case managers, legal advocates, and judges (Roberts, 1996b). Professionals in the legal system often focus on conviction as the primary means for accomplishing justice. The pain that the abuser has caused the female survivor, her children, and her family can be minimized or overlooked. The social worker therefore has a twofold task: the social worker needs, first, to educate people in the legal system about the dynamics and issues within the abusive situation and, second, to remind everyone to address the psychosocial effects that have occurred regardless of the legal outcome (Green & Roberts, 2008).

From assessment to treatment, the third role that the social worker can assume is to be a "safe individual" whom the survivor can trust and feel comfortable with. It is crucial for the professional helper to communicate clearly to the client the purpose of the therapy and to see the sessions as a safe place that is violence- and judgment-free (Walker, 2009). One dynamic in abusive relationships is for women to become isolated from their family and friends. They have often been taught to fear and avoid contact with others outside the abusive relationship. This isolation is problematic even when a woman has started to receive relief from the legal system. This woman must face her abuser and others who may threaten retaliation if the abuser faces conviction and possible incarceration. Anticipating this outcome of the legal process may leave the survivor feeling a mixture of relief and guilt, and these contradictory emotions can hamper her testimony and make her look like an unreliable witness. To represent herself in the best possible light the survivor needs to feel supported in this process. The prosecutor is usually rushed, however, and cannot build the rapport needed to get the survivor to trust her; therefore, the social worker can be a critical bridge between the prosecutor and the survivor.

Activity...It is important to understand the difference between physical and psychological abuse and how best to handle the two types of situations. Break into groups and take the two case examples below. Decide whether they involve physical abuse or psychological abuse. As a social worker presented with this situation, how would you best intervene to help? What referrals would you make in each situation and for whom would the referral be made?

Scenario 1: A verbal dispute between a husband and wife resulted in the husband threatening to get a knife and stab the wife if she tried to leave the house with the children. For fear that her husband might act on the threat, the wife did not leave.

Scenario 2: During an altercation a husband and wife yelled and pushed each other repeatedly. Upon being pushed down the husband hit his head, cutting it on an end table, and the wife later developed bruises on her shoulder and arms where her husband had grabbed her in anger.

The fourth role the social worker embraces is that of advocate. This role has always been critical for social work professionals, and advocating for the survivor within the legal system through all stages of the criminal process is essential. Social workers have the right to serve as advocates for the survivor, even before an arrest is made or while a case is awaiting trial or on appeal (Mullarkey, 1988). The role of the survivor's advocate (a.k.a. victim's advocate) is to assist the client in acting as her own representative whenever possible (Martin, 1988). When it is not possible—perhaps because the survivor is too distraught or incapacitated by the fear of retribution—the advocate can speak with the client's permission. Many states now permit the survivor or the survivor's advocate to address the judge at sentencing (Mullarkey, 1988). When situations are highly lethal, the professional helper has a responsibility to share and be honest about concerns for the client's safety, especially when planning to return to the abusive situation (Walker, 2009).

The successful advocate for a domestically abused woman must address not only a safety plan to help keep the client safe but also recognize and prepare the client for the complexities of the legal system that may be encountered. The social worker needs to be aware of the variety of system components that are involved—

in particular, law enforcement procedures, prosecution, and corrections. The second task is advocacy with family members and the support system to which the client will return. Many myths and beliefs about the survivors of domestic violence are ingrained in our society (Roberts, 1996c), and clients may be forced to confront myths subscribed to by family and friends.

The social worker can assist the survivor in this by telling people in the support system 1) about the strengths of the survivor, 2) the reason it was necessary for her to leave the abusive relationship, and 3) the reason she should put a formal end to abuse and request legally sanctioned punishment for the abuser.

The fifth role the social worker plays is expert witness. The social worker can provide professional information to clarify the meaning of the survivor's behavior (Martin, 1988; Saunders, 1992). Although social workers welcome any opportunity to assist their clients, they may worry that acting as a witness will compromise their duty to protect their client's legal rights. Counseling sessions and written notes may contain information that the social worker does not want to share because its disclosure might harm the survivor's case. For example, many times the survivor is angry with the abuser and voices this anger in an attempt to gain emotional distance from the abuser. The social worker should nevertheless always take careful case notes, though well aware that these notes can be subpoenaed by a court of law. "The constitutional guarantee to confront accusers provided by the sixth amendment can be interpreted by any competent court to over-ride any privacy statute or shield law" (Mullarkey, 1988, p. 49).

Without a court order, social workers are not required to speak to defendants, attorneys, or investigators outside of the courtroom. Mullarkey (1988) recommended that when social workers are summoned to court they recognize the importance of 1) appearing and being professional and nonpartisan, 2) answering all questions directly or fully, 3) immediately asking for clarification of unclear questions, 4) going over possible questions with the prosecutor before testifying, and 5) ensuring that every note, professional conversation, and report they have prepared is discoverable by the defendant and his legal representatives.

Activity...In the classroom, break into small groups of three or more students. As a group look at the six goals for domestic violence programs listed below and choose the three most important goals. Compare your group's choices with those of the other groups. Was it difficult for your group to agree? Why? Why not?

Goals for Domestic Violence Programs

    1. To ensure safe surroundings for survivors and their children
    2. To increase access to material resources—income, housing, food, etc.
    3. To establish and enhance legal supports
    4. To build social contacts and support networks for survivors and their children
    5. To change societal beliefs about domestic violence
    6. To create a model for relationships of shared power and leadership (adapted from Roche & Sadoski, 1996).

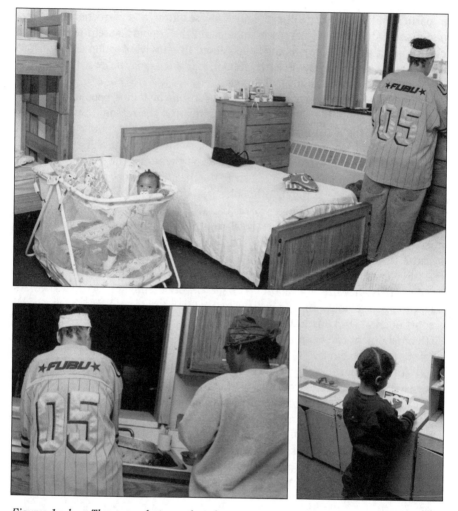

Figures 1a, b, c: These are photographs taken in a shelter for women and children who are victims of domestic abuse. The bedroom with two beds and two bunk beds may be used for one or two families. The women are cleaning up after lunch in the communal kitchen. The child is in a play area. The center is staffed by childcare workers who care for the children while mothers go to work, look for work, or go to counseling.

PRACTICE APPLICATION: THE ROLE OF THE WOMEN'S SHELTER SOCIAL WORKER

Susan and her husband have been together for ten years. During that time she has been beaten severely and treated in the local hospital emergency room. Much of the abuse between the couple is reported to be mutual; however, Susan's husband has never been hospitalized for her return attacks. On several occasions, Susan has called the police to intervene, but when they arrived on the domestic violence scene, she usually refuses to press charges. Susan has stated that she once began to press charges but soon dropped them when her husband called from jail to tell her that he loved her and to beg her forgiveness. The police are being dispatched to the scene so often that they refer to Susan and her husband by their first names.

Susan has tried to leave her husband several times but he always tracks her down and persuades her to return. Susan's family is well aware of the abuse. Both Susan's mother and her sister have started to refuse her calls asking for help. Susan often calls them when she and her husband are fighting, asking for an "understanding ear or a safe place to stay." Her family is frustrated because no matter what they do Susan always seems to return to the abusive situation. Also, whenever they do take Susan in, her husband arrives and tries to intimidate her mother. Susan's mother doesn't think her health is strong enough to handle the repeated stress.

On a referral from her employer, Susan called the shelter from a pay phone near her home after an altercation with her husband. Upon arrival at the shelter she confided in a shelter social worker that she feels lost and abandoned. During the second session Susan told the social worker that she wants to kill her husband. When asked how she would do it, Susan immediately breaks down and cries that she would probably be better off killing herself. Although when questioned further, she says she has not planned to harm herself, but that ending her life would make it easier for all. The event that precipitated Susan's crisis is a fight that she and her husband had the previous night. Susan's husband insisted that she climb a ladder and help him paint the house. Susan refused because she is four months pregnant and is afraid of heights. Her husband then hit her with the ladder across her back.

Based on the information Susan provides the social worker is able to make the following assessment. First, Susan is being beaten regularly. Second, she fears for her life, is threatening to take the life of another, and might also take her own life if she could. Third, Susan has alienated her family and has no support system available to her. Since she has made vague threats to hurt herself, this needs to be addressed immediately. The social worker feels that immediate intervention is essential to help Susan to adjust to her current situation without violence to herself or others. First, the social worker explores the possibility of getting her a formal assessment to check for any medical concerns to her unborn child and for her suicidal thoughts. After assessment, the hospital staff determine she is not in need of admission but should be watched for the potential of suicidal thoughts. Since Susan has no medical insurance and no support system, she has nowhere to go, so the social worker helps her formulate a plan.

The social worker helps Susan gain admission to the local shelter for abused women. Shelter personnel are notified of Susan's possible desire to end her life and a suicide watch is implemented. Intensive individual and group counseling resources are made available. With the help and support of the social worker an order of protection is filed. Susan decides to press charges against her husband, and asks the social worker to help her to state her case to an attorney; the social worker agrees. Susan does press charges this time and her husband is sentenced to two years in prison with the possibility of parole in six months. After she regains the recognition and assistance of her family, Susan moves to another city and stays with her aunt. Before leaving, Susan has started making plans to give up her child for adoption.

Discussion. Clevenger and Roe-Sepowitz (2009) reported that most women utilize shelter services if they have children to care for at the time of the abusive incident, call for assistance from a place other than their home, do not have a current order of protection in place, and were injured during the domestic violence incident. In this case the social worker played a twofold role. First, the social worker found a safe environment where the client received help in dealing with her crisis. The social worker also provided counseling and supportive services. Second, the social worker helped the client to create and carry out a plan of action in her dealings with the legal system. Women who have been abused by their spouses or partners need supportive services. In addition, they need the assistance of this country's legal institutions. These women need to know the following: 1) that legal services are available to them, 2) that supportive services such as those provided by a social worker are available, and 3) that the combined use of these services will alleviate and eventually resolve the situation. The role of the social work professional is crucial. Whether working within the criminal justice system itself or outside the system in an ancillary agency, the social worker can make a true difference for a survivor of domestic abuse.

SUMMARY

The survivors of domestic violence need all the services and protection that law enforcement can provide (Walker, 2009). They also need to be treated with respect and dignity and to be active in planning a course of action to protect all involved, including the children. In domestic violence, substance abuse is often a problem for males, whereas concerns about child maltreatment exist for both males and females (Johnston, Rodeby, & Kuehnle, 2009). The children are often the innocent victims. The perpetrators of the violence also need to be treated with respect. When morally objectionable behavior has occurred, it is important not to encourage supporting views that the abuser is a monster incapable of change (Knoll, 2009).

Social workers play a crucial role by providing the following services to survivors of abuse. First, they complete detailed assessments that give information about the type of abuse, the history of abuse, and the circumstances and repercussions of the abuse. Second, they actively educate and are educated by law enforcement and justice system participants and people directly involved, such as survivors, abusers, and family and support system members. Third, they act as safe individuals whom survivors can trust. Fourth, they advocate for survivors through all stages of the criminal prosecution (Green & Roberts, 2008). Last, they assist prosecutors and aid survivors by acting as expert witnesses.

Social workers must strive to develop a team approach with the legal professionals involved. These professionals must be trained to view domestic assault situations as appropriate and routine targets of police intervention. Representatives of the legal system and social workers can work together, each an integral part of the intervention team. The criminal justice system can be an effective force in decreasing violence against women. Both short-term emergency support and long-term support services are needed (Davis, Hagen, & Early, 1994). Counseling, social service assistance, and protection must be carefully coordinated and available to the abuse survivor twenty-four hours a day (Fusco, 1989; Green & Roberts, 2008; Roberts, 1996a). Morning or next-day referrals are a poor substitute for an immediate response to the crisis. Social work professionals need to be available to work directly with police and to start intervention services at the crisis scene or as soon after the incident as possible. Our current system of referral "after the fact" is not meeting the needs of many survivors of abuse.

The domestic violence shelter can offer an "immediate" safe place for women who wish to escape an abusive situation. Unfortunately, however, the number of existing shelters is far from adequate (Dziegielewski, Campbell, & Turnage, 2005; Dziegielewski et al., 1996). There are few shelters convenient for women in rural areas, and attempts to establish emergency shelters for battered women in cities still meet a variety of obstacles. Before a facility is granted approval a review of proposed property use by community boards and city planners is required in many cities. However, this requirement may compromise the confidentiality of the women and children who depend on the emergency shelter for services and so risk their safety. In addition, many community residents object to having emergency shelters in their neighborhoods because they believe such facilities are disruptive (Mullins, 1994).

Social workers must participate in and help to establish brief time-limited practice strategies (Dziegielewski, 2008a, 2008b). Also, schools of social work must address this topic and help the beginning social work professional to feel academically prepared (Danis, 2003). The purpose of these programs and policies is to immediately ease the severity of domestic violence as well as to develop long-term solutions to the need for emergency housing and financial support systems. One advance in this direction was the 1994 Violence Against Women Act.

Until recently, our society and our laws have treated the preservation of the family as paramount. Fortunately, this is changing. We must break from our history of preserving the family at any cost—even the cost of exposing women to abuse. Because social workers practice across the public and private sectors, they have enormous potential for influencing approaches to the problem of violence against women (Martin, 1988; NASW, 2003). The profession must demand changes in our laws and legal system that will prevent domestic violence. Social workers clearly recognize the importance of counseling and supportive services. However, to plan for the future, they must never lose sight of the importance of social policy change in assisting the survivors of domestic violence.

Chapter 13

The Political Arena

THINK FOR A MOMENT ABOUT POLITICS AND THE GLAMOUR OF being an elected politician. Think about the movie *Mr. Smith Goes to Washington*, ok it's a bit old, yes black and white, but still a fun movie, in which Jimmy Stewart plays a young, idealistic politician who goes to Washington to represent the people and do what is right. He embraces his new job wrapped by a simple ideal—government is the friend of all the people, works for all the people, and represents all the people. He believes that elected leaders are simply an extension of our neighbors who act on our behalf and place the community's need above their personal interests. Their overriding purpose is to help achieve what is best for the country. Do you hold this view of politics and the government? We suspect not. It's likely that few people today believe that Mr. Smith's idealistic vision accurately depicts the motivations of politicians in the late twentieth and early twenty-first centuries. Rather, the view of a recent president, Ronald Reagan, is more widely held: "Government is not the friend of the people." Even so, we believe that all social workers should and must be actively engaged in their political environments.

For many social workers the political arena is not an enticing place. Politics may conjure up ideas of backroom deal making, abuses of rank and power, payoffs, and other unethical activities. Political scandals and allegations of wrongdoing over the past few years have reached every level of political office and branch of the government. It's not surprising if you hold politics in low esteem.

Yet the days and months leading up to the November 2008 national election seemed different from previous elections. There was an energy in the air and no matter one's beliefs or party affiliation, there was a shared national excitement and a sense of political renewal. What had typically been quiet conversations ignited into almost frenzied debates in the hallways, lounges, and classrooms. Everyone had their own list of candidates, some wore buttons, yards were littered with campaign signs, and many social workers' cars made for an interesting bumper sticker read. Almost everywhere we turned, friends, colleagues, and students were in a full, open, and animated debate mode.

Now we must continue with our passions and directly engage in the political process, no matter if it is at the national, state, or local level of government. We social workers are obligated to work on behalf of our clients and promote social policies that strengthen our communities, our neighborhoods, and our nation.

Name: Jacqueline Richardson-Melecio

Place of Residence: Albany, NY

College/University Degrees: BA, MA, PhD Candidate in Social Work, University at Albany, Albany, NY

Present Position and Title: Assistant Executive Director, National Association of Social Workers, New York State Chapter; President, New Heights Consulting

Previous Work/Volunteer Experience: Managing Director, Mental Health Association New York State; Program Director, Hispanic Outreach Services Catholic Charities; Member of New York State Office of Mental Health, Multicultural Advisory Committee; Training Consultant; Adjunct Instructor, University at Albany, St. Rose College, Schenectady Community College

Why did you choose social work as a career? What is your favorite social work story? My favorite social work story occurs prior to my career as a social worker. When I reflect upon my community and the people who surrounded me my whole life, I do not have any doubt about what inspired me to be a social worker. My community, while predominately Hispanic, included a wonderful mix of various ethnic and racial groups. The early evenings of hot summer days were made up of unscheduled gatherings of young and old on the building steps. The crowd would usually extend out into the sidewalk and parked cars would sometimes be used as benches and folding chairs and steps would also serve as seats. The grown-ups chattered while they rested from a long day at work. Some children played hopscotch; others played games like catch or hide-and-seek, while a few sat and talked and shared a joke or two. All the laughter, talking, screaming, music, and pitter patter of little feet served as the backdrop to what I deem social work in its most natural state—resource sharing. At these gatherings, one saw resource sharing in many forms: referrals, housing assistance, job coaching and employment services, and counseling. It all happened so naturally everyday and just because you were a part of the community, a neighbor in need, another human being. So my favorite social work story is also my inspiration for being a social worker. Being part of a profession committed to making a difference in the lives of others, because it is the right thing to do—being a good neighbor.

What is one thing you would change in the community if you had the power to do so? It is challenging to think of just "one" thing to change. Access to healthcare, homelessness, and hunger are all things at the top of my list. If I had the power to do so, I would aim to address each of these basic need areas. I would address the quality of services, access to care, and would work toward ending hunger and homelessness in the world.

Before going any further, let's clarify what we mean by politics. Certainly, politics and the political arena include all elected offices and the officials who fill them, at the local, county, state, and federal levels. This arena is often referred to as "electoral politics." Electoral politics doesn't include what some would call "informal" or "day-to-day" politics, which involves politically charged or motivated behavior in organizations, agencies, and even on social work practice teams. How often have you heard someone say "the politics here stink" or "they're just playing politics" or "you have to understand the politics of the situation"? Therefore, what we refer to as "politics" is diverse and embraces many of our day-to-day activities. Indeed, Haynes and Mickelson (1991) have gone further, contending that all social work activities are political. In this chapter we look at electoral politics and its relation to social work practice. Our discussion examines political strategies that we hope can serve as a primer for social workers on politics and political activities.

WHY POLITICS AND SOCIAL WORK?

First, let's take a brief look at the political arena and its relation to social service agencies. What guides the activities of social workers in agencies? Workers are not able to take liberties in their practice and provide any type of service they see fit. An agency's function clearly dictates what the practitioner can do with and on behalf of a client. Let's say, for example, that a practitioner in a child welfare agency wants to offer group therapy to senior citizens in a local housing project. The intervention may be worthy, but the agency is likely to decide that a senior's group falls outside its purpose and function.

An agency's function is set forth in its mission statement and operationalized by its policies. Policies do not just spring forth; rather they are the result of a political process, be it an agency board of directors or an elected body such as a state legislature. And who are these people? Are they social workers? Are they really expert enough in human services that they should be shaping social work practice? Unfortunately, many people who develop social policies have little, if any, direct social work experience, and few have an educational background in social work. When professional social workers choose to avoid the political aspects of the field, one outcome is inevitable: people who are not social workers will govern social work practice.

Activity...Find out how many social workers there are in your state legislature, both the house and senate. You can do this by checking with your state's secretary of state's office. Then look at the house and senate committees that oversee social problems; they may have titles like Committee on Health and Human Services. Now, look to see how many committee members are social workers. Now look at their staffs; how many staff members are social workers? What do your findings tell you about the development of social policies in your state?

SOCIAL WORK VALUES AND POLITICAL ACTIVITY

Some social workers allow negative images of politics and political activity to outweigh their responsibility to engage in the political arena. Yet the NASW Code of Ethics clearly states our obligations and political responsibilities in two separate places in section 6, "the social worker's ethical responsibilities to society":

Social workers should facilitate informed participation by the public in shaping social policies and institutions. (sec. 6.02)

Social workers should . . . advocate for changes in policy and legislation to improve social conditions in order to . . . promote social justice. (sec. 6.04(a))

The Educational Policy and Accreditation Standards (EPAS) (CSWE, 2009) also support the profession's political involvement. The EPAS states specifically:

Educational Policy 2.1.8—Engage in policy practice to advance social and economic well being and to deliver effective social work services.

Social work practitioners understand that policy affects service delivery, and they actively engage in policy practice. Social workers know the history and current structures of social policies and services; the role of policy in service delivery; and the role of practice in policy development. Social workers analyze, formulate, and advocate for policies that advance social well-being; and collaborate with colleagues and clients for effective policy action.

Why do the Code of Ethics and the CSWE accreditation standards emphasize practitioner involvement in the political arena? First and foremost, remember that the definition of social work includes working to bring about a just community built on the tenets of social and economic equality. Second, many of the problems experienced by clients are created by forces external to the client and can be remedied only through amended social policy or additional funding for social services. Third, the best advocates for change are those who deal with problems day in and day out. Through direct practice, social workers see firsthand the debilitating effects of problems on clients.

Now this is where it can get a bit messy for social workers. Some groups contend that the social work profession is nothing more than a "left wing" group of ideologues who want nothing more than socialist-style programs and a "big" government. So right now, let's be clear: there is no accusation that is more unfounded and untrue. Just take a look at where social work educational programs are located; some are in our nation's most conservative faith-based universities while others are found in the most liberal universities. In other words, social work crosses the political and ideological spectrum. The social work tent includes conservatives and liberals; Democrats, Republicans, Greens, Independents, and others from the dozens of political parties that are active in politics. In other words, the social work ideology of justice for all people is not owned by one political party. Our political ideologies and philosophies merely frame different pathways to achieve justice for all.

The political diversity in social work can be difficult to accept, but if we use our critical thinking approaches, we can engage in thoughtful debate that will result in answers that benefit the greater good. And that is ultimately what politics is about—doing what is right for the greater good.

A HISTORICAL OVERVIEW OF POLITICAL ACTIVITY BY SOCIAL WORKERS

Social work has had three separate but significant waves of political involvement: the Progressive Era of the nineteenth century, the 1930s New Deal, and the

1960s War on Poverty. In each of these periods, social work's involvement in politics mirrored the profession's growth and internal conflict over mission, scope, and function. In all three periods, leaders disagreed about the causes of social problems and how best to solve them. The Progressive movement was attractive to many social workers and provided a political focus for their philosophical beliefs and commitments. Jane Addams and Florence Kelley, among others, used the political system to address social problems. Settlement house workers seemed to be more partisan than other social workers. Weismiller and Rome (1995) have noted that settlement workers ran political campaigns, organized neighborhoods to support particular candidates, lobbied, and worked on welfare reform. On the other hand, Mary Richmond, a leader in the COS movement, believed that social workers should be nonpartisan and confine their efforts to helping clients to resolve their individual issues (Weismiller & Rome, 1995).

The Great Depression of the 1930s created ample opportunity for social workers to again venture into the political arena. Schools of social work were more organized than their forerunners during the Progressive Era and macro-content, which touched on political concerns, was included in the curriculum. The federal government's Children's Bureau and Women's Bureau provided social workers with a setting in which to address social issues. In fact, many parts of the Economic Security Act of 1935 were written by social workers (Weismiller & Rome, 1995). The profession was beginning to accept political activism as an appropriate response to crisis; however, it still did not embrace political activity as an appropriate long-term social work methodology (Haynes & Mickelson, 1991).

The third wave of political activism by social workers came in the 1960s. With the emergence of the Peace Corps and VISTA, a domestic version of the Peace Corps program, and the burgeoning civil rights movement, social workers actively promoted a political agenda. Community organization, both as a practice and an educational specialization, took shape in the late 1950s and 1960s. This activity challenged social workers to view systems from the much broader macroperspective. Federal dollars were funneled to initiatives that encouraged neighborhoods and local people to engage in problem solving and community action.

Did You Know...A social worker, Senator Barbara Mikulski (D-Maryland), was a keynote speaker during the 1992 Democratic National Convention.

Within the profession, debate continued on the role and scope of political activity. Weismiller and Rome (1995) have reported that NASW members in one study agreed to pay increased dues if it brought about greater political activity by members. Yet this somewhat overzealous characterization didn't nearly affect the entire profession, and members continued to debate the merits of efforts at the political level, particularly in light of the massive problems facing individuals and families.

In 1976, NASW organized its first conference on politics, in Washington, DC. Aimed primarily at social work political activists, the meeting gathered NASW members from around the country for a political training institute. NASW then supplemented this national meeting with regional institutes. By the end of the twentieth century, NASW discontinued these gatherings and left training to the state chapters and other professional associations.

The 1990s seemed to be a watershed decade for social workers involved in electoral politics. Never before in the profession's history were social workers and their professional organizations as active in political campaigns as in the last decade of the twentieth century. "Lift Up America" was the NASW's 1992 Presidential Project theme, augmented by numerous national, regional, and state election activities (Landers, 1992); and NASW's political action committee, Political Action for Candidate Election (PACE), endorsed more than one hundred candidates for national office (Hiratsuka, 1992) and contributed approximately $200,000 to national campaigns while state PACE committees dispensed in excess of $160,000 to state and local candidates (D. Dempsey, personal communication, November 30, 1992; Dempsey, 1993).

In 1991, NASW reported that 113 social workers held elected office (Weismiller & Rome, 1995); by 1992, 165 known social workers in forty-three states had won a variety of races (NASW, 1992); and by 1998, there were more than 200 known social workers holding political office in the nation! They held elected office at all levels of government from city council to the U.S. Senate. With each succeeding election, individual social workers and their professional associations gained new experiences, built on previous knowledge, and strengthened themselves as active players in the political arena. In 2003, 175 social workers nationwide held a variety of local, state, and federal offices and the most current information (February 2009) available by NASW reports 177 social workers holding elected office (see table 1).

All too often social workers do not think of themselves as "politicians" being elected to a political office. Yet, men and women (see table 1) and people of color (see table 2) hold a variety of offices. Although most elected social workers hold the MSW degree (82%), BSWs hold state and local offices as well (see table 3).

Table 1: Social Workers in Elected Offices by Gender/Office, 2003

	Women	Men	Total
U.S. Congress	5	1	6
State Legislature	39	30	69
County/Borough	21	9	30
City/Municipal	32	12	44
School Board	12	16	28
Other	—	—	—
Total	109	68	177

Table 2: Social Workers in Elected Offices by Race/Ethnicity/Office, 2003

	African American	Asian American/ Pacific Islander	Caucasian	Hispanic/ Latino	Unknown
U.S. Congress	2		14		
State Legislature	16	1	47	5	
County/Borough	5	4	17	4	
City/Municipal	7		33	3	1
School Board	6	2	17	1	2
Other					
Total	36	7	118	13	3

Table 3: Social Workers in Elected Offices by Credential/Office, 2003

	BSW	MSW	DSW	Unknown
U.S. Congress		6		
State Legislature	8	58	3	1
County/Borough	4	22		4
City/Municipal	5	37		1
School Board		22	2	4
Other				
Total	17	145	5	10

A quick point of information. In 2009, the "dean" of women in the United States Senate, Barbara McCloskey (Democrat, Maryland), is a social worker who was first elected in 1986.

ELECTORAL AND LEGISLATIVE POLITICS

Critical thinking is the overarching skill set necessary for successful policy work (Colby, 2008, p. 422). Political social work has two sides that also need to be critically analyzed as both sides are intricately related and are central to the social work profession's realization of its goals. First, social workers identify and support candidates who are friends of the profession and support our issues. By making contributions and working in candidates' campaigns, social workers are able to help pro-human service candidates to win elections. We call this phase "electoral politics." Second, social workers collaborate with elected officials on policy proposals during the legislative process. We call this phase "lobbying."

Political activity is generally viewed through the lobbying lens. Richman (1991), Haynes and Mickelson (1991), Mahaffey and Hanks (1982), and Wolk (1981), among others, emphasize the lobbying side of politics. Little attention is paid to electing candidates to public office. Deemphasizing electoral politics violates two important legislative lessons, however:

Lesson 1: Lobbying is much easier with supporters and friends of social work than with its detractors and antagonists.

Lesson 2: Lobbying for prevention proposals is a much better use of energy than lobbying against negative proposals and rectifying previous legislative errors.

You might view the political process as a cycle (see box 1). In a rational model, the political life cycle begins with candidate identification, then progresses through participation in electoral politics, educating the candidate on social work issues and advocating certain positions, lobbying the candidate to support the profession's stance, and back to candidate identification and reelection. The real-life political cycle is not so rational, and you may in fact enter the process and begin your efforts at any given point. Suppose, for example, that legislation regarding abortion is up for debate in the state senate. First, you attempt to educate your legislator on the issue from a social work perspective; the representative decides not to support your view. You soon realize that a new elected official is needed to better serve the interests of your district and the profession, and you begin to seek an alternative candidate for the next election. And the cycle continues.

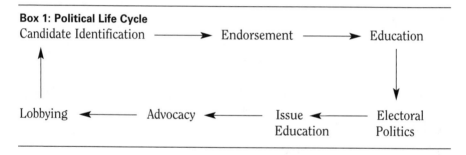

Box 1: Political Life Cycle

Elected officials, while primarily responsible to their constituencies, are also open to input from their campaign supporters. Active campaign support establishes a positive relation between the office holder and the social work community. When this is achieved, rather than having to adopt a defensive lobbying posture—protecting what we have from social work antagonists—social workers are able to influence the development and enhancement of social services through public policy. Conversely, when we don't have friends in the legislative body, social workers must put most of their efforts into attempting to block or modify coercive public policies.

Social Work Organizations and Electoral Politics

Nonprofit organizations, such as those in which social workers are most typically employed, are not allowed to campaign directly, lobby, or give money to a political candidate. Further, campaign financing laws severely restrict the amount of money a person or group can give to a candidate, campaign, or a political party.

Political action committees (PACs) evolved as a mechanism organized to spend money for the election or defeat of a candidate. The first PAC was created in 1944 by the Congress of Industrial Organizations (CIO) so contributions could be made to pro-union candidates while skirting the federal law that precluded unions giving money to candidates. In 2009, there are thousands of PACs registered with the Federal Election Commission; PACs represent every interest you can think of: welfare rights to automakers, environmentalists to veterans.

PACs are required to file with the Federal Election Commission (FEC) within ten days of opening. Campaign finance restrictions state that PACs can give $5,000 to a candidate committee per election (primary, general, or special), up to $15,000 annually to any national party committee, and $5,000 annually to any other PAC. PACs may receive up to $5,000 from any one individual, PAC, or party committee per calendar year.

Opensecrets.org reports that between 1988 and 2008, the top donor PAC was American Telephone and Telegraph (AT&T), which contributed slightly more than $40.8 million to candidates and parties (retrieved February 27, 2009). And Opensecrets.org reports that in 2008, another $3.24 billion was spent on lobbying efforts!

Although most political action committees would be considered either conservative or liberal—Republican or Democrat—many are nonpartisan, favoring neither political party, and focus on issues rather than party affiliation.

Education Legislative Network. In 1971, the *Education Legislative Network* (ELAN) was organized by NASW as a vehicle to bring together divergent and often contentious social work groups, in particular, clinical and macrolevel social workers. The premise of ELAN was that a united work community would strive together for the good of the whole and as it did so separate groups would become more friendly toward each other, thus creating broader support for each group's issues.

As a beginning effort, ELAN was successful in educating NASW members on a number of national policy issues. ELAN used a progressive strategy in which NASW members were 1) informed on issues and 2) encouraged to lobby their elected representatives in Washington. It became obvious, however, that more friendly elected leaders were needed. Concurrent with the association's first organized political efforts, political action committees took on greater importance in American politics overall. In 1976, NASW organized PACE, which served as the association's national effort to raise money and endorse candidates for national office who supported the profession's agenda. In other words, PACE was NASW's PAC.

Political Action for Candidate Election. PACE has a threefold purpose. First, it endorses those candidates who are most supportive of social work issues. Second, PACE sometimes makes campaign contributions to endorsed candidates. And third, PACE educates NASW members about candidates and encourages electoral participation.

National PACE is limited to endorsing and contributing to national candidates, that is, candidates for the presidency, the U.S. House of Representatives, and the U.S. Senate. A board of trustees, each of whom is appointed by the national NASW president, governs PACE. The board, with consultation from NASW members and state chapters, screens candidates for national elections, endorses candidates, and in some but not all instances makes financial contributions. Following endorsement of a candidate, NASW members in the candidate's state or district are encouraged to work in the candidate's campaign and make additional campaign contributions.

Even as the national PACE effort grew in strength, NASW recognized the truth of former House Speaker Tip O'Neill's (D-Massachusetts) statement "All politics is local." NASW therefore encouraged state chapters to organize their own PACE units to endorse local and statewide candidates and raise funds for their campaigns.

By 1998, every state had a PACE unit working to help candidates who support social work positions. The state PACE units are structured in a manner similar to the national PACE: each has a board of trustees, appointed by the state chapter president, and each screens and endorses candidates. The efforts and activities of the state PACE units are separate from each other and from the national PACE; there is no formal mechanism or means for accountability to the national professional association.

In theory, a state PACE unit could work against the interests of NASW by endorsing candidates who do not support the social work positions outlined at the national level. If this happened there would be no recourse for the NASW or the chapter membership. As trustees, the board members are ultimately responsible for all endorsements and for disbursements of campaign contributions, and they are accountable only to themselves. Nevertheless, the nationwide network of social work PACE units provides an important opportunity to identify, support, and work to elect individuals who can be advocates for social work issues and friends of the profession.

According to the Political Affairs Office of NASW, national PACE contributions placed PACE in the top ten of the more than 2,000 PACs contributing to that year's election (D. Dempsey, personal communication, November 30, 1992; Dempsey, 1993). While the national PACE's level of activity seems impressive, Colby and Buffum (1998) did not find the NASW membership to be especially active or concerned with PACE activities, and few dollars were raised by the association outside of the money collected as part of membership dues. (PACE dollars are raised by a "negative dues check-off" that requires NASW members to check off on their annual dues bills that they do not want $10.00 of their dues to be donated to PACE. If the box is left unchecked, $10.00 is transferred to PACE.)

Did You Know...A number of graduate and undergraduate academic programs offer courses focusing on politics and social work. The University of Houston School of Social Work implemented a graduate specialization in politics and social work, and the University of Connecticut sponsors an institute on political social work.

PACE Endorsement Process. Each state unit as well as the national PACE develops its own endorsement process and procedures. Remember that the state PACE units are not tied to each other or to the national PACE; they are separate entities, each with its own set of by-laws. A state's PACE unit is separate even from the state's NASW chapter.

Colby and Buffum (1998) found what seems to be a typical format for state endorsement (but recognize that not all states follow this procedure). The board puts together a survey that is distributed to all candidates (see box 2). Candidates are given a specified period in which to respond; if a survey is not returned a telephone call to the candidate's office is made asking to have the survey completed. If the candidate is seeking reelection, the board will also review the incumbent's voting record. Finally, members of local NASW units are asked to provide input to the process. Some state PACE units also hire professional lobbyists to help assess candidates. Professional lobbyists work the legislative halls every day, attempting to convince legislators to vote one way or another on specific legislation. As a result they often have a more detailed understanding of candidates than PACE trustees.

Based on the information it accumulates from the survey, the board decides which candidates to endorse. Once endorsements are made, the board then determines whether a financial contribution will be made. The board looks at many issues in deciding whether to make a contribution: Is the candidate opposed in the election? Does the candidate need the money? If unopposed, does the candidate need help in retiring a campaign debt? There are no correct answers to these questions; they simply serve as discussion points to help the trustees to make a final decision.

Financial contributions are governed by state law. Typically states cap the amount an organization may contribute to a candidate for a specific election or election cycle. Also, the level of office—for example, state representative versus governor—affects the limits on contribution size.

Did You Know… "Bundling" is a campaign loophole that allows organizations to get around legal financial caps on contributions. For example, a state PACE unit may contribute the maximum amount for a person running for the state house, say $500.00. When presenting the PACE check, additional checks from individual NASW chapter members are given at the same time (thus the idea of a bundle of checks). So a candidate may receive $500.00 from the organization and, say, thirty checks each for $50.00, for a total of $2,000. In effect, the organization, with member support, has increased its level of financial support to the candidate. And the candidate is more likely to remember a $2,000 contribution than individual $50.00 checks.

Once endorsements are made and the level of contributions determined, NASW members are informed of the PACE decisions. Checks are presented directly to the candidate by social workers from the candidate's district; this provides an opportunity for local social workers to make a direct connection with the candidate and to strengthen the relations for future lobbying efforts.

Box 2: Examples of Candidate Survey

Currently, Texas is ranked 49th of the 50 states and the District of Columbia in the delivery of health and human services. At the same time, Texas also ranks near or at the top of all states in terms of severity of many health and social problems, including teen pregnancy, school dropouts, the number of AIDS cases, infant mortality, and the lack of rural health care.

During the Spring Texas Legislative Session, numerous bills were introduced to address these issues. As with most states, however, the ongoing state deficit forced cuts in social services. Public education to housing and health care were all cut. Yet the legislature spent three special sessions, at a cost of $1.5 million per session, to redraw Congressional district maps in order to eliminate Congressional seats held by Democrats and increase the number of Republicans in the U.S. House of Representatives. Obviously the majority of the members in the Texas Legislature were more concerned about political self-interests rather than providing for the public good.

Do you support or oppose the following initiatives?

Support	Oppose	
_____	_____	1. Legislation that would allow parents to take up to three months' leave without pay from their jobs to care for a seriously ill child, spouse, or parent or for the birth or adoption of a child.
_____	_____	2. Increased funding for Aid to Families with Dependent Children (AFDC).
_____	_____	3. Legislation ensuring that all at-risk students have access to pupil services (including school social workers, school psychologists, and counselors).
_____	_____	4. Legislation that would prohibit the use of corporal punishment in Texas public schools.
_____	_____	5. Legislation that would ensure that pregnant women have full access to prenatal care.
_____	_____	6. Legislation that would ensure that children in need receive regular preventive health care and treatment.
_____	_____	7. Include funding in Texas' budget to supplement federal funds for Head Start.
_____	_____	8. Include funding to supplement federal funds for the Supplemental Food Program for Women, Infants and Children (WIC).
_____	_____	9. Legislation increasing the availability of affordable, quality childcare, preschool, and early childhood development programs.

_____   _____ 10. Legislation that opposes mandatory HIV testing of all health care workers who perform invasive procedures.

_____   _____ 11. A state income tax in order to adequately fund state services.

_____   _____ 12. Increased funding for the Texas Department of Human Services Child Protective Services Unit to hire professional social workers in order to provide higher quality services to children at risk and raise the minimum standards of training and qualifications for frontline workers.

_____   _____ 13. In the event the Supreme Court overturns Roe v. Wade, legislation protecting the freedom of choice and access to reproductive health care for women and families.

_____   _____ 14. Legislation that increases the availability of affordable housing in the state.

_____   _____ 15. Legislation amending the Texas Commission on Human Rights Act of 1991 and requiring state agencies to implement Affirmative Action programs and workforce diversity programs.

_____   _____ 16. Making a substantial investment in initiatives to reform and improve services to children and families involved in protective services, mental health, and the juvenile justice system.

On a separate piece of paper, please answer the following questions:

1. If elected, (a) what would be your main legislative priorities, and (b) what committee assignments would you seek?
2. Are you, any member of your family, or a close personal friend a professional social worker?
3. Many of the health care licensing and certification acts are under Sunset Review, and the legislature will have to re-enact these laws during the next regular session. Social work certification is one of the laws under Sunset Review. NASW/Texas is interested in strengthening this law by refining the definition of social work practice and regulating under the law only those practitioners who hold BSW and MSW degrees. Will you support the continued regulation of social workers? Would you support the narrowing of the law to only regulate social workers who hold professional degrees? Would you support a license for social workers?
4. Why are you seeking our endorsement? If endorsed, how would you use our endorsement?

Source: National Association of Social Workers/Texas PACE Candidate Questionnaire, 1992.

Social Workers and Political Campaigns

Volunteers and paid campaign staff provide critical support to a candidate's electoral bid. Commitments to a candidate and her ideas is the only prerequisite. It doesn't matter where the individual's competence lies: a campaign has room for a volunteer to perform an array of tasks—answering phones, preparing bulk mailings, putting up yard signs, and canvassing neighborhoods.

Social workers, in particular, can contribute many skills typical of their profession to a political campaign. These include planning, decision-making, consensus building, group management, research, assessment, relationship building, crisis intervention, and communication. In terms of roles, or functions, that social workers perform, eight are appropriate for political campaigns:

Role	Tasks
Advocate	Speaks on behalf of the candidate and represents his position to various constituent groups
Teacher/educator	Instructs staff and volunteers about campaign strategy and issues; in conjunction with advocacy, educates potential supporters about the candidate
Mobilizer	Energizes staff and volunteers; prioritizes and assigns individuals to needed campaign activities
Consultant	Provides expertise in problem solving and strategizing; helps candidate and staff to develop strategies for the campaign
Planner	Identifies key community players and activities; assesses strengths of potential relationships and overall prospects for electoral victory
Caregiver	Provides emotional support to candidate, his family, friends, staff, and supporters (relations can become strained)
Data manager	Develops and implements a data structure that allows for quick and easy access; designs a user-friendly system for staff, volunteers, and candidate
Administrator	Develops and implements a well-operating campaign structure that is functional and not overwhelming; keeps the structure simple, efficient, and consistent with the candidate's best interests

The following are a few simple things that social workers can do to strengthen the presence of the social work profession in a political campaign.

Spend time at a campaign office. Traditionally a campaign begins on Labor Day and concludes with the general election in November, generally a ten- to eleven-week period. But now it seems that this traditional election cycle has been thrown away. The day after President Obama won the November 2008 presidential election, political pundits were already predicting who would be in the running for the Republican presidential nomination in 2012!

Name: Anita C. Cruzan, LCSW, CCM

Place of residence: Springfield, Missouri

College/university degrees: Southwest Missouri State University, BSW

Present position: Community Resource Coordinator/Trainer, Special Health Care Needs Unit of the Missouri Department of Health and Senior Services. I provide training, technical assistance, and mentoring to contracted service coordinators who work with children with special health care needs.

Previous work/volunteer experience: Service Coordinator for children with special health care needs, Service Coordinator for individuals with HIV/AIDS, and Service Coordinator for disabled adults and the elderly.

Why did you choose social work as a career? My introductory sociology class in college was the first class that I truly enjoyed and seemed to understand completely—it all made sense to me. From that beginning I took the introductory social work class and decided this career was a perfect fit for me and it remains so after twenty-five years. Social work allows me to have a positive impact on the lives of others, and at the same time, it reminds me of how fortunate I am to have the life I do.

What is your favorite social work story? I worked as an investigator of elderly abuse and neglect hotline calls. I received a report of an elderly woman with a gun who was upset with her husband. I met two police officers at the home and stood behind them as they knocked on the front door. The officers appeared casual, as if this were a routine matter. The woman came to the door and admitted she did have a gun and was having marital problems. The officers asked to see the gun and she readily complied. The officers continued to act nonchalant, possibly because the woman appeared so calm. The woman returned to the front door carrying a shotgun! The officers came to full attention and asked to see the gun. When they opened it up they discovered it was indeed loaded. The woman voluntarily allowed the officers to remove the gun. I began to provide social work services to this family to assist with the stress that triggered this event. The lesson I learned was that for your own safety you should always be aware of your surroundings and what is going on around you; situations may change rapidly and you need to be prepared to respond.

What would be the one thing you would change in our community if you had the power to do so? Have people redefine their priorities. We all seem to be rushing here and there because we think we need to do so much and have so much. We all need to stop and smell the roses more.

A campaign relies on volunteers to staff an office, with much of the work taking place during evenings and on weekends. Organize ten to fifteen social workers and commit to providing a volunteer for one night each week at the campaign office for the duration of the campaign. Say you selected Tuesday evening; this can become known as Social Work Night to the candidate and key staff. The potential value to future lobbying efforts of even such a brief commitment is incalculable. The candidate will be much more open and sympathetic to a group that worked throughout the campaign.

Use buttons and t-shirts. Make a modest investment to purchase buttons or t-shirts printed with a simple slogan. Social workers for (candidate's name)—what an effective message! Be sure to wear the buttons or t-shirts on Social Work Night/Day at the campaign office. Let others know who you are and where you stand.

Host a fundraiser. All candidates need money to run a campaign. A bare-bones, efficient run for the state house costs at least $25,000. Plan a fundraising event with other social workers. Be sure to coordinate the event with the candidate's campaign staff—there is usually one person who is responsible for scheduling the candidate's time. Make the event brief—the candidate has no extra time during the heat of a campaign and often needs to be in four places at once. Try to make the event fun as well. Be creative. For example, one interesting fundraiser was a "non-event fundraiser" that people donated $25.00 *not* to attend! If you host an event with the candidate present, be sure to wear your buttons or t-shirts.

Realize the importance of election day. Election day is the longest day in the campaign. With polls opening as early as 6:00 a.m. in some states and closing as late as 8:00 p.m., campaign volunteers work up to eighteen hours! Volunteers are needed to work near the polling places, passing out candidate literature; put up last-minute candidate yard signs; provide voters with transportation to the polls (be sure to wear your buttons or t-shirts and to talk about your candidates with those you are driving); and staff the campaign office answering phones and dealing with last-minute glitches and crises. When the polls close, go to the candidate's headquarters or wherever the party is being held. You deserve to celebrate after all the energy you've put into the campaign. And be sure to wear your buttons or t-shirts.

Activity...Contact your state PACE unit through NASW. Find out who serves on the PACE board of trustees. What is the track record of PACE endorsements? Do endorsed candidates get elected? How many Republicans, Democrats, or candidates from other political parties were endorsed in the last election? How much money was contributed to the candidates?

Lobbying for Social Work Legislation

Lobbying is an act of persuasion in which you educate someone about an issue with the goal of gaining their active support. According to Opensecret.org (retrieved March 1, 2009), 15,150 lobbyists were registered to "pursuade" and "educate" the U.S. Congress and the various federal agencies. That's 28.3 lobbyists for each of the 535 members of the U.S. Congress (100 Senators and 435 members of the House of Representatives). And this is just for the federal government! Every state, county, and city/town government also has its own lobbyists. In Texas, for example, 1,625 lobbyists were registered with the state's Ethics Commission for the spring 2009 legislative session. So what is it that all these individuals, who are paid hundreds of millions of dollars by their clients to lobby, have in common? They are the experts with key information. You, too, can be a lobbyist with specialized information around a specific social issue.

Lobbying takes many different forms. Typical activities include writing letters, making telephone calls, making personal visits, and giving public testimony. Each is an effective and important part of the lobbying process. With computer technology, letter writing is not very difficult—a mass mailing to the legislature doesn't take too much longer to compose than a single letter. Telephone calls may be more costly, especially if you don't live in the state capital, but they take far less time. Personal visits are expensive if you don't live in or near the state capital, and they also require a great deal of time for what are generally brief meetings; but face-to-face meetings are effective. No matter which form of lobbying you select be sure to be brief, dignified, sincere, and, most important, respectful.

Letter writing. Write early, before the legislator has made up her mind. Make the letter one page or less, legislators don't have time to read dissertations! Get to the point quickly and be concise. Attach handouts to support the key points. Make sure you educate, educate, and educate the legislator on the issue. If you are writing about a specific bill, be sure to include the bill number. Note how the legislation will affect the legislator's district, mention the names of key supporters of your position from the district or from the legislator's campaign, provide reasons to support the bill, and request an answer to your letter indicating how she plans to vote on the issue. Be sure to say thank you at the beginning and the end of the letter, and be sure to use the appropriate salutation (see box 3).

A typical BUT not useful letter-writing strategy is the postcard approach—this involves preparing preaddressed postcards with a prewritten message that only requires the person to sign her or his name. This does not work, nor does the strategy of using duplicated copies of the same letter with a signature line. Politicians know that people have not taken time to share their views and this is a "quick" and dirty mail method. The basic lesson—mass duplicated mailings are a 100 percent waste of time and energy. Have your people write a personal handwritten note; this is your most effective strategy and best bet to be heard.

Telephone calls. You'll probably talk with a legislative aide, so don't take it personally if you don't speak with the legislator. Also, if there is a phone blitz on the bill you're calling about, the aide may be rather short with you and may cut you off in the middle of your presentation. Again, don't take it personally.

Be brief and to the point; try to take less than three minutes. Make notes before you call and practice what you want to say. Introduce yourself and mention your address, especially if you are from the legislator's home district. Follow the same principles as in letter writing: identify the bill number and describe how it will affect the legislator's district. Ask how the legislator plans to vote on the issue; if the person you speak to doesn't know, ask when you can call back to learn of the decision. End by thanking the legislator or aide for his time and support.

Box 3: Salutations for Letter Writing

Governor
1. Writing:
   The Honorable (full name)
   Governor of (State)
   Address

   Dear Governor (last name)

2. Speaking: "Governor (last name)"

Lieutenant Governor
1. Writing:
   The Honorable (full name)
   Lieutenant Governor of (state)
   Address

   Dear Lieutenant Governor (last name)

2. Speaking: "Lieutenant Governor (last name)"

Speaker of the House
1. Writing:
   The Honorable (full name)
   Speaker of the House
   Address

   Dear Mr./Madame Speaker:

2. Speaking: "Mr./Madame Speaker"

State Senator
1. Writing:
   The Honorable (full name)
   The (State) State Senate
   Address

   Dear Senator (last name)

2. Speaking: "Senator (last name)"

State Representative
1. Writing:
   The Honorable (full name)
   The (State) House of Representatives
   Address

   Dear Mr./Ms. (last name)

2. Speaking: "Representative (last name)" or "Mr./Ms. (last name)"

E-mail. All elected officials now have Web sites that post a variety of information, including a "contact us" section. This are useful if you organize a large group to send a series of e-mails in concert with a letter-writing campaign. But if you plan on writing one e-mail to let off steam, well that's about all that will happen—you'll let off steam but nothing much will come of it. Oh, you will probably get two e-mail responses. The first one will come back almost immediately thanking you for writing "Senator So and So" or "Representative So and So." You might get a second e-mail a month or so later, maybe sooner, that again thanks you "for sharing your views." You might be fortunate enough to get the personal e-mail address of an elected official. If so, use it sparingly, unless the elected person tells you otherwise, and certainly do not give it out to others.

Personal visits. Personal visits are probably the most time-consuming, frustrating, and potentially the most effective form of lobbying. Meetings are as a rule very brief, lasting from a few to no more than fifteen minutes. They usually take place in the legislator's office, but don't be surprised if you find yourself walking down the hall accompanying the representative or senator to a meeting while you lobby for a few short minutes. Most often you'll meet with an aide, but if you have a good relationship with the legislator—in particular, if you were a good campaign volunteer—you'll probably be able to meet with the elected official. You'll need to be pleasant, brief, concise, and convincing. Discuss only one legislative issue during your meeting. Be sure to follow up with a phone call and a letter of appreciation.

These meetings may be short in time, but many a social worker has found that they have been able to change a politician's stance on an issue as a result of a face-to-face meeting. Your sincerity, knowledge, and compassion about the issue speak volumes to politicians.

Check with your faculty to have them invite elected officials to your school, maybe for a class lecture or a noon-hour presentation. Most elected officials enjoy visiting with college students and try to work in the time if at all possible. Such visits provide a wonderful opportunity to develop a relationship with an elected official as well as for him/her to learn more about social work. There is one basic rule of thumb for such visits—do not get into arguments. Listen, be courteous, and most of all remember you are representing the social work profession.

Public testimony. In general, when considering legislation a committee must allow opportunities for public input. Such testimony usually lasts less than five minutes per speaker. The committee will have rules that govern the testimony's length—check them out beforehand by contacting the committee's staff person in the legislative offices.

Be sure your testimony is in a typed or word processed format, distribute copies to the committee members, and be sure to have a few extra copies available for others who are interested in your comments. Make sure your name, address, and phone numbers are easily found on the cover page of your testimony in case someone wishes to get in touch with you after the hearing.

Don't be surprised if the legislators ask you no questions after your presentation. There may be twenty to thirty people offering testimony, each speaking three to five minutes. Asking questions only prolongs the process. If a question is asked, be sure of your answers. Don't make up an answer; if you aren't sure what the answer is, tell the committee you'll find out and get back to their staff person within twenty-four hours. And be sure you do! Nothing is more damaging to your credibility in the legislature than to give inaccurate or misleading information or to make a promise and not follow up.

Finally, *don't argue with the legislators!* You are a guest in their workplace. You are there to convince and make friends, not to argue and make enemies. Your legislative opponent today may be your key supporter tomorrow on another issue. Don't burn your bridges.

COMMUNITY ORGANIZATION: LINKING THE POLITICAL TO THE COMMUNITY

To best link the political to the needs of the community, a strategy must first be outlined. By "strategy" we mean the action options that are open to the social worker to help reach the change goals identified. Rothman, Erlich, and Tropman, (1995) remind us that this must start by researching the history and the evolution of strategies that have been applied in the past. After all, the old adage "history can repeat itself" could complicate any type of intervention plan. Second, the social worker must explore the societal climate or environment. What is important to the individuals that live in the community? What are the values, the norms, and the expectations of the constituents to be served? To discover this, the community itself must be examined. The stakeholders must be identified. Small groups, both formal (such as church members) and informal (such as neighborhood support systems) within this community will affect the change efforts to be implemented. These players must be identified and all efforts must be ensured to make sure that their needs are addressed. In community organization, the needs and wishes of the community always provide the cornerstone for all helping efforts. Therefore, it is important not to have helping efforts thwarted by individual or institutional agendas that do not operate for the best efforts of the community. To completely describe the fundamentals of this type of practice is beyond the scope of this chapter. Although it is a critical part of social work macro practice, more specialized training and education is encouraged before a beginning social worker should embark in this type of practice.

SUMMARY

"Despite residual skepticism about the appropriateness of political work, there has been a resurgence of political action in recent years" among social workers (Weismiller & Rome, 1995, p. 2312). Courses in schools of social work, ongoing efforts by national and state PACE units, direct participation in political campaigns, and the election of social workers to political office are among the many ways social workers are developing much-needed political savvy.

We have learned through many, often painful, experiences that attempts to influence the development of public policy must begin well before the legislative process. Identifying and working for the election of people who are in favor of human services initiates the lobbying effort; having the right people in place makes lobbying that much easier.

Moreover, elected officials are influenced by groups that "vote regularly and are active in the electoral process" (Parker & Sherraden, 1992, p. 27). Social workers and their membership organizations are making significant contributions to political campaigns. As campaign workers, social workers are able to translate their agency-based practice expertise to the political arena.

In 2008, an economic tsunami swept the world and overshadowed all efforts, no matter the profession or ideological beliefs. The trillions of dollars that are being set aside to reenergize the American economy will certainly influence legislative decisions for years to come.

The question is, to what extent?

Will universal health care be set aside once more? Will full funding for public education continue to be kept at bay? Will the economic crisis divert Congress's attention from strengthening civil rights enforcement and expanding hate crime statutes? Will Congress once again find reason not to create new jobs that offer a living wage rather than a minimum wage? Will Congress shy away from strengthening immigration laws that will allow people to come out of the shadows to participate fully in society?

Social work students, too, will be challenged when they move into the practice world. Current and future social workers must have knowledge and skills in economic and financial literacy, not just around macro policy issues, but in the day-to-day work with those whose homes are in foreclosure, or those who have lost their jobs, or with retirees whose fixed incomes and pension plans have been devastated.

Even with the daunting economic crisis swirling around us, social workers must pursue our legislative agenda for social work education. Social work education must advocate for new ways to increase and broaden access to higher education through new fellowship and scholarship programs; seek ways to strengthen existing and create new loan forgiveness programs, advocate for the full and complete funding of Pell Grants, and repair the faulty federal student loan assistance program; and argue for the deepening and expansion of funding streams to our colleges and universities, to ensure that the necessary financial support is available for our programs to address their missions in the education of undergraduate and graduate social work students.

Social work practice is directly affected by politics. Who can call themselves social workers and practice as such, program eligibility requirements, and the types and levels of services are but a few of the critical decisions made by elected politicians. Taking part in elections is critical—people must vote—and there are elections every year throughout the United States. For example, let's look to the year 2011. There will be elections for governors in Kentucky and Mississippi and Louisiana; state or territorial elections will be held in four states—Louisiana, Mississippi, New Jersey, and Virginia—and one U.S. territory, the Northern Mariana Islands; and there are cities, counties, school boards, special districts, and others that will elect members to their governing bodies. These elected officials are for the most part not social workers. While the number of social workers holding elected office increased by over 90 percent in the 1990s, decisions made by non-social workers continue to have enormous impact on social workers and clients alike. Social workers face a simple choice: remain on the sidelines while others make decisions that determine how the social service community operates, or participate aggressively at all levels of political activity in order to open the door for progressive lobbying efforts. Simply put, social workers can sit in the audience watching others or can be pivotal actors who build on the rich experiences of political campaigns.

Part **IV**

Expanding Horizons for Social Work

Chapter 14

International Social Welfare

OUR WORLD IS A GLOBAL COMMUNITY. WE MUST THINK ON A LARGE scale about our interests, concerns, influences, and obligations, for the community in which we live stretches far beyond the confines of our geographic neighborhood. Today, we call this phenomenon globalization, the creation of an international system that affects domestic economies, politics, and cultures (Midgley, 1997).

Most of us would agree that we live in a global neighborhood. Friedman's (2005) classic work, *The World Is Flat,* vividly describes the shrinking world and how our nations' borders have virtually disappeared. Technology has opened the doors to new possibilities for peoples throughout the world. E-mail allows us to communicate in a manner unthought-of at the beginning of the 1990s. Now we can only wonder what the world will look like by 2025.

Twentieth-century history has shown how regional conflicts and disasters can quickly escalate into global ones. The Great Depression of the 1930s, for example, was felt worldwide and not only in the United States where the early effects were concentrated. Later in the 1930s, after the German and Japanese war machines had conquered many of their neighbors, the United States, which had originally assumed an isolationist position, became one of the leading allied nations. The collapse of the Berlin Wall in November 1989 signaled upheavals in many communist bloc nations that have had significant social and economic consequences around the world. In 1998, weakening in the Asian and Russian economies led to stock market gyrations in the financial centers of the world. And in late 2008 and well into 2009, the weakening global economy fueled by any number of issues reverberated throughout the world. Certainly, other examples of global effects exist, but the message is clear: what happens across the oceans affects all of us, no matter where we live.

> *Did You Know...That in 2009 more than 14.4 million people have tuberculosis and there were 247 million cases of malaria. Malaria kills one child every 30 seconds.*

We also can learn from other societies and cultures about how to strengthen our own approach to social living. We can study how other countries approach social problems and think about how their successes may work in our communities. Some people believe that the United States has nothing to learn from the rest of the world about technology, education, and other social advancements. But this is not true! "Social scientists agree that knowledge can be increased by

Name: Matthew Colton

Place of residence: Swansea, Wales, United Kingdom

College/university degrees: Keele University; BA with honors (First Class) in Applied Social Studies, Diploma in Applied Social Studies, Certificate of Qualification in Social Work, Oxford University, D.Phil.

Present position: Professor and Head of Applied Social Studies (Social Work), University of Wales, Swansea

Previous work/volunteer experience: Social work teacher and researcher, social worker mainly with children and families

What do you do in your spare time? I don't have any spare time as such. Outside of my work, most of my time is spent with my wife, two children, and extended family. I really enjoy family activities and take an active interest in my children's hobbies and interests.

Why did you choose social work as a career? From an early age, my parents nurtured and encouraged me to have respect and concern for others, particularly those who are troubled or oppressed. My mother died when I was 9 years old. I think that this experience deepened my compassion and empathy for those whose lives are especially difficult, and my concern for social justice.

What is your favorite social work story? There are so many! For example, I was once called to the home of a client who wished to make a complaint about her social worker. Having introduced myself on the doorstep, I was beckoned in by the old woman whom I was there to see. The house was dimly lit and overrun with cats.

"How can I help?," I asked when we were seated.

"She [the social worker] doesn't like my cats," complained the woman. "Wants me to kill them all. Told me to hit them with a spade."

"Hit them with a spade?" I asked, somewhat puzzled. Then it dawned on me. My colleague had, in fact, advised the woman to have the cats spayed.

What would be the one thing you would change in our community if you had the power to do so? I would like to see a genuine commitment to tackling social exclusion. This would include practical measures to reverse the increasing polarization in British society between the poor and the affluent as well as measures to combat child poverty—which has tripled over the past two decades—and institutional racism.

investigating phenomena in other societies and by testing propositions in different social, economic, and cultural contexts" (Midgley, 1995, p. 1490). The study of international social welfare is an imperative that will move us beyond our many self-imposed barriers and allow all of us to be better off in a cooperative, world community.

Even within the ever-changing world community and the recognition of its importance in our daily lives, American social workers have been ambivalent in their commitment to the international arena. In fact, Midgley (1997, p. 63) has contended that the profession is not "fully prepared" to meet international challenges and opportunities and must be more aggressive in benefiting from international opportunities. In other words, just as the world experiences globalization and the realization grows that we are all connected, progressive community organization will continue to evolve as a critical part of social work advocacy and practice (Pyles, 2009).

Did You Know...The global population was 2.8 billion in 1955 and is 5.8 billion now. It will increase by nearly 80 million people a year to reach about 8 billion by the year 2025.

In this chapter, we touch on the many international facets of social work. Though we cannot delve into details of cultural differences and economic and demographic trends, we hope to raise your awareness of these issues. By the end of the chapter you'll recognize that social work is a global profession, facing the persistent challenge of promoting social and economic justice.

HOW DO WE COMPARE DIFFERENT NATIONS?

A general question that, on the surface, seems simple enough to answer: how many nations do you think there are in the world? We could look at the United Nations but not all nations are UN members. We could perform an Internet search and see what comes up—why not do that now and see what number you find. For example, when this sentence was being written on March 1, 2009, a Google search came up with a number of answers ranging from 192 (United Nations count) to 243!

A second point to consider is that the world's nations are not static but susceptible to change. A nation emerges in any number of ways, from the spoils of war to a nation giving up its governance over land. Enriquez (2005, pp. 22–23) reminds us that in 1909, about 100 years ago, the British Empire included 11.5 million square miles, which was 20 percent of the world's land mass—this gave way to the saying that the sun never sets on the British Empire. Yet, within fifty years, the British Empire shrank by more than 11.4 million square miles to about 94,248 square miles. And let's not forget when in 1991 the Union of Soviet Socialist Republics splintered into Russia and fourteen other republics. And who is to say that the United States will always be comprised of fifty states; maybe Puerto Rico will join the Union at some point in time. Remember, Hawaii and Alaska joined the United States in 1959. Illustrating the point of changing borders and new countries forming, Enriquez (2005, p.25) notes that there has yet to be a U.S. president born and buried under the same flag; in other words, the addition of new states changed the number of stars on the U.S. flag.

When making international comparisons, it is helpful to have a framework for grouping nations based on similarities. Otherwise, comparisons may not be meaningful and can lead to inaccurate conclusions. For example, very little can be learned from comparing the economic systems of the United States and Nepal. The vast political, economic, social, historical, and cultural differences between these two nations make such a comparison virtually impossible.

Did You Know...More than 50 million people live today in countries with a life expectancy of less than 45 years.

One framework is based on a nation's technological level, which incorporates three tiers, identified as preindustrial, industrial, and postindustrial (Bell, 1973). This framework can be visualized as a core with circles, "concentric zones," surrounding the center. Core nations include those in Western Europe and North America. A middle zone surrounds the core and includes former communist nations and selected nations in Asia and South America. The periphery includes the remaining Asian and South American countries and Africa. Chatterjee (1996) called these three groups of nations the first world, the second world, and the third world (see box 1).

Box 1: The World System

First World: Also known as the core, it includes North America, western Europe, Australia, and Japan. It is wealthy, capitalist, industrial, and based on the traditions of a market economy and individualism.

Second World: Somewhat outside the core, it consists of eastern Europe, central and northern Asia, and Cuba. It is neither wealthy nor poor, socialist, selectively industrial, and based on the traditions of a planned economy and collectivism. A substantial part of the second world has been attempting to convert to a market economy since 1991.

Third World: It includes nations mostly in Africa, southern and Southeast Asia, and South America. It is mostly poor, often nationalist, selectively industrial to preindustrial, and based on a mixed economy and regional loyalty.

Source: Chatterjee (1996, p. 46).

The World Bank, an international organization that promotes economic development and productivity to raise the standard of living in less-developed nations, uses a different framework. The World Bank categorizes nations into six regions: South Asia, Middle East and North Africa, Latin America and the Caribbean, Europe and Central Asia, East Asia and the Pacific, and the Africa Region (see box 2).

At the same time, we must be sensitive to our use of words and how they may be interpreted by others. For example, what does it mean to be called "developed" versus "undeveloped"? Even more important, what are we implying when calling a nation "undeveloped"? Are we holding that country to our standards or their standards? We create a messy situation when referring to a country as "undeveloped." At best, it is paternalistic and at its worst, it suggests cultural elitism.

Box 2: Regions of the World as Defined by the World Bank

South Asia: Afghanistan, Bangladesh, Bhutan, India, Maldives, Nepal, Pakistan, Sri Lanka.

Middle East and North Africa: Algeria, Bahrain, Egypt, Iran, Jordan, Kuwait, Lebanon, Morocco, Oman, Qatar, Saudi Arabia, Syrian Arab Republic, Tunisia, Yemen, United Arab Emirates.

Latin America and the Caribbean: Antigua and Barbuda, Argentina, Belize, Bolivia, Chile, Colombia, Costa Rica, Dominica, Dominican Republic, Ecuador, El Salvador, Grenada, Guatemala, Guyana, Haiti, Honduras, Jamaica, Mexico, Nicaragua, Panama, Paraguay, Peru, St. Kitts and Nevis, St. Lucia, St. Vincent and the Grenadines, Suriname, Trinidad and Tobago, Uruguay, Venezuela.

Europe and Central Asia: Albania, Armenia, Azerbaijan, Belarus, Bosnia and Herzegovina, Bulgaria, Croatia, Czech Republic, Estonia, Georgia, Hungary, Kazakhstan, Kyrgyz Republic, Latvia, Lithuania, Former Yugoslav Republic of Macedonia, Moldova, Poland, Romania, Russian Federation, Slovak Republic, Slovenia, Tajikistan, Turkey, Turkmenistan, Ukraine, Uzbekistan.

East Asia and the Pacific: Cambodia, China, Fiji, Indonesia, Kiribati, Korea, Lao People's Democratic Republic, Malaysia, Marshall Islands, Federated States of Micronesia, Mongolia, Myanmar, Palau, Papua New Guinea, Philippines, Samoa, Solomon Islands, Thailand, Tonga, Vanuatu, Vietnam.

Africa: Angola, Benin, Botswana, Burkina Faso, Burundi, Cameroon, Cape Verde, Central African Republic, Chad, Comoros, Congo, Democratic Republic of Congo, Republic of Côte d'Ivoire, Djibouti, Equatorial Guinea, Eritrea, Ethiopia, Gabon, The Gambia, Ghana, Guinea, Guinea-Bissau, Kenya, Lesotho, Liberia, Madagascar, Malawi, Mali, Mauritania, Mauritius, Mozambique, Namibia, Niger, Rwanda, São Tomé and Principe, Senegal, Seychelles, Sierra Leone, Somalia, South Africa, Sudan, Swaziland, Tanzania, Togo, Uganda, Zambia, Zimbabwe.

Question: What countries are missing from the list and why? Connect with the World Bank's web page (www.worldbank.org) for additional information and read the organization's purpose for the answer.

Source: www.worldbank.org.

We've described two frameworks here, but there are a number of alternative approaches to comparing nations. You might hear some describe the world as "developed, undeveloped, and underdeveloped" nations; another model speaks to nations in "north and the south," using the equator as a global dividing line. What we want to accomplish is to organize the world's countries in such a manner as to facilitate discussions that are consistent and appropriate. In other words, we want to compare apples with apples, not apples with peaches!

Let's use Chatterjee's classification to demonstrate how a framework can be applied to make international comparisons. As shown in box 3, Chatterjee identified social issues and then tabulated how the first, second, and third worlds respond to them. Chatterjee also took the application a step further by asking the following questions about the three worlds and then compiling responses, listed in box 4.

Box 3: Welfare Trends on Selected Issues in the Three Worlds

Issue	First World	Second World	Third World
Housing	Public housing for the poor; some rent control or subsidy	Rationed housing for all	No such concept
Education	State supported; uneven in the United States	State supported	State efforts do not reach all
Income maintenance	Almost all countries	Almost all countries	Almost none except in Singapore, South Korea, Taiwan, and Hong Kong
Health care	Almost all countries except the United States; rising costs	Almost all countries; supplies and equipment problematic	Crisis-based care to the poor from charitable clinics or hospitals

Did You Know…The World Bank estimates that 900 million adults worldwide are illiterate. Four hundred million 6- to 17-year-olds are not in school and 225 million of them are girls.

1. Once a person has been socially defined as not employable, can he/she ask the state for help?

2. Once a person has been socially defined as employable but is unemployed, can he/she ask the state for support?

3. Once a person has been socially defined as employed but is marginally employed, can he/she ask the state for support?

4. If the state is providing support, is it means tested?

5. If the state is providing support, it is related to past or potential future earnings?

6. If the state is providing support, it is a flat rate or with a minimum or maximum, or is it linked to an index of fluctuating living costs?

7. Is the state committed to seeing that each citizen receives a basic package of health care, or has it engaged other qualified parties to do so?

8. Is the state committed to seeing that each citizen receives a basic education? If so, has it set up a formal structure to provide such education itself, or has it engaged other qualified parties to do so?

9. Is the state committed to seeing that each citizen receives basic housing? If so, has it set up a formal structure to provide such housing, or has it engaged other parties to do so?

10. Is the state committed to providing protection to various vulnerable groups (children, elderly, developmentally disabled, and mentally ill)? If so, has it set up a formal structure to provide such protection, or has it engaged other qualified parties to do so?

11. Have one or more occupational groups emerged within the state, which are self-appointed advocates for vulnerable groups and are seeking increased professionalization? (1996, p. 78)

Box 4: Comparison of Eleven Welfare State Variables

Question	First World	Second World	Third World
1.	Yes	Mostly yes	Mostly no
2.	Yes	Mostly yes	No
3.	Mostly yes	Mostly yes	No
4.	Mostly yes	Mostly yes	Does not apply
5.	Mostly yes	Mostly yes	Does not apply
6.	Mostly yes	Mostly yes	Does not apply
7.	Yes except in US	Yes	No
8.	Mostly yes	Mostly yes	No
9.	Mostly yes	Yes	No
10.	Yes	Mostly yes	No
11.	Yes	Partially yes	Partially yes

Source: Chatterjee (1996, p. 80).

RECENT HAPPENINGS AND THE WORLD TODAY

The September 11, 2001, attacks on the United States remain unprecedented in American history. The American people have traditionally been expected to adjust to new social environments, maintain good personal and occupational standing, and face pressures related to supporting friends and family. Americans, along with people around the world, were shocked and stunned as the terrorist attacks of September 11, 2001, unfolded. Following the attacks, debates relating to terrorist activity within the United States and the vulnerabilities inherent within American society began to emerge. Fears that terrorists could cross our extensive borders, the relative ease with which immigrants can disappear into American society, and the global and open nature of lifestyles Americans have come to depend upon leave the society susceptible to terrorist threats and attacks (Dziegielewski & Sumner, 2002). Furthermore, the threat of biological warfare abounded. New measures were put in place ranging from color coding threat levels in U.S. airports to eavesdropping on phone calls of suspected terrorists.

But the fear of terrorism is not limited to the United States and is felt in nation after nation around the world.

Did You Know...At least two million a year of the deaths under age 5 could be prevented by existing vaccines. Most of the rest are preventable by other means.

There are people in Middle East who live in fear of terrorist threats each day. There are those in Israel who believe the Hamas, a political group that believes Israel is an illegal nation, will at any moment attack and kill Israelis. The January 2009 Israeli-Hamas war illustrates the level of fear and hatred felt on both sides. Israel attacked Gaza because Hamas continued to fire rockets into Israel. Hamas said the rockets were fired because Israel closed Gaza's borders to Israel; Israel justified its invasion because of the constant rocket attacks.

Since the astronauts first circled the moon and took one of the most exciting pictures of the planet Earth, there has been a growing awareness of the complexities that exist in all people and nations as we become more economically and technologically connected.

The earth is a very large home to some 6.7 billion people (retrieved March 2, 2009, U.S. Census Bureau World Population Clock). There is great diversity among the earth's people, governments, and experiences. And yet within this great diversity, despite the looming threats, there are common social problems that afflict people day in and day out. Poverty, homelessness, mental illness, inadequate housing, hunger, poor health care, physical violence, and neglect are among the many problems that know no geographic borders.

Did You Know...Among the premature deaths are those of 585,000 young women who die each year in pregnancy or childbirth. Most of these deaths are preventable. Where women have many pregnancies, the risk of related death over the course of a lifetime is compounded. While the risk in Europe is just one in 1,400, in Asia it is one in 65, and in Africa, one in 16.

Social problems are enormous from a worldwide perspective. According to the World Bank, 1.4 billion people live on less than $1.25 each day (retrieved March 2, 2009, http://web.worldbank.org). The World Bank also notes that the impact of the 2008 and 2009 global economic crisis will impact every nation, not surprisingly stating that those nations with stronger economic structures will be less affected than those whose economies are weak to begin with. Thus, the underdeveloped and developing nations in the world, those with the largest percentages of people in poverty, will be much more adversely impacted.

Consider, for example, that poverty prior to the economic crisis of 2009 declined in parts of South Asia and the Middle East and North Africa, where three billion people lived on less than $2 a day. About one-third of the world's developing population is poor. According to the United Nations Africa Recovery Program, 172 of every 1,000 African children died before reaching age 5, 2.4 million African children under age 15 are HIV positive, and 12.1 million African children are AIDS orphans (Fleshman, 2002). In most countries, social exclusion is closely linked to economic, health, and educational disparities.

Did You Know...The World Bank estimates that 70 percent of women infected with HIV are between ages 15 and 25.

Infant mortality rate is an indicator of a nation's health care, in particular, of its comprehensiveness and ability to cover the poor and nonpoor alike. It counts the number of children under age 1 who die per 1,000 live births. According to the United Nations–sponsored UNICEF, the number of children dying before their fifth birthday fell below 10 million to 9.7 million; Sub Saharan nations accounted for 4.8 million deaths compared to 100,000 in the industrialized nations. The top three major causes of infant death include neonatal causes (37%), pneumonia (19%), and diarrhea (17%); AIDS accounted for 3% of the worldwide infant deaths.

Some sobering numbers for you to consider. In 2008, Angola's infant mortality rate was estimated to be 183 per 1,000 births; Sierra Leone's rate was 156 children per 1,000; Afghanistan was 154; and Liberia 143. Compare these numbers to Singapore, Sweden, and Japan, each with less than 3 deaths per 1,000 (retrieved March 2, 2009 https://www.cia.gov/library/publications/the-world-factbook/rankorder/2091rank.html) and the United States—6.3 deaths per 1,000 births in 2008 (see table 1).

Life expectancy is a second indicator of a nation's well-being. Life expectancy is a numerical estimate of the average age a group of people will reach. Macau has the oldest life expectancy of 84 years, followed by Andorra and Japan of approximately 82 years; life expectancy in the U.S. in 2008 was 78—forty-five nations have higher life expectancies (retrieved March 2, 2009 https://www.cia.gov/library/publications/the-world-factbook/rankorder/2102rank.html). On the other extreme, Swaziland's life expectancy is the lowest in the world at 31 years, followed by Angola (37) and Zambia (38) (see table 2).

Death rates, the number of deaths per 1,000 people, also provide an important glimpse into a nation's well-being. Swaziland and Angola lead the world in this tragic category with 30 and 24 deaths respectively; on the other hand, United Arab Emirates, Northern Mariana Islands, Kuwait, Qatar, Saudi Arabia, and Jordan each report less then 3 deaths per 1,000 persons (retrieved March 2, 2009 https://www.cia.gov/library/publications/the-world-factbook/rankorder/2066rank.html).

To be honest, it is sometimes very hard to fully understand and comprehend the meaning of such numbers. For a moment, let's say you are in a university that totals 15,000 students. During one year, 95 students die—what do you think will be the public outcry? Clearly this would be a national and probably an international story, with all sorts of investigations taking place. But what is special about 95 deaths? That number reflects the United States infant mortality rate. But what if

Table 1: National Infant Mortality Rates Lower than U.S. Rate (6.30), 2009

Rank	Nation	Rate per 1,000
181	United States	6.30
182	Cuba	5.93
183	Isle of Man	5.62
184	Italy	5.61
185	Taiwan	5.45
186	San Marino	5.44
187	Greece	5.25
188	Monaco	5.18
189	Ireland	5.14
190	Canada	5.08
191	Jersey	5.01
192	New Zealand	4.99
193	United Kingdom	4.93
194	Gibraltar	4.91
195	Portugal	4.85
196	Australia	4.82
197	Netherlands	4.81
198	Luxembourg	4.62
199	Guernsey	4.53
200	Liechtenstein	4.52
201	Belgium	4.50
202	Austria	4.48
203	Denmark	4.40
204	Slovenia	4.30
205	Korea, South	4.29
206	Israel	4.28
207	Spain	4.26
208	Switzerland	4.23
209	Germany	4.03
210	Czech Republic	3.83
211	Malta	3.79
212	Andorra	3.68
213	Norway	3.61
214	Anguilla	3.54
215	Finland	3.50
216	France	3.36
217	Iceland	3.25
218	Macau	3.23
219	Hong Kong	2.93
220	Japan	2.80
221	Sweden	2.75
222	Singapore	2.30

Source: Central Intelligence Agency (2003). World Factbook.
(https://www.cia.gov/library/publications/the-world-factbook/rankorder/2091rank.html)

Table 2: National Life Expectancies at Birth, Greater Than U.S. Expectancy (78.14), 2009

Rank	Country	Life expectancy at birth (years)
1	Macau	84.33
2	Andorra	82.67
3	Japan	82.07
4	Singapore	81.89
5	San Marino	81.88
6	Hong Kong	81.77
7	Australia	81.53
8	Canada	81.16
9	France	80.87
10	Sweden	80.74
11	Switzerland	80.74
12	Guernsey	80.65
13	Israel	80.61
14	Iceland	80.55
15	Anguilla	80.53
16	Cayman Islands	80.32
17	New Zealand	80.24
18	Italy	80.07
19	Gibraltar	80.06
20	Monaco	79.96
21	Liechtenstein	79.95
22	Spain	79.92
23	Norway	79.81
24	Jersey	79.65
25	Greece	79.52
26	Austria	79.36
27	Malta	79.30
28	Faroe Islands	79.29
29	Netherlands	79.25
30	Luxembourg	79.18
31	Germany	79.10
32	Belgium	79.07
33	Guam	78.93
34	Virgin Islands	78.92
35	Saint Pierre and Miquelon	78.91
36	United Kingdom	78.85
37	Finland	78.82
38	Isle of Man	78.80
39	Jordan	78.71
40	Korea, South	78.64
41	Puerto Rico	78.58
42	Bosnia and Herzegovina	78.33
43	Bermuda	78.30
44	Saint Helena	78.27
45	Cyprus	78.15

Source: Central intelligence Agency (2009). World Factbook.
https://www.cia.gov/library/publications/the-world-factbook/rankorder/2102rank.html

there were 2,745 deaths in the same university of 15,000 students? The outcry would be horrific, people labeling this a national scandal and calling for immediate safeguards and measures to be put in place so this never happens again. And what do the 2,745 deaths represent? The infant mortality rate for Angola.

For whatever reason most Americans and social workers do not consider the impact of the world's health to be "our issue." Why? There is any number of possible reasons, but we must at least take a first step and recognize the scope and depth of social issues around the world. Once we develop this beginning awareness, we can then begin to initiate discussions with our global colleagues to determine what we can do together. But the first step rests with each of us to look outside the borders of the United States to gain as full an understanding of the human condition as possible.

HOW DO WE LOOK AT INTERNATIONAL SOCIAL WELFARE?

The literature detailing international social welfare issues is, to say the least, interesting and stimulating. Themes that you'll find consistently in international

Figure 1: Chona and her grandmother at their home in the mountains of Northern Luzon in the Philippines. They live with the bare necessities and medical help is scarce. The grandmother's feet show the effects of a lifetime of work in the rice fields.

social welfare journals include peace and social justice, human rights, and social development. These areas are critical for all social workers to understand. In fact, CSWE accreditation standards require that these topics be included in both baccalaureate and graduate social work programs. Our fascination with international issues transcends our educational mandates, however, and is evident in our day-to-day conversations. How often have we heard people compare the United States with other countries? Typically, the conversation will include a statement such as "The poor in the United States have it easy compared with the poor in India." Statements of this sort form the basis of comparative social welfare discussions.

Midgley identified five basic types of international social welfare studies:

◆ Comparative studies of social need
◆ Comparative studies of social policies and human services
◆ Typologies of welfare states
◆ Studies of the genesis and functions of social policy
◆ Studies of the future of the welfare state (1995).

Comparative studies of social need are reports that collect and assess a variety of social and economic data from different countries. These reports are usually quantitative in nature and present tabular data on a variety of topics. Typical studies include data on income, education, birthrates, poverty, and migration.

Figure 2: Girls on their way home from school in a remote mountain area of the Philippines where the New People's Army is rebelling against the government. Roads are almost nonexistent in this part of the country.

Figure 3: Japanese students in a school for persons with developmental disabilities. Like most Japanese students, they wear uniforms. The school teaches trade skills (woodworking, plumbing, bricklaying) as well as life skills. Art, music, and physical education are taught. The school has a large gym and swimming pool. Many of the students train for the Special Olympics.

Comparative studies of social policies and human services are most often qualitative or descriptive presentations of issues. The topics explored are similar to those addressed by comparative studies of social needs, but the discussion includes analysis of political issues, funding patterns, eligibility standards, types of services, and provision or delivery of services.

Typologies of welfare states discuss the ideological and philosophical bases for the welfare systems of different countries. Typology studies, which are generally qualitative or descriptive, can shed light on a nation's view of people and social issues and, at the same time, provide important insight into the direction of its social welfare program. According to Midgley (1995), the most common typology is the Wilensky and Lebeaux conceptual model of residual versus institutional social welfare (see chapter 2 for a discussion of this framework).

Did You Know…Each year, according to the World Bank, 2 million or more girls are subjected to genital mutilation with upwards of 115 million girls worldwide having undergone genital mutilation. This practice is found in 26 African countries (including the Middle East), a few Asian countries, and is increasingly practiced in Europe, Canada, Australia, and the United States. Egypt, Ethiopia, Kenya, Nigeria, Somalia, and the Sudan account for 75 percent of all cases. In Djibouti and Somalia, 98 percent of girls are mutilated.

Studies of the genesis and functions of social policy are closely related to welfare typology studies. They focus on three areas: how welfare organizations emerged, what forces affect the development of social policy, and what are the functions of social policy in the society (Midgley, 1995). Such studies may be either quantitative or qualitative. They form the theoretical basis for social welfare endeavors.

Studies of the future of the welfare state have become more common recently. Midgley (1995) believed this happened in response to international criticism of social welfare and worldwide attempts to rethink national social welfare commitments and responsibilities. Such reports integrate the other four types of welfare studies and forecast the future.

INTERNATIONAL SOCIAL WELFARE ASSOCIATIONS

Many social work practitioners and students are surprised to learn that numerous, long-standing social welfare associations exist around the world. The number of international social welfare associations greatly expanded following World War II, primarily to help rebuild war-torn countries and to assist poor countries in gaining greater economic stability (Healy, 1995). Healy (1995) classified international associations into three groups: 1) United Nations structures, 2) U.S. government agencies, and 3) private voluntary bodies.

United Nations Structures

The United Nations was originally organized in 1945 by fifty-one nations to provide a forum to help stabilize and maintain international relations and to give peace among nations a more secure foundation. By 2006, 192 nations were members, with an increase of thirty-three new members since 1990 (http://www.un.org/members/growth.shtml). The newest member to join the UN was Montenegro, in 2006, which separated from Serbia in the same year.

The United Nations is probably most recognized for its peacekeeping forces, which have been deployed throughout the world to help mediate conflict. In addition to its peacekeeping mission, however, the United Nations conducts a variety of activities listed as fifty different areas on its Web page, with 80 percent of the work taking place in developing nations. Typical of these services are programs for AIDS, children, women, environmental protection, persons with disabilities, human rights, health and medical research and services, poverty and economic development, agricultural development, family planning, emergency and disaster relief, air and sea travel, use of atomic energy, and labor and workers' rights.

Did You Know...The United Nations spends about $10 billion each year or $1.70 for each of the world's inhabitants. At the end of March 2003, member nations owed the UN $1.182 billion for previous years' dues, of which the United States alone owed $532 billion (47 percent in total and 45 percent of the regular budget).

While the United Nations is involved in an array of activities, seven specific agencies address social welfare issues:

United Nations Children's Fund: Probably the best known UN social welfare program, it provides a variety of child-directed services in such areas as health, child abuse, neglect and exploitation, child nutrition, education, and water and sanitation. UNICEF received the Nobel Peace Prize in 1965 for its efforts on behalf of children.

World Health Organization: This specialized UN agency focuses on world-wide health issues. It works to establish international health standards in a variety of areas, including vaccines, research, and drugs; it monitors and attempts to control communicable diseases; and it has a special focus on primary health care.

UN High Commission for Refugees: The commission oversees protection, assistance, and resettlement aid. In 1981, it was awarded the Nobel Peace Prize for its work with Asian refugees.

Economic and Social Council: The council coordinates a number of economic and social activities, with specific commissions for focusing on social development, human rights, population, the status of women, and drugs.

Department of Policy Coordination and Sustainable Development: Under the auspices of the UN Secretariat, the leading body of the United Nations, this department coordinates the development of welfare policies and activities.

UN Development Programme: This program provides technical assistance grants to developing member nations. Its primary area of support is in agriculture, though grants also support health, education, population, employment, and other related human service programs.

UN Population Fund: This agency collects worldwide population data and implements family programs, including education and contraception.

Did You Know...The United Nations and its organizations have been awarded the Nobel Peace Prize on six separate occasions—1954, 1965, 1969, 1981, 1988, and 2001. In addition, seven people affiliated with the United Nations have received the Nobel Peace Prize—1945, 1949, 1950, 1957, 1961, 1974, and 2001.

The United Nations provides many other social welfare services. Typical activities include scores of annual conferences and conventions, as well "special years" dedicated to a specific issue. Conferences focus on very specific themes. In 1990, for example, the United Nations sponsored the World Summit for Children; in 1992, the UN Conference on the Environment; in 1995, the Fourth World Conference on Women; in 1997, Earth Summit; the 1999 conference on fighting land-mines; the 2002 World Food Summit; the 2006 Forum on the Eradication of World Poverty; and in 2008, a special conference on indigenous populations. Special years included the 1994 International Year of the Family, 1996 International Year for the Eradication of Poverty, the 1999 International Year of Older Americans, International Year of Mobilization against Racism, Racial Discrimination, Xenophobia and Related Intolerance in 2001, International Year to Commemorate the Struggle against Slavery and Its Abolition (2004), and in 2009 the International Year of Reconciliation.

Of particular interest to social work is the United Nation's sponsorship of Social Work Day at the UN. Typically held in the spring, this annual meeting brings together about 1,000 social workers to discuss and advocate on global human issues. Social work students from around the United States participate at the UN event; check with your social work program to see if a student delegation may be attending the next UN social work day.

Did You Know…The headquarters for IFSW is located in Berne, Switzerland, and can be reached at Tel (41) 31 382 6015, Fax (41) 31 381 1222, or via e-mail: secr.gen@ifsw.org

U.S. Government Agencies

The United States carries out a variety of international social welfare efforts through federal agencies:

Administration for Children and Families: A subsection of the Office of Public Affairs, this agency is the primary conduit for international affairs and social work. Activities include meetings, research, professional exchanges, and co-sponsorship of welfare programs. (See http://www.acf.hhs.gov/)

Office of Refugee Resettlement: This office coordinates resettlement of refugees in the United States. Since 1975 over 2.6 million people, with nearly 77 percent being either Indochinese or citizens of the former Soviet Union, have been assisted in the United States because of persecution in their homelands due to race, religion, nationality, or political or social group membership (retrieved March 1, 2009, http://www.acf.hhs.gov/programs/orr/about/history.htm).

Social Security Administration: This agency examines social insurance programs worldwide. (See www.ssa.gov.)

U.S. International Development Corporation: This corporation has two responsibilities: international private investment and operating the Agency for International Development (AID). AID provides funding for international projects and is very concerned about AIDS, child welfare, population growth, and basic education. AID has given money to welfare groups, including NASW, to sponsor international programs. (See www.info.usaid.gov.)

Peace Corps: First organized in 1961, the Peace Corps sends American volunteers to different nations to assist in a variety of social, economic, and agricultural projects. (See www.peacecorps.gov.)

U.S. Information Agency: This agency sponsors international leaders from around the world to participate with their colleagues in the United States. The agency also sponsors Americans to study abroad. (Healy, 1995).

Private Voluntary Bodies

Private or nongovernmental groups provide a variety of services and activities throughout the world. Human service organizations such as the YMCA and YWCA sponsor direct services and programs. In addition, nonprofit organizations consult with international agencies and groups about human service issues.

INTERNATIONAL PROFESSIONAL SOCIAL WELFARE ORGANIZATIONS

There are a variety of international social welfare organizations around the world. Some are social work membership associations, similar to the NASW. Others are national and regional educational associations, similar in purpose and function to CSWE.

Three primary worldwide organizing bodies cross national boundaries and encourage partnerships: the International Federation of Social Workers, the International Association of Schools of Social Work, and the International Council on Social Welfare.

International Federation of Social Workers

The International Federation of Social Workers (IFSW) was founded in 1956 to promote social work on the world stage. IFSW is divided into five geographical regions: Africa, Asia and the Pacific, Europe, Latin America and the Caribbean, and North America. Membership is open to one professional social work association in each country. In 2009, 90 countries with more than 745,000 members reported belonging to the Federation (see box 5). Individuals and organizations may join IFSW as well as take part in the Friends Program. As a friend, a social worker receives the IFSW newsletter, published three times annually, policy papers, and a discount on registration for IFSW international and regional conferences.

With the International Association of Schools of Social Work (see below), IFSW generated a definition of social work that is used around the world. The global definition took a number of years to write and reach consensus from the various member associations. For a moment think how difficult it is in your class to reach agreement on some items; now transpose this to a worldwide discussion that involves a variety of cultural frameworks and different meanings of words set within historical patterns of mistrust between regions and nations. The idea that people from around the world were able to find common ground speaks volumes to the authenticity and commitment of social workers no matter where they live and work. Reflecting sensitivity to the diversity of languages and its membership, IFSW posts the "definition" in several languages on its Web site (see box 6).

IFSW sponsors meetings throughout the world (see box 7). In addition to its biennial international meetings, IFSW sponsors regional meetings that focus on specific area issues; participant costs are much lower for these meetings. Between 1966 and 2009, there have been nineteen regional meetings in Europe, sixteen

Box 5: Members of the IFSW, 2003

Argentina	Hungary	Palestine
Armenia	Iceland	Papua New Guinea
Australia	India	Peru
Austria	Ireland	Philippines
Bahrain	Israel	Poland
Bangladesh	Italy	Portugal
Belarus	Japan	Romania
Benin	Kenya	Russian Federation
Bolivia	Korea	Rwanda
Brazil	Kuwait	Sierra Leone
Bulgaria	Kyrgyz Republic	Singapore
Canada	Latvia	Slovak Republic
Chile	Lebanon	South Africa
China	Lesotho	Spain
Colombia	Liberia	Sri Lanka
Croatia	Libya	Sudan
Cuba	Lithuania	Swaziland
Cyprus	Luxembourg	Sweden
Czech Republic	Malaysia	Switzerland/Liechtenstein
Denmark	Malta	Tanzania
Dominican Republic	Mauritius	Thailand
F.Y.R.o. Macedonia	Mongolia	Turkey
Faeroe Islands	Morocco	Uganda
Fiji	Netherlands	Ukraine
Finland	Netherlands Antilles	United Kingdom
France	New Zealand-Aotearoa	United States of America
Germany	Nicaragua	Uruguay
Ghana	Niger	Zambia
Greece	Nigeria	Zimbabwe
Hong Kong	Norway	

meetings in Asia and the Pacific, and seven meetings in Africa. Both regional and worldwide gatherings provide social workers from around the world with a chance to share research findings as well as program ideas.

IFSW also provides critical leadership in the pursuit of human rights for individual social workers, social work students, and social service workers. In 1988, IFSW established a Human Rights Commission with members representing each region. The commission works with a number of international human rights groups including Amnesty International.

Another noteworthy activity of IFSW is its research and publication of policy papers that explore social issues that social workers face day in and day out. In

---

Box 6: Global Definition of Social Work

Global definitions as posted in various languages by the International Federation of Social Workers. See website for the definition in other languages such as Russian, Spanish, and German (retrieved September 20, 2009 from http://www.ifsw .org/f38000138.html).

English—The social work profession promotes social change, problem solving in human relationships and the empowerment and liberation of people to enhance well-being. Utilising theories of human behaviour and social systems, social work intervenes at the points where people interact with their environments. Principles of human rights and social justice are fundamental to social work.

French—La profession d'assistant social ou de travailleur social cherche à promouvoir le changement social, la résolution de problèmes dans le contexte des relations humaines et la capacité et la libération des personnes afin d'améliorer le bien-être général. Grâce à l'utilisation des théories du comportement et des systèmes sociaux, le travail social intervient au point de rencontre entre les personnes et leur environnement. Les principes des droits de l'homme et de la justice sociale sont fondamentaux pour la profession.

Box 7: Meetings Sponsored by IFSW

1966	Helsinki	1992	Washington, DC
1970	Manila	1994	Colombia
1974	Nairobi	1996	Hong Kong
1976	Puerto Rico	1998	Jerusalem
1978	Tel Aviv	2000	Montreal
1980	Hong Kong	2002	Harare
1982	Brighton	2004	Australia
1984	Montreal	2006	Germany
1986	Tokyo	2008	Brazil
1988	Stockholm	2010	Hong Kong—joint meeting with
1990	Buenos Aires		IASSW and ICSW

---

addition to the following issues, policy papers are planned to explore indigenous people and international adoptions:

Advancement of women
Child Welfare
HIV-AIDS
Migration
Protection of personnel
Rural communities
Youth

Welfare of elderly people
Health
Human rights
Peace and disarmament
Refugees
Self-help

International Association of Schools of Social Work

As the name suggests, the International Association of Schools of Social Work (IASSW) is the focal point for social work education around the world. IASSW does not set international accreditation standards for social work education; rather it promotes social work education and the development of high-quality educational programs around the world. In a 1928 worldwide meeting, attended by more than 3,000 people from forty-two different nations, the participants agreed that social work was a mechanism that could professionalize and achieve better outcomes from charitable activities (Hokenstad & Kendall, 1995). The following year IASSW was organized, and today membership is open to national associations, such as CSWE, and their specific educational programs. By 1995 IASSW membership totaled 450 schools from 100 countries (Hokenstad & Kendall, 1995) and in 2009 membership had grown to over 600 programs in more than 115 nations. Member schools are divided into four regions—Asia-Pacific; Africa, Europe and Middle East; Latin America, and the Caribbean; and North America—which facilitates development of regional educational initiatives.

Did You Know…The journal International Social Work *is sponsored jointly by the International Association of Schools of Social Work, the International Federation of Social Workers, and the International Council on Social Welfare.*

IASSW sponsors a biennial meeting, the International Conference of Schools of Social Work, and supports a variety of educationally directed projects. In addition, the association publishes a newsletter and texts. IASSW has also published, with CSWE, a very useful guide to social work programs around the world. The guide—Rao and Kendall (1984)—lists social work programs in different countries, admission standards, and an overview of curricula. While this publication is out of date, it does provide an interesting look at the diversity of social work education around the world. For example, in some African countries you'll find a "certificate" or "state diploma" awarded after the completion of three years of postsecondary study. In Asia, undergraduate and graduate programs are similar in structure to those in America. Hokenstad and Kendall (1995) have written that national traditions and ideologies make it impossible to generalize about social work education in Europe. Structures differ greatly, from length of time to complete a degree program to the content studied.

International Council on Social Welfare

The International Council on Social Welfare (ICSW) is a "global nongovernmental organization which represents a wide range of national and international member organizations that seek to advance social welfare, social justice and social development" (www.icsw.org). The primary thrust of the council is to promote social and economic development activities that will reduce poverty, hardship, and vulnerability. The council was founded in Paris in 1928, and today its office is located in London, England. Like IFSW and IASSW, the council holds a biennial conference as well as regional meetings.

ICSW is subdivided into five regions—Africa, Asia and Pacific, Latin America and Caribbean, North America, and Europe. In 2009 ICSW was active in more than forty countries and included six different international social welfare associations and associations in twenty-seven different countries (retrieved March 1, 2009, www.icsw.org).

NASW AND CSWE INTERNATIONAL INITIATIVES

National Association of Social Workers

NASW is active in pursuing and promoting international relations. The association is guided by its International Activities Committee, which was formed in 1986. The international committee seeks to adopt a variety of mechanisms to increase the globalization of NASW.

As part of its international outreach activities, NASW has sponsored international meetings and travel opportunities. For example, in 1992 NASW, as part of that year's annual meeting, co-hosted the World Assembly, the biannual international conclave of social workers, in Washington, D.C. During the 1980s and 1990s, many state NASW chapters forged partnerships with social workers and associations in other countries. In fact, by 1992 twenty-one state chapters had formal relationships with other associations around the world. In addition, the national association and a number of state chapters have sponsored study tours in various countries around the world.

Council on Social Work Education

CSWE is also extremely active in international circles. Organizationally, the council includes the Commission on Global Social Work Education. The commission works with other international organizations, including the International Association of Schools of Social Work, to promote international programs and projects and to develop the international dimension of the social work curricula (see box 8). The commission also is responsible for advising the Foreign Equivalency Determination Service and for maintaining relationships with foreign students and schools. While linking CSWE with international groups, the commission strongly advocates that schools internationalize curricula and provide students with worldwide opportunities. The commission also sponsors the Katherine A. Kendall Institute for International Social Work Education, which serves as a conduit for the generation of educational materials for social work educators. For example, the Kendall Institute sponsored a "disaster management" meeting in the Caribbean with educators and relief workers from around the world. This led to the development of curriculum programs on social workers and disaster relief. The Kendall Institute sponsored similar meetings that were held in South Africa and China. The Kendall Institute is also leading social work educators in curriculum development around immigration.

A number of social work programs offer international student exchanges, field placement opportunities, and study tours. These opportunities are usually open to students and faculty from different programs; check with your social work faculty

---

Box 8: Sample of International Social Welfare Organizations and Their Web Sites

HelpAge International	www.helpage.org
Inclusion International	www.inclusion-international.org
International Catholic Migration Commission	www.icmc.net
International Council of Jewish Women	www.icjw.org.uk
International Council on Jewish Social and Welfare Services	(no web; phone: 41-22-344-9000)
International Federation of Aging	www.ifa-fiv.org
International Federation of Red Cross and Red Crescent Services	www.ifrc.org/what/health/archi/homepage.htm
International Federation of Settlements and Neighborhood Centers	http://datenbanks.spinnenwerk.de/ifs
International Organization for Migration	www.iom.int
International Planned Parenthood Federation	www.ippf.org
International Social Service	www.iss-ssi.org/index.htm
Salvation Army	www.salvationarmy.org

---

to learn more about recent and upcoming international study opportunities either in your program or in other programs (remember, you can transfer credit back to your home college or university!). The following list is just a small sample of the activities that social work programs have undertaken; check directly with your own social work program about any international opportunities it offers:

University of North Carolina–Chapel Hill: study tour of Ireland, Wales, and Scotland

University of Houston: academic exchange program with City University of Hong Kong and travel courses to Wales, Turkey, South Africa, Mexico, and China.

University of Central Florida: summer course in Mexico

Florida State University: summer course in England and Spain

East Carolina State University: summer course in Bristol, England

University of South Carolina: study tour of Greece

SUMMARY

The events of September 11, 2001, and the fear of terrorism have created a climate never before experienced in this country. Terrorism and fear of differences, however, cannot be used as an excuse to turn away from the issues so germane to the globalization of our society. Problems of substance abuse, child abuse and neglect, spouse battering, poverty, inadequate mental health and health care, and the 'isms' of race, age, and gender continue to be found in every region of the world. And social workers too are found throughout the world,

---

Box 9: International Acronyms

EC	European Community
ECE	Economic Commission of Europe
EFTA	European Free Trade Association
EU	European Union
Eurostat	European Statistical Office
FAO	Food and Agriculture Organization
GATT	General Agreement on Tariffs and Trade; succeeded by WTO
IBRD	International Bank for Reconstruction and Development; usually called the World Bank
IDA	International Development Association
IFAD	International Fund for Agricultural Development
IFC	International Finance Corporation
IMF	International Monetary Fund
NATO	North Atlantic Treaty Organization
OPEC	Organization of Petroleum Exporting Nations
UNDP	United Nations Development Programme
UNESCO	United Nations Educational, Scientific, and Cultural Organization
UNICEF	United Nations Children's Fund
UNIDO	United Nations Industrial Development Organization
USAID	United States Agency for International Development
WFP	World Food Programme
WHO	World Health Organization
WTO	World Trade Organization

---

helping individuals, families, and communities to confront these and other social issues. We experience globalization every day. We can cross the oceans in a matter of hours; we can talk to a friend in another nation simply by dialing a telephone. Through e-mail we can send messages around the world to any number of people in mere milliseconds. As Kottler and Marriner (2009) outlined so beautifully in their book, reaching out to help others that are the victims of injustice can be in itself curative. In helping others, we grow stronger and more intent on creating a path for social justice within a global community.

Social work and social welfare are part of this fast-paced, ever-changing world. Yet social work students in the United States have limited exposure to international issues (Hokenstad & Kendall, 1995). Certainly, CSWE and NASW encourage, in a variety of ways, exposure to the international scene as part of the professional experience. But should we be doing more? And if so, how?

The social work educational curriculum is already packed with required content. It is easy to say "International content is required in all social curricula," but at what expense? Will existing content need to be dropped or modified? Are social work educators and practitioners willing to decide whether international content, while important in our world today, is necessary for effective social work practice?

Social work practitioners often claim that they are stretched to the limit by work obligations and wonder how they could continue to manage the rigors of work if required to move into the international arena. As one practitioner stated:

> Don't get me wrong, I'm very concerned about poverty in India and the clear mistreatment of people based on a caste system. BUT I just don't have enough time in a day to do what needs to be done for my child welfare clients. What is important for me is that my kids are able to get back with their families and no longer feel the pain of abuse and neglect.

Attending an international meeting is often a surprise for the American social worker. It's not uncommon to hear social workers from around the world speak in negative terms about the American social work community. Many believe that American social workers do not value the international experience. Whether true or not, they perceive that American social welfare journals discriminate against international authors by declining to publish their manuscripts. They feel that U.S. social work programs do not value international journals and texts, an idea reinforced by the absence of international materials among required readings in social work courses.

There is some truth to allegations that American social workers are ignorant of the international social welfare arena. We are surprised to learn that there are social work organizations similar to NASW and CSWE throughout the world. Yes, we are surprised to discover that social work extends beyond the borders of North America and some parts of Europe.

But rather than berate the profession and each other, we need to commit ourselves to professional globalization. In the classroom, we need to look at issues and conduct discussions in an international context. That doesn't mean that the focus of all efforts should be international, but it does mean that we should consider topics through an international lens, when appropriate.

But what are some specific things we can do? First, we can support NASW in its organizational efforts on a national level as well as in the state chapters and local units. Dedicating one monthly meeting to an international issue with either a guest speaker or a film will enhance our efforts. Second, while more ambitious than looking for a guest speaker, we can try to organize with NASW or utilize a study-travel tour offered by a social work program. Third, we can work to develop a sister program with an international social welfare association or school that can lead to professional exchanges for practitioners and students alike. Fourth, each year most colleges sponsor an "international week" on their campuses. The local social work student group can sponsor an activity that highlights international social welfare.

International experiences have a way of changing who we are and how we approach our work and daily life circumstances. One of this text's authors wrote the following to the college's alumni, describing a trip he took to Israel in January 2009 during the height of the Gaza war.

> For ten days in early January I traveled around Israel as part of a five-person delegation invited by the Israeli Foreign Ministry. Other delegation

members came from Harvard, Georgetown University, Virginia Commonwealth University, and the University of Illinois-Chicago. We met a variety of people including Knesset members, the Minister for Social Welfare, former ambassadors, think tank professionals, educators, lawyers, and leaders of social agencies. The war in Gaza was in its full fury during our visit and framed the majority of our conversations. I was particularly impacted by a meeting with a colleague who teaches at Sapir College, located in S'derot approximately 4.8 kilometers from Gaza. She described classrooms built like bomb shelters, the air raid sirens going off 15 to 20 times in a typical class; students and faculty know a siren means a rocket will hit within 15 seconds—everyone falls to the floor and waits for the rocket blast. Everyone then gets back in their chairs and resumes class until the next siren goes off. The morning of our discussion she described the College reopening after being closed for three weeks; she described the constant buzz of helicopters flying over the campus while watching smoke rising in the near distance. She said that women do not wear heels—they need to be able to run as fast as possible to a bomb shelter; or people do not use bathrooms all day simply because they are not bomb proof. My colleague noted that approximately 3,000 of the 7,000 students suffer from PTSD.

I cannot imagine teaching a class in an environment similar to my colleague in S'derot. How do you literally pick yourself up off the floor and resume teaching as if nothing happened? How different my life would be knowing that at any moment a siren may go off and I would have 15 seconds to find a safe place. As our evening together concluded I said to her that I was having a very difficult time trying to fully understand what she was describing. She interrupted me and said, "I pray you never have to experience what I am in order to understand what our lives are like."

Most certainly I came away from Israel with a greater understanding of the Middle East conflict and all of its complexities. While that is important, I also no longer take for granted the safe and secure environments that many of us enjoy both at work and at home. I hope that my colleague's wish is realized and that I, we, will never have to experience an air raid siren or dive to the floor for safety.

But even more than that, this one international experience only serves to reinforce my profound respect and admiration for those who teach and work in war-torn and unsafe areas. They are true heroes and remind us all that our mission in social work, the promotion of justice for all, is important and necessary. As the Reverend Dr. Martin Luther King Jr. said, the hopes for a livable world rest with those who strive for peace and justice.

What we do is limited only to our creativity and our willingness to grow. But before doing anything we must first commit to the belief that we live in a global community. We need to embrace the notion that our work influences and is influenced by the global community. Then, and only then, will we be able to confront the social ills that plague the world and have any chance of achieving social justice for all people no matter where they live or what their social and economic status.

Chapter 15

Conclusions

THE TITLE OF A BOOK CAN TELL THE READER A GREAT DEAL ABOUT its contents and the views of its authors. Margaret Truman's *Murder at the CIA,* for example, is a murder mystery set within the government. Woodward and Bernstein's *All the President's Men* is a work exploring a president, Nixon in this case, and his staff. On the other hand, titles may mislead you. *Hunt for Red October* is not a story about fall in New England. Salinger's classic *Catcher in the Rye* is not a baseball story about the exploits of Yankee legend Yogi Berra.

In social work, you can also tell a lot from book titles. Look at the following titles from the 1960s to the present and think about what they say to you:

- *The Professional Altruist* (Lubove, 1965)
- *Social Work, the Unloved Profession* (Richan & Mendelsohn, 1973)
- *The Drama of Social Work* (Bloom, 1990)
- *Unfaithful Angels* (Specht & Courtney, 1994)
- *Maneuvering the Maze of Managed Care* (Corcoran & Vandiver, 1996)
- *Economics for Social Workers: Social Outcomes of Economic Globalization with Strategies for Community Action* (Prigoff, 2000)
- *The Changing Face of Health Care Social Work: Professional Practice in Managed Behavioral Health Care* (Dziegielewski, 2004)
- *Cognitive-Behavioral Interventions: Empowering Vulnerable Populations* (Eamon, 2008)
- *Combating Violence and Abuse of People with Disabilites: A Call to Action* (Fitzsimons, 2009)
- *Taking Charge: A School-Based Life Skills Program for Adolescent Mothers* (Harris & Franklin, 2008)
- *Social Work, a Profession of Many Faces,* 11th edition (Morales, Sheafor, & Scott, 2009)
- *Social Work: The People's Profession* (Colby & Dziegielewski, 2010)

Each title should tell you something about the authors' view of the profession and the population they seek to serve. Lubove (1965) recognizes social workers as people who want to help others but looks beyond the philanthropic model, to someone who is professionally trained in this important art and science. *Social Work, the Unloved Profession* depicts the somewhat negative view that the larger

Name: Carrie Marie Sullivan

Place of residence: Boston, Massachusetts

College/university degrees: Florida International University, BA; Boston College, MSW

Present position: Community Affairs Director for Massachusetts State Senator Dave Magnani.

Previous work/volunteer experience: Mentor at Miami-Dade Halfway House, and at a Child Enrichment Center for foster care children in Miami, Florida, Community Liaison at a childcare resource center in Cambridge, Massachusetts, volunteer cook at a soup kitchen for the homeless in Ft. Lauderdale, Florida.

What do you do in your spare time? Almost five years ago, I became actively involved with saving abandoned dogs from shelters throughout the eastern United States. Three years ago, I began my own rescue organization specializing in saving and re-homing dogs, mostly, Labrador Retrievers. To date, I have placed over 300 dogs, that were destined to die in shelters, into loving homes.

Why did you choose social work as a career? The study of human relations has always interested me and I really enjoy working with people. When I found out that I could obtain an MSW concentrating in community organization and public policy, I knew immediately that I wanted to work in public office. As a social worker, I understand social problems and I am committed to social justice. I know how policies affect individuals and communities and I see the opportunity to make changes on a broader scale. Social workers make the best politicians because they are committed to improving the quality of life for people.

What is your favorite social work story? Every day, I speak with people who feel helpless. When I first started working in government, I received a call from an elderly woman who could no longer afford to pay her bills. Like most senior citizens, this woman was on a fixed income and because of rising property taxes, she was being taxed right out of her home. After hearing the fear in her voice, I made a few phone calls and was able to put her in touch with a local agency that, in turn, was able to help her. A few weeks later, I received a thank-you card from this woman thanking me for helping her maintain her dignity and independence.

What would be the one thing you would change in our community if you had the power to do so? There are so many people who lack empowerment and do not know that they have a voice. I would empower these people to speak their feelings and to fight for what they believe in. People also seem to have a limited perception of the social work profession, therefore, I would also encourage people to be more open-minded and to realize that the profession of social work is within every facet of life.

community holds of social work, one in which the profession's activities are not held in high regard. *The Drama of Social Work* by Bloom (1990) unfolds the many struggles that social workers face in providing care. *Unfaithful Angels* is a critical look by two social workers at the social work profession in which the authors strongly assert that professionals have abandoned advocacy efforts on behalf of the poor in favor of for-profit and private psychotherapeutic services.

As can be seen by the title, *Maneuvering the Maze of Managed Care* by Corcoran and Vandiver (1996) explores the struggles that social workers have in a fragmented system of delivery that highlights time-limited interventions and clearly defined and measured clinical outcomes with the ultimate responsibility being to the funding source. *Economics for Social Workers* by Prigoff (2000) speaks clearly to the need to recognize economic concerns and the movement toward globalization and how it relates to community action. *The Changing Face of Health Care Social Work* by Dziegielewski (2004) outlines the many roles that social workers can assume in health care and the flexibility that is needed to embrace what is often termed behavioral managed care. Eamon (2008) highlights the strong focus many schools of social work are taking in terms of cognitive behavioral therapy and assisting and empowering vulnerable populations. Other books call to action social workers to help vulnerable populations, from combating violence and abuse for people suffering from disabilites (Fitzsimons, 2009) to calling adolescent mothers to take charge of their lives through empowerment and skill building (Harris & Franklin, 2008).

Finally, consider the work of Morales, Sheafor, and Scott (2009), who see social work as a profession of many faces with numerous varied roles and contributions to society. And, lastly, the authors of this book deliberately chose the title *Social Work: The People's Profession* because similar to the other authors mentioned we see the field of practice as an exciting, fascinating, although at times frustrating, way to approach life as a helping professional.

Each of these titles, whether taken collectively—or viewed as a whole—can inspire an interesting, thought-provoking discussion. And while the main purpose of each of these texts is to educate, advocate, and inform, a text should also get its readers to think about the subject matter in a more critical, insightful manner.

After reading this book, we hope you can see why we chose the title *Social Work: The People's Profession*. After reading the chapters, have you learned something new about the social work profession? Do you have a better understanding of the profession, its varied practice methodologies, and the issues faced by today's practitioners? We hope so, as the primary purpose of this book is to do just that by helping the reader to develop a better understanding of social work as a profession, while outlining the many intriguing areas of practice and advocacy that social work involves. In providing a reality-based approach to practice, we hope to give the beginning social work professional a tool-kit for examining person-in-environment relations, and how to assist by making this a better place for all.

THE TIME TO DECIDE IS APPROACHING

From the outset, we've made some assumptions about you as the reader of this text and as a beginning social work professional. First, we believe you are reading this book because it's assigned for a class. We realize this isn't the evening, weekend, or vacation book of choice! Second, we think you are taking a social work course that's called "Introduction to Social Work," or something similar, because you're interested in learning more about the field. Actually, whatever the course title may be, the class you are taking is probably one of the first social work courses in a series of prospective majors. Third, we've assumed that while you or some of your classmates may have had some experience with social work professionals, for the most part you agreed when we said that most people do not really have a detailed understanding of the social work profession, including its mission, purpose, and function. Fourth, some of you are seriously exploring social work as a possible career and have registered for this course with that purpose in mind. For others of you, however, this may have been the course that was available at the time or you may have heard that the instructor was really interesting.

Trying to address all of the needs implicit in these assumptions was sometimes daunting, but it was an effort we enjoyed making. It feels good to have put together a text that meets the social work accreditation standards, helps people to gain a clear understanding of the social work profession, supports the faculty member's direction in a course, and helps the individual student to make a career decision: is social work for me?

Making a career decision is not easy, nor should it be. We'll be very forthright with our advice to you: Don't make yourself miserable with worry. What you decide today doesn't obligate you for the rest of your life, or even through next week! You can change your mind at any time about your career goals. It's not unusual for college students to change majors a number of times before completing their baccalaureate studies.

To be fair, it's true that family, friends, and college teachers and counselors put unnecessary pressure on today's students. Why is it so important to select a major by the end of your sophomore year? When you say that you're going to college, why is the first question you hear "What's your major?"

The reasons vary. Family and friends are probably excited that you're pursuing a college education, and naturally they're interested in what courses you plan to take and what career path you'll follow. Those of us who teach in higher education see the potential major as a means to sustain the field. Academic programs are under constant pressure, in many institutions intense pressure, to maintain student enrollments. Declining student enrollments jeopardize continuation of a major. Look at what happened to sociology at a number of colleges in the 1980s: it was discontinued as a major, non-tenured faculty were released from their jobs, and tenured faculty members were moved to other departments.

Only a few years ago, the preference was for a student to get a liberal arts education as an undergraduate. To be considered educated a person must have studied a variety of subjects in the arts, sciences, and humanities in an effort to develop a broad, worldly view of people and their settings. The idea was that a liberal thinker, in the literal rather than the political sense, is better suited to participate in society. Some occupations were satisfied with this broad-based education. People could get good jobs without having majored in a specific area. Training for a specific position or workplace happened on the job. People who chose to continue their studies in a specialized field did so in graduate programs.

By contrast, today undergraduate students, some even at the time of application, are asked to declare their majors. Is it fair to ask someone who is just beginning her college education to select a career? Well, we could argue the merits and drawbacks of this practice till we're all blue in the face. The fact is that you must select a major or be cast into the land of the general major (different colleges have different terms for this group; it usually captures all students who haven't chosen a career path).

Most readers of this text have probably made some decisions about social work by this point. We won't take sole credit for influencing the decision-making process. In your course, class discussions, guest speakers, and other instructional strategies, in addition to this text, have helped you to make your decision, or at least a partial decision.

The Non-Social Work Major

We want to offer a few words to those of you who have decided that social work is not for you. First, we're glad you've made a decision that is right for you at this time. Don't be disappointed that social work is not your profession of choice as you may have thought originally. By looking at yourself in the light of information gleaned from this course, you are taking a very important step in your life. And you can always revisit your decision. In career choices the door never closes for good: you can always reconsider your options.

We hope you have a better understanding and appreciation of social work and the issues that drive our profession. While you feel social work is not your career choice, you can nevertheless help to increase the understanding of different people. You have learned how to better communicate with them as well as know the strengths and weaknesses of our social welfare system, and thereby you can initiate a positive change-related strategy. You are better informed about a number of social issues and a number of myths that shroud public policy. When you hear others attack social welfare, listen carefully to what is being said and respond with accurate information. Or at least, be slow to judge and be sure to look up or research what others say if it does not sound like what we have discussed thus far. You can be part of the myth-busting squad that dispels misinformation. Let people know the facts about poverty, child welfare, mental health, and the many other areas discussed in the text. Stay informed about the issues: read the daily newspapers and visit social welfare Web sites for updated information. Information and facts are among the most powerful tools you can have at your disposal. You can also be invaluable as a social service volunteer. The vast majority of social agencies need people of one kind or another. All it takes is one phone call to a specific agency asking if it needs help. Or if you just want to volunteer a few hours a week and the agency setting doesn't matter, call your local volunteer service agency. You will most likely be placed in the areas of greatest need at which your awareness of the profession and what is needed will help you to make a meaningful client-empowered contribution.

The Social Work Major

Well, you are about to enter a very structured educational experience. Remember what we learned about CSWE accreditation demands in chapter 2? (If not, you may want to reread that chapter, especially before your final examination!) With restrictions and expectations related to accreditation and professional practice you can plan on your academic schedule being outlined for you for the remainder of the program. Since the coursework is so prescribed be sure you meet with an advisor to discuss the courses you plan to take. This way there will not be any surprises as you get ready to graduate. Be sure you are aware of how the courses in your program are sequenced by semester or quarter. You can look at your program's student handbook or ask the course instructor or your academic advisor to review the academic program.

Based on certain restrictions some aspects of your program are set in granite with little room for modification or negotiation. We also want to raise some considerations for you to keep in mind.

1. The program will take two years of full-time study and oftentimes courses are sequenced in a certain order. You cannot take these classes out of order and there is no possible way to double up and be able to graduate in one year. We have found over the years that some students spend an inordinate amount of time challenging and trying to change a structured educational program. They often become angry with the faculty and program, calling them inflexible, yet so many of these events are beyond instructor and program control. Before signing on the dotted line and making the decision to become a social work major, be sure to check the curriculum model and its specific requirements. This includes mapping out a course of study and accepting the length of time that will be needed to complete the program. Be sure to explore all aspects that may affect your ability to meet these financial and structural requirements. If you are concerned about the requirements, meet with a social work advisor and determine whether your needs can be accommodated. Don't select the major without planning out the time you will need to complete the degree and exploring all possible scenarios. Plan your schedule carefully and make any necessary arrangements, such as childcare or employment, in order to complete all the program requirements (see item 3 below on field placement). If you feel you cannot commit to the full-time option, check to see if there is a part-time option. It may take you twice as long to complete the program but living and working between classes may warrant a slower although steady pace for your course of study.

2. Academic credit will not be given for any life experiences, according to CSWE accreditation standards. There are no ifs, ands, or buts on this point. Academic credit is awarded for successful completion of specific college courses and activities only. It doesn't matter if you have lots of experience in the field, were in the Peace Corps for two years, or worked in a human service agency for five years—no credit can be awarded for these activities.

3. In social work there is an expectation that each graduate will have supervised work in the field upon graduation. Therefore, you will have a field placement, which is strategically scheduled in your academic program to allow demonstration of specific knowledge and skills learned in the classroom. Your field experience will be sequenced after you have had certain courses and you will not be able to take the field course any sooner in the program. Nor can your field course be waived in recognition of previous work experience. Remember, since CSWE does not accept experience in lieu of class work, the life credit requirement applies to all facets of the educational program, including the field placement. Check with the field coordinator to discuss any worries you may have; if you cannot or prefer not to work in any agency or require special considerations in your placement options, it is best to let the field coordinator know as early as possible. Most programs will be as flexible as possible to help meet your needs. You'll also need to be flexible in field placement selection. A program will work with you to find the best site to meet your academic needs, but the final field assignment rests with the social work program and what is available in the community. We've heard students say that their placement must be in a certain agency, in order to get a job. While programs are concerned about your prospective employment, the primary issue in field assignment is your learning—employment comes later. Be careful to work closely with your field placement director and always take into account that some programs may have limited resources to meet all or even some of your field placement needs. Remember what we said about planning in advance and making sure it is doable. It is very sad when a student cannot receive a BSW or MSW degree simply because they did not complete their field placement hours. Although programs and agency placements try to be flexible, it may not be possible to get an evening or weekend placement and it would be a shame if noncompletion of the field hours stopped you from graduating.

4. Remember: Your peers in social work courses are in the same place you are. Although everyone's circumstances are different—some are older or younger, some have agency experience while others have none—these differences really have minimal importance in the educational setting as all of you are evolving as you begin the process of becoming a professional social worker. No one is better off than anyone else as a result of life experiences. Don't be intimidated by what others say or do or how they come across in class. Try to listen objectively to what others say and process accordingly as you start to question your own assumptions. Allow yourself to expand your previous assumptions as you embrace this professional perspective.

5. The purpose of your educational program is to prepare you for entry-level generalist social work practice. It is not to prepare you for a specialization. At this level of your academic career your course instructor and academic advisor care primarily about your development as a beginning social worker.

6. Don't approach an instructor and say that you need an A in the course for your own personal satisfaction or in order to get into graduate school. There's a saying in Texas that fits this type of situation: That dog won't hunt! You certainly have the right to talk with a faculty member about a grade and how it was reached, but it doesn't do any good to be argumentative. The instructor's responsibility is to assess your answers and summarize the quality of your responses with a grade. Grading is not easy—to say the least—and many teachers struggle to ensure that their grades are fair and consistent. Rather than arguing your position, be a social worker: clarify the situation and seek a remedy if you feel one is needed. Can you redo the assignment? Is there extra credit work you can do for the course? What changes can you make to do better next time? And so on. If you feel that your grade is incorrect, check out the student grievance policy in the program. But, we emphasize, use this only as a last resort.

Remember that your faculty members were once students and, like you, at one time or another felt that an instructor had graded them unfairly. We also know that the vast majority of the time, the instructor's assessment is correct; it's just that as students we don't like to get negative information. The key is to look at what the assessment is saying: What didn't you do on the assignment? What could you have done to get your point across more clearly?

Remember, your goal should be the same as your faculty's goal for you: to develop competence and expertise in entry-level generalist social work practice. Your energy should be directed toward developing critical knowledge and skills necessary for effective practice. Learning to be a professional is not easy; it means re-looking at your old ways of doing things and applying this new professional strategy. You are a student striving to learn, and if mistakes are made, this is the place you want to make them.

Two questions, then, to ask around grades: 1) How will my challenging a grade for a paper, test, or final exam make me a better social work practitioner? 2) Is there an error in the grading that I can demonstrate to the course instructor that justifies the assignment of another grade?

THE FUTURE AND YOU

We are now in a new century and the second hundred years of social work practice. As an up-and-coming social worker, the foundation for the twenty-first century will be laid by your efforts. You represent our future and what you do and say will shape the profession for years to come. As we bring the text to a close, we want to spend our remaining time looking at two questions. First, applying the knowledge you have learned about social work, explore how you can use this knowledge in the years to come. And second, how can you use these skills to work with clients individually and collectively to provide client-centered care and system level advocacy?

Social Work as a Profession: Future Considerations

You've seen how social work evolved from volunteer effort geared toward the poor to a multifaceted profession working with a variety of client groups. Education was initially limited to on-the-job training, with no oversight of work other than the agency's internal safeguards. Men were the supervisors while women were the caseworkers. Today, social work education is formal and for some too rigid, as to get this professional designation, it must be provided within colleges and universities. There is public regulation in every state for some, but not all, levels of social work practice. Many states are seeking or already have title protection, wherein you simply cannot use the title unless you have the professional training and qualifications to do so. Social work remains a female-dominated profession. Therefore, it comes as no surprise that women, throughout the first hundred years of the profession, made critical contributions to the theory, practice, and politics making social work what it is today. In the twenty-first century, we find women holding critical positions, leading the profession in academic institutions, professional associations, and in social welfare agencies.

The profession's first century required commitment, passion, and vision in order to achieve its current stature. While we've come a long way, as the poet Robert Frost wrote, we have miles to go before we sleep. So what are some areas the profession should move into more aggressively? Let's put forth a few ideas to consider:

1. Social work is not just designed to help the individual family or small group. With all the societal upheaval and changes around us the twenty-first century provides fertile ground for social workers to assume a pivotal position to create positive social change. To empower all individuals, Eamon (2008) identifies four goals: 1) accessing and enhancing social resources; 2) acquiring and increasing economic resources; 3) increasing self-determined behavior; and 4) influencing the social policies and organizational and community practices that affect the lives of vulnerable groups. To achieve these goals, providing services at the micro level only can fall short; therefore, it is critical to also focus helping efforts at the macro level. Macro level interventions require social change and advocacy that can be most easily accomplished by recognizing the importance of holding elective office at the local, state, and national levels. We need more of our colleagues to take this chance and run for office and to advocate for policy change. Richan (2006) states that social problems follow a logical sequence. First the social problem must be recognized and analyzed. Once this is completed, the policy is formalized and later implemented. Once it is in effect, an evaluation of the expected results and consequences is monitored. This stepwise process creates an interlocking cycle where one step leads to the next. In creating policy, whether in the formulation or the evaluation stage, who is better to write laws about families, children, the poor, the sick, and those at risk than social workers? Social workers

and lawyers make a great team. Therefore, we should never be afraid of being called a "bleeding heart liberal." Be proud of it. If assuming the role of a bleeding heart liberal means that we stand for health care for all people, shelter for the homeless, food for the hungry, and education for all children, then stand proudly as we do represent that term. Wouldn't you love to run against an opponent who claims to oppose care of sick children, to want homeless seniors to live unprotected on the streets, to want people, in particular children, to starve, and to oppose making all of our children the best educated in the world? In other words, the profession must use its assets. If we are a "people's profession," our assets start with our attention to human rights striving to protect the rights of all people.

2. The profession of social work needs to recognize the importance of unification and work together, especially on critical issues, presenting a unified front. Social work is a diverse field and there are those that believe we need special interest groups and membership associations in order to focus on specialized practice matters. But we are fast approaching, if we haven't already reached, a crossroad where practice membership associations are in conflict with each other and with the overall interests of the profession. A case in point is public regulation of social work practice. NASW is a staunch advocate of regulation for BSW and MSW levels of practice. The national and state clinical social work membership groups generally oppose licensing of practice other than clinical practice. Why? Could it be that these clinical practitioners feel if licensing were opened up to all social workers, it would hurt the clinical practice distinction and therefore decrease the ability to secure fee-paying clients? Some would deny this and point to other factors, but if that is the case, why would they oppose licensing designed to protect all members of the public, not just those who are insured?

How do we bridge the gulf between these two groups? NASW, nationally and in the states, is an important power than can help clinical social worker membership societies achieve their goals. Tension between members of these two groups is not healthy for the profession or, more important, for the public and the clients we serve. Social work membership groups must find common ground if we are to become even more effective in our public efforts.

3. The entry degree in the field of social work is the BSW, yet there are far too few active in professional membership organizations such as NASW. BSWs make important contributions to the field and their voices need to be heard. We must seek out more BSWs to join NASW. Since there are too few BSW members in the association, their practice interests are not fully represented at all levels of the association. Annual membership dues certainly are expensive—in particular, for lower-paid BSWs—and NASW has tried to address this by taking this into account in the dues structure. But efforts to attract BSWs must go far beyond lower dues. MSWs must make BSWs feel like accepted and important members of the profession. Elitism and professional ethnocentrism will only weaken our efforts.

Social work programs can play a critical role by involving BSW students in NASW. First, programs can promote membership. Student dues are relatively inexpensive and are far outweighed by the association's benefits. Second, social work programs, together with state chapters and local units, can look at developing student units that hold meetings on campus. Third, social work programs can work with local NASW units to hold meetings on campus—many students are placebound and have no way to get to a meeting.

The key is for professional groups and social work programs to be aggressive in recruiting students, then to value BSW students as future members, and finally to involve them in association activities.

4. In chapter 14, we spent time exploring the international social welfare arena. Social work is a worldwide profession that helps people, families, communities, and social systems to deal with issues that cut across national boundaries. Each of these groups comes from a different culture, which requires that a social worker be able to understand and integrate the differences that occur. It is through this understanding that the social worker helps to interpret how all these individuals view the world (Johnson & Grant, 2005). As we grow closer together and the boundaries become more easily crossed practitioners in the twenty-first century, are challenged more than at any other time in the world's history to understand the influence and be influenced by the international community. The phrase "think globally, act locally" probably best captures the direction we must go. Yet social workers, for the most part, have little exposure to international social welfare. International course content is sparse in both undergraduate and graduate programs. There are exceptions, of course; some schools sponsor study-abroad programs, offer educationally directed travel programs, or have a greater international emphasis. Yet most social work programs do little more than offer brief mentions as part of a course or courses.

Professional associations also work to promote international issues. Again through study tours and publications, we become more aware of the international community. But is this enough? We don't think so. We support the goal of global understanding and activism. Expanding our understanding will help us to be knowledgeable members of the world community. Our global learning and understanding of others will help us to better appreciate the strength and potential of seemingly different people while developing greater awareness of the struggles that will need to be engaged. Global activism builds on knowledge. Once we understand others, we are in a better position to offer effective assistance and support.

There are many mechanisms we can implement to pursue the goal of global understanding and activism. Obviously, the expansion of BSW and MSW curriculum content would help us toward this goal. International content in each course and an additional specific international course would help enhance our knowledge base. We can also become more creative in our approach. Social work educational programs can sponsor annual activities that highlight one or two aspects of international social welfare. Professional associations, both at the national and state levels, can sponsor international activities each year. Hosting continuing education workshops, dedicating parts of association newsletters to international issues, and developing dedicated international handouts and brochures will help us to become more global.

The American Social Welfare System: The Future

What a fascinating history we have in social welfare! The overview in chapter 2 was just that, an overview. Even from that brief foray, we can see emerging the beliefs that underpin the current U.S. social welfare system.

First is the myth that poor people and people in need are "different" from the rest of us. Some say the poor are morally inferior and lazy; others might say the poor are poorly educated and lack the motivation to change. This negative stereotyping can justify the lack of attention and service provision the system affords. Second, welfare services are best organized by nongovernmental entities. Americans have always been reluctant to support federal involvement in the social welfare system. Social agencies, churches, volunteer associations, and informal networks are more acceptable vehicles for social welfare. Yet, as a society we must be careful to not discriminate against others based on lifestyle or religious preference, and this makes suspect service provision provided by those motivated by religious custom and dogma (Blackwell & Dziegielewski, 2005).

Third, social welfare is not an entitlement but rather a temporary support given only to the most worthy. Over time, women, infants, children, the aged, and people with disabilities have fallen into the category of the "worthy" poor. Fourth is the myth that work is the primary way to achieve self-sufficiency. All anyone needs is a job, not even a good-paying job at first, because the early experience will lead to future, higher paying jobs.

Now, these views are not necessarily those of most social workers, but they do express the expectations of much of the American public. In chapter 2 we discussed the modern welfare system and, in chapter 7, the 1990s welfare reform package. And with the presidential election of 2000, a new welfare concept came across the national scene: "compassionate conservatism." These discussions showed how well ingrained into the American welfare system these four beliefs are.

So, where does the American welfare system go? Is the current system working? Here are some proposed changes to the welfare system:

1. The welfare system must be just and treat all people with respect and dignity. How do we explain compassion for the less fortunate when we have in each state a federally mandated and binding welfare program known as Temporary Assistance to Needy Families (TANF). This program only allows a maximum of five years of assistance in a lifetime. Some people, no matter what we do, just won't be able to care for themselves. Why do we penalize an unborn baby by denying it welfare benefits because the mother was already on assistance? What kind of life are we promising that child? A comprehensive welfare system embraces people and their strengths. We should move away from a punitive system to one based on hope.

2. American welfare carries an enormous stigma. Every day politicians, radio talk show hosts and callers, and newspaper columnists, among others, rail against the poor. With this constant barrage, it would be a wonder if welfare clients didn't hide from the general public. Being poor and receiving public assistance is not the fulfillment of a lifelong ambition. We should work to remove the stigma associated with public aid.

3. The goal of the welfare system should be to help all people with adequate benefits and supports. If the system works, then people who are capable of doing so will move to sustainable work. The purpose of the welfare system's benefits and supports is simple: help clients to meet their daily needs in order to focus their energies on becoming self-sufficient. The welfare system should concentrate on meeting basic needs: food, shelter, and protection. The level of these benefits must be sufficient. A second tier of services, which includes high-quality health care and childcare, supports adults in their efforts to work. A third tier of programs focuses on developing knowledge and skills necessary to become self-sufficient in a technological society. Transportation and education and training programs are the two principal components of this tier. Reliable transportation is needed to ensure that people can get to the training programs; not everyone has a car and not all cities and towns have public transportation. The fourth and final tier of the welfare system includes access to permanent, good-paying jobs that offer upward mobility and self-sufficiency. Once employed, the client is able to receive workplace benefits and no longer needs public welfare support.

4. A comprehensive welfare system is expensive. But if we care for the poor and less fortunate, the price tag should not matter. Funding decisions for programs are made in a political context. The decision to fund roads and highways at one level and after-school childcare at a much lower level is a statement about our beliefs. Funds are available to support a comprehensive welfare system, either by changing government spending patterns or by raising taxes. Throughout the text we have referred directly and indirectly to the influence of the political system on social welfare, and in chapter 13 we outlined the role that social workers can assume in politics. As we consider the role of politics in social welfare and questions related to funding, we must first answer two questions: What is the goal of our welfare system? What commitments are we willing to make to achieve that goal?

5. Social welfare and social work should do no harm to any person, group, or community. The "do no harm" philosophy is a fundamental value embraced by the medical community and its ideas should resonate throughout our helping systems. Do we want to create social policies that harm people? Of course we would never want to do this. Yet most agree that the first thrust of TANF is to make it clear that women (particularly unwed teen mothers) do not take personal responsibility for having children (Day, 2003). To overcome this and place responsibility for the loss of support on the mother, TANF has a lifetime limit in place on the number of months a person can receive federal assistance. Why do we allow millions of our children not to be fully immunized?

Under a "do no harm" philosophy, we would ensure that ALL children would be fully immunized. "Do no harm" is a core concept that serves as a pivotal girder in the foundation of a just, compassionate society.

SOCIAL WORK PRACTICE

Of all the practice professions, social work has one of the most comprehensive code of ethics. The profession makes statements such as "once a client, always a client" and "start where the client is," where individual worth and dignity of each client is held paramount. Moreover, social workers, no matter how experienced, are often alone when they make these difficult decisions, and oftentimes there are no easy clear-cut answers (Dolgoff, Moewenberg, & Harrington, 2005). Or they may be part of a multidisciplinary or interdisciplinary team. When working as part of a team, a social worker may note an ethical problem—when no one else does. Having such a comprehensive code of ethics can be both a blessing and a curse, especially when other professionals do not view the problem in the same way. This can make ethical practice decision difficult for the new social worker, especially when faced with an environment of cost containment and behavioral-based managed care strategies. To practice in this competitive environment, social workers must either accept this challenge for change or lose the opportunity to be players. Regardless, whether making the decision alone or as part of a team, social workers must be able to show that what they do is necessary and effective while maintaining their own ethical and moral standards for the helping relationship.

As discussed is several chapters of this book, culturally sensitive practice is essential, and the distinction is made that the nuances of culture can range in subtlety from the difference in meaning behind certain nonverbal gestures to the differences in perception for the roles and responsibilities of the practitioner (Arden & Linford, 2009).

All social workers must take a PROACTIVE stance regardless of their practice area. This book is designed to serve as a practical guide for understanding and applying this philosophy in our social work practice environment.

Simply stated, all social workers need to embrace the following imperatives at all levels of practice:

P PRESENT and POSITION themselves as competent professionals with POSITIVE attitudes in all service settings, whatever the type of practice.

R RECEIVE adequate training and continuing education in the current and future practice area of social work.
   RESEARCH time-limited treatment approaches that can provide alternatives for social workers struggling to provide high-quality services while cutting costs.

O ORGANIZE individuals and communities to help themselves to access safe and affordable services.
   ORGANIZE other social workers to prepare for the changes that are occurring and develop strategies to continue to provide ethical, cost-effective service.

A   ADDRESS policies and issues relevant to providing ethical, effective, efficient service.

C   COLLABORATE with other helping professionals to address client concerns and needs utilizing a client-centered and culturally-sensitive approach.

COMPLEMENT orthodox practices by utilizing holistic practices and alternative strategies that can help clients achieve increased well-being.

T   TEACH others about the value and the importance of including social work services and techniques.

TAKE TIME to help ourselves holistically by preventing professional burnout, thus remaining productive and receptive and serving as good role models for clients and other professionals.

I   INVESTIGATE and apply INNOVATIVE approaches to client care problems and issues.

INVOLVE all social workers in the change process that needs to occur in traditional social work.

V   VISUALIZE and work toward positive outcomes for all clients and potential clients.

VALUE the roles of all other helping professionals and support them as they face similar challenges and changes.

E   EXPLORE supplemental therapies and strategies that clients can self-administer at little or no cost to preserve and enhance well-being.

EMPOWER clients and ourselves by stressing the importance of EDUCATION for self-betterment as well as individual and societal change (adapted from Dziegielewski, 2004).

We will need to face the many changes that are in store for helping professionals, and we need to remember that in this area of budget cutting and cost containment we can be viable players. The NASW Code of Ethics (National Association of Social Workers [NASW], 2008) encourages us to charge reasonable fees and base our charges on ability to pay. This means that the fees social work professionals charge are very competitive with those of psychiatrists, psychologists, family therapists, psychiatric nurses, and mental health counselors, who provide similar services. This fact could entice health and other service delivery agencies to contract with social workers instead of other professionals to provide services that have traditionally fallen in the domain of social work practice. In this era of competition between the helping disciplines, no aspect of taking a proactive stance can be underestimated.

SPECIAL TOPIC: REGULATION OF PROFESSIONAL SOCIAL WORK PRACTICE

In practice we are expected to be accountable professionals, especially since we work with vulnerable populations (Gelman, 2009). To help ensure accountability, the government regulates all professions throughout the United States. Regulation is important to ensure that the public is protected from harm caused by unqualified persons. Credentialing is generally a part of the government's regulatory functions and licensing rules are maintained in the administrative code (Marks & Knox, 2009). Licensing is designed to ensure the public is protected (DeAngelis, 2009).

Why do we regulate occupations? What does credentialing do for us in the long run? First, a regulated occupation's activities are such that the average citizen may be harmed physically, emotionally, or financially if he is exposed to the practice of an unqualified person. Second, credentialing suggests that a specific educational background is needed to make a person qualified to carry out the tasks in a regulated occupation. Third, the public is assured that all regulated persons meet minimum standards of competence as set forth by the state. Finally, the public is assured that mechanisms are available for the pursuit of grievances against regulated workers.

> *Activity…Contact your state's social work licensing board or regulatory body and ask for information about the regulation of social work practice. Are all levels of social work practice licensed? Does the board seem to reflect the social work profession's broad range of work, or is its membership restricted to one or two types of practice? Attend a licensing board meeting (they are open to the public), and determine how the board protects the public interest. Finally, how does the local social work community perceive licensing? (Check this out at a local NASW unit meeting.)*

Think for a moment about the types of occupations that are regulated by the government. Decisions to regulate professions are left to state governments, so you'll find that some occupations are licensed in one state but not in another. Even when a profession is regulated by more than one state, the criteria that must be met for certification may differ. Types of educational degrees and years of experience required and the use of exams to test competence vary by state and occupation.

The list of occupations that states regulate seems endless. Each state oversees a wide array of occupations that can affect people's lives for good or bad (see box 1, for regulated professions in Florida).

Box 1: Partial List of Occupations Regulated by the State of Florida

Architect	Interior designer	Barber
Public Accountant	Pool contractor	Solar contractor
Building Contractor	Chiropractor	Nail specialist
Cosmetologist	Hair braiders	Dental hygienist
Dentist	Electrical contractor	Alarm system contractor
Embalmer	Talent agency	Physician
Optometrist	Podiatrist	Veterinarian
Nurse	Auctioneer	Athletic trainer
Respiratory therapist	Midwife	Nutrition counselor
Surveyor and mapper	Audiologist	School psychologist
Mental health counselor	Asbestos contractor	Physical therapist
Occupational therapist	Liquor salesperson	Building inspector

The profession of social work is regulated in all fifty states. By that we mean that some form of social work practice is licensed or certified by each state government. For the most part, regulation does not have two levels that mirror the two levels of social work practice, the BSW (generalist practice) and the MSW (specialist practice). For example, some states license both BSW and MSW practitioners together, while other states limit licensing to MSW practitioners who specialize in clinical social work. Most, but not all, states require passage of a written examination; and most, but not all, states require ongoing continuing education after being licensed.

The regulation of social work practice is subject to a number of complications. First, it is tied to the intricacies of the political process. As with any law passed by a state legislature, it reflects political interests. What seems to be a logical, straightforward piece of legislation may end up being defeated for any number of reasons. Some social workers are against formal licensure for the profession, but if we license and regulate hair braiders and surveyors, doesn't it make sense also to regulate a profession that is concerned with the emotional and psychological well-being of people?

Second, licensing requires social work professionals to overcome their own biases and act in the best interests of the profession. Unfortunately, this is easier said than done. Many social work special interest groups are most concerned with protecting their own members. Once a group feels its interests are enhanced and not compromised, it will support the legislation. You can imagine what happens to a licensing bill that must satisfy any number of social work interest groups, and what can result when ten or more interest groups are all actively lobbying at any given time.

Third, once the profession has pieced together a compromise proposal, it must then meet the demands of other human service professions and organizations.

Typically, these groups feel that their activities will be affected by the social work licensing act. As a result, these groups work to ensure that the final legislation will not interfere with their day-to-day activities or finances.

Finally, licensing BSW and MSW practice can become very cumbersome and confusing. While licensing protects the public from nonprofessional practice, state regulation also carves out specific practice areas or "turf" for professions. And "turf battles" can be hard fought. In Texas, for example, the state legislature in 2003 amended the licensing law to allow BSW degreed individuals to conduct "independent" practice. For some, this is very confusing—could one interpret "independent practice" as being similar to "private practice"? According to the Texas law, this is not the case. But will the public understand the "legal" definition—probably not, given that most social workers themselves are not able to differentiate between independent and private practice.

FINAL THOUGHTS

You should be writing this chapter. As future social workers and members of the global community, you will ultimately be responsible for the social welfare system of the twenty-first century. The types of programs, levels of assistance, and the clients eligible for benefits will all be issues that you will address.

The social work profession will always be part of our community as long as complex human social problems remain. As social workers, our challenge is to remain relevant to our nation's goals and our clients' needs. We can do this by vigorously pursuing competence in practice, by discovering and validating innovative interventions, and by ensuring that our educational and training programs continue to excel.

As you tackle social welfare issues be passionate in your convictions, ethical in your actions, knowledgeable about your information, and, above all, committed to the view that social justice is due to all people. Our community will be a better place because of people like you. We hope you will find what has fueled us over the multiple years in this field and that you too will feel as strongly and passionately about this profession as we do after many years of practice.

Glossary

absolute poverty qualitative measure of poverty that compares a person's situation with a numerical standard that usually reflects bare subsistence; cf. relative poverty.

abuse improper behavior that can result in physical, psychological, or financial harm to an individual, family, group, or community. In social work the term is most often related to acts against children, the elderly, the mentally impaired, or spouses or used in relation to drug or other substance abuse.

accreditation professional recognition that a social work program meets explicit standards; voted on by the CSWE Commission on Accreditation after it reviews the program's self-study documents, the site visitors' written report, and the program's written response to the site visit.

advocacy professional activities aimed at educating, informing, or defending and representing the needs and wants of clients through direct intervention or empowerment.

ageism (agism) stereotyping or generalization based on a person's age. This is considered a form of discrimination that is commonly directed toward older individuals.

agency organization that provides social services and is typically staffed by social service professionals, including social workers. Public, private, and not-for-profit agencies provide an array of services, usually to a target population. Policy is set by a board of directors and is implemented by administrators.

agency-based occurring in an agency. Agency-based practice can include a few specific practice methodologies or can span the continuum of social work practice, depending on the agency's size, mission, and purpose.

Aid to Families with Dependent Children (AFDC) a means-tested program that provided financial aid to children in need due to parental disability, absence, or death. It was administered nationally through the Administration for Children and Families division of the U.S. Department of Health and Human Services; state and county departments of public welfare provided local administration. AFDC ended in 1996 with the creation of Temporary Assistance for Needy Families.

almshouse (also know as **poorhouse**) place of refuge for the poor, medically ill, and mentally ill of all ages; considered the forerunner of the hospital.

assessment process of determining the nature, cause, progression, and prognosis of a problem and identifying the personalities and situations involved; process of reasoning from facts to tentative conclusions about their meaning.

at-risk populations (also known as vulnerable populations) groups with increased exposure to potential harm due to specific characteristics. Examples are infants born to drug-using mothers, who are at risk for birth defects; minorities, who are at risk for oppression; and poor children, who are at risk for malnutrition.

biopsychosocial approach   a perspective to social work practice, especially in health care and mental health, that assesses and places appropriate emphasis on the biological, psychological, and social or environmental aspects of the client's situation.

blended family   a term applied to a family unit when two previously separate families are joined together in a union and portray traditional family roles. Often referred to as a stepfamily.

block grant   lump sum of funds given to a state by the federal government. The state has authority over expenditure of block grants and may supplement them with state funds.

BSW (baccalaureate in social work)   undergraduate degree in social work from a CSWE-accredited program; the entry-level social work qualification. BSW and BA or BS in social work are equivalent degrees.

candidacy pre-accreditation   status for a social work program, which generally lasts two years; signifies that an educational program meets general criteria to conduct a self-study for accreditation.

charity assistance   aid given to the poor in the 1600s; viewed as a mechanism that reinforced dependent lifestyles.

charity organization society (COS)   privately or philanthropically funded agency that delivered social services to the needy in the mid- to late nineteenth century; considered the forerunner of the nonprofit social service agency.

child welfare   series of human service and social welfare programs designed specifically to promote the protection, care, and health development of children; found at the national, state, and local levels.

client   an individual, couple, family, group, or community that is the focus of intervention.

codependency   a relationship between two or more persons that is based on dependence of the other to meet and provide needs. For the most part, this is considered unhealthy as one individual is dependent on the other taking control and manipulation is highly probable and difficult to avoid.

Commission on Accreditation   CSWE committee of twenty-five social work educators and practitioners who oversee the accreditation process. The commission establishes educational standards and reviews programs to ensure that they meet the standards.

continuing education   training acquired after the completion of a degree program. NASW and state licensure boards require specified hours of continuing education in order to maintain a license or certification.

Council on Social Work Education (CSWE)   sole national accreditation board for schools of social work; founded in 1952 from the merger of the American Association of Schools of Social Work (founded 1919) and the National Association of Schools of Social Administration (founded 1942).

delirium   this is a state of mind that often presents itself as a disturbance in one's thinking and attention, often evidenced by hallucinations and anxiety. There can be multiple causes for this, from organic damage to the brain to drug or alcohol use.

diagnosis   process of identifying a problem—social, mental, or medical—and its underlying causes and formulating a solution.

disadvantaged   term used to describe individuals, groups, communities, and the like, that are unable to access the resources and services needed to maintain a minimal standard of living.

discharge planning   service provided by health care social workers to assist clients in, for example, securing placement and services to support a timely transition from a health care facility to home or to another less restrictive environment.

discrimination   the prejudgment and negative treatment of a person or a group of people based on known characteristics. Common areas where this can occur include race, gender, ethnicity, religion, or sexual identity.

domestic violence   violent acts toward another person perpetrated in a domestic situation.

door-knob communication   a term applied when a person in therapy shares something significant just as the therapy session is about to end. This can range from something the client felt uncomfortable about that was either mentioned or not mentioned in the session. Often it is considered a "stall tactic" to prolong the session.

DSM-IV-TR (Diagnostic and Statistical Manual, 4th edition, Text Revision)   manual that presents a classification system designed to assist in reaching formal diagnoses. It uses five "axes": Axis I, the first level of coding, records such categories as major clinical syndromes, pervasive developmental disorders, learning disorders, motor skills disorders, communication disorders, and other disorders that may be the focus of clinical treatment. Axis II records personality disorders and mental retardation. Axis III records general medical conditions that can affect mental health. Axis IV records psychosocial and environmental problems/stressors. Axis V records level of functioning.

DSW (doctor of social welfare or social work)   one of the highest social work degrees; typically requires two years of full-time post-master's course work, passage of comprehensive examinations, and successful completion of a dissertation. There is also a PhD in social work or social welfare that often has similar requirements.

educable   means one is capable of being educated. Professionals often use this term in regard to individuals with mental retardation who have the ability to learn certain social or academic skills.

Educational Policy and Accreditation Standards (EPAS)   written document that outlines the purpose and framework of social work education programs. The CSWE Commission on Accreditation is responsible for oversight of the EPAS.

empirically based social work practice   type of intervention in which the professional social worker uses research as a practice and problem-solving tool. Data are collected systematically, and problems and outcomes are stated in measurable terms.

entitlement programs   these are governmental programs offered to all individuals that meet the predetermined criteria.

ethics   system of moral principles used in decision making to discern right from wrong or to choose between two or more seemingly equal alternatives.

ethical practice in social work   adhering to the standards and principles set forth in the profession and acting in a way that highlights the core values and expectations of the profession.

field placement   work in an agency during the BSW or MSW educational experience, supervised by a social worker. The agency and the educational institution jointly train and monitor the students during placement.

Food Stamp Program   program that distributes to people in need "stamps" that can be used to purchase basic food items; implemented in 1964 and administered by the U.S. Department of Agriculture until 1996; now administered by states under the Personal Responsibility and Work Opportunity Reconciliation Act of 1996.

friendly visitor   volunteer from a charity organization society who visited poor families to offer aid and to serve as a role model.

generalist practice   practice underpinned by knowledge and skills across a broad spectrum and by comprehensive assessment of problems and their solutions; includes coordination of activities of specialists.

hallucination   an imagined perception of an object or idea that is not really present. This is often a symptom of psychosis and can include auditory (hearing), visual (seeing), olfactory (smelling), gustatory (tasting), and tactile or haptic (touching) things that are not present. This may most likely be seen in a mental disorder called schizophrenia.

Head Start   program intended to help preschool children of disadvantaged families to overcome or offset problems related to social deprivation; established in 1965 and administered by Child Youth and Families within the U.S. Department of Health and Human Services.

home care   in this type of health care, social work services are provided to individuals and families in their home or community and/or other homelike settings.

hospice care   this type of care involves providing services to individuals who are considered to be terminally ill and their family members. In this type of care there is open acknowledgment that no cure is expected for client's illness, and to support the process of dying in a dignified manner, physical, emotional, social, and spiritual care are provided.

hospital social worker   social worker who practices in hospitals and health care facilities; focuses on assessments, discharge planning, preventive services, interdisciplinary coordination, and individual and family counseling.

human rights   universal social rights all persons share without distinction to race, gender, language, or religion. An example of this are civil rights.

indoor relief   assistance provided during colonial times to the "unworthy" poor in poorhouses.

in kind   benefit in the form of food, clothing, education, and so forth, in place of, or in addition to, cash.

institutional social welfare   social programs available to all as a part of well-being in the modern state; cf. residual social welfare.

interdisciplinary team   variety of health care professionals brought together to provide a client with effective, better coordinated, and improved quality of services.

International Federation of Social Workers (IFSW)   international association of social workers comprising members through their national organizations; founded in 1928 in Paris; promotes social work, establishes standards, and provides a forum for exchange among associations throughout the world.

intervention   treatment, services, advocacy, mediation, or any other practice action, performed for or with clients, that is intended to ameliorate problems.

label   in mental health, it is generally referred to as a clinical diagnosis of a client that stays with the client indefinitely, possibly to the client's detriment.

macrosystem   community, administrative, and environmental forces that affect the human condition. Political action, community organizing, and administration of large public welfare agencies are examples of macropractice.

managed care   a form of health care delivery within a specific framework with specific rules, requirements, and expectations for the delivery of service.

Meals on Wheels   delivery of meals to the homes of people unable to meet their own nutritional needs, usually due to physical or mental impairment. The providers of service are usually community agencies, such as senior citizen councils, local human service departments, and private agencies.

means-tested program   a means-tested program involves evaluating a potential program recipient's resources and whether the need is great enough for eligibility within a predetermined criteria set.

Medicaid   program established in 1965 that funds hospital and other medical services to people who meet means tests; administered by the federal Health Care Financing Administration.

Medicare   national health insurance program established in 1965. Eligibility is universal, with attainment of age 65 the criterion for most people; however, there are allied programs for the disabled among others. Medicare is funded through employee and employer contributions and administered by the Social Security Administration and the Health Care Financing Administration.

mezzosystem   system that connects micro- and macrosystems.

microsystem   individual, family, or small group. Direct intervention and casework are examples of micropractice.

MSW (master of social work)   degree requiring approximately sixty hours of post baccalaureate education, including 900 hours of field placement, in a CSWE-accredited program. MSSW and MA or MS in social work are equivalent degrees.

multidisciplinary team   mix of health and social welfare professionals, with each discipline working, for the most part, on an independent or referral basis.

National Association of Social Workers (NASW)   world's largest social work membership association with approximately 160,000 members in 1999; established in 1955 through the merger of five special interest organizations; chapters exist in all fifty states and the District of Columbia, New York City, Puerto Rico, and the Virgin Islands, in addition to an international chapter.

nativism   the idea that certain personality factors are present at birth and are not learned.

needs assessments (NA)   made on behalf of the client by agencies to evaluate their clients' needs and establish priorities for service.

New Deal   set of social welfare programs and legislation implemented during President Franklin D. Roosevelt's administration in response to the Great Depression. Examples include the Economic Security Act of 1935, Works Progress Administration, and Federal Emergency Relief Act.

outdoor relief   minimal assistance provided during the colonial period to the "worthy" poor in their own homes.

overseer of the poor   individual responsible during colonial times for identifying the poor, assessing their needs, and coordinating a community response by levying and collecting taxes; considered a colonial version of a social worker.

parens patriae   principle under which children can become wards of the state. Related to children's rights as this principle has allowed children's advocates to argue that children should be viewed differently from adults and has been used to support the creation of a range of juvenile services.

Person-in-Environment Classification System (PIE)   systematic approach to classifying social functioning. It employs four levels to aid in the systematic collection of data about clients and in planning interventions. Level I is social functioning problems. Level II is environmental problems. Level III is mental disorders—DSM-IV Axes I and II. Level IV is physical health problems.

person-in-situation (also called **person-in-environment**)   casework concept that focuses on the interrelation between problem, situation, and the interaction between them.

PhD (doctorate in philosophy)   highest social work degree, emphasizing research, knowledge expansion, and advanced clinical practice; similar, often identical to, DSW. See DSW for requirements.

policy   plan that an agency, organization, or governmental institution follows as a framework; includes formal written policies and unwritten (informal) policies.

political lens   political context—often candidates for public office and their campaigns—that influences how society defines a term, for example, "family."

poor laws   codified in 1601; redefined welfare as no longer a private affair but rather a public governmental responsibility.

poverty   general term used to describe a state of deprivation. See absolute poverty and relative poverty.

poverty threshold   level of income below which a person is living in poverty. This level is based on the cost of securing the basic necessities of living.

projection   a defense mechanism one uses when rejecting or attributing unacceptable aspects of one's personality to another person.

psychosocial history   systematic compilation of information about a client; encompasses family, health, education, spirituality, legal position, interpersonal relations, social supports, economic status, environment, sexual orientation, and culture.

rapport   an important part of the therapeutic relationship that results in harmony, compatibility, and empathy, fostering mutual understanding and a working relationship between the client and social worker.

reaffirmation   confirmation of CSWE accreditation, for which an accredited program must undergo the self-study and review process every seven years.

relative poverty   subjective measure of poverty that compares a person's situation with a normative standard; cf. absolute poverty.

residual social welfare   social programs activated only when normal structures of family and market are not sufficient; cf. institutional social welfare.

role culturally expected behavior associated with a person or status.

sanction 1) formal or informal authorization to perform services; 2) penalty imposed for noncompliance with policies and procedures. NASW sanctions members who have violated the Code of Ethics with membership suspension or removal of certification.

selective eligibility (also called means-tested eligibility) eligibility based on demonstrating need or inability to provide for one's needs; cf. universal eligibility.

site visit visit to a social work educational program by a site team composed of social work educators and, for graduate programs, an MSW practitioner. The site team makes a written report to the CSWE Commission on Accreditation that is considered during the commission's deliberations on the program's accreditation.

social justice a core social work value that involves efforts to confront discrimination, oppression, and other social inequities.

social welfare 1) society's specific system of programs to help people to meet basic health, economic, and social needs; 2) general state of well-being in society.

specialist practice practice focused in approach and knowledge on a specific problem or goal or underpinned by highly developed expertise in specific activities.

strengths-based assessment this type of assessment relies on the social worker's ability to critically analyze the positive aspects, attributes, or strengths in a client or client system and utilize these strengths in every aspect of the problem-solving process.

stigma negative connotation attached to individuals, or groups of individuals, based on characteristics that may include economic status, health, appearance, education, sexual orientation, and mental health.

Temporary Assistance for Needy Families (TANF) program established in 1996 to replace AFDC; subject to strict eligibility requirements, which mandate employment, and to a lifetime limit on benefits of five years; funded through federal block grants to states, which administer the program.

universal eligibility availability to all people regardless of income or social support; cf. selective eligibility.

unworthy poor see worthy poor.

victim blaming a philosophy or orientation that attributes blame and responsibility to the person who is harmed by a social circumstance. An example of this would be a female who is raped but publically accused of dressing seductively and thereby seducing her attacker.

Violence Against Women Act (VAWA) passed in 1994, a comprehensive federal response to the problems of domestic violence that promotes preventive programs and victim's services.

worthy poor category of people "deserving" of public aid introduced by the 1601 poor laws; included the ill, the disabled, orphans, the elderly—people viewed as having no control over their life circumstances—as well as people who were involuntarily unemployed. The unworthy poor consisted of the vagrant or able-bodied who, while able to work, did not seek employment.

Appendix A

National Association of Social Workers, Code of Ethics

Preamble

The primary mission of the social work profession is to enhance human wellbeing and help meet the basic human needs of all people, with particular attention to the needs and empowerment of people who are vulnerable, oppressed, and living in poverty. A historic and defining feature of social work is the profession's focus on individual wellbeing in a social context and the wellbeing of society. Fundamental to social work is attention to the environmental forces that create, contribute to, and address problems in living.

Social workers promote social justice and social change with and on behalf of clients. "Clients" is used inclusively to refer to individuals, families, groups, organizations, and communities. Social workers are sensitive to cultural and ethnic diversity and strive to end discrimination, oppression, poverty, and other forms of social injustice. These activities may be in the form of direct practice, community organizing, supervision, consultation administration, advocacy, social and political action, policy development and implementation, education, and research and evaluation. Social workers seek to enhance the capacity of people to address their own needs. Social workers also seek to promote the responsiveness of organizations, communities, and other social institutions to individuals' needs and social problems.

The mission of the social work profession is rooted in a set of core values. These core values, embraced by social workers throughout the profession's history, are the foundation of social work's unique purpose and perspective:

–service
–social justice
–dignity and worth of the person
–importance of human relationships
–integrity
–competence.

This constellation of core values reflects what is unique to the social work profession. Core values, and the principles that flow from them, must be balanced within the context and complexity of the human experience.

PURPOSE OF THE NASW CODE OF ETHICS

Professional ethics are at the core of social work. The profession has an obligation to articulate its basic values, ethical principles, and ethical standards. The *NASW Code of Ethics* sets forth these values, principles, and standards to guide social workers' conduct. The *Code* is relevant to all social workers and social work students, regardless of their professional functions, the settings in which they work, or the populations they serve.

The *NASW Code of Ethics* serves six purposes:

1. The Code identifies core values on which social work's mission is based.
2. The *Code* summarizes broad ethical principles that reflect the profession's core values and establishes a set of specific ethical standards that should be used to guide social work practice.
3. The *Code* is designed to help social workers identify relevant considerations when professional obligations conflict or ethical uncertainties arise.
4. The *Code* provides ethical standards to which the general public can hold the social work profession accountable.
5. The *Code* socializes practitioners new to the field to social work's mission, values, ethical principles, and ethical standards.
6. The *Code* articulates standards that the social work profession itself can use to assess whether social workers have engaged in unethical conduct. NASW has formal procedures to adjudicate ethics complaints filed against its members.[1] In subscribing to this *Code*, social workers are required to cooperate in its implementation, participate in NASW adjudication proceedings, and abide by any NASW disciplinary rulings or sanctions based on it.

The *Code* offers a set of values, principles, and standards to guide decision making and conduct when ethical issues arise. It does not provide a set of rules that prescribe how social workers should act in all situations. Specific applications of the *Code* must take into account the context in which it is being considered and the possibility of conflicts among the *Code's* values, principles, and standards. Ethical responsibilities flow from all human relationships, from the personal and familial to the social and professional.

Further, the *NASW Code of Ethics* does not specify which values, principles, and standards are most important and ought to outweigh others in instances when they conflict. Reasonable differences of opinion can and do exist among social workers with respect to the ways in which values, ethical principles, and ethical standards should be rank ordered when they conflict. Ethical decision making in a given situation must apply the informed judgment of the individual social worker and should also consider how the issues would be judged in a peer review process where the ethical standards of the profession would be applied.

Ethical decision making is a process. There are many instances in social work where simple answers are not available to resolve complex ethical issues. Social workers should take into consideration all the values, principles, and standards in this *Code* that are relevant to any situation in which ethical judgment is warranted. Social workers' decisions and actions should be consistent with the spirit as well as the letter of this *Code*.

In addition to this *Code*, there are many other sources of information about ethical thinking that may be useful. Social workers should consider ethical theory and principles generally, social work theory and research, laws, regulations, agency policies, and other relevant codes of ethics, recognizing that among codes of ethics social workers should consider the *NASW Code of Ethics* as their primary source. Social workers also should be aware of the impact on ethical decision making of their clients' and their own personal values and cultural and religious beliefs and practices. They should be aware of any conflicts between personal and professional values and deal with them responsibly.

[1] For information on NASW adjudication procedures, see *NASW Procedures for the Adjudication of Grievances*.

For additional guidance social workers should consult the relevant literature on professional ethics and ethical decision making and seek appropriate consultation when faced with ethical dilemmas. This may involve consultation with an agencybased or social work organization's ethics committee, a regulatory body, knowledgeable colleagues, supervisors, or legal counsel.

Instances may arise when social workers' ethical obligations conflict with agency policies or relevant laws or regulations. When such conflicts occur, social workers must make a responsible effort to resolve the conflict in a manner that is consistent with the values, principles, and standards expressed in this Code. If a reasonable resolution of the conflict does not appear possible, social workers should seek proper consultation before making a decision.

The *NASW Code of Ethics* is to be used by NASW and by individuals, agencies, organizations, and bodies (such as licensing and regulatory boards, professional liability insurance providers, courts of law, agency boards of directors, government agencies, and other professional groups) that choose to adopt it or use it as a frame of reference. Violation of standards in this *Code* does not automatically imply legal liability or violation of the law. Such determination can only be made in the context of legal and judicial proceedings. Alleged violations of the *Code* would be subject to a peer review process. Such processes are generally separate from legal or administrative procedures and insulated from legal review or proceedings to allow the profession to counsel and discipline its own members.

A code of ethics cannot guarantee ethical behavior. Moreover, a code of ethics cannot resolve all ethical issues or disputes or capture the richness and complexity involved in striving to make responsible choices within a moral community. Rather, a code of ethics sets forth values, ethical principles, and ethical standards to which professionals aspire and by which their actions can be judged. Social workers' ethical behavior should result from their personal commitment to engage in ethical practice. The *NASW Code of Ethics* reflects the commitment of all social workers to uphold the profession's values and to act ethically. Principles and standards must be applied by individuals of good character who discern moral questions and, in good faith, seek to make reliable ethical judgments.

Ethical Principles

The following broad ethical principles are based on social work's core values of service, social justice, dignity and worth of the person, importance of human relationships, integrity, and competence. These principles set forth ideals to which all social workers should aspire.

Value: Service

Ethical Principle: Social workers' primary goal is to help people in need and to address social problems.

Social workers elevate service to others above selfinterest. Social workers draw on their knowledge, values, and skills to help people in need and to address social problems. Social workers are encouraged to volunteer some portion of their professional skills with no expectation of significant financial return (pro bono service).

Value: Social Justice

Ethical Principle: Social workers challenge social injustice.

Social workers pursue social change, particularly with and on behalf of vulnerable and oppressed individuals and groups of people. Social workers' social change efforts are focused primarily on issues of poverty, unemployment, discrimination, and other forms of social injustice. These activities seek to promote sensitivity to and knowledge about oppression and cultural and ethnic diversity. Social workers strive to ensure access to needed information, services, and resources; equality of opportunity; and meaningful participation in decision making for all people.

✳ Value: Dignity and Worth of the Person

Ethical Principle: Social workers respect the inherent dignity and worth of the person.

Social workers treat each person in a caring and respectful fashion, mindful of individual differences and cultural and ethnic diversity. Social workers promote clients' socially responsible selfdetermination. Social workers seek to enhance clients' capacity and opportunity to change and to address their own needs. Social workers are cognizant of their dual responsibility to clients and to the broader society. They seek to resolve conflicts between clients' interests and the broader society's interests in a socially responsible manner consistent with the values, ethical principles, and ethical standards of the profession.

✳ Value: Importance of Human Relationships

Ethical Principle: Social workers recognize the central importance of human relationships.

Social workers understand that relationships between and among people are an important vehicle for change. Social workers engage people as partners in the helping process. Social workers seek to strengthen relationships among people in a purposeful effort to promote, restore, maintain, and enhance the wellbeing of individuals, families, social groups, organizations, and communities.

✳ Value: Integrity

Ethical Principle: Social workers behave in a trustworthy manner.

Social workers are continually aware of the profession's mission, values, ethical principles, and ethical standards and practice in a manner consistent with them. Social workers act honestly and responsibly and promote ethical practices on the part of the organizations with which they are affiliated.

Value: Competence

Ethical Principle: Social workers practice within their areas of competence and develop and enhance their professional expertise.

Social workers continually strive to increase their professional knowledge and skills and to apply them in practice. Social workers should aspire to contribute to the knowledge base of the profession.

Ethical Standards

The following ethical standards are relevant to the professional activities of all social workers. These standards concern (1) social workers' ethical responsibilities to clients, (2) social workers' ethical responsibilities to colleagues, (3) social workers' ethical responsibilities in practice settings, (4) social workers' ethical responsibilities as professionals, (5) social workers' ethical responsibilities to the social work profession, and (6) social workers' ethical responsibilities to the broader society.

Some of the standards that follow are enforceable guidelines for professional conduct, and some are aspirational. The extent to which each standard is enforceable is a matter of professional judgment to be exercised by those responsible for reviewing alleged violations of ethical standards.

1. Social Workers' Ethical Responsibilities to Clients

✳ 1.01 Commitment to Clients

Social workers' primary responsibility is to promote the wellbeing of clients. In general, clients' interests are primary. However, social workers' responsibility to the larger society or specific legal obligations may on limited occasions supersede the loyalty owed clients, and clients should be so advised. (Examples include when a social worker is required by law to report that a client has abused a child or has threatened to harm self or others.)

1.02 SelfDetermination

Social workers respect and promote the right of clients to selfdetermination and assist clients in their efforts to identify and clarify their goals. Social workers may limit clients' right to selfdetermination when, in the social workers' professional judgment, clients' actions or potential actions pose a serious, foreseeable, and imminent risk to themselves or others.

1.03 Informed Consent

(a) Social workers should provide services to clients only in the context of a professional relationship based, when appropriate, on valid informed consent. Social workers should use clear and understandable language to inform clients of the purpose of the services, risks related to the services, limits to services because of the requirements of a thirdparty payer, relevant costs, reasonable alternatives, clients' right to refuse or withdraw consent, and the time frame covered by the consent. Social workers should provide clients with an opportunity to ask questions.

(b) In instances when clients are not literate or have difficulty understanding the primary language used in the practice setting, social workers should take steps to ensure clients' comprehension. This may include providing clients with a detailed verbal explanation or arranging for a qualified interpreter or translator whenever possible.

(c) In instances when clients lack the capacity to provide informed consent, social workers should protect clients' interests by seeking permission from an appropriate third party, informing clients consistent with the clients' level of understanding. In such instances social workers should seek to ensure that the third party acts in a manner consistent with clients' wishes and interests. Social workers should take reasonable steps to enhance such clients' ability to give informed consent.

(d) In instances when clients are receiving services involuntarily, social workers should provide information about the nature and extent of services and about the extent of clients' right to refuse service.

(e) Social workers who provide services via electronic media (such as computer, telephone, radio, and television) should inform recipients of the limitations and risks associated with such services.

(f) Social workers should obtain clients' informed consent before audiotaping or videotaping clients or permitting observation of services to clients by a third party.

1.04 Competence

(a) Social workers should provide services and represent themselves as competent only within the boundaries of their education, training, license, certification, consultation received, supervised experience, or other relevant professional experience.

(b) Social workers should provide services in substantive areas or use intervention techniques or approaches that are new to them only after engaging in appropriate study, training, consultation, and supervision from people who are competent in those interventions or techniques.

(c) When generally recognized standards do not exist with respect to an emerging area of practice, social workers should exercise careful judgment and take responsible steps (including appropriate education, research, training, consultation, and supervision) to ensure the competence of their work and to protect clients from harm.

1.05 Cultural Competence and Social Diversity

(a) Social workers should understand culture and its function in human behavior and society, recognizing the strengths that exist in all cultures.

(b) Social workers should have a knowledge base of their clients' cultures and be able to demonstrate competence in the provision of services that are sensitive to clients' cultures and to differences among people and cultural groups.

(c) Social workers should obtain education about and seek to understand the nature of social diversity and oppression with respect to race, ethnicity, national origin, color, sex, sexual orientation, gender identity or expression, age, marital status, political belief, religion, immigration status, and mental or physical disability.

✳ 1.06   Conflicts of Interest

(a) Social workers should be alert to and avoid conflicts of interest that interfere with the exercise of professional discretion and impartial judgment. Social workers should inform clients when a real or potential conflict of interest arises and take reasonable steps to resolve the issue in a manner that makes the clients' interests primary and protects clients' interests to the greatest extent possible. In some cases, protecting clients' interests may require termination of the professional relationship with proper referral of the client.

(b) Social workers should not take unfair advantage of any professional relationship or exploit others to further their personal, religious, political, or business interests.

(c) Social workers should not engage in dual or multiple relationships with clients or former clients in which there is a risk of exploitation or potential harm to the client. In instances when dual or multiple relationships are unavoidable, social workers should take steps to protect clients and are responsible for setting clear, appropriate, and culturally sensitive boundaries. (Dual or multiple relationships occur when social workers relate to clients in more than one relationship, whether professional, social, or business. Dual or multiple relationships can occur simultaneously or consecutively.)

(d) When social workers provide services to two or more people who have a relationship with each other (for example, couples, family members), social workers should clarify with all parties which individuals will be considered clients and the nature of social workers' professional obligations to the various individuals who are receiving services. Social workers who anticipate a conflict of interest among the individuals receiving services or who anticipate having to perform in potentially conflicting roles (for example, when a social worker is asked to testify in a child custody dispute or divorce proceedings involving clients) should clarify their role with the parties involved and take appropriate action to minimize any conflict of interest.

✳ 1.07   Privacy and Confidentiality

(a) Social workers should respect clients' right to privacy. Social workers should not solicit private information from clients unless it is essential to providing services or conducting social work evaluation or research. Once private information is shared, standards of confidentiality apply.

(b) Social workers may disclose confidential information when appropriate with valid consent from a client or a person legally authorized to consent on behalf of a client.

(c) Social workers should protect the confidentiality of all information obtained in the course of professional service, except for compelling professional reasons. The general expectation that social workers will keep information confidential does not apply when disclosure is necessary to prevent serious, foreseeable, and imminent harm to a client or other identifiable person. In all instances, social workers should disclose the least amount of confidential information necessary to achieve the desired purpose; only information that is directly relevant to the purpose for which the disclosure is made should be revealed.

(d) Social workers should inform clients, to the extent possible, about the disclosure of confidential information and the potential consequences, when feasible before the disclosure is made. This applies whether social workers disclose confidential information on the basis of a legal requirement or client consent.

(e) Social workers should discuss with clients and other interested parties the nature of confidentiality and limitations of clients' right to confidentiality. Social workers should review with clients circumstances where confidential information may be requested and where disclosure of confidential information may be legally required. This discussion should occur as soon as possible in the social workerclient relationship and as needed throughout the course of the relationship.

(f) When social workers provide counseling services to families, couples, or groups, social workers should seek agreement among the parties involved concerning each individual's right to confidentiality and obligation to preserve the confidentiality of information shared by others. Social workers should inform participants in family, couples, or group counseling that social workers cannot guarantee that all participants will honor such agreements.

(g) Social workers should inform clients involved in family, couples, marital, or group counseling of the social worker's, employer's, and agency's policy concerning the social worker's disclosure of confidential information among the parties involved in the counseling.

(h) Social workers should not disclose confidential information to thirdparty payers unless clients have authorized such disclosure.

(i) Social workers should not discuss confidential information in any setting unless privacy can be ensured. Social workers should not discuss confidential information in public or semipublic areas such as hallways, waiting rooms, elevators, and restaurants.

(j) Social workers should protect the confidentiality of clients during legal proceedings to the extent permitted by law. When a court of law or other legally authorized body

orders social workers to disclose confidential or privileged information without a client's consent and such disclosure could cause harm to the client, social workers should request that the court withdraw the order or limit the order as narrowly as possible or maintain the records under seal, unavailable for public inspection.

(k) Social workers should protect the confidentiality of clients when responding to requests from members of the media.

(l) Social workers should protect the confidentiality of clients' written and electronic records and other sensitive information. Social workers should take reasonable steps to ensure that clients' records are stored in a secure location and that clients' records are not available to others who are not authorized to have access.

(m) Social workers should take precautions to ensure and maintain the confidentiality of information transmitted to other parties through the use of computers, electronic mail, facsimile machines, telephones and telephone answering machines, and other electronic or computer technology. Disclosure of identifying information should be avoided whenever possible.

(n) Social workers should transfer or dispose of clients' records in a manner that protects clients' confidentiality and is consistent with state statutes governing records and social work licensure.

(o) Social workers should take reasonable precautions to protect client confidentiality in the event of the social worker's termination of practice, incapacitation, or death.

(p) Social workers should not disclose identifying information when discussing clients for teaching or training purposes unless the client has consented to disclosure of confidential information.

(q) Social workers should not disclose identifying information when discussing clients with consultants unless the client has consented to disclosure of confidential information or there is a compelling need for such disclosure.

(r) Social workers should protect the confidentiality of deceased clients consistent with the preceding standards.

1.08 Access to Records

(a) Social workers should provide clients with reasonable access to records concerning the clients. Social workers who are concerned that clients' access to their records could cause serious misunderstanding or harm to the client should provide assistance in interpreting the records and consultation with the client regarding the records. Social workers should limit clients' access to their records, or portions of their records, only in exceptional circumstances when there is compelling evidence that such access would cause serious harm to the client. Both clients' requests and the rationale for withholding some or all of the record should be documented in clients' files.

(b) When providing clients with access to their records, social workers should take steps to protect the confidentiality of other individuals identified or discussed in such records.

1.09 Sexual Relationships

(a) Social workers should under no circumstances engage in sexual activities or sexual contact with current clients, whether such contact is consensual or forced.

(b) Social workers should not engage in sexual activities or sexual contact with clients' relatives or other individuals with whom clients maintain a close personal relationship when there is a risk of exploitation or potential harm to the client. Sexual activity or sexual contact with clients' relatives or other individuals with whom clients maintain a personal relationship has the potential to be harmful to the client and may make it difficult for the social worker and client to maintain appropriate professional boundaries. Social workers—not their clients, their clients' relatives, or other individuals with whom the client maintains a personal relationship—assume the full burden for setting clear, appropriate, and culturally sensitive boundaries.

(c) Social workers should not engage in sexual activities or sexual contact with former clients because of the potential for harm to the client. If social workers engage in conduct contrary to this prohibition or claim that an exception to this prohibition is warranted because of extraordinary circumstances, it is social workers—not their clients—who assume the full burden of demonstrating that the former client has not been exploited, coerced, or manipulated, intentionally or unintentionally.

(d) Social workers should not provide clinical services to individuals with whom they have had a prior sexual relationship. Providing clinical services to a former sexual partner has the potential to be harmful to the individual and is likely to make it difficult for the social worker and individual to maintain appropriate professional boundaries.

1.10 Physical Contact

Social workers should not engage in physical contact with clients when there is a possibility of psychological harm to the client as a result of the contact (such as cradling or caressing clients). Social workers who engage in appropriate physical contact with clients are responsible for setting clear, appropriate, and culturally sensitive boundaries that govern such physical contact.

1.11 Sexual Harassment

Social workers should not sexually harass clients. Sexual harassment includes sexual advances, sexual solicitation, requests for sexual favors, and other verbal or physical conduct of a sexual nature.

1.12 Derogatory Language

Social workers should not use derogatory language in their written or verbal communications to or about clients. Social workers should use accurate and respectful language in all communications to and about clients.

*1.13   Payment for Services

(a) When setting fees, social workers should ensure that the fees are fair, reasonable, and commensurate with the services performed. Consideration should be given to clients' ability to pay.

(b) Social workers should avoid accepting goods or services from clients as payment for professional services. Bartering arrangements, particularly involving services, create the potential for conflicts of interest, exploitation, and inappropriate boundaries in social workers' relationships with clients. Social workers should explore and may participate in bartering only in very limited circumstances when it can be demonstrated that such arrangements are an accepted practice among professionals in the local community, considered to be essential for the provision of services, negotiated without coercion, and entered into at the client's initiative and with the client's informed consent. Social workers who accept goods or services from clients as payment for professional services assume the full burden of demonstrating that this arrangement will not be detrimental to the client or the professional relationship.

(c) Social workers should not solicit a private fee or other remuneration for providing services to clients who are entitled to such available services through the social workers' employer or agency.

*1.14   Clients Who Lack DecisionMaking Capacity

When social workers act on behalf of clients who lack the capacity to make informed decisions, social workers should take reasonable steps to safeguard the interests and rights of those clients.

*1.15   Interruption of Services

Social workers should make reasonable efforts to ensure continuity of services in the event that services are interrupted by factors such as unavailability, relocation, illness, disability, or death.

*1.16   Termination of Services

(a) Social workers should terminate services to clients and professional relationships with them when such services and relationships are no longer required or no longer serve the clients' needs or interests.

(b) Social workers should take reasonable steps to avoid abandoning clients who are still in need of services. Social workers should withdraw services precipitously only under unusual circumstances, giving careful consideration to all factors in the situation and taking care to minimize possible adverse effects. Social workers should assist in making appropriate arrangements for continuation of services when necessary.

(c) Social workers in feeforservice settings may terminate services to clients who are not paying an overdue balance if the financial contractual arrangements have been made clear to the client, if the client does not pose an imminent danger to self or others, and if the clinical and other consequences of the current nonpayment have been addressed and discussed with the client.

(d) Social workers should not terminate services to pursue a social, financial, or sexual relationship with a client.

(e) Social workers who anticipate the termination or interruption of services to clients should notify clients promptly and seek the transfer, referral, or continuation of services in relation to the clients' needs and preferences.

(f) Social workers who are leaving an employment setting should inform clients of appropriate options for the continuation of services and of the benefits and risks of the options.

2.   Social Workers' Ethical Responsibilities to Colleagues

2.01   Respect

(a) Social workers should treat colleagues with respect and should represent accurately and fairly the qualifications, views, and obligations of colleagues.

(b) Social workers should avoid unwarranted negative criticism of colleagues in communications with clients or with other professionals. Unwarranted negative criticism may include demeaning comments that refer to colleagues' level of competence or to individuals' attributes such as race, ethnicity, national origin, color, sex, sexual orientation, gender identity or expression, age, marital status, political belief, religion, immigration status, and mental or physical disability.

(c) Social workers should cooperate with social work colleagues and with colleagues of other professions when such cooperation serves the wellbeing of clients.

2.02   Confidentiality

Social workers should respect confidential information shared by colleagues in the course of their professional relationships and transactions. Social workers should ensure that such colleagues understand social workers' obligation to respect confidentiality and any exceptions related to it.

2.03   Interdisciplinary Collaboration

(a) Social workers who are members of an interdisciplinary team should participate in and contribute to decisions that affect the wellbeing of clients by drawing on the perspectives, values, and experiences of the social work profession. Professional and ethical obligations of the interdisciplinary team as a whole and of its individual members should be clearly established.

(b) Social workers for whom a team decision raises ethical concerns should attempt to resolve the disagreement through appropriate channels. If the disagreement cannot be resolved, social workers should pursue other avenues to address their concerns consistent with client wellbeing.

2.04   Disputes Involving Colleagues

(a) Social workers should not take advantage of a dispute between a colleague and an employer to obtain a position or otherwise advance the social workers' own interests.

(b) Social workers should not exploit clients in disputes with colleagues or engage clients in any inappropriate discussion of conflicts between social workers and their colleagues.

2.05   Consultation

(a) Social workers should seek the advice and counsel of colleagues whenever such consultation is in the best interests of clients.

(b) Social workers should keep themselves informed about colleagues' areas of expertise and competencies. Social workers should seek consultation only from colleagues who have demonstrated knowledge, expertise, and competence related to the subject of the consultation.

(c) When consulting with colleagues about clients, social workers should disclose the least amount of information necessary to achieve the purposes of the consultation.

2.06   Referral for Services

(a) Social workers should refer clients to other professionals when the other professionals' specialized knowledge or expertise is needed to serve clients fully or when social workers believe that they are not being effective or making reasonable progress with clients and that additional service is required.

(b) Social workers who refer clients to other professionals should take appropriate steps to facilitate an orderly transfer of responsibility. Social workers who refer clients to other professionals should disclose, with clients' consent, all pertinent information to the new service providers.

(c) Social workers are prohibited from giving or receiving payment for a referral when no professional service is provided by the referring social worker.

2.07   Sexual Relationships

(a) Social workers who function as supervisors or educators should not engage in sexual activities or contact with supervisees, students, trainees, or other colleagues over whom they exercise professional authority.

(b) Social workers should avoid engaging in sexual relationships with colleagues when there is potential for a conflict of interest. Social workers who become involved in, or anticipate becoming involved in, a sexual relationship with a colleague have a duty to transfer professional responsibilities, when necessary, to avoid a conflict of interest.

2.08 Sexual Harassment

Social workers should not sexually harass supervisees, students, trainees, or colleagues. Sexual harassment includes sexual advances, sexual solicitation, requests for sexual favors, and other verbal or physical conduct of a sexual nature.

2.09 Impairment of Colleagues

(a) Social workers who have direct knowledge of a social work colleague's impairment that is due to personal problems, psychosocial distress, substance abuse, or mental health difficulties and that interferes with practice effectiveness should consult with that colleague when feasible and assist the colleague in taking remedial action.

(b) Social workers who believe that a social work colleague's impairment interferes with practice effectiveness and that the colleague has not taken adequate steps to address the impairment should take action through appropriate channels established by employers, agencies, NASW, licensing and regulatory bodies, and other professional organizations.

2.10 Incompetence of Colleagues

(a) Social workers who have direct knowledge of a social work colleague's incompetence should consult with that colleague when feasible and assist the colleague in taking remedial action.

(b) Social workers who believe that a social work colleague is incompetent and has not taken adequate steps to address the incompetence should take action through appropriate channels established by employers, agencies, NASW, licensing and regulatory bodies, and other professional organizations.

2.11 Unethical Conduct of Colleagues

(a) Social workers should take adequate measures to discourage, prevent, expose, and correct the unethical conduct of colleagues.

(b) Social workers should be knowledgeable about established policies and procedures for handling concerns about colleagues' unethical behavior. Social workers should be familiar with national, state, and local procedures for handling ethics complaints. These include policies and procedures created by NASW, licensing and regulatory bodies, employers, agencies, and other professional organizations.

(c) Social workers who believe that a colleague has acted unethically should seek resolution by discussing their concerns with the colleague when feasible and when such discussion is likely to be productive.

(d) When necessary, social workers who believe that a colleague has acted unethically should take action through appropriate formal channels (such as contacting a state licensing board or regulatory body, an NASW committee on inquiry, or other professional ethics committees).

(e) Social workers should defend and assist colleagues who are unjustly charged with unethical conduct.

3. Social Workers' Ethical Responsibilities in Practice Settings

3.01 Supervision and Consultation

(a) Social workers who provide supervision or consultation should have the necessary knowledge and skill to supervise or consult appropriately and should do so only within their areas of knowledge and competence.

(b) Social workers who provide supervision or consultation are responsible for setting clear, appropriate, and culturally sensitive boundaries.

(c) Social workers should not engage in any dual or multiple relationships with supervisees in which there is a risk of exploitation of or potential harm to the supervisee.

(d) Social workers who provide supervision should evaluate supervisees' performance in a manner that is fair and respectful.

⚹ 3.02   Education and Training

(a) Social workers who function as educators, field instructors for students, or trainers should provide instruction only within their areas of knowledge and competence and should provide instruction based on the most current information and knowledge available in the profession.

(b) Social workers who function as educators or field instructors for students should evaluate students' performance in a manner that is fair and respectful.

(c) Social workers who function as educators or field instructors for students should take reasonable steps to ensure that clients are routinely informed when services are being provided by students.

(d) Social workers who function as educators or field instructors for students should not engage in any dual or multiple relationships with students in which there is a risk of exploitation or potential harm to the student. Social work educators and field instructors are responsible for setting clear, appropriate, and culturally sensitive boundaries.

⚹3.03   Performance Evaluation

Social workers who have responsibility for evaluating the performance of others should fulfill such responsibility in a fair and considerate manner and on the basis of clearly stated criteria.

⚹3.04   Client Records

(a) Social workers should take reasonable steps to ensure that documentation in records is accurate and reflects the services provided.

(b) Social workers should include sufficient and timely documentation in records to facilitate the delivery of services and to ensure continuity of services provided to clients in the future.

(c) Social workers' documentation should protect clients' privacy to the extent that is possible and appropriate and should include only information that is directly relevant to the delivery of services.

(d) Social workers should store records following the termination of services to ensure reasonable future access. Records should be maintained for the number of years required by state statutes or relevant contracts.

⚹3.05   Billing

Social workers should establish and maintain billing practices that accurately reflect the nature and extent of services provided and that identify who provided the service in the practice setting.

⚹ 3.06   Client Transfer

(a) When an individual who is receiving services from another agency or colleague contacts a social worker for services, the social worker should carefully consider the client's needs before agreeing to provide services. To minimize possible confusion and conflict, social workers should discuss with potential clients the nature of the clients' current relationship with other service providers and the implications, including possible benefits or risks, of entering into a relationship with a new service provider.

(b) If a new client has been served by another agency or colleague, social workers should discuss with the client whether consultation with the previous service provider is in the client's best interest.

⚹3.07   Administration

(a) Social work administrators should advocate within and outside their agencies for adequate resources to meet clients' needs.

(b) Social workers should advocate for resource allocation procedures that are open and fair. When not all clients' needs can be met, an allocation procedure should be developed that is nondiscriminatory and based on appropriate and consistently applied principles.

(c) Social workers who are administrators should take reasonable steps to ensure that adequate agency or organizational resources are available to provide appropriate staff supervision.

(d) Social work administrators should take reasonable steps to ensure that the working environment for which they are responsible is consistent with and encourages compliance with the *NASW Code of Ethics*. Social work administrators should take reasonable steps to eliminate any conditions in their organizations that violate, interfere with, or discourage compliance with the *Code*.

3.08 Continuing Education and Staff Development

Social work administrators and supervisors should take reasonable steps to provide or arrange for continuing education and staff development for all staff for whom they are responsible. Continuing education and staff development should address current knowledge and emerging developments related to social work practice and ethics.

3.09 Commitments to Employers

(a) Social workers generally should adhere to commitments made to employers and employing organizations.

(b) Social workers should work to improve employing agencies' policies and procedures and the efficiency and effectiveness of their services.

(c) Social workers should take reasonable steps to ensure that employers are aware of social workers' ethical obligations as set forth in the *NASW Code of Ethics* and of the implications of those obligations for social work practice.

(d) Social workers should not allow an employing organization's policies, procedures, regulations, or administrative orders to interfere with their ethical practice of social work. Social workers should take reasonable steps to ensure that their employing organizations' practices are consistent with the *NASW Code of Ethics*.

(e) Social workers should act to prevent and eliminate discrimination in the employing organization's work assignments and in its employment policies and practices.

(f) Social workers should accept employment or arrange student field placements only in organizations that exercise fair personnel practices.

(g) Social workers should be diligent stewards of the resources of their employing organizations, wisely conserving funds where appropriate and never misappropriating funds or using them for unintended purposes.

3.10 LaborManagement Disputes

(a) Social workers may engage in organized action, including the formation of and participation in labor unions, to improve services to clients and working conditions.

(b) The actions of social workers who are involved in labormanagement disputes, job actions, or labor strikes should be guided by the profession's values, ethical principles, and ethical standards. Reasonable differences of opinion exist among social workers concerning their primary obligation as professionals during an actual or threatened labor strike or job action. Social workers should carefully examine relevant issues and their possible impact on clients before deciding on a course of action.

4. Social Workers' Ethical Responsibilities as Professionals

4.01 Competence

(a) Social workers should accept responsibility or employment only on the basis of existing competence or the intention to acquire the necessary competence.

(b) Social workers should strive to become and remain proficient in professional practice and the performance of professional functions. Social workers should critically examine and keep current with emerging knowledge relevant to social work. Social workers should routinely review the professional literature and participate in continuing education relevant to social work practice and social work ethics.

(c) Social workers should base practice on recognized knowledge, including empirically based knowledge, relevant to social work and social work ethics.

4.02   Discrimination

Social workers should not practice, condone, facilitate, or collaborate with any form of discrimination on the basis of race, ethnicity, national origin, color, sex, sexual orientation, gender identity or expression, age, marital status, political belief, religion, immigration status, or mental or physical disability.

4.03   Private Conduct

Social workers should not permit their private conduct to interfere with their ability to fulfill their professional responsibilities.

4.04   Dishonesty, Fraud, and Deception

Social workers should not participate in, condone, or be associated with dishonesty, fraud, or deception.

4.05   Impairment

(a) Social workers should not allow their own personal problems, psychosocial distress, legal problems, substance abuse, or mental health difficulties to interfere with their professional judgment and performance or to jeopardize the best interests of people for whom they have a professional responsibility.

(b) Social workers whose personal problems, psychosocial distress, legal problems, substance abuse, or mental health difficulties interfere with their professional judgment and performance should immediately seek consultation and take appropriate remedial action by seeking professional help, making adjustments in workload, terminating practice, or taking any other steps necessary to protect clients and others.

4.06   Misrepresentation

(a) Social workers should make clear distinctions between statements made and actions engaged in as a private individual and as a representative of the social work profession, a professional social work organization, or the social worker's employing agency.

(b) Social workers who speak on behalf of professional social work organizations should accurately represent the official and authorized positions of the organizations.

(c) Social workers should ensure that their representations to clients, agencies, and the public of professional qualifications, credentials, education, competence, affiliations, services provided, or results to be achieved are accurate. Social workers should claim only those relevant professional credentials they actually possess and take steps to correct any inaccuracies or misrepresentations of their credentials by others.

4.07   Solicitations

(a) Social workers should not engage in uninvited solicitation of potential clients who, because of their circumstances, are vulnerable to undue influence, manipulation, or coercion.

(b) Social workers should not engage in solicitation of testimonial endorsements (including solicitation of consent to use a client's prior statement as a testimonial endorsement) from current clients or from other people who, because of their particular circumstances, are vulnerable to undue influence.

4.08   Acknowledging Credit

(a) Social workers should take responsibility and credit, including authorship credit, only for work they have actually performed and to which they have contributed.

(b) Social workers should honestly acknowledge the work of and the contributions made by others.

5. Social Workers' Ethical Responsibilities to the Social Work Profession

5.01 Integrity of the Profession

(a) Social workers should work toward the maintenance and promotion of high standards of practice.

(b) Social workers should uphold and advance the values, ethics, knowledge, and mission of the profession. Social workers should protect, enhance, and improve the integrity of the profession through appropriate study and research, active discussion, and responsible criticism of the profession.

(c) Social workers should contribute time and professional expertise to activities that promote respect for the value, integrity, and competence of the social work profession. These activities may include teaching, research, consultation, service, legislative testimony, presentations in the community, and participation in their professional organizations.

(d) Social workers should contribute to the knowledge base of social work and share with colleagues their knowledge related to practice, research, and ethics. Social workers should seek to contribute to the profession's literature and to share their knowledge at professional meetings and conferences.

(e) Social workers should act to prevent the unauthorized and unqualified practice of social work.

5.02 Evaluation and Research

(a) Social workers should monitor and evaluate policies, the implementation of programs, and practice interventions.

(b) Social workers should promote and facilitate evaluation and research to contribute to the development of knowledge.

(c) Social workers should critically examine and keep current with emerging knowledge relevant to social work and fully use evaluation and research evidence in their professional practice.

(d) Social workers engaged in evaluation or research should carefully consider possible consequences and should follow guidelines developed for the protection of evaluation and research participants. Appropriate institutional review boards should be consulted.

(e) Social workers engaged in evaluation or research should obtain voluntary and written informed consent from participants, when appropriate, without any implied or actual deprivation or penalty for refusal to participate; without undue inducement to participate; and with due regard for participants' wellbeing, privacy, and dignity. Informed consent should include information about the nature, extent, and duration of the participation requested and disclosure of the risks and benefits of participation in the research.

(f) When evaluation or research participants are incapable of giving informed consent, social workers should provide an appropriate explanation to the participants, obtain the participants' assent to the extent they are able, and obtain written consent from an appropriate proxy.

(g) Social workers should never design or conduct evaluation or research that does not use consent procedures, such as certain forms of naturalistic observation and archival research, unless rigorous and responsible review of the research has found it to be justified because of its prospective scientific, educational, or applied value and unless equally effective alternative procedures that do not involve waiver of consent are not feasible.

(h) Social workers should inform participants of their right to withdraw from evaluation and research at any time without penalty.

(i) Social workers should take appropriate steps to ensure that participants in evaluation and research have access to appropriate supportive services.

(j) Social workers engaged in evaluation or research should protect participants from unwarranted physical or mental distress, harm, danger, or deprivation.

(k) Social workers engaged in the evaluation of services should discuss collected information only for professional purposes and only with people professionally concerned with this information.

(l) Social workers engaged in evaluation or research should ensure the anonymity or confidentiality of participants and of the data obtained from them. Social workers should inform participants of any limits of confidentiality, the measures that will be taken to ensure confidentiality, and when any records containing research data will be destroyed.

(m) Social workers who report evaluation and research results should protect participants' confidentiality by omitting identifying information unless proper consent has been obtained authorizing disclosure.

(n) Social workers should report evaluation and research findings accurately. They should not fabricate or falsify results and should take steps to correct any errors later found in published data using standard publication methods.

(o) Social workers engaged in evaluation or research should be alert to and avoid conflicts of interest and dual relationships with participants, should inform participants when a real or potential conflict of interest arises, and should take steps to resolve the issue in a manner that makes participants' interests primary.

(p) Social workers should educate themselves, their students, and their colleagues about responsible research practices.

6. Social Workers' Ethical Responsibilities to the Broader Society

6.01   Social Welfare

Social workers should promote the general welfare of society, from local to global levels, and the development of people, their communities, and their environments. Social workers should advocate for living conditions conducive to the fulfillment of basic human needs and should promote social, economic, political, and cultural values and institutions that are compatible with the realization of social justice.

6.02   Public Participation

Social workers should facilitate informed participation by the public in shaping social policies and institutions.

6.03   Public Emergencies

Social workers should provide appropriate professional services in public emergencies to the greatest extent possible.

6.04   Social and Political Action

(a) Social workers should engage in social and political action that seeks to ensure that all people have equal access to the resources, employment, services, and opportunities they require to meet their basic human needs and to develop fully. Social workers should be aware of the impact of the political arena on practice and should advocate for changes in policy and legislation to improve social conditions in order to meet basic human needs and promote social justice.

(b) Social workers should act to expand choice and opportunity for all people, with special regard for vulnerable, disadvantaged, oppressed, and exploited people and groups.

(c) Social workers should promote conditions that encourage respect for cultural and social diversity within the United States and globally. Social workers should promote policies and practices that demonstrate respect for difference, support the expansion of cultural knowledge and resources, advocate for programs and institutions that demonstrate cultural competence, and promote policies that safeguard the rights of and confirm equity and social justice for all people.

(d) Social workers should act to prevent and eliminate domination of, exploitation of, and discrimination against any person, group, or class on the basis of race, ethnicity, national origin, color, sex, sexual orientation, gender identity or expression, age, marital status, political belief, religion, immigration status, or mental or physical disability.

Appendix B

International Federation of Social Workers, The Ethics of Social Work: Principles and Standards

1 Background

Ethical awareness is a necessary part of the professional practice of any social worker. His or her ability to act ethically is an essential aspect of the quality of the service offered to clients.

The purpose of IFSW's work on ethics is to promote ethical debate and reflection in the member associations and among the providers of social work in member countries.

The basis for the further development of IFSW's work on ethics is to be found in *Ethics of Social Work: Principles and Standards* which consists of two documents, *International Declaration of Ethical Principles of Social Work* and *International Ethical Standards for Social Workers*. These documents present the basic ethical principles of the social work profession, recommend procedures when the work presents ethical dilemmas, and deal with the profession's and the individual social worker's relation to clients, colleagues, and others in the field. The documents are components in a continuing process of use, review and revision.

2 International Declaration of Ethical Principles of Social Work

2.1 Introduction

The IFSW recognises the need for a declaration of ethical principles for guidance in dealing with ethical problems in social work.

The purposes of the *International Declaration of Ethical Principles* are:

1. to formulate a set of basic principles for social work, which can be adapted to cultural and social settings,
2. to identify ethical problem areas in the practice of social work (below referred to as "problem areas"), and
3. to provide guidance as to the choice of methods for dealing with ethical issues/problems (below referred to as "methods for addressing ethical issues/problems").

Compliance

The *International Declaration of Ethical Principles* assumes that both member associations of the IFSW and their constituent members adhere to the principles formulated therein. The IFSW expects each

Published by International Federation of Social Workers, P.O. Box 4649, Sofienberg, N-0506 Oslo, Norway; October 1994. Adopted by the IFSW General Meeting, Colombo, Sri Lanka, July 6–8, 1994.

member association to assist its members in identifying and dealing with ethical issues/problems in the practice of their profession.

Member associations of the IFSW and individual members of these can report any member association to the Executive Committee of the IFSW should it neglect to adhere to these principles. National associations who experience difficulties adopting these principles should notify the Executive Committee of IFSW. The Executive Committee may impose the stipulations and intentions of the *Declaration of Ethical Principles* on an association which neglects to comply. Should this not be sufficient the Executive Committee can, as a following measure, suggest suspension or exclusion of the association.

The *International Declaration of Ethical Principles* should be made publicly known. This would enable clients, employers, professionals from other disciplines, and the general public to have expectations in accordance with the ethical foundations of social work.

We acknowledge that a detailed set of ethical standards for the member associations would be unrealistic due to legal, cultural and governmental differences among the member countries.

2.2   The Principles

Social workers serve the development of human beings through adherence to the following basic principles:

2.2.1.   Every human being has a unique value, which justifies moral consideration for that person.

2.2.2.   Each individual has the right to self-fulfilment to the extent that it does not encroach upon the same right of others, and has an obligation to contribute to the well-being of society.

2.2.3.   Each society, regardless of its form, should function to provide the maximum benefits for all of its members.

2.2.4.   Social workers have a commitment to principles of social justice.

2.2.5.   Social workers have the responsibility to devote objective and disciplined knowledge and skill to aid individuals, groups, communities, and societies in their development and resolution of personal-societal conflicts and their consequences.

2.2.6.   Social workers are expected to provide the best possible assistance to anybody seeking their help and advice, without unfair discrimination on the basis of gender, age, disability, colour, social class, race, religion, language, political beliefs, or sexual orientation.

2.2.7.   Social workers respect the basic human rights of individuals and groups as expressed in the *United Nations Universal Declaration of Human Rights* and other international conventions derived from that Declaration.

2.2.8.   Social workers pay regard to the principles of privacy, confidentiality, and responsible use of information in their professional work. Social workers respect justified confidentiality even when their country's legislation is in conflict with this demand.

2.2.9.   Social workers are expected to work in full collaboration with their clients, working for the best interests of the clients but paying due regard to the interests of others involved. Clients are encouraged to participate as much as possible, and should be informed of the risks and likely benefits of proposed courses of action.

2.2.10.   Social workers generally expect clients to take responsibility, in collaboration with them, for determining courses of action affecting their lives. Compulsion which might be necessary to solve one party's problems at the expense of the interests of others involved should only take place after careful explicit evaluation of the claims of the conflicting parties. Social workers should minimise the use of legal compulsion.

2.2.11. Social work is inconsistent with direct or indirect support of individuals, groups, political forces or power structures suppressing their fellow human beings by employing terrorism, torture or similar brutal means.

2.2.12. Social workers make ethically justified decisions, and stand by them, paying due regard to the *IFSW International Declaration of Ethical Principles* and to the *International Ethical Standards for Social Workers* adopted by their national professional association.

2.3   Problem Areas

2.3.1. The problem areas raising ethical issues directly are not necessarily universal due to cultural and governmental differences. Each national association is encouraged to promote discussion and clarification of important issues and problems particularly relevant to its country. The following problem areas are, however, widely recognized:

1. *When the loyalty of the social worker is in the middle of conflicting interests*
   - between those of the social workers own and the clients
   - between conflicting interests of individual clients and other individuals
   - between the conflicting interests of groups of clients
   - between groups of clients and the rest of the population
   - between systems/institution and groups of clients
   - between system/institution/employer and social workers
   - between different groups of professionals
2. *The fact that the social worker functions both as a helper and controller*
   The relation between these two opposite aspects of social work demands a clarification based on an explicit choice of val-

ues in order to avoid a mixing-up of motives or the lack of clarity in motives, actions and consequences of actions. When social workers are expected to play a role in the state control of citizens they are obliged to clarify the ethical implications of this role and to what extent this role is acceptable in relation to the basic ethical principles of social work.

3. *The duty of the social worker to protect the interests of the client will easily come into conflict with demands for efficiency and utility*
   This problem is becoming important with the introduction and use of information technology within the fields of social work.

2.3.2. The principles declared in section 2.2 should always be at the base of any consideration given or choice made by social workers in dealing with issues/problems within these areas.

2.4   Methods For The Solution of Issues/ Problems

2.4.1. The various national associations of social workers are obliged to treat matters in such a way that ethical issues/problems may be considered and tried to be solved in collective forums within the organization. Such forums should enable the individual social worker to discuss, analyse and consider ethical issues/problems in collaboration with colleagues, other expert groups and/parties affected by the matter under discussion. In addition such forums should give the social worker opportunity to receive advice from colleagues and others. Ethical analysis and discussion should always seek to create possibilities and options.

2.4.2. The member associations are required to produce and/or adapt ethical standards for the different fields of work, especially for those fields where there are complicated ethical issues/problems as well as areas where the ethical principles of social work may come into conflict with the respective country's legal system or the policy of the authorities.

2.4.3. When ethical foundations are laid down as guidelines for actions within the practice of social work, it is the duty of the associations to aid the individual social worker in analysing and considering ethical issues/problems on the basis of:

1. The basic *principles* of the Declaration (section 2.2)
2. The ethical/moral and political *context* of the actions, i.e. an analysis of the values and forces constituting the framing conditions of the action
3. The *motives* of the action, i.e. to advocate a higher level of consciousness of the aims and intentions the individual social worker might have regarding a course of action
4. The *nature* of the action, i.e. help in providing an analysis of the moral content of the action, e.g. the use of compulsion as opposed to voluntary co-operation, guard-ianship vs participation, etc.
5. The *consequences* the action might have for different groups, i.e. an analysis of the consequences of different ways of action for all involved parties in both the short and long term.

2.4.4. The member associations are responsible for promoting debate, education and research regarding ethical questions.

3 International Ethical Standards for Social Workers

(This section is based on the *International Code of Ethics for the Professional Social Worker* adopted by the IFSW in 1976, but does not include ethical principles since these are now contained in the new separate International Declaration of Ethical Principles of Social Work in section 2.2 of the present document.)

3.1 Preamble

Social work originates variously from humanitarian, religious and democratic ideals and philosophies and has universal application to meet human needs arising from personal-societal interactions and to develop human potential. Professional social workers are dedicated to service for the welfare and self-fulfilment of human beings; to the development and disciplined use of validated knowledge regarding human and societal behaviour; to the development of resources to meet individual, group, national and international needs and aspirations; and to the achievement of social justice. On the basis of the *International Declaration of Ethical Principles of Social Work,* the social worker is obliged to recognise these standards of ethical conduct.

3.2 General Standards of Ethical Conduct

3.2.1. Seek to understand each individual client and the client system, and the elements which affect behaviour and the service required.

3.2.2. Uphold and advance the values, knowledge and methodology of the profession, refraining from any behaviour which damages the functioning of the profession.

3.2.3. Recognise professional and personal limitations.

3.2.4. Encourage the utilisation of all relevant knowledge and skills.

3.2.5. Apply relevant methods in the development and validation of knowledge.

3.2.6. Contribute professional expertise to the development of policies and programs which improve the quality of life in society.

3.2.7. Identify and interpret social needs.

3.2.8. Identify and interpret the basis and nature of individual, group, community, national, and international social problems.

3.2.9. Identify and interpret the work of the social work profession.

3.2.10. Clarify whether public statements are made or actions performed on an individual basis or as representative of a professional association, agency or organisation, or other group.

3.3 Social Work Standards Relative to Clients

3.3.1. Accept primary responsibility to identified clients, but within limitations set by the ethical claims of others.

3.3.2. Maintain the client's right to a relationship of trust, to privacy and confidentiality, and to responsible use of information. The collection and sharing of information or data is related to the professional service function with the client informed as to its necessity and use. No information is released without prior knowledge and informed consent of the client, except where the client cannot be responsible or others may be seriously jeopardized. A client has access to social work records concerning them.

3.3.3. Recognise and respect the individual goals, responsibilities, and differences of clients. Within the scope of the agency and the client's social milieu, the professional service shall assist clients to take responsibility for personal actions and help all clients with equal willingness. Where the professional service cannot be provided under such conditions the clients shall be so informed in such a way as to leave the clients free to act.

3.3.4. Help the client—individual, group, community, or society—to achieve self-fulfilment and maximum potential within the limits of the respective rights of others. The service shall be based upon helping the client to understand and use the professional relationship, in furtherance of the clients legitimate desires and interests.

3.4 Social Work Standards Relative to Agencies and Organizations

3.4.1. Work and/or cooperate with those agencies and organizations whose policies, procedures, and operations are directed toward adequate service delivery and encouragement of professional practice consistent with the ethical principles of the IFSW.

3.4.2. Responsibly execute the stated aims and functions of the agency or organizations, contributing to the development of sound policies, procedures, and practice in order to obtain the best possible standards or practice.

3.4.3. Sustain ultimate responsibility to the client, initiating desirable alterations of policies, procedures, and practice, through appropriate agency and organization channels. If necessary remedies are not achieved after channels have been exhausted, initiate appropriate appeals to higher authorities or the wider community of interest.

3.4.4. Ensure professional accountability to client and community for efficiency and effectiveness through periodic review of the process of service provision.

3.4.5. Use all possible ethical means to bring unethical practice to an end when policies, procedures and practices are in direct conflict with the ethical principles of social work.

3.5 Social Work Standards Relative to Colleagues

3.5.1. Acknowledge the education, training and performance of social work colleagues and professionals from other disciplines, extending all necessary cooperation that will enhance effective services.

3.5.2. Recognise differences of opinion and practice of social work colleagues and other professionals, expressing criticism through channels in a responsible manner.

3.5.3. Promote and share opportunities for knowledge, experience, and ideas with all social work colleagues, professionals from other disciplines and volunteers for the purpose of mutual improvement.

3.5.4. Bring any violations of professional ethics and standards to the attention of the appropriate bodies inside and outside the profession, and ensure that relevant clients are properly involved.

3.5.5. Defend colleagues against unjust actions.

3.6 Standards Relative to the Profession

3.6.1. Maintain the values, ethical principles, knowledge and methodology of the profession and contribute to their clarification and improvement.

3.6.2. Uphold the professional standards of practice and work for their advancement.

3.6.3. Defend the profession against unjust criticism and work to increase confidence in the necessity for professional practice.

3.6.4. Present constructive criticism of the profession, its theories, methods and practices

3.6.5. Encourage new approaches and methodologies needed to meet new and existing needs.

IFSW Homepage General Directory Activities Publications Partnerships information
    Contact IFSW: secr.gen@ifsw.org
    Last updated 13 September 2000
    Designed and produced by X Kommunikation

Appendix C

National Association of Black Social Workers, Code of Ethics

Web link: http://www.nabsw.org/mserver/CodeofEthics.aspx

In America today, no Black person, except the selfish or irrational, can claim neutrality in the quest for Black liberation nor fail to consider the implications of the events taking place in our society. Given the necessity for committing ourselves to the struggle for freedom, we as Black Americans practicing in the field of social welfare, set forth this statement of ideals and guiding principles.

If a sense of community awareness is a precondition to humanitarian acts, then we as Black social workers must use our knowledge of the Black community, our commitments to its determination, and our helping skills for the benefit of Black people as we marshal our expertise to improve the quality of life of Black people. Our activities will be guided by our Black consciousness, our determination to protect the security of the Black community, and to serve as advocates to relieve suffering of Black people by any means necessary.

Therefore, as Black social workers we commit ourselves, collectively, to the interests of our Black brethren and as individuals subscribe to the following statements:

I regard as my primary obligation the welfare of the Black individual, Black family, and Black community and will engage in action for improving social conditions.

I give precedence to this mission over my personal interest.

I adopt the concept of a Black extended family and embrace all Black people as my brothers and sisters, making no distinction between their destiny and my own.

I hold myself responsible for the quality and extent of service I perform and the quality and extent of service performed by the agency or organization in which I am employed, as it relates to the Black community.

I accept the responsibility to protect the Black community against unethical and hypocritical practice by any individual or organizations engaged in social welfare activities.

I stand ready to supplement my paid or professional advocacy with voluntary service in the Black public interest.

I will consciously use my skills, and my whole being as an instrument for social change, with particular attention directed to the establishment of Black social institutions.

Appendix D

North American Association of Christian Social Workers, Statement of Faith and Practice

Web link: http://www.nacsw.org/2008/2008_about.htm#Statement

The following statement of faith and practice appears in NACSW's Bylaws: Article II, Section 2

Tenets emphasizing Christian beliefs:

1 There is one God, who created and sustains everything that exists, and who continues to be active in human history.

2 Humanity is the highest creation of God, but rebelled against its Creator, and is in need of forgiveness and reconciliation.

3 God became incarnate in Jesus Christ, who died on the cross, who was raised bodily from the dead to reconcile human beings to their Creator, and who has promised to return personally in judgment to complete the establishment of His kingdom.

4 God works in and through people in the person of the Holy Spirit.

5 The character and purposes of God are revealed in the Bible, the Word of God, which is the basis for what Christians are to believe and how they are to live.

6 Jesus Christ calls all Christians to be a caring community and a corporate witness to faith in Him.

Tenets emphasizing human relationships and responsibilities:

7 Every individual is a person of worth, with basic human rights and essential human responsibilities.

8 The uniqueness of each human being and the distinctiveness of social groups derive from factors such as age, gender, race, ethnicity, national origin, life philosophy, family, culture, and economic and social structures.

9 Human beings are interdependent with each other and with their social and physical environments.

10 Jesus Christ is Lord over all areas of life, including social, economic and political systems.

Tenets emphasizing vocation:

11 A dynamic relationship exists between the Christian life and social work practice.

12 Christians in social work ought not to be motivated by temporal wealth, power or security.

13 Christians in social work ought to examine and evaluate all human ideologies and social work theories and methods as to their consistency with the Bible, their consciences, social laws, and professional codes of ethics.

14 Christians in social work ought to work for the temporal and eternal well-being of all human beings, and for the redemption of human communities and social institutions.

15 Christians in social work ought to support and submit themselves to the highest standards of professional education, practice, and ethics.

16 Christians in social work ought to use the insights of their faith in helping people, and to treat everyone as Jesus Christ would have them treated.

Appendix E

Council on Social Work Education Educational Policy and Accreditation Standards

PURPOSE: SOCIAL WORK PRACTICE, EDUCATION, AND EDUCATIONAL POLICY AND ACCREDITATION STANDARDS

The purpose of the social work profession is to promote human and community well-being. Guided by a person and environment construct, a global perspective, respect for human diversity, and knowledge based on scientific inquiry, social work's purpose is actualized through its quest for social and economic justice, the prevention of conditions that limit human rights, the elimination of poverty, and the enhancement of the quality of life for all persons.

Social work educators serve the profession through their teaching, scholarship, and service. Social work education—at the baccalaureate, master's, and doctoral levels—shapes the profession's future through the education of competent professionals, the generation of knowledge, and the exercise of leadership within the professional community.

The Council on Social Work Education (CSWE) uses the Educational Policy and Accreditation Standards (EPAS) to accredit baccalaureate- and master's-level social work programs. EPAS supports academic excellence by establishing thresholds for professional competence. It permits programs to use traditional and emerging models of curriculum design by balancing requirements that promote comparability across programs with a level of flexibility that encourages programs to differentiate.

EPAS describe four features of an integrated curriculum design: (1) program mission and goals; (2) explicit curriculum; (3) implicit curriculum; and (4) assessment. The Educational Policy and Accreditation Standards are conceptually linked. Educational Policy describes each curriculum feature. Accreditation Standards (*in italics*) are derived from the Educational Policy and specify the requirements used to develop and maintain an accredited social work program at the baccalaureate (B) or master's (M) level.

1. Program Mission and Goals

Educational Policy 1.0— Program Mission and Goals

The mission and goals of each social work program address the profession's purpose, are grounded in core professional values (EP 1.1), and are informed by context (EP 1.2).

Educational Policy 1.1—Values

Service, social justice, the dignity and worth of the person, the importance of human relationships, integrity, competence,[1] human rights, and scientific inquiry are among the core values of social work. These values underpin the explicit and implicit curriculum and frame the profession's commitment to respect for all people and the quest for social and economic justice.

Educational Policy 1.2—Program Context

Context encompasses the mission of the institution in which the program is located and the needs and opportunities associated with the setting. Programs are further influenced by their historical, political, economic, social, cultural, demographic, and global contexts and by the ways they elect to engage these factors. Additional factors include new knowledge, technology, and ideas that may have a bearing on contemporary and future social work education and practice.

Accreditation Standard 1.0—
Mission and Goals

The social work program's mission and goals reflect the profession's purpose and values and the program's context.

1.0.1 The program submits its mission statement and describes how it is consistent with the profession's purpose and values and the program's context.

1.0.2 The program identifies its goals and demonstrates how they are derived from the program's mission.

2. Explicit Curriculum

Educational Policy 2.0—The Social Work Curriculum and Professional Practice

The explicit curriculum constitutes the program's formal educational structure and includes the courses and the curriculum. Social work education is grounded in the liberal arts, which provide the intellectual basis for the professional curriculum and inform its design. The explicit curriculum achieves the program's competencies through an intentional design that includes the foundation offered at the baccalaureate and master's levels and the advanced curriculum offered at the master's level. The BSW curriculum prepares its graduates for generalist practice through mastery of the core competencies. The MSW curriculum prepares its graduates for advanced practice through mastery of the core competencies augmented by knowledge and practice behaviors specific to a concentration.

Educational Policy 2.1—Core Competencies

Competency-based education is an outcome performance approach to curriculum design. Competencies are measurable practice behaviors that are comprised of knowledge, values, and skills. The goal of the outcome approach is to demonstrate the integration and application of the competencies in practice with individuals, families, groups, organizations, and communities. The ten core competencies are listed below [EP 2.1.1–EP 2.1.10(d)], followed by a description of characteristic knowledge, values, skills, and the resulting practice behaviors that may be used to operationalize the

---

[1] These six value elements reflect the National Association of Social Workers Code of Ethics. National Association of Social Workers (approved 1996, revised 1999). Code of Ethics for Social Workers. Washington, D.C.: NASW.

curriculum and assessment methods. Programs may add competencies consistent with their missions and goals.

Educational Policy 2.1.1—Identify as a professional social worker and conduct oneself accordingly

Social workers serve as representatives of the profession, its mission, and its core values. They know the profession's history. Social workers commit themselves to the profession's enhancement and to their own professional conduct and growth. Social workers

- advocate for client access to the services of social work;
- practice personal reflection and self-correction to assure continual professional development;
- attend to professional roles and boundaries;
- demonstrate professional demeanor in behavior, appearance, and communication;
- engage in career-long learning; and
- use supervision and consultation.

Educational Policy 2.1.2—Apply social work ethical principles to guide professional practice

Social workers have an obligation to conduct themselves ethically and to engage in ethical decision-making. Social workers are knowledgeable about the value base of the profession, its ethical standards, and relevant law. Social workers

- recognize and manage personal values in a way that allows professional values to guide practice;
- make ethical decisions by applying standards of the National Association

of Social Workers Code of Ethics[2] and, as applicable, of the International Federation of Social Workers/International Association of Schools of Social Work Ethics in Social Work, Statement of Principles;[3]

- tolerate ambiguity in resolving ethical conflicts; and
- apply strategies of ethical reasoning to arrive at principled decisions.

Educational Policy 2.1.3—Apply critical thinking to inform and communicate professional judgments

Social workers are knowledgeable about the principles of logic, scientific inquiry, and reasoned discernment. They use critical thinking augmented by creativity and curiosity. Critical thinking also requires the synthesis and communication of relevant information. Social workers

- distinguish, appraise, and integrate multiple sources of knowledge, including research-based knowledge, and practice wisdom;
- analyze models of assessment, prevention, intervention, and evaluation; and
- demonstrate effective oral and written communication in working with individuals, families, groups, organizations, communities, and colleagues.

Educational Policy 2.1.4—Engage diversity and difference in practice

Social workers understand how diversity characterizes and shapes the human experience and is critical to the formation of identity. The dimensions of diversity are understood as the intersectionality of multiple factors including age, class, color, culture, disability, ethnicity, gender, gender

---

[2]National Association of Social Workers (approved 1996, revised 1999). *Code of Ethics for Social Workers*. Washington, DC: NASW.
[3]International Federation of Social Workers and International Association of Schools of Social Work. (2004). *Ethics in Social Work, Statement of Principles*. Retrieved January 2, 2008 from http://www.ifsw.org

identity and expression, immigration status, political ideology, race, religion, sex, and sexual orientation. Social workers appreciate that, as a consequence of difference, a person's life experiences may include oppression, poverty, marginalization, and alienation as well as privilege, power, and acclaim. Social workers

- recognize the extent to which a culture's structures and values may oppress, marginalize, alienate, or create or enhance privilege and power;
- gain sufficient self-awareness to eliminate the influence of personal biases and values in working with diverse groups;
- recognize and communicate their understanding of the importance of difference in shaping life experiences; and
- view themselves as learners and engage those with whom they work as informants.

Educational Policy 2.1.5— Advance human rights and social and economic justice

Each person, regardless of position in society, has basic human rights, such as freedom, safety, privacy, an adequate standard of living, health care, and education. Social workers recognize the global interconnections of oppression and are knowledgeable about theories of justice and strategies to promote human and civil rights. Social work incorporates social justice practices in organizations, institutions, and society to ensure that these basic human rights are distributed equitably and without prejudice. Social workers

- understand the forms and mechanisms of oppression and discrimination;
- advocate for human rights and social and economic justice; and
- engage in practices that advance social and economic justice.

Educational Policy 2.1.6—Engage in research-informed practice and practice-informed research

Social workers use practice experience to inform research, employ evidence-based interventions, evaluate their own practice, and use research findings to improve practice, policy, and social service delivery. Social workers comprehend quantitative and qualitative research and understand scientific and ethical approaches to building knowledge. Social workers

- use practice experience to inform scientific inquiry and
- use research evidence to inform practice.

Educational Policy 2.1.7—Apply knowledge of human behavior and the social environment

Social workers are knowledgeable about human behavior across the life course; the range of social systems in which people live; and the ways social systems promote or deter people in maintaining or achieving health and well-being. Social workers apply theories and knowledge from the liberal arts to understand biological, social, cultural, psychological, and spiritual development. Social workers

- utilize conceptual frameworks to guide the processes of assessment, intervention, and evaluation; and
- critique and apply knowledge to understand person and environment.

Educational Policy 2.1.8—Engage in policy practice to advance social and economic well-being and to deliver effective social work services

Social work practitioners understand that policy affects service delivery, and they actively engage in policy practice. Social workers know the history and current structures of social policies and services; the role of policy in service delivery; and the role of practice in policy development. Social workers

- analyze, formulate, and advocate for policies that advance social well-being; and
- collaborate with colleagues and clients for effective policy action.

Educational Policy 2.1.9—Respond to contexts that shape practice

Social workers are informed, resourceful, and proactive in responding to evolving organizational, community, and societal contexts at all levels of practice. Social workers recognize that the context of practice is dynamic, and use knowledge and skill to respond proactively. Social workers

- continuously discover, appraise, and attend to changing locales, populations, scientific and technological developments, and emerging societal trends to provide relevant services; and
- provide leadership in promoting sustainable changes in service delivery and practice to improve the quality of social services.

Educational Policy 2.1.10(a)–(d)— Engage, assess, intervene, and evaluate with individuals, families, groups, organizations, and communities

Professional practice involves the dynamic and interactive processes of engagement, assessment, intervention, and evaluation at multiple levels. Social workers have the knowledge and skills to practice with individuals, families, groups, organizations, and communities. Practice knowledge includes identifying, analyzing, and implementing evidence-based interventions designed to achieve client goals; using research and technological advances; evaluating program outcomes and practice effectiveness; developing, analyzing, advocating, and providing leadership for policies and

services; and promoting social and economic justice.

Educational Policy 2.1.10(a)— Engagement

Social workers

- substantively and affectively prepare for action with individuals, families, groups, organizations, and communities;
- use empathy and other interpersonal skills; and
- develop a mutually agreed-on focus of work and desired outcomes.

Educational Policy 2.1.10(b)— Assessment

Social workers

- collect, organize, and interpret client data;
- assess client strengths and limitations;
- develop mutually agreed-on intervention goals and objectives; and
- select appropriate intervention strategies.

Educational Policy 2.1.10(c)— Intervention

Social workers

- initiate actions to achieve organizational goals;
- implement prevention interventions that enhance client capacities;
- help clients resolve problems;
- negotiate, mediate, and advocate for clients; and
- facilitate transitions and endings.

Educational Policy 2.1.10(d)— Evaluation

Social workers critically analyze, monitor, and evaluate interventions.

Educational Policy B2.2— Generalist Practice

Generalist practice is grounded in the liberal arts and the person and environment construct. To promote human and social well-being, generalist practitioners use a range of prevention and intervention methods in their practice with individuals, families, groups, organizations, and communities. The generalist practitioner identifies with the social work profession and applies ethical principles and critical thinking in practice. Generalist practitioners incorporate diversity in their practice and advocate for human rights and social and economic justice. They recognize, support, and build on the strengths and resiliency of all human beings. They engage in research-informed practice and are proactive in responding to the impact of context on professional practice. BSW practice incorporates all of the core competencies.

Educational Policy M2.2— Advanced Practice

Advanced practitioners refine and advance the quality of social work practice and that of the larger social work profession. They synthesize and apply a broad range of interdisciplinary and multidisciplinary knowledge and skills. In areas of specialization, advanced practitioners assess, intervene, and evaluate to promote human and social well-being. To do so they suit each action to the circumstances at hand, using the discrimination learned through experience and self-improvement. Advanced practice incorporates all of the core competencies augmented by knowledge and practice behaviors specific to a concentration.

Educational Policy 2.3—Signature Pedagogy: Field Education

Signature pedagogy represents the central form of instruction and learning in which a profession socializes its students to perform the role of practitioner. Professionals have pedagogical norms with which they connect and integrate theory and practice.[4] In social work, the signature pedagogy is field education. The intent of field education

is to connect the theoretical and conceptual contribution of the classroom with the practical world of the practice setting. It is a basic precept of social work education that the two interrelated components of curriculum—classroom and field—are of equal importance within the curriculum, and each contributes to the development of the requisite competencies of professional practice. Field education is systematically designed, supervised, coordinated, and evaluated based on criteria by which students demonstrate the achievement of program competencies.

Accreditation Standard B2.0— Curriculum

The 10 core competencies are used to design the professional curriculum. The program

B2.0.1 *Discusses how its mission and goals are consistent with generalist practice as defined in EP B2.2.*

B2.0.2 *Identifies its competencies consistent with EP 2.1 through 2.1.10(d).*

B2.0.3 *Provides an operational definition for each of its competencies used in its curriculum design and its assessment [EP 2.1 through 2.1.10(d)].*

B2.0.4 *Provides a rationale for its formal curriculum design demonstrating how it is used to develop a coherent and integrated curriculum for both classroom and field (EP2.0).*

B2.0.5 *Describes and explains how its curriculum content (knowledge, values, and skills) implements the operational definition of each of its competencies.*

Accreditation Standard M2.0— Curriculum

The 10 core competencies are used to design the foundation and advanced curriculum. The advanced curriculum

---

[4]Shulman, L. S. (2005, Summer). Signature pedagogies in the professions. *Daedelus*, 52-59.

builds on and applies the core competencies in an area(s) of concentration. The program

M2.0.1 Identifies its concentration(s) (EP M2.2).

M2.0.2 Discusses how its mission and goals are consistent with advanced practice (EP M2.2).

M2.0.3 Identifies its program competencies consistent with EP 2.1 through 2.1.10(d) and EP M2.2.

M2.0.4 Provides an operational definition for each of the competencies used in its curriculum design and its assessment [EP 2.1 through 2.1.10(d); EP M2.2].

M2.0.5 Provides a rationale for its formal curriculum design (foundation and advanced), demonstrating how it is used to develop a coherent and integrated curriculum for both classroom and field (EP 2.0).

M2.0.6 Describes and explains how its curriculum content (relevant theories and conceptual frameworks, values, and skills) implements the operational definition of each of its competencies.

Accreditation Standard 2.1—
Field Education

The program discusses how its field education program

2.1.1 Connects the theoretical and conceptual contribution of the classroom with the practice setting, fostering the implementation of evidence-informed practice.

B2.1.2 Provides generalist practice opportunities for students to demonstrate the core competencies.

M2.1.2 Provides advanced practice opportunities for students to demonstrate the program's competencies.

2.1.3 Provides a minimum of 400 hours of field education for baccalaureate programs and 900 hours for master's programs.

2.1.4 Admits only those students who have met the program's specified criteria for field education.

2.1.5 Specifies policies, criteria, and procedures for selecting field settings; placing and monitoring students; maintaining field liaison contacts with field education settings; and evaluating student learning and field setting effectiveness congruent with the program's competencies.

2.1.6 Specifies the credentials and practice experience of its field instructors necessary to design field learning opportunities for students to demonstrate program competencies. Field instructors for baccalaureate students hold a baccalaureate or master's degree in social work from a CSWE-accredited program. Field instructors for master's students hold a master's degree in social work from a CSWE-accredited program. For cases in which a field instructor does not hold a CSWE-accredited social work degree, the program assumes responsibility for reinforcing a social work perspective and describes how this is accomplished.

2.1.7 Provides orientation, field instruction training, and continuing dialog with field education settings and field instructors.

2.1.8 Develops policies regarding field placements in an organization in which the student is also employed. To ensure the role of student as learner, student assignments and field education supervision are not the same as those of the student's employment.

3. Implicit Curriculum

Educational Policy 3.0— Implicit Curriculum: The Learning Environment

The implicit curriculum refers to the educational environment in which the explicit curriculum is presented. It is composed of the following elements: the program's commitment to diversity; admissions policies and procedures; advisement, retention, and termination policies; student participation in governance; faculty; administrative structure; and resources. The implicit curriculum is manifested through policies that are fair and transparent in substance and implementation, the qualifications of the faculty, and the adequacy of resources. The culture of human interchange; the spirit of inquiry; the support for difference and diversity; and the values and priorities in the educational environment, including the field setting, inform the student's learning and development. The implicit curriculum is as important as the explicit curriculum in shaping the professional character and competence of the program's graduates. Heightened awareness of the importance of the implicit curriculum promotes an educational culture that is congruent with the values of the profession.[5]

Educational Policy 3.1—Diversity

The program's commitment to diversity—including age, class, color, culture, disability, ethnicity, gender, gender identity and expression, immigration status, political ideology, race, religion, sex, and sexual orientation—is reflected in its learning environment (institutional setting; selection of field education settings and their clientele; composition of program advisory or field committees; educational and social resources; resource allocation; program leadership; speaker series, seminars, and special programs; support groups; research and other initiatives; and the demographic make-up of its faculty, staff, and student body).

Accreditation Standard 3.1—Diversity

3.1.1 The program describes the specific and continuous efforts it makes to provide a learning environment in which respect for all persons and understanding of diversity and difference are practiced.

3.1.2 The program describes how its learning environment models affirmation and respect for diversity and difference.

3.1.3 The program discusses specific plans to improve the learning environment to affirm and support persons with diverse identities.

Educational Policy 3.2— Student Development

Educational preparation and commitment to the profession are essential qualities in the admission and development of students for professional practice. To promote the social work education continuum, BSW graduates admitted to MSW programs are presented with an articulated pathway toward a concentration. Student participation in formulating and modifying policies affecting academic and student affairs are important for the student's professional development.

Accreditation Standard 3.2— Student Development: Admissions; Advisement, Retention, and Termination; and Student Participation

Admissions

B3.2.1 The program identifies the criteria it uses for admission.

---

[5]Eisner, E. W. (2002). *The educational imagination: On the design and evaluation of school programs* (3rd ed.). New York: Macmillan.

M3.2.1 *The program identifies the criteria it uses for admission. The criteria for admission to the master's program must include an earned bachelor's degree from a college or university accredited by a recognized regional accrediting association.*

3.2.2 *The program describes the process and procedures for evaluating applications and notifying applicants of the decision and any contingent conditions associated with admission.*

M3.2.3 *BSW graduates entering MSW programs are not to repeat what has been mastered in their BSW programs. MSW programs describe the policies and procedures used for awarding*

Advisement, retention, and termination

3.2.6 *The program describes its academic and professional advising policies and procedures. Professional advising is provided by social work program faculty, staff, or both.*

3.2.7 *The program spells out how it informs students of its criteria for evaluating their academic and professional performance, including policies and procedures for grievance.*

3.2.8 *The program submits its policies and procedures for terminating a student's enrollment in the social work program for reasons of academic and professional performance.*

Student participation

3.2.9 *The program describes its policies and procedures specifying students' rights and responsibilities to participate in formulating and modifying policies affecting academic and student affairs.*

3.2.10 *The program demonstrates how it provides opportunities and encourages students to organize in their interests.*

Educational Policy 3.3—Faculty

Faculty qualifications, including experience related to the program's competencies, and an appropriate student-faculty ratio are essential for developing an educational environment that promotes, emulates, and teaches students the knowledge, values, and skills expected of professional social workers. Through their teaching, scholarship, and service—as well as their interactions with one another, administration, students, and community—the program's faculty models the behavior and values expected of professional social workers.

Accreditation Standard 3.3—Faculty

3.3.1 The program identifies each full and part-time social work faculty member and discusses her/his qualifications, competence, expertise in social work education and practice, and years of service to the program. Faculty who teach social work practice courses have a *master's degree in social work from a CSWE-accredited program and at least two years of social work practice experience.*

3.3.2 *The program discusses how faculty size is commensurate with the number and type of curricular offerings in class and field; class size; number of students; and the faculty's teaching, scholarly, and service responsibilities. To carry out the ongoing functions of the program, the full-time equivalent faculty-to-student ratio is usually 1:25 for baccalaureate programs and 1:12 for master's programs.*

B3.3.3 The baccalaureate social work program identifies no fewer than two full-time faculty assigned to the program, with full-time appointment in social work, and whose principal assignment is to the baccalaureate program. The majority and no fewer than two of the full-time faculty has either a master's degree in social work from a CSWE-accredited program, with a doctoral degree preferred, or a baccalaureate degree in social work from a CSWE-accredited program and a doctoral degree preferably in social work.

M3.3.3 The master's social work program identifies no fewer than six full-time faculty with master's degrees in social work from a CSWE-accredited program and whose principal assignment is to the master's program. The majority of the full-time master's social work program faculty has a master's degree in social work and a doctoral degree preferably in social work.

3.3.4 The program describes its faculty workload policy and discusses how the policy supports the achievement of institutional priorities and the program's mission and goals.

3.3.5 Faculty demonstrate ongoing professional development as teachers, scholars, and practitioners through dissemination of research and scholarship, exchanges with external constituencies such as practitioners and agencies, and through other professionally relevant creative activities that support the achievement of institutional priorities and the program's mission and goals.

3.3.6 The program describes how its faculty models the behavior and values of the profession in the program's educational environment.

Educational Policy 3.4— Administrative Structure

Social work faculty and administrators, based on their education, knowledge, and skills, are best suited to make decisions regarding the delivery of social work education. They exercise autonomy in designing an administrative and leadership structure, developing curriculum, and formulating and implementing policies that support the education of competent social workers.

Accreditation Standard 3.4— Administrative Structure

3.4.1 The program describes its administrative structure and shows how it provides the necessary autonomy to achieve the program's mission and goals.

3.4.2 The program describes how the social work faculty has responsibility for defining program curriculum consistent with the Educational Policy and Accreditation Standards and the institution's policies.

3.4.3 The program describes how the administration and faculty of the social work program participate in formulating and implementing policies related to the recruitment, hiring, retention, promotion, and tenure of program personnel.

3.4.4 The program identifies the social work program director. Institutions with accredited BSW and MSW programs appoint a separate director for each.

B3.4.4(a) The program describes the BSW program director's leadership ability through teaching, scholarship, curriculum development, administrative experience, and other academic and professional activities in social work. The program documents that the director has a master's degree in social work from a CSWE-accredited program with a doctoral degree preferred or a baccalaureate degree in social work from a CSWE-accredited program and a doctoral degree, preferably in social work.

B3.4.4(b) The program provides documentation that the director has a full-time appointment to the social work program.

B3.4.4(c) The program describes the procedures for determining the program director's assigned time to provide educational and administrative leadership to the program. To carry out the administrative functions of the program, a minimum of 25% assigned time is required at the baccalaureate level. The program demonstrates this time is sufficient.

M3.4.4(a) The program describes the MSW program director's leadership ability through teaching, scholarship, curriculum development, administrative experience, and other academic and professional

activities in social work. The program documents that the director has a master's degree in social work from a CSWE-accredited program. In addition, it is preferred that the MSW program director have a doctoral degree, preferably in social work.

M3.4.4(b) The program provides documentation that the director has a full-time appointment to the social work program.

M3.4.4(c) The program describes the procedures for determining the program director's assigned time to provide educational and administrative leadership to the program. To carry out the administrative functions of the program, a minimum of 50% assigned time is required at the master's level. The program demonstrates this time is sufficient.

3.4.5 The program identifies the field education director.

3.4.5(a) The program describes the field director's ability to provide leadership in the field education program through practice experience, field instruction experience, and administrative and other relevant academic and professional activities in social work.

3.4.5(b) The program documents that the field

education director has a master's degree in social work from a CSWE-accredited program and at least 2 years of postbaccalaureate or postmaster's social work degree practice experience.

B3.4.5(c) The program describes the procedures for determining the field director's assigned time to provide educational and administrative leadership for field education. To carry out the administrative functions of the field at least 25% assigned time is required for baccalaureate programs. The program demonstrates this time is sufficient.

M3.4.5(c) The program describes the procedures for determining the field director's assigned time to provide educational and administrative leadership for field education. To carry out the administrative functions of the field at least 50% assigned time is required for master's programs. The program demonstrates this time is sufficient.

3.4.5(d) The program provides documentation that the field director has a full-time appointment to the social work program.

Educational Policy 3.5—Resources

Adequate resources are fundamental to creating, maintaining, and improving an educational environment that supports the development of competent social work practitioners. Social work programs have the necessary resources to support learning and professionalization of students and program improvement.

Accreditation Standard 3.5—Resources

3.5.1 The program describes the procedures for budget development and administration it uses to achieve its mission and goals. The program submits the budget form to demonstrate sufficient and stable financial supports that permit program planning and faculty development.

3.5.2 The program describes how it uses resources to continuously improve the program and address challenges in the program's context.

3.5.3 The program demonstrates sufficient support staff, other personnel, and technological resources to support itself.

4. Assessment

Educational Policy 4.0—Assessment

Assessment is an integral component of competency-based education. To evaluate the extent to which the competencies have been met, a system of assessment is central to this model of education. Data from assessment continuously inform and promote change in the explicit and implicit curriculum to enhance attainment of program competencies.

Accreditation Standard 4.0—Assessment

4.0.1 The program presents its plan to assess the attainment of its competencies. The plan specifies procedures, multiple measures, and benchmarks to assess the attainment of each of the pro-

gram's competencies (AS B2.0.3; AS M2.0.4).

4.0.2 The program provides evidence of ongoing data collection and analysis and discusses how it uses assessment data to affirm and/or make changes in the explicit and implicit curriculum to enhance student performance.

4.0.3 The program identifies any changes in the explicit and implicit curriculum based on the analysis of the assessment data.

4.0.4 The program describes how it makes its constituencies aware of its assessment outcomes.

4.0.5 The program appends the summary data for each measure used to assess the attainment of each competency for at least one academic year prior to the submission of the self-study.

References

Abramowitz, M. (1983). Everyone is on welfare: "The role of redistribution in social policy" revisited. *Social Work, 28*(6), 440–445.

Adoption of Safe Families Act (ASFA). (1997). Public Law 105-89, Federal Register, January 7, 1997. Retrieved December 24, 2008 from: http://frwebgate.access.gpo.gov/cgi-bin/getdoc .cgi?dbname=105_cong_bills&docid=f:h867enr.txt.pdf

Alexander, C. (1995). Distinctive dates in social welfare history. In R. Edwards et al. (Eds.), *Encyclopedia of social work* (19th ed., pp. 2631–2647). Washington, DC: NASW Press.

Alexander, C. A. (1997). Distinctive dates in social welfare history. In R. Edwards et al. (Eds.), *Encyclopedia of social work, 1997 supplement* (19th ed.). Washington, DC: NASW Press.

American Assembly. (1989, November). *The future of social welfare in America.* New York: Columbia University, Barnard College.

American Association for Long Term Health Insurance. (2008). Long-term care: important information for women. Retrieved December 29, 2008 from: http://www.aaltci.org/long-term-care-insurance/learning-center/for-women.php

Americans for Divorce Reform. (n.d.). Divorce statistics collection: Summary of findings so far. Retrieved June 5, 2009 from http://www.divorcereform.org/results.html

American Psychiatric Association. (2000). *Diagnostic and statistical manual of mental disorders* (4th ed.) Text revision. Washington, DC: Author.

Anderson, F., & Williams, B. (1989). *Practical management of the elderly.* Boston: Blackwell.

Andrade, J. T. (Ed.). (2009). *Handbook of violence risk assessment and treatment: New approaches for mental health professionals.* New York, NY: Springer Publishing Company, LLC.

Arden, J. B., & Linford, L. (2009). *Brain-based therapy with adults: Evidence-based treatment for everyday practice.* Hoboken, NJ: John Wiley & Sons.

Arnone, W. J., Kavouras, F., & Nissenbaum, M. (2001). *Ernst and Young's retirement planning guide: New tips and strategies for building wealth* (2nd ed.). New York: John Wiley & Sons.

Atchley, R. (1976). *The sociology of retirement.* New York: Halsted.

Austin, C. D., & McClelland, R. W. (2009). Case management with older adults. In A. R. Roberts, *Social workers' desk reference* (2nd ed., pp. 797–801). New York: Oxford University Press.

Austrian, S. G. (2009). Guidelines for conducting a biopsychosocial assessment. In A. R. Roberts, *Social workers' desk reference* (2nd ed., pp. 376–380). New York: Oxford University Press.

Axinn, J., & Levin, H. (1982). *Social welfare: A history of the American response to need* (2nd ed.). New York: Harper and Row.

Ban, T. A. (1987). Pharmacological perspectives in therapy of depression in the elderly. In G. L. Maddox & E. W. Busse (Eds.), *Aging: The universal experience* (pp. 127–131). New York: Springer.

Barker, R. L. (2003). *The social work dictionary* (5th ed.). Washington, DC: NASW Press.

Bartels, S. J., Drake, R. E., & McHugo, G. J. (1992). Alcohol abuse, depression, and suicidal behavior in schizophrenia. *American Journal of Psychiatry, 149,* 394–395.

Bartels, S. J., Teague, G. B., Drake, R. E., Clark, R. E., Bush, P., & Noordsy, D. L. (1993). Substance abuse in schizophrenia: Service utilization and costs. *Journal of Nervous Mental Diseases, 181,* 227–232.

Barth, R. P. (1995). Adoption. In R. Edwards et al. (Eds.), *Encyclopedia of social work* (19th ed., pp. 48–59). Washington, DC: NASW Press.

Bartle, E. E., Couchonnal, G., Canda, E. R., & Staker, M. D. (2002). Empowerment as a dynamically developing concept for practice: Lessons learned from organizational ethnography. *Social Work, 47*(1), 32–44.

Baugher, E., & Lamison-White, L. (1996). *Poverty in the United States, 1995 (Current Population Reports, Series pp. 60–194).* Washington, DC: U.S. Department of Commerce, Bureau of the Census.

Beck, A., & Maruschak, L. (2001). *Mental health treatment in state prisons, 2000.* Washington, DC: U.S. Department of Justice, Office of Justice Programs, Bureau of Justice Statistics.

Beder, J. (2006). *Hospital social work: The interface of medicine and caring.* New York: Routledge/Taylor and Francis Group.

Begly, C. (1985). Are DRGs fair? *Journal of Health and Human Resources Administration, 8,* 80–89.

Beless, D. W. (1995). Council on social work education. In A. Edwards et al. (Eds.), *Encyclopedia of social work* (19th ed., pp. 632–636). Washington, DC: NASW Press.

Bell, D. (1973). *The coming of post-industrial society.* New York: Basic Books.

Belsky, J. (1988). *Here tomorrow: Making the most of life after fifty.* Baltimore: Johns Hopkins University Press.

Bergeron, L. R. (2006). Self-determination and elder abuse: Do we know enough? *Journal of Gerontological Social Work, 46*(3/4), 81–102.

Berkman, B. (1996). The emerging health care world: Implications for social work practice and education. *Social Work, 41*(5), 541–549.

Berkman, B., & Abrams, R. (1986). Factors related to hospital readmission of elderly cardiac patients. *Social Work, 31*(2), 99–103.

Berkman, B., Chauncey, S., Holmes, W., Daniels, A., Bonander, E., Sampson, S., & Robinson, M. (1999). Standardized screening of elderly patients' needs for social work assessment in primary care: Use of the SF-36. *Health and Social Work, 24*(1), 9–17.

Berzin, S. C., Thomas, K. L., & Cohen, E. (2007). Assessing model fidelity in two family group decision-making programs: Is this child welfare intervention being implemented as intended? *Journal of Social Service Research, 34*(2), 55–71.

Biggerstaff, M. (1995). Licensing, regulation, and certification. In R. L. Edwards et al. (Eds.), *Encyclopedia of social work* (19th ed., pp. 1616–1624). Washington, DC: NASW Press.

Bishaw, A., & Semega, J. (2008). U.S. Census Bureau, American Community Survey Reports, ACS-09, *Income, Earnings, and Poverty Data from the 2007 American Community Survey.* Washington, DC: U.S. Government Printing Office.

Blackwell, C. W., & Dziegielewski, S. F. (2005). The privatization of social services from public to sectarian: Negative consequences for America's gays and lesbians. *Journal of Human Behavior and the Social Environment, 11*(2), 25-43.

Blazyk, S., & Canavan, M. (1985). Therapeutic aspects of discharge planning. *Social Work, 30,* 489–495.

Bloom, M. (1990). *Introduction to the social work drama.* Itasca, IL: Peacock.

Blumenfield, S., & Epstein, I. (2001). Introduction: promoting and maintaining a reflective professional staff in a hospital-based social work department. *Social Work in Health Care, 33*(3/4), 1–13.

Boehm W. (Ed.). (1959). *Social Work Curriculum Study* (Vol. 1). Washington, DC: Council on Social Work Education.

Boes, M., & McDermott, V. (2005). Crisis intervention in the hospital emergency room. In A. R. Roberts (Ed.), *Crisis intervention handbook* (3rd ed., pp. 543–565). New York: Oxford University Press.

Bomba, P. A. (2006). Use of a single page elder abuse assessment tool: A practical clinician's approach to identifying elder mistreatment. *Journal of Gerontological Social Work, 46*(3/4), 103-122.

Booth, B. M., Cook, C. A. L., & Blow, F. C. (1992). Co-morbid mental disorders in patients with AMA discharges from alcoholism treatment. *Hospital and Community Psychiatry, 43,* 730–731.

Boyer, P. (1978). *Urban classes and moral order in America, 1820–1990.* Cambridge, MA: Harvard University Press.

Brace, C. L. (1872). *The dangerous classes of New York and twenty years' work among them.* New York: Wynkoop and Hallenbeck.

Braus, P. (1996, February). Who will survive managed care? *American Demographics, 18,* 16.

Brennan, E. M., Evans, M. E., & Spencer, S. A. (2008). Mental health services and support for families. In J. M. Rosenzweig & E. M. Brennan (Eds.), *Work, life, and mental health system of care* (pp. 3–26). Baltimore, MD: Paul H. Brooks Publishing.

Brieland, D., Costin, L. B., & Atherton, C. R. (1980). *Contemporary social work* (2nd ed.). New York: McGraw-Hill.

Bristow, D., & Herrick, C. (2002). Emergency department: The roles of the nurse case manager and the social worker. *Continuing Care, 21*(2), 28–29.

Bronson, D. E. (2009). Critically appraising studies for evidence-based practice. In A. Roberts (Ed.), *Social workers' desk reference* (2nd ed., pp. 1137–1141). New York: Oxford University Press.

Browning, C. H., & Browning, B. J. (1996). *How to partner with managed care: A "do-it-yourself-kit" for building working relationships & getting steady referrals,* expanded edition. New York: John Wiley.

Brunner, B. (Ed.). (1997). *1998 Information please almanac.* Boston: Information Please, LLC.

Bruster, B. E. (2009). Transition from welfare to work: Self-esteem and self-efficacy influence on the employment outcome of African women. *Journal of Human Behavior in the Social Environment, 19*(4), 375–393.

Burger, W. R., & Youkeles, M. (2004). *Human services in contemporary America.* Belmont, CA: Brooks Cole.

Burke, T. N. (2008). Nonprofit service organizations: Fidelity with strategic plans for financial survival. *Journal of Human Behavior in the Social Environment, 18*(2), 204–221.

Butterfield, F. (1998, March 5). Prisons replace hospitals for the nation's mentally ill. *New York Times,* pp. A1, A26.

Cabot R. C. (1913). Letter. *Journal of the American Medical Association, 60,* 145.

Cabrera, E., & Raju, N. (2001). Utility analysis: Current trends and future directions. *International Journal of Selection and Assessment, 9,* 92–102.

Calsyn, R., Morse, G., Klinkenberg, W., Trusty, M., & Allen, G., (1998). The impact of assertive community based treatment on the social relationships of people who are homeless and mentally ill. *Community Mental Health Journal, 34,* 6, 579.

Canetto, S. S. (1992). Gender and suicide in the elderly. *Suicide and Life Threatening Behavior,* *22*, 80–97.

Caper, P. (1995). The next shift: Managed care. *Public Health Reports, 110*, 682–683.

Capriotti, T. (2006). Update on depression and anitdepresssant medications. *Medsurg Nursing,* *15*(4), 241–246.

Carlton, T. O. (1984). *Clinical social work in health care settings: A guide to professional practice with exemplars.* New York: Springer.

Carlton-LaNey, I. B. (2008). Diversity. In K. M. Sowers & C. N. Dulmus (Series Eds.) & B. W. White (Vol. Ed.), *Comprehensive handbook of social work and social welfare: Vol. 1. The profession of social work* (pp. 395–417). Hoboken, NJ: John Wiley & Sons, Inc.

Carter, J. (2000). Reducing poverty: It can be done. *New Perspectives Quarterly, 17*(1), 41–44.

Casas, J. M. (1984). Policy, training, and research in counseling psychology: The racial/ethnic minority perspective. In S. D. Brown & R. W. Lent (Eds.), *Handbook of counseling psychology* (pp. 785–831). New York: Wiley.

Centers for Disease Control and Prevention [CDC]. (June 25, 2003). U.S. Department of Health and Rehabilitative Services. *National Vital Statistics Reports, 51*(11), 1–20.

Centers for Disease Control and Prevention [CDC]. (2007). CDC HIV/AIDS Surveillance Report: Cases of HIV Infection and AIDS in the United States and Dependent Area, 2006. Department of Health and Human Services. Retrieved December 27, 2008 from http://www.cdc.gov/hiv/topics/surveillance/basic.htm#hivest.

Chambers, C. A. (1967). *Seedtime of reform: American social service and social action,* *1918–1933.* Ann Arbor: University of Michigan Press.

Chan, C. L. W., & Law, C. K. (2008). Advocacy. In K. M. Sowers & C. N. Dulmus (Series Eds.) & W. Rowe, & L. A. Rapp-Paglicci (Vol. Eds.), *Comprehensive handbook of social work and social welfare: Vol. 3. Social work practice* (pp. 161–178). Hoboken, NJ: John Wiley & Sons, Inc.

Chapman, D. G., & Toseland, R. W. (2007). Effectiveness of advanced illness care teams for nursing home residents with dementia. *Social Work, 52*(4), 321–329.

Chatterjee, P. (1996). *Approaches to the welfare state.* Washington, DC: NASW Press.

Chelf, C. P. (1992). *Controversial issues in social welfare policy: Government and the pursuit of happiness.* Newbury Park, CA: Sage.

Children's Bureau. (2003). *Child maltreatment 2001.* U.S. Department of Health and Human Services. Washington, DC: U.S. Government Printing Office. Retrieved November 13, 2003, from http://www.acf.hhs.gov/programs/cb/publications/cm01/outcover.htm.

Children's Defense Fund. (1998). *The state of America's children: Yearbook, 1997.* Washington, DC: Author.

Children's Defense Fund. (2008). *The state of America's children 2008.* Washington, DC: Author.

Children's Defense Fund. (August 2008). Child poverty in America. Retrieved June 30, 2009 from: http://www.childrensdefense.org/child-research-data-publications/data/child-poverty-in-america.pdf

Children's Defense Fund. (November 2008). Children's Defense Fund: Children in the United States. Retrieved June 30, 2009 from: http://www.childrensdefense.org/child-research-data-publications/data/state-data-repository/cits/children-in-the-states-2008-unitedstates.pdf

Child Welfare League of America. (2006). *CWLA survey of post-adoption services.* Washington, DC: Author. Available online at: www.cwla.org/programs/adoption/adoptionsurvey.htm

Child Welfare league of America. (2009). National Fact Sheet 2009. Retrieved July 2, 2009 from http://www.cwla.org/advocacy/nationalfactsheet09.htm

Choi, N. G., & Mayer, J. (2000). Elder abuse, neglect, and exploitation: Risk factors and prevention strategies. *Journal of Gerontological Social Work, 33*(2), 5–25.

Christ, W. R., Clarkin, J. F., & Hull, J. (1994). A high risk screen for psychiatric discharge planning. *Health and Social Work, 19*(4), 261–270.

Christian Coalition. (1995). *Contract with the American family.* Nashville, TN: Moorings.

Clark, R. E. (1994). Family costs associated with severe mental illness and substance use: A comparison of families with and without dual disorders. *Hospital and Community Psychiatry, 45*, 808–813.

Clevenger, B. J., & Roe-Sepowitz, D. (2009). Shelter service utilization of domestic violence victims. *Journal of Human Behavior in the Social Environment, 19*(4), 359–374.

Cohen, L. R., Hien, D. A., & Batchelder, S. (2008). The impact of cumulative maternal trauma and diagnosis on parenting behavior. *Child Maltreatment, 13*, 27–38.

Cohen-Liebman, M. S. (1999). Draw and tell: Drawings within the context of child sexual abuse. *Arts in Psychotherapy, 26*, 185–194.

Colby, I. (1990). The throwaway teen. *Journal of Applied Social Sciences, 14*(2), 227–294.

Colby, I. C. (2008). Social welfare policy as a form of social justice. In K. M. Sowers & C. N. Dulmus (Series Eds.) & I. C. Colby (Vol. Ed.), *Comprehensive handbook of social work and social welfare: Vol. 4. Social policy and policy practice* (pp.113–128). Hoboken, NJ: John Wiley & Sons, Inc.

Colby, I., & Buffum, W. (1998). Social work and political action committees. *Journal of Community Practice, 5*(4), 87–103.

Cole, B. (1973). *Perspectives in public welfare: A history* (3rd printing). Washington, DC: Government Printing Office.

Cole, E. S. (1985). Adoption: History, policy, and program. In J. Laird & A. Hartman (Eds.), *A handbook of child welfare: Context, knowledge, and practice* (pp. 638–666). New York: Free Press.

Comer, R. J. (2002). Forward. In Sifton, D.W. (Ed.) *PDR: Drug guide for mental health professionals* (pp. v–vi). Montvale, NJ: Thompson Medical Economics.

Congress, E. P. (1994). The use of culturagrams to assess and empower the culturally diverse families. *Families in Society, 75*, 531–540.

Congress, E. P. (1997). *Multicultural perspectives in working with families.* New York: Springer.

Congress, E. P. (2009). The culturagram. In A. Roberts (Ed.), *Social workers desk reference* (2nd ed., pp. 969–975). New York: Oxford University Press.

Conly, C. (1999). *Coordinating community service for mentally ill offenders: Maryland's community criminal justice treatment program.* Washington, DC: US Department of Justice, Office of Justice Programs, National Institute of Justice.

Constable, R., & Lee, D. B. (2004). *Social work with families: Content and process.* Chicago, IL: Lyceum.

Constantino, C. (1981). Intervention with battered women: The lawyer social worker team. *Social Work, 26*(6), 456–460.

Convention on the Rights of the Child. (2003). Child maltreatment summary 2001: Key findings. United Nations Children's Fund UNICEF: Status of the Ratification. Retrieved November 13, 2003, from www.unicef.org

Conway-Giustra, F., Crowley, A., & Gorin, S. H. (2002). Crisis in caregiving: A call to action. *Health and Social Work, 27*(4), 307–311.

Cook, R. E., & Sparks S. N. (2008). *The art and practice of home visiting: Early intervention for children with special needs & their families.* Baltimore, MD: Paul H. Brooks Publishing Co.

Corcoran, K., Gingerich, W. J., & Briggs, H. E. (2001). Practice evaluation: Setting goals and monitoring change. In Briggs & Corcoran (Eds.), *Social work practice: Treating common client problems* (pp. 66–85). Chicago, IL: Lyceum.

Coulton, C., & Chow, J. (1995). Poverty. In R. Edwards et al. (Eds.), *Encyclopedia of social work* (19th ed., pp. 1867–1878). Washington, DC: NASW Press.

Council on Social Work Education/SAGE SW. (2001). *Strengthening the impact of social work to improve the quality of life for older adults and their families: A blueprint for the new millennium.* Alexandria, VA: Council on Social Work Education.

Council on Social Work Education [CSWE]. (1994). *Handbook of accreditation standards and procedures.* Alexandria, VA: Author.

Council on Social Work Education [CSWE] (2004/2001). *Educational Policy and Accreditation Standards.* Alexandria, VA: Council on Social Work Education, Inc.

Council on Social Work Education [CSWE]. (2007). *2006 statistics on social work education in the United States, a summary.* Alexandria, VA: Council on Social Work Education.

Council on Social Work Education [CSWE]. (2009). www.cswe.org.

Council on Social Work Education [CSWE]. (June 26, 2009). Accreditation. Retrieved June 30, 2009 from: http://www.cswe.org/CSWE/accreditation/

Cournos, F., Empfield, M., Horwath, E., McKinnon, K., Meyer, I., Schrage, H., Currie, C., & Agosin, B. (1991). HIV seroprevalence among patients admitted to two psychiatric hospitals. *American Journal of Psychiatry, 148,* 1225–1230.

Corcoran, K., & Vandiver, V. (1996). *Maneuvering the maze of managed care: Skills for mental health practitioners.* New York: The Free Press.

Cowdry, E. V. (Ed.). (1942). *Problems of aging: Biological and medical aspects.* Baltimore: Williams and Wilkins.

Cowles, L. A., (2003). *Social work in the health field: a care perspective* (2nd Edition). Florence, KY: Routledge.

Craig, Y. (1998, August 19). Victim dived from La Madeline lunches to homeless. Star-Telegram.com.

Crosson-Tower, C. (1998). *Exploring child welfare: A practice perspective.* Boston: Allyn and Bacon.

CSWE Commission on Accreditation. (2009). Educational policy and accreditation standards. Alexandria, VA: CSWE. Retrieved June 2009 from www.CSWE.org

Cumming, E., & Henry, W. (1961). *Growing old: The process of disengagement.* New York: Basic Books.

Daley, D. C., & Zuckoff, A. (1998). Improving compliance with the initial outpatient session among discharged inpatient dual diagnosis clients. *Social Work, 43*(5), 470–474.

Dammeyer, M. D. (1998). The assessment of child sexual abuse allegations: Using research to guide clinical decision-making. *Behavioral Sciences and the Law, 16,* 21–34.

Damron-Rodriquez, J. (2008). Developing a competence for nurses and social workers. *Journal of Social Work Education, 44*(3), 27–37.

Danis, F. S. (2003). Social work response to domestic violence: Encouraging news from a new look. *Affilia, 18,* 177–191.

Darby, M. R. (1996). Facing and reducing poverty. In M. R. Darby (Ed.), *Reducing poverty in America: Views and approaches* (pp. 3–12). Thousand Oaks, CA: Sage.

Darkness to Light. (2009). Statistics surrounding child sexual abuse. Retrieved July 2, 2009 from: http://www.darkness2light.org/KnowAbout/statistics_2.asp

Davidson, K. W. (1990). *Social work for health care: A handbook for practice.* New York: The Haworth Press.

Davidson, W. R., & Kunze, K. (1979). Psychological, social and economic meanings of work in modern society: Their effects on the worker facing retirement. In W. C. Sze (Ed.), *Human life cycle* (pp. 690–717). New York: Jason Aronson.

Davis, K. (2008). The mental health field of practice. In K. M. Sowers & C. N. Dulmus (Series Eds.) & B. W. White (Vol. Ed.), *Comprehensive handbook of social work and social welfare: Vol. 1. The profession of social work* (pp. 253–282). Hoboken, NJ: John Wiley & Sons, Inc.

Davis, L., Hagen, J., & Early, T. (1994). Social services for battered women: Are they adequate, accessible, and appropriate? *Social Work, 39*(6), 695–704.

Dawes, S. (1996) Interagency information sharing, expected benefits, manageable risks. *Journal of Policy Analysis and Management, 15*(3), 377–394.

Day, P. J. (2003). *A new history of social welfare* (4th ed.). Belmont, CA: Allyn and Bacon.

DeAngelis, D. (2009). Social work licensing examinations in the United States and Canada. In A. Roberts (Ed.), *Social workers desk reference* (2nd ed., pp. 136–147). New York: Oxford University Press.

Deblinger, E., & Heflin, A. (1996). *Treating sexually abused children and their non-offending parents: A cognitive-behavioral approach.* Thousand Oaks, CA: Sage Publications.

Dempsey, D. (1993, March 10). *Letter to chapter presidents.* Washington, DC: NASW.

DeNavas-Walt, C., Proctor, B. D., & Smith, J. C. (2008, August). U.S. Census Bureau, Current Population Reports, P60-235, *Income, Poverty, and Health Insurance Coverage in the United States: 2007.* U.S. Government Printing Office, Washington, DC.

Department of Children and Family Services. (2003). DCFS Foster Care, Illinois Department of Children and Family Services. Retrieved November 13, 2003, from: http://www.state.il.us .dcfs/fc_foster.shtml.

Department of Human Services. (2007). A guide for mandatory reporters. Social Services Division, Child Welfare Services Branch. Retrieved May 12, 2009 from http://hawaii.gov/dhs/ protection/social_services/child_welfare/MANDATED%20REPORTER%20HANDBOOK.pdf

Diller, J. V. (2004). *Cultural diversity: A primer for human services* (2nd ed.). Belmont, CA: Brooks/Cole.

Ditton, P. (1999). *Mental health and treatment of inmates and probationers.* Washington, D.C., US Department of Justice, Office of Justice Programs, Bureau of Justice Statistics Special Reports NCJ 174463. Washington DC: Department of Justice.

Dobelstein, A. W. (1996). *Social welfare: Policy and analysis* (2nd ed.). Chicago: Nelson-Hall.

Dodd, S. J., & Booker, L. C. (2008). Social work practice with lesbian individuals. In G. P. Mallon (Ed.), *Social work practice with lesbian, gay, bisexual, and transgender people* (2nd ed., pp. 113–140). New York: Taylor & Francis Group/Routledge.

Dolgoff, R., Lowenberg, F. M., & Harrington, D. (2005). *Ethical decisions for social work practice* (7th ed.), Belmont, CA: Brooks Cole.

Drifthnery, F. (2000). Work history and U.S. elders. *Transitions into Poverty,* November 30, 2000.

Dubble, C. (2006). A policy perspective on elder justice through APS and law enforcement collaboration. *Journal of Gerontological Social Work, 46*(3/4), 35–55.

Duckworth, M. P. (2009). Cultural awareness and culturally competent practice. In W. T. O'Donohue & J. E. Fisher (Eds.), *General principles and empirically supported techniques of cognitive behavior therapy* (pp. 63–76). Hoboken, NJ: John Wiley & Sons, Inc.

Duke, W. M., Barton, L., & Wolf-Klein, G. P. (1994). The chief complaint: Patient caregiver and physician's perspectives. *Clinical Gerontologist, 14*(4), 3–11.

Dupper, D. (1992). Separate schools for black males. *Social Work in Education, 14*(12), 75–76.

Dwyer, D. C., Smokowski, P. R., Bricout, J. C., & Wodarski, J. S. (1996). Domestic violence and woman battering: Theories and practice implications. In A. R. Roberts (Ed.), *Helping battered women: New perspectives and remedies* (pp. 67–82). New York: Oxford University Press.

Dziegielewski, S. F. (1990). The institutionalized dementia relative and the family member relationship. Unpublished PhD dissertation. Florida State University, Tallahassee.

Dziegielewski, S. F. (1991). Social group work with family members of elderly nursing home residents with dementia: A controlled evaluation. *Research on Social Work Practice, 1*(4), 358–370.

Dziegielewski, S. F. (1996). Managed care principles: The need for social work in the health care environment. *Crisis Intervention and Time Limited Treatment, 3*(2), 97–110.

Dziegielewski, S. F. (1997). Time limited brief therapy: The state of practice. *Crisis Intervention and Time-Limited Treatment, 3*(3), 217–228.

Dziegielewski, S. F. (2002). *DSM-IV-TR™ in action.* New York: Wiley and Sons.

Dziegielewski, S. F. (2004). *The changing face of health care social work: Professional practice in managed behavioral health care.* (2nd Edition). New York: Springer.

Dziegielewski, S. F. (2006). *Psychopharmacology for the non-medically trained.* New York: Norton.

Dziegielewski, S. F. (2008a). Brief and intermittent approaches to practice: The state of practice. *Journal of Brief Treatment and Crisis Intervention,* Advance Access on-line version, published April 11, 2008. For on line version: http://brief-treatment.oxfordjournals.org

Dziegielewski, S. F. (2008b). Problem identification, contracting, and case planning. In K. M. Sowers & C. N. Dulmus (Series Eds.) & W. Rowe, & L. A. Rapp-Paglicci (Vol. Eds.), *Comprehensive handbook of social work and social welfare: Vol. 3. Social work practice* (pp. 78–97). Hoboken, NJ: John Wiley & Sons, Inc.

Dziegielewski, S. F., Campbell, K., & Turnage, B. (2005). Domestic violence: Focus groups from the survivor's perspective. *Journal of Human Behavior in the Social Environment, 11*(2), 9–24.

Dziegielewski, S. F., & Harrison, D. F. (1996). Counseling the aged. In D. F. Harrison, B. A. Thyer, & J. Wodarski (Eds.), *Cultural diversity in social work practice* (2nd ed.). Springfield, IL: Thomas.

Dziegielewski, S. F., & Holliman, D. (2001). Managed care and social work: Practice implications in an era of change. *Journal of Sociology and Social Welfare. XXVIII,* 2, 125–138.

Dziegielewski, S. F., & Leon, A. M. (1998). Psychopharmacology and the treatment of major depression. *Research on Social Work Practice, 8*(4), 475–490.

Dziegielewski, S. F., Leon, A., & Green, C. (1998). African American children: A model for culturally sensitive group practice. *Early Child Development and Care, 147*(44), 83–97.

Dziegielewski, S. F., & Powers, G. T. (2000). Procedures for evaluating time-limited crisis intervention. In A. Roberts (Ed.), *Crisis intervention handbook* (2nd ed.). New York: Oxford University Press.

Dziegielewski, S. F., & Resnick, C. (1996). Crisis intervention in the shelter setting. In A. R. Roberts (Ed.), *Crisis management and brief treatment* (pp. 123–141). Chicago: Nelson Hall.

Dziegielewski, S. F., Resnick, C., & Krause, N. B. (1996). Shelter based crisis intervention with abused women. In R. Roberts (Ed.), *Helping battered women: New perspectives and remedies* (pp. 159–171). New York: Oxford University Press.

Dziegielewski, S. F., & Ricks, J. (2000, July–September). Adult daycare for mentally impaired elderly and measurement of caregiver satisfaction. *Activities, Adaption and Aging, 24*(4), 51–64.

Dziegielewski, S. F., & Roberts, A. R. (2004). Evidence-based practice. In A. Roberts & K. Yeager (Eds.), *Handbook of practice-focused research and evaluation*. New York: Oxford University Press.

Dziegielewski, S. F., Shields, J., & Thyer, B. A. (1998). Short-term treatment: Models and methods. In J. Williams & K. Ell (Eds.), *Advances in mental health research: Implications for practice*. Washington, D.C.: NASW Press.

Dziegielewski, S. F., & Sumner, K. (2002). An examination of the American response to terrorism: Handling the aftermath through crisis intervention. *Brief Treatment and Crisis Intervention, 2*(4), 287–300.

Eamon, M. K. (2008). *Empowering vulnerable populations*. Chicago, IL: Lyceum Books.

Earner, I. A., & Garcia, G. (2009). Social work practice with Latinos. In A. Roberts (Ed.), *Social workers desk reference* (2nd ed., pp. 959–962). New York: Oxford University Press.

Edleson, J. L. (1991, June). Note on history: Social worker's intervention in woman abuse, 1907–1945. *Social Service Review*, pp. 304–313.

Edleson, J. L., & Tolman, R. M. (1992). *Intervention with men who batter: An ecological approach*. Newbury Park, CA: Sage.

Edna McConnell Clark Foundation. (n.d.). *Keeping families together: Facts on family preservation services*. New York: Author.

Ekerdt, D. J. (1986). The busy ethic, moral continuity between work and retirement. *Gerontology, 26,* 239–244.

Ellis, R. A. (2008). Policy practice. In K. M. Sowers & C. N. Dulmus (Series Eds.) & I. C. Colby (Vol. Ed.), *Comprehensive handbook of social work and social welfare: Vol. 4. Social policy and policy practice* (pp. 129–143). Hoboken, NJ: John Wiley & Sons, Inc.

Enriquez, J. (2005). *The untied states of America*. New York: Crown Publishers.

Epstein, M. W., & Aldredge, P. (2000). *Good but not perfect*. Boston: Allyn and Bacon.

Erikson, E. (1959). Identity and the life cycle. In *Papers by Erik H. Erikson*. New York: Universities Press.

Erlangsen, A., Jeune, B., Bille-Brahe, U., & Vaupel, J. W. (2004). Loss of partner and suicide risks among oldest old: A population-based register study. *Age and Ageing, 33*(4), 378–383.

Ethics meet managed care. (1997, January). *NASW News, 42*(1), 7.

Everett, J. E. (2008). Child foster care. In R. Edwards et al. (Eds.), *Encyclopedia of social work* (20th ed., pp. 375–389). Washington, DC: NASW Press.

Everhart, K., & Wandersman, A. (2000). Applying comprehensive quality programming and empowerment evaluation to reduce implementation barriers. *Journal of Educational and Psychological Consultation, 11,* 177–191.

Facts and Figures. (2008). *National Hospice and Palliative Care Organization*. Abstract retrieved July 4, 2009 from http://www.nhpco.org/files/public/Statistics_Research/NHPCO_facts-and-figures_2008.pdf

Falck, H. S. (1990). Maintaining social work standards in for-profit hospitals: Reasons for doubt. *Health & Social Work, 15,* 76–77.

Fanger, M. T. (1995). Brief therapies. In R. Edwards et al. (Eds.), *Encyclopedia of social work* (19th ed., pp. 323–334). Washington, DC: NASW Press.

Favor, C. A., & Strand, E. B. (2003). Domestic violence and animal cruelty: Untangling the web of abuse. *Journal of Social Work Education, 39*(2), 237–253.

Federal Interagency Forum on Aging-Related Statistics. (2000, August). *Older Americans 2000: Key indicators of well-being*. Federal interagency forum on aging-related statistics, Washington, D.C.: U.S. Government Printing Office.

Finkelhor, D., Hotaling, G., & Yllo, K. (1988). *Stopping family violence*. Newbury Park, CA: Sage.

Fischer, J. (1978). *Effective casework practice: An eclectic approach*. New York: McGraw-Hill.

Fitzsimons, N. M. (2009). *Combating violence & abuse of people with disabilities: A call to action*. Baltimore, MD: Paul H. Brooks Publishing Co., Inc.

Fleshman, M. (2002). A troubled decade for Africa's children. *Africa Recovers, 16*(1), 6.

Florida Administrative Code, 409.166 Special needs children; subsidized adoption program (2002).

Fong, R. (2009). Overview of working with vulnerable populations and persons at risk. In A. R. Roberts (Ed.), *Social workers desk reference* (2nd ed., pp. 925–927). New York: Oxford University Press.

Forbes, H. T., & Dziegielewski, S. F. (2003). Issues facing adoptive mothers of children with special needs. *Journal of Social Work, 3*(3), 301–320.

Forder, A. (2008). Social work and system theory. *British Journal of Social Work, 6*(1), 23–42.

Fox, R. D. (2009). The essential elements of private practice social work. In A. R. Roberts (Ed.), *Social workers' desk reference* (2nd ed., pp. 53–60). New York: Oxford University Press.

Frank, L. (1946). Gerontology. *Journal of Gerontology, 1,* 1.

Franklin, C. (2001). Coming to terms with the business of direct practice social work. *Research on Social Work Practice, 11,* 2, 235–244.

Franklin, C., Jordan, C., & Hopson, L. (2008). Intervention with families. In K. M. Sowers & C. N. Dulmus (Series Eds.) & W. Rowe, & L. A. Rapp-Paglicci (Vol. Eds.), *Comprehensive handbook of social work and social welfare: Vol. 3. Social work practice* (pp. 423–446). Hoboken, NJ: John Wiley & Sons, Inc.

Freud, S., & Krug, S. (2002a). Beyond the code of ethics, part 1: Complexities of ethical decision making in social work practice. *Families in Society*, Sept.-Dec., 474–482.

Freud, S., & Krug, S. (2002b). Beyond the code of ethics, part 2: Dual relationships revisited. *Families in Society*, Sept.-Dec., 483–493.

Friedlander, W. (1955). *Introduction to social welfare*. Englewood Cliffs, NJ: Prentice-Hall.

Friedman, T. (2005) *The world is flat*. New York: Farrar, Straus & Girox.

Frisch, L. A., & Caruso, J. M. (1996). In A. R. Roberts (Ed.), *Helping battered women: New perspectives and remedies* (pp. 102–131). New York: Oxford University Press.

Fusco, L. J. (1989). Integrating systems: Police, courts and assaulted women. In B. Pressman, G. Cameron, & M. Rothery (Eds.), *Intervening with assaulted women: Current theory, research and practice* (pp. 125–135). Hillsdale, NJ: Erlbaum.

Galambos, C. M., & Rosen, A. (2000). The aging are coming and they are us. In S. M. Keigher, A. E. Fortune, & S. L. Witkin (Eds.), *Aging and social work: The changing landscapes* (pp. 13–19). Washington, DC: NASW Press.

Ganley, A. L. (1989). Integrating feminist and social learning analyses of aggression: Creating multiple models for intervention with men who batter. In P. L. Caesar & L. K. Hamberger (Eds.), *Treating men who batter*. New York: Springer.

Gardellia, L. G. (1997). Baccalaureate social work. In R. Edwards et al. (Eds.), *Encyclopedia of social work, 1997 supplement* (19th ed., pp. 37–46). Washington, DC: NASW Press.

Gelles, R. J. (1979). Violence in the American family. *Journal of Social Issues, 35*(1), 15–39.

Gelles, R. J. (1987). *The violent home*. Thousand Oaks, CA: Sage.

Gelles, R. J., & Cornell, C. P. (1990). *Intimate violence in families*. Thousand Oaks, CA: Sage.

Gelles, R. J., & Harrop, J. W. (1989). Violence, battering, and psychological distress among women. *Journal of Interpersonal Violence, 4*(4), 400–420.

Gellis, Z. D. (2009). Evidence-based practice in older adults with mental health disorders. In A. R. Roberts, *Social workers' desk reference* (2nd ed., pp. 376–380). New York: Oxford University Press.

Gelman, S. R. (2009). On being an accountable profession: The code of ethics, oversight by boards of directors, and whistle-blowers as a last resort. In A. R. Roberts, *Social workers' desk reference* (2nd ed., pp. 156–162). New York: Oxford University Press.

Gibelman, M., & Schervish, P. H. (1997). *Who we are, a second look.* Washington, DC: NASW Press.

Gil, D. (1985). The ideological context of child welfare. In J. Laird & A. Hartman (Eds.), *A handbook of child welfare: Context, knowledge, and practice* (pp. 11–33). New York: Free Press.

Gil, E. (1996). *Treating abused adolescents.* New York: Guilford Press.

Gilbelman, M. (2003). So how far have we come? Pestilent and persistent gender gap in pay. *Social Work, 48,* 1, 22–32.

Gilbert, N., & Specht, H. (1981). *The emergence of social welfare and social work* (2nd ed.). Itasca, IL: Peacock.

Gilgun, J. (2005). The four cornerstones of evidence-based practice in social work. *Research on Social Work Practice, 15*(1), 52–61.

Gillespie, E., & Schellhas, B. (Eds.). (1994). *Contract with America.* New York: Times.

Ginsberg, L. (1998). *Conservatives social welfare policy: A description and analysis.* Chicago: Nelson-Hall.

Glicken, M. D., & Sechrest, D. K. (2003). *The role of helping professionals in treating victims and perpetrators of violence.* New York: Pearson Education.

Glisson, C. (2008). Interventions with organizations. In K. M. Sowers, & C. N. Dulmus (Series Eds.) & W. Rowe, & L. A. Rapp-Paglicci (Vol. Eds.), *Comprehensive handbook of social work and social welfare: Vol. 3. Social work practice* (pp. 556–581). Hoboken, NJ: John Wiley & Sons Inc.

Gonzalez-Ramos, G. (1990). Examining the myth of Hispanic families' resistance to treatment: Using the school as a site for services. *Social Work in Education, 12*(4), 261–274.

Goode, R. A. (2000). *Social work practice in home health care.* Binghamton, NY: Haworth.

Gray, J. (1992). *Men are from Mars, women are from Venus.* New York: HarperCollins.

Green, D. L., & Macaluso, B. (2009). The social worker in a domestic violence shelter. In A. R. Roberts, *Social workers' desk reference* (2nd ed., pp. 95–102). New York: Oxford University Press.

Green D. L., & Roberts, A. R. (2008). *Helping victims of violent crime: Assessment, treatment and evidence-based practice.* New York: Springer Publishing Company, LLC.

Grigorenko, E. L. (Ed.). (2009). *Multicultural psychoeducational assessment.* New York: Springer Publishing Company, LLC.

Grob, G. (July/August, 1995). The paradox of deinstitutionalization. *Society, 32,* 51–59.

Gross, R., Tabenkin, H., Heymann, A., Greenstein, M., Matzliach, R., Portah, A., & Porter, B. (2007). Physician's ability to influence the life-style behaviors of diabetic patients: Implications for social work. In S. Dumont & M. St.-Onge, (Eds.), *Social work health and international development: Compassion in social policy and practice* (pp. 191–204). Binghamton, NY: Haworth Publishing.

Group for the Advancement of Doctoral Education [GADE]. (n.d.). Purpose of GADE. Retrieved June 30, 2009 from: http://www.gadephd.org/

Groze, V. (1996). A 1 and 2 year follow-up study of adoptive families and special needs children. *Children and Youth Services Review, 18*(1/2), 57–82.

Gurteen, H. (1882). *A handbook of charity organization.* Buffalo, NY: Charity Organization Society.

Gustavsson, N. S., & Segal, E. A. (1994). *Critical issues in child welfare.* Thousand Oaks, CA: Sage.

Gutierrez, L. M. (1987, Summer), Social work theories and practice with battered women: A conflict-of-values analysis. *Affilia,* pp. 36–52.

Hansen, R. A., Gartlehner, G., Lohr, K. N., Gaynes, B. N., & Carey, T. S. (2005). Efficacy and safety of second generation antidepressants in the treatment of major depressive disorder. *Annals of Internal Medicine, 143*(6), 415–426.

Harrington, M. (1962). *The other America: Poverty in the United States.* New York: Macmillan.

Harrington, S. (May/June, 1999). New bedlam: Jails not psychological hospitals now care for the indigent mentally ill. *Humanist, 59,* 9–13.

Harris, M. B., & Franklin, C. (2008). *Taking charge: A school-based life skills program for adolescent mothers.* New York: Oxford University Press.

Harris, V., & Koespell, T. (1998). Re-arrest among mentally ill offenders. *Journal of the American Academy of Psychiatry and the Law, 26,* 3, 393–402.

Hawkins, J., Veeder, N., & Pearce, C. (1998). *Nurse social worker collaboration managed care: A model of community case management.* New York: Springer.

Haynes, K., & Mickelson, J. S. (1991). *Affecting change, social workers in the political arena.* New York: Longman; 5th ed., Boston, MA: Allyn & Bacon, 2003.

Healy, L. (1995). International social welfare: Organizations and activities. In R. L. Edwards et al. (Eds.), *Encyclopedia of social work* (19th ed., pp. 1499–1510). Washington, DC: NASW Press.

Heffernan, J., Shuttlesworth, G., & Ambrosino, R. (1988). *Social work and social welfare: An introduction.* St. Paul, MN: West.

Heffner, W. (1913). *History of poor relief legislation in Pennsylvania, 1682–1913.* Cleona, PA: Holzapfel.

Helms, J. E. (Ed). (1990). *Black and white racial identity: Theory, research, and practice.* Westport, CT: Praeger.

Henry, M. J., & Pollack, D. (2009). *Adoption in the United States: A reference for families, professionals, and students.* Chicago: Lyceum Books, Inc.

Hepworth, D. H., Rooney, R. H., & Larsen, J. (2002). *Direct social work practice: Theory and skills.* Pacific Grove, CA: Brooks/Cole.

High, D. (1978). Quality of life and care of the dying person. In M. Blaes & D. High (Eds.), *Medical treatment and the dying: Moral issues* (pp. 65–84). Salem, MA: Hall.

Hiller, M., & Knight, K. (June, 1996). Compulsory community-based substance abuse treatment and the mentally ill criminal offender. *Prison Journal, 76*(2), 180–185.

Hiratsuka, J. (1990). Managed care: A sea of change in health. *NASW News, 35,* 3.

Hiratsuka, J. (1992). 114 more races backed. *NASW News, 37*(9), 1, 10.

Hodge, D. H. (2003). Value differences between social workers and members of the working and middle class. *Social Work, 48*(1), 107–119.

Hodges, J. Q., & Anderson, K. M. (2005). What do social workers need to know about mental health courts? *Social Work in Mental Health, 4*(2), 17–30.

Hoeffer, R., & Colby, I. (1998). Private social welfare expenditures. In R. Edwards et al. (Eds.), *Encyclopedia of social work update.* Washington, DC: NASW Press.

Hokenstad, M. C., & Kendall, K. A. (1995). International social work education. In R. L. Edwards et al. (Eds.), *Encyclopedia of social work* (19th ed., pp. 1511–1520). Washington, DC: NASW Press.

Holliman, D. (1998). Discharge planning in Alabama hospitals. DAI-59-09A 3647. Ann Arbor: UMI, unpublished dissertation.

Holliman, D., Dziegielewski, S. F., & Datta, P. (2001). Discharge planning and social work practice. *Social Work in Health Care, 32*(3), 1–19.

Hopps, J. G., & Collins, P. M. (1995). Social work profession overview. In R. Edwards et al. (Eds.), *Encyclopedia of social work* (19th ed., pp. 2266–2282). Washington, DC: NASW Press.

Hopps, J. G., & Lowe, T. B. (2008). The scope of social work practice. In K. M. Sowers & C. N. Dulmus (Series Eds.) & B. W. White (Vol. Ed.), *Comprehensive handbook of social work and social welfare: Vol. 1. The profession of social work* (pp. 37–64). Hoboken, NJ: John Wiley & Sons, Inc.

Hoyt, D. R., Kaiser, M. A., Peters, G. R., & Babchuk, N. (1980). Life satisfaction and activity theory: A multi-dimensional approach. *Journal of Gerontology, 35,* 935–981.

Iftekhar, A. (2008-07-31). *Retirement of U.S. Elderly in Foreign Countries: Social and Health Care Issues.* Paper presented at the annual meeting of the American Sociological Association Annual Meeting, Sheraton Boston and the Boston Marriott Copley Place, Boston, MA. Retrieved June 19, 2009, from http://www.allacademic.com/meta/p242458_index.html

Jacobs, M. A., Bruhn, C., & Graf, I. (2008). Methodological and validity issues involved in collection of sensitive information from children in foster care. *Journal of Social Service Research, 34*(4), 71–83.

Jansson, B. S. (2004). *The reluctant welfare state: American social welfare policies past, present, and future* (5th ed.). Pacific Grove, CA: Brooks/Cole.

Johnson, J. L., & Grant, G. (2005). A multi-systemic approach to practice. In Johnson, J. L., & Grant, G. (Eds.), *Adoption* (pp.1–28). New York: Allyn and Bacon.

Johnson, L. C., & Schwartz, C. L. (1988). *Social welfare: A response to human need.* Boston: Allyn and Bacon.

Johnston, J., Roseby, V., & Kuehnle, K. (2009). *In the name of the child: A developmental approach to understanding and helping children of conflicted and violent divorce* (2nd Ed.). New York: Springer Publishing Company, LLC.

Jones, A. (1994). *Next time she'll be dead: Battering and how to stop it.* Boston: Beacon.

Jordan, C., & Franklin, C. (2009). *Clinical assessment for social workers: Quantitative and qualitative methods* (3rd Ed.). Chicago: Lyceum Books.

Kadushin, A. (1976). *Supervision in social work.* New York: Columbia University Press.

Kadushin, A., & Martin, J. A. (1988). *Child welfare services* (4th ed.). New York: Macmillan.

Kadushin, G., & Kulys, R. (1994). Patient and family involvement in discharge planning. *Journal of Gerontological Social Work, 22,* 171–199.

Kamradt, B., Gilbertson, S. A., & Jefferson, M. (2008). Services for high risk populations in systems of care. In Stroul, B. A., & Blau, G. M. (Eds.), *The system of care handbook: Transforming mental health services for children, youth and families* (pp. 469–490). Baltimore, MD: Paul H. Bookes.

Kantrowitz, B., & King, P. (1991). Foster care can protect children from abuse. In C. Wekesser (Ed.), *America's children: Opposing viewpoints* (pp. 96–99). San Diego, CA: Greenhaven.

Karger, H. J., & Stoesz, D. (2010). *American social welfare policy: A pluralist approach* (6th ed.). Boston, MA: Pearson Education, Inc./Allyn Bacon.

Karls, J. M., & O'Keefe, M. E. (2008). *The PIE Manual.* Washington, DC: NASW Press.

Karls, J. M., & O'Keefe, M. E. (2009). Person in environment system. In A. R. Roberts (Ed.), *Social workers' desk reference* (2nd ed., pp. 371–376). New York: Oxford University Press.

Karls, J. M., & Wandrei, K. M. (Eds.). (1996a). *Person-in-environment system: The PIE classification system for social functioning problems.* Washington, DC: NASW Press.

Karls, J. M., & Wandrei, K. M. (1996b). *PIE manual: Person-in-environment system: The PIE classification system for social functioning problems.* Washington, DC: NASW Press.

Karp, C., & Butler, T. (1996). *Treatment strategies for abused children: From victim to survivor.* Thousand Oaks, CA: Sage.

Kastenbaum, R., & Coppedge, R. (1987). Suicide in later life: A counter trend among the old-old. In G. L. Maddox & E. W. Busse (Eds.), *Aging: The universal human experience*. New York: Springer.

Katz, M. B. (1986). *In the shadow of the poorhouse: A social history of welfare in America*. New York: Basic Books.

Kendall, K. (1984). *World guide to social work education*. New York: CSWE.

Knoll, J. (2009). Treating the morally objectionable. In J. T. Andrade (Ed.), *Handbook of violence risk assessment and treatment: New approaches for mental health professionals* (pp. 311–346). New York: Springer Publishing Company, LLC.

Knox, K. S., & Roberts A. R. (2009). The social worker in a police department. In A. R. Roberts (Ed.), *Social workers' desk reference* (2nd ed., pp. 85–94). New York: Oxford University Press.

Koerner, K., & Linehan, M. M. (2009). Validation principles and strategies. In W. T. O'Donohue & J. E. Fisher (Eds.), *General principles and empirically supported techniques of cognitive behavior therapy* (pp. 674–680). Hoboken, NJ: John Wiley & Sons, Inc.

Kottler, J. A., & Marriner, M. (2009). *Changing people's lives while transforming your own: Paths to social justice & global human rights*. Hoboken, NJ: John Wiley & Sons, Inc.

Lanci, M., & Spreng, A. (2008). *The therapist's starter guide: Setting up and building your practice, working with clients and managing personal growth*. Hoboken, NJ: John Wiley & Sons.

Landers, S. (1992). NASW steps up efforts to elect Clinton. *NASW News, 37*(9), 1.

Landon, P. S. (1995). Generalist and advanced social work practice. In R. Edwards et al. (Eds.), *Encyclopedia of social work* (19th ed., pp. 1101–1108). Washington, DC: NASW Press.

Landrine, H., & Klonoff, E. A. (1997). *Discrimination against women: Prevalence, consequences, remedies*. Newbury Park, CA: Sage.

LaRue, G. A. (1985). *Euthanasia and religion*. Eugene, OR: Hemlock Society.

Leach, M. M. (2006). *Cultural diversity and suicide: Ethnic, religious, gender and sexual orientation perspectives*. Binghamton, NY: Haworth Press.

Lee, E., Forthofor, R., & Taube, C. (1985). Does DRG mean disastrous results for psychiatric hospitals? *Journal of Health and Human Services Administration, 8*, 53–78.

Leighninger, L. (1987). *Social work: Search for identity*. Westport, CT: Greenwood.

Leighninger, L. (2008). The history of social work and social welfare. In K. M. Sowers & C. N. Dulmus (Series Eds.) & B. W. White (Vol. Ed.), *Comprehensive handbook of social work and social welfare: Vol. 1. The profession of social work* (pp. 1–24). Hoboken, NJ: John Wiley & Sons, Inc.

Leipzig, R. M., Hyer, K., Ek, K., Wallenstein, S., Vezina, M. L., Fairchild, S., Cassel, C. K., & Howe, J. L. (2002). Attitudes toward working on interdisciplinary healthcare teams: A comparison by discipline. *Journal of Geriatric Society, 50*(6), 1141–1148.

Lemon, B. L., Bengston, V. L., & Peterson, J. A. (1972). An exploration of activity of aging: Activity types and life satisfaction among in-movers to a retirement community. *Journal of Gerontology, 27*, 511–583.

Lennon, T. (2002). *Statistics in social work education in the United States, 2000*. Alexandria, VA: CSWE.

Lens, V. (2002). Managed care and the judicial system: Another avenue for reform? *Health and Social Work, 27*(1), 27–36.

Leon, A. M., & Dziegielewski, S. F. (1999). The psychological impact of migration: Practice considerations in working with Hispanic women. *Journal of Social Work Practice, 13*(1), 69–82.

Levin, R., & Herbert, M. (1995). Differential work assignments of social work practitioners in hospitals. *Health and Social Work, 20*(1), 21–30.

Ligon, J. (2009). Fundamentals of brief treatment. In A. Roberts (Ed.), *Social workers' desk reference* (2nd ed., pp. 215–220). New York: Oxford University Press.

Linderman, D. S. (1995). Child welfare overview. In R. Edwards et al. (Eds.), *Encyclopedia of social work* (19th ed., pp. 424–433). Washington, DC: NASW Press.

Lindsey, D. (1994). *The welfare of children*. New York: Oxford University Press.

Linsley, J. (2003). Social work salaries: Keeping up with the times? *The New Social Worker, 10*, 1, 1–5.

Litsky, M. (1994). Reforming the criminal justice system can decrease violence against women. In B. Leone, B. Szumski, K. de Koster, K. Swisher, C. Wekesser, & W. Barbour (Eds.), *Violence against women*. San Diego, CA: Greenhaven.

Liutkus, J. F. (1994, April). Wife assault: An issue for women's health. *Internal Medicine, 7*, 41–53.

Lockery, S., Dunkle, R., Kart, C., & Coulton, D. (1994). Factors contributing to the early re-hospitalization of elderly people. *Health and Social Work, 19*(3), 182–191.

Logan, M. L. (2009). Social work with African Americans. In A. Roberts (Ed.), *Social workers' desk reference* (2nd ed., pp. 962–969). New York: Oxford University Press.

Lovell, D., & Rhodes, L. (1997). Mobile consultation, crossing correctional boundaries to cope with disturbed offenders. *Federal Probation, 61*(35), 40–45.

Lowry, L. (1979). *Social work with the aging: The challenge and promise of later years*. New York: Harper and Row.

Lubove, C. (1965). *The professional altruist*. Cambridge, MA: Harvard University Press.

Lyons, J. S., Howard, K. I., O'Mahoney, M. T., & Lish, J. D. (1997). *The measurement and management of clinical outcomes in mental health*. New York: Wiley.

Mackelprang, R. W., & Salsgiver, R. O. (2009). *Disability: A diversity model approach in human service practice* (2nd ed.). Chicago: Lyceum Books, Inc.

Maddox, G. (1964). Disengagement theory: A critical evaluation. *Gerontologist, 4*, 80–82.

Mahaffey, M., & Hanks, J. (Eds.). (1982). *Practical politics and social work and political responsibility*. Silver Spring, MD: NASW.

Maldonado, D. (1987). Aged. In A. Minahan (Ed.), *Encyclopedia of social work* (pp. 95–106). Silver Spring, MD: NASW Press.

Mallon, G. P. (2008). Social work practice with LGBT parents. In G. P. Mallon (Ed.), *Social work practice with lesbian, gay, bisexual, and transgender people* (2nd ed., pp. 269–312). New York: Taylor & Francis Group/Routledge.

Mankita, S., & Alalu, R. (1996, Spring). Hospital social work: Challenges, rewards. *New Social Worker*, pp. 4–6.

Marks, A. T., & Knox, K. S. (2009). Social work regulation and licensing. In A. R. Roberts, *Social workers' desk reference* (2nd ed., pp. 148–155). New York: Oxford University Press.

Marshall, T. B., & Solomon, P. (2009). Working with families of persons with severe mental illness. In A. R. Roberts (Ed.), *Social workers' desk reference* (2nd ed., pp. 491–494). New York: Oxford University Press.

Marsiske, M., Franks, M. M., & Masat, B. T. (1998). Psychological perspectives on aging. In L. Morgan & S. Kunkel (Eds.), *Aging: The social context* (pp. 145–182). Thousand Oaks, CA: Pine Forge Press.

Martin, M. (1988). A social worker's response. In N. Hutchings (Ed.), *The violent family: Victimization of women, children, and elders*. New York: Human Science Press.

Matas, M., Staley, D., & Griffin, W. (1992). A profile of the noncompliant patient: A thirty-month review of outpatient psychiatry referrals. *General Hospital Psychiatry, 14*, 124–130.

Mattaini, M. A. (2001). The foundation of social work practice. In Briggs & Corcoran (Eds.), *Social work practice: Treating common client problems* (pp. 15–35). Chicago: Lyceum.

McAdoo, H. (1997). *Black families.* Thousand Oaks, CA: Sage.

McDonald, D., & Teitelbaum, M. (1994). *Managing mentally ill defendants in the community.* Washington, D.C., US Department of Justice, Office of Justice Programs, National Institute of Justice, 11.

McLeod, E., & Bywaters, P. (2000). *Social work, health and equality.* New York: Routledge.

McPhee, D. M., & Bronstein, L. R. (2003). The journey from welfare to work: Learning from women living in poverty. *Affilia, 18*(1), 34–38.

McSkimming, S., Myrick, M., & Wasinger, M. (2000). Supportive care of the dying: A coalition for compassionate care-conducting an organizational assessment. *American Journal of Hospice & Palliative Care, 17*(4), 245–252.

Mechanic, D. (November/December, 1998). Emerging trends in mental health policy and practice: Managed care provides the potential for a more balanced system in the post-institutional era of mental health care. *Health Affairs, 17,* 82–98.

Mechanic, D., & McAlpine, D. (September/October, 1999). Mission unfulfilled: Potholes on the road to mental health parity. *Health Affairs, 18*(5), 7–21.

Meyer, C. (1976). *Social work practice* (2nd ed.). New York: Free Press.

Miall, C. E. (2000). Adoption as family form. *Family Relations: Journal of Applied Family & Child Studies, 49*(4), 359–362.

Midgley, J. (1995). International and comparative social welfare. In R. L. Edwards et al. (Eds.), *Encyclopedia of social work* (19th ed., pp. 1490–1499). Washington, DC: NASW Press.

Midgley, J. (1997). Social work in international context: Challenges and opportunities for the 21st century. In M. Reisch & E. Gambrill (Eds.), *Social work in the 21st century* (pp. 59–67). Thousand Oaks, CA: Pine Forge Press.

Miley, K. K., O'Melia, M., & Dubois, B. L. (1998). *Generalist social work practice: An empowering approach.* Boston: Allyn and Bacon.

Miller, L. (2008). *Counseling crime victims: Practical strategies for mental health professionals.* New York: Springer Publishing Company, LLC.

Miller, P. J. (2008). Health-care policy: Should change be small or large? In K. M. Sowers & C. N. Dulmus (Series Eds.) & I. C. Colby (Vol. Ed.), *Comprehensive handbook of social work and social welfare: Vol. 4. Social policy and policy practice* (pp. 219–236). Hoboken, NJ: John Wiley & Sons, Inc.

Miller, J., & Garran, A. M. (2009). The legacy of racism for social work practice today and what to do about it. In A. Roberts (Ed.), *Social workers' desk reference* (2nd ed., pp. 928–923). New York: Oxford University Press.

Miller, T., Veltkamp, L., & Raines, P. (1998). The trauma of family violence. In Miller, T., *Children of Trauma: Stressful life events and their effects on children and adolescents* (pp. 61–76). Madison, CT: International Universities Press, Inc.

Mills, R. J., & Bhandari, S. (2003). Health insurance coverage in the United States: 2002. Current Population Reports. U.S. Census Bureau (pp. 60–223). U.S. Department of Commerce, Economics and Statistics Division. Issued September 2003. Retrieved October 12, 2003, from www.census/gov/pubs

Mizrahi, T. (1995). Health care: Reform initiatives. In R. Edwards et al. (Eds.), *Encyclopedia of social work* (19th ed., Vol. 2, pp. 1185–1198). Silver Spring, MD: NASW Press.

Moggi, F., Ouimette, P. C., Finney, J. W., Moos, & Rudolf, H. (1999). Effectiveness of treatment for substance abuse and dependence for dual diagnosis patients: A model of treatment factors associated with one-year outcomes. *Journal of Studies on Alcohol, 60*(6), 856.

Moniz, C., & Gorin, S. (2003). *Health and health care policy*. Boston: Allyn and Bacon.

Monroe, I. (2003). Becoming what we ought to be: We cannot separate our efforts to heal the world from the difficult work of healing ourselves. *The Other Side, 39*(1), 43–45.

Montana, P. (1985). *Retirement programs: How to develop and implement them*. Englewood Cliffs: NJ: Prentice-Hall.

Moore, K. A., Redd, Z., Burkhauser, M., Mbwana, K., & Collins, A. (2009). Children in poverty: Trends, consequences, and policy options. *Trends Child Research Brief, #2009-11*. Retrieved June 30, 2009, from: http://www.childtrends.org/Files/Child_Trends-2009_04_07_RB_ChildreninPoverty.pdf

Morales, A. T., & Sheafor, B. W. (2006). *The many faces of social work clients*. Boston: Allyn and Bacon.

Morales, A. T., Sheafor, B. W., & Scott, M. E. (2009). *Social work: A profession of many faces*. Boston: Allyn & Bacon.

Morgan, L., & Kunkel, S. (1998). *Aging: The social context*. Thousand Oaks, CA: Pine Forge Press.

Morris, R. (1993). Do changing times mean changing agendas for the elderly? *Journal of Aging and Social Policy, 5*(3), 1–6.

Morrison, M. (1982). *Economics of aging: The future of retirement*. New York: Van Nostrand Reinhold.

Mosher-Ashley, P. M. (1994). Diagnoses assigned and issues brought up in therapy by older adults receiving outpatient treatment. *Clinical Gerontologist, 15*(2), 37–64.

Mueller, S. L., & Overmann, M. (2008). *Working world: Careers in international education, exchange and development*. Washington, DC: Georgetown University Press.

Mullahy, C. (1998). *The case manager's handbook*. Gaithersburg, MD: Aspen Publishers.

Mullarkey, E. (1988). The legal system for victims of violence. In N. Hutchings (Ed.), *The violent family: Victimization of women, children, and elders* (pp. 43–52). New York: Human Science Press.

Mullins, G. P. (1994). The battered woman and homelessness. *Journal of Law and Policy, 3*(1), 237–255.

Mulroy, E. (2004). Theoretical perspectives on the social environment to guide management and community practice: An organizational-in-environment approach. *Administration in Social Work, 28*(1), 77–96.

Munson, C. E. (2009). Guidelines for the diagnostic and statistical manual of mental disorders (DSM-IV-TR) multiaxial system diagnosis. In A. R. Roberts (Ed.), *Social workers' desk reference* (2nd ed., pp. 334–342). New York: Oxford University Press.

Mushlin, M. B. (1991). Foster care cannot protect children from physical abuse. In C. Wekesser (Ed.), *American children: Opposing viewpoints* (pp. 100–104). San Diego, CA: Greenhaven.

Nacman, M. (1977). Social work in health setting: A historical review. *Social Work in Health Care, 2*(4), 407–418.

Nadir, A., & Dziegielewski, S. F. (2001). Called to Islam: Issues and challenges in providing ethnically sensitive social work practice with Muslim people. In M. Hook, B. Hugen & M. Aguilar (Eds.), *Spirituality within religious traditions in social work practice* (pp.144–166). Pacific Grove, CA: Brooks/Cole.

National Association for Home Care. (2000). *Basic statistics about home care* (pp. 1–25). Retrieved February 11, 2002, from www.nach.org.Consumer/hcstats.html

National Association of Social Workers [NASW]. (1990). *NASW clinical indicators for social work and psychosocial services in the acute psychiatric hospital* [pamphlet]. Washington, DC: Author.

National Association of Social Workers [NASW]. (1993). *Choices: Careers in social work.* Washington, DC: Author.

National Association of Social Workers [NASW]. (1995). *A brief look at managed mental health care* [brochure]. Washington, DC: NASW Press.

National Association of Social Workers [NASW]. (1996, August). Code of Ethics (adopted by the NASW National Delegate Assembly, August 1996). Washington, DC: NASW Press.

National Association of Social Workers [NASW]. (1998). *Centennial information: Celebrating 100 years of social work practice* [pamphlet]. Washington, DC: Author.

National Association of Social Workers [NASW]. (2000). *Code of ethics for the national association of social workers.* Washington, DC: NASW Press.

National Association of Social Workers [NASW]. (2003). Family violence policy statement. In *Social work speaks.* Washington, D.C.: NASW Press.

National Association of Social Workers [NASW]. (2008). HIV/AIDS: General overview. Retrieved December 27, 2008, from http://www.socialworkers.org/practice/hiv_aids/aidsday.asp

National Association of Social Workers [NASW]. (Revised, 2008). *Code of Ethics of the National Association of Social Workers.* Washington, DC: Author, retrieved June 30, 2009, from http://www.socialworkers.org/pubs/code/code.asp

NASW Political Affairs Office. (1992, April). *The political social worker.* Washington, DC: NASW.

National Bureau of Economic Research, (n.d.). Medicare and its impact. Retrieved December 28, 2008, from http://www.nber.org/digest/apr06/w11609.html

National Center for Children in Poverty [NCCP]. (2008). United States: Demographics of low-income children. Retrieved June 30, 2009, from http://www.nccp.org/profiles/US_profile_6.html

National Resource Center on Domestic Violence and the Battered Women's Justice Project. (1994). *The Violence Against Women Act 1994.* Available from the National Resource Center, 6400 Flank Drive, Suite 1300, Harrisburg, PA 17112-2778.

Nelson, J., & Powers, P. (2001). Community case management for frail, elderly clients: The nurse case manager's role. *Journal of Nursing Administration, 31*(9), 444–450.

Nemeroff, C. B. (2007). The burden of severe depression: A review of diagnostic challenges and treatment alternatives. *Journal of Psychiatric Research, 41,* 89–206.

Nerenberg, L. (2006). Communities respond to elder abuse. *Journal of Gerontological Social Work, 46*(3/4), 5–33.

Nesvisky, M. (2006). Medicare and its impact. National Bureau of Economic Research (NBER). Retrieved June 5, 2009, from https://nber15.nber.org/digest/apr06/w11609.html

Netting, F. E., Kettner, P., & McMurtry, S. (1993). *Social work macro practice.* New York: Longman.

Neuman, K. (2000). Understanding organizational reengineering in health care: Strategies for social work's survival. *Social Work in Health Care, 31*(1), 19–32.

Nicholas, D. B., Darch, J., McNeill, T., Brister, L., O'Leary, K., Berlin, D., & Koller, D. (2007). Perceptions of online support for hospitalized children and adolescents. In S. Dumont & M. St.-Onge, (Eds.), *Social work health and international development: Compassion in social policy and practice* (pp. 205–224). Binghamton, NY: Haworth.

Nolan, K. (1987). In death's shadow: The meanings of withholding resuscitation. *Hastings Center Report, 17,* 9–14.

Novick, K. K., & Novick, J. (2005). *Working with parents makes therapy work*. Lanham, MD: Rowman & Littlefield Publishers, Inc.

Ofahengaue-Vakalahi, H. F., & Fong, R. (2009). Social work practice with Asian and Pacific Island Americans. In A. Roberts (Ed.), *Social workers desk reference* (2nd ed., pp. 954–958). New York: Oxford University Press.

O'Gorman, A. (2002). Playing by the rules and losing ground. *America, 187*(3), 12–16.

O'Hare, T. (2009). *Essential skills of social work practice: Assessment, intervention, and education*. Chicago: Lyceum Books, Inc.

O'Hare, T., & Sherrer, M. V. (2009). Impact of the most frequently reported traumatic events on community mental health clients. *Journal of Human Behavior in the Social Environment, 19*(2), 186–195.

Olson, M. E. (2006). Family and network therapy training for a system of care. In A. Lightburn & P. Sessions (Eds.), *Handbook of community-based practice* (pp. 135–152). New York: Oxford University Press.

Palmer, J., & Sawhill, I. (1984). *The Reagan record*. Cambridge, MA: Ballinger.

Parker, M., & Sherraden, M. (1992). Electoral participation of social workers. *New England Journal of Human Services, 11*(3), 23–28.

Paterson, S. L., Baker, M., & Maeck, J. P. (1993). Durable powers of attorney: Issues of gender and health care decision making. *Journal of Gerontological Social Work, 21,* 161–177.

Pavao, J. M. (1998). *The family of adoption*. Boston: Beacon Press.

PDR Medical Dictionary (3rd ed.). (2005). Montvale, NJ: Physician's Desk Reference.

Pence, E., & Paymar, M. (1993). *Education groups for men who batter*. New York: Springer.

Perkins, K., & Tice, C. (1994). Suicide and older adults. The strengths perspective in practice. *Journal of Applied Gerontology, 13,* 438–454.

Peterson, M. (1994). Physical aspects of aging: Is there such a thing as normal? *Geriatrics, 49*(2), 45–49.

Petretic-Jackson, P. A., & Jackson, T. (1996). Mental health interventions with battered women. In A. R. Roberts (Ed.), *Helping battered women: New perspectives and remedies* (pp. 188–221). New York: Oxford University Press.

Pike, C. K. (2009). Developing client focused measures. In A. R. Roberts (Ed.), *Social workers' desk reference* (2nd ed., pp. 351–357). New York: Oxford University Press.

Podnieks, E. (2006). Social inclusion: An interplay of health: New insights into elder abuse. *Journal of Gerontological Social Work, 46*(3/4), 57–79.

Poertner, J., & Rapp, C. A. (2007). *The textbook of social administration: The consumer centered approach*. Binghamton, NY: Haworth Press, Inc.

Ponto, J. M., & Berger, W. (1992). Social work services in the emergency department: A cost benefits analysis of an extended coverage program. *Health & Social Work, 17,* 1, 67–75.

Poole, D. (1995). Health care: Direct practice. In R. Edwards et al. (Eds.), *Encyclopedia of social work* (19th ed., Vol. 2, pp. 1156–1167). Washington, DC: NASW Press.

Popple, P., & Leighninger, L. (1990). *Social work, social welfare and American society*. Needham, MA: Allyn and Bacon.

Pratt, C., Wright, S., & Schmall, V. (1987). Burden, coping and health status: A comparison of family caregivers to community dwelling institutionalized Alzheimer's patients. *Social Work, 10,* 99–112.

Prigoff, A. (2000). *Economics for social workers: Social outcomes of economic globalization with strategies for community action*. Belmont, CA: Wadsworth/Thomson Learning.

Pyles, L. (2009). *Progressive community organizing: A critical approach for a globalizing world.* New York: Routledge/Taylor & Francis Group.

Quam, J. (1995). Charles Loring Brace (1826–1890). In R. Edwards et al. (Eds.), *Encyclopedia of social work* (19th ed., p. 2575). Washington, DC: NASW Press.

Queralt, M. (1996). *The social environment and human behavior: A diversity perspective.* Boston: Allyn and Bacon.

Ragg, D. M. (2001). *Building effective helping skills: The foundation of generalist practice.* Needham Heights, MA: Allyn & Bacon.

Rao, V., & Kendall, K. (Eds.). (1984). *World guide to social work education.* New York: CSWE.

Reamer, F. G. (2001). Ethics and values in clinical and community social work practice. In Briggs & Corcoran (Eds.), *Social work practice: Treating common client problems* (pp. 85–106). Chicago: Lyceum.

Reamer, F. G. (2009). Ethical issues in social work. In A. Roberts (Ed.), *Social workers' desk reference* (2nd ed., pp. 115–120). New York: Oxford University Press.

Reddon, J. R., Hoglin, B., & Woodman, M. (2008). Immediate effects of a 16-week life skills education program on the mental health of adult psychiatric patients. *Social Work in Mental Health, 6*(3), 21–40.

Rehman, T. F., & Dziegielewski, S. F. (2003). Women who choose Islam: Issues, changes and challenges in providing ethnically diverse practice. *International Journal of Mental Health, 32*(3), 31–50.

Reid, P. N. (1995). Social welfare history. In R. Edwards et al. (Eds.), *Encyclopedia of social work* (19th ed.). Washington, DC: NASW Press.

Reinberg, S. (2007). Teen birth rates up for the first time in 14 years, U.S. reports, Health, U.S. News and World reports, USnews.com, retrieved December 26, 2008, from http://health.usnews.com/usnews/health/healthday/071205/teen-birth-rates-up-for-first-time-in-14-years-us-reports_print.htm

Rennison, C. M., & Welchans, S. (2000). *Intimate partner violence.* Retrieved August 3, 2003, from http:///www.ojp.usdoj.gov/bjs/pub/pdf/ipv.pdf

Resnick, C., & Dziegielewski, S. F. (1996). The relationship between therapeutic termination and job satisfaction among medical social workers. *Social Work in Health Care, 23*(3), 17–35.

Reynolds, C. F., Small, G. W., Stein, E. M., & Teri, L. (1994, February). When depression strikes the elderly patient. *Patient Care,* pp. 85–101.

Rhodes, C. (1988). *An introduction to gerontology: Aging in American society.* Springfield, IL: Thomas.

Richan, W. C. (2006). *Lobbying for social change* (3rd ed.). New York: Haworth Press.

Richan, W., & Mendelsohn, A. R. (1973). *Social work, the unloved profession.* New York: Franklin Watts.

Richardson, V. E. (2009). Clinical social work with older adults. In A. R. Roberts, *Social Workers' Desk Reference* (2nd ed., pp. 938–954). New York: Oxford University Press.

Richman, W. (1991). *Lobbying for social change.* New York: Haworth.

Ridley, C. R. (1995). *Overcoming unintentional racism in counseling and therapy.* Thousand Oaks, CA: Sage.

Rife, J. C., & Belcher, J. R. (1994). Assisting unemployed older workers to become reemployed: An experimental evaluation. *Research of Social Work Practice, 4,* 3–13.

Risley, M. (1961). *The house of healing.* London: Hale.

Rizk, M. (1988, April). Domestic violence during pregnancy. In *Proceedings Family Violence: Public Health Social Work's Role in Prevention* (pp. 19–31). Pittsburgh, PA: Department of Health and Human Services, Bureau of Maternal and Child Health.

Robbins, J. M. (2008, February 22). *The Costs of Rising Divorce Rates Across The US.* Retrieved December 24, 2008, from http://ezinearticles.com/?The-Costs-of-Rising-Divorce-Rates-Across-The-US&id=1003126

Roberts, A. R. (1996a). Police responses to battered women: Past, present and future. In A. R. Roberts (Ed.), *Helping battered women: New perspectives and remedies* (pp. 85–95). New York: Oxford University Press.

Roberts, A. R. (1996b). Court responses to battered women. In A. R. Roberts (Ed.), *Helping battered women: New perspectives and remedies* (pp. 96–101). New York: Oxford University Press.

Roberts, A. R. (1996c). Introduction: Myths and realities regarding battered women. In A. R. Roberts (Ed.), *Helping battered women: New perspectives and remedies* (pp. 3–12). New York: Oxford University Press.

Roberts, A. R., & Dziegielewski, S. F. (1995). Basic forms and applications of crisis intervention and time-limited cognitive therapy. In A. R. Roberts (Ed.), *Crisis intervention and time-limited cognitive treatment* (pp. 5–30). Newbury Park, CA: Sage Publications.

Roche, S. E., & Sadoski, P. J. (1996). Social action for battered women. In A. R. Roberts (Ed.), *Helping battered women: New perspectives and remedies.* New York: Oxford University Press.

Rosenberg, G. (2008). Social determinants of health: Twenty-first-century social work priorities. In K. M. Sowers & C. N. Dulmus (Series Eds.) & I. C. Colby (Vol. Ed.), *Comprehensive handbook of social work and social welfare: Vol. 4. Social policy and policy practice* (pp. 237–247). Hoboken, NJ: John Wiley & Sons, Inc.

Rosenthal, J. A. (1993). Outcomes of adoption of children with special needs. *The Future of Children, 3*(1), 77–88.

Rosenthal, J. A., & Groze, V. (1990). Special-needs adoption: A study of intact families. *Social Service Review, 64,* 475–505.

Rosenzweig, J. M., & Brennan, E. M. (2008). The intersection of children's mental health and work-family studies. In J. M. Rosenzweig & E. M. Brennan (Eds.), *Work, life, and mental health system of care* (p. 3–26). Baltimore: Paul H. Brooks Publishing.

Ross, J. (1993). Redefining hospital social work: An embattled professional domain [Editorial]. *Health and Social Work, 18,* 243–247.

Rossi, P. (1999). *Case management in healthcare.* Philadelphia: W. B. Saunders.

Rothman, D. (1971). *The discovery of the asylum social order and disorder in the new republic.* Boston: Little, Brown.

Rothman, J., Erlich, J. L., & Tropman, J. E. (1995). *Strategies for community intervention.* Itasca, IL: Peacock.

Rubin, A., & Babbie, E. (2008). *Research methods for social work* (6th Ed.). Belmont, CA: Brooks/Cole.

Rubinstein, R. L., Lubben, J. E., & Mintzer, J. E. (1994, March). Social isolation and social support: An applied perspective. *Journal of Applied Gerontology, 13*(1), 58–72.

Ryff, C. D. (1982). Self-perceived personality change in adult-hood and aging. *Journal of Personality and Social Psychology, 42,* 108–115.

Sackett, D., Rosenberg, W., Gray, J., Haynes, R., & Richardson, W. (1996). Evidence based medicine: What it is and what it isn't. *British Medical Journal, 312*(7023), 71–72.

Sadavoy, J., Jarvik, L. F., Grossberg, G. T., & Meyers, B. S. (Eds). (2004). *Comprehensive textbook of geriatric psychiatry* (3rd ed.). New York: W. W. Norton & Company.

Sakamoto, I., & Pitner, R. (2005). Use of critical consciousness in anti-oppressive social work practice: Disentangling power dynamics at personal and structural levels. *British Journal of Social Work, 35,* 435–452.

Satcher, D. (2000). Foreword. In *U.S. Public Health Service, Report of the Surgeon General's Conference on Children's Mental Health: A National Action Agenda* (pp. 1–2). Washington, DC: U.S. Department of Health and Human Services.

Saunders, D. G. (1992). Woman battering. In R. T. Ammerman & M. Hersen (Eds.), *Assessment of family violence: A clinical and legal source book*. New York: Wiley.

Sawhill, I. V. (2001). What can be done to reduce teen pregnancy and out-of-wedlock births? CCF Briefs, Number 8. The Brookings Institute. Retrieved May 28, 2009, from http://www.brookings.edu/papers/2001/10childrenfamilies_Sawhill.aspx

Scharlach, A. E., Mor-Barak, M. E., & Birba, L. (1994). Evaluation of a corporate sponsored health care program for retired employees. *Health and Social Work, 19,* 192–198.

Scheyett, A., Kim, M., Swanson, J., Swartz, M., Elbogen, E., Dorn, R. V., & Ferron, J. (2009). Autonomy and the use of directive intervention in the treatment of individuals with serious mental illnesses: A survey of social work practitioners. *Social Work in Mental Health, 7*(4), 283–306.

Schnapp, W. B., & Cannedy, R. (March, 1998). Offenders with mental illness: Mental health and criminal justice best practices. *Administration and Policy in Mental Health, 25*(4), 463–466.

Schneider, E. M. (1994). Society's belief in family privacy contributes to domestic violence. In B. Leone, B. Szumski, K. de Koster, K. Swisher, C. Wekesser, & W. Barbour (Eds.), *Violence against women*. San Diego, CA: Greenhaven.

Segal-Engelchin, D., & Kaufman, R. (2008). Micro and macro orientation: Israeli students' career choices in an antisocial era. *Journal of Social Work Education, 44*(3), 139–157.

Segal, W., & Brzuzy, S. (1998). *Social welfare policy, programs, and practice*. Itasca, IL: Peacock.

Segrin, C. (1994). Social skills and psychological problems among the elderly. *Research on Aging, 16,* 301–321.

Sheafor, B. W., Horejsi, C. R., & Horejsi, G. A. (1997). *Techniques and guidelines for social work practice* (4th ed.). Needham Heights, MA: Allyn and Bacon.

Sheikh, J. I., Cassidy, E. L., Doraiswamy, M. P., Salomon, R. M., Hornig, M., Holland, P. J., Mandell, F. S., et al. (2004). *Journal of American Geriatrics Society, 52,* 86–92.

Sherman, A., & Shapiro, I. (2005). *Social security lifts 13 million seniors above the poverty line: A state by state analysis*. Washington, DC: Center on Budget and Policy Priorities (February 24).

Shernoff, M. (2008). Social work practice with gay individuals. In G. P. Mallon (Ed.), *Social work practice with lesbian, gay, bisexual, and transgender people* (2nd ed., pp. 141–178). New York: Taylor & Francis Group/Routledge.

Shlonsky, A. (2009). Evidence-based practice in social work education. In A. Roberts (Ed.), *Social workers desk reference* (2nd ed., pp. 1169–1176). New York: Oxford University Press.

Shock, N. W. (1987). The International Association of Gerontology: Its origins and development. In G. L. Maddox & E. W. Busse (Eds.), *Aging: The universal experience* (pp. 21–43). New York: Springer.

Shortell, S. M., & Kaluzny, A. D. (1994). Foreword. In S. M. Shortell & A. D. Kaluzny (Eds.), *Health care management: Organizational behavior and design* (3rd ed., p. xi). Albany, NY: Delmar.

Shulman, L. (1992). *Interactional supervision*. Washington, DC: NASW Press.

Shulman, L. (2002). Developing successful therapeutic relationships. In A. R. Roberts & G. J. Greene (Eds.), *Social workers' desk reference*. (pp. 375–378). New York: Oxford University Press.

Siegler, R. T. (1989). *Domestic violence in context: An assessment of community attitudes.* Lexington, MA: Heath.

Sills, J. S. (1980). Disengagement reconsidered: Awareness of finitude. *Gerontologist, 20,* 457–462.

Simon, E. P., Showers, N., Blumfield, S., Holden, G., & Wu, X. (1995). Delivery of home care services after discharge: What really happens. *Health and Social Work, 20,* 5–14.

Skidmore, R. A., Thackeray, M. G., & Farley, O. W. (1997). *Introduction to social work* (7th ed.). Boston: Allyn and Bacon.

Smallegan, M. (1985). There was nothing else to do: Needs for care before nursing home admission. *Gerontologist, 25,* 364–369.

Smith, S. L., & Howard, J. A. (1999). *Promoting successful adoptions: Practice with troubled families.* Thousand Oaks, CA: Sage Publications.

Sorenson, S. B. (2003). Funding public health: The public's willingness to pay for domestic violence prevention programming. *American Journal of Public Health, 93*(11), 1934–1938.

Sousa, L., & Eusebio, C. (2005). When multi-problem poor individuals' values meet practitioners' values! *Journal of Community & Applied Social Psychology, 15,* 353–367.

Southwell, P. (2009). The measurement of child poverty in the United States. *Journal of Human Behavior in the Social Environment, 19*(4), 317–329.

Specht, H., & Courtney, M. (1994). *Unfaithful angels.* New York: Free Press.

Spitzer, W. J., & Kuykendall, R. (1994). Social work delivery of hospital-based financial assistance of services. *Health and Social Work, 19,* 4, 295–298.

Srinivasan, M., & Davis, L. V. (1991). A shelter: An organization like any other? *Affilila, 6*(1), 38–57.

Starr, P. (1982). *The social transformation of American medicine.* New York: Basic Books.

State Policy Documentation Project. (2005). Findings in brief: Child care assistance. Retrieved June 29, 2009, from http://www.spdp.org/tanf/childcare/childcaresumm.htm

Statman, J. B. (1990). *The battered woman's survival guide: Breaking the cycle.* Dallas: Taylor.

Sterns, H. L., Barrett, G. V., Czaja, S. J., & Barr, J. K. (1994). Issues in work and aging. *Journal of Applied Gerontology, 13,* 7–19.

Stith, S. M., Williams, M. B., & Rosen, K. (1990). *Violence hits home: Comprehensive treatment approaches to domestic violence.* New York: Springer.

Storey, J. R. (1982). Income security. In J. Palmer & I. Sawhill (Eds.), *The Reagan experiment* (Vol. 5, pp. 361–392). Washington, DC: Urban Institute Press.

Straus, M. (1980). A sociological perspective on the causes of family violence. In M. R. Green (Ed.), *Violence and the family* (pp. 7–31). Boulder, CO: Westview.

Strawbridge, W. J., Camacho, T. C., Cohen, R. D., & Kaplan, G. A. (1993). Gender differences in factors associated with change in physical functioning in old age: A six-year longitudinal study. *Gerontologist, 33*(5), 603–609.

Strom-Gottfried, K. J. (2007). *Straight talk about professional ethics.* Chicago: Lyceum.

Strom-Gottfried, K. (2008). *The ethics of practice with minors: High stakes, hard choices.* Chicago: Lyceum.

Strom-Gottfried, K. (2009). Enacting the educator role: Principles for practice. In A. R. Roberts (Ed.), *Social workers' desk reference* (2nd ed., pp. 720–725). New York: Oxford University Press.

Sue, D. W., & Sue, D. (2008). *Counseling the culturally diverse: Theory and practice.* Hoboken, NJ: John Wiley & Sons.

Summers, N. (2001). *Fundamentals of case management practice.* Belmont, CA: Brooks/Cole.

Tabenkin, H. (2004). *Israeli Task Force recommendations on health promotion and disease prevention.* Israel Medical Association. (In Hebrew).

Taber's cyclopedia medical dictionary. (1977). Philadelphia: Davis.

Talbott, J. (1988). Taking issue. *Hospital and Community Psychiatry, 39,* 115.

Tan, J. (2009). Measurement issues of service use among elders. *Journal of Human Behavior in the Social Environment, 19*(2), 171–185.

The President's health security plan. (1993). New York: Times Books/Random House.

Thyer, B. (2001). Evidence-based approaches to community practice. In Briggs & Corcoran (Eds.) *Social work practice: Treating common client problems* (pp. 54–65). Chicago: Lyceum.

Thyer, B. A. (2004). What is evidence-based practice? *Brief Treatment and Crisis Intervention, 4*(2), 167–176.

Thyer, B. A. (2008). Practice evaluation. In K. M. Sowers & C. N. Dulmus (Series Eds.) & W. Rowe & L. A. Rapp-Paglicci (Vol. Eds.), *Comprehensive handbook of social work and social welfare: Vol. 3. Social work practice* (pp. 98–119). Hoboken, NJ: John Wiley & Sons, Inc.

Thyer, B. A., & Meyers, L. L. (2007). *The social worker's guide to evaluating practice outcomes.* Alexandria, VA: CSWE Press.

Titmus, R. (1959). *Essays on the welfare state.* New Haven, CT: Yale University Press.

Titmus, R. (1965). The role of redistribution in social policy. *Social Security Bulletin, 28*(6), 34–55.

Tolman, R. M., & Bennett, L. W. (1990). A review of quantitative research on men who batter. *Journal of Interpersonal Violence, 5*(1), 87–118.

Tourse, R. W. C. (1995). Special-interest professional associations. In R. Edwards et al. (Eds.), *Encyclopedia of social work* (19th ed., pp. 2314–2319). Washington, DC: NASW Press.

Tracy, E. M. (1995). Family preservation and home-based services. In R. Edwards et al. (Eds.), *Encyclopedia of social work* (19th ed., pp. 973–983). Washington, DC: NASW Press.

Trattner, W. (1989). *From poor law to welfare state: A history of social welfare in America* (4th ed.). New York: Free Press.

Twohig, M. P., & Crosby, J. M. (2009). Values clarification. In W. T. O'Donohue & J. E. Fisher (Eds.), *General principles and empirically supported techniques of cognitive behavior therapy* (pp. 681–686). Hoboken, NJ: John Wiley & Sons, Inc.

UNAIDS (2002). *Adults and children estimated to be living with HIV/AIDS as of end of 2002.* Retrieved October 5, 2003, from http://www.who.int/hiv/facts/en/plwha_m.jpg

UNAIDS, World Health Organization (WHO). (December 2007). 2007 AIDS Epidemic update. Retrieved June 5, 2009, from http://data.unaids.org/pub/EPISlides/2007/2007_epiupdate_en.pdf

United Nations. (1989, November 20). *United Nations convention on the rights of children.* New York: Author.

U.S. Census Bureau. (1994). *Population Projections of the United States, by Age, Sex, Race, and Hispanic Origin: 1993 to 2050,* Current Population Reports, P25-1104, U.S. Government Printing Office, 1993. Retrieved December 29, 2004, from http://www.census.gov/population/www/pop-profile/elderpop.html

U.S. Census Bureau. (2001). *Aging in the United States: Past, Present, and Future.* Washington, DC: U.S. Government Printing Office.

U.S. Census Bureau. (2003). Children's living arrangements and characteristics: March 2002. U.S. Department of Commerce, Economics and Statistics Administration. Retrieved October 7, 2003, from www.census.gov/prod/2003pubs/p20-547.pdf

U.S. Census Bureau. (2006). Estimates of child population levels. Information retrieved December 23, 2008, from U.S. Census Bureau at http://www.census.gov/popest/states/asrh/

U.S. Census Bureau. (2007). Table 19, US Census data by age 55 years and older by region, age and sex. Retrieved December 29,2008, from http://www.census.gov/population/socdemo/age/2006older_table19.xls

U.S. Census Bureau. (2008). 2006 American Community Survey; B16001. Language Spoken at Home by Ability to Speak English for the Population 5 Years and Over; using American. Retrieved June 5, 2009, through FactFinder®; http://factfinder.census.gov

U.S. Census Bureau. (2008). Current Population Survey [CPS]: A joint effort between the Bureau of Labor Statistics and the Census Bureau. Retrieved June 30, 2009, from http://pubdb3.census.gov/macro/032008/pov/new01_200_01.htm

U.S. Census Bureau. (2008). Income, poverty and health insurance in the United States: 2007. Retrieved December 26, 2008, from http://www.census.gov

U.S. Census Bureau. (November 17, 2008). Public Information Office. Retrieved December 23, 2008, from http://www.census.gov/Press-Release/www/releases/archives/income_wealth/007419.html

U.S. Census Bureau, Statistical Abstracts for the United States. (2009). American fact finder. Retrieved June 5, 2009, from http://factfinder.census.gov/servlet/DatasetMainPageServlet?_program=ACS&_lang=en&_ts=143471788982

U.S. Census Bureau, Population Division. (2008). Income poverty and health insurance coverage in the United States, Current Population Reports.U.S. Department of Commerce, Economics and Statistics Administration, U.S. Census Bureau. Release date August 2008, Retrieved December 21, 2008, from www.census.gov/prod/208pubs/p60-235.pdf and www.census.gov/prod/2008pubs/09statab/pop.pdf

U.S. Department of Health and Human Services, Administration for Children and Families, Administration on Children, Youth and Families, Children's Bureau. (2007). *AFCARS report #13: Preliminary FY 2005 estimates as of September 2006.* Washington, DC: U.S. Department of Health and Human Services. Retrieved June 9, 2009, from http://www.acf.hhs.gov/programs/cb/stats_research/afcars/tar/report13.htm

U.S. Department of Health and Human Services, Administration on Children, Youth and Families. (2007). *Chapter 6 Services, Child Maltreatment 2007.* Washington, DC: U.S. Government Printing Office. Retrieved June 9, 2009, from http://www.acf.hhs.gov/programs/cb/pubs/cm07/chapter6.htm#removed

U.S. Department of Health and Human Services, Administration on Children, Youth and Families. (2008). *Child Maltreatment 2006.* Washington, DC: U.S. Government Printing Office. Retrieved June 9, 2009, from http://www.acf.hhs.gov/programs/cb/pubs/cm06/table4_2.htm

U.S. Department of Health and Human Services, Administration on Children, Youth and Families. (2009). *Child Maltreatment 2007.* Washington, DC: U.S. Government Printing Office. Retrieved June 9, 2009, from http://www.acf.hhs.gov/programs/cb/pubs/cm07/chapter3.htm#child

U.S. Department of Health and Human Services. (2007). Child maltreatment, 2005. Administration for Children and Families. Retrieved July 6, 2009, from http://www.acf.hhs.gov/programs/cb/pubs/cm05

U.S. Department of Health and Human Services, Health Resources and Services Administration. (2003). *The AIDS Epidemic and the Ryan White CARE Act Past Progress, Future Challenges 2002–2003.* Health Resources and Services Administration, HIV/AIDS Bureau 301.443.1993. Retrieved October 5, 2003, from http://hab.hrsa.gov

U.S. Department of Labor. (2008). *Occupational Outlook Handbook, 2008–09 Edition,* Retrieved December 27, 2008, from http://www.bls.gov/oco/ocos060.htm

U.S. Senate Special Committee on Aging. (1981). *Development in aging, 1981 (Vol 1)*. Washington, DC: U.S. Government Printing Office.

U.S. Social Security Administration. (n.d). SSI Monthly Statistics, January 2009. Retrieved June 30, 2009, from http://www.ssa.gov/policy/docs/statcomps/ssi_monthly/2009-01/table01.html

Van Wormer, K., & Boes, M. (1997). Humor in the emergency room: A social work perspective. *Health and Social Work, 22*(2), 87–92.

Vass, A. (1996). *New directions in social work competencies, core knowledge, values, and skills*. Thousand Oaks, CA: Sage.

Walker, J. S., Bruns, E. J., & Penn, M. (2008). Individualized services in systems of care: The wrap-around process. In Stroul, B. A. & Blau, G. M. (Eds.), *The system of care handbook: Transforming mental health services for children, youth and families* (pp. 127–155). Baltimore, MD: Paul H. Bookes.

Walker, L. E. A. (2009). *The battered women syndrome* (3rd edition). New York: Springer Publishing Company, LLC.

Wallerstein, N. (2002). Empowerment to reduce health disparities. *Scandinavian Journal of Public Health, 30*, 72–77.

Walsh, J. (2009). Psychoeducation. In A. R. Roberts (Ed.), *Social workers' desk reference* (2nd ed., pp. 474–478). New York: Oxford University Press.

Walsh, J., & Holton, V. (2008). Case management. In K. M. Sowers & C. N. Dulmus (Series Eds.) & W. Rowe & L. A. Rapp-Paglicci (Vol. Eds.), *Comprehensive handbook of social work and social welfare: Vol. 3. Social work practice* (pp. 139–160). Hoboken, NJ: John Wiley & Sons, Inc.

Watkins, S. A. (1990). The Mary Ellen myth: Correcting child welfare history. *Social Work, 35*(6), 500–503.

Watkins, J. M., & Holmes, J. (2008). Educating for social work. In K. M. Sowers & C. N. Dulmus (Series Eds.) & B. W. White (Vol. Ed.), *Comprehensive handbook of social work and social welfare: Vol. 1. The profession of social work* (pp. 25–36). Hoboken, NJ: John Wiley & Sons, Inc.

Wegar, K. (2000). Adoption, family ideology, and social stigma: Bias in community attitudes, adoption research, and practice. *Family Relations, 49*, 363–370.

Weismiller, T., & Rome, S. H. (1995). Social workers in politics. In R. L. Edwards et al. (Eds.), *Encyclopedia of social work* (19th ed., pp. 2305–2313). Washington, DC: NASW Press.

Wells, R. A., & Phelps, P. A. (1990). The brief psychotherapies: A selective overview. In R. A. Wells & V. J. Giannetti (Eds.), *Handbook of the brief psychotherapies* (pp. 3–26). New York: Plenum.

Wells, R. A. (1994). *Planned short-term treatment* (2nd ed.). New York: Free Press.

When violence hits home. (July 4,1994). *Time Magazine, 144*(1). Retrieved June 9, 2009, from http://www.time.com/time/magazine/article/0,9171,981054,00.html

White House Conference on Children in a Democracy (1942). *Final Report*, Washington, D.C., January 18–20, 1940 (Publication No. 272). Washington, DC: U.S. Government Printing Office. Reprinted in *Children and Youth: Social Problems and Social Policy*. New York: Arno Press.

Whiting, L. (1996). Foreword. In J. M. Karls & K. M. Wandrei (Eds.), *Person-in-environment system: The PIE classification system for social functioning problems* (pp. xiii–xv). Washington, DC: NASW Press.

Whittaker, J. K. (1995). Children: Group care. In R. Edwards et al. (Eds.), *Encyclopedia of social work* (19th ed., pp. 448–460). Washington, DC: NASW Press.

Wilensky, H., & Lebeaux, C. (1958). *Industrial society and social welfare*. New York: Russell Sage Foundation.

Wilensky, H., & Lebeaux, C. (1965). *Industrial society and social welfare*. New York: Free Press.

Wilke, D. J., & Vinton, L. (2003). Domestic violence and aging: Teaching about their intersection. *Journal of Social Work Education, 39*(2), 225–235.

Williams, H. (1944). Benjamin Franklin and poor laws. *Social Service Review, 18,* 77–84.

Williams, J. B. (2009). Using the diagnostic and statistical manual of mental disorders, fourth edition, text revision. In A. R. Roberts (Ed.), *Social workers' desk reference* (2nd ed., pp. 325–334). New York: Oxford University Press.

Willison, J. S., & Lutter, Y. L. (2009). Contextualizing women's violence: Gender-responsive assessment and treatment. In J. T. Andrade (Ed.), *Handbook of violence risk assessment and treatment: New approaches for mental health professionals* (pp. 121–155). New York: Springer Publishing Company, LLC.

Wineman, D. (1995). Children's rights. In R. Edwards et al. (Eds.), *Encyclopedia of social work* (19th ed., pp. 465–475). Washington, DC: NASW Press.

Witkin, S. L., & Iversen, R. R. (2008). Issues in social work. In K. M. Sowers & C. N. Dulmus (Series Eds.) & B. W. White (Vol. Ed.), *Comprehensive handbook of social work and social welfare: Vol. 1. The profession of social work* (pp. 467–496). Hoboken, NJ: John Wiley & Sons, Inc.

Wolinsky, F. D., & Arnold, C. L. (1988). A different perspective on health and health services utilization. In G. L. Maddox & M. P. Lawton (Eds.), *Annual review of gerontology and geriatrics* (Vol. 8, pp. 77–94). New York: Springer.

Wolk, J. (1981). Are social workers politically active? *Social Work, 26*(4), 283–288.

Woo, S. M., & Keatinge, C. (2008). *Diagnosis and treatment of mental disorders across the lifespan*. Hoboken, NJ: John Wiley & Sons.

Woods, T. A., & Kurtz-Cortes, B. (2007). Race identity and race socialization in African American families: Implications for social workers. *Journal of Human Behavior and the Social Environment, 2*(3), 99–116.

Worden, M. (1999). *Family therapy basics* (2nd ed.). Pacific Grove, CA: Brooks/Cole.

Yeager, K. R., & Latimer, T. R. (2009). Quality standards and quality assurance in health settings. In A. R. Roberts (Ed.), *Social workers' desk reference* (2nd ed., pp. 194–203). New York: Oxford University Press.

Yeager, K. R., Roberts, A. R., & Saveanu, R. (2009). Optimizing the use of patient safety standards, procedures, and measures. In A. R. Roberts (Ed.), *Social workers' desk reference* (2nd ed., pp. 174–186). New York: Oxford University Press.

Zabora, J. R. (2009). Development of a proactive model of health care versus a reactive system of referrals. In A. R. Roberts (Ed.), *Social workers' desk reference* (2nd ed., pp. 826–832). New York: Oxford University Press.

Zarit, S. H., & Zarit, J. M. (2007). *Mental disorders in older adults: Fundamentals of assessment and treatment* (2nd Ed.). New York: The Guilford Press.

Index

Note: Pages numbers followed by "f" or "t" denote figures or tables respectively. Page numbers in **boldface** *refer to glossary terms.*